Between Reform and Revolution

Between Reform and Revolution

German Socialism and Communism from 1840 to 1990

Edited by

David E. Barclay and Eric D. Weitz

NEW YORK • OXFORD

First published in 1998 by

Berghahn Books

Library of Congress Cataloging-in-Publication Data

Between reform and revolution : German socialism and communism from
1840 to 1990 / edited by David E. Barclay, Eric D. Weitz.
p. cm.
Includes bibliographical references and index.
ISBN 1-57181-000-5 (alk. paper)
1. Socialism—Germany—History. 2. Communism—Germany—History. I.
Barclay, David E., 1948- . II. Weitz, Eric D. HX273.B557 1997 335'.00943—
dc21

97-22088
CIP

British Library Cataloguing in Publication Data

A catalogue record for this book is available from the
British Library.

Printed in the United States on acid-free paper.

Contents

List of Abbreviations

ADAV	Allgemeiner Deutscher Arbeiterverein
ADGB	Allgemeiner Deutscher Gewerkschaftsbund
AfA	Arbeitsgemeinschaft freier Angestelltenverbände
AOFAA	Archive de l'Occupation française en Allemagne et Autriche
APZ	*Aus Politik und Zeitgeschichte*
AsD	Archiv der sozialen Demokratie der Friedrich-Ebert-Stiftung, Bonn-Bad Godesberg
ASPD	Alte Sozialdemokratische Partei Deutschlands
BAK	Bundesarchiv Koblenz
BAK, RSH	Bundesarchiv Koblenz, Reichssicherheitshauptamt
BAP	Bundesarchiv, Abteilungen Potsdam
BT	*Berliner Tageblatt*
CDU	Christlich Demokratische Union Deutschlands
Comintern	Communist International
CPSU	Communist Party of the Soviet Union
CSU	Christlich Soziale Union
DA	*Deutschland Archiv*
DAF	Deutsche Arbeitsfront
DDR	Deutsche Demokratische Republik
DFD	Demokratischer Frauenbund Deutschlands
DFDA	Demokratischer Frauenbund Deutschlands Archiv
DG	*Die Gesellschaft*
DGB	Deutscher Gewerkschaftsbund
DGB	Archiv beim DGB-Bundesvorstand
DNVP	Deutschnationale Volkspartei
DR	*Deutsche Republik*
DVP	Deutsche Volkspartei

D Z	*Dresdner Volkszeitung*
ECCI	Executive Committee of the Communist International
ECSC	European Coal and Steel Community
EDC	European Defense Community
FW	*Das Freie Wort*
GARF	State Archives of the Russian Federation
GlavPURKKA	Main Political Administration of the Red Army
GPS	*German Politics and Society*
GR	Gewerkschaftsrat
GSR	*German Studies Review*
GStAPK (M)	Geheimes Staatsarchiv Preußischer Kulturbesitz, Berlin: former Merseburg archives
GZ	Gewerkschaftliches Zonensekretariat
HIA	Hoover Institution Archives
HICOG	[United States] High Commissioner in Germany
HStAD	Hauptstaatsarchiv Düsseldorf
IISG	Internationaal Instituut voor Sociale Geschiedenis, Amsterdam
IRA	International Ruhr Authority
IWK	*Internationale wissenschaftliche Korrespondenz zur Geschichte der deutschen Arbeiterbewegung*
KAPD	Kommunistische Arbeiterpartei Deutschlands
KPD	Kommunistische Partei Deutschlands
KPO	Kommunistische Partei-Opposition
LAB	Landesarchiv Berlin
LADAV	Lassallescher Allgemeiner Deutscher Arbeiterverein
LDP	Liberal-Demokratische Partei Deutschlands
MKF	*Mitteilungen aus der kulturwissenschaftlichen Forschung*
MSEUEE	Mouvement Socialiste pour les États-Unis d'Europe
MSPD	Mehrheitssozialdemokratische Partei Deutschlands
NATO	North Atlantic Treaty Organization
NB	*Neue Blätter für den Sozialismus*
NHStAH	Niedersächsisches Hauptstaatsarchiv Hanover
NKFD	Nationalkomitee "Freies Deutschland"
NKVD	People's Commissariat of Internal Affairs
NL	Nachlaß (papers)
NSDAP	Nationalsozialistische Deutsche Arbeiterpartei (Nazi Party)
NSDAP HA	Nationalsozialistische Deutsche Arbeiterpartei, Hauptarchiv
NV	*Neuer Vorwärts*

NWStAM	Nordrhein-Westfälisches Staatsarchiv Münster
PDS	Partei des Demokratischen Sozialismus
RTsKhIDNI	Russian Center for the Preservation and Study of Historical Documents, Moscow
RWW	Rheinisch-Westfälisches Wirtschaftsarchiv
SA	Sturmabteilung (Nazi Storm Troopers)
SAP	Sozialistische Arbeiterpartei
SAPD	Sozialistische Arbeiterpartei Deutschlands
SAPMO-BA	Stiftung Archiv der Parteien und Massenorganisationen der DDR im Bundesarchiv, Berlin
SBZ	Sowjetische Besatzungszone
SDAP	Sozialdemokratische Deutsche Arbeiterpartei
SED	Sozialistische Einheitspartei Deutschlands
SFIO	French Socialist Party
SFIO/CD	French Socialist Party/Directing Committee
SM	*Sozialistische Monatshefte*
SMAD	Sowjetische Militäradministration in Deutschland
Sopade	Sozialdemokratische Partei Deutschlands/Exilvorstand
SOWI	*Sozialwissenschaftliche Information*
SPD	Sozialdemokratische Partei Deutschlands
SPD/PV	Sozialdemokratische Partei Deutschlands/Parteivorstand
SStAD	Sächsisches Staatsarchiv Dresden
StAD	Stadtarchiv Düsseldorf
StAHH	Staatsarchiv Hamburg
StAKö	Stadtarchiv Köln
StBKAH	Stiftung Bundeskanzler-Adenauer-Haus
UEM	United Europe Movement
USPD	Unabhängige Sozialdemokratische Partei Deutschlands
UW	*Unser Weg*
VDAV	Verband (or Vereinstag) Deutscher Arbeitervereine
VIHK-NRW	Archiv der Vereinigung der Industrie- und Handelskammern des Landes Nordrhein-Westfalen
WTB	Woytinsky-Tarnow-Baade Plan
WWI	Wirtschaftswissenschaftliches Institut
ZfS	*Zeitschrift für Sozialismus*
ZK	Zentralkomitee
ZPA	Zentrales Parteiarchiv

INTRODUCTION

David E. Barclay and *Eric D. Weitz*

1. Socialism in Modern Germany

For some one hundred and fifty years, from the first glimmers of industrialization to the present day, socialism has constituted a central element in the historical development of Germany. From the League of the Just and the General German Workers Association in the middle decades of the nineteenth century to the Social Democratic and Communist parties in the twentieth, socialist parties in Germany have claimed to represent the finest ideals of human liberty and to offer the route to material riches for all. They have professed to represent the interests of the industrial working class and the population as a whole in a society often wrenched by intense class, religious, and regional conflicts. The ideology of socialism has served as a central theme of intellectual and political conflict, one fought out in the array of arenas – legislatures and the press, universities and the streets – that constituted the public sphere. Although their programs have never come close to fulfillment, the socialists and communist parties have decisively shaped the character of Germany's politics and society in the modern era – both by their own actions, and by the intense hostility that they have often engendered from liberals, conservatives, Catholics, and fascists. Socialists played a major, perhaps the key, role in the democratization of German politics, contributed greatly to the expansion of the social welfare state, promoted women's participation in politics and the economy, and gave to German society a more open and liberal tenor. They also helped engender the bureaucrati-

Notes for this chapter begin on page 28.

zation and regulation of modern Germany, were often blind to forms of oppression that were only partly rooted in the class character of industrial society, and, in the case of the German Democratic Republic, built an authoritarian order that systematically violated political liberties.

Faced at times with the most severe political repression, Socialists and Communists nonetheless built vibrant movements that established a socialist presence in the political arena, in the workplace, in neighborhoods and communities and even a few villages, and in the social and cultural lives of their members. As popular movements, the socialist parties provided workers with the ideological and organizational tools to contest employers and governments and to lay claim to political and economic rights and cultural opportunities. The rhetoric of socialism constituted, for many working-class Germans, the linguistic terrain upon which their social and political identities were formed. Narratives of class constructed out of daily experience and socialist ideology enabled workers to make sense of their present and to envisage a more just, prosperous, and inclusive future.

And German socialism had resonance far beyond Germany's shifting borders. Karl Marx, of course, began to develop his system of thought in the context of German philosophy and politics in the first half of the nineteenth century. German socialist émigrés and exiles from the 1840s onward carried their ideas with them to such far-flung places as Milwaukee, Mexico City, and Shanghai. By the turn of the twentieth century, the Social Democratic Party (SPD) had established itself as the "model party" of the Second International, the beacon of ideological clarity and mentor of less powerful organizations.[1] In the Third International, the Communist Party of Germany (KPD) ranked just behind the Russian party. Strategic decisions turned on evaluations of German affairs, and Communists around the world expected the KPD to realize the next stage of the proletarian revolution.

2. Socialism and the Proletarian Milieu

Socialism, then, never merely signified a political party that contested elections. For much of its life, socialism has been an ideal and a movement, and it has proved capable of inspiring the deepest commitments from its supporters. As a movement, socialism became firmly anchored in the proletarian "milieu" of Germany, yet the relationship between party and movement on the one side, and milieu on the other, has always been complex and at times fraught with tension. The socialist parties drew sustenance and support from the proletarian milieu, but they also tried to shape it in their own image. They were not always successful, however, because the milieu was itself shaped by a myriad of constantly shifting historical forces. Religious issues, the generally conservative tenor of German politics and society, understandings of gender, the attractions of twentieth-century mass culture, rival political movements that included Nazism, the poverty and discriminations of proletarian life, the nature of the proletarian family, the changing character of work: all these factors shaped the proletarian milieu as much as did the socialist and communist parties. The proletarian milieu was, then, malleable, changing, and elusive. Only with great effort and never completely were socialists able to shape it as they desired, while in an often subterranean manner the milieu also shaped the nature of the socialist movement in Germany.[2]

In its origins around the middle of the nineteenth century, that milieu was, for the most part, still an artisanal one. Socialism found support in few factories and among very few factory workers. In the Revolution of 1848, only scattered glimmers of socialist politics appeared among the largely liberal and guild-oriented programs that dominated the Revolution. But in the 1860s, socialism began to appear as a defined movement in a number of communities, and preeminently in the kingdom of Saxony, the early center of industrialization in Germany. Spurred along by the first organized workers' party, Ferdinand Lassalle's General German Workers Association (ADAV), socialism remained a minority movement, that was nonetheless vigorous enough to inspire deep-seated fears among Germany's established elites. In a sharp break from many of the '48ers, Lassalle, like Marx, embraced industrialization while developing a devastating critique of the private ownership of capital and the exploitation of workers. Lassalle's program registered the seismic shift from artisanal to industrial production and the formation of the proletariat as a class even while many of the members of the ADAV were skilled craftsmen. They experienced the pressures of the advance of a market-driven economy, if not yet the rigors of factory labor. In his advocacy of a male family wage – that is, the model of the male breadwinner earning enough for his wife to stay at home – Lassalle both reflected and advanced the patriarchal family structure that was so much a part of bourgeois and proletarian life.

By the end of the 1860s socialism had progressed enough that it experienced a series of controversies and divisions, culminating in the formation of new parties and associations – a seemingly fixed feature of socialist politics. In 1869 August Bebel and Wilhelm Liebknecht formed an explicitly Marxist socialist party, which in 1875 merged with the Lassalleans to create the Social Democratic Party of Germany (its name after the 1890s). And it was the SPD that would first reap the benefits of the full-fledged formation of the proletarian milieu in Germany. Driven underground or into exile by Bismarck's Anti-Socialist Law from 1878 to 1890, socialism took on its heroic cast, a movement of faith and progress propagated by a persecuted minority. When the law lapsed more or less concurrently with Germany's powerful drive into the first rank of industrial nations, the SPD was well poised to recruit supporters from the ever growing numbers of industrial workers. By the late nineteenth century, the proletarian milieu that made the SPD a mass party was composed largely of skilled and semi-skilled urban, Protestant industrial workers.

The specifically social democratic component of the proletarian milieu never constituted a majority of Germany's industrial working class, and many more people voted for than joined the SPD. Nor was the milieu revolutionary in character, despite the SPD's tornadic rhetoric and immersion in the fine points of Marxist ideology. By the turn of the twentieth century the SPD had become largely reformist in practice – an orientation that inspired intense political controversy within the party, but which seemed to suit better the aspirations of its own supporters who were in most instances less fixated upon revolution and more concerned with acquiring political rights, economic well-being, and a sense of social dignity while dealing with the officials of a semi-authoritarian state and repressive employers who continually violated all three aspirations.

The working-class milieu, overcrowded, over-worked, geographically mobile, and patriarchal, provided sustenance for the SPD while the party also sought to guide and discipline workers. The party ideal around 1900 – the sober, skilled, and dedicated male worker, who provided for his family and struggled for the cause in the factory and community – perfectly embodied this sensibility. He agitated for the party, represented his union to the employers, attended evening lectures, and instructed his wife and children in the ideals of socialism. For recreation he might join the workers' gymnastics association, bicycle club, or choir. Women, until 1908 legally banned from participation in political organizations, might be involved in their own association attached to the local party or, more rarely, in the socialist women's organization headed by Clara Zetkin. The men and, more rarely, women who became members of the SPD entered, if they so desired, an all-encompassing world involving endless rounds of meetings, leaflet distributions, demonstrations, and lectures, accompanied by leisure-time pursuits within the range of party-linked cultural and sports associations. On Sundays the entire family, after an outing at the zoo or a demonstration, might retire to the party or trade union hall for beer and bratwurst.

In 1890 the milieu helped the SPD become Germany's largest single political party, though because of inequities in the apportionment of electoral districts, it was not until 1912 that the party acquired the largest single representation in the Reichstag. Then, in one of the most scrutinized decisions in modern political history, the SPD voted to support Germany's war effort in 1914. The party became more firmly integrated into the nation's politics, though was still not accepted or trusted by the elites.

At the same time, the proletarian milieu was radically transformed in the course of the war by the enormously high death rate, incessant mobility, and, not least, the intense immiseration suffered by the population. Incremental change seemed a rather unsatisfying program as food supplies and official rations plummeted and working hours increased. A great divide opened between the moderate course of the SPD, still supported by a large segment of German workers, and those increasingly impatient with the travails of wartime at home and at the front. The impatience would erupt in the last days of the war into the German Revolution of 1918 to 1919 and the foundation of the Weimar Republic.

The SPD served as the bastion of the Republic. Even when shut out of the Reich government, it staffed many of the leading positions in the *Land* and municipal administrations. Social democracy gave the Republic its decisive – though deeply contested – democratic and social welfare content, epitomized in the legally guaranteed recognition of trade unions, the expansion of welfare benefits, free and equal suffrage, introduction of unemployment insurance, construction of municipal housing estates, the eight-hour day, and many other reforms beneficial to workers. Weimar came also to represent the high point of a specifically socialist culture in Germany. Mass working-class cultural organizations, from the rock-searching and mountain-hiking Friends of Nature to bicycle and radio clubs to choirs and theatrical groups, attracted the participation of hundreds of thousands of workers. Socialists and Communists alike promoted women's involvement in the polity and economy, albeit within a larger patriarchal world view, and contributed decisively to the flourishing sex reform movement of the Weimar years.

But in Weimar the proletarian milieu was also shattered by social, political, and economic factors of wide-ranging consequence. Radical workers and intellectuals built in Germany the first mass-based communist party outside of the Soviet Union. A political gulf opened up in the proletarian milieu as the two socialist parties competed for workers' loyalties. After the wild inflation of 1923, German employers instituted a rationalization program designed to reassert managerial authority and raise labor productivity. Workers lost many of the social benefits gained in the Revolution, while sustained unemployment came to characterize the lives of those rendered "useless" by both rationalization and the enormous and devastating Depression that began in 1929. Never homogeneous and now further divided politically between Communists and Socialists, the proletarian milieu shattered into rival social camps – those with work who benefited from publicly supported housing and state arbitration of labor disputes, and the long-term unemployed who received barely enough to exist from the vaunted Weimar welfare state, between those who sought to build a "respectable" work and home life based on the family wage and skill, and those who inhabited the rough-and-tumble world of the casual long-term unemployed and claimed neighborhood streets as their terrain. The social divide turned the political distance between socialism and communism into an increasingly violent and intransigent political chasm.

Additional cracks emerged in the edifice of the proletarian milieu in Weimar even as socialist culture, in both its KPD and SPD versions, attained its greatest penetration of working-class life. Alongside its longtime opponents among Germany's conservative elites, Catholics, small property owners, and the thousands of workers who remained distant from socialist ideas and programs, two new and even more powerful challenges to socialist culture appeared in the 1920s: mass, commercial culture and National Socialism. Against the immensely popular world of film and fashion, Social Democrats and Communists alike generally had little to offer except a prudish call for socialist morality and discipline, and the hope that demonstrations and organized hikes in the countryside would keep youth immersed in the struggle and oblivious to sex and the dream world of cinema. National Socialism proved a more murderous if less enduring opponent, one that drew upon the techniques of mass organization that socialists had pioneered and then turned them against Socialists and Communists under the shrill cries of nation and race, the leader and the people. Communists engaged the Nazis in street battles, while Social Democrats fought a rearguard action to defend the legal norms and social rights of the Weimar Republic. Both parties vastly underestimated the intentions and brutality of the Nazis, yet they would be the first victims once Hitler attained the chancellorship on 30 January 1933. Social Democrats and Communists found themselves driven into concentration camps or exile; tens of thousands were murdered by the regime.

As individuals, Communists and Social Democrats suffered appallingly from the repressive practices of the Nazi regime. As organizations, both the KPD and SPD were ripped from the proletarian milieu that had sustained them as mass movements. Some Socialists and communists maintained a heroic but ultimately hopeless resistance against Nazism; for most, activism was reduced to fleeting and furtive meetings of a few comrades at a bar or in a living room. Many more workers, including one-time Social Democrats and Communists, were won over to the Third Reich by the Nazis' cult of race and leader and by imperial aggrandizement, economic revival, and social welfare measures that bestowed honor – if not real material benefits – upon work and motherhood.

In short, National Socialism went a long way toward radically restructuring the proletarian milieu that had once sustained both the SPD and the KPD as mass movements. The specifically socialist-influenced proletarian milieu barely survived the Third Reich. Reconstituted after 1945, it was much altered yet again by the lingering impact of National Socialism and total war, by Allied occupation, and by the experience in exile of many Socialists and Communists. In the west, despite initial calls for socialization, Social Democrats moved rather quickly toward accommodation with other social and political groups and with the Atlantic orientation that culminated in the mid-1950s in West German rearmament and membership in NATO. The burgeoning consumer culture of the 1950s enabled workers to pursue more privatized forms of pleasure, weakening further the old solidaristic, proletarian milieu. In a striking – some would say long overdue – recognition of both postwar realities and its own, long prevalent reformist practice, the SPD in 1959 finally abandoned its Marxist and exclusively working-class orientation in favor of democracy, social welfare, and the stature of a *Volkspartei* (people's party) rather than a *Klassenpartei* (class party). The SPD's self-transformation paved the way for its electoral triumphs in the 1960s and 1970s and, under the chancellorships of Willy Brandt and Helmut Schmidt, the further expansion of the welfare state, ever tighter connections to the Atlantic alliance coupled with *Ostpolitik* and détente, and, perhaps most enduringly, the liberalization of German society. At the same time, the SPD's metamorphosis into a *Volkspartei* sounded the death knell of the "classic" proletarian milieu of the industrial age and of the tight links between the party and its working-class base. Left-wing politics came to be defined increasingly by the student protests of the late 1960s and the flurry of new social movements that emerged in their wake, notably environmental and feminist groups.

In the German Democratic Republic, a rather different pattern unfolded. In some senses the old proletarian milieu survived much longer than in the west, a result of the resistance to western, especially American, cultural influences and the far more straitened living conditions of the population. However, the milieu that had once been the setting for independent working-class organizations and associations and popular protests now became the object of manipulation from above. In Weimar the KPD had come increasingly under the sway of the Soviet Union. Those German Communists who had survived exile and the Stalin terror in the Soviet Union came back to Germany even more determined to impose the Soviet model of central state direction in their area of influence. The partly autonomous and self-created organizations of workers and the labor movement, rooted in the proletarian milieu, were replaced by hierarchical organizations created by the party-state. The proletarian milieu in the east also met its demise, though by a different route than in the west. It was replaced by the "niche society," the small groups of like-minded friends and family within which people sought to carve out some autonomy away from the ever-watchful eyes of the state and from which would emerge the vigorous protest movement of 1989 to 1990.

3. At the Margins: The Historiography of the German Labor Movement to 1945

For many decades the historiography of the German labor movement was intimately bound up with its own history. Just as social democratic labor organizations were regarded as pariahs and political outcasts before 1918, so too was the history of German labor confined to the margins of the country's cultural, academic, and intellectual life. Roger Chickering has written that historians were "the most politically active group of scholars in [I]mperial Germany," and their devotion to the existing Imperial state and to a vision of history as a narrative of *große Politik* excluded the very possibility of taking labor history or related topics as serious objects of study.[3] Karl Lamprecht's fruitless efforts in the 1890s to incorporate the study of economic, social, and comparative approaches into the writing of academic history were symptomatic. His proposals resulted in a fierce controversy that almost ruined Lamprecht and left him isolated within the historical profession. To be sure, some established academics, most notably the so-called *Kathedersozialisten* or "professorial socialists" associated with middle-class movements for social reform, did undertake a number of important studies that are still of interest to modern labor historians. But these writers – who included economists and sociologists like Gustav Schmoller, Adolph Wagner, Lujo Brentano, Max Weber, or, with some reservations, Werner Sombart – were not historians, and were moreover largely interested in what was for them the analysis of contemporary social issues: the conditions of working-class life or the ideological roots of contemporary social movements.[4] For the most part, Germany's first labor historians were non-academics, and several were actively involved in the labor movement themselves. Two especially notable examples were Franz Mehring and Eduard Bernstein.[5]

Born into a conservative, middle-class family in 1846, Franz Mehring was attracted to radical-democratic causes while still a university student. In 1891 he joined the resuscitated, newly legalized Social Democratic Party, and until his death in 1919 he devoted his career to the socialist cause by serving as one of the party's most prominent and prolific journalists, especially as editor of the influential *Leipziger Volkszeitung*.[6] Toward the end of his life he was active on the radical left wing of the socialist movement. Although Mehring wrote many works, including a still-useful biography of Karl Marx that appeared in 1918, his most significant contribution was a pathbreaking history of German social democracy that first appeared in 1898 and by 1904 had been thoroughly re-edited and expanded to four volumes.[7] Notable for its stylistic verve, its narrative detail, its polemical edge, and its thorough command of available sources, Mehring's work quickly established itself as a classic, and almost a century after its first publication it is still worth reading. Mehring tries to locate the evolution of German socialism within the broader context of German history, describing the political and ideological development of German socialism from the July Revolution of 1830 to the end of the Anti-Socialist Law in 1890 and the SPD's Erfurt Program of 1891. It contained a number of themes which later became staples of socialist historiography in Germany, such as the alleged "betrayal" of parliamentary values by the bourgeoisie during the Revolution of 1848. According to Mehring and subsequent generations of socialist historians, that betrayal in turn helped to accelerate the birth of an autonomous socialist movement in Germany: "Because the German bourgeoisie politically abdicated and threw away the rights of the people, the German proletariat took up the rights of the people and asserted its claims to political power."[8] The real hero of Mehring's history, despite the radicalism of his later years in the SPD, is Ferdinand Lassalle, to whom the author devotes the entire third part of his six-part study. For Mehring it was Lassalle who responded to the failures of the German bourgeoisie in 1848 by paving the way for a new kind of social democracy. One of the major aims of his history, as he put it, was to show how "on the one hand, German social democracy was the natural-born child of the German working class, but also, on the other hand, how Lassalle performed invaluable and enduring services by helping to give it birth."[9]

Eduard Bernstein (1850 to 1932) was Mehring's ideological rival and opposite. Although he is best known for his embrace of "revisionism" and of an "evolutionary" socialism after the 1890s, he too can be counted, like Mehring, as one of the first great historians of the German labor movement. During his long life as a party journalist and activist, he devoted a vast amount of effort to accumulating and editing the extant historical record of the labor movement, from obscure newspapers to the writings of Lassalle and the multivolume correspondence between Marx and Engels.[10] But his best-known and most important historical work was his lavishly illustrated, superbly researched three-volume history of the Berlin labor movement that appeared between 1907 and 1910. This study remains extremely useful for the student of German labor history, as does Bernstein's 1910 introductory survey of the labor movement, *Die Arbeiterbewegung*, originally published for a bourgeois reading public.[11]

Most early Social Democratic Party and trade-union activists were practical people, skilled craft workers with little formal education and comparatively little time to concern themselves with the history of the movement with which they were themselves so actively engaged. Still, quite a few socialist and trade-union activists published semi-official or commemorative histories of their own native regions or their own organizations, and many of those works were of rather high quality.[12] Memoirs and the biographies of close friends and comrades also represented important contributions to the historiography of the labor movement before 1933. Examples of the latter two genres includes the extremely important memoirs of August Bebel, the grand old man of social democracy; the memoirs of the Weimar politician Philipp Scheidemann; or the biography of the pioneering union leader Carl Legien published in 1928 by Theodor Leipart, his successor as head of the SPD-oriented "free" trade union federation.[13] Among the few party and union activists who did find time to devote themselves to in-depth historical study was Rudolf Wissell (1869 to 1962), a veteran trade unionist and social democratic politician who received an honorary doctorate from the University of Kiel for a pathbreaking, two-volume history of artisanal and guild practices from the Middle Ages to the nineteenth century. Wissell's book was not primarily an organizational or political history. In fact, it was one of the few histories written by a labor historian before 1933 that focused mainly on the activities of "ordinary" working men and women.[14] But before 1945, examples like Wissell were comparatively rare.

Interestingly, the real pioneer of "academic" labor history in Germany before 1933 was a man who was neither a socialist nor an academic. Gustav Mayer (1871 to 1948) was a left-liberal journalist of bourgeois origin who worked as a correspondent for Leopold Sonnemann's *Frankfurter Zeitung* before settling down in 1905 as a financially independent, freelance historian. Despite his growing sympathies with the SPD, he never joined the party and never became a political activist.[15] Like Mehring and also like his close friend Bernstein, Mayer was especially interested in the contributions of Lassalle and the Lassalleans to the history of the organized labor movement in Germany. Indeed, his doctoral dissertation of 1894 focused on Lassalle's economic views, while his first major book-length publication on the labor movement was a 1909 study of Johann Baptist von Schweitzer, who had succeeded Lassalle after the latter's death in 1864 and who, according to Mayer, had to be regarded as the real founder of the "Lassallean" tradition in German social democracy.[16] Although Mayer always emphasized that he was an outsider, his book on Schweitzer and his subsequent writings demonstrated that he deeply regretted what he called the "separation between proletarian and bourgeois democracy" that had taken place in Germany in the late 1860s. Like a number of left-wing liberals just before World War I, Mayer hoped – in vain, as it turned out – to create a united front of democratic forces against the authoritarian *Obrigkeitsstaat* that led the country into war in 1914.

Mayer's most enduring contributions to the historiography of the German labor movement are probably his six-volume edition of Lassalle's letters and publications and his two-volume biography of Friedrich Engels. Indeed, the latter remains unsurpassed, and is still required reading for anyone interested in the history of Marxism and the early history of German social democracy.[17] The second volume of Mayer's biography only appeared in 1934, and had to be published by Martinus Nijhoff in The Hague. By that date it had become impossible to publish anything of either a sympathetic or a scholarly nature about the labor movement in Germany, and the labor movement itself faced the darkest hours of its history.

4. Silences and Breakthroughs in Postwar Historiography

In exile from Nazi Germany, a few socialists continued to write the history of their times and movement. But sustained historical reflection and scholarship were hardly the order of the day for exiles outside the country or "inner emigrants" and active resisters inside Germany.[18] And after the defeat of National Socialism, many Social Democrats in the western zones of occupation and Communists in the eastern zone were too preoccupied with the enormous tasks of economic, political, social, and moral reconstruction to concern themselves very much with the writing of history. To be sure, many veterans of the labor movement published useful and important memoirs after 1945. But these sorts of things were barely noticed in West German universities, where labor history continued to be marginalized until the dramatic breakthroughs of the 1960s. The profession remained deeply conservative with an almost ingrained prejudice against social democracy as an "alien," anti-national political formation. Social historical investigations in the forms developed by Eckart Kehr and Hans Rosenberg had little resonance among the established historians of the late 1940s and 1950s. Innovative analyses, when they occurred, revolved around the issue of National Socialism and its place in the long course of German history.[19]

But at Heidelberg in the late 1950s, Werner Conze instituted pathbreaking seminars and colloquia under the rubric of "structural" history. With somewhat tainted roots in Nazi *Volksgeschichte*, the structural history of Conze, Otto Brunner, and others entailed an effort at a unified social and economic account of past time somewhat akin to the *Annales* school in France.[20] In his series *Industrielle Welt*, Conze began publishing many innovative studies on the social and economic conditions of working-class life. His own essay, "Vom 'Pöbel' zum 'Proletariat,'" was itself a landmark examination of the transition in social position and consciousness of the proletariat that accompanied the emergence of the industrial age.[21]

Furthermore, a number of pioneering monographs were published in the 1950s and early 1960s in Germany and the United States. Two of the most important – Gerhard A. Ritter's *Die Arbeiterbewegung im Wil-*

helminischen Reich and Carl Schorske's *German Social Democracy 1905-1917: The Development of the Great Schism* – remain in print to this day, a sign of their enduring value.[22] Although both scholars' sympathies with their subject were not difficult to discern, their works were notable for their nuanced treatment of social democracy as a topic worthy of serious historical investigation, rather than an object in partisan political warfare. Schorske's book only received a German translation in the 1970s, but its interpretation of the later communist-socialist split as prefigured in the factional conflicts of the pre-war SPD long prevailed. While not explicitly a work of social history, at least as the term would come to be understood by the end of the 1960s, Ritter's work was notable for placing the SPD in the context of Imperial German society. Implicitly, both works, as well as other important studies by Helga Grebing, Hedwig Wachenheim, Vernon Lidtke, and Shlomo Na'aman, legitimized socialism as a topic of historical investigation and contested the pariah status of the SPD – a view that continued to prevail in some quarters of German society, and the historical profession in particular, into the 1960s.[23]

Two other pathbreaking studies deserve mention. Hans Mommsen, a student of Hans Rothfels and Werner Conze, produced a major work on social democracy in the Habsburg Monarchy. Mommsen's topic lay outside Germany proper, but like Ritter, he demonstrated the rootedness of the party in its particular milieu, in this case the multinational character of the Austro-Hungarian Empire, and legitimized the historical study of social democracy.[24] Eberhard Kolb published in 1962 one of the first serious studies of the Revolution of 1918 to 1919, a topic that would soon become central to the historiography of the socialist movement in Germany.[25] Also notable from this period were two works on the KPD. Ossip K. Flechtheim's *Die KPD in der Weimarer Republik* was for many years the only serious historical study of the party. Not only the absence of competition made this an important work. Flechtheim presented not just a political history of the party but also sought to ground the character of the KPD in the social and political conditions of the Weimar Republic.[26] In the early 1960s an émigré to the United States, Werner Angress, published a detailed history of the KPD in the first years of the Weimar Republic.[27]

In the DDR a different kind of historiography unfolded. As one arrow in the quiver of campaigns designed to promote the legitimacy of the party-state, the Socialist Unity Party (SED) early in the 1950s began to encourage historical studies of the labor movement. Under the direction of Leo Stern at the Martin-Luther-Universität Halle-Wittenberg, a small group of researchers began turning out collections of documents and then articles and monographs on the history of the SPD and of industrialization in the nineteenth century.[28] Later, they began to move into the more recent, and politically sensitive, periods of Weimar and the Third Reich. At the Sixth Party Congress in 1963, these tasks were elevated into a major campaign under the nominal direction of Walter Ulbricht, and culminated with the publication of the eight-volume *Geschichte der deutschen Arbeiterbewegung* in 1966.[29]

Interpretatively these works were tendentious. They all sought to justify the actions of the KPD and the socialist state and to vilify the "treasonous" SPD. The communist movement and the foundation of the DDR were presented as the "crowning [achievement] of the more than hundred-year struggle of the German labor movement," the DDR as the state in which "the ideas of the Communist Manifesto had now realized their complete victory."[30] The Bolshevik Revolution and Soviet Union were held up as models that inspired German workers to engage in their own activism. Yet if one reads past the interpretations, important empirical detail can still be found, even in some of the works produced in the 1950s at the height of Stalinism. Especially useful are the hundreds of works published from the 1960s to the late 1980s under the auspices of the various SED Commissions for Research on the History of the Local Labor Movement. Often difficult to locate, these brochures and books consist of both document collections and historical analyses and provide a wealth of detail on the labor movement in the localities.[31]

5. Labor History and "Historical Social Science"

By the 1960s, a new generation of historians began to challenge the assumptions and attitudes that had prevailed in West German universities after 1945. Sustained by the democratic reforms of that decade, they were also profoundly influenced by the "Fischer controversy" that shook German historiography out of its complacency after 1961. Fritz Fischer, a Hamburg professor of the older generation, argued in his now-classic *Griff nach der Weltmacht* (translated into English under the innocuous title *Germany's Aims in the First World War*) that Germany did indeed bear major responsibility for the outbreak of World War I; that, in fact, the conflict was to a large extent an outgrowth of domestic conflicts, especially the desire of powerful elite groups to maintain their own domestic political hegemony and to resist pressures for democratic reforms.[32] Although Fischer's book and the bitter debate that it engendered did not directly touch on the history of German labor, they profoundly altered the terms of German historiography and, thus, helped to create an environment in which labor history could gradually move into the mainstream of academic scholarship. Among other things, Fischer's work called into question the traditional "primacy of foreign policy" (*Primat der Außenpolitik*) in

German history, suggesting that historians should focus instead on the history of social classes, social groups, and social conflict within Germany. One of the first young historians to heed this call was Hans-Ulrich Wehler.

Born in 1931, Wehler studied history and, not coincidentally, sociology before completing his doctorate in Cologne. Moreover, like many scholars of his generation he spent a great deal of time in the English-speaking world and was strongly influenced by Anglo-American approaches to the social sciences. He was not a student of Fritz Fischer, and differed with him in many respects; rather, he was more powerfully shaped by the examples of two other historians of the older generation, Eckart Kehr and Hans Rosenberg, whose writings on social and economic themes encouraged him to think of history not simply as a narrative or literary text but as an "historical social science" *(historische Sozialwissenschaft)*. Historians should move beyond the narrative of events, of *große Politik* (grand politics) and individual personalities, and focus instead on the *structural* continuities and discontinuities that had shaped German historical development, including the evolution of the working class and the labor movement. Moreover, history had an obligation to be a *critical* social science. West Germans should be encouraged to confront the traumas and shortcomings of their national past, and critical social history, thus, had a central, democratic, emancipatory role to play in contemporary German life.[33] Although Wehler's first book, published in 1962, concerned social democracy and the nationalities question before 1914, his subsequent writings rarely dealt specifically with the labor movement.[34] Many concerned the Imperial period and the ways in which powerful elite groups, using techniques of "negative integration," inflamed social conflict and inhibited Germany's progress toward political modernization and democratization. Wehler and like-minded colleagues argued, on the basis of a series of theoretical and comparative studies, that Germany had followed a "distinctive path" (*Sonderweg*) toward modernity. It had never experienced a truly bourgeois revolution and, as a result, its historical experiences diverged in fundamental respects from those of the Western European parliamentary democracies. Thus, Imperial Germany had remained an authoritarian *Obrigkeitsstaat*, despite the rise of mass movements like social democracy, and those authoritarian traditions in turn helped to undermine Germany's fragile experiment in democracy after 1918 to 1919.

Wehler's vision of a critical, interdisciplinary, comparative, theoretically informed, "structural" social history was shared by many younger contemporaries; indeed, Wehler himself was one of the central figures in what came to be known as the "Bielefeld school," so called after the university where Wehler taught. There he was joined by historians like Jürgen Kocka, Hans-Ulrich Puhle, and, later, Klaus Tenfelde and Christoph

Kleßmann, and together the "Bielefelders" and their allies at other universities – people like Heinrich August Winkler, Hans Mommsen, Hans-Christoph Schröder, Dieter Groh, Hans-Josef Steinberg, Gerhard A. Ritter, and others – helped to establish a new "social history of politics." Their writing – vigorous, detailed, engaged, self-confident, and brimming with new insights and arresting conclusions – reflected a heady enthusiasm and a conviction that German academic scholarship could finally escape from methodological provincialism and from the embrace of an outdated historicism.

In this context the writing of German labor history flourished as never before, and the 1960s, 1970s, and 1980s witnessed a spate of new publications by English- and French-speaking scholars as well as by German historians. Some, like the works of the Americans Richard Hunt, Robert Wheeler, and David Morgan, the Franco-German writer Joseph Rovan, the British historian W.L. Guttsman, or the German scholars Dieter Groh and Susanne Miller, represented new, richly detailed organizational and structural histories of socialist political movements.[35] Similarly, those decades also saw the publication of new organizational, political, and structural histories of Germany's trade-union movements.[36] At the same time, significant numbers of "traditional" biographies of labor leaders continued to be published during those years. Other studies, like those produced by the Bielefelder Jürgen Kocka or the Berkeley historian Gerald D. Feldman, considered the interactions among labor, the state, and other social groups, especially during the era of World War I and thereafter.[37] And still other historians, like Klaus Tenfelde, concerned themselves not so much with organizational and political history as with the social history of both white- and blue-collar workers, including such matters as workplace socialization, workers' culture, wage levels, consumption patterns, and protest behavior.[38] In short, the history of German labor was being incorporated in new and important ways into the writing of German history as a whole.

While the Bielefelders were developing their own contributions to a "social history of politics," many historians in the English-speaking world were approaching the social history of modern Germany from a somewhat different angle of vision. Inspired by the example of E.P. Thompson's monumental history of the making of the English working class and also, in part, by American social historians like Stephan Thernstrom and Herbert G. Gutman, they increasingly came to be interested in social history viewed "from the bottom up" rather than "from the top down."[39] In the United States, historians like David F. Crew or Mary Nolan published pioneering social histories that focused on social structure, social mobility, working-class life, social conflict, and political radicalism in the cities of Bochum and Düsseldorf.[40] And in Great Britain, Richard J. Evans and his colleagues launched a vigorous reconsideration of German working-class life under the auspices of the Social Science Research Council's Research Seminar Group in Modern German Social History. Other historians active in the United Kingdom, such as Dick Geary and Eve Rosenhaft, published important contributions on topics like comparative labor protest or communist violence in the later years of the Weimar Republic.[41]

One measure of the new importance of labor history and of the Bielefelders' critical-emancipatory "social history of politics" was the emergence in West Germany of journals that reflected these concerns. As early as 1960 the annual *Archiv für Sozialgeschichte* had introduced a new public forum for historians of the labor movement; it was supplemented after 1964 by the quarterly *Internationale wissenschaftliche Korrespondenz zur Geschichte der deutschen Arbeiterbewegung* (IWK). And in 1975 the Bielefelders established the pathbreaking journal *Geschichte und Gesellschaft* ("History and Society") as a forum for the study of history as an "historical social science." Like the work of the Bielefelders themselves, this journal did not confine itself to the study of labor and working-class history, but it quickly became (and remains) indispensable reading for all students of that history. Similarly, in 1972 the Bielefelders began to produce a series of critically acclaimed monographs and essay collections called *Kritische Studien zur Geschichtswissenschaft*. Many of these volumes also dealt with themes of importance to scholars of working-class and labor history.

For the most part, historiography in the DDR was little affected by the new ferment that was transforming the writing of labor and working-class history in the Federal Republic. To be sure, some major publications did appear after the 1960s, especially important reference works like Dieter Fricke's handbook on the history of German labor between 1869 and 1914, or Jürgen Kuczynski's continuing stream of massive, statistics-laden writings on the living conditions of workers throughout the industrial world.[42] DDR historians also established their own labor history journal, the *Beiträge zur Geschichte der Arbeiterbewegung*. Only a few exceptional works in the DDR clearly did show the effects of the kinds of structural social history that were being written in the west, most notably Hartmut Zwahr's pioneering analysis of the origins of the working class in nineteenth-century Leipzig.[43]

6. New Pathways

By the 1980s, the heady, sharply honed thrust of the Bielefeld school had lost much of its edge. The vibrant young rebels of West German historiography had become a new historical establishment ensconced in professorial chairs and with access to research funds, international conferences, and armies of doctoral students. Their writings had changed forever the character of historical scholarship on Germany, and the leading practitioners of the Bielefeld school – along with some only loosely associated with it – began to produce massive works of synthesis. In 1987 Wehler himself published the first of a planned four-volume history of German society since 1700, while Kocka, Tenfelde, Ritter, and Winkler turned to a multivolume series on workers and the labor movement since the end of the eighteenth century.[44] These volumes are among the most comprehensive and learned examples of German historical scholarship, but they represent the culmination of an historiographical trend. The innovations and the most interesting recent work now come from beyond the realm of "historical social science."

In terms of the history of German socialism, the structuralist inclinations of the Bielefelders had left largely unexamined the life worlds of the proletariat. In the Bielefeld version, history was never made by the subjects themselves, only by elites at the top of society.[45] Moreover, the girders of the Bielefeld building were forged essentially from politics and economics; the structuring impact of other social factors, gender in particular, lay beyond the grasp of most of the Bielefeld partisans, and many of them were profoundly resistant to the insights emerging from feminist-inspired historiography.[46] Furthermore, the leading generation of West German historians, as mentioned, had deep professional ties to the United States and Great Britain. Many of them had spent extensive periods as students and guest professors in the U.S. in particular, and were notably open to American historiography on Germany and American social science methods – both of which had been pioneered to a significant extent by German émigré scholars in the United States, whose achievements were then re-exported to West Germany in the 1950s and 1960s. Apparently, the greater the geographical distance, the more profound the intellectual influence: German historians were far less receptive to currents emanating from neighboring France, which, beginning in the 1960s, were to have a profound influence on historical scholarship in the U.S. and U.K. Historians of workers and the socialist movement who were influenced by the *annaliste* effort at total history began to move their studies away from the formal organizations of the labor movement to the patterns of daily life at the local level. Beginning in the 1980s, poststructuralist theorists influenced historians to make language and culture the central categories of their investigations. Many labor historians in the U.S. and U.K abandoned the classic narrative of industrial development and the class formation of the proletariat. Instead, they began to assess critically the way that workers, women, and other subordinate groups creatively deployed such key terms as "man," "woman," "skill," and even "work" itself, and in the process forged their own narratives of identity.[47]

The leading practitioners of the German historical profession remained largely closed to these developments. Yet partly in conjunction with the historiographical departures in the U.S. and U.K., partly indigenously developed, new approaches emerged in West Germany in the 1980s, and they vastly broadened the terrain of labor history. Three trends, which often overlapped, are notable: women's history and gender studies, oral history, and *Alltagsgeschichte*, the history of everyday life. All three were rooted in a reaction to the overly structuralist interpretation of the Bielefelders, and, politically, in the international social and political upheavals that erupted in 1968 and the subsequent development of new social movements. Insofar as they related to the history of socialism in Germany, the three trends sought to recapture the lives of historical subjects, including those outside the formal organizations of the labor movement. For more recent topics, the methodology of oral history proved of central importance.[48] The new approaches also sought to grasp the nature of the social institutions and networks within which people lived – that is, not just the party or trade union, but the local bar, marketplace, and family. Often influenced by anthropology, a discipline that had long been tainted in postwar Germany because of its misuse under the Third Reich, they were attentive to the importance of cultural symbols and practices and to the general effort by workers to carve out spheres of autonomy in their daily lives.[49] Inspired by the feminist movement, many of the newer works uncovered the role of women in the socialist movement and, at the same time, the barely hidden misogyny that governed many of the practices of the SPD, KPD, and trade unions. The effort to uncover a distinctively female past soon led – as in the U.S. and U.K. – to an analysis of the way the labor movement absorbed and strengthened the patriarchal family and the gender inequities of modern society.[50]

Little of this, however, carried over into the DDR. Cultural distance and political resistance resulted in little echo of the feminist- and post-structuralist-inspired work that had such a profound influence on historical writing in the U.S., U.K., and, finally, the Federal Republic. Indeed, it is probably fair to say that as the legitimacy of the regime came increasingly under question in the latter part of the 1980s, the recourse to a stagnant and stultifying historiography – to the legitimizing function of the KPD and SED as the embodiment of "all that was progressive in the history of the German people" – only intensified.

7. Contemporary Agendas

Historical writing on German labor, originating within the socialist movement, has become rich and multilayered. The vein of significant research and writing runs deeply, yet no single overarching approach, no particular methodology, any longer defines the field. The various chapters in the present volume capture the methodological and thematic diversity and richness of current historical work. Some are written in the Bielefeld vein, others with a more "traditional" intellectual or political history approach. A number of chapters are written very much in the context of feminist- and poststructuralist-inspired critiques of an older historiography; others are eclectic in approach. All the chapters explore the deep and varied meaning of socialism for the course of modern German history.

In the strikingly original essay that opens this volume, Warren Breckman reminds us that the emerging discourses of radicalism and socialism during the Vormärz years were chronologically coterminous with debates on the national question and national identity in Germany. Issues of "Germanness" and German national character, of "cosmopolitanism" and "philistinism," were hotly debated by early German socialist writers. Breckman shows that the self-understanding and self-perception of the German Left in its earlier years were deeply rooted in discussions about the deficiencies of the Germans and the putative historical mission of the German nation. It was in the context of these debates that Marx and Engels developed their materialist critique of utopian moralism and of the relative backwardness of the German nation. From these debates, the author suggests, emerged an ambivalence toward the national question and issues of national identity that complicated the political work of German socialists for decades.

The next three contributions provide divergent perspectives both on the historic significance of the Lassallean labor movement in Germany and on the fateful split between liberalism and the nascent socialist labor movement in the 1860s. During that decade, Hermann Beck writes, national and constitutional issues became commingled with urgent social issues that reflected Germany's explosive industrialization. The coincidence of those issues created a climate in which liberals and conservatives as well as socialists vied for working-class support. The same decade also witnessed the creation of the country's first working-class parties, beginning with Lassalle's General German Workers Association in 1863, which sprang from dissatisfaction with older, liberal-supported "worker educational associations." Among other things, Beck notes that Lassalle's own alienation from liberalism led to an "astounding congruence" between his ideas and those of prominent social conservatives. Moreover, he argues that the breach between liberalism and socialism was not so much a reflection of the weakness of liberalism as of the volatility of the times.

Where Beck reflects on the larger context that led to the formation of working-class parties during the 1860s, Toni Offermann turns to a detailed analysis of the inner life, structure, and composition of the two

Lassallean parties themselves, the General German Workers Association and its offshoot and rival, the Lassallean General German Workers Association (LADAV). Offermann shows how these organizations were rooted in older German associational *(Verein)* traditions and how, despite endless organizational difficulties that were compounded by the repressive realities of an authoritarian police state, they successfully articulated the real grievances of ordinary people in Germany, especially in areas north of the Main River. Offermann concludes his remarks by emphasizing the extreme importance of Lassalle's contribution to a distinctive form of root-and-branch radicalism and to the creation of the first truly modern socialist party in Germany.

Ralf Roth evaluates the vexed relationship between liberals and socialists after the 1860s from another angle of vision. Germany's cities, he points out, had for centuries constituted a social space that had been dominated by a self-conscious *Bürgertum* around which a whole range of customs, political norms, and varieties of associational life had evolved. The emergence of a new kind of labor movement confronted the *Bürgertum* with equally unprecedented challenges at the local level. Attempts to incorporate workers into a system based on old notions of "civic law" *(Bürgerrecht)* and *bürgerlich* respectability were inappropriate to the circumstances of the 1860s. Still, just as Germany's cities were changing, so too was the *Bürgertum* radically transformed in the last decades of the nineteenth century. And though the "social liberalism" of the years between 1840 and 1870 may have been utopian, it would be a grievous error, the author insists, to assume that the estrangement between middle-class liberalism and the labor movement was preordained or that it necessarily persisted past the 1860s. In fact, Roth presents compelling evidence of liberal and labor cooperation at the municipal level, especially in the years leading up to World War I. Frankfurt am Main, which he examines in some detail, is a particularly important case in point, though by no means the only one.

Mary Jo Maynes initiates the very significant reconsideration of the SPD that runs through many of the chapters of this book. Beginning her study in 1890, Maynes notes that no models existed for a socialist party that could now operate in the open amid the semi-democratic conditions of Imperial Germany. The SPD, she argues, created a new model of militancy, a "movement culture" that allowed men and women to imagine themselves as committed activists, a key feature in the SPD's rapid growth. In contrast to much of the recent historical literature, Maynes finds that the party in the 1890s was highly attentive to women's concerns and to the need to organize women. By focusing on the almost routine, day-to-day activities of socialist militants, Maynes finds not a bureaucratized party, the lament of so many historical accounts of the

SPD, but a vibrant, innovative movement that helped define the nature of mass politics and provided the setting in which working-class women and men forged their identities.

Jonathan Sperber continues the volume's reassessment of the SPD by looking in provocative new ways at the social democratic electorate in Imperial Germany. Using a sophisticated set of statistical methods, Sperber challenges many older assumptions about the social composition of that electorate and the ways in which it changed over time. Especially noteworthy among his several important contributions are his ability to determine political party voting patterns from one election to the next and the effects of confession and social class on the population's electoral proclivities. Thus, for example, he demonstrates that it is incorrect to describe the SPD as a party of previous non-voters, especially after 1890. Many voters swung back and forth between the SPD and the liberal parties, and during the Wilhelmine years the Social Democrats extended their appeal to people who had previously voted for conservative or minority parties. Although the SPD never garnered more than twelve percent of Germany's Catholic vote, Sperber shows that the Social Democrats appealed quite successfully to middle-class as well as working-class Protestants. Thus, the author concludes that at no general election in Wilhelmine Germany was the SPD "exclusively, or even heavily, a party of blue-collar workers." Rather, it was a party that garnered electoral support from all social groups, and significant support from several. In short, the Wilhelmine SPD – and not, as much of the historical literature has suggested, the Nazi party – was Germany's first real "people's party."

While Sperber examines the SPD on a national scale, Adelheid von Saldern penetrates the internal life of the party in the provincial town of Göttingen. Like Maynes, von Saldern is not content simply to bring to life social democratic activists; she shows how social democracy as a mass movement was shaped from below by the activities and attitudes of workers. Using an extraordinary source, the minutes of local party meetings, and police reports, von Saldern depicts the deeply held and often contradictory attitudes and conceptions of Göttingen's Social Democrats. She finds that they had little understanding of formal Marxian theory and demonstrated an almost submissive attitude to party leaders in Hanover and Berlin. But they felt deeply the injustices and inequities of capitalism and the Imperial political system. They believed strongly in egalitarianism, a fair wage, and political rights, but shared in a patriarchal understanding of gender roles. Von Saldern shows how socialist reformism developed not only from the writings of party ideologues, but also from the character of everyday life and the subjective perspectives of workers in provincial towns like Göttingen.

David F. Crew shifts the focus to the social welfare state, one of the vaunted achievements of the Weimar Republic and of the SPD in particular. Social Democrats, Crew explains, viewed the state as an agent that could ameliorate the harsh regimen of capitalism and prepare society for the transition to socialism. But welfare policy became a highly contested terrain and the SPD found itself battered from right and left. While the SPD viewed welfare as a set of enlightened and progressive social policies, welfare practices fundamentally entailed heightened state intervention in the lives of the population. Social Democrats staffed many of the local welfare offices, and they brought their own disciplinary and scientistic attitudes to bear in the effort to "reform" the poor. Means testing led to investigations into the private lives not only of recipients, but of their entire extended families as well. Yet welfare clients were not passive recipients of bureaucratic decisions; they challenged the injustices they perceived in the administration of welfare policy and made welfare offices a new locus of popular protest. Their discontents made them an appealing group to Communists, who used the insufficiencies of welfare as a highly effective organizing tool.

The ultimate failure of the Weimar Republic and the rise to power of the Nazis has often been seen as the failure, especially, of the Weimar SPD. As Germany's largest party until it was surpassed by the Nazis in the summer of 1932, the SPD provided the key support for the Republic. Even when out of power at the national level, Social Democrats dominated many state *(Land)* and local governments. Yet by 1932, with Germany's economy engulfed in depression, its Republic subject to unrelenting attacks from all sides, the SPD could no longer summon the strength and enthusiasm to defend its proudest achievement. Or so it has seemed. Donna Harsch, challenging received understandings, radically recasts the picture of the SPD in the end phase of the Republic. She shows how the Iron Front, a coalition of the SPD and its ancillary organizations, adopted new techniques of political organization, an aesthetic and psychological modernism modeled on the NSDAP's tactics and, in a less suspect fashion, modern social psychology. For a brief moment, the new strategy regenerated the SPD rank and file and drove the Nazis on the defensive. The SPD was not simply a bureaucratized, moribund organization, and its commitment to political liberties and social egalitarianism could still inspire the profound sense of enthusiasm that marked the party from its very beginning. Weimar social democracy, Harsch suggests, responded creatively to the threats posed by the Nazis.

Eric D. Weitz turns to the other major party of German labor in the Weimar Republic, the KPD. German communism, he argues, developed amid the highly contested, intensely active public spheres of the Republic. The democratic contours of the polity, the associational traditions of the German labor movement, economic rationalization and depression, and mass, popular culture all contributed to the forging of the KPD's particularly intransigent, masculinized political culture. Like many of the other contributors, Weitz contends that the everyday patterns of social life decisively shaped the nature of German socialism and communism. He thereby challenges the prevailing tendency to define the KPD as a mere appendage of the Soviet Union.

In his contribution to this volume, William Carl Mathews reminds us again of the importance of regional factors in the history of German socialism. His essay focuses on the fate of social democracy in Saxony, the heartland of socialism in Germany since the 1860s. The working-class milieu that figures so prominently in several of this book's essays was especially vivid and especially vigorous in Saxony. At the same time, the Saxon SPD had gained substantial middle-class support, especially from people employed in the public sector. Moreover, during the early Weimar years the Saxon SPD served as a party of government without the burden of bourgeois coalition partners. Thus, the steady decline of Saxon social democracy after the hyperinflation of 1923 was particularly dramatic. Mathews convincingly attributes that decline to a complex array of factors, among them the difficulties of carrying out far-reaching reforms with a narrow support base, the complexities of coalition politics, structural crises within the Saxon industrial economy, and the transformation of the socialist milieu itself.

The emancipatory claims of socialism and communism have given the movements their mass support and dynamic character. Yet the socialist labor movement never organized a majority of German workers, and the competition with conservatives and liberals, Catholics and Protestants, was intense. In the twentieth century, the SPD and KPD/SED also found that mass, commercial culture provided an even more beguiling competitor, a problem Geoff Eley explores in his chapter. The Left, far from recognizing its emancipatory potential, archly condemned and even anathematized popular culture. The Left's hostility to cultural and social experimentation, its unceasing efforts to intervene and reshape popular life in a uniform and partly repressive manner, reveals the underlying disciplinary tendencies of both the SPD and KPD. More fatally, their disastrous shortcomings in this area enabled the fascists to lay successful claim to the worlds of pleasure and desire. In this analysis of popular culture and the Left, Eley also develops an incisive critique of Jürgen Habermas's highly influential concept of the public sphere, which, Eley contends, has to be seen as a site of conflict imbued with gendered understandings of politics and the family. Moreover, the boundaries of the public sphere need to be radically broadened beyond the "classical" bourgeois universe that Habermas depicted to include the broad, messy arenas of popular politics. The public sphere is never singular and is always replete with exclusions. To understand adequately its workings – including those in which the German Left operated – Eley advocates adding to Habermas the theoretical contributions of Antonio Gramsci, Michel Foucault, modern social history, and contemporary feminism.

The Nazi assumption of power in January 1933 led to the almost immediate repression of the socialist and communist parties. Thousands upon thousands of activists were imprisoned, killed, or driven into exile, while the parties themselves were forcibly separated from the working-class milieus that had given them their dynamic character. Many activists sustained an heroic if ultimately unsuccessful resistance against the Third Reich. Gerd-Rainer Horn examines resistance at the base level in the first years of the dictatorship. Creatively using SPD underground and Gestapo reports, he finds widespread potential for labor unity despite the long-standing bitterness of the socialist-communist split. Horn also finds a great deal of conflict between social democratic activists in Germany and the Sopade, the exiled leadership in Prague. The activists were far more militant, far more intent on resistance against the Nazis and cooperation with the Communists than the Sopade, which remained encased in the outlook of the Weimar SPD.

Beatrix Herlemann explores the nature of communist resistance in the Third Reich. Like Horn's study of the SPD, she finds significant conflicts between underground KPD activists in Germany and the exiled leadership. The leaders held on longer to the completely illusory and disastrous notion that the Nazis would not long remain in power and would soon be succeeded by the communists. Moreover, the KPD's hierarchical structure made the party relatively easy prey for the Gestapo. Rank-and-file activists, those who experienced Nazi terror first hand, helped force a change in party strategy in 1935 that accorded with the decisions of the Seventh Comintern Congress. The KPD finally decentralized its structure and began advocating unity of action with the SPD. But even these decisive departures could not dent Nazi hegemony, nor forestall the leadership's almost inevitable return to its more centralized and authoritarian tendencies.

The catastrophe of 1933 encouraged many German socialists – including members of the social democratic "establishment" in exile – to think in new ways about the past, the future, and the adequacy of the socialist project itself. Among those exiles, as David E. Barclay describes in his contribution to this volume, was Rudolf Hilferding, who before 1933 had enjoyed a deserved reputation as German social democracy's most important theorist after Karl Kautsky. Before his arrest and tragic death in Gestapo custody in 1941, Hilferding had begun to sketch out important ideas about the nature of the modern state, the relationship between democracy and socialism, and the future reorganization of Europe. Hilferding's writings in exile, thus, represent a kind of intellectual bridge between the older SPD of Bebel and Kautsky and the postwar party of Brandt and Schmidt.

The utter defeat of Nazi Germany in 1945 brought no *tabula rasa*, no "zero hour," as Germans labeled it. Germany had been devastated and twelve years of National Socialist rule had wrought immense transformations. But when Socialists and Communists began to rebuild their movements, they inevitably drew on long standing traditions even as their own varied trajectories during the twelve years of the Third Reich – exile in the west or in the Soviet Union, underground resistance, concentration camps – and the unprecedented postwar situation led them toward new ideas and forms of organization. Diethelm Prowe explores the mix of tradition and innovation in the policies of the trade unions amid the catastrophic social and economic conditions of the immediate postwar years. The union leaders were not shortsighted bureaucrats who could barely move beyond their Weimar perspectives, nor the saps of German and U.S. capital. They were remarkably flexible, sure-footed leaders whose specific policy adaptations all rested on the underlying, and ultimately successful, determination to play a central role in the reconstruction of the country and in the shaping of postwar German society. They abandoned their initial commitment to economic planning, that hallowed element of social democratic ideology, for the famed "social market economy." In return, they won an implicit commitment to rising wages, an extensive social welfare program, and the ongoing voice of the unions in the councils of the state and economy.

Norman Naimark turns to the eastern zone of occupation and the interactions between German communists and their Soviet mentors. Using Soviet and German archives that have been open to scholars only in the last few years, Naimark provides a panoramic view of Soviet policies and of the myriad elements of the German Left, many of whom were Weimar Communists who had emerged from concentration camps and the underground in the waning days of the war. Isolated from the larger currents of Allied politics and Soviet directives, they sought to revive the intransigence of Weimar communism with its emphasis on hard-fought, proletarian class struggle. Yet such revolutionary efforts undoubtedly would have alienated large segments of the population and, most importantly, hardly accorded with the aims of the Soviets and their German dependents. Instead, the communist leadership in the eastern zone moved quickly to secure administrative powers and leveled the free-floating charge of "sectarianism" against all those who refused to fall in line behind the circumscribed understanding of "socialism" promoted by the Soviet Administration in Germany and the KPD/SED.

Weimar Germany's vibrant political and cultural life had included very intense, public debates over gender and reproductive rights. Weimar's sex reformers, including many associated with the SPD and KPD, had been driven into exile or concentration camps as the Nazis instituted their own particularly brutal version of gender politics. But immediately at war's end, the politics of reproduction re-emerged as a central element in the debate on the shaping of postwar society. As Atina Grossmann shows, the decimation of the population in the war and the intense misery of the immediate postwar years lent new urgency to long-standing fears about the declining birthrate. In the eastern zone, the focus of Grossmann's attention, the huge incidence of rape made reproductive issues even more trenchant. Many veterans of the Weimar labor and sex reform movements returned to the eastern zone in the hope of implementing at long last their public health and reproductive commitments. They set to work immediately – ironically, alongside many Nazi physicians – performing thousands of abortions, and also campaigned for the abolition of paragraph 218, the law that largely criminalized abortions. In 1947, the states and provinces of the SBZ passed liberal abortion laws, but shortly after the foundation of the DDR abortion was again criminalized. Even Communists, Grossmann points out, joined in a broad pronatalist consensus that granted the state – in this case, a "workers' and peasants' state" – the right to "protect" the *Volkskörper* through intervention and restriction of reproductive rights.

Dietrich Orlow explores the contradictory, at times self-defeating character of SPD policies toward European unity. The longtime advocates of a supranational order found themselves continually stymied by their own ideologically based vision of a specifically socialist Europe, the realities of Cold War politics, and the adroit maneuvers of their domestic opponents, Konrad Adenauer and the Christian Democrats, in alliance with the United States. In the end, the SPD, along with its historic abandonment of Marxism at Bad Godesberg in 1959, also became reconciled to a more conservative form of European unity – a reconciliation that paved the way for the SPD's emergence as a ruling party in the late 1960s.

Ironically, the gender codes of the DDR were not all that different from those that prevailed in the Federal Republic, as Anna-Sabine Ernst demonstrates in her chapter. Drawing on the hugely popular etiquette books published in the 1950s and 1960s, Ernst shows how the SED advocated very traditional, hierarchical, and sexist models of behavior. The party hoped thereby to win the support of the middle classes in particular and to promote an orderly, productive society. Ernst's chapter demonstrates that the SED as a ruling party had abandoned the disruptive strategy of Weimar communism, but also shows how deeply the party-state was rooted in German cultural traditions of order and discipline.

Slow to adapt to the shifting discourse on European unity, as Dietrich Orlow notes in his chapter, the SPD was even slower to adapt to women's concerns and the transformations of women's status in postwar society. Skillfully interweaving policy analysis, social history, and women's narratives, Hanna Schissler depicts the contradictions embedded in the SPD's formal commitment to women's equality alongside its active support for the patriarchal culture of domesticity that dominated West Germany in the 1950s. Only very belatedly and under pressure from a new generation of educated women did the SPD begin to undertake reforms both within the party and in society that recognized the new status of women in affluent West Germany and lessened their rigid subordination.

Two concluding chapters ponder the destiny of the historic Social Democratic and Communist parties. In a thoughtful reflection on the recent evolution of the SPD, Peter Lösche describes the party's trajectory from what he calls an older "community of solidarity" during the Weimar years – a community based on the proletarian milieu that has figured so prominently in this volume – to its current condition of "loosely coupled anarchy." In Western Europe, North America, and Australasia, large political parties like the SPD have become "decentralized and fragmented service organizations in the political marketplace." The party is now exceptionally heterogeneous, and composed of a variety of pressure groups, interest groups, and semi-autonomous local groups. These trends reflect long-term shifts in occupational structures, demographic transformations, the role of the welfare state, educational reforms, and the steady secularization of the larger society. Although, as Lösche emphasizes, Social Democrats continue to be held together by a variety of shared political values, many of them rooted in the old labor movement, the SPD itself is no longer a labor party.

Eric D. Weitz provides an overview of the collapse of the DDR and the fate of the Party of Democratic Socialism (PDS), the SED's successor. He argues that despite the electoral achievements of the PDS in the new federal states, the epoch of communism is over. The PDS will retain support as a party of protest, but the working-class milieu that created the mass communist movement is now long gone, destroyed by war, the party dictatorship, and the enormous social and economic transformations of the late twentieth century. The labor movement no longer defines left-wing politics, and the PDS's future can only lie in a tension-filled alliance between the new social movements and the descendants of the working-class-based parties of the classic labor movement.

Notes

1. See the classic articles by Annie Kriegel, "Le parti modèle (La Social-Démocratie allemande et la IIe Internationale), in idem, *Le Pain et les roses: Jalons pour une histoire des socialismes* (Paris, 1968), 159-73, and J.P. Nettl, "The German Social Democratic Party 1890-1914 as a Political Model," *Past & Present* 30 (1965): 65-96.
2. For the concept of "milieu," see the classic essay by M. Rainer Lepsius, "Parteiensystem und Sozialstruktur: Zum Problem der Demokratisierung der deutschen Gesellschaft," in *Wirtschaft, Geschichte und Wirtschaftsgeschichte: Festschrift zum 65. Geburtstag von Friedrich Lütge*, ed. Wilhelm Abel (Stuttgart, 1966), 371-93. While the idea has been immensely fruitful, in its original version it was rather too pat; the formulation of an immediate and direct connection between milieu and party overlooked the many fault lines between the two. For a recent effective and critical appropriation of the concept, see Klaus-Michael Mallmann, *Kommunisten in der Weimarer Republik: Sozialgeschichte einer revolutionären Bewegung* (Darmstadt, 1996).
3. Roger Chickering, *Karl Lamprecht: A German Academic Life (1856-1915)* (Atlantic Highlands, NJ, 1993), 394.
4. For an excellent survey, see the "Einleitung" in Klaus Tenfelde and Gerhard A. Ritter, eds., *Bibliographie zur Geschichte der Arbeiterschaft und Arbeiterbewegung 1863 bis 1914: Berichtszeitraum 1945 bis 1975* (Bonn, 1981), 39-48.
5. Paul Kampffmeyer, an important SPD activist, should also be briefly mentioned here. Rather like Mehring, he wrote a pioneering general history of class relationships and class conflict in modern German history, attempting to locate the development of German socialism in the context of those larger conflicts. Paul Kampffmeyer, *Geschichte der modernen Gesellschaftsklassen in Deutschland: Ein politisch-wirtschaftliches und sozialkulturelles Bild deutscher Entwicklung*, 3d ed. (Berlin, 1921).
6. For a biographical sketch, see Christoph Stamm's entry in the *Neue Deutsche Biographie*, vol. 16 (Berlin, 1990), 623-25.
7. Mehring's history was republished in the German Democratic Republic as volumes 1 and 2 of Mehring's *Gesammelte Schriften*: Franz Mehring, *Geschichte der deutschen Sozialdemokratie*, 2 vols. (Berlin, 1980). His biography of Marx, *Karl Marx: Geschichte seines Lebens* (Berlin, 1979), is volume 3 in the same series.
8. Ibid., 1: 695.
9. Ibid., 2: 707.
10. Eduard Bernstein, ed., *Intime Briefe Lassalles* (Berlin, 1905); idem, ed., *Gesammelte Reden und Schriften Ferdinand Lassalles* (Berlin, 1919-20); idem, ed., *Briefwechsel zwischen Marx und Engels*, 4 vols. (Berlin, 1919).
11. Eduard Bernstein, *Die Geschichte der Berliner Arbeiter-Bewegung: Ein Kapitel der Geschichte der deutschen Sozialdemokratie*, 3 vols. (Berlin, 1907-10); idem, *Die Arbeiterbewegung* (Frankfurt am Main, 1910). Peter Gay's study of Bernstein's revisionism, *The Dilemma of Democratic Socialism: Eduard Bernstein's Challenge to Marx* (New York, 1952), remains indispensable.
12. See the discussion and extensive bibliography in Tenfelde and Ritter, *Bibliographie*, 85-89.
13. August Bebel, *Aus meinem Leben*, 3 vols. (Stuttgart, 1911-14); Philipp Scheidemann, *Memoiren eines Sozialdemokraten*, 2 vols. (Dresden, 1928); Theodor Leipart, *Carl Legien* (Berlin, 1929; reprinted Cologne, 1981).
14. Rudolf Wissell, *Des alten Handwerks Recht und Gewohnheit*, 2 vols. (Berlin, 1929); new edition edited by Ernst Schraepler, 6 vols. (Berlin, 1971-88).

15. Gustav Mayer, *Erinnerungen: Vom Journalisten zum Historiker der deutschen Arbeiterbewegung*, ed. Gottfried Niedhart (Hildesheim, 1993; orig. published 1949).
16. Gustav Mayer, *Johann Baptist von Schweitzer und die Sozialdemokratie: Ein Beitrag zur Geschichte der deutschen Arbeiterbewegung* (Berlin, 1909; reprinted Glashütten im Taunus, 1970).
17. Ferdinand Lassalle, *Nachgelassene Briefe und Schriften*, ed. Gustav Mayer, 6 vols. (Berlin, 1921-25; reprinted Osnabrück 1967); Gustav Mayer, *Friedrich Engels: Eine Biographie*, 2 vols. (Berlin and The Hague, 1920, 1934).
18. Among the writings published by prominent pre-1933 Social Democrats in exile, see esp. Friedrich Stampfer, *Die vierzehn Jahre der ersten deutschen Republik* (Karlsbad, 1936). Although not explicitly a history of the labor movement, it nevertheless places that history within the broader context of the history of the Weimar Republic.
19. Notably, Karl Dietrich Bracher, *Die Auflösung der Weimarer Republik: Eine Studie zum Problem des Machtverfalls in der Demokratie* (Stuttgart, 1955), and Fritz Fischer, *Griff nach der Weltmacht* (Düsseldorf, 1961), in English as *Germany's Aims in the First World War* (New York, 1967). The subject matter of the latter concerned the First World War, but the implication of continuity in German war aims between the two world wars inspired much of the controversy.
20. For a thorough account and analysis, see a number of the essays in James Van Horn Melton and Hartmut Lehmann, eds., *Paths of Continuity: Central European Historiography from the 1930s to the 1950s* (Cambridge, 1994).
21. Werner Conze, "Vom 'Pöbel' zum 'Proletariat': Sozialgeschichtliche Voraussetzungen für den Sozialismus in Deutschland," *Vierteljahrschrift für Sozial-und Wirtschaftsgeschichte* 41 (1954): 333-64. An English version, "From 'Pöbel' to 'Proletariat': The Socio-Historical Preconditions of Socialism in Germany," can be found in *The Social History of Politics: Critical Perspectives in West German Historical Writing since 1945*, ed. George Iggers (Leamington Spa, 1985), 49-80.
22. Gerhard A. Ritter, *Die Arbeiterbewegung im Wilhelminischen Reich: Die Sozialdemokratische Partei und die Freien Gewerkschaften 1890-1900* (Berlin, 1959), and Carl E. Schorske, *German Social Democracy 1905-1917: The Development of the Great Schism* (Cambridge, Mass., 1955). Note also Gay, *Dilemma of Democratic Socialism*.
23. Helga Grebing, *Geschichte der deutschen Arbeiterbewegung: Ein Überblick* (Munich, 1966); Hedwig Wachenheim, *Die deutsche Arbeiterbewegung 1844 bis 1914* (Cologne, 1967); Vernon Lidtke, *The Outlawed Party: Social Democracy in Germany, 1878-1890* (Princeton, 1966); Shlomo Na'aman, *Lassalle*, (Hanover, 1970).
24. Hans Mommsen, *Die Sozialdemokratie und die Nationalitätenfrage im habsburgischen Vielvölkerstaat* (Vienna, 1963).
25. Eberhard Kolb, *Die Arbeiterräte in der deutschen Innenpolitik* (Düsseldorf, 1962).
26. Ossip K. Flechtheim, *Die KPD in der Weimarer Republik* (Hamburg, 1986; orig. published 1948).
27. Werner Angress, *Stillborn Revolution: The Communist Bid for Power in Germany, 1921-1923* (Princeton, 1963).
28. See the series *Archivalische Forschungen zur Geschichte der Deutschen Arbeiterbewegung*, ed. Forschungsgemeinschaft "Dokumente und Materialien zur Geschichte der Deutschen Arbeiterbewegung," Leitung Prof. Dr. Leo Stern (Berlin, 1955ff.).
29. *Geschichte der deutschen Arbeiterbewegung*, 8 vols., ed. Institut für Marxismus-Leninismus beim Zentralkomitee der SED (Berlin, 1966).
30. *Geschichte der Deutschen Arbeiterbewegung*, vol. 1, 4.

31. For just a couple of examples, *Dokumente und Materialien zur Geschichte der KPD-Bezirksorganisation Halle-Merseburg bis 1933*, ed. Bezirksleitung Halle der SED, Kommission zur Erforschung der Geschichte der örtlichen Arbeiterbewegung (Halle, 1982); Irmtraud Dalchow, "Die Hallesche Maschinenfabrik und Eisengiesserei AG von ihrer Gründung bis zum Jahre 1918," *Aus der Geschichte der halleschen Arbeiterbewegung*, vol. 7, ed. Stadtleitung Halle der SED (Halle, n.d.).
32. Fischer, *Germany's Aims*.
33. For an excellent, brief discussion of these matters, see James Retallack, *Germany in the Age of Kaiser Wilhelm II* (New York, 1996), 9-13.
34. Hans-Ulrich Wehler, *Sozialdemokratie und Nationalstaat: Die deutsche Sozialdemokratie und die Nationalitätenfragen in Deutschland von Karl Marx bis zum Ausbruch des Ersten Weltkrieges* (Würzburg, 1962). Among his more important subsequent works were *Bismarck und der Imperialismus* (Cologne, 1969) and *Das deutsche Kaiserreich 1871-1918* (Göttingen, 1973), available in English as *The German Empire, 1871-1918* (Leamington Spa, 1985).
35. Richard N. Hunt, *German Social Democracy, 1918-1933* (New Haven, Conn., 1964); Robert F. Wheeler, *USPD und Internationale: Sozialistischer Internationalismus in der Zeit der Revolution* (Frankfurt am Main, 1975); David W. Morgan, *The Socialist Left and the German Revolution: A History of the German Independent Social Democratic Party, 1917-1922* (Ithaca, NY, 1975); Joseph Rovan, *Histoire de la Social-Démocratie allemande* (Paris, 1978); W.L. Guttsman, *The German Social Democratic Party, 1875-1933: From Ghetto to Government* (London, 1981); Dieter Groh, *Negative Integration und revolutionärer Attentismus: Die deutsche Sozialdemokratie am Vorabend des Ersten Weltkrieges* (Frankfurt am Main, 1973); Susanne Miller, *Burgfrieden und Klassenkampf: Die deutsche Sozialdemokratie im Ersten Weltkrieg* (Düsseldorf, 1974); idem, *Die Bürde der Macht: Die deutsche Sozialdemokratie 1918-1920* (Düsseldorf, 1978).
36. Among many titles, see Ulrich Engelhardt, *"Nur vereinigt sind wir stark": Die Anfänge der deutschen Gewerkschaftsbewegung 1862/63 bis 1869/70*, 2 vols. (Stuttgart, 1977); Heinrich Potthoff, *Gewerkschaften und Politik zwischen Revolution und Inflation* (Düsseldorf, 1979); idem, *Freie Gewerkschaften 1918-1933: Der Allgemeine Deutsche Gewerkschaftsbund in der Weimarer Republik* (Düsseldorf, 1987); Klaus Schönhoven, *Expansion und Konzentration: Studien zur Entwicklung der freien Gewerkschaften im Wilhelminischen Deutschland 1890 bis 1914* (Stuttgart, 1980); John Anthony Moses, *Trade Unionism in Germany from Bismarck to Hitler, 1869-1933*, 2 vols. (London, 1982); Ulrich Borsdorf, ed., *Geschichte der deutschen Gewerkschaften von den Anfängen bis 1945* (Cologne, 1987); Michael Schneider, *Kleine Geschichte der Gewerkschaften: Ihre Entwicklung in Deutschland von den Anfängen bis heute* (Bonn, 1989). Written from a much more aggressively "leftist" position is Frank Deppe, Georg Fülberth, and Jürgen Harrer, eds., *Geschichte der deutschen Gewerkschaftsbewegung*, 2nd ed. (Cologne, 1978).
37. Jürgen Kocka, *Klassengesellschaft im Krieg: Deutsche Sozialgeschichte 1914-1918* (Göttingen, 1973); Gerald D. Feldman, *Army, Industry, and Labor in Germany, 1914-1918* (Princeton, 1966); idem, *Iron and Steel in the German Inflation, 1916-1923* (Princeton, 1977); idem, *The Great Disorder: Politics, Economics, and Society in the German Inflation, 1914-1924* (New York and Oxford, 1993).
38. Again, among many works by many authors see Klaus Tenfelde, *Sozialgeschichte der Bergarbeiterschaft an der Ruhr im 19. Jahrhundert* (Bonn-Bad Godesberg, 1977); idem, *Proletarische Provinz: Radikalisierung und Widerstand in Penzberg/Oberbayern 1920-1945* (Munich, 1982); Gerhard A. Ritter, ed., *Arbeiterkultur* (Königstein/Taunus, 1979); Klaus Tenfelde and Heinrich Volkmann, eds., *Streik:*

Zur Geschichte des Arbeitskampfes in Deutschland während der Industrialisierung (Munich, 1981).

39. Among many works, see E.P. Thompson, *The Making of the English Working Class* (New York, 1963); Stephan Thernstrom's important work on social mobility, such as *Poverty and Progress: Social Mobility in a Nineteenth-Century City* (Cambridge, Mass., 1964); or Herbert G. Gutman, *Work, Culture, and Society and Industrializing America: Essays in American Working-Class and Social History* (New York, 1976).
40. David F. Crew, *Town in the Ruhr: A Social History of Bochum, 1860-1914* (New York, 1979); Mary Nolan, *Social Democracy and Society: Working-Class Radicalism in Düsseldorf, 1890-1920* (Cambridge, Mass., 1981).
41. See such collections as Richard J. Evans and W.R. Lee, eds., *The German Family: Essays on the Social History of the Family in Nineteenth- and Twentieth-Century Germany* (London, 1981); Richard J. Evans, ed., *The German Working Class, 1888-1933: The Politics of Everyday Life* (London, 1982); Richard J. Evans and Dick Geary, eds., *The German Unemployed: Experiences and Consequences of Mass Unemployment from the Weimar Republic to the Third Reich* (Beckenham, Kent, 1987). See also Evans's subsequent work, such as *Death in Hamburg: Society and Politics in the Cholera Years 1830-1910* (Oxford, 1987); *Comrades and Sisters: Feminism, Socialism, and Pacifism in Europe, 1870-1945* (Brighton, 1987); and the work of other historians active in the U. K., including Dick Geary, *European Labour Protest 1848-1939* (London, 1981), and Eve Rosenhaft, *Beating the Fascists? The German Communists and Political Violence, 1929-1933* (Cambridge, Mass., 1983).
42. Jürgen Kuczynski, *Die Geschichte der Lage der Arbeiter unter dem Kapitalismus*, 38 vols. (Berlin, 1960ff.); Dieter Fricke, *Die deutsche Arbeiterbewegung 1869 bis 1914: Ein Handbuch über ihre Organisation und Tätigkeit im Klassenkampf* (Berlin, 1976); idem, *Handbuch zur Geschichte der deutschen Arbeiterbewegung 1869 bis 1917*, 2 vols. (Berlin, 1987).
43. Hartmut Zwahr, *Zur Konstituierung des Proletariats als Klasse: Strukturuntersuchung über das Leipziger Proletariat während der industriellen Revolution* (Berlin, 1978).
44. Hans-Ulrich Wehler, *Deutsche Gesellschaftsgeschichte*, 3 vols. to date (Munich, 1987). The following have so far appeared in the series edited by Gerhard A. Ritter, "Geschichte der Arbeiter und der Arbeiterbewegung in Deutschland seit dem Ende des 18. Jahrhunderts": Jürgen Kocka, *Weder Stand noch Klasse: Unterschichten um 1800* (Bonn, 1990); idem, *Arbeitsverhältnisse und Arbeiterexistenzen: Grundlagen der Klassenbildung im 19. Jahrhundert* (Bonn, 1990); Gerhard A. Ritter and Klaus Tenfelde, *Arbeiter im deutschen Kaiserreich 1871 bis 1914* (Bonn, 1992); Heinrich August Winkler, *Von der Revolution zur Stabilisierung: Arbeiter und Arbeiterbewegung in der Weimarer Republik 1918 bis 1924* (Berlin, 1984); idem, *Der Schein der Normalität: Arbeiter und Arbeiterbewegung in der Weimarer Republik 1924 bis 1930* (Berlin, 1985); idem, *Der Weg in die Katastrophe: Arbeiter und Arbeiterbewegung in der Weimarer Republik 1930 bis 1933*, 2nd ed. (Bonn, 1990).
45. For the most thoroughgoing critique, though not specifically from the vantage of labor and socialism, see David Blackbourn and Geoff Eley, *The Peculiarities of German History: Bourgeois Society and Politics in Nineteenth-Century Germany* (New York, 1984).
46. For a critique, see Kathleen Canning, "Gender and the Politics of Class Formation: Rethinking German Labor History," *American Historical Review* 97:3 (1992): 736-68.
47. For one excellent example, see Lenard Berlanstein, ed., *Rethinking Labor History: Essays on Discourse and Class Analysis* (Urbana, 1993), as well as Joan Wal-

lach Scott, *Gender and the Politics of History* (New York, 1988). For some early efforts to attend to the everyday in working-class life, see Evans, *German Working Class*, and a number of the subsequent volumes on family life and crime co-edited by Evans.

48. For the pathbreaking work, see Lutz Niethammer and Alexander von Plato, eds., *Lebensgeschichte und Sozialkultur im Ruhrgebiet 1930 bis 1960*, 3 vols. (Berlin, 1983-85), and more recently, Lutz Niethammer, Alexander von Plato, and Dorothee Wierling, *Die Volkseigene Erfahrung: Eine Archäologie des Lebens in der Industrieprovinz der DDR* (Berlin, 1991).
49. See especially Alf Lüdtke's many important articles, now collected in *Eigen-Sinn: Fabrikalltag, Arbeitererfahrungen und Politik vom Kaiserreich bis in den Faschismus* (Hamburg, 1993), as well as various issues of the journal *WerkstattGeschichte*. See also Alf Lüdtke, ed., *The History of Everyday Life: Reconstructing Historical Experiences and Ways of Life*, trans. William Templer (Princeton, 1995). For very positive assessments in English, Geoff Eley, "Labor History, Social History, *Alltagsgeschichte*: Experience, Culture, and the Politics of the Everyday – A New Direction for German Social History?" *Journal of Modern History* 61:2 (1989): 297-343, and David F. Crew, "*Alltagsgeschichte*: A New Social History from Below?" *Central European History* 22:3/4 (1989): 394-407.
50. Important early works are various chapters in Annette Kuhn et al., eds., *Frauen in der Geschichte* (Düsseldorf, 1979ff.); Karin Hausen, ed., *Frauen suchen ihre Geschichte: Historische Studien zum 19. und 20. Jahrhundert* (Munich, 1982); Renate Bridenthal, Atina Grossmann, and Marion Kaplan, eds., *When Biology Became Destiny: Women in Weimar and Nazi Germany* (New York, 1984); and Ruth-Ellen Joeres and Mary Jo Maynes, eds., *German Women in the Eighteenth and Nineteenth Centuries: A Social and Literary History* (Bloomington, Ind., 1986). Note also Heinz Niggemann, *Emanzipation zwischen Sozialismus und Feminismus: Die sozialdemokratische Frauenbewegung im Kaiserreich* (Wuppertal, 1981); Jean Quataert, *Reluctant Feminists in German Social Democracy, 1885-1917* (Princeton, 1979); and Richard J. Evans, *The Feminist Movement in Germany, 1894-1933* (London, 1976). For more recent works, see Karen Hagemann, *Frauenalltag und Männerpolitik: Alltagsleben und gesellschaftliches Handeln von Arbeiterfrauen in der Weimarer Republik* (Bonn, 1990); and Kathleen Canning, *Languages of Labor and Gender: Female Factory Work in Germany, 1850-1914* (Ithaca, NY, 1996).

Chapter 1

DIAGNOSING THE "GERMAN MISERY"

Radicalism and the Problem of National Character, 1830 to 1848

Warren Breckman

Although liberals, republican-democrats, and the tiny number of Germans who might retrospectively be called "socialist" were not oblivious to their differences in the 1830s, they all acknowledged common membership in the *Bewegungspartei*, the party of movement. Even by the standards of the loose factional groupings that acted politically in the German states of that time, however, the *Bewegungspartei* was less a real party than an invisible assembly of conscientious opponents of the reactionary monarchies of Germany. By the early 1840s, Karl Marx was not alone in recognizing that the crude division of German politics into opposing parties of "movement" and "resistance" had become untenable and was no longer adequate to a more complex reality. "Without parties there is no development," he wrote in 1842, and "without demarcation there is no progress."[1] In that same year, the progressive poets Georg Herwegh and Ferdinand Freiligrath quarreled publicly over the proper relationship between poets and party politics. Prompted by this debate, the prominent editor of the Left Hegelian *Hallische Jahrbücher*, Arnold Ruge, contended that the interests of the *Zeitgeist* were served neither by reactionaries who denied parties nor by an undifferentiated party of progress. The real aim of the question posed in the title of Ruge's article "Who Is and Who Is Not a Party?" was to discover *the* party which could carry the banner of the progressive spirit of the age.[2]

Notes for this chapter begin on page 57.

German radical politics during the 1840s was dominated by this question. No single party emerged as the clear leader of the Left in that decade, but by the time of the revolution in 1848, the relatively undifferentiated *Bewegungspartei* had split into groups that saw nearly as much to oppose in each other as in the princely regimes. Moreover, not only had the socialist Left recognized its grievance with liberalism, but Marx and Engels had swept away their rivals for the leadership of the far Left in Germany. Knocked out of contention were the republican-democrats, the Young Hegelians, and the "True Socialists," those utopians who based their socialism on the philosophic humanism of Ludwig Feuerbach. Of course, it was not until the 1880s, after the many bleak years following the failed Revolution of 1848, that Marxism came to dominate socialist politics in Germany; but Marx and Engels's success prior to 1848 may be measured by the conversion of the radical German exiles in Paris, London, Brussels, and Switzerland from Jacobinism and Christian or utopian socialism to "scientific" communism. They changed the name of their "League of the Just" to the "League of Communists" and appointed Marx and Engels to write their party manifesto in 1847.

That famous text declares that the global spread of capitalism has stripped the proletariat of every trace of national character. Though the *Communist Manifesto* deemed the proletarian conquest of national power a tactical necessity, it reasoned that communist revolution must inevitably be international since the universal force of capitalism may only be overturned by the universal class which is its product. Radical internationalism was the most historically fateful claimant to the banner of progressive politics in the 1840s. However, this essay will show that socialist internationalism was itself channeled in the tracks of a specific German left-wing discourse about the problems of German national character. Consider the following portraits of national character drawn by men who were on the left of the political spectrum in their respective eras. In 1800, Friedrich Schiller wrote that the Germans are "chosen by the world spirit, in the midst of ephemeral struggles, to work on the eternal edifice of humanity."[3] Decades later, Ferdinand Lassalle declared it the mission of the German *Volk* to lead the way to the universal freedom of all humanity.[4] On the other hand, Heinrich Heine observed in the 1830s that "a German's patriotism means that his heart contracts and shrinks like leather in the cold, and a German then hates everything foreign, no longer wants to become a citizen of the world, a European, but only a provincial German."[5] Or, again, Engels described the Germans as the "philistines of world history"; and, in 1890, he claimed that the German "*Spießbürgertum* ... remains stuck even as the movement of history again seizes Germany; [this character] was strong enough to impress upon all German classes a general German type."[6] How should one make sense of the conflict between these representations of Germanness within the German Left? One answer, of course, would be to distinguish between a nationalist and an internationalist Left in nineteenth-century Germany. That was Marx and Engels's strategy when they criticized the Lassallean socialists in the 1860s and 1870s. Yet that poses the alternatives too sharply. These conflicting representations of German national character should be understood, rather, as dynamically interrelated aspects of the self-understanding of the German Left in the nineteenth century.

This essay will show how the tension and interplay between these images of Germanness coalesced into a defining feature of German radicalism after the defeat of revolutionary hopes in the early 1830s. During the 1840s, the ambiguity of the left-wing perception of German character underlay a vital positional strategy in the German Left's internecine struggles for self-clarification and differentiation. In each of the key ideological confrontations in that crucial decade, the relationship between the "universal" and merely "parochial" elements of German character was a crucial point of contention. Through the answers that radicals gave to this question, they claimed for themselves the "universal" content of the German character while accusing their rivals of embodying the parochial qualities of Germanness. Hence, the left-wing discourse about national character became a powerful rhetorical vehicle for the substantive discussion of radical strategies and goals that defined the German Left in the 1840s. Contrary to much of the earlier scholarship on the history and theory of early socialism, then, this essay is less concerned with the pronouncements of left-wing intellectuals on the nationality problem than with the role played by the diagnosis of national character in the process of theoretical development and political identity-formation.

1.

By the early nineteenth century, the image of Germany as the land of poets and philosophers, of spirit and inwardness, had gained a firm hold over the imaginations of both Germans and foreigners. This was the representation of Germanness popularized by Madame de Staël throughout Europe, and it survived long into twentieth-century literature and historiography in the figure of the "unpolitical German." Chauvinist "anti-revolutionary" nationalists could find solace in this portrait of the German character, since it appeared to promise an obedient citizenry. Surprisingly, progressive Germans also viewed these characteristics as Germany's greatest virtues, not as political liabilities. So, for instance, it was a common assumption of the Prussian Reform Era that these qualities of soulful introspection and reflection had helped Germans to avoid the violence of revolution and civil war, while still allowing them to embark on an ambitious course of reform.

Philosophers divined an even more illustrious meaning in the Germans' special affinity for spirit. At the end of the eighteenth century, rationalist universalism was the common coin of the German Enlightenment. The cosmopolitan humanism of Herder, Kant, Lessing, and other *Aufklärer* did not utterly vanish with the Romantic reaction against the Enlightenment, but in the first years of the nineteenth century there was a noticeable tendency to identify universalism as a particularly German trait. Schiller was not alone in his belief that Germany was chosen by the World Spirit to fulfill the potential of all humanity. Novalis assigned a special role to Germany in the restoration of universal Christendom because of what he thought was Germany's greater immunity to the corrosive atheism of western Europe. Others seized upon Herder's claims for the purity of the German language to insist on Germany's special status.[7] This could quickly slide into chauvinism, as it did in Ernst Moritz Arndt, Joseph Görres, and Friedrich Ludwig Jahn; but for Schiller and even for Fichte in his *Addresses to the German Nation*, German specialness was expected to serve the general cause of humanity. For many progressive-minded Germans, the idea that Germany had a unique cosmopolitan mission was not incompatible with the goal of a national – even a democratic-national – state. Nonetheless, it is also easy to see this representation of Germanness as a consolation for the absence of a unified German state. Universality of spirit cancelled out political fragmentation and particularity; indeed, the celebrated universality of the Germans depended precisely on the obstacles to forming narrower political identities in Germany.[8]

It was Hegel's conception of German universality that proved most influential among German progressives in the early nineteenth century. According to Hegel, the German Protestant Reformation had demonstrated the essential freedom of the Christian message by creating a religion of free individualism. Freedom became identical with the "Protestant principle," the emergence and development of which formed the core and content of Hegel's idea of modern history. Hegel did not tie this Protestant ideal to a narrow national or confessional context, for he traced two paths in the modern history of freedom. One path culminated in the critical rationalism of Kant, the theoretical liberation of the human intellect from all received beliefs; but it was the French Revolution, albeit in an imperfect and problematic way, that made the Protestant principle the standard of the world, the principle on which all true political and social order must be built. Hegel, thus, insisted on a parallel between the German revolution in spirit and the French revolution in politics that was to have a long career among German progressives in the early nineteenth century.[9] The parallel was not perfect, however, because both paths finally converged once again in Germany, or, to be more precise, in Hegel himself. That is, the full realization of the Protestant principle was to be found in Hegel's mediation of the inner and exterior, German and French, histories of freedom.

2.

The identification of Germany with universality was never without its critics, who included both ethnic nationalists and monarchists. By the early 1830s, some German radicals had also begun to question the representation of German identity celebrated by progressive Germans since the 1790s. Their disaffection stemmed from growing frustration with the failure of the German states to grant civic freedoms after Napoleon's defeat. This disillusionment deepened in the years after the French Revolution of 1830, when reactionary governments and indifferent publics derailed radical hopes for revolutionary change in Germany. The July Revolution did much to rekindle republican and democratic sentiment in Germany, suppressed since the Carlsbad Decrees of 1819 by rigorous censorship and bans on political organization.[10] Like the German Jacobins of the 1790s or the democratic-nationalist *Burschenschaftler* of the late 1810s, the democrats of the 1830s identified the German *Volk* as the indivisible sovereign power that transcends the fragmentation and particularism of old-regime Germany.[11] They combined nationalist demands for a unified German republic with cosmopolitan respect for human and civil rights and a utopian vision of a future brotherhood of nations. Both themes figured prominently in the speeches delivered to the great crowd gathered at the Hambach Festival in May 1832 and in the writings of young democrats like Jakob Venedey, Georg Büchner, Ludwig Börne, Heine, or the Young Germans.[12]

If the republicans of the early 1830s embraced the populist-democratic language of Jacobin nationalism, however, circumstances undermined the synthesis of democratic nationalism and cosmopolitanism. In the years of struggle against Napoleon, many of the leading German nationalists had renounced their hopes for a democratic *Volk* in favor of an ethnic and linguistic-cultural concept of national identity that could neutralize revolutionary impulses and rally rulers and subjects, aristocrats and commoners, to the defense of a shared German identity. The dominance of demagogic, anti-democratic, and virulently anti-French nationalism in Germany by 1830 meant that republicans had to fight not only princes and aristocrats but also nationalists who claimed to speak for the genuine interests and aspirations of the *Volk*. Under the strain of this two-front war, some of the greatest democratic publicists of the 1830s grew skeptical of the possibility of uniting a benign love of Fatherland with a cosmopolitan, democratic orientation. Compounding this skepticism, the new German democrats had to contend with the cumulative disappointments of two revolutions, 1789 and 1830, that had now come and gone without stirring the German people.

Although republicans continued to address the German *Volk*, often from foreign exile, their appeals were deeply ambivalent. Like many eighteenth-century critics of despotism, the radicals of the 1830s held potentially conflicting views on the relationship between national character and political change. On the one hand, it was commonly believed that political systems determine a people's character. Hence, it was argued, because the existing *Volk* languished under despotism, its character had been corrupted and stood in urgent need of redemption. Radical democratic appeals to the *Volk* were directed less to this present reality than to a potentiality for action that slumbered in the subjects of tyrannous regimes. The real *Volk* would emerge only as it stirred into political action, and its moral and political virtues would be cultivated only as it struggled for political rights.[13] On the other hand, theorists of republicanism since at least Montesquieu and Rousseau had believed that republics depend upon the virtue of the people.[14] The relationship of national character to republicanism was conceived in two different ways, as cause and as effect; that is, the *Volk* was considered simultaneously as the agent of revolution and also as its product. The experiences of German history since 1789 brought this ambiguity into the foreground of republican rhetoric, and so the hortatory tone of the republicans of the 1830s mingled with despair. Either the revolutionary writer could accept the burden of embodying all the latent virtues of the *Volk* while waiting for the leviathan to awaken; or, as Theodor Mundt speculated, he could take in the "defects of the German nationality like a poison" in the hopes of purifying the German national character through the strength of his own immunity.[15]

Radicals continued to blame the corruption of the *Volk* on the crippling effects of foreign and domestic tyrants, but the evidence of the past fifty years suggested that the people's apathy was due to a flaw in character, rather than a deficit of liberty. With this disturbing possibility clearly posed, the democrats appealed to a *Volk* that seemed increasingly distant from the real people of the real Germany. For example, Heine wrote that "the German is by nature servile, and the concerns of the *Volk* are never popular concerns in Germany."[16] Likewise, when the conservative historian Friedrich Raumer complained that among Europeans, Germans had cultivated a unique taste for attacking their homeland, Ludwig Börne conceded that the exiles of France, Spain, and Poland did not accuse their homelands, but only their governments. In those countries, he wrote, "the entire *Volk* fights for its freedom," whereas in Germany the defenders of freedom are betrayed by the people. "The German patriots will be defeated," he predicted, "not by their enemies, but by the cowardice of their friends."[17]

In seeking an explanation for the failure of the Germans that went beyond merely blaming governments, some radicals began to challenge the dominant representation of the German national character. What had appeared as positive virtues to Schiller, Hegel, or Schlegel were now recast as severe liabilities. This revaluation is forcefully presented in Börne's famous *Menzel, der Franzosenfresser*, published in 1837 to rebut the anti-French and anti-democratic nationalism of the literary critic Wolfgang Menzel. In the crucible of Börne's anger, the positive virtues of the Germans were recast as severe liabilities:

> *With a people that, despite its spiritual power and its spiritual freedom, does not know how to free itself from a censor that destroys this power and this freedom; a people that subjects itself to those most weak in spirit; a people that despite a prosperity that lifts all the cares of life; a people that despite its virtue and morality has never achieved what other peoples without spiritual power, spiritual freedom, virtue, or prosperity knew how to gain ... such a people must be an entirely unique case.*

Börne underlined the clear limitations of an excessive valorization of spiritual freedom: "What is there to extol in spiritual freedom? Who is not spiritually free? One is free in this sense everywhere and at all times, whether in jail, on the stake, in the wilderness of exile, in a horde of fools, or at the table of cruel, bloodthirsty, and drunken tyrants."[18] Börne demanded for Germans the less exalted freedom that might come with rights and a constitution. Yet here he was deeply skeptical about the chances of Germans winning such liberties for themselves. After all, he was a man who attributed the passivity of Shakespeare's Hamlet to the Danish Prince's study of German philosophy at Wittenberg.[19] Surveying German history, Börne saw only a story of failure, beginning with the Protestant Reformation, that quintessential German event. Instead of accepting the older narrative that ascribed universal significance to the Reformation, he denounced Luther as "the very model of the German philosopher, with all the virtues and faults of his nationality." Whereas Hegel had identified the Protestant principle with the course of freedom itself, Börne blamed the Reformation's personalistic spiritualism for the Germans' political incapacities.[20]

Radicals of the 1830s reinterpreted the features of the German national character not as universal, but as private attributes. Private virtues became public vices in the estimation of republicans who hoped to create a genuine public life in Germany, with publicly shared sovereignty, civic virtue, openness, and freedom of the press. Republican ideology had long perceived a tension between the private and the public, literally understood as the *res publica*; but only among German republicans did privacy become synonymous with a specific national trait. The dichotomy of public and private was to play a powerful role in the rhetoric of democrats and socialists in the 1840s, but here we must note that in the 1830s the Germans' alleged obsession with privacy and personal security, even at the expense of political liberty and public virtue, became synonymous with "philistinism" and "*Spießbürgerlichkeit.*" From being the "philosopher" and "poet," the spiritually endowed and poetically soulful German became the philistine or "*Spießbürger.*" The German "type" to which Engels referred in 1890 was essentially invented when disillusioned republicans in the 1830s applied these epithets to the German character. Since the mid-1700s, when philistinism had been used polemically at Halle to designate people not associated with the university, the philistine had been associated with narrowness of mind, but generally its meaning was restricted to matters of intellectual cultivation and artistic taste. Now, it was directly applied to political narrowness. The term *Spießbürger* had entered German usage in historical writing to describe the spear-carrying infantry-citizen of ancient Sparta. The term was quickly translated from an antiquarian to a contemporary reference; by 1800, *Spießbürgerlichkeit* denoted plebeianism in social contexts and philistinism in cultural contexts. The term also took on more explicit political connotations. So, for example, Jean Paul distinguished in 1804 between the *Spießbürger* and the *Staatsbürger*. Still, it was only in the 1830s that the contrast of the *Spießbürger*, the servile private subject of a despotic regime, to the *Staatsbürger*, the proud citizen of a free state, became common to the rhetoric of German social and political critics.

This process of disillusionment and rethinking did not, however, mean the total abandonment of the older association of the German identity with the universal task of emancipating humankind. Radicals like Börne, Heine, and Moses Hess maintained that the German spiritual revolution, begun by Luther and consummated by the critical idealism of Kant and Hegel, did indeed have a universal meaning, because the Germans had liberated the intellect from the bondage of received beliefs. It was this conviction that underlaid a counterfactual view of Germany as the ultimate seedbed of all revolutions.[21] But they each considered this spiritual revolution inadequate when measured against their desire to translate theory into practice, inward freedom into political and social freedom. This orientation toward the practical led many radicals in the 1830s to look to France for the salvation of Germany. That is, the presumed strength of the French national character, its political activism, would supplement the passivity of the German character and bring German spiritualism into the world. So profound was Börne's belief that the French democrats, the "guardians of Europe's peoples," would remedy the German malady that he gauged true German patriotism by the extent to which Germans loved France.[22]

Numerous others, notably Heine and some of the Young Germans, like Karl Gutzkow, Heinrich Laube, and Ludolf Wienbarg, began to question the relevance of the French Revolution's political ideals to an age of industrialism and increasing pauperism; but here, too, the first German advocates of social revolution found in the new French social thought, particularly Saint-Simonianism, a key to the transition from German spiritual radicalism to a new political and social order.[23] The need for a mutually reinforcing alliance of French social thought and the German philosophical avant-garde became a central theme in Moses Hess's *Holy History of Humanity* (1837), the obscure work that has been called the first socialist book written in Germany; such an alliance informs August Cieszkowski's *Prolegomena zur Historiosophie* (1838); and, of course, it became a preoccupation of radicals like Ludwig Feuerbach, Arnold Ruge, and Karl Marx who wanted to forge links between the Hegelian Left and French socialism. Right up to 1848, the German Left, including Marx and Engels to an extent, never fully freed itself from what one commentator calls a "metaphysic of character," whereby the alleged "principle" of each leading nation of the world made a unique contribution to the emancipation of humanity.[24] Yet it is essential to note that the circumstances of the 1830s exposed an ambiguity that had always been latent in the paradoxical identification of Germanness with universality. That is, in the 1830s, the positive ideal of German universality became increasingly detached from any real reference to Germany, which was now branded the land of philistines and *Spießbürger*. Radicals claimed for themselves one portion of the German affinity for "spirit," while condemning Germans precisely for their preoccupation with personal spirituality and private virtue. This unstable image of the German national character proved a volatile element in the series of ideological confrontations that transformed the German Left in the 1840s.

3.

In the late 1830s and early 1840s, the Young Hegelians played a vital role in defining the course of German radicalism. The Hegelian philosophers David Friedrich Strauß, Bruno Bauer, and Ludwig Feuerbach first gained notoriety in the late 1830s for their fundamental critique of Christianity.[25] Strauß's *The Life of Jesus* (1835) established the two crucial features of the Young Hegelian critique of religion: the exposure of humanity as the real object of religious devotion and the employment of alienation and recovery of human essence through the critical exposure of the anthropological truth of religion. The Young Hegelians' relentlessly critical spirit soon led them from critiques of religion to a rejection of speculative philosophy, including that of Hegel, the autonomy of which they denied by tracing philosophy's deepest impulses to the illusions of religion. The collapse of Hegelian metaphysics scattered the Young Hegelians. Bauer adopted a promethean stance as the "terrorist of reason," determined to negate all constraints on the expression of human self-consciousness. Feuerbach looked for the true essence of humanity in a philosophy of social and material life. Still others sought to exit philosophy altogether, to replace theory with practice, spiritualism with materialism, metaphysics with sociology.

Articulated within a political culture that was still deeply Christian, Young Hegelian theological and philosophical radicalism was unavoidably political,[26] but during the late 1830s the connection between philosophical and political critique became increasingly explicit. In part, this was the result of the furious controversy sparked by *The Life of Jesus*, a dispute which had the effect of linking religious questions to politics. Overt politicization was also a response to an increasingly reactionary climate during a decade that witnessed setbacks to constitutionalism throughout Germany and, in 1840, the accession to the Prussian throne of Frederick William IV, a ruler deeply committed to reactionary policies and surrounded by a coterie of Pietists, mystics, and Romantics. The mounting harassment of Hegelians by the champions of the so-called "Christian-German" states helped to crystallize political opposition in the main journal of the "Left" Hegelians, Arnold Ruge's *Hallische Jahrbücher*, published in Halle from 1838 until it was closed by government order in 1841, whereupon it was printed in Saxony as the *Deutsche Jahrbücher* until its suppression there in 1843.

Initially, the Young Hegelians responded to these circumstances by accusing conservatives of deviating from the progressive course set in the enlightened Prussia of the Reform Era. This was the image of Prussia that Hegel had presented, and it remained a powerful ideal for the Hegelians of the 1830s. In upholding this image, Hegelians made common cause with a broad front of liberal Germans committed to constitutionalism, individual rights, and freedom of the press. Notwithstanding the differences between east Prussian and southwest German liberalism, liberals and progressive Hegelians shared more than a range of concerns. Individuals like Eduard Gans in Berlin and Karl Rosenkranz in Königsberg were regarded as champions both of Hegelianism and of liberalism.[27] A unified "party of movement" became increasingly untenable, however, as political repression within the German states intensified. In place of the

Bewegungspartei, some of the left-wing Hegelians began to distinguish their own democratic republicanism from German liberalism. They did this, essentially, by incorporating German liberalism into an Hegelianized narrative of the flawed national German character.

The path taken by Arnold Ruge, the most prominent of the Hegelian political radicals, best illustrates the defection of the Hegelian Left from liberalism. In the years after he founded the *Hallische Jahrbücher*, Ruge moved rapidly toward the conviction that neither monarchic absolutism nor the bureaucratically administered *Rechtsstaat* could satisfy his ideals of political openness and participation.[28] In 1841, he condemned the present Prussian state as a "*res privata*," the antithesis of a "*res publica*" in which each citizen shares in "public life."[29] Excluded from public life, Germans languished in a state of political ignorance, content with private security and comfort. Ruge charged that as a result Germany, led by Prussia, was a land of *Spießbürgertum*, a crippling legacy of Germany's long history of despotic regimes and the quietism, resignation, and servility bred into Germans by Protestant culture.[30] He praised the Reform Era for trying to mobilize the people in order to convert them from "*Spießbürger* into *Staatsbürger*," but he believed that the monarchy had subsequently regressed. It was now content to rule over "*Spießbürger* and egoists" instead of "republicans and free men."[31] Ruge was not alone in describing the task of radical politics as overcoming the dichotomy of private and public life. The same impulse inspired Feuerbach to attack "*Spießbürgerliche* virtue" in favor of the public virtues of "political republicanism."[32] It lay at the heart of Edgar Bauer's praise for the French Jacobins, who had heralded what he called a "new civilization" that rejected anything "private." This principled rejection of all privacy, Bauer believed, must even lead beyond the achievements of the Jacobins to the abolition of private property and all forms of representative government.[33] Finally, the young Marx located the source of alienation in the modern separation of civil society from the state, of private from public life.[34]

In 1841, Ruge equated "liberalism" literally with "the emancipation of *Spießbürgertum*" from the narrowness of private life.[35] However, liberalism was an unlikely ally for a movement that sought to abolish the division between political and civil life. When liberals seemed willing to compromise with the repressive German monarchies, the Hegelian radicals began to suspect liberalism of being indifferent to the form of the state so long as it guaranteed the security of the private sphere.[36] Ruge brought this conflict into sharp focus in early 1843 with his "Self-Critique of Liberalism," the essay that finally led the Saxon government to yield to Prussian pressures to ban the *Deutsche Jahrbücher*. Significantly, Ruge did not seek the roots of liberalism's indifference to public life in the general nature of liberal ideology as it had developed in western Europe. Rather, he denounced liberalism as a product of "the old moralistic Spirit of Protestantism, the empty good will," that is, of a fatal German incapacity for politics. "Right at the time when the realization of democracy in Germany was made impossible by the German Federation," he claimed, "there arose liberalism, i.e., this good German intention, this pious wish for freedom, this 'free-thinking *mood*,' or this sympathy with democracy 'in intention.'"[37]

Notwithstanding the strong Hegelian cast of Ruge's thought, his critique of German "*Spießbürgerlichkeit*" echoed that of earlier republicans like Börne, whom Ruge praised as the German "Tacitus." But he went further than critics from the 1830s by detailing a continuum of dysfunctional Germanness that begins with the servile philistine *Bürger*, incorporates the German Idealist philosophers from Kant to Hegel, and runs through to the self-deceiving liberals, whose pursuit of freedom stops at the demand for private spiritual liberty. "Political liberalism," Ruge wrote in a key passage, "is to be derived from our perverse, deeply, and unspeakably confused Germanness, from the Germanness that wants to have everything different from the 'Franks,' and that, with its powerful originality, has derived from them nothing but the pure appearance of everything that they have attained."[38] Here again is the contrast between German passivity and French activism, only now the comparison is deployed in order to isolate elements within the German Left itself. Thus, Ruge demanded that "Liberalism be dissolved into Democratism."[39] The Left must translate liberalism's theoretical demand for freedom into revolutionary praxis, and convert the anemic "privacy" of Germans into a robust public life. In other words, the Left must renounce the "perverse" Germanness to which liberalism had fallen prey and embrace the "one, great, infinitely profitable purpose of causing the breakup of boneheaded philistine consciousness and the engendering of a living, sensitive, political spirit."[40]

Ruge's criticism of German liberalism crystallized the disaffection of left-wing intellectuals from their erstwhile allies in the *Bewegungspartei*. The incorporation of German liberalism into the negative narrative of German-Protestant national identity immediately became a *leitmotiv* of radical democratic polemics, seen in Edgar Bauer's writings of 1843 and 1844 and encountered repeatedly in Marx's works from late 1842 to 1848.

Still, the radicals faced the same dilemma as the republicans of the 1830s. How were the Germans to be liberated from their own narrowness? The Young Hegelians placed inordinate faith in the power of political enlightenment to transform philistines into citizens. As Feuerbach wrote, "the Germans are political children; they must first be educated."[41] For the Young Hegelians, this meant essentially an education in the most advanced findings of German philosophy, that is, the new demystified humanism of the Young Hegelians themselves. Nonetheless, despite their belief in the power of critical thought to redirect human devotion from the illusions of religion and metaphysics to its proper object, humanity itself, they could not ignore the apathy of the Germans. Ruge succumbed to resentment when he finally acknowledged the breach between his ideal of the people and the failure of the real people to recognize their putative rational interests. "Our *Volk* is not a *Volk*," Ruge complained.[42] When Germans remained unmoved while the Prussian and Saxon governments banned Left Hegelian journals at the beginning of 1843, Ruge concluded bitterly that "no one can make a revolution with the German philistines." In a letter of 1843, he wrote, "this entirely liberal and rational *Volk* is politically incapable. Well? What then? We must make another *Volk*, and I suspect that will cost much time."[43] Marx, who had claimed a year earlier that "*res publica* is quite untranslatable into German," likewise remarked in 1843 that in contrast to his own "shame" at his homeland, "in Germany even shame is not felt; on the contrary, these miserable people are still patriots."[44]

While Ruge took a leap into the political imaginary, Bruno Bauer turned against republicanism altogether. His defection is reflected in his changing estimation of the French Revolution. In 1841, Bauer had declared that the Hegelians "are Germans no more ... they are French revolutionaries"; and he counseled Arnold Ruge to "consider the revolution – whose history cannot be studied enough – it is the codex of all the laws of historical movements."[45] From enthusiastic Jacobinism, however, Bauer moved to "the terrorism of reason," a struggle that pitted the solitary critic against all threats to the sovereignty of self-consciousness, including the *Volk* and the nation. In 1844, he dismissed the Revolution as an "experiment of the eighteenth century" and lamented the emergence of the "masses," the "most significant product of the Revolution .... [The masses] are the detritus of the abolition of feudal oppositions; the phlegm that remained after the egotism of the nationalities exhausted itself in the revolutionary wars ... the natural enemy of theory."[46] In place of all political philosophies that relied on the debased "crowd" or "mass," whether Feuerbachian humanism or French socialism, Bauer championed the idea of "pure criticism," a concept so sterile that it ensured almost universal defection from the Bauerian camp, including Bauer himself by 1848. The same trajectory carried Max Stirner away from democratic engagement toward the extreme anarchistic individualism of his only significant work, *Der Einzige und sein Eigenthum*.[47]

Bruno Bauer wryly observed in 1844 that just as the "German enlighteners were suddenly disappointed in their hopes of 1842, and in their predicament knew not what to do, news of the latest French systems came to them."[48] Bauer was referring to the effects of Lorenz von Stein's

Der Socialismus und Communismus des heutigen Frankreichs.[49] Knowledge of French socialism did not arrive quite as abruptly as Bauer suggested. A German book on Charles Fourier had already appeared in 1834, and, more importantly, Saint-Simonianism was widely discussed in the German press in the early 1830s.[50] Saint-Simonianism had influenced not only the writers of Young Germany but also prominent political thinkers like Eduard Gans and Friedrich Buchholz.[51] Moreover, the German receptiveness to French socialist thought in the early 1840s was not simply the product of their own ideological impasse. During the late 1830s, social observers, journalists, bureaucrats, and intellectuals had begun to comment on a steadily worsening problem of mass impoverishment and homelessness. The pauperism crisis was to deepen even further in the mid-1840s, but by 1842 many German intellectuals were acutely aware of the plight of the poor.[52] In this context, Stein's book, which was intended to warn Germans of the threats of impending social revolution, had the ironic effect of reviving German interest in the Saint-Simonians and Fourierists and popularizing the ideas of a younger generation of French socialists like Louis Blanc, Pierre-Joseph Proudhon, Etienne Cabet, George Sand, Victor Considérant, and Pierre Leroux. For numerous Left Hegelians, the new French social thought did offer a way to redeem the setbacks to their cause and to overcome their disillusionment with the *Volk*.[53]

German radicals began to define the proletariat, the "fourth estate," as the "actual *Volk*." Even in 1842 both Edgar Bauer and Arnold Ruge had still defined the *Volk* in classic democratic-republican style as the nation minus the ruler. By 1843, Bauer and Ruge castigated the liberals for excluding the poor from their definition of the *Volk*.[54] The turn to the poor in part recapitulated the Jacobin romanticization of the poor as the purest, most virtuous segment of the people; however, it was also inspired more directly by the French socialists, above all by Louis Blanc.[55] Edgar Bauer, moving in the opposite direction from his brother Bruno, became the first Left Hegelian to identify the poor as the agent of a world-historical revolution. In *Der Streit der Kritik mit Kirche und Staat* he turned against the French Revolution as a mere half-step on the path to freedom, because the political revolution left private property in place. The "propertyless," the true *Volk*, would be the heroes of a total revolution that would finally abolish all private property along with the state that had been erected to preserve it. Yet, even as Bauer redefined the *Volk*, he questioned the legitimacy of the word itself. Although he claimed to be writing in the interests of the people, he ended his major book by rejecting the idea of the *Volk* altogether as an outmoded "political concept." The *Volk* is a "trusting crowd that allows itself to be led," and it is irredeemably associated with "national arrogance." "In a free society," he predicted, "there will no longer be an exclusive *Volk*."[56] Other examples abound of this simultaneous redefinition and delegitimation of the category of the *Volk*, as in Engels's claim that in Germany "proletarians, small peasants and urban petty bourgeoisie ... constitute the 'people'"; or in Marx's more precise specification: "The people, or, to replace this broad and vague expression by a definite one, the proletariat."[57]

The reconceptualization of the *Volk* directed the attention of radicals away from the failed idea of national political community to an idea of cosmopolitan social community. Moses Hess registered the abrupt shift of German radicals from Jacobin-democratic republicanism to socialism when he declared in an 1844 essay that, since 1843, the "best minds in Germany have been won over to socialism .... What was earlier merely national, liberal, philosophical, or political radicalism, is now more or less socialistic."[58] It must also be noted that in the context of Germany in the 1840s, with its limited industrialization and the virtual non-existence of a modern working class, the redefinition of the *Volk* as the proletariat deepened the gap between real Germans and Germans as perceived agents of the anticipated social revolution in that country. The "class with radical *chains*" that Marx identified so famously at the end of 1843 scarcely existed in Germany.[59] Marx was not alone in preferring this image of a redemptive heroic class, assumed to have privileged access to universal truths because of its "universal suffering," to the less encouraging complexities of German society. Such a choice was made at the cost of elevating a static conception of class and revolutionary agency over more dynamic and sociologically grounded accounts of Germany's revolutionary possibilities.[60] Although Marx, Engels, and other German socialists were to evolve more flexible insights into the relationship between class formation and revolutionary activity, the heated clashes within the German Left before 1848 tended to favor formalistic definitions of class as the blunt instrument of polemics.

4.

Even as some of the leading German radicals embraced a cosmopolitan socialist ideal, the ambivalent image of Germany once again proved crucial to their self-understanding and to their attempts to distinguish themselves from rival progressives. Nearly all the new German socialists regarded their new creed as the necessary consequence of German philosophical radicalism. For instance, Edgar Bauer deduced the world-historical role of the propertyless from his own reworking of his brother's philosophy of self-consciousness, even though he disagreed with Bruno's retreat from the masses. That is, Edgar was convinced that the dialectical evolution of human self-consciousness had reached a point that demanded the reappropriation of, and mastery over, all alienating abstractions, including the state and private property. He was, however, relatively isolated in his attempt to base socialism on a philosophy of self-consciousness. By contrast, Feuerbachian humanism became the basis for "True Socialism," perhaps the most prominent socialist creed in *Vormärz* Germany.[61] Moses Hess, the leading True Socialist, believed that all German philosophy and political thought before Feuerbach shared the endemic weaknesses of the Germans, their abstractness and theoretical fixation on spirit. At the same time, he argued that German thought had prepared the way for the advent of socialism through the transformation of German philosophy into the philosophic humanism of Ludwig Feuerbach. That is, the spiritual liberation begun in German thought had culminated in what Feuerbach had himself called "the fundamental, German dissolution" of the essence of Christianity.[62] According to Hess, Feuerbach's radical claim that humanity had mistakenly worshiped its own virtues in the form of an alien divinity created the basis for recognizing the true social nature of human essence. If anthropology is the secret of religion, as Feuerbach had declared, then Hess went one further to declare that socialism is the secret of anthropology.[63] Because of the apparent capacity of German philosophy to transform itself into humanism, Hess could echo a familiar refrain: "We Germans are the most universal, the most European *Volk* in Europe."[64]

Numerous other Germans also recognized Feuerbach's philosophical anthropology as truly expressing the social nature of humanity, the creative role of work in producing human *species-being*, and the need to socialize labor in order to meet human needs and overcome alienation. Ruge, who ultimately remained aloof from communism, wrote several articles between 1843 and 1846 defending democratic socialism from the standpoint of Feuerbachian humanism; his simultaneous defense of cosmopolitan humanism against German patriotism severely harmed his reputation in that country.[65] For a brief time, the young Marx and Engels were equally impressed by the connection between Feuerbach's humanism and communism. Much later, Engels recalled that when Feuerbach's major work, *The Essence of Christianity*, had appeared in 1842, "at once we all became Feuerbachians";[66] and Marx assured Feuerbach in a letter of August 1844 that "you have provided … a philosophical basis for socialism and the Communists."[67] For both Ruge and Marx, moreover, the German dissolution of religion had elevated German over French socialism, which still remained fettered by religious illusions, as they discovered to their surprise upon arriving in Paris in 1844.

The socialist implications of Feuerbachian humanism seemed to vindicate the true, progressive legacy of German universality. However, these radicals were in virtually unanimous agreement that German contemplativeness must strike an alliance with French activism in order to achieve what Moses Hess called "perfect socialism." Hess aligned the transition from philosophy to communism with the move from contemplation to practice, from spiritual to social liberation, from German passivity to French activism. Distrust of Germany, as well as an administration of the long history of left-wing francophilism, led the advance guard of the German Left once again to stake its own legitimacy on its capacity to place German universality under the sign of the French national principle. In this way, Engels made the question of communism the pivotal measure of the entire German nation: "Our party has to prove that either all the philosophical efforts of the German nation, from Kant to Hegel, have been useless – worse than useless; or, that they must end in Communism; that the Germans must either reject their great philosophers, whose names they hold up as the glory of their nation, or that they must adopt Communism."[68]

As in the immediate past, the accusation of unreconstructed Germanness remained the weapon of choice in the internecine polemics of the Left. In 1844, Engels informed an English readership that "a war has been declared against those of the German philosophers who refuse to draw from their mere theories practical inferences, and who contend that man has nothing to do but to speculate upon metaphysical questions." Engels referred the English to his first collaborative work with Marx, *The Holy Family*, which polemicized against Bruno and Edgar Bauer, Max Stirner, and the Berlin *Freien*, some of whom had, ironically, turned to communism earlier than Marx or Engels. These thinkers, Engels continued, are "the representatives of the ultimate consequences of *abstract* German philosophy, and, therefore, the only important philosophical opponents of Socialism – or rather Communism."[69] Engels also praised the efforts of Moses Hess, whose essay "The Last Philosophers" attacked Bruno Bauer and Stirner's subjectivist fixation on merely idealistic negation. Hess's 1844 tract neatly reversed the enthusiastic evaluation of Young Hegelianism that he had offered in 1841, when he praised the critical negation of existing relations as itself a species of praxis.[70] It appears that the 1844 diagnosis of the German vice of contemplativeness in the Young Hegelians and the Berlin *Freien* had an effect even among the *Freien* themselves. Edgar Bauer's biographer contends that competition from Hess's communism – along with press censorship, Bauer's imprisonment, and the isolation of these intellectual radicals from Berlin workers – contributed to the disintegration of the *Freien*.[71]

The same year also witnessed the opening of a campaign against another significant tendency within Left Hegelianism, the democratic-socialist humanism of Arnold Ruge. In May 1844, Hess fired the first salvo at Ruge.[72] Although Hess and Ruge had shared editorial duties on the *Deutsch-Französische Jahrbücher* just months earlier, the seeds of their disagreement had been planted at the time of their first meeting. Hess, who had been one of the first Germans to embrace communism, had no patience for Ruge's interest in moral persuasion and political education.[73] In contrast to the more radical Hess, Ruge held to the conviction that the struggle for political equality must take priority over the attempt to create a *Gütergemeinschaft*, a community of *property*.[74] This unreconstructed stubbornness tagged him as irremediably "German" and, therefore, a retrograde element to be purged from the Left. "As a Young Hegelian, as a *revolutionary* philosopher, as a man of progress," Hess wrote, "[Ruge] embraced the newest movement, the newest advance, including socialism. As a *German* philosopher, however, he discovered no philosophy in the socialist movement." Because Ruge, like the other Left Hegelians, had proved himself incapable of self-criticism, he remained stuck in an allegedly typical German impasse: "German philosophy shatters against praxis, for which it has no understanding." The result, Hess concluded, is an irreconcilable conflict between "socialism" and the German "philosophical *Bewegungspartei*."[75]

Marx published an even more devastating critique of Ruge later that summer. Ruge had been Marx's closest collaborator since the two had gone into exile after the closing of the *Rheinische Zeitung* and the *Deutsche Jahrbücher*. Nonetheless, their months of work together on the *Deutsch-Französische Jahrbücher* were strained by the same disagreement that had divided Ruge from Hess. An article published anonymously by Ruge on the Silesian weavers' revolt of June 1844 brought their quarrel fully into the open. In that piece, Ruge had described the revolt as an uprising of the desperately hungry poor. Further, he expressed deep pessimism about the possibility of such disturbances effecting change in "an unpolitical land" like Germany.

> *The German poor are no wiser than the poor Germans, i.e., they never see beyond their own hearth, their factory, their district. The whole question until now still lacks the all-pervading political spirit. All uprisings which break out in this unholy isolation of men from the commonwealth and of their thoughts from social principles, will smother in blood and ignorance .... A social revolution without a political spirit ... is impossible.*[76]

Ruge's pessimism about revolution in Germany still rested on the familiar image of German philistinism and privacy, which he now extended further to include the German poor. What all Germans lacked, according to Ruge, was political understanding and the courage to act. Marx rejected this "old story about *unpolitical* Germany" and emphasized instead the reality of class interest and the intractability of class antagonism.[77] More significantly, from our perspective, he exempted the German workers from the German stereotype by devaluing the political criteria by which the German Left had long evaluated national character. The German poor no longer needed political understanding, since their interest lay in social revolution. Education for social revolution did not derive from the political culture of the nation, but from the discipline of the marketplace, which by 1844 Marx had recognized as supranational. He could thereby turn the charge of Germanness back on Ruge himself and knock his *bon mot* on its ear: "The wisdom of the German poor, therefore, is in inverse ratio to the wisdom of poor Germans."[78]

Surprisingly, however, even as Marx subverted the familiar left-wing analysis of Germanness, he fully employed the metaphysics of national character: "the German proletariat is the *theoretician* of the European proletariat, just as the English proletariat is its *economist*, and the French proletariat its *politician*."[79] Like Hess at this time, Marx used the rhetoric of Germanness both to distance himself from a rival and to legitimize the claim of the German working class, and its theoretical spokesmen, to a role in the coming European social revolution.[80] Further, the metaphysics of national character furnished him with an answer to a question that he had not yet clearly posed. Could a proletarian revolution occur in a "backward" country, or must each country progress through necessary stages? He was to return to this question periodically over the years, both in relation to the situation in Germany and, later, in Russia; and he was to formulate numerous theories about how backwardness might actually facilitate revolution. In 1844, his belief that Germany is "*classically* destined for a *social* revolution" because a "philosophical people can find its corresponding practice only in socialism" was decidedly metaphysical.[81] It was also distinctly out of touch with German realities. In this regard, Ruge was actually closer to the truth when he called the Silesian weavers' revolt an uprising of the hungry, and not the opening act in the German proletarian revolution.

By 1845, Ruge found himself ostracized by the German communists in Paris, an affiliation which he had, at any rate, already rejected. Despite his advocacy of Rousseauian "democratism" in 1843 and his interest in addressing the social problem through the social organization of work, Ruge had grown skeptical of the possibility of totally revolutionizing civil society. Furthermore, he began to worry that a full *Gütergemeinschaft* would erase individual rights altogether, which would be self-defeating for the emancipatory goals of socialism. Between 1845 and 1848, Ruge tried to develop a conception of social democracy that remained true to Hegel's insights into the "state of absolute terror," that is, the dangers of attempts to collapse the distinction between state and civil society into a monistic identity.[82] Ruge did not produce a clear or compelling alternative to communism, and, by his own admission, these scruples made him a "reactionary" within the context of a radical politics that dreamed of creating the whole man precisely by overcoming the division between state and civil society, public and private, community and individual.[83] Ruge's criticisms, voiced from within the broad front of socialism, might have occasioned discussion in a movement that was, after all, committed to discovering the adequate conditions of emancipation; but instead, Marx, Hess, and Engels summarily dismissed him by intoning the charge that Ruge remained fettered by idealist, German thinking. Except for a brief period of influence as a deputy for Breslau in the National Assembly in Frankfurt, Ruge's rejection of communism marked his irrevocable fall from significance. Subsequently, he surfaced only as a "philistine" in Marx and Engels's criticism of German republicans like Karl Heinzen.[84]

If Ruge had been discredited largely by identification with German philistinism, his own parting shot at the communists leveled the same charge at them: evidence, perhaps, of the strength of that discourse. As he reflected on his personally disastrous years in Paris, he blamed his rough handling on the apparent aberrations of German communism. He accused the German communists of falling prey to German backwardness, which had the effect of driving them into a particularly zealous partisanship. They lacked the tolerance and humaneness of the French communists, because the Germans simply imported doctrine from France, where those ideas had been forged in the tempering medium of political action.[85] Because neither political action nor the social question existed in Germany in anything like the concrete forms found in France or England, communism in Germany "translates ... the practical problems of the French and English into drunken metaphysics and makes a new religion from politics. Even this movement places itself in the speculative dreamworld of the Germans .... they mock the political freedom of thought, speech and action, as well as the norms of human behavior, because no political freedom, no guarantee of civil rights, removes poverty."[86] Ruge's depiction of his erstwhile friends distorted their views almost as much as their attacks distorted his, but he was neither the first nor the last critic of German communism to attempt to discredit it by tying it to national peculiarity.[87] One could, evidently, be just as German for going too far as for not going far enough.

Marx and Engels made common cause with Moses Hess in the campaign against the social democratic Left, but they were in fact preparing to distance themselves from True Socialism. Both Marx and Engels had tempered their enthusiasm for Feuerbachian philosophical communism with a strong empirical bent toward concrete analyses of politics, society, and economics. From the beginning of Marx and Engels's collaboration on *The Holy Family* in 1844, they sought to ground communism not in a philosophical ideal of human essence but in an analysis of the social and economic relations of capitalism.[88] Of course, it seems clear that one of the most powerful themes of communism, alienation and its overcoming, would remain unintelligible without a specific ideal of human essence. To recognize this retrospectively, however, does not deny the extent to which Marx and Engels's empirical shift did actually distinguish them from other contemporary leftists. Moses Hess clearly recognized the importance of this shift and tried to keep pace; but, like the other True Socialists, he remained too closely tied to the categories of Feuerbachian humanism.

From 1845 and early 1846, when Engels and Marx prepared the manuscript of *The German Ideology*, to *The Communist Manifesto* of 1847, they mounted a sustained polemic against the True Socialists. Their criticism relentlessly pursued the strategy of exposing the parochial reality behind the universal claims of the True Socialists. In *The German Ideology*, Marx identified this paradox in the German philosophic and socialistic radicals' concern for the universal emancipation of humanity. Their activity, wrote Marx, is "a purely *national* affair of the Germans and has merely *local* interest for Germany .... These pompous and arrogant hucksters of ideas, who imagine themselves infinitely exalted above all national prejudices, are, thus, in practice far more national than the beer-swilling philistines who dream of a united Germany."[89] Early in 1847, Engels complained that "German socialist literature grows worse from month to month. It increasingly confines itself to the broad effusions of those *true socialists* whose whole wisdom amounts to an amalgam of German philosophy and German-philistine sentimentality with a few stunted communist slogans."[90] Later that year, he ridiculed the universalistic pretensions of the True Socialists. Whereas Karl Grün, one of the leading True Socialists, had made familiar claims that "the German nation is not a 'national' nation, but the nation 'of all that is human,'" Engels sarcastically countered that as he examined the German discovery of the universally human, he recognized that "'man,' who, as we have already seen, is *German* by birth, is gradually beginning to turn into the spit image of a *German petty bourgeois*." The "man" of True Socialism is "a man of conscience, an honorable, virtuous, German philistine."[91] It is telling that among the forms of mistaken socialism criticized in *The Communist Manifesto*, only "True, or German Socialism" is labeled with a national designation and identified with a national deviation.

5.

"Germanness" during the 1840s had become a loose signifier that could be applied polemically and to good effect to virtually any group or individual, including radicals who had themselves aided in the construction of the negative image of the "German." Successively, the potent and highly flexible distinction between universal and parochial Germanness had served to distinguish the *Bewegungspartei* from the German *Spießbürgertum*, radical democrats from liberals, socialists from democrats, and finally, the historical materialists from the "holy family" of would-be German radicals. The discourse of dysfunctional national character helped to articulate substantive differences among competing visions of progressive politics; but it also helped to elide similarities and points of fruitful disagreement. In the rather rarefied atmosphere of socialist "politics" in the 1840s, when the political groupings of workers were little more than minute sects and theoretical debates were a greater preoccupation than political organization, the charge of "Germanness" drew its persuasive power from the conjunction of philosophical and socio-political criticism, utopian hopes, and the real experience of political alienation and repression.

When Marx and Engels extended the national character flaw to the German socialists, they availed themselves of a standardized gesture in the repertoire of German radicalism. However, even if they tapped a relatively static rhetorical vein, they also significantly refined the analysis of German national character. Right up to Moses Hess and the other True Socialists, radicals blamed the failings of the German character on moral and political factors – on Protestant inwardness, egotism, the corrupting influence of despotism, and so forth. Marx and Engels sought the answer to the problem of German identity in their growing understanding of the material basis of history. They replaced the categories of moral critique with those of a socioeconomic analysis based on the model of political and economic modernity that they derived from their studies of France and England.

Measured by those norms, Germany was neither abjectly backward nor fully modern. Marx first articulated this analysis in the introduction to his critique of Hegel's philosophy of law. Not only did he diagnose Germany's philosophical modernity as a compensation for its thwarted social and political development,[92] he also explored the general effects of Germany's suspension between two worlds, between the old regime and the modern state, between feudalism and capitalism. Germany's in-between status, Marx argued, meant that it contained "all the sins of all political forms," while its hybrid economy ensured that, unlike in France or England, no particular class had the social power to reshape politics in its own image.[93] Drawing on Marx's analysis, Engels traced Germany's "philistine" and "civic mediocrity" to the general lack of capital in Germany, which prevented the formation of fully modern markets and modern class relations. As a result, Engels claimed, the petty bourgeoisie is the "standard class of Germany," and it has "imparted to all other classes their specific depression and their concern over their existence."[94] In the light of this new social analysis, the epithets of national character took on double meaning. Now "philistinism" and "*Spießbürgerlichkeit*" referred not only to the depoliticized "subject" of the German-Christian monarchies but also to the "bourgeois" of civil society, in his specific German form. Privacy, passivity, and egotism became the ascribed attributes of Germany's socioeconomic, as well as its political, life. The "philistine" and the "*Spießbürger*" could, therefore, embody what Engels and Marx took to be the unique German interpenetration of old regime forms and nascent industrial society.[95]

Given their analysis of Germany's socioeconomic situation, they denied the power of moral appeals, education, or even political action to correct the defects of Germanness. The apparent intractability of German social conditions caused Engels considerable pessimism in the months before the outbreak of revolution in 1848. Not only was he more convinced than Marx that even the German working classes were dominated by petty bourgeois consciousness,[96] his pessimism also extended to German intellectuals, whose limitations he now traced to the social structure of which they were a part.[97] Nonetheless, for both Engels and Marx, short-term pessimism was compensated by optimism in the longer view. Their shift from moral and political to social and economic phenomena afforded them the hope that the "German misery" would be corrected by the universal history of civil society, that is, the global history of economic transformation. The dynamic tension between the universal and the parochial within the German character that had structured left-wing discourse about national identity gave way to the tension between national peculiarity *per se* and a universal modernization process that promised eventually to efface all national difference. As Engels said in 1890, only the German working class, a product of that global process, had succeeded in breaking through the "narrow limits" of the "general German type."

With the articulation of this supranational perspective, Marx and Engels did not cease to discuss national issues, nor did their analysis of the German situation cease to evolve. Nor, on the other hand, did they entirely abandon a claim to the "universal" content of Germanness, or, at least, of German thought. As we have already suggested, their dependence on the categories of totality and alienation and their continued use of Hegel's dialectical logic testifies to that fact, as does their lifelong belief in the superiority of German philosophy over other national philosophical traditions. These are complicated aspects of Marx and Engels's subsequent development that cannot be explored here. It is more immediately relevant to emphasize that from the vantage point of historical materialism, Engels and Marx could claim an exemption for their constituents from the burden of national identity; they could also exempt themselves from the

"German" weaknesses of their rivals on the Left and the deep pessimism that had haunted earlier German radicals. Their theoretical achievements before 1848 furnished a kind of resolution to the problem of national character, but they left in place the deeply ambivalent view of German character that had formed within the Left during the 1830s and 1840s.

That ambivalence created a difficult legacy for German socialism. To be sure, the followers of Ferdinand Lassalle were quite willing in the 1860s and 1870s to link socialism to a democratic conception of German nationalism; and even the old image of the Marxian socialists as "*vaterlandslose Gesellen*," comrades without a fatherland, has been challenged by studies that present a more nuanced picture of socialist participation in issues of national concern, even revealing the development of something like social democratic "patriotism" in the face of foreign threats – though it might be observed that support for the idea of a defensive war against a potential Russian invasion was a hesitant form of patriotism.[98] Moreover, the German Left was not alone in experiencing tensions between internationalism and nationalism, as well as alienation from the narratives of national history and identity proffered by the dominant classes. Still, German socialists faced greater troubles than their English or French counterparts in claiming positive affiliations with aspects of their national history. This had much to do with that history itself, which could boast neither of revolutions nor of parliamentary rule, as well as with the ongoing experience of state-sanctioned repression; but the Germans' deeper alienation also stemmed from the persistent power of a discourse of national deviation. We have seen that this discourse presented both an opening and a constraint in the development of radical theory in the 1840s: an opening, because it provided a means for ordering the substantive differences among leftists; a constraint, because its polemical power could pre-empt a more searching discussion of the theory and practice of emancipation. At times of challenge in the decades of the late-nineteenth and early-twentieth centuries, German socialists and communists frequently felt compelled to reaffirm their identity by repeating the founding act of German socialism, the rhetorical denial of their own German provenance and destiny. That was a problematic and at times deluded self-understanding for a radical politics that always operated first and foremost within a national political context, despite its internationalist profession and the significance of the Second and Third Internationals.

Notes

1. Karl Marx, "The Leading Article in No. 179 of the *Kölnische Zeitung*," in *Collected Works* (New York, 1975), 1:202 (hereafter cited as CW).
2. Arnold Ruge, "Wer ist und wer ist nicht Partei?," in *Die Hegelsche Linke. Dokumente zu Philosophie und Politik im deutschen Vormärz*, ed. Heinz and Ingrid Pepperle (Leipzig, 1985), 399-408.
3. Schiller, "Deutsche Größe," in *Schillers Werke*, vol. 2/1, ed. Norbert Öllers (Weimar, 1983), 433.
4. Ferdinand Lassalle, "Die Philosophie Fichte's und die Bedeutung des deutschen Volksgeistes," in *Gesammelte Reden und Schriften*, vol. 6, ed. Eduard Bernstein (Berlin, 1919-20), esp. 141-42.
5. Heinrich Heine, *The Romantic School and Other Essays*, ed. Jost Hermand and Robert C. Holub (New York, 1985), 21.
6. Engels quoted in Hermann Strobach, "Zum Volksbegriff bei Marx und Engels" in *Das geschichtswissenschaftliche Erbe von Karl Marx*, ed. Wolfgang Küttler (Berlin, 1983), 176.
7. See Harold Mah, "The Epistemology of the Sentence: Language, Civility, and Identity in France and Germany, Diderot to Nietzsche," *Representations* 47 (Summer 1994): 64-84.
8. For a recent treatment of these themes, see Hinrich Seeba, "'Germany – A Literary Concept': The Myth of National Literature," *German Studies Review* 17: 2 (May 1994): 353-69.
9. See Harold Mah, "The French Revolution and the Problem of German Modernity: Hegel, Heine, and Marx," *New German Critique*, no. 50 (Spring/Summer 1990): 3-20; and Hermann Lübbe, "Die politische Theorie des hegelschen Rechte," *Archiv für Philosophie* 10: 3-4 (1962): 191-92.
10. On the persistence of Jacobin sentiments in early nineteenth-century Germany, see Walter Grab, "Die Kontinuität der demokratischen Bestrebungen 1792-1848," in *Die demokratische Bewegung in Mitteleuropa im ausgehenden 18. und frühen 19. Jahrhundert: Ein Tagungsbericht*, ed. Otto Büsch (Berlin, 1980), 439-52; and Jonathan Sperber, *Rhineland Radicals: The Democratic Movement and the Revolution of 1848-1849* (Princeton, 1991), 6. Peter Wende questions the existence of a "vertical tradition" of radicalism stemming from the Jacobinism of the 1790s and emphasizes the more immediate legacy of the left wing of the German *Burschenschaften* in *Radikalismus im Vormärz: Untersuchungen zur politischen Theorie der frühen deutschen Demokratie* (Wiesbaden, 1975), 20-23.
11. See Heinrich Scheel, ed., *Jakobinische Flugschriften aus dem deutschen Süden Ende des 18. Jahrhunderts* (Vaduz/Liechtenstein, 1980).
12. On the Hambach festival, see Thomas Nipperdey, *Deutsche Geschichte 1800-1866: Bürgerwelt und starker Staat*, 6th ed. (Munich, 1993), 370; and, more generally, James Sheehan, *German History 1770-1866* (Oxford, 1991), 610-13.
13. See, for example, Georg Büchner, "Der Hessische Landbote," in *Dichtungen* (Leipzig, 1990), 184.
14. This view is discussed in Moses Hess, "The Philosophy of the Act," in *Socialist Thought: A Documentary History*, ed. Albert Fried and Ronald Sanders (New York, 1964), 274.
15. Theodor Mundt, "Über Bewegungsparteien in der Literatur," *Literarischer Zodiacus* (January 1835), 14.

16. Heine quoted in Klaus Briegelb, "Der 'Geist der Gewalthaber' über Wolfgang Menzel," in *Demokratisch-revolutionäre Literatur in Deutschland: Vormärz*, ed. Gert Mattenklott (Kronberg, 1973), 126.
17. Ludwig Börne, *Schriften zur deutschen Literatur* (Leipzig, 1987), 270.
18. Börne, *Schriften*, 276.
19. Ibid., 153-71.
20. Ibid., 248-50. On the broader background of this type of anti-Protestantism, see Laurence Dickey, "Saint-Simonian Industrialism as the End of History: August Cieszkowski on the Teleology of Universal History," in *Apocalypse Theory and the Ends of the World*, ed. Malcolm Bull (Oxford, 1995), 184-85.
21. See, for example, Börne, *Schriften*, 238; and Heine, *Religion and Philosophy in Germany*, trans. John Snodgrass (Albany, NY, 1986).
22. Börne, *Schriften*, 225.
23. Still fundamental on this issue is E.M. Butler, *The Saint-Simonian Religion in Germany: A Study of the Young Germany Movement* (Cambridge, Mass., 1926). See also Charles Rihs, *L'école des jeunes hegeliens et les penseurs socialistes français* (Paris, 1978).
24. Wolfgang Mönke, "Einleitung," in *Moses Hess: Philosophische und Sozialistische Schriften, 1837-1850* (Vaduz/Liechtenstein, 1980), xxvii.
25. On the Young Hegelians, see especially John Toews, *Hegelianism: The Path Toward Dialectical Humanism, 1805-1841* (New York, 1985).
26. On the overlap of politics and religion in Young Hegelianism, see Walter Jaeschke, "Urmenschheit und Monarchie: Eine politische Christologie der Hegelschen Rechten," *Hegel-Studien* 14 (1979): 73-107; Marilyn Chapin Massey, *Christ Unmasked: The Meaning of The Life of Jesus in German Politics* (Chapel Hill, NC, 1983); and Warren Breckman, "Ludwig Feuerbach and the Political Theology of Restoration," *History of Political Thought* 13: 3 (Autumn 1992): 437-62.
27. On the relations between Hegelians and German liberals, the classic essays by Gustav Mayer remain fundamental. See "Die Anfänge des politischen Radikalismus im vormärzlichen Preußen," *Zeitschrift für Politik* 6 (1913): 1-113, and "Die Junghegelianer und der preußische Staat," *Historische Zeitschrift* 121 (1920): 413-40. See also Wolfgang Eßbach, *Die Junghegelianer: Soziologie einer Intellektuellengruppe* (Munich, 1988), 207-8.
28. See Arnold Ruge and Theodor Echtermeyer, *Der Protestantismus und die Romantik*, ed. Norbert Öllers (Hildesheim, 1972), 23; and Ruge, "Karl Streckfuß und das Preußentum," in *Die Hegelsche Linke*.
29. Ruge, "Vorwort zum Jahrgang 1841 der *Hallischen Jahrbücher*," in *Die Hegelsche Linke*, 204.
30. Ruge, "Der preußische Absolutismus und seine Entwicklung," *Gesammelte Schriften* 4: 46.
31. Ibid., 20.
32. See Feuerbach, "[Über] Dr. Karl Bayer," *Gesammelte Werke*, ed. Werner Schuffenhauer (Berlin, 1969), 8: 95; and "The Necessity of a Reform of Philosophy," in *The Fiery Brook: Selected Writings of Ludwig Feuerbach*, trans. Zawar Hanfi (New York, 1972), 152.
33. See by Edgar Bauer: *Georg Herwegh und die literarische Zeitung* (Leipzig, 1843), 32; and "*Geschichte Europas seit der ersten französischen Revolution* von Archibald Alison," and "Der Streit der Kritik mit Kirche und Staat," both in *Die Hegelsche Linke*, 522-46, 651.
34. See Marx, "Contribution to the Critique of Hegel's Philosophy of Law," and "On the Jewish Question," in *CW*, vol. 3.

35. Ruge, "Der preußische Absolutismus," 48-49.
36. Edgar Bauer, *Die liberalen Bestrebungen in Deutschland*, vol. 1, *Die Irrthümer der Ostpreußischen Opposition* (Zürich und Winterthur, 1843), 26; and [Edgar Bauer,] *Staat, Religion und Partei* (Leipzig, 1843), 9-10.
37. Ruge, "Liberalism," 250, 242.
38. Ibid., 246.
39. Ibid., 259.
40. Ibid., 257.
41. Feuerbach to Ruge, mid-April 1844, *Briefwechsel*, vol. 2, ed. Werner Schuffenhauer and Erhard Voigt (Berlin, 1988), 339.
42. Ruge, "Vorwort zur Verständigung der Deutschen und Franzosen, von einem deutschen Publizisten in der Fremde," in Louis Blanc, *Geschichte der zehn Jahre, 1830 bis 1840*, trans. Gottlob Fink (Zürich, 1843), xxviii.
43. Ruge to Fleischer, 18 June 1843, *Briefwechsel und Tägeblätter*, ed. Paul Nerrlich (Berlin, 1886), 311.
44. Marx to Ruge, 5 March 1842, CW, 1; and Marx, "Letters from the *Deutsch-Französische Jahrbücher*," CW 3: 133.
45. Bruno Bauer, *The Trumpet of the Last Judgement against Hegel the Atheist and Antichrist*, trans. Lawrence S. Stepelevich (Berkeley, 1989), 141; and Bruno Bauer to Arnold Ruge, 19 October 1841, in *The Philosophical Forum* 8: 2-4 (1978): 124.
46. Bruno Bauer, "Was ist jetzt der Gegenstand der Kritik?" *Allgemeine Literatur-Zeitung* 2: 8 (July 1844): 25.
47. Stirner, *The Ego and His Own*, trans. Steven T. Byington (London, 1912).
48. Ibid., 25.
49. Lorenz von Stein, *Der Socialismus und Communismus des heutigen Frankreichs* (Leipzig, 1842).
50. See Friedrich Tappehorn, *Die vollkommene Association als Vermittler in der Einheit des Vernunftstaats und der Lehre Jesu: Ein Beitrag zur ruhigen Lösung aller großen Fragen dieser Zeit* (Augsburg, 1834). For a bibliography of works on Saint-Simonianism in the German press from 1830-34, see Butler, *Saint-Simonian Religion*, 52-59.
51. Rütger Schäger, *Friedrich Buchholz – ein vergessener Vorläufer der Soziologie*, 2 vols. (Göttingen, 1972); and Norbert Waszek, "Eduard Gans on Poverty: Between Hegel and Saint-Simon," *The Owl of Minerva* 18: 2 (1987): 167-78.
52 See Carl Jantke and Dietrich Hilger, eds., *Die Eigentumslosen: Der deutsche Pauperismus und die Emanzipationskrise in Darstellungen und Deutungen der zeitgenössischen Literatur* (Munich, 1965).
53. See, for example, Ruge, *Der Patriotismus*, ed. Peter Wende (Frankfurt am Main, 1968), 14.
54. Edgar Bauer, "Der Streit der Kritik," 707; and Ruge, "Liberalism," 248.
55. The Jacobin provenance of Marx's turn to the poor has been emphasized recently by Paul Thomas, *Alien Politics: Marxist State Theory Retrieved* (New York, 1994), 45-46.
56. Bauer, "Der Streit der Kritik," 700-1.
57. Marx, "The Communism of the *Rheinischer Beobachter*," CW 6: 222, and Engels, "The Communists and Karl Heinzen," CW 6: 294. See also Theodor Oelckers, *Die Bewegung des Socialismus und Communismus* (Leipzig, 1844), 59; and anon., *Über den vierten Stand und die socialen Reformen* (Augsburg, 1844), 55.
58. Moses Hess, "Über die sozialistische Bewegung in Deutschland," in *Philosophische und Sozialistische Schriften*, 304. See also David Gregory, "Karl Marx's and

Friedrich Engels's Knowledge of French Socialism in 1842-43," *Historical Reflections/Réflexions Historiques* 10: 1 (1983): 143-93.

59. Marx, "Contribution to the Critique of Hegel's Philosophy of Law: Introduction," *CW* 3: 186.
60. Thomas makes a similar argument in *Alien Politics*, 47.
61. See, for example, Sperber, *Rhineland Radicals*, 122-23.
62. Feuerbach to Ruge, mid-April 1844, *Briefwechsel*, vol. 2: 338.
63. Hess, "Über die sozialistische Bewegung in Deutschland," 293.
64. Hess, "Die europäische Triarchie," in *Philosophische und Sozialistische Schriften*, 118.
65. See Ruge, "Freiheit, befreite Natur," "Freiheit und Recht," and "Der Mensch, eine Skizze," in *Sämmtliche Werke*, vol. 6 (Mannheim, 1848); and *Der Patriotismus*. On the self-destructive effects of Ruge's denunciation of German patriotism, see A. Stahr, *Kleine Schriften zur Literatur und Kunst* (Berlin, 1871), 1: 448. In the mid-1840s, Ruge described his position as humanism or democratism, but not as social democracy. A conceptual evolution is evident in Ruge's *Die Gründung der Demokratie in Deutschland, oder der Volksstaat und die social-demokratische Freiheit* (Leipzig, 1849), which defends the idea of "social democratic republicanism."
66. Engels, *Ludwig Feuerbach and the End of Classical German Philosophy*, 14.
67. Marx to Feuerbach, 11 August 1844, *CW* 3: 354.
68. Engels, "Progress of Social Reform on the Continent," *CW* 3: 406.
69. Engels, "Rapid Progress of Communism in Germany," *CW* 4: 240.
70. Hess, "Gegenwärtige Krisis der deutschen Philosophie," in *Philosophische und sozialistische Schriften*, 169-71.
71. Gamby, *Edgar Bauer*, 20.
72. See Hess, "Als die deutsch-franzosische Jahrbücher in Paris gegründet wurden, ließ ich mir von Fröbel und Graziano" [Graziano = Ruge], in *Die Gesellschaft: Internationale Revue für Sozialismus und Politik*, vol. 1; and Hess, *Philosophische und sozialistische Schriften*, 401-24.
73. See the conversation with Hess recounted in Ruge, *Zwei Jahre in Paris: Studien und Erinnerungen aus den Jahren 1843 bis 1845* (Leipzig, 1846), 39.
74. Ibid., 431-33.
75. Hess, "Über die sozialistische Bewegung in Deutschland," 300.
76. Ruge, "Der König von Preußen und die Sozialreform: Von einem Preußen," *Vorwärts*, 27 July 1844.
77. Marx, "Critical Marginal Notes on the Article 'The King of Prussia and Social Reform. By a Prussian,'" *CW* 3: 204.
78. Ibid., 202.
79. Ibid.
80. See also Marx, "Contribution to the Critique of Hegel's Philosophy of Law: Introduction," *CW* 3: 180, where Marx validates German participation in the "problems of the present" because "we are *philosophical* contemporaries of the present without being its *historical* contemporaries."
81. Ibid., 202.
82. See Ruge to Fleischer, 27 May 1845, *Ruges Briefwechsel*, vol. 1: 395-97; "Freiheit und Recht," *SW*, vol. 6; *Die Gründung der Demokratie in Deutschland, oder: Der Volksstaat und der sozial-demokratische Freistaat* (Leipzig, 1849).
83. Ruge quoted in Mesmer-Strupp, *Arnold Ruges Plan*, 144.
84. See, for example, Engels, "The Communists and Karl Heinzen," and Marx, "Moralising Criticism and Critical Morality: A Contribution to German Cultural History," *CW*, vol. 6: 291-306, 312-40.

85. Ruge, *Zwei Jahre in Paris*, 105-11.
86. Ibid., 431-32.
87. A similar argument was made in 1844 by Lorenz von Stein, "Blicke auf den Sozialismus und Communismus in Deutschland und ihre Zukunft," *Deutsche Vierteljahrsschrift* 2 (1844): 1-61.
88. For a good discussion of this development, particularly Engels' role, see Terrell Carver, *Marx & Engels: The Intellectual Relationship* (Sussex, 1983), esp. Chaps. 2-3.
89. Marx and Engels, *The German Ideology* (Moscow, 1976), 63-65.
90. Engels, *CW* 6: 75.
91. Ibid., 6: 257, 267, 272.
92. Mah, "The French Revolution and the Problem of German Modernity," offers a very good discussion of this aspect of Marx's text.
93. Marx, "Contribution to the Critique of Hegel's Philosophy of Law: Introduction," 184-85.
94. Engels, "The Constitutional Question in Germany," *CW* 6: 85.
95. See, for example, Marx, "Draft of an Article on Friedrich List's Book *Das national System der politischen Oekonomie*," *CW*, vol. 4: 265-93.
96. Engels, "The Constitutional Question in Germany," 6: 85.
97. Ibid., "German Socialism in Verse and Prose," *CW* 6: 249.
98. See Dieter Groh and Peter Brandt, "*Vaterlandslose Gesellen*": *Sozialdemokratie und Nation, 1860-1990* (Munich, 1992); and, earlier, Werner Conze and Dieter Groh, *Die Arbeiterbewegung in der nationalen Bewegung: Die deutsche Sozialdemokratie vor, während und nach der Reichsgründung* (Stuttgart, 1966).

Chapter 2

Working-Class Politics at the Crossroads of Conservatism, Liberalism, and Socialism

Hermann Beck

Not only national and constitutional issues hung in the balance during the 1860s. Due to northern Germany's rapid industrialization, social problems had also assumed a pressing urgency that demanded an expeditious, long-term political solution. Vital problems and issues that in countries like Britain and France had worked themselves out gradually, often over the course of centuries, frequently had to be resolved within the span of a decade in the states of the German Confederation. This unusual array of problems may well have represented the most important aspect of the peculiarities in Germany's development, for solutions to the interconnected national, constitutional, and social questions were bound to influence each other in a multitude of ways. The late unification of Germany and the specific features of the German nation-state, as well as the pronounced particularism of the various territorial units that composed the nation, would all have a formative impact on the only viable political solution to the social question – namely, the formation of working-class parties. These parties emerged during the short period between the resurgence of political life in 1858 to 1859 and the Franco-Prussian War of 1870 to 1871. During this time the advocates of socialism were not alone in vying for the working man's favor. Liberals and Prussian conservatives had equally high and, considering the political situation of the

Notes for this chapter begin on page 82.

age, justified hopes of winning over the emerging proletariat and using it for their own political ends.

1.

The "New Era" in Prussia, which commenced when the future William I assumed the regency for his ailing brother in 1858, ended a decade of reactionary rule and with it the manipulation of elections, previously a common practice designed to keep liberal forces from wielding decisive influence in the Prussian Landtag. The buoyant mood of optimism that surfaced in the wake of William I's regency concentrated less on social or constitutional affairs than on the question of German unity, which had already been a prominent issue during the Revolution of 1848, only to be buried during the reaction that followed it. The 1859 war between France and Austria over Italy, when the question of Prussian intervention on behalf of Austria was hotly debated, as well as the *Schillerfeiern* of the same year, when Schiller's one hundredth birthday was celebrated by liberal and national-minded Germans throughout the country, had once again pushed the national issue to the forefront.[1] Grass-roots political life, so exuberant during the revolution but stifled thereafter, was resuscitated at the same time, so that by the beginning of the 1860s an ever-growing number of political associations had emerged, among them many "worker education associations" *(Arbeiterbildungsvereine)* in which members of the working classes eagerly participated.

These *Arbeiterbildungsvereine* were initially liberal-bourgeois organizations for the working class, presided over mostly by members of the liberal bourgeoisie and imbued with liberal principles. Their founders were also intrigued by the idea of creating a mass basis for their own liberal opposition against aristocratic rule and the bureaucratic, neo-absolutist form of government that predominated in Prussia and most other states of the German Confederation. In the political cauldron of the early 1860s, when politically aware Germans, eagerly following the spellbinding developments of the Prussian constitutional conflict, rapidly grew in number and determination, the number of associations doubled from year to year: where a mere fifty associations existed in 1860, that number had risen to well over a hundred at the end of the following year.[2]

In some locations, such as the Prussian Rhine Province, the workers associations had not been founded by members of the bourgeoisie, but by the scions of the erstwhile League of Communists (*Bund der Kommunisten*). The Prussian Rhineland had already been a breeding ground for radical movements before and during the Revolution of 1848. Communist groups had been among them.[3] Now radical associations that included communists were founded in Solingen, Cologne, and Düsseldorf.[4] Those kinds of associations underline the political continuity of the workers' movement from the *Vormärz* through the Revolution into the 1860s. The remnants of the pre-revolutionary workers movement had withstood the political repression of the reactionary 1850s. In several German regions, such as the Bergisches Land and the Rhine-Main area, in Württemberg, and in Hamburg, associations founded during the Revolution had often lived on under different names.

Although the 1860s are generally regarded as the founding period of working-class associations, there existed a structural and programmatic continuity from the *Vormärz* to the Revolution and beyond. In some cases that continuity was represented by some hard-core members who remained faithful to the associations throughout their various political transmutations. Important social and political notions prevalent in 1848, such as demands for political rights and social democracy, had remained alive among journeymen and skilled laborers alike. In terms of social composition, the early workers' movement consisted mainly of apprenticed journeymen from smaller establishments as well as trained and skilled laborers, who were among the first workers to develop the consciousness of belonging to the new industrial working class.[5] In the early days of the movement workers still aspired to bourgeois social status: the "Herr" mode of address that they used with each other testifies to that. Unskilled laborers originally had little interest in participating in the *Arbeiterbildungsvereine*. They remained largely unorganized because, given working conditions, they remained too preoccupied with sheer survival and the task of feeding themselves. The better trained stratum of laborers, however, enthusiastically embraced the *Bildungsideal* of the bourgeoisie.

In the spirit of the national awakening of the late 1850s and early 1860s, the majority of workers organized in *Arbeiterbildungsvereine* not only considered themselves as a part of the greater bourgeois-liberal movement of freedom from absolute rule but also as ardent advocates of German unity and the creation of a national state. They were unanimous in believing that German unity along democratic-constitutional lines had to be realized before the social question could be tackled. Most skilled laborers, like members of the bourgeoisie, had an emotional stake in their desire to create a national state.[6]

From the viewpoint of the liberals, who initially dominated the *Arbeiterbildungsvereine*, social problems appeared to be nothing more than fleeting and transitional phenomena that could be gradually eliminated by the self-healing forces inherent in societal development. Education (*Bildung*) would not only improve the laborer as a human being and facilitate integration into bourgeois society but also blunt the dangerous edge of the working classes, whose revolutionary rebelliousness was still vividly and anxiously recalled. Liberals were convinced that their own goals, such as freedom of movement and freedom of trade, also lay in the interest of the working classes, a group they, thus, came to consider as a potential standard-bearer and ally against a common conservative foe. Paradoxically, some in the camp of that common foe – social conservatives like Josef Maria von Radowitz, Carl Rodbertus, Viktor Aimé Huber and, during the 1860s, Hermann Wagener – had based their own political considerations on similar assumptions; for they, too, intended to use first the rural and then the urban proletariat as foot soldiers in their fight against the growing might of insidious liberalism. Both liberals and conservatives in their instrumental policy conceptions had come to regard the working classes as a tool to be used against the other; indeed, among the conservatives this tradition was of a longer standing. But the working classes soon came to demonstrate their own independence. One by-product of the *Arbeiterbildungsvereine*, unintended by their liberal founders, was that workers' self-confidence grew in proportion to their increasing knowledge and newly acquired skills. To many who participated in the instructional advancement courses regularly offered by the *Arbeiterbildungsvereine*, the workings of the world around them and the political forces in operation within it became less mysterious, while their desire and ability to strike out on their own became stronger. The liberals' own creations, thus, made many a skilled laborer more conscious of his own class interests, alienating him from these very liberals.

This was a dangerous development for political liberalism in northern Germany, which at the time was locked in the life-and-death struggle of the Prussian constitutional conflict. For liberals like Hermann Schulze-Delitzsch, the spokesman for social liberalism, a united front with the growing working class was imperative because a secession of the *Arbeiterbildungsvereine* would necessarily result in a further weakening of the liberal movement against what seemed the overpowering might of the established conservative-bureaucratic state. During the early 1860s, the phase of the constitutional conflict in Prussia when another revolution appeared to be a distinct possibility, achieving at least the semblance of a united front was of central importance. A secession would clearly mean a perilous loss of blood vital for the survival of political liberalism. Nevertheless, it was the liberals' behavior which provoked the split by effectively barring workers from joining the great organization created to encourage national unity, the *Nationalverein*. When, in early 1863, the *Nationalverein* held its general assembly in Leipzig, Hermann Schulze-Delitzsch lavished praise upon those workers who used their savings to improve their situation, for "workers are so badly off, living from hand to mouth, that they have neither the time nor the inclination to concern themselves with public affairs."[7] It soon became obvious that the workers' economic condition would effectively exclude them from actual membership in the organization, given that payment of the substantial membership fee, either in monthly installments or an annual basis, was essentially unaffordable. Thus, it had become clear that the working classes would be shunted to the sidelines in what had hitherto been the great common cause of unification. This symbolic exclusion from the national political struggle anticipated a more concrete social division between the classes.

Many liberals tended to underestimate class conflicts based on actual material conflicts of interest. Even liberals like the social-minded Schulze-Delitzsch dreaded political demands such as universal suffrage for fear that they might be used to mobilize the masses on behalf of reactionary goals, which they had seen successfully translated into practice in the contemporary French state of Napoleon III. To this fear was added (though unmentioned in political discourse) the ever-present reservoir of natural mistrust felt by liberal notables *(Honoratioren)* toward unkempt laborers. Based on notions of harmony, the labor policy of liberalism eschewed controversial themes such as wages, and minimized the intrinsic conflict of interest between liberals and the working class. It was inevitable, however, that the ranks of the growing working class would evince anti-liberal tendencies: *Heimarbeiter* (outworkers) and journeymen, fearing the erosion of their working conditions by rising industrialization, could naturally muster little enthusiasm for a liberal party which endorsed and fostered this very same industrial development. Anti-capitalism, vehement resistance against industrialization, and a concomitant anti-liberalism mutually reinforced each other, and were bound to estrange the working classes from their liberal masters.

2.

Originally a majority of the liberal *Arbeiterbildungsvereine* were apolitical and strenuously avoided addressing the burning political issues of the time. Political debate would only have laid bare the contradictions between their working-class membership and their bourgeois sponsors. In February 1863 members of the central committee of the *Arbeiterbildungsvereine* in Leipzig, dissatisfied with the political vacuity of the associations and the dominance of liberal notables, turned to Ferdinand Lassalle, a man whose interest in the lower classes and critical attitude toward liberalism were well known.[8] The committee, which included Friedrich W. Fritzsche, Julius Vahlteich, and Otto Dammer, was outspoken in its opposition to the principles of the liberals' labor policy and demanded instead the direct political participation of the working classes. Given the standards of the age, the committee's letter requesting that

Lassalle become the leader of the workers' movement was an audacious step, for the view was still prevalent that workers lacked the education and the leisure for political involvement.

As a public figure Lassalle was known for his uncompromising views on democracy. Unlike other revolutionaries he had not been exiled after 1848, because, ironically, a short-term imprisonment at that time had prevented him from becoming active during the Revolution itself. Thus, Lassalle was spared not only the experience of a decade-long emigration but also the resulting trials of embitterment and alienation endured by so many other Forty-Eighters who returned to Germany in the 1860s. And theirs was often a bitterness that rendered them unable to act. Lassalle, however, remained an activist. Even at the beginning of the reactionary 1850s, he resurfaced in the police files of the Düsseldorf district as a supposedly revolutionary organizer and head of a dangerous "party of revolution" (*Umsturzpartei*).[9] And in contrast to their attitude of a decade later, Marx and Engels in their English exile found words of praise for the aspiring revolutionary.[10] His role in the divorce trials of Countess Hatzfeldt, the cause célèbre of the decade, gained Lassalle notoriety and financial independence in the form of a hefty pension which gave him the leisure to develop his own interests. In 1857 he was able to acquire a reputation as a brilliant young intellectual through the publication of his *Heraklit*, an attempted reconstitution of the philosopher's political system based on assorted fragments and scraps, which caused quite a splash in the salons as well as in the world of academic scholarship. Alexander von Humboldt and August Böckh paid him high tribute. Lassalle's reputation as an intellectual became his *entrébillet* into society and opened doors that money alone would have been unable to unbolt.

Lassalle was convinced that none of the liberals' panacea neither thrift, the foundation of consumer cooperatives and trade unions, nor disability relief funds (as suggested by Schulze-Delitzsch), nor the right of association – would be able to improve decisively the fate of the working class. As the size of the work force was regulated by the law of supply and demand, average wages would always be limited to the absolute minimum so that workers would never earn more than what was necessary to eke out a miserable existence. Lassalle, thus, deemed it imperative to escape from the yoke of this "iron law of wages." An ardent admirer of Hegelian philosophy, Lassalle was a strong believer in the state's obligation to support the poor, and consequently he demanded that the state fulfill its destiny and take up the cause of the laboring poor. He also remained convinced, however, that the practical implementation of key political demands, notably universal manhood suffrage, had to precede social ones, for only a truly democratized state would willingly shoulder its social commitment. But this democratic state could be created only if the working class

(Arbeiterstand) participated in the representative political bodies of Germany, which in turn necessitated the creation of a working-class party. Universal suffrage, the most important point in Lassalle's political program, represented an especially risky, well-nigh monstrously radical demand, even for more progressive German workers; at the beginning of the 1860s it was widely argued that workers had not yet reached an appropriate level of political maturity to justify universal manhood suffrage.[11]

The appearance of Lassalle destroyed virtually overnight the unity between the workers' movement and liberalism. Lassalle's belief in the high moral purpose of the state, his affinity for authoritarian systems based on a plebiscitary Bonapartism, his belief that the state was the ultimate instrument of socialism, and his ingrained opposition to liberal individualism explain why he regarded liberals (and not conservatives) as his main enemy.[12] The liberals fought back ferociously: Lassalle's penchant for state intervention, they suggested, was essentially reactionary. Hermann Schulze-Delitzsch's *Arbeiterkatechismus* became one of the most popular books of the age. The liberal press, more influential in shaping public opinion than ever before or afterwards during the whole duration of the Empire, lashed out at Lassalle. Personal slanders, imputations, and defamation of character had become the order of the day. Many among the working class lent an open ear to these criticisms, for Lassalle's biting attacks on *Bildungsvereine*, cooperatives, and self-help had alienated those who had profited from the instructional advancement they offered. Not only Lassalle's call for state intervention but also his implacably hostile attitude toward the Progressive party, whose courageous struggle for constitutional rights against Bismarck had won over even former democrats, smacked of reaction. It, thus, became a standard liberal reproach that Lassalle drove workers into the camp of political reaction and was secretly in league with Bismarck. The latter criticism was not without foundation.

In many regards Lassalle's ideas were paradoxically similar to the ideas of a "social kingdom" propagated by conservatives such as Josef Maria von Radowitz and Hermann Wagener. In his correspondence, the conservative Carl Rodbertus called a spade a spade when he wrote to Lassalle: "With respect to today's party struggle and to how you approach the social question in Germany, I have increasingly come to the conclusion that your solution is closer to Caesarism than to the Republic."[13] That Rodbertus's assessment was on target is borne out by one of Lassalle's letters to Bismarck, dated 8 June 1863, into which Lassalle had enclosed a copy of the statutes of his recently founded *Allgemeiner Deutscher Arbeiterverein* (ADAV):

> *from this miniature painting [the enclosed statutes] you will clearly arrive at the conviction how true it is that the* Arbeiterstand *instinctively gravitates toward*

> *dictatorship once it [the* Arbeiterstand*] can be rightly convinced that this dictatorship will be carried out in its own interest, and how much it, as I have just told you recently, will be inclined, despite all its republican persuasions – or maybe because of them – to accept the crown as the natural champion of a social dictatorship, provided the crown itself … will come to the resolution to pursue a true revolutionary and national policy and turn from a kingdom for the privileged estates into a true social and revolutionary* Volkskönigtum.[14]

Bismarck was used to receiving similar advice from his long-time friend and adviser in social issues, the *Justizrath* Hermann Wagener. In a memorandum to Bismarck which, as Bismarck's notes in the margin betray, had been diligently studied by him, Wagener wrote that "the European monarchy … only has a future as a social monarchy."[15] Therefore, it lay in the interest of the conservative party "to acquire and secure the good will of the bulk of the population by dint of active intercession on behalf of their material and moral interests."[16] Wagener also tried to convince Bismarck that the opposition of the liberal bourgeoisie could be broken only

> *by satisfying the justified material demands … of the middle classes* [Bürgerthum] *and, thus, possibly winning it over; on the other hand, by creating a political counterweight … among small tradesmen and the* Arbeiterstand, *whose social and political interests have, thus far, lacked the proper foundations and whose political wants always gravitate toward monarchical power.*[17]

Wagener also suggested that the king should prove himself to be the "king of beggars" and become a savior of the wide masses of the people.[18] To win over the hearts of the people, Bismarck should be prepared to grant substantial concessions and not shy away from introducing universal suffrage. Wagener rejected Prussia's three-class suffrage system, for he believed it unduly favored the liberal parties, whereas universal suffrage could well be accepted as a counterpart to universal conscription. Due to the lower classes' inherent conservatism, which he never doubted, the cause of conservative politics was ultimately bound to profit by it.

Lassalle might have given the very same advice. In a letter to Hermann Wagener of March 1864, Lassalle proved himself astonishingly receptive toward the notion of a "royal dictatorship," since he, too, was convinced that any additional strengthening of state power would contribute to the solution of the social question.[19] And on 12 June 1864, two months before Lassalle's death in a duel, Wilhelm Liebknecht reported to Karl Marx in his London exile that Lassalle referred to the bourgeoisie as "the sole enemy" and that he did not even flinch "from an alliance with the monarchy."[20]

This astounding congruence with social conservatism is one of the hallmarks of Lassalle's thought. The main point of convergence between Lassalle's socialism and Prussian social conservatism was the notion of a social kingdom. But there were other similarities. A corollary of the social kingdom was the consolidation of the central state power, without which neither Lassalle nor the conservative Wagener believed themselves able to redress social grievances. In addition, there was the struggle by socialists against the increasing atomization of modern society and its "*Bindungslosigkeit*," its lack of commitment, a criticism also leveled by conservatives such as Josef Maria von Radowitz and Hermann Wagener. To these conservatives liberalism posed by far the greater danger to the future of society, since socialists made at least a commendable effort to install a new community in the place of the one that had been lost. It was above all the yearning to recapture a lost community that socialists had in common with the conservatives. Both shared a collectivist outlook and the belief that the needs and wants of the individual had to be subordinated to those of the larger whole. Both preferred state intervention to the free play of market forces which, they were convinced, produced dubious advantages for their common enemy, the liberal entrepreneur. That was why both were in favor of replacing the liberal economic system with a more planned, state-directed organization of labor. Both shared a predilection for organization and the concomitant rejection of the liberal caretaker state with its belief in self-help. Virulent anti-liberalism constituted a final common denominator between Lassalle and the social conservatives.

Yet, despite Lassalle's common ground with conservatism and his favorable predilection toward a "royal dictatorship," his contacts with Bismarck remained without immediate political effect. After 1866, the fourth estate became politically dispensable, because Bismarck had found a new ally in the National Liberals. But already by the time of Lassalle's death in 1864 it had become clear that, through his foreign policy, Bismarck was prepared to make concessions to the liberal program of unification in order to undermine the initially implacable antagonism of his liberal opponents. The main reason for the failure of the collaboration between Lassalle and Bismarck, however, was stark in its simplicity: at the time, Lassalle had nothing to offer; he had no mass organization behind him.

When Lassalle died on 31 August 1864, his *Allgemeiner Deutscher Arbeiterverein*, founded in May 1863, had a mere 4,600 members. Even Lassalle's charismatic personality, admired by the most steadfast of opponents, together with the religious overtones evinced by his movement, had not been sufficient to build a mass organization. At the time of its founder's death, the ADAV had only thirty-five members in Berlin, 208 in Silesia, 2,669 in the Prussian Rhineland, and 1,693 in other German states. The lack of favor Lassalle's policy found with the working class was due in no small measure to his anti-liberalism and his hatred of the bourgeoisie, a sentiment workers during this period did not unequivocally share. For his own age, Lassalle's program was too radical; and his obstinate opposition to liberalism hurt him especially during the constitutional conflict, when opponents of Prussian absolutism heralded the Progressive party as the precursor of a freer age.

Originally, the ADAV represented but a small secession from the vast movement of liberal *Arbeiterbildungsvereine*, because the founders of the ADAV consisted only of about five hundred members.[21] Among them were the remnants of the democratic movement of 1848, socialists, and erstwhile members of the League of Communists, as well as workers who increasingly chafed at their chains, such as weavers, masons, carpenters, or those engaged in outworking activities.[22] More highly qualified and better-trained and -paid urban workers, such as the engine construction workers at the Borsig locomotive factories in Berlin, remained under the sway of the Progressive party until the end of the 1860s.[23]

The strength of the ADAV was regionally centered: its points of concentration were in the industrially more developed parts of northern Germany, whereas in the south, especially in Baden and Württemberg, where industrialization set in only at the beginning of the 1860s, associations under liberal influence were still being founded until well after 1871. The ADAV was especially successful in industrialized regions outside the major urban centers, that is, in regions where liberal organizations and workers' associations were still non-existent or in the western regions of Rhine and Ruhr, where industrialization had begun early in places like Duisburg, Solingen, Barmen, Elberfeld, and Düsseldorf, as well as in cities where a traditionally high degree of political freedom contrasted all too sharply with conservative trade regulations. The concurrence of these two factors had made skilled laborers and journeymen more radical there than elsewhere. Where confrontations between workers and a liberal city government had become acrimonious, as in Leipzig or in the Rhine Province with its communist traditions, the ADAV was successful as well. Very soon after its inception the ADAV developed into a centrally-directed party which, in its earliest phase, opposed the establishment of trade unions and rejected strikes. Like its successor, the SPD, it was a party of integration that enveloped all aspects of the individual's life.

3.

In its claim to encompass every facet of existence, the ADAV was distinctly different from the *Verband Deutscher Arbeiter-Vereine* (VDAV), the union of the liberal *Arbeiterbildungsvereine*, founded in June 1863 as a response to the rival ADAV.[24] It was led by Leopold Sonnemann, a democrat and the founder of the liberal *Frankfurter Zeitung*, which was soon to evolve into a press organ of European-wide reputation. It had been Sonnemann's original intention that the VDAV would primarily safeguard the worker's economic interest (to the exclusion of politics) and, thereby, solidify the liberals' position among the laboring classes. At its first *Vereinstag* in Frankfurt the organization was represented mostly by republican democrats who favored a *großdeutsch* German solution: that is, they were pro-Austrian and anti-Prussian. Members of Prussia's Progressive party as well as moderate adherents of the *Nationalverein* were also present. It is not without irony that the most ardent advocate of a *kleindeutsch* German solution, the German *Nationalverein*, originally sponsored the VDAV, which so vehemently opposed Prussian predominance in Germany. From the first, Lassalle, clearly intent on organizing the workers strictly along class lines, was the natural enemy, since his movement seemed to undermine the liberal and democratic cause. The VDAV, by contrast, made a strenuous effort to keep the working classes within the liberal-democratic movement. It held annual *Delegiertenversammlungen* and included more than a hundred branches with over two thousand members by 1865. The organization underwent a major change in 1866, when delegates renounced their own initial political quiescence, increasingly supporting strikes and demanding higher wages and better working conditions. At its party conference in Mannheim on 10 June 1866, the executive committee decided to sever ties with the liberals and merge with the People's Party *(Volkspartei)*, a democratic organization adamantly opposed to Prussian aggrandizement.

The VDAV's estrangement from its liberal comrades-in-arms had been unavoidable due to real conflicts of interest. After 1866, this process of mutual alienation was accelerated by both sides, especially since liberals, particularly in Prussia, were generally satisfied with what had been accomplished on the road to unification. Nevertheless, the elite group of skilled laborers and craftsmen, who made up a sizable portion of the membership of the VDAV, adhered to their original radical liberal orientation even in the years after 1866.[25] The VDAV had its geographical strongholds in areas where liberals had organizational networks, such as in Berlin and the industrially advanced state of Saxony (where Lassalle's movement was also well represented), or in places with an established liberal-democratic tradition, such as Württemberg. In southern Germany, where status distinctions among craftsmen, workers, and the *Bürgertum* were less pronounced than in the north, the VDAV was generally well represented.

The political ideas of the leaders of the VDAV, men such as Leopold Sonnemann, Friedrich A. Lange, Ludwig Büchner, Ludwig Eckhardt (who, in 1865, had organized the *Deutsche Volkspartei*), and Johann Peter Eichelsdörfer, differed markedly from those of Prussia's Progressive party.

Sonnemann and the others were republicans, opposed to Prussian domination of Germany; as a rule they favored universal suffrage and demanded a parliament that was politically accountable. Before 1866, they had little difficulty in protecting their organization from socialist ideas, as most politically active workers had already participated in the *Arbeiterbildungsvereine* and their political exertions during the years of the constitutional conflict were primarily directed against Bismarck.

To the contemporary observer the most obvious difference between the ADAV and the VDAV – apart from the latter's more critical attitude toward the state – was their contrasting position on the national question. Thus, it was not a social issue, but different visions of the resolution of the German question that divided the workers' movement. Both branches of the workers' movement strongly favored national unity. Indeed, the demand that all Germans be unified in a federated, liberal, and democratic state was a cornerstone of the VDAV's program even at the time of its foundation in June 1863. From its very inception the organization claimed a close connection to the democratic ideals of the Revolution of 1848 and displayed a concomitant distrust of Prussia. For the VDAV, national unity and social democracy were inseparable twin goals. Conservatives were their main enemy. In stark contrast to the pro-Prussian, *kleindeutsch* orientation of the ADAV which, in 1866, hoped for the victory of Prussian arms, the VDAV was intent on creating a greater German state, dominated by Austria.

Wilhelm Liebknecht, one the leaders of the VDAV and later to emerge as one of the driving forces in the growth of German social democracy, was known for his hatred of Prussia. For him as for other former revolutionaries, Prussia was the incarnation of reaction, having bloodily suppressed the Revolution and driven thousands into a miserable existence as homeless migrants in foreign lands. In the other German states, notably in the south and in Saxony, the broad masses of the population considered Prussia to be a counterrevolutionary power that had smothered in blood the revolutionary uprisings of Saxony and Baden. Since the eruption of the constitutional conflict, which had brought the semi-absolutist traits of the Prussian state to the fore and had, thus, re-emphasized its reactionary nature, the much-vaunted "moral conquests" in Germany made by the Prussian government at the beginning of the New Era had quickly been dispelled. With the approach of war in 1866, this well-nourished hatred of Prussia intensified. Liebknecht and his comrades-in-arms were convinced that a Prussian victory might mean the loss of German borderlands, which, in Liebknecht's view, Bismarck had secretly pledged to France, not to mention the complete domestic triumph of reaction. Such fears were generally widespread in Saxony and southern Germany. The outbreak of war and the Prussian victory at Königgrätz, thus, became a caesura in the history of German political parties and also a decisive date for the political development of working-class parties.

Directly following Königgrätz, August Bebel and Wilhelm Liebknecht founded the *Sächsische Volkspartei,* which served as a branch of the *Deutsche Volkspartei* on the one hand and the political arm of the VDAV on the other. This radical democratic party in Saxony emerged at a time when the national question had begun to pervade even the most divisive of socio-political disputes. Respective positions on national orientation clearly overshadowed any common perception or universal resolution of social problems. When push came to shove, the workers' associations in Saxony voted with the conservative Saxon particularists, just as in Prussia Lassalle's workers' movement had allied itself with Bismarck.

4.

In the other German states party formation was even more decisively influenced by national considerations than in Prussia. Bismarck's policies and Prussia's struggle for predominance in Germany had fundamentally altered the nature of liberalism and political democracy. In 1861 and 1862 most of the liberal factions and groups in the smaller and medium-sized German states had followed the lead of Prussia's Progressive party and adopted the name *Fortschrittspartei.* What was more, the initially uncompromising struggle for constitutional rights against the absolutism of the crown made even some former radical democrats join the Prussian Progressives. At the beginning of the 1860s, the party was celebrated by all liberal and democratic elements in Germany. But as Bismarck emerged as the only viable executor of the liberal program, and as it became clear that even the *Nationalverein,* with its close ties to the Prussian Progressive party, would simply follow in his wake, it was natural that the reputation of the latter began to suffer among all those who looked askance at Prussia's semi-absolutist governmental structure. Mistrust was especially pronounced among former revolutionary democrats who demanded that a new democratic *Volkspartei* with an orientation to the left of the Progressives be founded. The foundation of such a party was beset with problems because the notion of "democrat" had acquired a purely negative connotation after the Revolution; even at the time of the constitutional conflict terms such as "democracy" and "*Volkspartei*" were likely to encounter deep popular resentment.[26] In the first half of the 1860s, political democracy distinguished itself from the liberalism of the Progressive party by its advocacy of universal manhood suffrage, a distinction that had naturally become obsolete after 1866. The program of the Progressive party, by contrast, was dominated by demands for constitutional reform and national unification. With respect to social policy it offered next to nothing. Its exclusive orientation toward a *kleindeutsch* solution kept those who might have enriched its social program, people such as Carl Rodbertus and Lothar Bucher, for example, at bay.[27] And Hermann Schulze-Delitzsch, the standard-bearer of the party's social ideas, would be fully propelled into action only by the appearance of Lassalle. The politics of the Progressive party were also shaped by ideals regarding free trade, so that curtailing state intervention and liberating economic life from the police state's restraining fetters occupied center stage. Innate mistrust toward social-policy legislation became an inevitable corollary. What was more, Prussia's three-class franchise deprived Progressives of all political incentives to woo voters of the third class who, for the most part, did not bother to participate in public elections. With the Progressive party's credit on the decline, the chance for a viable, more socially conscious *Volkspartei* improved.

Yet, in the eyes of many, Bismarck's unexpected and complete triumph of 1866 had depreciated the high-flown ideals of democrats and Left liberals who yet again had failed miserably to translate their ideals into practice. The success of Bismarck's policy signified a general change of opinion to the disadvantage of political democracy, a conversion that was especially blatant in the case of erstwhile radical revolutionaries who eagerly went over into the camp of reaction or at least to that of National Liberalism.[28] Those who had resided in England and France for long periods and who had chafed at what they perceived as a contempt for German and Prussian military impotence were now especially inclined to gloat over Prussian military exploits. In addition, the introduction of universal manhood suffrage on the territory of the North German Diet had fulfilled one of political democracy's main demands, so that only a small circle of democrats was loath to accept the changes that had come in the wake of the Austro-Prussian War.

In Saxony, the creation of a *Volkspartei* had been a direct consequence of the threatening preponderance of Prussian power following the war of 1866, because the bulk of the working class, artisanate, and small tradesmen there were democratic and anti-Prussian. And in the south, it was in Württemberg that the democratic movement in the second half of the 1860s was strongest. But in both cases it was obvious from the first that the new party would offer a viable alternative only if supported by the masses of the working class. The *Württemberger Volkspartei*, mindful of its need for mass support, assiduously endeavored to accommodate the interests of laborers, and, thus, vociferously promoted protective legislation for workers and even legal claims for material support.[29] In Saxony, where the Saxon *Volkspartei* was closely affiliated with the VDAV, Bebel and Liebknecht were careful to keep socialist program elements out of the

Volkspartei's Chemnitz Program for fear of alienating the liberal *Arbeiterbildungsvereine*. It was in their own interest not to overemphasize class differences between the bourgeoisie and working class so as not to weaken the united front of all anti-Prussian forces and out of consideration for democrats in southern Germany whose assistance was indispensable in tackling the hegemony of Prussia. For the time being, the conflicts between democracy and socialism, two forces that had been such seemingly close allies against Prussia after 1866, remained latent. Toward the end of the 1860s, however, the inevitable showdown could no longer be postponed, and the result was a separation between "pure" political democracy and social democracy.[30] At the time it was clear that the future would belong to the socialists, for traditional democracy, when deprived of its mass basis, had little chance to survive. Already in 1866 it had been weakened first by the enthusiasm accompanying the outbreak of war and then by the Prussian victory. In 1870 it would meet with the same fate; in fact, the consequences were now even graver, as the Franco-Prussian War rendered the *großdeutsch* democratic course of the *Volkspartei* obsolete. In the Empire the ideals of traditional "pure" democracy began to pale, and 1848 was essentially recalled as an ill-conceived, youthful prank best forgotten.

For the ADAV the results of 1866 spelled the end of collaboration with Bismarck. Although this link had already been suspended before Lassalle's death, it was revived under a different leadership later on. Lassalle's immediate successor as president was Bernhard Becker, formally appointed at the Düsseldorf Congress in November 1864; but he soon proved unsuitable, especially when compared to his charismatic predecessor, and was forced to step down. Becker was succeeded by Karl Wilhelm Tölcke, though it might be noted that the organization's second man, Johann Baptist von Schweitzer, editor of the party paper *Social-Demokrat*, wielded greater power. In 1866, Countess Hatzfeldt, Lassalle's confidante, intimate friend, and admirer, attempted to replace Tölcke with her own protegé Hugo Jillmann. The attempt failed and August Perl, who had been nominated by Schweitzer, was appointed president. Finally, in May 1867 Schweitzer himself came into the leadership. Outraged at Schweitzer's election, about one fifth of the movement's members, representing party sections in Saxony, Schleswig-Holstein, and Bremen, broke away from the ADAV with Countess Hatzfeldt's encouragement. These dissidents soon formed a separate party, the *Lassallesche Allgemeine Deutsche Arbeiterverein*, soon to become known as the "female" line of Lassalle's movement due to the Countess's financial domination. Though internal developments during the two years of its separate existence may be of little intrinsic interest, its very existence was undeniably important, as it later helped to determine Schweitzer's own tactics.

Neither Schweitzer nor Bernhard Becker had been averse to collaborating with the government, if only as a means of pushing through universal manhood suffrage. In a rare and self-serving gesture of generosity by the Prussian government, Schweitzer had been granted furlough from prison in May 1866 so that he could mobilize the masses of the working men for universal suffrage. Even after Königgrätz, Schweitzer supported Bismarck; he condoned Prussian annexations, the Nikolsburg Peace, and Prussian leadership in the North German Diet. As late as 1867 the ADAV called on voters in the Elberfeld constituency in the Rhine Province to vote not for the liberal candidate but for Bismarck in run-off elections. Yet when Bismarck made peace with the liberal bourgeoisie Schweitzer had to realize that he had backed the wrong horse. In addition to his old enemy, the liberals, he was now forced to attack the government as well. What was more, the VDAV remained unappeased, because Schweitzer had so willingly acknowledged Prussian leadership in the North German Confederation. Movement toward a possible union with the VDAV or the anti-Prussian *Volkspartei* had, thus, become virtually impossible. On the contrary: the more the VDAV grew into a working-class party, the more vigorous became its rivalry with the ADAV. And Schweitzer was unrelenting in his (often public) professions that the VDAV was no real working-class party at all, given its alliance with the *Volkspartei.*

This was a weighty accusation, since in Prussia's new provinces, annexed after the 1866 war, reactionary and conservative supporters of former legitimate, sovereign princes had joined the *Volkspartei* to demonstrate their anti-Prussian pique; the result was a paradoxical alliance of democracy and reactionary particularism. Prussia's triumph and the events of 1866 had also radicalized the VDAV and the newly founded Saxon *Volkspartei* affiliated with it. Their leadership was divided between liberal democrats like Leopold Sonnemann, Ludwig Büchner, and Ludwig Eckardt on the one hand, and socialists like Wilhelm Liebknecht and August Bebel on the other. Until 1868 the socially diverse VDAV, an amalgamation of anti-Prussian and *großdeutsch* elements, remained ideologically uncommitted.[31]

5.

The radicalization of the VDAV was hurried along by the mere existence of the ADAV and accelerated further by Schweitzer's allegation that it lacked the qualities of a true working-class party. The competition of both organizations eventually involved even the First International, founded by Karl Marx in 1864, since unquestioning compliance with its principles served as a litmus test for true socialism. In 1868, both ADAV and VDAV subscribed to the program of the International.[32] When Bebel, president of the VDAV since 1867, suggested at the Nuremberg *Vereinstag* in September 1868, where representatives of 130 *Arbeitervereine* had assembled, that his organization should adhere to the program of the International, he pointed out that in August the ADAV had already done so at its Hamburg General Assembly. Even the liberal bourgeois deputies of the VDAV were not openly opposed to the connection with the International. Sonnemann, anxious to avoid a conflict between the VDAV and the *Volkspartei*, even supported the rapprochement with Marx's International Working Men's Association. At the Nuremberg Congress the predominance of the VDAV's radical wing forced a minority of associations, close to Prussian liberalism, to withdraw from the organization, while the majority increasingly fell under the sway of Liebknecht and Bebel. Although at this point both men were still loath to cut existing links with the *Volkspartei*, a new workers' party, composed of the VDAV's remaining radical majority and a group of renegades from Schweitzer's ADAV, soon emerged. This was the *Sozialdemokratische Deutsche Arbeiter-Partei* (SDAP), founded in August 1869 in Eisenach.

Again it had been Schweitzer who was indirectly responsible for developments that ran counter to his own interests. Up to the Nuremberg *Vereinstag*, Schweitzer refused to admit the existence of a second working-class party, but further obtuseness in the matter became impossible after his rival organization joined the International. In vehement public attacks on Liebknecht's and Bebel's movement, Schweitzer was careful to blur any distinction between their socialist left wing and the reactionary-particularist right wing of the *Volkspartei*. He could, thus, engage in a wholesale condemnation of the entire *großdeutsch* democratic movement.[33] But toward the end of 1868 Schweitzer's own position had become precarious; in September, the Leipzig headquarters of the ADAV had been closed by the police, and, in December, Schweitzer himself was taken into custody. Liebknecht and Bebel were quick to capitalize on Schweitzer's absence. In March 1869 they put in an appearance at the ADAV's annual congress, charging that Schweitzer was in the pay of Bismarck. These allegations did not remain without effect and jeopardized Schweitzer's own standing within the ADAV. When Liebknecht and Bebel renewed their attack in June, Schweitzer himself went on the offensive. Knowing that he could count on the support of Fritz Mende, president of the Hatzfeldt splinter group which had left the ADAV when Schweitzer had been elected president, he now hoped to reunite the *Lassallesche Allgemeine Arbeiterverein* with his own organization. But when Schweitzer proclaimed reunification without first consulting with other ADAV leaders – he had always reveled in emulating Lassalle's dictatorial style – a number of leading members from northern Germany dissociated themselves from him.[34] Together with Liebknecht the secessionists called upon socialists from all of Germany to send delegates to a general assembly in Eisenach, where a new unitary party was to be created. The group that had split from the ADAV left no doubt about the fact that it would join only an unambiguously socialist organization which, in turn, forced Liebknecht and Bebel to stop camouflaging their own socialist persuasions.[35] When the VDAV, founded six years previously by Sonnemann, merged into the new SDAP, the majority of traditional "pure" democrats were compelled to distance themselves from their own creation, even though the program of the SDAP, an amalgam of the principles of the Chemnitz program of the Saxon *Volkspartei* with those of the Nuremberg program of the VDAV, contained no communist demands.

The geographical strongholds of the SDAP were in Saxony, Thuringia, Franconia, Württemberg, Baden, and the Palatinate, while the new party had almost no support in Prussia. The SDAP did not consider itself part of the *Deutsche Volkspartei,* though existing affiliations remained in operation. Due to the influx of the group of uncompromising socialists from the ADAV it had become a true working-class party, so that on the eve of German unification two working-class parties confronted each other: the ADAV with about 14,000 members in northern Germany and the SDAP with about 10,000 members in the south (including Saxony).[36] The new party naturally remained loyal to international socialism; it was this tight mooring at the dock of the International that would eventually spell doom for its alliance with liberalism.

Because the SDAP had acknowledged the political leadership of the International, the *Volkspartei* was bound to follow the further development of international socialism with interest. Grave concern was, thus, inevitable when, at the International's 1869 Basel Congress, an overwhelming majority of deputies favored the abolition of private property in land and its transformation into common property.[37] Leading democrats were now fearful that if the resolution were adopted by the SDAP, the working classes would automatically incur the hostility of all other classes of society. Jacob Venedey, democrat and revolutionary of 1848, argued that endorsement would drive other classes of the population into the camp of reaction: Bismarck and Napoleon III, thus, had good reason to be grateful for the International's untimely extremism.[38]

Even though Liebknecht and Bebel deemed the Basel demands too provocative, it proved impossible to disclaim them before their own party. The leaders of the SDAP found themselves in an inescapable predicament: on the one hand, they did not want to destroy all links with the *Volkspartei,* but on the other their reluctance to acknowledge the Basel resolution made them subject to constant attacks from Schweitzer and radicals within their own party. Promptings of the Württemberg *Volkspartei* to reject the Basel resolution once and for all compounded their dilemma, as critics within their own ranks grew more vigorous. The most trenchant criticism was voiced by the group of secessionists from the ADAV, who had made a break with Schweitzer and now demanded an unequivocal profession to the socialist faith. Their unease was kept alive by Schweitzer's unrelenting attacks that cast aspersions on the socialist character of the SDAP.[39] Liebknecht and Bebel delayed the matter as long as possible. It was only when a group of Bavarian socialists, dissatisfied with Schweitzer's leadership style, declared their readiness to secede from the ADAV and join the SDAP that they were prepared to risk the final break with the *Volkspartei.*[40] The Bavarian group, deeply suspicious of the SDAP's links with the *Volkspartei,* made it clear that they would join only if the SDAP unambiguously subscribed to the socialist creed.

When the resolution was officially adopted at the SDAP's Stuttgart Congress, the break had become inevitable. Only weeks later, the outbreak of the Franco-Prussian War destroyed the two groups' common anti-Prussian, *großdeutsch* orientation. In the camp of the democratic *Volkspartei,* Sonnemann deeply regretted that theoretical differences had undermined a united front on practical political issues. Dismay over the separation was naturally much greater among the ranks of the *Volkspartei,* whose leaders clearly realized that the erosion of their traditional mass base, the industrial working class, had made their party's decline but a matter of time.

6.

In the wake of the great changes of the 1860s, a buoyant mood of optimistic activity permeated the system of German political parties; new parties were being founded and existing ones were being rapidly transformed. In their annual assemblies they were forced to work out theoretical problems and, thus, could not avoid – as happened in the case of the *Volkspartei* and SDAP – commenting upon and reacting to the burning and divisive issues of the day, such as the Basel resolution. In the contemporary context of German development this great divide between working-class movements and bourgeois democracy was, therefore, unavoidable. One might argue that it was a break that occurred twice: first in the spring of 1863, with the foundation of the *Allgemeine Deutsche Arbeiterverein,* and then again in June 1870, when the *Volkspartei* and the SDAP went their separate ways. It would be idle to regret this division and speculate whether liberals in the 1860s might have fought more ardently for constitutional reform if only they had not had to face another enemy on their left, or if the authoritarian political system of the German

Empire, so clearly foreshadowed in the constitution of the North German Diet, had borne a more visibly liberal-democratic stamp. Arguing along these lines, one is bound to say that the very fact that socialist parties came into being at an early date in Germany contributed to the erosion of the Empire's liberal-democratic potential, for liberals became more willing to compromise and conservatives became more adamant in refusing to consider change and adaptation. One might also remember that the separation between bourgeois democratic liberalism and social democracy had already been anticipated during the Revolution of 1848, and that German liberals – in contrast to some of their conservative opponents – were little bothered about the social question. The development of scientific socialism by Marx and Engels in their exile in England had nothing to do with this great division. Schweitzer was probably more familiar with Marx's theoretical writings than Liebknecht, who so willingly deferred to the master's authority. Through their early connection with the First International and by agreeing to make the resolutions of that body binding on their development, German socialists knowingly became political outcasts. Both ADAV and VDAV eagerly sought to claim the International as a higher authority and as a source of legitimacy to emphasize the superiority of their own brand of socialism. The most obvious and important reason for the early separation of democrats and liberals from socialists undoubtedly lies in the coincidence of constitutional, national, and social problems during the decade of the *Reichsgründung* and not in what has often been called the traditional weakness of German liberalism.

Notes

1. On the history of the period in general see Thomas Nipperdey, *Deutsche Geschichte 1800-1866: Bürgerwelt und starker Staat* (Munich, 1983), as well as idem, *Deutsche Geschichte 1866-1918: Machtstaat vor der Demokratie* (Munich, 1992), 11-84; Wolfram Siemann, *Gesellschaft im Aufbruch: Deutschland 1849-1871* (Frankfurt, 1990); Hans-Ulrich Wehler, *Deutsche Gesellschaftsgeschichte 1849-1914* (Munich, 1995), 7-492, and, among the older histories, Johannes Ziekursch, *Politische Geschichte des neuen deutschen Kaiserreiches: Die Reichsgründung* (Frankfurt, 1925).
2. On the regional distribution and strength of the *Arbeiterbildungsvereine*, see Toni Offermann's informative and well-documented *Arbeiterbewegung und liberales Bürgertum in Deutschland 1850-1863* (Bonn, 1979), esp. 515-56.

3. Jonathan Sperber, *Rhineland Radicals: The Democratic Movement and the Revolution of 1848-1849* (Princeton, 1991).
4. Helga Grebing, *Arbeiterbewegung: Sozialer Protest und kollektive Interessenvertretung bis 1914* (Munich, 1985), 53.
5. See especially Shlomo Na'aman, *Demokratische und soziale Impulse in der Frühgeschichte der deutschen Arbeiterbewegung der Jahre 1862/63* (Wiesbaden, 1969). On the issue of continuity, see Frolinde Balser, *Sozialdemokratie 1848/49-1863*, 2 vols. (Stuttgart, 1963).
6. Werner Conze and Dieter Groh, *Die Arbeiterbewegung in der nationalen Bewegung* (Stuttgart, 1966).
7. August Bebel, *Ausgewählte Reden und Schriften*, 6: *Aus meinem Leben* (Berlin, 1983), 57-58. Schulze-Delitzsch welcomed workers as "spiritual members, as honorary members of the *Nationalverein*."
8. Grebing, *Arbeiterbewegung*, 58-59; Bebel, *Aus meinem Leben*, 60-77; Vernon L. Lidtke, *The Outlawed Party: Social Democracy in Germany* (Princeton, 1966), 18-27; Shlomo Na'aman, *Lassalle* (Hanover, 1970); Arno Herzig, *Der Allgemeine Deutsche Arbeiter-Verein in der deutschen Sozialdemokratie: Dargestellt an der Biographie des Funktionärs Carl Wilhelm Tölke, 1817-1893* (Berlin, 1979); and, for an informed East German synopsis, see Rolf Weber, "Der Kampf zwischen demokratischen und antirevolutionären Kräften um die Bildung des bürgerlichen Nationalstaates (1859-1871)," in *Deutsche Geschichte*, ed. Walter Schmidt et al. (Berlin, 1984), 4: 422-511.
9. "Polizeilicher Wochenbericht aus Düsseldorf vom 29. Dezember 1851," BAP, Rep. 30, C-Titel 94, Lit. W, no. 296. See also Hans-Jürgen Friederici, *Ferdinand Lassalle: Reden und Schriften* (Berlin, 1985), 14.
10. Marx deemed Lassalle "trotz der vielen 'Abers' … dur und energisch" (10 March 1853); Engels also praised his usefulness. Karl Marx and Friedrich Engels, *Der Briefwechsel, 1844-1883* (Munich, 1983), 1: 456-57.
11. In his recollections, August Bebel tells us that while freedom of trade and freedom of movement were demands fully supported by most workers, universal suffrage did not appear to be an "indispensable right" (*unentbehrliches Recht*). Bebel, *Aus meinem Leben*, 60.
12. Heinz Gollwitzer, "Der Cäsarismus Napoleons III. im Widerhall der öffentlichen Meinung Deutschlands," *Historische Zeitschrift* 173 (1952): 23-78, esp. 71-73.
13. Ferdinand Lassalle, *Nachgelassene Briefe und Schriften*, ed. Gustav Mayer (Stuttgart and Berlin, 1922), 6: 295.
14. Gustav Mayer, *Bismarck und Lassalle: Ihr Briefwechsel und Ihre Gespräche* (Berlin, 1928), 60.
15. "Denkschrift von Justizrath Wagener vom 1. März 1864," GStAPK (M), Rep. 92, Nachlaß Zitelmann, Nr. 91, Bl. 1.
16. Ibid, Bl. 9-10.
17. Ibid., Bl. 2.
18. Hermann Wagener, *Die Lösung der sozialen Frage* (Berlin, 1878), 66.
19. Lassalle to Hermann Wagener, 3 March 1864, BAP, Rep. 90 Wa 3, Nachlaß Hermann Wagener, Nr. 1, Bl. 175.
20. Mayer, *Bismarck und Lassalle*, 53.
21. Grebing, *Arbeiterbewegung*, 60.
22. Jürgen Kocka, *Lohnarbeit und Klassenbildung* (Bonn, 1983), 190. See also Roger P. Morgan, *The German Social Democrats and the First International, 1864-1872* (Cambridge, Mass., 1965), 4.
23. Herzig, *Der Allgemeine Deutsche Arbeiter-Verein*.

24. The acronym VDAV is used interchangeably for *Verband Deutscher Arbeiter-Vereine and Vereinstag Deutscher Arbeiter-Vereine* (e.g., Grebing and Wehler use *Vereinstag*, while Rolf Weber and Roger Morgan use *Verband*).
25. See Shlomo Na'aman, ed., *Von der Arbeiterbewegung zur Arbeiterpartei: Der fünfte Vereinstag der deutschen Arbeitervereine zu Nürnberg im Jahr 1868* (Berlin, 1976).
26. In his memoirs of the 1848 Revolution, Jacodus Temme tells the reader that "Demokrat" and "Demokratie" had become terms viewed with loathing. No one wanted to be considered a democrat, for it was widely held that they had been responsible for the Revolution and had pushed the country into misery in 1849. See J.D. Temme, *Erinnerungen*, ed. Stefan Born (Leipzig, 1883).
27. Gustav Mayer, "Die Trennung der proletarischen von der bürgerlichen Demokratie in Deutschland," in idem, *Radikalismus, Sozialismus und bürgerliche Demokratie*, ed. Hans-Ulrich Wehler (Frankfurt, 1969), 108-78, esp. 112.
28. Some of the more prominent names include Arnold Ruge (1802 to 1880), Friedrich Karl Hecker (1811 to 1881), Friedrich Kapp (1824 to 1884), Ludwig Bamberger (1823 to 1899), Karl Hillebrand (1829 to 1884), and Lothar Bucher (1817 to 1892). The former Left Hegelian Bruno Bauer (1809 to 1882) had earlier been attracted to Bonapartist ideas; he avidly collaborated with Bismarck's adviser Hermann Wagener on the project of a conservative encyclopedia, the *Staats- und Gesellschaftslexikon*. One forgets too easily that even in the early 1840s Left Hegelians had been Prussian patriots and were favorably disposed toward the Prussian state, but were then deprived of the chance to participate.
29. The Stuttgart Program of the *Volkspartei* did include a social program. See Mayer, "Trennung," 108-79, esp. 149-52.
30. On liberalism, democracy, social democracy, and the eventual division, see S.W. Armstrong, "The Social Democrats and the Unification of Germany 1863 to 1871," in *Journal of Modern History* 12 (1940): 485-509; Ernst Schraepler, "Linksliberalismus und Arbeiterschaft in der preußischen Konfliktzeit," in *Forschungen zu Staat und Verfassung: Festgabe für Fritz Hartung*, ed. Richard Dietrich und Gerhard Oestreich (Berlin, 1958), 385-401; the essays in Jürgen Kocka, *Europäische Arbeiterbewegungen im 19. Jahrhundert* (Göttingen, 1983); Wolfgang Schieder, "Das Scheitern des bürgerlichen Radikalismus und die sozialistische Parteibildung in Deutschland," in *Sozialdemokratie zwischen Klassenbewegung und Volkspartei*, ed. Hans Mommsen (Frankfurt, 1974), 17-34; Raymond H. Dominick, *Wilhelm Liebknecht and the Founding of the German Social Democratic Party* (Chapel Hill, NC, 1982); and Mayer, "Trennung."
31. For a summary of this anti-Prussian attitude, see Wilhelm Liebknecht to Friedrich Engels, 11 December 1867, quoted in Gustav Mayer, *Friedrich Engels: Eine Biographie*, 2 vols. (The Hague, 1934), 2: 161.
32. The International had been explicitly working-class from the outset, advocating trade unionism, an eight-hour day, and public education. Initially these goals were acceptable to non-socialist democrats like Leopold Sonnemann. The early growth of the International in Germany had been due largely to the propaganda of Johann Philipp Becker, and soon it became clear that allegiance to its program would be a source of prestige for the emerging working-class parties. See the excellent study by Roger P. Morgan, *The German Social Democrats and the First International 1864-1872* (Cambridge, Mass., 1965).
33. Particularism was especially widespread in southern Germany. Despite their adulation of local dynasties, particularist movements in Württemberg and Hesse were democratic, while they displayed strong clerical overtones in the Catholic regions of Bavaria and in Southern Baden. The April 1868 elections to the *Zoll-*

parlament gave an impressive demonstration of the potential political clout of particularism. See Johannes Ziekursch, *Politische Geschichte des Deutschen Kaiserreiches* (Frankfurt, 1925), 1: 247; and Ernst Rudolf Huber, *Deutsche Verfassungsgeschichte seit 1789*, 3rd ed. (Stuttgart, 1988), 3: 629-41.

34. These were, among others, Wilhelm Bracke (1842 to 1880) from Braunschweig, Samuel Spier (1828 to 1903) from Wolfenbüttel, and the Hamburg leaders Wilhelm Geib (1842 to 1879), August Perl, and Theodor Yorck (1830 to 1875).
35. See Gustav Mayer, *Johann Baptist von Schweitzer und die Sozialdemokratie* (Jena, 1909), 357-59.
36. Figures in Ziekursch, *Politische Geschichte*, 1: 250-51.
37. Even though he anticipated difficulties with the *Volkspartei*, Liebknecht, who went to Basel as an SDAP deputy, voted for the resolution as well.
38. See Mayer, "Trennung," 157-58.
39. Schweitzer alleged that Liebknecht and Bebel were far from being true socialists: their radicalism merely sprang from anti-Prussian resentments. Liebknecht's and Bebel's seeming ambiguity lent credence to these charges.
40. See Morgan, *Social Democrats*, 193-99.

Chapter 3

The Lassallean Labor Movement in Germany

Organization, Social Structure, and Associational Life in the 1860s

Toni Offermann

1. Introduction: Lassalle and Lassalleanism

A decade after the defeat of the democratic and labor movements in 1849 to 1850, a network of "worker educational associations" began to reconstitute itself with the vigorous assistance of the left wing of the bourgeois national movement. By 1862 to 1863 efforts were again being launched to centralize associational *(Verein)* activities at the national level. Asked by a group in Leipzig to help them achieve this goal, the radical democrat Ferdinand Lassalle (1825 to 1864) outlined a social and political plan of action in his "Official Response" *(Offizielles Antwortschreiben)* that called for workers to distance themselves from the liberal bourgeoisie and to assert their own organizational and ideological autonomy. For the working class, he asserted, the liberal bourgeoisie represented the real political and economic enemy. Probably for tactical reasons, Lassalle embraced the older idea of "associational socialism" – that is, the appropriation of the products of labor by workers organized in producer cooperatives – and combined it with the fundamental democratic demand for universal male suffrage. The state, which was nothing more than "the grand association of the working classes," should provide credits to finance such cooperatives or

Notes for this chapter begin on page 109.

"associations." But the state could only be forced to undertake such measures if workers exercised a decisive influence over its politics, and that in turn required the introduction of universal suffrage. Both ideas – state-supported producers' cooperatives and universal suffrage – contributed to divergent interpretations of "Lassalleanism" in the 1860s. These ranged from state-socialist ideas of a "social kingdom" to reformist conceptions of a "legal" transformation of society to radical democratic, petty-bourgeois, anti-capitalist ideas of revolutionary change. The theory of the "iron law of wages," which Lassalle had incorporated into his program, suggested that the average wage would always remain at the levels necessary only for bare survival. Accordingly, trade-union activity could never fundamentally or permanently improve the situation of the working class.

On 23 May 1863 the General German Workers Association (*Allgemeiner Deutscher Arbeiterverein*, or ADAV) was founded in Leipzig to "enlighten workers about their class situation" and to press for universal, equal, and direct male suffrage. In this way it would be possible, it was hoped, to establish state-financed producer associations and, thus, transform the existing class society peacefully and legally. Its highly centralized, even dictatorial organizational structure corresponded to Lassalle's own Jacobin understanding of democracy. Although Lassalle himself was repellent to many democratically inclined workers, members of the Association were convinced that his views were both a necessary precondition for effective mass organization and a guarantee of success in political agitation. Some ADAV members were recruited in 1863 to 1864 from the worker education associations that bore the stamp of artisanal attitudes toward work and morality: that is, they tended to come from urban areas with democratic associational traditions. Other members, though, came from rural regions based on proletarianized cottage labor without any kind of democratic or labor-movement tradition, and it was there that "the real, historically significant ADAV arose."[1] In that same year, however, most of the worker education associations organized themselves, with strong middle-class support, into a Congress of German Workers Associations (*Vereinstag Deutscher Arbeitervereine*) in opposition to the anti-bourgeois ADAV. In its first years this new organization was indebted to Hermann Schulze-Delitzsch and his ideas of educational and cooperative self-help. But within six years a slight majority of its member associations had become socially and politically radicalized and had transformed themselves into the Social Democratic German Workers Party (*Sozialdemokratische Deutsche Arbeiterpartei*, or SDAP), which in turn became the ADAV's most vigorous competitor.

After Lassalle's early death in 1864, "Lassalleanism" itself came to have three primary characteristics. First, Lassalleans believed workers must maintain an unconditional ideological and organizational independence vis-à-vis the liberal bourgeoisie. Workers were the only social class that pursued no special interests, and in their support for social democracy they were working for the common good. Second, Lassalleans insisted that the ADAV should remain an agitational organization that pressed for equal and universal manhood suffrage. The ADAV's organizational structure was a necessary prerequisite for success in the struggle, and it, thus, had to be maintained in its unsullied purity, true to the principles of Lassalle himself. Third, Lassalleans continued to regard trade unions as incapable of permanently improving the condition of workers.

Although it had become clear by 1866 that Lassalle's ideas could not sustain a long-term strategy for German labor, his fundamental critique of existing social-political relationships remained powerful and served as the basis of class-conscious labor politics in Germany.[2] His popular, vividly written agitational brochures continued to convince industrial workers and small-scale artisans that labor was the source of all value, that the appropriation of the full product of one's work should replace wage labor, and that this condition was attainable only in a social democratic state which in turn could only be established through the common struggle of the working class.[3] During the period following the Anti-Socialist Law of 1878, however, Lassalleanism largely lost its influence within social democracy, although Lassalle's views continued to be used on behalf of state-socialist tendencies within the SPD, especially after 1914.[4]

The following remarks will focus on two Lassallean organizations, the ADAV and the Lassallean General German Workers Association (*Lassallescher Allgemeiner Deutscher Arbeiterverein*, or LADAV). Historians have usually treated these two organizations separately, and have unfairly regarded the LADAV as a kind of sect.[5] Composed of various oppositional groups, the LADAV was established in Dresden on 16 June 1867, three years after Lassalle's death. To the extent that ideological differences underlay the split between the two Lassallean organizations, the LADAV was even stricter in its rejection of strikes and of trade unions in general. Although both organizations were guided by Lassalle's writings, the LADAV insisted dogmatically on maintaining Lassalle's statutes to the letter, especially as far as the organization's leadership structure was concerned. For tactical reasons the two organizations fused briefly in 1869. After its last general assembly in July 1871, remnants of the LADAV persisted at least until January 1873.

2. Organization of the Lassallean Party

Both before and after 1871, the laws on political association in Germany's individual states prohibited any kind of union or alliance between or among "political" associations. Any organization was regarded as "political" if it concerned itself with "public affairs," an intentionally vague formulation. In order to get around the possibility of intervention and prohibition by the police, Lassalle had originally turned to the model of the bourgeois-liberal *Nationalverein,* founded in 1859. The ADAV's original statutes did not provide for autonomous local or branch associations. Rather, all members belonged directly to the central association with its seat in Leipzig. The president named association officials to represent him at the municipal level, but they were not permitted any autonomy at all. An insoluble dilemma was the result. On the one hand, the Association needed local organizational structures to carry out local agitation and administration; but, on the other hand, such activity could threaten the existence of the local branches by enabling the police to categorize them as separate, "independent" political associations which could then be broken up, its members prosecuted for maintaining illegal contacts with other political associations.

The ADAV and the LADAV were undeniably political parties in the modern sense of the term: that is, they were organized on the basis of a dues-paying membership and attempted to influence legislation by participating in parliamentary elections. They made use of party statutes and rules for conducting business, and they had a president and an executive committee. To be sure, neither organization developed an official party program, and at the beginning they did not have much of a general sense of what they wanted to achieve politically. Lassalle's writings served as substitutes for these things, though in 1867 the ADAV did develop a kind of programmatic statement in response to the suffrage reforms that accompanied the establishment of the new North German Confederation.[6]

At the summit of the Lassallean organization stood a president with virtually dictatorial powers. According to the organization's statutes, he had to be elected by all the members of the organization. This originally took place by a vote of the delegates at the ADAV's founding congress, but Lassalle insisted that his election be confirmed by a poll of the entire membership. His successor, Bernhard Becker, was selected by a vote of the local branches *(Gemeinden)*, an arrangement that was slightly modified in 1867 and again in 1869.[7] The LADAV continued to insist on the president's direct election by the members.

The executive committee *(Vorstand)* was supposed to support and, where necessary, control the president. The twenty-four members of the executive were chosen for one-year terms at the general assembly *(Generalversammlung)*. Because the members of the executive were scattered all over Germany, they in fact could not effectively control or question the president's actions. In fact, the ADAV's highly centralized, highly dictatorial structure remained deeply controversial, but it persisted, especially during the presidency of Johann Baptist von Schweitzer.[8] Only after his resignation did the general assembly limit the president's powers. Indeed, it was this annual assembly that represented the organization's democratic qualities. Delegates to the assembly were elected at the local-branch level, and their decisions were binding on the president.

The agitational and political backbone of the Lassallean organizations was provided by the official agents *(Bevollmächtigte)* who represented the president at the local level. Lassalle had stipulated in March 1864 that members of each local organization should nominate three candidates for this position, one of whom would then be selected by the president himself.[9] Lassalle also required them to be responsible "for increasing and spreading the association's membership" at the local level.[10] This requirement often overstretched these officials' capacities, as they were often simple factory workers or artisans with little formal education and a lot of personal responsibilities.

Of course, the ranks of the local agents included many competent individuals, and their ability to deal with the problems we have just described was often quite remarkable. To a large extent they had to limit their agitational activities to public readings of Lassalle's own writings or articles from association newspapers.[11] They often had to improvise because of the absence of clearly delineated propaganda publications and policy statements; and the Lassallean newspapers – the *Nordstern*, the *Social-Demokrat*, and the *Freie Zeitung* – could only partially fill this gap. Among other things, these newspapers' range was rather limited. In 1867 to 1868, for example, a maximum of 52 to 59 percent of all ADAV locals received the *Social-Demokrat*, and it was mostly the small locals that were unable to subscribe.[12]

3. The Spread of the Lassallean Movement

The ADAV quickly learned that its centralized structure did not offer much protection against official chicanery or legal prohibitions. The organization constantly tried to emphasize to officials that it was a single, unitary organization. Its dues, however, were collected and often spent at the local level, which seemed to suggest that it was not in fact one big organization but a collection of smaller, separate associations. Accordingly, the ADAV leadership called for dues to go directly to the organization's central account.[13] It also maintained membership data for the entire organization and had to present hair-splitting arguments about the "local" uses of national funds in order to convince the authorities that it was not using these funds illegally for "local purposes." Similarly, in order to maintain the guise of a single, national organization, the president himself was required to report the election of local agents directly to officials at the local level.[14]

Despite all these efforts to ensure the continued legality of Lassallean organizations, local and state officials in Germany never doubted that the Lassallean labor movement represented a threat to the existing order; and they always attempted to repress it, despite occasional attempts to use it opportunistically as a means of breaking up the unified opposition of liberal-democratic forces. After 1865, in other words, a regionally diverse form of political warfare developed between Lassallean functionaries and representatives of the state, and these conflicts simply proved to many members that Lassalle's thesis about the nature of class society had been amply confirmed, not only at the workplace but in the behavior of the state toward its citizens. For the first two years of the ADAV's existence, officials in the various German states rarely proceeded against the Lassalleans, for the opportunistic political reasons we have just mentioned.[15] This situation changed as the ADAV's significance began to grow and the political situation within the German Confederation began to deteriorate.

In Saxony, the ADAV's seat, government officials were punctilious in their observation of the Association's activities, but uncertain about how to deal with them. In trying to devise a strategy to deal with the Lassalleans, the Saxon government sometimes asked officials in neighboring states how they dealt with their own Lassalleans, and sometimes they simply waited to see how the courts would respond to anti-Lassallean actions taken by their own lower-level authorities.[16] Some municipal authorities in Saxony, especially in the region of Zwickau, simply declared that the Lassallean locals in their jurisdictions were illegal branches of the larger national organization. And, finally, in September 1868 police officials in Leipzig unilaterally dissolved the ADAV in the city where it had been officially registered. But ADAV President von Schweitzer reestablished the organization in Berlin – that is, outside Saxony – in October, and Saxon officials themselves remained unable to develop a systematic policy toward the Lassallean groups within their own borders.[17] On the whole, general assemblies or gatherings of workers were less stringently controlled; and the uncertain, unsystematic responses of Saxon authorities toward the new labor movement found parallels in other German states.

Even where official efforts to ban the Lassalleans did not hold up in court, such litigation could incapacitate these organizations for months. And even where the authorities did not proceed directly against the Lassalleans, they could use other kinds of repressive measures to harass their opponents: e.g., by barraging them with bans on individual meetings, by accusing them of slander or libel, or by prosecuting them for alleged violations of press laws or laws of association and assembly. Such measures convinced many Lassalleans that they were indeed the victims of a merciless class justice, and they often responded to this situation in imaginative ways. So, for example, if ADAV meetings were banned, they would simply declare their meetings to be general "public assemblies" that were not prohibited by the law.[18]

Just how large and extensive were the ADAV and the LADAV? Official statements by these organizations concerning their memberships were inflated for propaganda or internal political purposes and, thus, met with justified skepticism. Still, enough reliable material was made available by the Lassalleans themselves to permit us to reach some conclusions about the number of their local associations, their regional extent, and their strength. The historian Hartmut Zwahr has already calculated figures of this sort for the year 1875, when the ADAV and the Social Democratic Workers Party (SDAP) merged.[19] The following remarks will be based on similar figures published by the ADAV and LADAV themselves.

One rather obvious source is the official statistical information presented at general assemblies between 1863 and 1874, but this material is extremely problematical. Between 1864 and 1866 from twenty-nine to fifty-seven locals were represented at Lassallean assemblies, but exact membership figures were not available. Between 1867 and 1874 the number of locals represented at the general assemblies ranged from forty-five to 180 in 1873, and the number of members represented varied from 2,508 in 1867 to 17,523 in 1874. By comparison, in 1871 the German Empire contained 2,528 municipalities with more than two thousand inhabitants, and 271 with more than ten thousand.[20] And in 1862, the year of its greatest significance, the liberal *Nationalverein* numbered between twenty and twenty-five thousand members, despite its relatively high annual dues.[21] Only in 1875 was the united workers' party able to achieve comparable membership levels. Similarly, some internal ADAV statistics paint a rather critical picture of the organization's membership. Its second president, Bernhard Becker, reported that at the time of Lassalle's death in 1864 the organization consisted of thirty-one functioning locals with a total membership of about 4,610. But even this number seems greatly inflated.[22] More reliable figures can be found in materials concerning the designation of ADAV officials between 1867 and 1871.[23] According to this information, sixty-five ADAV locals were functioning in July 1867. By April 1868 this number had increased to ninety-two, by May 1869 to 139, and by late 1869 (after the fusion with the LADAV) to 260. In mid-1871 the number was sixty-two. These numbers point to three conclusions. First, under Schweitzer's leadership the ADAV grew notably up until its merger with the LADAV. Second, the secession of the ADAV opposition after Schweitzer's organizational coup and the subsequent creation of the

SDAP did not have as dramatic an effect as has heretofore been supposed, at least as far as the actual number of locals themselves is concerned.

The Franco-Prussian War represented a more significant organizational catastrophe for the ADAV than the establishment of the SDAP a year earlier. The example of the ADAV organization in Görlitz is typical:

> With one blow the war of 1870 to 1871 destroyed everything that we had built up with such effort. Most of our comrades were conscripted for the army, and only six members remained behind. The military successes and the jingoistic mood that they engendered did not permit the members to develop political agitation .... They placed their hopes on the return of the comrades from the war, but this turned out to be a false calculation. In fact, these people came back either wounded, sick, or with military decorations, and as a result they had exchanged their ideals for jingoism.[24]

The high rate of fluctuation in membership figures becomes quite clear when one looks at the minutes of the general assembly of 23 August 1868, where it is proudly noted that sixty-three new locals had been founded since the beginning of the year.[25] However, only thirty-four of these local groups seem to have paid their dues between March 1869 and July 1871. It is safe to assume that the growing number of local groups also corresponds to a rapid turnover in members whose ties to the ADAV were of short duration. The reorganization of the ADAV after the Franco-Prussian War also points to high fluctuation levels in the membership. Only twenty out of the sixty-two locals listed in the summer of 1871 also show up in figures for 1867.

Table 1 Payments to the ADAV April 1868 – July 1871[26]

Month	Total	Complete		Partial		Not paid		Exempted		a*	b*
April 1868	78	45	57.69%	4	5.13%	15	19.23%	14	17.95%		
March 1869	118	64	54.24%	6	5.08%	32	27.12%	16	13.56%		
April 1869	131	65	49.62%	1	0.76%	56	42.75%	9	6.87%		
August 1869	141	54	38.30%	1	0.71%	81	57.45%	5	3.55%		
September 1869	190	82	43.16%			108	56.84%				
October 1869	213	85	39.91%			122	57.28%			6	
June 1870	153	66	43.14%			87	56.86%				
July 1870	169	29	17.16%			140	82.84%				
August 1870	142	33	23.24%			109	76.76%				
September 1870	144	32	22.22%			112	77.78%				
October 1870	153	27	17.65%			125	81.70%				1
May 1871	80	40	50.00%			40	50.00%				
June 1871	83	35	42.17%			48	57.83%				
July 1871	83	36	43.37%			47	56.63%				

*a = payment confirmation present b = dues payment unclear

An especially useful source of membership information is the list of receipts of dues payments from the individual locals published in the *Social-Democrat* between 1868 and 1871. These data mention all the individual localities that maintained contact with the central office during these years. The amount and the regularity of dues payments also permit some conclusions about the organizational strength of those local organizations. When the data are controlled to exclude identifiable LADAV locals during the period of the unification with the ADAV, the following figures result for the months from August to October 1869:

August 1869	113	53	46.90%	1	0.88%	54	47.79%	5	4.42%	
September 1869	158	76	48.10%			82	51.90%			
October 1869	175	78	44.57%			92	52.57%			6

Only thirteen locals appear in all the balance sheets, and only four of these paid the total amount due. This also illustrates just how miserably the ADAV's vaunted centralism functioned when it had to confront the twin realities of official harassment and its own local organizations' chronic financial weakness. Moreover, the creation of the SDAP had resulted in the loss of active, strong (and financially sound) *Gemeinden*, which in turn were replaced by unstable new organizations at the local level.

But how large was the number of *active* members of the association, that is, those who participated regularly in local meetings and, thus, in presidential elections? The constant complaints about low levels of participation in these meetings can lead us to conclude that only an activist core regularly took part. Police harassment tended to discourage participation even more. Two presidential elections are illustrative in this respect. Writing of the election of April 1868, the *Social-Demokrat* noted: "Electoral participation has been small. In practically all locations not even half of the association's members turned out .... In many places not even a third voted. And of the ninety-six locations in which the association is represented, only sixty-one took part in the election."[27] These remarks reflect general complaints about the indifference of the membership as a whole. The presidential election of February 1869, in which 17,734 members from eighty-three localities took part, elicited another rebuke from the *Social-Demokrat*: "In the end I have to note that about forty localities do not seem to have participated in the election .... On the whole, electoral participation was weak in most places."[28]

A political party's public success can of course be measured not only on the basis of its membership levels, especially under the conditions of a repressive police state, but also according to its electoral success. The German states did not employ a secret ballot, and, thus, a public vote for a candidate from the ADAV or the LADAV was tantamount to a public declaration. Still, in the Reichstag elections of March 1871 more than sixty thousand voters, or about 1.6 percent of the total, voted for the two Lassallean parties, including more than forty-six thousand in Prussia and about 2,200 in Saxony.[29] But the Lassalleans' initial electoral successes turned out to be unstable. Only four years earlier, in September 1867, the Lassallean candidate Friedrich Wilhelm Emil Försterling had garnered 5,512 votes in just one electoral district, Chemnitz in Saxony; and in March 1869 another Lassallean candidate, Fritz Mende, gained 5,615 votes in the Saxon constituency of Freiberg.[30] Election campaigning often had variable effects. Thus, members could sometimes mobilize their energy to an extraordinary extent, but often they overextended themselves. Electoral results were on the whole disappointing, which in turn frustrated precisely those members who had put a lot of their time and monetary resources into a campaign that had not brought them closer to their political goal.

The limited availability of sources makes it difficult to construct reliable statistics for the LADAV. Certainly official data presented at the LADAV's general assemblies should be regarded with great caution. The first general assembly, in June 1867, reported a total of 2,929 members, of whom 1,332 came from Dresden.[31] President Fritz Mende later spoke of 3,200 association members, though by September 1868 only 1,800 remained.[32] Twenty-three locals with about 1,200 members can be identified in internal LADAV documents from the end of 1867 and early 1868.[33] Seventy-nine local organizations with 8,818 members officially took part in the general assembly of November 1868.[34] At the end of 1869 the association launched a new membership campaign that included paid agitators, and these efforts enjoyed some success, especially in localities that did not have any kind of labor-movement tradition. These new local groups, though, tended to be short-lived. Moreover, this intensified recruitment campaign finally foundered on the shoals of the Franco-Prussian War, which, as we have seen, also had serious consequences for the ADAV. President Mende's attempt to revive the movement by traveling through the country and demanding that French reparations be used to finance producer cooperatives failed completely.[35] But despite these problems, one should not underestimate the LADAV's organizational strength. Indeed, available evidence suggests that during its existence the LADAV encompassed 130 localities with more than ten thousand members, even though most of these members only remained in the organization briefly. As Dieter Dowe has written, during its heyday in 1868 to 1869 the LADAV was a "relatively strong, internally vigorous workers' organization that was capable of expansion." Like the ADAV and the SDAP, it "did not cover all Germany equally";

rather, its organizational strength varied significantly from region to region.[36] This leads us to the next problem: the regional distribution of both the ADAV and the LADAV.

In considering this matter, we should begin with the situation of the ADAV under Lassalle himself. According to Bernhard Becker's figures, some 4,610 individuals had joined the organization by August 1864. Of that number, 2,674 (58 percent) came from the Rhineland; 670 (14.5 percent) were from Saxony; 675 (14.6 percent) came from Hamburg and its environs; and, finally, another 208 members (4.5 percent) were from Silesia. Individual memberships were also reported from Asch, Augsburg, Mainz, Frankfurt am Main, Berlin, and Bremen.[37]

Becker concluded his term of office at the general assembly of November-December 1865 by critically reviewing the organization's geographic spread.[38] Since Lassalle's death, he noted, the organization had almost tripled in size to about 5,500 members, but it had not yet penetrated new regions of Germany. There were a few new local groups in Saxony, Silesia, the Rhineland, Schleswig-Holstein, Braunschweig, and in a few locations in Prussia's Saxon province. The list of local agents from July 1867 shows no significant changes. Original centers of the movement, like the Rhineland and Saxony, were also the areas that showed the strongest growth in membership. In addition, a few new locals had emerged in the industrial region of the Mark in Westphalia, but serious ADAV agitation only began in this area after 1867. In north Germany, too, the association had gained some strength, with new local groups in the Kingdom of Hanover, the lower Weser, and the Duchy of Braunschweig. Permanent memberships were reported from Thuringia, the Saxon duchies, and Kassel in northern Hesse. The Schleswig-Holstein locals that were established between 1864 and 1866 tended to oscillate between the ADAV and the LADAV. On the whole, the Lassallean movement tended to be an affair of Germany's north, with the Main river essentially serving as the ADAV's southern boundary. Augsburg was the only place in southern Germany where the Lassalleans were able to strike deep roots. At the end of 1868 a new local group emerged in Mannheim, in the Grand Duchy of Baden. The agitation that followed led to the establishment of a number of short-lived organizations, and only in Karlsruhe did the Lassalleans achieve some long-term success. ADAV data from May 1869 show that, in addition to the old Lassallean bastions in Prussia and Saxony, a number of new locals had taken root in Schleswig-Holstein, Thuringia, and Hesse; the ADAV had also managed to regain control of certain powerful local groups, like those in Mainz and Kiel, that had temporarily gone over to the LADAV.

When it was founded in June 1867, the LADAV was largely limited to Saxony, Schleswig-Holstein, and Bremen. In 1868 to 1869 it managed to extend its activities to the regions around Halle, Zeitz, and then to the lower Weser and the Catholic textile-producing areas on the left bank of the lower Rhine around Mönchengladbach, Düsseldorf, and Krefeld. As we have also seen, the Lassallean locals in Schleswig-Holstein also temporarily joined the LADAV. Apart from these organizations, the LADAV only included a few scattered groups in Marburg and Breslau.

The ADAV in particular availed itself of several techniques in its efforts to expand the organization. The public assembly was especially effective.[39] For agitational purposes, meetings of the members could be opened to the public, although guests did not enjoy the right to speak or to vote. Moreover, the laws that governed the right of association prohibited women, children, or apprentice workers from attending such meetings. In addition to opening their own meetings to non-members, established Lassallean locals would often organize public rallies and meetings in nearby towns, and anyone could speak or otherwise take part in these sorts of gatherings, which remained an especially effective form of mass propaganda. In addition, the ADAV was able to take good advantage of the country's railroad network in its attempts to spread its membership and its message.

For the most part, the spread of Lassallean propaganda depended upon the personal activities of individual agitators. So, for example, the ADAV's local agents liked to organize weekend rallies in neighboring, politically unorganized areas, and these meetings were often attended by members of the nearby local. These rallies were often preceded by attempts to encourage a few individuals from these neighboring localities to join the existing local.[40] Practices of this sort tended to take place in regions with a homogeneous social milieu and fairly high levels of industrial or artisanal activity. They were especially effective in proto-industrial, textile-producing regions in which traditional, export-oriented forms of cloth manufacture had moved from the city to the village and in which artisanal workers found themselves moving from decentralized cottage industry-based to centralized, factory-based modes of production. Examples include the area around Düsseldorf and the mountainous Erzgebirge region close to Chemnitz.[41] Other regions were also important targets of Lassallean recruitment efforts. The Bergisches Land, on the right bank of the Rhine, was one important example, with export-oriented textile and small-scale iron industries and a more heavily proletarianized social structure than the areas just mentioned.[42]

Like the ADAV, the LADAV also tried to use "core" locals as bases for an extension of the association's activities into neighboring regions, especially after September 1868 in the environs of Halle, Chemnitz, and Mönchengladbach. They also used paid agitators to spread their message. In the 1860s the ADAV and the LADAV both used a system of "flying" agitators, in which certain representatives from particularly active local organizations were designated by the association's president and moved through certain regions, organizing workers' rallies along the way. This system was not without its disadvantages. It was not possible, for example, to train agitators in party doctrine. Instead, their success was measured by the number of new local branches that they helped to establish. Moreover, the "flying" agitators often moved through the countryside in an uncoordinated and unsystematic way, and as result many of the new local groups that they established turned out to be rather flimsy. Hence, one of the perennial issues at general assemblies concerned the question of who should select these agitators and whether or not they should be permanently assigned to certain regions. Finally, on 30 April 1868 ADAV President Johann Baptist von Schweitzer issued a decree that called for the "dispatching of paid agitators" into eight designated areas of Germany, and he called upon the members at the regional level to send him lists of suitable names for these positions.[43] And in the following year the Barmen general assembly ruled that a paid agitator should be designated for each association district *(Vereinsbezirk)*.[44]

The spread of Lassallean activities to previously unorganized regions served as the propagandistic backdrop to carefully prepared tours not only by association presidents like Schweitzer or Mende but also by particularly effective agitators like Wilhelm Kölsch, Hermann Haustein, or Leonhard von Bonhorst, who were active in southern Germany in the spring of 1869.[45] As we have seen, non-members could speak openly at the rallies that accompanied these tours, and, thus, members of rival organizations often attended these affairs and tried to disrupt them.

Lassalleans who moved from one place to another were quite successful at establishing new local branches or *Gemeinden*. This sometimes took place in a rather unsystematic or unpredictable fashion, as when Lassallean workers were cashiered for their political activities and had to seek employment elsewhere. On other occasions, however, the association's leadership ordered activists to return to their native regions and attempt to recruit new members there.[46] Even the ADAV's enemies had to admit that these tactics could be successful. As one wrote in 1875, "Whenever a particular area or industrial district is to be opened up for socialism, this usually takes the form at first not of a big 'people's rally.' Rather, a few comrades quietly enter the region, take up work, and at their workplaces and in the factories and in other places where they come in contact with their fellow workers they sow the seeds of socialism."[47] Newly-created locals of this sort often turned out to be quite stable.

Mass rallies that exposed the iniquities of the class system or called for general suffrage and producers' cooperatives were typical of the activism of the first years of the Lassallean movement. But the actual thematic content of these rallies was rather thin, and ultimately they represented a dead-end street – unless, that is, a new form of autonomous organizational life developed at the local level. Although Lassalle and his immediate successor, Bernhard Becker, had scorned such organizational life as a uselessly diverting "clubbiness" *(Vereinsspielerei)*, it nevertheless turned out to be very important for the development of an effective Lassallean movement. Moreover, by 1867 larger political and social issues were beginning to influence older and more "normal" forms of Lassallean agitation. The process of Germany's unification was especially significant in this regard. Thus, for example, legislation concerning election campaigns offered new possibilities for large public rallies, while "visits" to opponents' rallies provided new opportunities to agitate on behalf of Lassallean ideas. On such occasions even rank-and-file members often displayed great energy in distributing leaflets and broadsides.[48]

The Lassalleans' confrontation with the first great wave of strikes and with the developing trade-union movement posed a serious problem for the movement's official ideology; as we have seen, the Lassalleans rejected strikes as a means of resolving the "workers' question." Still, the strike wave of the early 1870s was an elemental movement that could sweep various organizations into it, even when, as in the case of existing Lassallean locals, they did not wish to be part of it. Even the LADAV could not distance itself from the strike movements that broke out in its strongholds, as in Mönchengladbach in 1871.[49] At the same time, though, its basic hostility to strikes and trade unions worked somewhat to its advantage whenever those movements failed.[50]

In assessing the content of the Lassalleans' public agitation, one of their opponents complained understandably that their speakers did everything in their power "to encourage dissatisfaction by a boundlessly exaggerated, negative criticism of prevailing conditions and of the foundations of the existing social order, and through these means to gain new adherents for the 'red flag.'"[51] Two general themes tended to dominate these public rallies: Who was responsible for the plight of the workers? And what would be the means of their liberation? By hearing about their own wretched conditions, listeners at these rallies were supposed to be stirred to action. The speakers talked in concrete terms about the miserable situation locally, about the general forms of class conflict, and about the ineffectiveness of liberal notions of individual self-help. The speakers often organized their remarks around concrete incidents, denouncing the perfidy and the blather of the bourgeoisie, who were betraying the workers by offering them nothing but palliatives. Examples were used to demonstrate how capital exploited workers, and then a description of the means by which workers could improve their lot would follow: membership in the Lassallean labor movement was described as the only possible road that could lead to the victory of social revolution. That revolution itself would result in a political settling of accounts and in the radical transformation of all social relations. Lassallean speakers tended to be vague about these latter notions, and not only in order to avoid legal prosecution. Many of their speeches, thus, tended to be chiliastic and eschatological, ending with an appeal to the audience to join and remain loyal to the organization. Julius Bruhns (1860 to 1927), a prominent representative of the tobacco workers' movement and a social democratic member of the Reichstag, vividly described these emotions in his memoir account of socialist cigar makers in the late 1860s and the early 1870s:

> Capitalism and its vile representative, the rotten bourgeoisie, were alone responsible for all the evils of the world, no matter what they were: the misery of the workers, floods, war, pestilence, bad weather, or any other calamity that took place anywhere on earth. The exaggeration and stubborn one-sidedness that characterized social democracy's relentless criticism of prevailing conditions was understandable and even necessary if those who were responsible for those conditions and those who had to suffer from them were both to be made aware of the terrible conditions for which capitalism was truly guilty and of the fervor with which that guilt was being exposed. And the derision of our opponents, especially the dominant city liberals who never took us seriously, poured oil onto the fire and fed social democratic criticism.[52]

And this form of agitation, the presentation of Lassalleanism as what Christian Gotthardt has called a "universal strategy to overcome the misery of everyday life," was eminently successful. Workers saw themselves represented in it. Thus, one official in Pirna (Saxony) commented that the LADAV's success in his region, which only had "a small population of workers," was "quite natural" because the Lassalleans were constantly hammering home the message that the workers' problems were not of their own making; and, even where workers were not willing to pay membership dues, they were certainly ready to vote for a movement that promised them the hope of improvement.[53]

4. Social Structure and "Ideology" of the Local Organizations

The difficulty of interpreting occupational categories from the membership lists of labor parties is well known. Categories like weaver, locksmith, or shoemaker do not allow for direct conclusions about the social position of the individual, who could be a well-situated craftsman, a middle-class employer, or a paid laborer, nor about the workplace, which could be an artisanal shop, a factory, or the home. It is vitally important to clarify such questions in order to explain the connection between particular social milieus and the attraction of distinctive political conceptions and organizations.

The nature of the sources – twelve membership lists and six statistical evaluations that cover 3,431 individuals in eighteen locals between 1863 and 1869 – permit only general conclusions concerning the membership of the ADAV and LADAV, and these will largely confirm existing theses.[54] As Shlomo Na'aman characterizes the ADAV in the summer of 1864: "The members [were] mostly proletarianized, semi-independent workers, masters and journeymen in small workshops, and home workers."[55] This picture of a membership socialized in an artisanal world did not significantly change until the successful agitation among construction workers in 1869 to 1870 and the rural population in Schleswig-Holstein after 1871. But this thesis does need to be refined. At the very least, one has to differentiate among the variety of ADAV organizations.

In the larger cities Lassallean groups were dominated by the classic mass craft occupations like tailors, shoemakers, and cabinetmakers. So far as we can tell, these members worked overwhelmingly in small and mid-sized workshops based on traditional "putting-out" modes of production. Typical for this pattern were ADAV locals in Frankfurt am Main, Berlin (55.2 percent shoemakers in 1864), Hamburg (27 percent tailors, 21.8 percent cabinetmakers, 12.2 percent shoemakers, and 18.6 percent cigarmakers in 1868), and Bremen (37.5 percent shoemakers, 34.6 percent tailors, and 7.7 percent carpenters in 1864-65). Alongside this profile were organizations in which a particular craft occupation dominated because of its leading role in the local economy, as in Altona (24.3 percent cabinetmakers, and 18.9 percent cigarmakers in 1864), Ansbach (50 percent cigarmakers in 1869), and Halberstadt (27.5 percent cigarmakers in 1868). In some instances, a high proportion of members was employed in factories, but they identified themselves by their craft occupation. Metalworkers dominated in places like Dortmund, where they constituted about one-fifth of the membership from 1870 to 1874. The high proportion of ADAV members identified as "factory worker" or "worker" is indicative of the progressive proletarianization of the society and of an emergent class consciousness. In the Halberstadt organization, for example, 27.5 percent of the members gave their occupation as cigarmakers, but fully 23.2 percent called themselves "worker" or "working man."

Another category of local organizations includes those with a high proportion of members involved in textile manufacturing, among them localities still dominated by the putting-out system in which masters worked in homes or small shops, as in the Silesian, Saxon, and Rhenish textile regions. Lassalleanism proved attractive in these areas because once-independent weavers were now threatened by an acute economic crisis, and banked their hopes upon state aid. A few scattered membership lists and other sources indicate that the membership profile of some local organizations shifted over time. In Munich, for example, the ADAV was at first dominated by printers and tailors, but later by members from the metal trades.

To sum up: in the 1860s the ADAV attracted individuals from occupational groups composed of proletarianized, semi-independent workers in a labor or social milieu that still bore a powerful artisanal stamp, along with those who can already be characterized as wage and factory workers. For both groups, the Lassallean slogans of full value for one's labor and state-financed associational socialism constituted an attractive alternative that could be variously understood and interpreted: either as the possibility of reviving old forms of independent production in a new cooperative pattern or as the path to a decent existence through a socialized workplace.

The social structure of the LADAV diverged only in a few particularities from that of the ADAV.[56] Through successful organizational efforts in the weaving and knitting district of the Chemnitz region and the textile region on the left bank of the Rhine, the textile occupations with 37 percent of the membership dominated the LADAV far more strongly than the ADAV. As a corollary, the classic mass craft trades were less well represented. In sixteen organizations "worker" or "factory worker" constituted the largest group. Further statistical investigation would indicate additional local particularities. In Brand, for example, an area with a long tradition of miners' protests and organization, the LADAV organization incorporated for a time a significant proportion of miners. The Bremen-Oldenburg Lower Weser area also had its particularities in that the LADAV, according to Gotthard, became "a movement of rural smallholders" and shipyard workers.[57] In general the LADAV had more local organizations defined by a particular occupational group, as in Pirna or Düsseldorf, where construction workers dominated, or in Mainz with its shoemakers, or in Wandsbeck with its tobacco workers.

Finally, a few comments are in order on the occupational composition of the leadership of both Lassallean associations. The LADAV experienced a greater fluctuation in the composition of its executive level: more members resigned, and President Mende claimed full powers and removed people he disliked. In both organizations textile workers composed the greatest proportion of the leaderships, with somewhat higher numbers in the LADAV (one-quarter to one-third) reflecting the higher proportion of textile workers in its membership at large. In general, individuals from the craft occupations dominated. In the ADAV, the mass craft occupations – again, shoemakers, tailors, and cabinetmakers – made up about one-fifth, and in the LADAV in 1867 to 1868 about one-third, of the executive level. Only the composition of the ADAV confirms the well-known claim that cigarmakers dominated in the leadership of the labor movement. In both associations individuals from middle-class professions played an important role. "Workers" or "factory workers," despite their high number in the membership at large, were rarely represented at the executive level.

Lassalle had intended the ADAV to be a pure, clearly defined agitational organization that did not need to develop any kind of associational life alongside its political efforts. The model of the strict centralization of all powers, designed to avoid splits and divisions, has been effectively described by Shlomo Na'aman as "the logic of a conspiratorial society taken over by a public organization." The Lassalleans strongly opposed every form of "clubbiness" that had become typical of the bourgeois worker education associations.[58] With this outlook, the ADAV became the self-fulfilling prophecy of a new kind of indissoluble, unitary labor organization.[59] Lassalle's successor, Bernhard Becker, attempted to implement thoroughly this concept of a strict, unitary organization without toleration of any kind of autonomy at the local level, and he just about managed to ruin the Association in the process.[60] In this view, the multifunctional character of the "association" as an organizational form – its diverse communal, sociable, and educational opportunities – hindered the development of a powerful, vigorous collection of members focused on continual political agitation.

Yet it is doubtful whether the organization could have survived at all without the development of an associational culture focused around local needs. Even the typical practice of holding organizational meetings in a local pub promoted elements of sociability. The essential goal of the Association could not really be separated from its purely sociable aspects, which expressed the sense of solidarity among its members who, following Lassallean theory, had deliberately cut themselves off from the liberal bourgeois public. From the very beginning a large number of local Lassallean groups absorbed many of the essential elements of the older worker associations, including those that had originated among the journeymen's movements, such as mutual aid funds, festivals, excursions, or libraries.[61] The Lassalle personality cult, which Lassalle himself had begun to encourage and which then blossomed after his death, served as the crystallization point of a festival culture that bound the members together and deeply shaped the life of the local organizations.[62]

It is notable that the LADAV received considerable support from women, and not just from a leading figure like Sophie von Hatzfeldt. Despite the law of association, which forbade women's participation in political groups, women were strongly encouraged to work with and support the LADAV. At Lassallean events women were sometimes featured speakers.[63] "The party as a huge family," as Arno Herzig has described it, entailed agitation designed to influence the members and have an impact on events beyond the organization.[64] A conservative Christian paper, a close observer of the LADAV scene in the Lower Rhine, wrote in 1872: "Presuming correctly that the dry handling of organizational business would put everyone to sleep, the Association provided for lively conversation to which members, women and children, and also friends were invited."[65] Otherwise, the women would keep their husbands from the Association since the men would be aroused by the agitation and would stay away from their families on the weekends. Instead, the Lassallean organizations managed to include women as well.

The much-discussed "subculture" of the German socialist labor movement is, then, in no way a product of the period after the establishment of the Reich in 1871. It emerged concurrently with the very founding of the labor movement. The subculture was formed out of elements of journeymen's social life and liberal bourgeois associational culture, both of which were taken over, partly reinterpreted, or brought together in a new functional union and welded to new, independently developed elements.

The associational culture did not, however, emerge without opposition, nor was it representative of all local organizations. In 1868, a debate broke out in the *Social-Democrat* about the ADAV's festival culture. Wilhelm Taute, a co-founder of the ADAV, criticized the "festivals that have suddenly bloomed … and which do not at all suit the dignity and the seriousness of our Association."[66] The only virtue to such events was that they brought some new supporters into the organization. In general, Taute argued, members had a right to festive entertainments only after the victory of the "struggle." In opposition, other members pleaded for the right to enjoyable times in the Association and emphasized the agitational value of such events. Yet Taute also found his supporters. These contributions indicate the breadth of conceptions about the Association and the variety of its internal organizational life. The ADAV never became the presidential, uniform party that Lassalle had imagined. The formation of a decisive, powerful organization, in which the members functioned as party soldiers who took orders from the executive level, never had a chance of success. Despite a certain dogmatic – and revered – Lassallean orthodoxy, the ADAV developed a varied and colorful associational life, one that emerged out of the independent learning process that the varied local organizations underwent.[67]

Thus, in regions with strong artisanal, anti-capitalist traditions, like Hamburg, Harburg, Frankfurt am Main, and a part of the Maingau, the radical anti-bourgeois and anti-liberal program expressed in Lassallean writings won support. Here Lassalleanism was interpreted in a social revolutionary and radical democratic manner, and the members lived at least until 1867 to 1868 in breathless expectation of a revolution and were addicted to what Gotthardt calls a "blood and barricades phraseology." Echoes of this approach were heard also in the "traditional regions of commercial export with declining household production, intensifying dependency of the producers on capital in the putting out system, and decentralized manufacturing," in the Chemnitz-Erzgebirge textile region, as well as in the textile and iron industry of the Bergland, where master craftsmen had endured proletarianization. The Bergland had become a deeply polarized society, and those inclined to Lassalleanism could draw upon a long tradition of independent organization and representation. They found in the state socialism of Lassalleanism ideas that resonated with their own commitment to producer associations.[68]

The ideological hinge for all party members was, above all else, the Lassallean agitational writings, along with the Association's newspaper. Lassallean ideas were disseminated especially at weekly rallies, as we know from the Association's correspondence in the newspapers and from police reports. In the first years the typical format consisted of the reading and explication of decisive passages from Lassalle's writings. Discussion of particular articles from the ADAV's newspaper soon supplemented, and even replaced, these recitations. The protocol book of the Augsburg organization, one of the major ADAV locals in south Germany, shows that the members also took notice of bourgeois newspapers, whose reaction to the Lassallean labor movement often served as a point of discussion. Individual members attempted to speak about historical events or presented independent, popular summaries of Lassalle's writings, which they also sought to bring to the bourgeois press. These discussions served to develop class consciousness, that is, to strengthen the sense of solidarity among workers by illuminating their social situation and their suppression by the bourgeoisie.

After 1865 to 1866, contemporary political issues became the major themes of discussion at meetings and rallies, which at times led to public actions and debates concerning strikes, the right to association, suffrage rights, and, of course, the process of national unification under Bismarck and the electoral battles for the North German and then the German Reichstag.[69] While the first meetings served mainly to establish the sheer presence of the local organizations, the regional and national themes led to more concrete formulations of the demand for a "people's state." In addition, from the middle of the 1860s a certain "regionalization" took place in many locals. For example, discussions in the Maingau of new Hessian factory regulations in October 1865 were followed by ADAV rallies that featured protests about usury laws and indirect taxes: issues that were of decisive importance to the predominantly artisanal audience in this region. Ultimately, the agitational themes promoted by the local organizations mirrored the character of their memberships.

In the 1860s neither the ADAV nor the LADAV engaged in basic, systematic educational work among their members. For the ADAV, which emerged in 1863 in sharp opposition to the enlightened, bourgeois ideal of worker education associations, political work sufficed.[70] Understanding and knowledge among workers were to be awakened by political agitation, notably the dissemination of Lassalle's writings. As conservative critics admitted, the diligent reading of the brochures did acquaint workers with the principles of the Association and provided them with a powerful reservoir of arguments that could be deployed in discussions.[71] Yet these methods sharpened the analytical understanding of the members in a very one-sided manner. They found themselves encased in a closed, immune, dogmatic world view that could explain all essential events in politics and economics. In *this* sense, the widely applied – and controversial – appellation of "sect" to the Lassallean labor movement has some validity. Yet this claim marked only one variant of Lassallean organizational life. The longer the movement persisted, the more a kind of independent analysis of everyday experiences took place. "We ... have found that we have to find an improvement of [our] situation nowhere else than in the transformation of our state. Only in the transformation ... of the sovereign, governing state to a people's state and the direction of this people's state through the representatives of a free people, through a parliament that is chosen by free, equal, and secret ballot, only then can we expect an improvement in our situation."[72]

5. Conclusion

Until the end of "real existing socialism" in Eastern Europe, scholarly interest in the Lassallean labor movement necessarily entailed political judgments and conflicts. Lassalle, after all, became the major rival of Karl Marx, and his impact upon the German labor movement was immense. Every evaluation of Lassalle and of the labor movement that he influenced became part of the dogmatic, ideological war between east and west, between Marxism-Leninism and social democracy, a part of the effort to establish lines of historical continuity and, thereby, political legitimation. This confrontation more or less marked all scholarly studies before 1990, but has now decisively receded. Of course, judgments about the Lassallean labor movement remain connected to one's own political values. But if one considers only the effective history of Lassalle and "his" labor movement, then the following conclusions are in order:

1. Lassalle took up and intensified the process, begun timidly in 1862 to 1863, in which the labor movement separated from the left wing of the bourgeois national movement. By making a radical break with received

tradition, an independent movement emerged with its own ideology and organization. With the ADAV a modern labor party was created.

2. The Lassallean movement formed its own theory through the somewhat artificial melding of two hitherto completely separate ideas – productive associations and universal, equal suffrage – along with the adoption of the "iron law of wages."

3. Through its agitational writings and its elaboration of the ideas of the *Communist Manifesto* as well as other socialist theses, the ADAV contributed mightily to the propagation and acceptance of socialist ideas in the German labor movement, as well as in neighboring countries.

4. The labor party shaped by the ADAV propagated a combative class consciousness. This sensibility joined together a consciousness of the creative and productive significance of labor with resentment at economic exploitation and social "de-classing." Out of this emerged a notion of class struggle, but also a valorization of the state, which the Lassalleans understood as a positive form of social organization. The charge of reformism is valid insofar as the daily political struggles of the Lassallean party were limited to the winning and extension of universal suffrage and the establishment, with state subsidies, of producer cooperatives. Hence, the Lassalleans founded that characteristic dualism of German social democracy – radical ideology and reformist practice.

5. Despite its numerical weakness, the founding of a separate labor party had a decisive impact on the domestic political scene within the German Confederation. From this point on, the liberal-democratic national movement found itself in a two-front war against the conservative-feudal government and the social democratic labor movement. Some have charged that what Gustav Mayer called the "separation of proletarian from bourgeois democracy in Germany" was premature and was not an insignificant precondition of Germany's "separate path" *(Sonderweg)* in Europe. In any case, from its beginnings the Lassallean labor movement developed its own internal "subculture," which extended and notably sharpened the political and economic differentiation of working-class from bourgeois Germany. The Lassalleans understood their movement as the legitimate heir and extension of the democratic ideals of the revolutionary period. With the Bismarckian foundation of the Reich and the marginalization of organized bourgeois democracy, this claim was also legitimate.

Translated by David E. Barclay and Eric D. Weitz

Notes

1. Shlomo Na'aman, *Die Konstituierung der deutschen Arbeiterbewegung 1862/63* (Assen, 1974), 136. See also Arno Herzig, *Der Allgemeine Deutsche Arbeiter-Verein in der deutschen Sozialdemokratie* (Berlin, 1979), 57; Christian Gotthardt, *Industrialisierung, bürgerliche Politik und proletarische Autonomie: Voraussetzungen und Varianten sozialistischer Klassenorganisationen in Nordwestdeutschland 1863 bis 1875* (Bonn, 1992), 230-31. For details on the social structure of the Lassallean movement, see the sources in Dieter Dowe and Toni Offermann, eds., *Materialien zur Sozialstruktur und Verbreitung von ADAV und LADAV 1867-1871* (forthcoming).
2. Cora Stephan, "Bemerkungen zur Rezeption Ferdinand Lassalles," in Bert Andreas, *Ferdinand Lassalle – Allgemeiner Deutscher Arbeiterverein: Bibliographie ihrer Schriften und der Literatur über sie 1840 bis 1975* (Bonn, 1981), 12.
3. On the power of Lassalle's message, see August Bebel to Friedrich Engels, May 1873, quoted in Hans-Josef Steinberg, *Sozialismus und deutsche Sozialdemokratie: Zur Ideologie der Partei vor dem I. Weltkrieg* (Bonn-Bad Godesberg, 1972), 20.
4. Ibid., 118-19; Stephan, "Bemerkungen," 17; Christiane Eisenberg, *Frühe Arbeiterbewgeung und Genossenschaften: Theorie und Praxis der Produktivgenossenschaften in der deutschen Sozialdemokratie und den Gewerkschaften der 1860er/1870er Jahre* (Bonn, 1985), 63ff.
5. See Dieter Dowe, "Einige Bemerkungen zur Berufsstruktur des Lassalleschen Allgemeinen Deutschen Arbeitervereins Ende der 1860er Jahre," in *"Der kühnen Bahn nur folgen wir …": Ursprünge, Erfolge und Grenzen der Arbeiterbewegung in Deutschland*, ed. Arno Herzig and Günter Trautmann, 2 vols. (Hamburg, 1989), 1: 135-36.
6. Dieter Dowe, *Protokolle und Materialien des Allgemeinen Deutschen Arbeitervereins (inkl. Splittergruppen)* (Berlin, 1980), 316; Dieter Fricke, *Handbuch zur Geschichte der deutschen Arbeiterbewegung 1869 bis 1917*, 2 vols. (Berlin, 1987), 1: 93-94, 102-3; Dieter Dowe and Kurt Klotzbach, *Programmatische Dokumente der deutschen Sozialdemokratie* (Bonn, 1990), 166-67.
7. Dowe, *Protokolle*, 76, 152; also Fricke, *Handbuch*, 1: 117. On the use of the term *Gemeinde*, see Bernhard Becker, *Geschichte der Arbeiter-Agitation Ferdinand Lassalle's* (Braunschweig, 1874; reprinted Berlin, 1978), 75.
8. Arno Herzig, "Diktatorische, bonapartistische und demokratische Tendenzen im Allgemeinen deutschen Arbeiterverein 1863-1869," *Jahrbuch des Instituts für Deutsche Geschichte* 10 (1981), 243-79.
9. SStAD, MdI 11144, Bl.343-44.
10. Becker, *Geschichte*, 75. See also the detailed stipulations in Carl Wilhelm Tölcke, *Zweck, Mittel und Organisation des Allgemeinen Deutschen Arbeiter-Vereins: Ein Leitfaden für Agitatoren, Bevollmächtigten und Mitglieder des Vereins*, 3 vols. (Berlin, 1873), 2: 26ff.
11. Becker, *Geschichte*, 141-42.
12. For 1867, see the *Social-Demokrat* from 21 July to 20 October of that year. For 1868, see the reports in the same paper on 3 April, 12 April, 17 April, and 6 September 1868.
13. *Freie Zeitung* 37 (10 October 1868), 151. These efforts largely failed: *Freie Zeitung* 40-41 (23 October 1868), 163.
14. *Freie Zeitung* 38-39 (17 October 1868): 158. On the naming of *Bevollmächtigte*, see SStAD, Amtshauptmannschaft Freiberg Nr.1605, Bl.54; and Walther Föhl, "Zur Geschichte der Arbeiterbewegung im Kreise Kempen," *Heimatbuch des Grenzkreises Kempen-Krefeld* 10 (1959): 39.

15. Toni Offermann, *Arbeiterbewegung und liberales Bürgertum in Deutschland 1850-1863* (Bonn, 1979), 502-5.
16. See the reports of such cases in SStAD, MdI 11144, Bl.252ff., KH Leipzig Nr.258, Bl.47ff., and KH Freiberg Nr.1605, Bl.35ff.
17. SStAD, MdI 11144, Bl. 310.
18. See the response of the Kreisdirektion Zwickau to these tactics in SStAD, MdI 11144, Bl. 280-81.
19. Hartmut Zwahr, "Die deutsche Arbeiterbewegung im Länder- und Territorienvergleich 1875," *Geschichte und Gesellschaft* 13 (1987): 448-507.
20. *Statistik des Deutschen Reichs*, vol. 25, part two.
21. Andreas Biefang, *Politisches Bürgertum in Deutschland 1857-1868* (Düsseldorf, 1994), 101.
22. Becker, *Geschichte*, 300. See also Bert Andreas, "Zur Agitation und Propaganda des Allgemeinen Deutschen Arbeitervereins 1863/64," *Archiv für Sozialgeschichte* 3 (1963): 300; Toni Offermann, "Einleitung," in Becker, *Geschichte*, xxiii-xxiv.
23. See the *Social-Demokrat* for 21 July 1867, 3 April 1868, 6 September 1868, 5 May 1869, 21 May 1869 (*Beilage*), 24 October 1869, 19 December 1869; and the *Neuer Social-Demokrat* for 14 July, 26 July, 11 August, and 27 August 1871.
24. Hugo Keller in the year 1909, quoted in Rudolf Gottscholl and Annelies Gottschol, *Die Görlitzer Arbeiterbewegung in der Zeit von 1871 bis 1903* (Görlitz, 1965), 45.
25. Dowe, *Protokolle*, 118.
26. This table is based on figures from the issues of the *Social-Demokrat* for 24 May 1868, 25 April 1869, 2 June 1869, 3 and 27 October 1869, 24 November 1869, 20 July 1870, 21 August 1870, 18 September 1870, 21 October 1870, 23 November 1870; and from the *Neuer Social-Demokrat* for 5 July, 19 July, and 20 August 1871.
27. *Social-Demokrat*, 24 May 1868.
28. *Social-Demokrat*, 14 February 1869.
29. The figures cited in the literature are contradictory. Fritz Specht and Paul Schwabe, *Die Reichstags-Wahlen von 1867 bis 1907* (Berlin, 1908), 318, report 60,466 votes, while Fricke, *Handbuch*, 2: 720, registers 62,952 votes. The latter, however, uses the unclear category "Stimmen für die Sozialdemokratie" in reporting these figures. The total sum that he indicates amounts to 124,655, while the number of votes for the SDAP and the Lassalleans, when added together from his figures, amounts to only 101,927.
30. Specht and Schwabe, *Reichstags-Wahlen*, 228, 224. Cf. Ernst Hofmann, "Die Chemnitzer Arbeiterbewegung 1862 bis 1867," (Ph.D. diss. Dresden, 1984), 193.
31. AsD, Abt. IV, Bestand ADAV Nr. 185, Bl. 630.
32. SAPMO-BA, II/139/2/8, Bl. 117.
33. SAPMO-BA, II/139/4/29, Bl. 109-18; see also Peter Pohlenz, "Entwicklung und Differenzierung im Allgemeinen Deutschen Arbeiterverein (1863 bis 1867)" (Ph.D. diss., Leipzig, 1986), 141.
34. Dowe, *Protokolle*, 576; SAPMO-BA, II/139/2/20, Bl. 3-5.
35. *Christlich-soziale Blätter* 3 (1 February 1872): 31.
36. Dowe, "Bemerkungen," 137.
37. Becker, *Geschichte*, 300.
38. Dowe, *Protokolle*, 17-18.
39. See Tölcke, *Zweck*, part two, 29-32; Gotthardt, *Industrialisierung*, 305.
40. See the evocative description of these activities in Düsseldorf and its environs in Heinrich Karl Schmitz, *Anfänge und Entwicklung der Arbeiterbewegung im Raum Düsseldorf* (Hanover, 1968), 39ff.

41. Hartmut Zwahr, "Arbeiterbewegung in Deutschland innerhalb der Trias von kapitalabhängigem Handwerk, Manufaktur und Fabrik," in Herzig and Trautmann, *Ursprünge*, 131-34.
42. Rudolf Boch, "Die Entstehungsbedingungen der deutschen Arbeiterbewegung: Das Bergische Land und der ADAV," in Herzig and Trautmann, *Ursprünge*, 108, 117-18.
43. *Social-Demokrat*, 1 May, 8 July 1868.
44. Herzig, *Allgemeine Deutsche Arbeiter-Verein*, 79. In the LADAV the designation of agitators was always the exclusive prerogative of the president.
45. Bayerisches Hauptstaatsarchiv, Munich, Minn Nr.46098, Bl. 64ff.; Hugo Eckert, *Liberal-oder Sozialdemokratie: Frühgeschichte der Nürnberger Arbeiterbewegung* (Stuttgart, 1968), 156ff.; Heinrich Hirschfelder, *Die bayerische Sozialdemokratie 1864-1914* (Erlangen, 1979), 78ff.; Klaus Schönhoven, *Zwischen Revolution und Sozialistengesetz: Die Anfänge der Würzburger Arbeiterbewegung 1848 bis 1878* (Würzburg, 1976), 26.
46. For examples, see Robert Kern, *Aus Vergangenheit und Gegenwart der Würzburger Arbeiterbewegung* (Würzburg, 1917), 6-7; Hirschfelder, *Sozialdemokratie*, 78; Wolfgang Schmierer, *Von der Arbeiterbildung zur Arbeiterpolitik: Die Anfänge der Arbeiterbewegung in Württemberg 1862/63-1878* (Hanover, 1970), 159.
47. Richard Schuster, *Die Social-Demokratie: Nach ihrem Wesen und ihrer Agitation* (Stuttgart, 1875), 7-8.
48. See, for example, the respectful comments from officials in the Amtshauptmannschaft Pirna, SStAD, MdI 1144, Bl. 329-30. See also Klaus Erich Pollmann, "Arbeiterwahlen im Norddeutschen Bund 1867-1870," *Geschichte und Gesellschaft* 15 (1989): 164-95.
49. In this connection, see the letters to Mende in SAPMO-BA, II 139/2/4, Bl. 50ff.
50. Gotthardt, *Industrialisierung*, 53 n. 155, and 274-75, attributes the LADAV's success in the lower Weser to this factor.
51. Schuster, *Social-Demokratie*, 5.
52. Julius Bruhns, *"Es klingt im Sturm ein altes Lied!" Aus der Jugendzeit der Sozialdemokratie* (Stuttgart and Berlin, 1921), 14.
53. Report of the III. Amtshauptmannschaft Pirna, 4 March 1869, SStAD, MdI 11144, Bl. 330-31.
54. For details, see Dowe and Offermann, *Materialien*.
55. Shlomo Na'aman, *Lassalle* (Hanover, 1970), 683; cf. Herzig, *ADAV*, 57ff.
56. Cf. for the following the evaluation of this material in Dowe, *Berufsstruktur*, 142-47.
57. Gotthardt, *Industrialisierung*, 236.
58. Becker, *Geschichte*, 48.
59. See Mende's rather confused comments to this effect: *Freie Zeitung* 1 (18 December 1867).
60. Bernhard Becker, *Enthüllungen über das tragische Lebensende Ferdinand Lassalle's und seine Beziehungen zu Helene von Dönniges* (Nuremberg, 1892), 225, 231.
61. See Offermann, "Vereinsmodell," 53ff.
62. Herzig, *ADAV*, 117-22, 135-39, and, in detail, idem, "Die Lassalle-Feiern in der politischen Festkultur der frühen deutschen Arbeiterbewegung," in *Öffentliche Festkultur: Politische Feste in Deutschland von der Aufklärung bis zum Ersten Weltkrieg*, ed. Dieter Düding, Peter Friedmann, and Paul Münch (Reinbek, 1988), 321-33.
63. Cf. the comments by Dowe, *Bemerkungen*, 138.
64. Herzig, *ADAV*, 135ff.
65. *Christlich-soziale Blätter* (Aachen) 11 (1 June 1872): 161.

66. *Social-Demokrat* 67 (10 June 1868); 71 (19 June 1868); 74A (26 June 1868); 78 (5 July 1868).
67. Cf. the stimulating considerations of Gotthardt, *Industrialisierung*, 230ff.
68. Zwahr, *Arbeiterbewegung*, 464; Broch, 117ff.
69. On ADAV responses to the threatened abrogation of the right to associate, see Thomas Parent, *"Passiver Widerstand" im preußischen Verfassungskonflikt: Die Kölner Abgeordnetenfeste* (Cologne, 1982), 322-48.
70. Peter Krug, *Gewerkschaften und Arbeiterbildung: Gewerkschaftliche Bildungsarbeit von ihren Anfängen bis zur Weimarer Republik* (Cologne, 1980), 109.
71. *Christlich-soziale Blätter* 11 (1 June 1872): 161.
72. So the worker Oscar Schmiedrich at a rally in Augsburg on 5 August 1866, cited by Hirschfelder, *Sozialdemokratie*, 69.

Chapter 4

BÜRGER AND WORKERS

Liberalism and the Labor Movement in Germany, 1848 to 1914

Ralf Roth

The relationship between "middle-class" *Bürger* and "workers" played a central role in nineteenth-century German history, and it is not surprising that recent social historians have devoted so much attention to it. Indeed, the breach between "bourgeois" and "proletarian" democracy in the 1860s is usually regarded as an especially fateful stage on Germany's allegedly "separate path" *(Sonderweg)* of historical development.[1] Virtually all studies of the relationship between *Bürger* and workers, however, have concentrated on developments at the national level. Thus, they almost uniformly come to the conclusion that the partnership between these two groups was only of short duration.[2] But in the years between 1848 and 1914 Germany was a country marked by powerful local and regional identities. Accordingly, these remarks will focus mainly on historical experiences at the local level. In this connection it is important to remember that middle-class and proletarian movements were urban movements. Both were rooted in a social space that had been shaped for centuries by a town-dwelling *Bürgertum*. An entire canon of behavioral norms, structures, rules, rights, and privileges conditioned the relations between the social strata of the towns. Fixed in laws that defined civic rights, they still decisively shaped the self-image of Germany's urban *Bürgertum* after 1848. Local developments and traditions are, thus, of essential importance when we consider liberal political responses to the emergence of the labor movement.[3]

Notes for this chapter begin on page 135.

1. "Civic Rights," "bürgerlich" Milieu, and Social Protest

In the late-eighteenth and early-nineteenth centuries, a number of German municipalities were in effect self-governing republics that regulated many of their affairs on a cooperative *(genossenschaftlich)* basis. Thus, local civic rights *(Bürgerrecht)* affected all groups contained within the organized society of the municipality, from merchants, manufacturers, and artisans to attorneys, teachers, doctors, municipal officials, scholars, and artists. It determined the rights and duties of every member of the municipal commonwealth; and it opened up possibilities for the acquisition of property and the practice of a trade or business. Membership in corporate bodies remained limited to those who fell under the purview of civic law, as was access to most relief institutions, such as hospitals, orphanages, or institutions for the poor or the aged. Above all, it was the civic laws of the towns that guaranteed political rights, including the right to vote and speak on matters that affected the common wealth. Theoretically, only those men who could demonstrate their economic independence could acquire citizenship rights. Acceptance into the ranks of citizens (*Bürger*), thus, represented the culmination of an entire phase in the lives of individual men. Of course, the practice of civic rights had often been altered or amended over the years. At the same time, however, in many regions the activities of larger territorial states often limited the prerogatives of municipal self-government, even leading, in places such as Prussia, to its complete abolition. In the nineteenth century, traditional civic law, thus, found itself in the midst of a complex process of delimitation and transformation that varied sharply from region to region and city to city. It is, therefore, of great significance that old-fashioned structures of municipal law and citizenship persisted into the *Kaiserreich*, where they controlled access to participation in municipal politics and helped to maintain the dominance of property-holding elites; the lower strata of society, thus, remained politically without rights in German cities.[4] As a result, traditional notions of civic law as well as the *Bürgertum*'s patriarchal self-perception persisted until the twentieth century, and both stood in sharp contrast to the concept of the citizen as passive "subject" that characterized the public law of the authoritarian central state.

Non-citizens were clearly distinguished from citizens in Germany's towns and cities. Non-citizens included servants and non-natives as well as all the lower orders that did not enjoy civic rights, were not economically independent, depended on the value of their own labor, had no fixed income, or were poor. In the nineteenth century poverty became a mass phenomenon, a collective fate bound up with uncertain work opportunities and the lack of any prospect of relief or improvement. These groups of people could be subdivided into a variety of distinctive categories, many of them defined by tradition, such as household servants, day laborers, and transport workers; but they also included new categories such as manufacturing and factory laborers. The modern factory system was, of course, still in its infancy. Only gradually did a new type of worker begin to emerge. But this new worker was barely represented in the early labor movement, for which the world of the artisanate and of handicraft (*Handwerk*) remained much more significant.[5] For a very long time indeed the rhythms of handicraft work continued to shape the realities of daily life in German cities; and although the old ties that bound the world of artisanal production and reproduction gradually dissolved, its value systems and behavioral patterns persisted well past the middle of the nineteenth century.

In contrast to servants and day-laborers, journeymen could hope to pass their masters' examinations and thereby acquire civic rights. As a result, the potential for protest only slowly began to build up among these people.[6] Although disorder and violent altercations between masters and artisans were frequent occurrences, protest activities among journeymen did not call into question the bases of urban government and society, nor did they embrace political demands.[7] It took the Revolution of 1848 to galvanize this social group politically. And only after the Revolution can one begin to see signs of a relationship between the *bürgerlich*-liberal movement and the movement of handicraft workers (*Handwerker-Arbeiter*).

During the Revolution itself, the German *Bürgertum* did not respond uniformly to the unprecedented, widespread political activities of the lower orders – although these activities represented a real cultural shock to them. Apart from the oft-cited conflicts between liberal and democrats, there were also major differences within the ranks of municipal citizenries themselves. Their responses, from integration to repression, seem largely to have been conditioned by the extent to which particular cities had retained or had moved away from their older corporative traditions. On the whole, scattered local attempts at social integration ended in failure; and so the years 1848 to 1849 witnessed the emergence, for the first time in German history, of a labor movement that stretched over the entire country. This took the form of local worker education associations (*Arbeiterbildungsvereine*), professional associations, unions, and journeymen's associations. Indeed, with centers in Cologne, Frankfurt am Main, Breslau, Hamburg, and Berlin, the "Workers' Brotherhood" (*Arbeiterverbrüderung*) established itself in more than four hundred locations, building an impressive if loosely-knit network of artisans' and workers' associations; in 1850 their membership was estimated at eighteen to twenty thousand. The movement consisted for the most part of journeyman carpenters, masons, joiners, shoemakers, and tailors, as well as representatives of highly skilled trades such as printers and compositors. A number of independent masters from the textile branch were also active.[8]

A well-known representative of the *Arbeiterverbrüderung* was the compositor Stephan Born, author of the movement's programmatic tracts. Apart from political demands which for the most part were borrowed from the radical democrats, Born emphasized two positions which were to be of decisive importance for the labor movement in the decades that followed. The first was the idea of *Bildung* or education, which an entire branch of the early labor movement had explicitly incorporated into its very name *(Arbeiterbildungsverein)*. The second was the idea of the *Association*, that is, the establishment of cooperatives. The *Arbeiterverbrüderung* itself thought that its principal object was to set up cooperative cash funds *(Associationskassen)*, "for they will make it possible for the poorest worker to stand up to the competition of capital."[9] Once they had been established, worker cooperatives would spread through the country of their own accord, organizing their own system of exchange and credit. Most scholars agree that Born's demands essentially embodied an old artisanal ideal, a utopia for skilled craft workers, an illusory opportunity collectively to preserve threatened forms of artisanal independence. To this extent they reflected the situation of Germany's workers in the transition from handicraft to wage labor.[10]

The early labor movement shared many of the ideas contained in the *bürgerlich*-liberal critique of modern social development. Liberals emphasized not only the destruction of feudalism, the modernization of agriculture and industry, and the establishment of a society based on middling incomes and equal rights, but in many cases they also criticized untrammeled capitalism. They opposed the estrangement of the country's various social strata, and proposed a more gradual process of industrial development. To bridge the structural crisis of small-scale business they proposed an entire system of self-help organizations. Many craft workers themselves rejected the idea of social segregation and embraced a *Vormärz* ideal of liberalism that had been strongly influenced by small-scale business interests.[11] It was important, in their view, to avoid the most serious consequences of English-style industrialization. Despite their confrontations with each other, the *bürgerlich* and the labor movements shared a number of common concerns and outlooks, most of them rooted in the world of old-fashioned urban society. Why, then, did the labor movement organize itself separately during the Revolution of 1848? Why did serious confrontations between *Bürger* and craft workers, including journeymen, arise? To answer these questions, it is not sufficient simply to point to the irreconcilability of their social and political ideals nor to the emergence of antagonism between bourgeoisie and proletariat. Above all, it seems, many *Bürger* continued to adhere to traditional patriarchal reservations regarding the lower orders and their demands for political participation, and these prejudices played a decisive role.

The emergence of the labor movement took place at a time when the major issue was the modernization of the political structures of the *Bürgertum* itself. The goal of the so-called "March demands" of 1848 was the establishment of economic and political conditions that in turn could create a society of individual citizens, active participants in the municipal community who would sweep away the remaining group-based distinctions among merchants, craft workers, confessions, and so on. But during the Revolution, the German *Bürgertum* was only willing to look with favor upon those members of the lower orders who regarded themselves as future *Bürger* and who were willing to accommodate themselves to traditional notions of spiritual and material independence. Otherwise the *Bürger* were not willing to countenance the idea of political equality or of a "downward" extension of the process of political emancipation.[12] This was the dividing line: at this point in the Revolution the integrative force of the liberal model of society had reached its end. But at this same point some tentative efforts were undertaken to develop a new politics of integration. Based on traditional notions of civic rights, these became the basis for a post-revolutionary labor politics. That politics in turn was caught up with the question of handicraft labor and its future.[13]

2. The Cooperative Movement and Education: The Utopias of Social Liberalism

As we have already noted, "association" and "education" were almost magical concepts for certain segments of the lower classes. The period from 1840 to 1870 witnessed a number of efforts to build on these concepts and, thus, introduce social principles into classical liberalism. In contrast to older views, which held that the state should intervene in the economy only to deal with the most extreme social misery and only when market forces had failed utterly, people like Karl Mathy argued that municipalities should undertake programs of municipal action and self-help. And it was Robert von Mohl who suggested that cooperatives and *Associationen* could work together against unemployment, sickness, and the miseries of old age. They could create public credit institutions and cooperative banks around the "crystallization points" of capital and labor. Hermann Schulze-Delitzsch played a central role in stimulating discussion of these issues. Influenced by the events of 1848, he, like Mohl, wanted to improve workers' social condition by establishing associations, which would include health insurance societies, burial societies, credit and savings associations, consumers' associations, and cooperatives to purchase and distribute goods at wholesale prices. Every member of a producers' cooperative would simultaneously be an owner and a worker, a master and a servant, and so these organizations would initiate a "true reconciliation between labor and capital, the just distribution of the fruits of production between both." As self-governing corporations, the cooperatives would revive one of the basic principles of traditional urban life in Germany: the idea that wage labor represented simply a transitional stage on the road to individual economic and financial independence.[14]

Central to liberal reflections on the problem of modern labor was the concept of *Bildung*, a word which is sometimes (if misleadingly) rendered into English as "education" or "cultivation." Though its exact meaning may sometimes be fuzzy to non-Germans, it became one of the defining characteristics of an awakening *bürgerlich* consciousness in the last third of the eighteenth century in Germany. The concept of *Bildung* was "multivalent," as James J. Sheehan has written;[15] and it cannot be reduced either to the ideals of neohumanist political reformers nor to the idea of the acquisition of knowledge for its own sake. In its original sense, it concerned the development of the individual personality. According to the proponents of *Bildung*, the *gebildete Bürger* – that is, the experienced and educated citizen, defined by achievement and by spiritual cultivation – should replace the incompetent aristocracies and patriciates that dominated Germany's towns and cities. The idea of *Bildung* also became caught up with another characteristic feature of *bürgerlich* social life after the late-eighteenth century: the emergence of new clubs, societies, and associations (*Vereine*) and, with them, new patterns of associational life. By 1800 new *Vereine* had been founded in most of the country's larger cities, devoting themselves not only to socializing but also to the pursuit of higher purposes such as the "acquisition and diffusion of useful knowledge."[16] After 1815, the number, variety, and social significance of *Vereine* grew dramatically, a process that was also connected with the popularization of the idea of *Bildung*. It is estimated that by the middle of the nineteenth century some fourteen thousand clubs, societies, and associations existed in Germany.[17] Most members were recruited from the commercial classes and the so-called *Bildungsbürgertum*. In these new associations the urban *Bürgertum* found a way to organize itself on a non-traditional, non-corporative basis; they, thus, constituted one of the structural ingredients of a new, still-evolving, dynamic civil society. Moreover, as the example of the labor movement shows, they were flexible enough to organize the lower strata as well. Above all, they were able to modify the idea of *Bildung*, itself so crucial to *bürgerlich* associational life, and adapt it to the needs of those strata. With the worker education associations they had created a model for the social and cultural integration of various non-*bürgerlich* groups.

After 1848 the idea of *Bildung* continued to be intimately associated with the idea of workers' emancipation and until the 1870s it remained an essential element of the labor movement itself. But it was based on the traditional categories of old German *Bürgerrecht*, with their emphasis on the importance of upward social mobility as a prerequisite for the acquisition of political rights. Thus, non-*bürgerlich* journeymen could be compared to under-age minors; just as the latter required the care of a responsible *paterfamilias*, the former would have to submit themselves to the tutelage of *bürgerlich* politicians. The middle-class founders of *Vereine* agreed that journeymen should be supported during the "transitional phase" to full participation as citizens, but journeymen should not be permitted to enjoy the rights and privileges of full citizenship until that process had been completed. All of these ideas and suppositions fit neatly into the general program of liberalism: a liberalism that was still informed by utopian notions of a classless society of equal citizens or *Bürger*, and which continued to use the categories and vocabulary of handicraft and artisanal work when addressing labor issues. With this program the liberal movement powerfully influenced the development of the German labor movement.

3. The Labor Movement as Part of the National Movement: Toward Political Marginalization

In 1859 the liberal opposition movement in Germany gained a new lease on life, most notably with the formation of the famous *Nationalverein*. A number of new worker education associations emerged at the same time, and immediately they were able to reestablish the communication links and the personal connections that the older labor and liberal-democratic movement had created in 1848.[18] By the end of the 1850s and in the 1860s it had become clear, especially to observers in southwestern and central Germany, that a new "people's party" (*Volkspartei*) to the left of the *Nationalverein* could only emerge if the laboring masses were included in it. Accordingly, 225 education societies for workers and artisans were quickly created in 218 locations. As in 1848, skilled craft workers (*Handwerker-Arbeiter*) constituted the bulk of their members; they tended to view the social problems of the time as transitional phenomena and, above all, they believed in the power of *Bildung*. Education and achievement would serve as the "entrance ticket" to *bürgerlich* society. *Bildung* represented the process of integration into civic society and the public realm and, quite concretely, it constituted the professional prerequisite for upward social mobility. And it was the educational programs of the various *Vereine* which determined the latter.[19]

An "educational process" *(Bildungsprozeß)* of this sort could not, however, permanently satisfy the movement of skilled craft workers and journeymen. For one thing, the promise of escaping from a dependent journeyman's existence increasingly seemed at variance with the realities of daily life. More and more journeymen found themselves unable to make the leap to economic independence and, thus, to the full rights of citizenship. Moreover, the kind of education or *Bildung* offered to craft workers was hardly the sort that could help them improve their economic situation. At the same time, the increasing politicization of the 1860s contributed to a significant decline of liberal influence among "lower" social groups. The unpolitical quality of the liberal message was becoming increasingly irrelevant.

Growing conflicts over political participation witnessed a clash between older, urban ideas of civic rights and citizenship *(Stadtbürgerrecht)* and newer ideas of civil rights and state citizenship *(Staatsbürgerrecht)*. The signal for this clash came from workers who wanted to join the *Nationalverein* but were discouraged by its high membership dues. Schulze-Delitzsch responded to their complaints with a bit of paternalistic advice: "You workers, think about yourselves; get a bit of prosperity for yourselves first, and improve your education. What good can political participation do for me if I have not acquired some modest prosperity?"[20] This answer was quite inappropriate in view of the increasingly heated political situation in which, following the example of the British labor movement, German workers were trying to create a general "workers' congress." The members of a committee in Leipzig who were laying the groundwork for such a congress asked Ferdinand Lassalle to prepare a "workers' program," and the result was his "Open Answer." He thereupon undertook a tour of Germany and achieved great acclaim with his programmatic ideas.

Lassalle's speech in Frankfurt am Main on 17 and 19 May 1863 really set the tone for subsequent developments, preparing the way for a triumphal visit to the Rhineland and the establishment of the General German Workers Association (*Allgemeiner Deutscher Arbeiterverein*, or ADAV).[21] Lassalle's programmatic position differs from the liberals' in one especially important respect. For Lassalle, the municipality disappears as a level of social organization with its own sphere of law. The political participation of workers, guaranteed by the state itself, would emerge in its place. The "duty and purpose of the state" was "to facilitate and to mediate the great cultural advances of humanity." Universal manhood suffrage would enable every male citizen to receive "an equal share of control over the state and of the capacity to shape its will and its purpose"; thus, the elected legislative body would be the "true image … of the people who elected it."[22] As we have already noted, the notion of universal manhood suffrage simply did not play a role in the imaginative universe of Germany's urban *Bürgertum*, and, thus, it represented the truly radical component of Lassalle's thesis. In virtually every other respect it remained wedded to the older ideas and goals of the liberal movement. To be sure, Lassalle argued that self-help, savings institutions, sickness and disability institutions, and the like were useless against the "competition of large-scale factory production." At the same time, however, he believed that the producers' cooperatives represented a solution to this competition; indeed, such organizations could create a society of free and autonomous citizens. "To make the working class its own entrepreneur": that was the means by which the worker could be freed from the fate that otherwise awaited him.[23] It was not at all a vision of the socialist future which separated Lassalle from liberalism. Rather, it was his breach with notions of politics that derived from the patriarchal forms of old-fashioned *Bürgerrecht*. The Lassallean program, thus, focused its attention on the complex contemporary problems of social change and political transformation; Lassalle had radically rejected the older formula of "education before politics," contending instead that universal manhood suffrage offered the key to the emancipation of labor. In 1863, as in 1848, it was not so much objective class differences or fundamentally incompatible social perceptions as divergent understandings of politics that divided the *Bürgertum*, rooted in its traditional urban milieu, from skilled craft workers and journeymen.

For many years the estrangement between "bourgeois" and "social" democracy was not terribly significant. The great mass of worker education associations remained loyal to the Frankfurt journalist Leopold Sonnemann's Assembly of German Worker Associations (*Vereinstag Deutscher Arbeitervereine*, or VDAV) and, thus, to continued liberal leadership.[24] In 1863, Lassalle's ADAV represented little more than a possible organizational focus for a movement that still lay essentially in the future. More than a decade was to pass before a labor party with a certain degree of political influence emerged in Germany, and that process in turn hinged upon three major political developments: the politicization of parts of the VDAV and the establishment of the Social Democratic Labor Party of Germany (*Sozialdemokratische Arbeiterpartei Deutschlands*, or SDAP); the development of a modern trade union movement; and the strike movement at the beginning of the 1870s. Although the first meetings of the VDAV largely dealt with non-political issues, the wars of unification served to intensify debates over questions such as universal suffrage or Prussian militarism. Indeed, debates about political issues led in 1869 to the split within the VDAV in Saxony and to the subsequent creation of the SDAP. At about the same time the German trade union movement began to develop, organized into professional associations which tended to be divided among politically neutral organizations, the Lassallean Workers Support Association, unions sympathetic to the SDAP, and liberal organizations called *Gewerkvereine*.[25]

Shortly thereafter the number of strikes increased dramatically. It is estimated that between 1871 and 1873 more than two hundred thousand workers participated in strike actions. For the first time, workers were responding not to crisis but to the desire to share in the opportunities of the boom that attended the establishment of the new Reich. Thanks to the unions' success, the labor movement was able to grow at a grass-roots level for the first time since 1848; and it was the two autonomous labor parties which were able to win over the unions and, thus, transform themselves into a significant political force. To be sure, at first the liberal-supported *Gewerkvereine* were able to register some notable successes. As late as 1878 they still constituted about a quarter of the total union movement, although their aloofness from the strike movement impaired their ability to benefit from the movement's growth. In the following two decades the liberal organizations dwindled into an ancillary branch of the larger trade-union movement.

In short, the increasingly autonomous labor movement of the 1860s was not yet unified. The development of such a movement was a process that took a number of years. The fusion of the ADAV and the SDAP into the Socialist Workers Party of Germany (*Sozialistische Arbeiterpartei Deutschlands*, or SAPD) in 1875 and then the Anti-Socialist Law of 1878 finalized the breach with the liberal movement. The SAPD was able to survive the repression of the 1880s and emerged in the 1890s at the forefront of a mass working-class movement of a more modern sort.

Influenced by the national movement and by the wars of unification, German society had been politicized to an unprecedented degree during the decade that led to the establishment of the new Reich. These new realities played a central role in the conflicts between the liberal movement and the early labor movement after the 1860s. "Middle-class" or *bürgerlich* society was in the process of emerging from its older, civic-urban traditions and was assuming a more modern, national character. Old-fashioned conflicts overlapped and became entangled with newer processes of social disintegration and class formation. In this situation old-style *bürgerlich* patriarchalism clashed with the emancipatory desires of journeymen and skilled craft workers. The result was a fragmentation of the various perspectives that shaped *bürgerlich* society, which may well explain the split in liberal ranks. Much the same was true for workers. Originally a heterogeneous collection of artisans, journeymen, cottage laborers, day laborers, and a few factory workers, they only became a modern, industrial working class as a result of a decades-long process of forced industrialization. In the long run, the labor parties that had emerged during the unification era represented a challenge to the liberal movement, even as they represented an impediment to the unity of those forces interested in a reform of German society.

4. "Die Welt im neuen Geleise": The New World of the Working Class

The *Kaiserreich* witnessed the development of the economic and social bases of modern bourgeois society, the rejection of superfluous traditions, and, at the level of cities and towns, the creation of a unitary municipal structure that in turn helped to create a homogeneous national bourgeoisie. At the same time, however, three decades of industrialization resulted in gigantic social upheavals. Within the course of a single generation, German society as a whole had to confront a monumental process of social transformation and reorientation. A portion of the country's "excess" population simply left the country in mighty waves of emigration, a movement of human beings that was paralleled by unprecedented levels of internal migration. Rural people from the eastern parts of the Reich poured into the new industrial regions; and the experience of moving over great distances was an integral feature of a collective transformation of values and customary outlooks that was more radical than in previous decades. The result was a new kind of worker, a person who was no longer connected to the traditions of urban handicraft and old-style urban structures.

The heterogeneity of the working class increased as a result of the tremendous process of industrialization. The journeyman could still be found in small-scale industry, and in many cases he had already become a *Gesellen-Arbeiter* and had adjusted himself to wage labor in factories. But after the 1880s the modern industrial laborer began to appear in massive numbers. Indeed, these workers represented a second generation of people who had become accustomed to the realities of modern urban living and of factory life. Many of these workers were still "skilled": that is, they had been trained in artisanal modes of production, in contrast to unskilled or semiskilled workers who had often been recruited from the ranks of rural immigrants. And there were other lines of division as well, based on gender, age, marital status, place of origin, confession, and levels of socialization. Still, in contrast to earlier times, three decades of rapid industrialization had created a new world of working-class experience.[26]

Factory workers' lives had become more settled, but they remained insecure. Despite the variety of jobs and working conditions that characterized working-class existence, most workers had to contend with hard exertion, monotony, early physical decline, and, above all, the insecurity of existence itself. Wretched living conditions and the exclusion of working-class children from advanced education made a mockery of the bourgeois ideal of education. Thus, the socialization of workers was largely a function of their own experiences with school, the church, and the military. Above all, though, from childhood they experienced the workplace as the site of a collective oppression that was fixed in a patriarchal system of labor discipline.[27]

This new lifestyle stood in sharp contrast to the promises of the disciples of progress. Scarcity combined with frustration to create a basis for socialist utopias and the belief that "general insecurity is the normal condition of society" and was rooted "in the essence of capitalist production."[28] Of course, things were gradually improving; slowly, ever so slowly, wages began to exceed the minimum needed for existence, and the quality of workers' nutrition also improved. Until the turn of the century, though, incomes were too low to provide adequately for workers' families, especially in times of emergency. Social insurance did represent a significant improvement in this respect. Workers were no longer covered by the old system of poor relief, and in its stead a new system of sickness, accident, disability, and old-age insurance was introduced between 1883 and 1889. The insured themselves could participate in the organization of the social insurance system, depending on the level of their contributions. Indeed, for a long time this remained the only area of social policy in which management and labor cooperated with government and actually managed to increase the benefits that were available to the insured.[29]

Where the 1860s had seen the creation of distinctive working-class political and trade union organizations, the period around the turn of the century witnessed the establishment of an array of working-class associations that paralleled middle-class *Vereine*. Located in virtually every German city, these new organizations were supposed to eliminate or at least alleviate the most serious problems that proletarian households faced. Where the middle classes had their home-building societies, the organized working class created its own building and savings societies. Working-class families began to do their daily shopping at consumer cooperatives, which grew from humble beginnings into gigantic enterprises with hundreds of thousands of members and a variety of ancillary commercial activities. Workers also began to appropriate the realms of education and culture for themselves by setting up educational associations and workers' libraries, and by organizing recreational activities and public festivals. Distinctive political, economic, and cultural organizations, thus, became a characteristic feature of the proletarian milieu and of a "workers' culture" that served as a collective device for the management of scarcity. In short, the proletarian milieu was a world in itself, defined and conditioned by the deprivations of working-class life.[30]

Half a century had now passed since the Revolution of 1848 and the first activities of the early, largely artisanal labor movement. Now, just as the workers had changed, so too had the workers' movement. By the turn of the century, unions had been set up in just about every branch of German industry. Before the Anti-Socialist Law of 1878 the craft trades, with their rather rudimentary journeyman traditions, had largely dominated the unions, but now larger organizations covering entire branches of industry were registering the highest growth rates. Older guild traditions had been set aside during the time of the Anti-Socialist Law, and now the unions were rapidly organizing the growing mass of industrial laborers. Thus, a new kind of union movement presented itself at the beginning of the 1890s; and between 1895 and 1907 it grew from 330,000 to 2.5 million members, despite the fact that large numbers of workers – government workers, white-collar employees, women, domestic servants, and agricultural laborers – could not be organized for legal or political reasons. At the same time the Social Democratic Party and its electorate also grew steadily. Where in 1877 the party of the working class had only gained half a million votes, by 1890 it had attracted three times as many voters, and in 1912 4.25 million. In the early 1870s it had been largely concentrated in a few centers such as Schleswig-Holstein, Hamburg, Bremen, Berlin, Saxony, and Thuringia; but now its organizational network had stretched over the entire Reich, with the exception of the East Elbian regions. Although the party's citadels remained powerful, the older north-south gap had become less important. After the turn of the century the Social Democrats began to penetrate Catholic milieus, though the typical social democratic voter remained relatively young, German-speaking, Protestant, urban, and, of course, working-class. The dynamic industrial development of the *Kaiserreich* and the emergence of a new generation of workers had increased the attractiveness of social democracy; and, as a result, both the SPD and the trade unions had become mass movements.[31] These trends created new possibilities, but also new complications.

5. The "Revisionism" Controversy: The Labor Movement as the Representative of Liberalism?

The incorporation of a new kind of industrial worker into the labor movement also affected its politics. What Rudolf Boch has described as "artisanal socialism" *(Handwerkersozialismus)* was increasingly replaced by a strategy that adapted itself to new forms of industrial production. New issues of social policy *(Sozialpolitik)* had now become more urgent than older ideas about the importance of education and of producers' cooperatives. Moreover, the labor movement's massive successes also provided support for the idea that, in the long run, some sort of compromise between workers and the middle classes might indeed be possible. The result was a kind of reformist policy that was immensely controversial within the labor movement itself and in turn precipitated the long strategic debate known to history as the "revisionism controversy." The older historical literature tended to regard this episode as evidence of the penetration of liberal ideas into the labor movement, based in turn on the alleged *embourgeoisement* of a particular group of workers, the so-called "labor aristocracy." More recently, however, historians have tended to suggest that revisionism was not so much an expression of the special interests of a particular group of workers; rather, it represented one of the results of an increasingly broad-based movement that had become aware of its real possibilities and was attempting to break out of the political ghetto to which it had been consigned since the Reich's foundation. A mass movement like social democracy and the trade unions had to adapt itself to the conditions of political and social work in the existing society. The movement simply had to attempt to overcome its political and social isolation if it were to seize the opportunity to improve the economic and social condition of working people.[32]

The unions became the major supporters of reformism within the labor movement, along with the south German wing of the SPD associated with people like Georg von Vollmar and Eduard Bernstein. Thus, union leaders like Carl Legien, Theodor Leipart, and Alexander Schlicke decisively shaped the destinies of their movement for decades, well into the Weimar years. Legien, chair of the General Commission of the so-called "free" trade unions, had become convinced that a successful *Sozialpolitik* was possible within the existing order. It could relieve the misery of workers and lead to their acceptance as equal citizens with equal rights; workers could achieve this result through effective organization and interest-group politics. He aspired to a "partnership role" and "an array of legally established arrangements in the area of social policy which could improve the condition of the working class and also integrate them into the state."[33] For Legien, then, the activities of the union movement extended beyond the struggle for better wages, working conditions, and educational opportunities. They also embraced the idea that unions should participate in a clearly defined system of negotiated social reform guaranteed and refereed by the state. The unions and some elements within the Social Democratic Party had, thus, opted for a reformist strategy, but it was informed less by the values of classical liberalism than by a pragmatic politics of social reform with state-socialist tendencies. At the same time, the unions failed to produce a parallel set of ideas to reform the *Kaiserreich* politically. Indeed, they tended to adopt a policy of neutrality toward the political forces that shaped the *Kaiserreich*, and they were not even necessarily hostile toward conservative policies of social reform. This strategic orientation toward the forces of the existing order encountered considerable resistance within the Social Democratic Party itself.[34] Still, Legien stuck to his guns and, assisted by a steady growth in union membership, maintained his position for a number of years.[35]

The year 1899 represented a turning point in several respects. The social-reformist wing of the liberals re-emerged with new energy, while the government itself eased a number of legal limitations that had restricted union activities and also began to develop proposals to reform workers' insurance and workers' protection. For their part, the unions demonstrated a cautious but growing readiness to engage in non-partisan efforts to alleviate social problems. Working-class reformers, liberal reformers, social conservatives, and state institutions, thus, began to collaborate with each other in complex ways, and their contributions to the social and political integration of the labor movement can hardly be underestimated.

6. The Liberal Middle Classes and the "Rediscovery" of the Social Question

The liberal middle classes had always been interested in reforming the authoritarian structures of the *Kaiserreich*, and at the end of the nineteenth century they "rediscovered" social issues that had been forgotten or overlooked during the years of Germany's massive economic transformation. To be sure, elements within the *Bürgertum* had concerned themselves with the social question for more than sixty years. Still, their social policies and programs largely reflected the ideals of an older *bürgerlich* society, and to a large extent they had concerned themselves with the plight of traditional journeymen. This concern was somewhat justified, because the traditional urban *Bürgertum* had been reasonably well acquainted with the social conditions of journeymen, traditional day-laborers, and cottage laborers. But by the end of the century an entirely new, socially uprooted group of people had moved into the new factory districts on the margins of Germany's cities. These people represented a world quite new and alien to the experiences of the country's upper classes.

Thus, the discovery of mass working-class poverty represented an immense form of culture shock for many Germans in the 1890s. The policy of official repression, embodied in the Anti-Socialist Law, had failed. Now, suddenly, middle-class writers reached a new public with socially critical novels that described the culture, the consumption patterns, the clothing, living and working conditions of factory workers; and they succeeded in reaching a public that had not been touched by the innumerable *exposés* produced by the working-class press itself. A vigorous, multifaceted literature of social criticism had developed by the end of the nineteenth century, with writers like Karl Henckel, Gerhart Hauptmann, Detlev von Liliencron, and the brothers Julius and Heinrich Hart depicting social misery in graphic prose reminiscent of American authors like Jack London. They all agreed that, as writers, it was no longer their obligation to entertain society's upper ten thousand; rather, they regarded their art as a form of "practical sociology" in which they could lay bare the "struggles and suffering" of the toiling masses.[36] But for all their good intentions, they in fact had little concrete experience of social reality, and they largely counted on the "horrified curiosity" of the middle-class reading public for their success.[37] They treated the world of the working class as though it were a far-off land in a contemporary travel account, full of mysterious aliens with unusual customs, peculiar rituals, and strange languages.[38]

Despite these limitations, they did manage to arouse a great deal of middle-class interest in workers' lives. Indeed, it is very likely that they inspired the young pastor Paul Göhre to undertake a real-life "expedition" into the alien world of the working class in 1890. Disguising himself as a factory worker, Göhre proposed to "uncover the full truth about the outlook of the working classes, their material wants, and their spiritual, moral, and religious character."[39] The response to his social reporting was enormous. Renowned newspapers reported on his experiences as though they were describing an exotic adventure, and they confessed their astonishment at having discovered that their own country was full of people whose ideas and feelings differed so radically from those of their fellow Germans.[40] Although Social Democrats responded derisively to this sort of naïveté, Göhre's work encouraged more and more socially engaged journalists to follow his example, until finally workers themselves began to write their own accounts of their experiences.[41] Not coincidentally, the impetus for the latter came from Göhre himself, who edited the first workers' autobiographies; he hoped that these accounts would be recognized as important "cultural documents," and indeed his publication of Carl Fischer's autobiography elicited a great deal of attention. In the words of several critics, Fischer's book represented a "piece of German cultural history," a "storehouse of information on the ethnography of the working class"; "important for social reformers," it was "the most important book of the year."[42] Similar accounts began to appear shortly thereafter, and soon social democratic publishers were producing workers' autobiographies to support their own political agitation.

A number of empirical studies also served to whet public interest in social issues after 1900, the best known being the famous investigations of the Association for Social Policy. So, for example, around 1910 the social scientist Adolf Levenstein posed a number of the same questions that Göhre had asked two decades earlier, this time, however, on a broadly empirical basis.[43] Such studies were based on innovative methodologies, and encouraged both a growing interest in modern social problems and a more vigorous discussion of those issues among the liberal middle classes.

In many cities the entrepreneurial bourgeoisie had become extremely influential and even, in some cases, the dominant social group. Now some of them attempted to deal with pressing social problems by developing their own social welfare and insurance initiatives at the factory or workshop level. Probably the best-known examples were the factory foundations that provided Alfred Krupp's twenty thousand workers with housing, shopping centers, dining halls, hospitals, sickness funds, and pensions. Krupp's foundations were designed to tie the worker to the firm; given the high and extremely costly turnover rates at German factories, this was a matter of great importance to management. At the same time management hoped to use foundations of this sort to influence workers' political opinions, and very often they banned union activity on their premises. Thus, they served to reinforce paternalistic relationships and thereby resist pressures for change.[44]

But programs like Krupp's were only one aspect of the new liberal discussion of social issues around the turn of the century. In fact, it was a discussion that was largely stimulated by the liberals' declining social and political influence. Both in the Reichstag and in state parliaments the liberals had been steadily losing seats; where in 1874 they still controlled 208 Reichstag seats, by 1912 that number had declined to 87. During the same period the Social Democrats had increased their parliamentary representation from nine to 110.[45] According to thoughtful observers like Fiedrich Naumann, liberals would have to develop new strategies if they were to prosper in the new age of mass politics.[46] Various left-liberal splinter groups like Naumann's own National Social Association *(Nationalsozialer Verein)* as well as parts of the Liberal People's Party *(Freisinnige Volkspartei)* and later of the Progressive People's Party *(Fortschrittliche Volkspartei)* regarded workers as especially valuable potential allies. This goal was even shared by some elements within the National Liberal Party, especially the Young Liberals. Liberals should break with the conservatives, these groups argued, and should instead forge a broad liberal alliance to promote a generous and expansive policy of social reform. They should support trade unions and cooperate with the Social Democrats. Such a policy could lead to the emergence of a Reichstag bloc that could stretch "from Bebel to Bassermann" and serve as an effective counterweight to the government and its parliamentary allies.[47] Arguments of this sort, however compelling, failed to gain the upper hand within liberal circles. A liberal politics of social reform always had to contend with a number of countervailing influences, and its potential attractiveness to the labor movement was reduced accordingly.[48] Germany's city governments were the only remaining political bastions of liberalism. Restrictive franchises had ensured the maintenance of *bürgerlich* majorities in the cities, and so it was only at the local level that liberals continued to control the structures of public administration. Only there could liberals seriously attempt to cooperate with the "lower" orders of society.

7. Germany's Cities: Centers of a "Liberal-Labor" Alliance?

Germany's cities were, of course, the places where the effects of the country's dramatic changes were most obvious and most problematic. At the same time, the institutions of local self-government offered municipal authorities an opportunity to undertake significant experiments in social reform.[49] A few weeks after the *Reichsgründung* in 1871, the new government pledged that every person in the Reich would be guaranteed the minimum necessary for survival. This burden was immediately transferred to municipal authorities, which began to produce new poor-relief measures that were largely run by public-relief officials on an unpaid, honorary basis. Thus, municipal administrations were only able to exercise a marginal influence on the actual implementation of these relief programs.[50] Moreover, new social insurance legislation required a significant expansion of hospitals in order to accommodate the needs of new social groups, while urban population increases necessitated significant investments in new housing.[51] At the same time that the urban middle classes and city administrations had to confront these challenges, they also had to create new public-education facilities, attempt to promote and popularize the arts and sciences, and establish new institutions like savings and loan associations, legal-advice bureaus, industrial courts and arbitration offices, employment offices, work-relief agencies, and municipal unemployment-insurance offices. In short, the urban *Bürgertum* was responsible for introducing a large number of pragmatic reforms that, taken together, can be regarded as a German version of the "municipal socialism" that emerged in Great Britain during those years: a "socialism" that contrasted sharply with the "state socialism" advocated by conservative social reformers. Many liberal urban politicians hoped that this kind of municipal socialism could forge new bonds between the middle classes and a labor movement that was willing to embrace certain bourgeois values, and they also hoped that this new cooperation at the local level would enable them to increase their own influence on state and society at the national level.[52]

Frankfurt am Main was one important center of social liberalism at the municipal level. Until 1867 it had been an autonomous city-state with a well-established tradition of local self-government; and as early as the 1860s it had become home to an especially vigorous form of liberalism of the sort that Leopold Sonnemann, socially conscious editor of the liberal *Frankfurter Zeitung*, embodied.[53] Like every other German city, Frankfurt had a distinctive workers' milieu that was sustained by a variety of self-help organizations. Here too the parties of the middle classes and of the workers had drifted apart. Around the turn of the century they had become mass organizations, with the center of gravity shifting in favor of the Social Democrats; within a ten-year period they had gained almost a third of the seats in the city parliament, despite the persistence of restrictions on workers' suffrage.[54] In contrast to numerous other cities, however, the contacts between liberals and socialists had never been fully disrupted in Frankfurt. As early as the mid-1880s, for example, liberal associations devoted to social welfare issues had already been established. Local organizations such as the *Freie Deutsche Hochstift*, the Social Museum, or the Central Association for Private Relief *(Centrale für private Fürsorge)* focused their efforts on empirical studies of the causes of urban poverty, and these materials served in turn as the basis for concrete reform policies. The Committee for Popular Lectures *(Ausschuß für Volksvorlesungen)* was responsible for reactivating collaborative educational measures with local trade unions. And one of Germany's most influential journals on welfare-related issues, the *Blätter für Soziale Praxis* (later *Soziale Praxis*), was founded in Frankfurt and edited by the Social Democrat Heinrich Braun. The prominent Frankfurt industrialist Wilhelm Merton, who supported the journal, also founded the Institute for Public Welfare *(Institut für Gemeinwohl)* and the Academy for the Social and Commercial Sciences *(Akademie für Sozial- und Handelswissenschaften)*. The latter became the basis for the modern University of Frankfurt, well known for its emphasis on the social sciences.

The chair of Frankfurt's Poor Relief Office, Karl Flesch, is usually regarded, with Hugo Sinzheimer, as the *spiritus rector* of modern German labor law. Flesch played a central role in merging the program of municipal social reform with the ideal of bourgeois self-determination and self-reliance, free of direct government intervention. Thus, he called for the creation of a labor court that would be composed equally of representatives of management and labor; this court was established in 1886 and provided the inspiration for a similar court system at the Reich level four years later. Flesch also advocated the introduction of a self-administered municipal employment office and a local system of unemployment insurance. The Committee for Popular Lectures was also supposed to encourage the integration of workers into the norms and manners of middle-class life; so too was an industrial adult-education school that included workers' representatives on its board. Both institutions were established in 1890. At the same time, private societies and institutions concerned themselves intensively with issues that the city administration did not directly address, including the numerous initiatives undertaken to support public housing projects.[55]

In short, at the national level the ideals of social liberalism remained unfulfilled; but in Frankfurt many aspects of the ideals of municipal socialism were translated into reality. Moreover, it was a system that directly engaged and involved workers themselves. Thus, between 1885 and 1914 a dense network of institutional relationships emerged that connected working-class representatives with representatives of a variety of politically divergent middle-class groups.[56]

But how effective were all these arrangements? Not everyone was convinced, including the Frankfurt Workers Secretariat, a free social insurance advice office run by the local trade unions under the direction of Eduard Gräf. The main hindrance to collaboration across social class lines, for Gräf's organization and for others, was the continued unwillingness of many liberals to grant equal political rights to workers. Domestic servants ordinances and factory rules continued to guarantee the patriarchal authority of the *Bürgertum* at home and in large factories, and the municipal franchise achieved the same result in the political arena. Although a modern and far-reaching system of municipal social welfare and social insurance attempted to bind the growing labor movement to liberal institutions, the persistence of a discriminatory, property-based franchise seriously undercut these efforts. But even where the suffrage system did not change, in the years before the First World War growing numbers of workers had become prosperous enough to qualify for the vote, which in turn explains the SPD's electoral success in many German cities. At the same time, just before the war some of the distinctions between the bourgeois milieu and the proletarian milieu were beginning to become a bit blurred.[57]

Of decisive importance, though, was the labor movement's loss of confidence in the state at the Reich level. Until the first years of the new century the unions, encouraged by small-scale government reforms, had generally backed the idea of state-sponsored welfare measures. When it became evident, though, that government proposals for a reform of the social insurance system were not going to take union suggestions into account, the unions themselves sharply altered their course and in 1907 began to denounce the "stagnation in social policy legislation" in the Reich. By the following year they were complaining that a number of alleged friends of social reform were guilty of "hypocrisy," and in fact were "closet opponents" of truly effective reform measures. At the same time, as their slogan "The Junkers have triumphed again!" suggests, they continued to reach out to the liberal *Bürgertum*.[58] That willingness to cooperate with the liberals manifested itself very clearly on 27 February 1910, when the largest pre-war demonstration in Frankfurt's history took place. The participants included not only labor organizations but also many local liberal groups.[59]

At this point, progress in social reform legislation at the local level began to accelerate, demonstrating that years of effort to develop structures of joint cooperation and collaboration had not been in vain. Union-sponsored employment offices for skilled workers merged with the municipal employment office. The local trade union office *(Gewerkschaftskartell)* began to talk with the legal-advice office that had been established by the Institute for Public Welfare. Only a few years earlier these unions had ignored Leopold Sonnemann's call for a system of municipal unemployment insurance, preferring to wait for action at the Reich level; but now the union *Kartell* and the city government jointly set up a system of the sort that Sonnemann had envisaged.[60] Political cooperation between liberals and labor also increased substantially in Frankfurt. In 1909 Social Democrats assumed offices in the city assembly, and in 1913 the city council (*Magistrat*) welcomed its first social democratic member.[61] The area of cultural policy also witnessed an upsurge of middle-class interest and engagement. Efforts to promote middle-class high culture among Frankfurt workers celebrated their most notable triumph in 1911, when an "artistic matinee" was organized in conjunction with a local union festival. Händel's oratorio *Judas Maccabaeus* was performed by more than a thousand musicians, including members of various workers' choirs, assorted soloists from the Frankfurt Opera, and the opera orchestra. Some twenty-five thousand workers observed the spectacle.[62] As these examples suggest, in Frankfurt a climate of political cooperation had halted and even partially reversed the estrangement between proletarian and middle-class lives. Indeed, liberals and Social Democrats in Frankfurt shared a common point of view on a wide range of issues, from support for electoral reform in Prussia to opposition to conservative blocs in Prussia and the Reich, and from support for joint social policy initiatives to growing harmony in the area of cultural policy.

Frankfurt was not an isolated case. Similar tendencies manifested themselves in Dresden and Munich, and can probably be identified in a number of developed urban regions, especially, but not only, in the south and southwest of the country.[63] Where at the turn of the century Social Democrats represented a *quantité négligeable* in local governments, by 1913 they held some twelve thousand local offices.[64] At the state level there were also signs of a new kind of cooperation between liberals and Social Democrats; in Baden and Bavaria, for instance, they established a political bloc directed against the center and the conservatives. Recent studies have also pointed to similar trends in Saxony.[65] Even there, in the very heartland of German socialism, there were signs of a new liberal willingness to cooperate with Social Democrats themselves. In short, historians have so far underestimated the extent to which, in the years before 1914, both liberals and Social Democrats were willing to return to the collaborative reform projects of the 1860s. To be sure, the worlds of the German working class and the German middle classes had changed dramatically since the 1860s, so that a full-scale return to the values, outlooks, and policies of that time was hardly possible.

8. Conclusion

Just when it seemed that a unified coalition for social reform was about to emerge, a special set of political circumstances interrupted that long-term process, much as in the 1860s. The outbreak of war in August 1914 brought a halt to the nascent cooperation between middle-class liberalism and the labor movement. Instead, the politics of *Burgfrieden* offered the trade unions an opportunity to pursue their own state-socialist inclinations. The creation of a great reform coalition of liberals and Social Democrats had to wait until the November Revolution of 1918. Such cooperation then came quite easily at the local level, where liberals and Social Democrats quickly picked up where they had earlier left off. Indeed, this kind of collaboration served as the basis for the Weimar Coalition at the Reich level.[66]

The history of the social relations between the "middle" and the proletarian classes evolved against the backdrop of the dissolution of an older, corporative style of urban existence and the emergence of modern forms of civil society. Social historians have tended to treat workers' history and the history of the *Bürgertum* as separate categories, thereby overlooking the ways in which these historical experiences were bound up with each other politically, socially, and culturally. The historical experience of Germany's cities offers a good opportunity conceptually to reintegrate both the *Alltagsgeschichte* and the political histories of the German *Bürgertum* and the working class. The political divorce between liberalism and the labor movement was a consequence not only of modern bourgeois fears of a "red republic" but also of the antiquated patriarchal structures and antidemocratic attitudes that had shaped the old-fashioned, preindustrial *Bürgertum*. As we have seen, in the 1860s modern notions of civil society and its rejuvenation coexisted with those older structures and attitudes. These contradictions became very visible in the overheated political climate of that decade, and the result was the secession of a part of the labor movement. But the political estrangement of the two camps was not irreversible. Despite much inconsistency and contradictoriness, a kind of reconciliation between liberalism and the labor movement did take place. The discussion of a new mass base for *bürgerlich* politics, the willingness to depart from a schematic "us-versus-them" approach to politics, and an escape both from the social democratic-proletarian and from the liberal-*bürgerlich* ghettos all helped to make it possible. In short, relations between liberalism and labor in Germany were marked not simply by a permanent split, but rather by a temporary tendency to drift apart, followed in the long run by a rapprochement which, however, only became an effective reality after World War I.

Translated by David E. Barclay

Notes

1. Gustav Mayer, *Radikalismus, Sozialismus und bürgerliche Demokratie* (Frankfurt am Main, 1969), 129-38. See also Karl Birker, *Die Deutschen Arbeiter-Bildungsvereine 1840-1870* (Berlin, 1973), 190-92; Werner Conze, *Möglichkeiten und Grenzen der liberalen Arbeiterbewegung in Deutschland: Das Beispiel Schulze-Delitzsch* (Heidelberg, 1965), 22-24; Christiane Eisenberg, "Arbeiter, Bürger und der 'bürgerliche Verein' 1820-1870: Deutschland und England im Vergleich," in *Bürgertum im 19. Jahrhundert: Deutschland im europäischen Vergleich*, ed. Jürgen Kocka, 3 vols. (Munich, 1988), 2: 217-18. See also John Breuilly, "Civil Society and the Labour Movement, Class Relations and the Law: A Comparison between Germany and England," in *Arbeiter und Bürger im 19. Jahrhundert: Varianten ihres Verhältnisses im europäischen Vergleich*, ed. Jürgen Kocka (Munich, 1986), 287-318, esp. 318. Terms like "*Bürgertum*," "*Bürger*," and "*bürgerlich*" are both vague and slippery, and their meanings changed over time. It is difficult to render them adequately into English; words like "middle class" or "bourgeoisie" fail to do justice to the specific qualities inherent in the German terms. Accordingly, this essay will frequently use the original German words.
2. John Breuilly, "Liberalism or Social Democracy? Britain and Germany, 1850-1875," *Labour and Liberalism in Nineteenth-Century Europe: Essays in Comparative History*, ed. John Breuilly (Manchester, 1992), 115-20.
3. On new directions in the study of the *Bürgertum*, see Lothar Gall, "Stadt und Bürgertum im Übergang von der traditionalen zur modernen Gesellschaft," in *Stadt und Bürgertum im Übergang von der traditionalen zur modernen Gesellschaft*, ed. Lothar Gall (Munich, 1993), 1-12.
4. Breuilly, "Society," 289.
5. Thomas Nipperdey, *Deutsche Geschichte 1800-1866: Bürgerwelt und starker Staat*, 2nd ed. (Munich, 1984), 219-48; Jürgen Kocka, *Lohnarbeit und Klassenbildung: Arbeiter und Arbeiterbewegung in Deutschland 1800-1875* (Berlin and Bonn, 1983), 71-123.

6. See Friedrich Lenger, *Sozialgeschichte der deutschen Handwerker seit 1800* (Frankfurt am Main, 1988), 58-63; idem, "Die handwerkliche Phase der Arbeiterbewegung in England, Frankreich, Deutschland und den USA – Plädoyer für einen Vergleich," *Geschichte und Gesellschaft* 13 (1987): 232-43; and Karl Ditt, "Fabrikarbeiter und Handwerker im 19. Jahrhundert in der neueren deutschen Sozialgeschichtsschreibung: Ein Zwischenbericht," *Geschichte und Gesellschaft* 20 (1994): 299-320.
7. See Arno Herzig, "Die politische Kultur der Unterschichten und ihre Bedeutung für die frühe Arbeiterbewegung," in *"Der kühnen Bahn nur folgen wir …": Ursprünge, Erfolge und Grenzen der Arbeiterbewegung in Deutschland*, ed. Arno Herzig and Günter Trautmann (Hamburg, 1989), 1: 83-100; and Wolfgang Kaschuba, "Vom Gesellenkampf zum sozialen Protest: Zur Erfahrungs- und Konfliktdisposition von Gesellen-Arbeitern in den Vormärz- und Revolutionsjahren," in *Handwerker in der Industrialisierung: Lage, Kultur und Politik vom späten 18. bis ins frühe 20. Jahrhundert*, ed. Ulrich Engelhardt (Stuttgart, 1984), 381-406.
8. On the *Arbeiterverbrüderung* see Max Quarck, *Die erste deutsche Arbeiterbewegung* (Leipzig, 1924); Birker, *Arbeiter-Bildungsvereine*, 39; Toni Offermann, "Die regionale Ausbreitung der frühen deutschen Arbeiterbewegung 1848/49-1860/64," *Geschichte und Gesellschaft* 13 (1987): 424-25; and Jürgen Kocka, "Traditionsbindung und Klassenbildung: Zum sozialhistorischen Ort der frühen deutschen Arbeiterbewegung," *Historische Zeitschrift* 243 (1986): 341-46.
9. Stephan Born, quoted in Quarck, *Arbeiterbewegung*, 382.
10. See Wolfgang Renzsch, *Handwerker und Lohnarbeiter in der frühen Arbeiterbewegung: Zur sozialen Basis von Gewerkschaften und Sozialdemokratie im Reichsgründungsjahrzehnt* (Göttingen, 1980), 97-102; Toni Offermann, "Mittelständisch-kleingewerbliche Leitbilder in der liberalen Handwerker- und handwerklichen Arbeiterbewegung der 50er und 60er Jahre des 19. Jahrhunderts," in Engelhardt, *Handwerker*, 533-35.
11. Lothar Gall, "Liberalismus und 'bürgerliche Gesellschaft': Zu Charakter und Entwicklung der liberalen Bewegung in Deutschland," in *Liberalismus*, ed. Lothar Gall (Königstein/Ts., 1980), 162-86.
12. Dieter Hein, "Die bürgerlich-liberale Bewegung in Baden 1800-1880," *Historische Zeitschrift*, Beiheft 19 (1995): 19-39, esp. 29; Manfred Hettling, "Bürgertum und Revolution 1848 – ein Widerspruch," in Puhle, *Bürger*, 219.
13. Gall, "Liberalismus," 175.
14. Hermann Schulze-Delitzsch, *Die arbeitenden Klassen und das Assoziationswesen in Deutschland als Programm zu einem deutschen Kongreß* (Leipzig, 1858), 59-60.
15. James J. Sheehan, *German History 1770-1866* (Oxford, 1989), 204.
16. "Gesetze und Anordnungen nebst den dazu gehörigen Berichtigungen und Zusätzen für die Casino-Gesellschaft in Frankfurt am Main, errichtet im Jahre 1802" (Frankfurt am Main, 1843), 1.
17. Eisenberg, *Arbeiter*, 193.
18. See Andreas Biefang, *Politisches Bürgertum in Deutschland 1857-1868: Nationale Organisation und Eliten* (Düsseldorf, 1994), 60-65; and Shlomo Na'aman, *Der deutsche Nationalverein: Die politische Konstituierung des deutschen Bürgertums 1859-1867* (Düsseldorf, 1987), 41-54.
19. Toni Offermann, *Arbeiterbewegung und liberales Bürgertum in Deutschland 1850-1863* (Bonn, 1979), 339-60.
20. Hermann Schulze-Delitzsch, in *Arbeiterzeitung Coburg*, 11 January 1863.
21. Ferdinand Lassalle, *Arbeiterlesebuch: Rede Lassalles zu Frankfurt am Main am 17. und 19. Mai 1863: Nach dem stenographischen Bericht*, 4th ed. (Leipzig, 1871). See

also Mayer, *Radikalismus*, 118; and Shlomo Na'aman, *Die Konstituierung der deutschen Arbeiterbewegung 1862/63: Darstellung und Dokumentation* (Assen, Netherlands, 1975), 21-107.

22. Ferdinand Lassalle, *Offenes Antwortschreiben an das Central-Comitee zur Berufung eines Allgemeinen Deutschen Arbeiter Congresses zu Leipzig* (Leipzig, 1869), 21; idem, *Arbeiterprogramm* (Stuttgart, 1973), 34, 36.
23. Lassalle, *Antwortschreiben*, 19.
24. Only a few weeks after the ADAV's creation, the majority of worker education associations opted for the VDAV instead. Birker, *Arbeiter-Bildungsvereine*, 59-62; Conze, *Möglichkeiten*, 17; Wolfgang Schieder, "Das Scheitern des bürgerlichen Radikalismus und die sozialistische Parteibildung in Deutschland," in *Sozialdemokratie zwischen Klassenbewegung und Volkspartei*, ed. Hans Mommsen (Frankfurt am Main, 1974), 29-30.
25. Willy Albrecht, *Fachverein – Berufsgewerkschaft – Zentralverband: Organisationsprobleme der deutschen Gewerkschaften 1870-1890* (Bonn, 1982), 89-94, 529-35; Ulrich Engelhardt, "Gewerkschaftliches Organisationsverhalten in der ersten Industrialisierungsphase," in *Arbeiter im Industrialisierungsprozeß: Herkunft, Lage und Verhalten*, ed. Werner Conze and Ulrich Engelhardt (Stuttgart, 1979), 390-91.
26. Hans-Ulrich Wehler, "Bürger, Arbeiter und das Problem der Klassenbildung 1800-1870: Deutschland im internationalen Vergleich," in Kocka, *Arbeiter*, 9. Cf. Gerhard A. Ritter and Klaus Tenfelde, *Arbeiter im Deutschen Kaiserreich 1871 bis 1914* (Bonn, 1992), 298-353; and Thomas Nipperdey, *Deutsche Geschichte 1866-1918*, 2 vols. (Munich, 1990), 1: 186-88, 291-334.
27. Gerhard A. Ritter, *Staat, Arbeiterschaft und Arbeiterbewegung in Deutschland: Vom Vormärz bis zum Ende der Weimarer Republik* (Berlin and Bonn, 1980), 26. For recent studies of the history of working-class experience, see the writings of Alf Lüdtke discussed in the introduction to this volume.
28. "Erfurter Programm der Sozialdemokratischen Partei von 1891," in *Programmatische Dokumente der deutschen Sozialdemokratie*, ed. Dieter Dowe and Kurt Klotzbach (Berlin, 1984), 188.
29. Cf. Volker Hentschel, *Geschichte der deutschen Sozialpolitik 1880 bis 1980* (Frankfurt am Main, 1983), 9, 23-24; Florian Tennstedt, *Vom Proleten zum Industriearbeiter: Arbeiterbewegung und Sozialpolitik in Deutschland 1800-1914* (Cologne, 1983), 182-83, 202-3, 245-46; Albin Gladen, *Geschichte der Sozialpolitik in Deutschland: Eine Analyse ihrer Bedingungen, Formen, Zielsetzungen und Auswirkungen* (Wiesbaden, 1974), 71-78; Gerhard A. Ritter, *Sozialversicherung in Deutschland und England: Entstehung und Grundzüge im Vergleich* (Munich, 1983), 37; Ritter and Tenfelde, *Arbeiter*, 679-716.
30. On the system of collective subsistence and its maintenance, see Wolfgang Kaschuba, *Lebenswelt und Kultur der unterbürgerlichen Schichten im 19. und 20. Jahrhundert* (Munich, 1990), 25-27, and Vernon L. Lidtke, "Die kulturelle Bedeutung der Arbeitervereine," in *Kultureller Wandel im 19. Jahrhundert*, ed. Günter Wiegelmann (Göttingen, 1973), 146-59. See also Dieter Langewiesche, "The Impact of the German Labor Movement on Workers' Culture," *Journal of Modern History* 59 (1987): 506-23.
31. On the development of the trade unions, see Albrecht, *Fachverein*, 470, 529; Klaus Schönhoven, "Gewerkschaftswachstum, Mitgliederintegration und bürokratische Organisation vor dem Ersten Weltkrieg," in *Arbeiterbewegung und industrieller Wandel*, ed. Hans Mommsen (Wuppertal, 1980), 16-37; idem, "Die regionale Ausbreitung der deutschen Gewerkschaften im Kaiserreich 1890-1918," in *Der Aufstieg der deutschen Arbeiterbewegung*, ed. Gerhard A. Ritter

(Munich, 1990), 345-78; idem, *Expansion und Konzentration: Studien zur Entwicklung der Freien Gewerkschaften im Wilhelminischen Deutschland 1890 bis 1914* (Stuttgart, 1980), esp. 120-21.

32. For recent research and a critical review of older interpretations, see Ritter and Tenfelde, *Arbeiter*, 463-66.
33. John Anthony Moses, "Carl Legiens Interpretation des demokratischen Sozialismus: Ein Beitrag zur sozialistischen Ideengeschichte" (Ph.D. diss., Erlangen, 1965), 111. See also ibid., 44-54; and *Protokoll der Verhandlungen des III. Kongresses der Gewerkschaften Deutschlands, abgehalten zu Frankfurt am Main-Bockenheim vom 8. bis 13. Mai 1899* (Hamburg, 1900), 99.
34. In October 1894 a major clash developed over this issue. Prominent members of the SPD accused the General Commission of forging "dark plans," and expressed their strong disapproval of this form of trade-union "collaboration." Carl Legien, "Adolf von Elm und die Gewerkschaftsbewegung," *Sozialistische Monatshefte* (21 October 1915): 1104. Cf. *Protokoll über die Verhandlungen des Parteitages der Sozialdemokratischen Partei Deutschlands, abgehalten zu Köln 1893* (Berlin, 1893), 201; Klaus Schönhoven, "Die Gewerkschaften als Massenbewegung im Wilhelminischen Kaiserreich 1890 bis 1918," in *Geschichte der deutschen Gewerkschaften: Von den Anfängen bis 1945*, ed. Klaus Tenfelde et al. (Cologne, 1987), 167-278, esp. 194-96; Gerhard A. Ritter and Klaus Tenfelde, "Der Durchbruch der Freien Gewerkschaften Deutschlands zur Massenbewegung im letzten Viertel des 19. Jahrhunderts," in *Vom Sozialistengesetz zur Mitbestimmung: Zum 100. Geburtstag von Hans Böckler*, ed. Heinz Oskar Vetter (Cologne, 1975), 103.
35. *Protokoll des III. Kongresses der Gewerkschaften*, 72, 83.
36. Quotations from anon., "Naturalisten und Sozialisten," *Berliner Volkstribüne* 4, no. 42 (1890); Klaus Michael Bogdal, *Schaurige Bilder: Der Arbeiter im Blick des Bürgers* (Frankfurt am Main, 1978), 41, 58; and Martin Halter, *Sklaven der Arbeit – Ritter vom Geiste: Arbeit und Arbeiter im deutschen Sozialroman zwischen 1840-1880* (Frankfurt am Main, 1983), 103-5.
37. Bogdal, *Bilder*, 43.
38. Ibid., 57-58.
39. Paul Göhre, *Drei Monate Fabrikarbeiter und Handwerksbursche: Sozialreportagen eines Pfarrers um die Jahrhundertwende* (Gütersloh, 1978), 15-16.
40. Dieter Schwarzenau, "Die frühen Arbeiterautobiographien," in *Beiträge zur Kulturgeschichte der deutschen Arbeiterbewegung 1848-1918*, ed. Peter von Rüden (Frankfurt am Main, 1979), 169.
41. Rudolf Lavant, "Drei Monate Fabrikarbeiter," in *Die deutsche Literatur in Text und Darstellung*, ed. Walter Schmähling, 16 vols. (Stuttgart, 1982), 12: 225-27; Friedrich G. Kürbisch, *Der Arbeitsmann, er stirbt, verdirbt, wann steht er auf*, 2 vols. (Berlin and Bonn, 1981); Wolfgang Emmerich, ed., *Proletarische Lebensläufe: Autobiographische Dokumente zur Entstehung der zweiten Kultur in Deutschland*, 2 vols. (Hamburg, 1974), 1: 19.
42. Carl Fischer, *Denkwürdigkeiten und Erinnerungen eines Arbeiters*, 2 vols. (Leipzig, 1903-4). Quotations from the journals *Rheinlande*, *Literarisches Echo*, *Christliche Welt*, and *Dresdener Anzeiger* in Schwarzenau, "Arbeiterautobiographien," 176.
43. Adolf Levenstein, *Die Arbeiterfrage: Mit besonderer Berücksichtigung der sozialpsychologischen Seite des modernen Großbetriebs und der psycho-physischen Einwirkung auf den Arbeiter* (Munich, 1912), 1.
44. Patrick Fridenson, "Herrschaft im Wirtschaftsunternehmen in Deutschland und Frankreich 1880-1911," in Kocka, *Bürgertum*, 2: 74-76.

45. Jürgen Kocka and Gerhard A. Ritter, eds., *Wahlgeschichtliches Arbeitsbuch: Materialien zur Statistik des Kaiserreichs 1871-1918* (Munich, 1980), 38-42.
46. Robert Michels, "Die deutsche Sozialdemokratie. I: Parteimitgliedschaft und soziale Zusammensetzung," *Archiv für Sozialwissenschaft und Sozialpolitik* 23 (1906): 474.
47. Dieter Langewiesche, *Liberalismus in Deutschland* (Frankfurt am Main, 1988), 133-64.
48. In 1913 only 106,000 workers were organized in the liberal Hirsch-Duncker associations, while the free trade unions could claim more than 2.5 million members. Albrecht, *Fachverein*, 464-65; Hans-Georg Fleck, *Sozialliberalismus und Gewerkschaftsbewegung: Die Hirsch-Dunckerschen Gewerkvereine 1868-1914* (Cologne, 1994), 352-64.
49. Dieter Langewiesche, "Deutscher Liberalismus im europäischen Vergleich: Konzeption und Ergebnisse," in *Liberalismus im 19. Jahrhundert: Deutschland im europäischen Vergleich*, ed. Dieter Langewiesche (Göttingen, 1988), 17; idem, "Liberalismus und Region," *Historische Zeitschrift*, Beiheft 19 (1995): 15. On the relationship between the urban *Bürgertum* and municipal social reform, see James J. Sheehan, *German Liberalism in the Nineteenth Century* (Chicago, 1978), 255, 269; and Hartmut Pogge von Strandmann, "The Liberal Power Monopoly in the Cities of Imperial Germany," in *Elections, Mass Politics, and Social Change in Modern Germany: New Perspectives*, ed. James Retallack and Larry Eugene Jones (New York, 1992), 99.
50. See Jürgen Reulecke and Adelheid Gräfin zu Castell Rudershausen, eds., *Stadt und Gesundheit: Zum Wandel von "Volksgesundheit" und kommunaler Gesundheitspolitik im 19. und frühen 20. Jahrhundert* (Stuttgart, 1991); and Christoph Sachße, "Frühformen der Leistungsverwaltung: Die kommunale Armenfürsorge im deutschen Kaiserreich," in *Bürokratisierung und Professionalisierung der Sozialpolitik in Europa, 1870-1918*, ed. Erk Volkmar Heyen (Baden-Baden, 1993), 7-16.
51. Franz Schrakamp, "Gesundheitspflege," in *Die deutsche Stadt und ihre Verwaltung: Eine Einführung in die Kommunalpolitik der Gegenwart*, ed. Otto Most, 3 vols. (Berlin and Leipzig, 1912), 1: 129. Cf. Florian Tennstedt, "Die Selbstverwaltung der Krankenkassen im deutschen Kaiserreich," in Heyen, *Bürokratisierung*, 89-92; Clemens Wischermann, "Wohnungsnot und Städtewachstum: Standards und soziale Indikatoren städtischer Wohnungsversorgung im späten 19. Jahrhundert," in Conze and Engelhardt, *Arbeiter*, 218-20.
52. On municipal socialism in Germany see, among several studies, Wolfgang R. Krabbe, "Munizipalsozialismus und Interventionsstaat: Die Ausbreitung der städtischen Leistungsverwaltung im Kaiserreich," *Geschichte in Wissenschaft und Unterricht* 30, no. 5 (1979): 265-83; idem, "Arbeitsmarkregulierung und Arbeiterschutz in den Städten des kaiserlichen Deutschland," in Heyen, *Bürokratisierung*, 39.
53. Ralf Roth, "Liberalismus in Frankfurt am Main 1814-1914: Probleme seiner Strukturgeschichte," *Historische Zeitschrift*, Beiheft 19 (1995): 67-73; idem, "Katholisches Bürgertum in Frankfurt am Main 1800-1914: Zwischen Emanzipation und Kulturkampf," *Archiv für mittelrheinische Kirchengeschichte* 46 (1994): 240. On Sonnemann, see Klaus Gerteis, *Leopold Sonnemann: Ein Beitrag zur Geschichte des demokratischen Nationalstaatsgedankens in Deutschland* (Frankfurt am Main, 1970); Siegbert Wolf, *Liberalismus in Frankfurt am Main: Vom Ende der Freien Stadt bis zum Ersten Weltkrieg, 1866-1914* (Frankfurt am Main, 1987), 67, 73-81.
54. John D. Rolling, "Liberals, Socialists, and City Government in Imperial Germany: The Case of Frankfurt am Main 1900-1918" (Ph. D. diss., University of Wisconsin, Madison, 1979), 176; Roth, "Liberalismus," 81-82.

55. Henriette Kramer, "Die Anfänge des sozialen Wohnungsbaus in Frankfurt am Main 1860-1914," *Archiv für Frankfurts Geschichte und Kunst* 56 (1978): 123-90.
56. Ralf Roth, *Gewerkschaftskartell und Sozialpolitik in Frankfurt am Main: Arbeiterbewegung vor dem Ersten Weltkrieg zwischen Restauration und liberaler Erneuerung* (Frankfurt am Main, 1992), 79-91, 198-220.
57. For all its inconsistencies, Frankfurt can, thus, be regarded as the best example of a German version of the alliance between liberals and labor, or, as the British call it, "lib-lab."
58. Eduard Gräf, "Landwirtschaftliche Unfallversicherung," *Jahresberichte des Arbeitersekretariats Frankfurt* 13 (1911): 97-98. Quotations in ibid. 9 (1907): 3; ibid. 10 (1908): 4.
59. Franz Neuland, *Zwischen Römer und Revolution 1869-1969: Hundert Jahre Sozialdemokraten in Frankfurt am Main* (Frankfurt am Main, 1969), 41-49.
60. *Jahresberichte des Arbeitersekretariats Frankfurt* 15 (1913): 44. See also ibid., 48. For these discussions, see also Rolling, "Liberals," 370-79; Gerteis, *Sonnemann*, 110.
61. *Sozialdemokratie und Stadtverwaltung: Ein Rückblick auf 10jährige Tätigkeit; zugleich Rechenschaftsbericht der sozialdemokratischen Stadtverordnetenfraktion für die Jahre 1909/10, zu den Stadtverordnetenwahlen 1910* (Frankfurt am Main, 1910), 127-30; John D. Rolling, "Das Problem der 'Politisierung' der kommunalen Selbstverwaltung in Frankfurt am Main 1900-1918," *Archiv für Frankfurts Geschichte und Kunst* 57 (1980): 179-82.
62. *Jahresberichte des Arbeitersekretariats Frankfurt* 13 (1911): 83-85.
63. See Karl Heinrich Pohl, *Die Münchener Arbeiterbewegung: Sozialdemokratische Partei, Freie Gewerkschaften, Staat und Gesellschaft in München 1890-1914* (Munich, 1992), 14.
64. Joachim Drogmann, "Grundlagen und Anfänge sozialdemokratischer Kommunalpolitik vor und nach dem Sozialistengesetz," *Die demokratische Gemeinde* 15 (1963): 998; Adelheid von Saldern, "Die Gemeinde in Theorie und Praxis der deutschen Arbeiterorganisationen 1863-1920: Ein Überblick," *IWK* 12: 3 (1976): 295-352.
65. James Retallack, "Antisocialism and Electoral Politics in Regional Perspective: The Kingdom of Saxony," in Retallack and Jones, *Elections*, 52-55; idem, "'What Is to Be Done?' The Red Specter, Franchise Questions, and the Crisis of Conservative Hegemony in Saxony, 1896-1909," *Central European History* 23:4 (1990): 275-76, 282-83; Karl Heinrich Pohl, "Die Nationalliberalen in Sachsen vor 1914: Eine Partei der konservativen Honoratioren auf dem Wege zur Partei der Industrie," *Historische Zeitschrift*, Beiheft 19 (1995): 211; idem, "Ein zweiter politischer Emanzipationsprozeß des liberalen Unternehmertums: Zur Sozialstruktur und Politik der Liberalen in Sachsen zu Beginn des 20. Jahrhunderts," in *Wege zur Geschichte des Bürgertums*, ed. Klaus Tenfelde and Hans-Ulrich Wehler (Göttingen, 1994), 241, 244-45.
66. In Frankfurt, the most visible expression of liberal-social democratic cooperation was in housing. See Gerd Kuhn, "Die kommunale Regulierung des Wohnungsmangels: Aspekte der sozialstaatlichen Wohnungspolitik in Frankfurt am Main," in *Wohnungspolitik und Städtebau 1900-1930*, ed. Wolfgang Hofmann and Gerd Kuhn (Berlin, 1993), 111-15; Dieter Rebentisch, "Frankfurt am Main in der Weimarer Republik und im Dritten Reich 1918-1945," in *Frankfurt am Main: Die Geschichte der Stadt* (Sigmaringen, 1991), 445.

Chapter 5

"Genossen und Genossinnen"

Depictions of Gender, Militancy, and Organizing in the German Socialist Press, 1890 to 1914

Mary Jo Maynes

1. Introduction

When in 1890 German Social Democratic Party (SPD) leaders reassembled after twelve years of exile and clandestine activity to build the newly re-legalized organization, they had no clear blueprints from which to work. The period between the party's founding in 1875 and its banning in 1878 had been too brief to establish an organizational culture.[1] Many previous forms of political protest and activity – whether the armed insurrections of the century's earlier decades or the secret meetings and smuggling of the outlaw period – no longer suited socialist visions and opportunities looking forward from 1890. The strategy of political mobilization that looked most promising centered on mass-membership organizations competing for power in the national electoral and economic arena.

The politically creative decades between the French Revolution and the Communes of 1870 to 1871 had produced important innovations in forms of popular protest across Europe, but most tended to be sporadic, local, and reactive.[2] German social democratic strategy, especially after the "outlaw" status of the party was ended, aimed instead toward building workers' organizations that would be permanent, national (even international), and pervasive embodiments of the power of institutional-

Notes for this chapter begin on page 164.

ized class solidarity. Indeed it can be argued that it was in the decade or so after 1890 that much of the modern repertoire of popular political mobilization – a repertoire that would dominate until the era of new social movement organizations of the 1960s – was elaborated.

The new organizing project required a new style of proletarian hero. The precedents – the *sans culottes*, '48ers, and *Communards* who engaged in armed battle in village protests or behind urban barricades, or the smugglers of the "Red Post Office" network who delivered contraband socialist literature into Germany during the outlaw years – were honored but outdated types. New conditions required new forms of activism and new definitions of heroism. German socialist memoirs of the Imperial era provide some evidence about how workers came to fashion themselves after a new image of heroism.[3] The autobiography of Julius Bruhns offers a particularly explicit example. Bruhns was born in a Hamburg suburb around 1860 and had begun working as a child in a cigar rolling shop in Hamburg. Assigned the job of reading newspapers aloud at work, he claims he had been converted to socialism by the time he was ten. More to the point, he recalls that the newspapers relayed to him a model of heroism he had not previously encountered:

> *Soon I tossed aside the monsters and giants, Indians and other enemies and after them the knights and heroes of the fist and dreamed only of becoming a leader of the people, of fighting for the rights of the people against their enemies with gripping articles and flaming speeches. To become a social democratic Reichstag deputy and, after a successful revolution, a leader, minister, even president of a social democratic republic, this appeared to me to be the epitome of all greatness, the single worthy goal of my ambition.*[4]

By the age of seventeen Julius was living out this image, doing party electoral work and writing and speaking as well. His life of commitment took a highly specific form defined by the political culture and strategies of the party, but it commenced according to his account with a leap of imagination based on newspaper representations of how a modern people's hero should behave.

Social democratic women also wrestled with the new possibilities, even if their numbers in the movement were far fewer than men's and even though models for them were more elusive.[5] Their historic legacy was also problematic: it was not only in conservative circles that the women of the insurrectionary crowds or the "petroleuses" of the Commune came to represent the worst excesses of revolution. And in popular traditions, women were often granted symbolic roles as goddesses of liberty or as mothers of the people rather than actual roles as political participants.[6]

So it is significant that women in central Europe also attempted to claim a space for themselves in the new politics of social democratic activism. Again, socialist memoirs are suggestive of the link between circulating images of activism and the decision to become a militant. One of the most popular of these memoirs – that of Adelheid Popp, published under the auspices of the SPD – offers an interesting counterpoint to Bruhns's recollection. In Vienna, half a continent away from Bruhns's home in Hamburg, Popp also struggled to make an imaginative leap into heroism through reading her brother's socialist newspapers. But to her the connection was not obvious: "Every single Social Democrat I got to know through the newspaper," Popp recalled, "appeared godlike to me. It never occurred to me that I could join with them in struggle. Everything I read about them seemed so high and lofty that it would have seemed like a fantasy even to think that I – ignorant, unknown and poor creature that I was – could actually one day take part in their endeavors."[7] Despite her initial inability to identify with these heroes, and the fact that even access to the papers was mediated through a male relative, Popp and other central European women workers would eventually find some ways of living out the fantasy of working-class heroism.

These two anecdotes provide a starting point for an examination of the role of gender in images of political activism in German social democracy. The memoirs suggest that the movement culture created space for both men and women to imagine themselves as and then become militants (indeed, recounting the process of becoming socialist is at the center of the plot of most socialist memoirs). Paths of men and women into and through the movement were different and the route for women certainly was "a rocky road."[8] But at least some version of militancy was imaginable by both men and women. The center of my attention in this chapter will be the historically innovative project of creating new activist identities in the social democratic movement in the period after 1890. My aim is to reconstruct the images of activism circulating in selected party publications and to discuss how gender was implicated in those representations.

Historians of the social democratic movement in Imperial Germany have taken it to task from a variety of perspectives. Early critics pointed to the bureaucratization that stifled the movement's democratic potential and the revisionism that marked socialist strategies in tension with the party's theoretical commitment to revolutionary Marxism. Critical attention has also underscored the leadership's concern for a respectability seemingly indistinct from that of the bourgeoisie, the socialist failure to combat the constraints of Wilhelmine gender roles, and the party's inability to comprehend or counter pernicious contemporary influences such as statism, nationalism, imperialism, and racism. Much effort has been spent demonstrating the extent to which rank-and-file members, socialist trade union leaders, or members of the women's movement were (or more typically were not) revolutionary or Marxist. Discussion has also focused on the extent to which the party's male leadership showed itself to be patriarchal despite the theoretical commitment to gender equity.[9]

These interpretations and criticisms are well founded; they highlight significant dimensions of the movement's history and contribute, as they were intended to do, to an explanation of the the impact and limitations of strategic choices of socialist leaders from the perspective of the longer run of German history. To emphasize, as I will in this chapter, the innovative character of the social democratic organizing project is to address a different kind of historical question. I will be stepping outside of the usual frameworks to problematize what is too often taken for granted or mentioned only in passing: from the perspective of the history of grass-roots political organizing, social democracy in late Imperial Germany represents a major breakthrough. As is well known, the movement produced both the largest and most highly disciplined workers' party of its time and a successful trade union movement; peripheral organizations such as socialist consumer cooperatives and party-affiliated social and cultural organizations also flourished. Through its various activities, the German socialist movement organized more fully, deeply, and permanently into the lower classes, including women of those classes, than any European movement had previously attempted to do. Nevertheless, relatively little close attention has been paid to the question of how it was actually organized on the ground and what legacy it left specifically in the realm of social movement organization.[10] My focus will be on what organized *Genossen* and *Genossinnen* (literally, male comrades and female comrades) did on a day-to-day basis, insofar as their grass-roots activism was reflected in the press.

2. Profiles of Militancy in the Socialist Press

Like Bruhns's and Popp's accounts mentioned above, many German-language workers' memoirs alluded to the role of the socialist press in their political formation. The press was significant not merely for providing information about social democracy's political program but also for depicting heroes at work. The press was a major site of circulation of concrete representations of the militant life. Moreover, if newspapers described the activities of the "godlike" party leaders, they also included rich information on the grass roots – that is, on the level of activity that was no doubt more imaginable or accessible to the movement's rank and file.

Throughout the Wilhelmine era the party's main national newspapers directed toward *Genossen* and *Genossinnen* respectively were *Vorwärts* and *Die Gleichheit*.[11] These papers served a variety of functions. They offered their readers an alternative perspective on the general news, for each covered political and social developments from a socialist perspective, and offered coverage of stories ranging from the latest Reichstag debates or political scandals along with exposes on housing conditions or health. In *Vorwärts* at least, even Berlin local news about crimes or neighborhood events were included if the story had a "social" angle to it.

But the papers also served as the main vehicle for broad internal communication within the party. Through them, leaders kept in touch with members, informed them of decisions and policies, and also publicized the activities of the many local chapters. Readers could follow national and local electoral successes, free trade union organizing, outreach efforts and even, by reading the fine print, the financial situation and organizational development of the movement in various localities.

I will focus my attention on the middle and back pages of the newspapers – on sections of *Vorwärts* with titles like "Korrespondenzen und Parteinachrichten" (Correspondence and Party Reports, later "Aus der Partei," or From the Party) or, in *Die Gleichheit*, "Aus der Bewegung" (From the Movement). Even if news of the SPD's larger-than-life electoral leaders held the front pages of both papers, in the articles and notices in many other sections of the papers readers could get a sense of what ordinary comrades like themselves were up to, of the concrete activities that party affiliation brought with it, and the specific roles members played in spreading the socialist movement. Both papers, thus, made it easy for readers to learn what an activist was and did.

Throughout the years between re-legalization and World War I, the pages of *Vorwärts* and *Die Gleichheit* relayed a sense of energetic militancy even if the specific activities portrayed changed in tandem with the party's tremendous development in these decades. Moreover, both publications talked explicitly to *Genossen* and *Genossinnen* to some degree, even if each addressed an audience primarily of one sex. In gender terms, both papers strategically employed gender-marked language of inclusivity, although not surprisingly *Die Gleichheit* was more insistent and more consistent on this score. As a late twentieth-century reader, I was struck by the evidence in *Vorwärts* of a deliberate effort to reach out to a female readership. At the same time, of course, the paper did not approach the record of *Die Gleichheit*, where virtually all the organizing news (with the exception of a small but increasing proportion of the trade union coverage) centered on activities that included or featured *Genossinnen*. (See Tables 1-3 for a quantitative summary of general reporting trends in sampled issues.) It can be argued that *Vorwärts*' coverage suggests a conscious editorial commitment to note and encourage female activism even if a comparison with *Die Gleichheit* makes clear the masculinist tendencies inherent in its reporting of activities, tendencies that in turn reflected party practices more generally. At the same time, both papers offer evidence of the specific ways in which, both because of deeply embedded notions of gender propriety and because of gender-explicit institutional constraints on organizing, the role of the *Genosse* and that of the *Genossin* remained somewhat distinctive. In addition, the papers' representations of militancy illustrate how larger trends – the movement's numerical growth, organizational development, changing legal frameworks, electoral and trade union successes – had gender-specific effects on grass-roots organizing and militants' activities.

3. The Categories of Activity

What did the papers suggest about the activities of *Genossen* and *Genossinnen*? Throughout the Wilhelmine epoch *Vorwärts* and *Die Gleichheit* provided an abundance of concrete detail of interest to party stalwarts (and historians) concerned about the nuts and bolts of organizing work. To start with *Vorwärts*, under the major headings of "Aus der Partei" and "Gewerkschaftliches" (Union News) readers could find the latest word on the activities of the party's electoral associations and their victories, the chapters' legal battles, and the activities of trade unions – strikes, boycotts, organizing drives. The section titled "Aus der Frauenbewegung" (From the Women's Movement) highlighted news of party and trade union activities of special concern to women activists. The "Versammlungen" (Meetings) sections of every issue left readers with a sense of tireless grass-roots activism. In the early 1890s various locals (both party chapters and unions) and affiliated organizations could announce their meetings. Although this practice became less common as the years went on and most routine meeting announcements were shifted into the advertising pages, these columns still continued to hold regular reports of selected meetings and at least occasional announcements about future meetings of special importance to comrades. Finally, since the paper also served Berlin area chapters as a local chapter organizing tool, their activities for the evening or near future were listed under a special section entitled "Parteiangelegenheiten" (Party Affairs). Here, in fact, we get closest to a sense of the day-to-day militant activities. Tables 1 through 3 show the distribution of movement activities according to the major categories that emerge from the reports: union organizing events, membership meetings of party-affiliated groups, legal challenges, party activities, public events, women's movement events, and participation in speaking tours.

Reports in these sections offered concrete detail about day-to-day party work. For example, an account in 1891 reported an assault on two *Genossen* who were distributing leaflets in the countryside around Bielefeld. The activity (distributing leaflets) was routine; the attack by conservative landowners added an element of heroism. Readers would also learn that these *Genossen* were rescued by their comrades and escaped with only minor injuries.[12] In an 1897 issue the Rheinland Organizing Committee published highlights of its 1896 organizing report: beyond the usual strike and electoral activities, its list of accomplishments for the year included the distribution of ninety thousand calendars, while the editors of its newspaper suffered eighteen separate charges, which resulted in a total of eleven months in prison plus 600 Marks in fines – an account that again combined the heroic and the routine.[13] A report of the 1906 annual meeting of the Magdeburg District Association boasted of raising its membership to 8,334 "organized *Genossen*" and accomplishing precinct-level ratios of members to total SPD vote of between .72 and 15.8 percent.[14]

The organization of *Die Gleichheit* also provided easy access to information about the organizing activities of movement activists, but in a simpler and shorter format than *Vorwärts*. News of events, meetings, and other movement activities comprised what soon settled into a routine middle section of a three-part format. That readers were members of the *Arbeiterinnenbewegung* (female workers' movement) was the paper's presumption, but the general title of the movement section was shortened and made correspondingly more general by the second half of the 1890s, when movement news was collected under the title "Aus der Bewegung" (From the Movement) and at least occasionally included items about activities even where there was no specific allusion to women. The third section of the paper was a series of items under the general rubric of "Kleine Nachrichten" (later "Notizentheil," both meaning Short Notices).[15] This section included both news items of specific pertinence to women and also routine updates on movement activities of interest to women under recurrent subsections, added just after the turn of the century, on political, union, and cooperative activities respectively. One 1906 issue, for example, contained articles on rates of illness among women workers in industry, a feature on women workers in the state tobacco factory in Spain, and the latest complaint of bourgeois feminists (*Frauenrechtlerinnen*) about relations between Imperial German troops and Chinese women.[16] Despite the particular focus on women's industries and activities, the categories in which *Die Gleichheit* portrayed movement activism differed very little from *Vorwärts*.

4. Gender and Profiles of Militancy

I will now turn to a more systematic analysis of the place of gender in the portrayal of movement activism in *Vorwärts* and *Die Gleichheit* from the early 1890s through the eve of World War I. I will discuss only the sections on movement organization described above and not the general news coverage. I will be using a sample of issues of each paper to assess both general trends over time in how militants' activites were portrayed in each paper and how the gender portrait varied by category of activity.[17]

Socialist activism as portrayed in *Vorwärts* was in every category male dominated. As Table 1 reveals, this male domination is particularly evident in the sections most reflective of leadership activities (this is the case even though the front section "news," concerning activities of elected officials, was not even included in the analysis) – namely *Todtenliste* that honored comrades who had died and reports of legal and police harassment cases that primarily affected socialist writers and editors. These categories rarely included mention of female activity (just eleven of 135 total items).

The editors of *Die Gleichheit* were quick to point to problems of gender equity at the leadership level. Their discussions of national party congresses, for example, provided the occasion for both gender-specific organizing and calling the male leadership to task for its failures to recruit women activists into prominent roles in the party organization. Moreover, the very language of their attack illustrates how gendered language worked to send signals to the readership. The 1896 announcement of the Gotha party congress offers a case in point. On the front page of an 1896 issue of *Die Gleichheit,* the lead article reproduced the meeting call and the provisional agenda. The call was addressed "Parteigenossen!" Agenda item number seven concerned "Die Frauenagitation" and listed the agenda's only woman speaker "Frau Klara Zetkin." The announcement then went on to call for the election of delegates from among "*Genossen*" and discussion between party members and local "*Vertrauensmänner*" (official party representatives) to set up election procedures.[18]

Die Gleichheit's editors were quick to demonstrate the announcement's shortcomings. Still on the front page, they followed up the call with an article of their own entitled "An die Genossinnen." They pointed to the significance of item number seven: "For the first time the representatives of social democracy are going to deliberate at a congress on the extremely important question: From what perspective and by what means are we to proceed so that the broad masses of proletarian women are won over to the idea of socialism?" They reiterated that this issue was crucial for their readers and for the movement, since socialists would not be able to succeed as trade unionists without organizing women workers. The implication was clear: "It's not only useful but necessary that the largest possible number of female delegates participate in the congress."[19] "*Genossinnen*" were called upon to take whatever steps were necessary to insure female representation from their localities. In particular, the editors advocated common delegations including both men and women wherever legally possible and told readers they should expect the serious support of their male colleagues in their efforts to secure female representation of their locals. The male party leaders were put on notice that use of the word *Genosse* was unacceptable in its linguistic exclusion of *Genossinnen*.

When we move from the activities of leadership closer to the grass roots, however, *Vorwärts* shows more evidence of concern for representing women among the activists, although unevenly across categories. It is possible to track sensitivity to the issue of gender-inclusive language, because (as the above-cited *Gleichheit* rejoinder to the call to the Gotha Congress demonstrates) in the German language the use of the feminine endings can be taken to signal a deliberate departure from the more typical use of the generic masculine. Reporters and correspondents from many locals made noticeable efforts to make readers aware of female presence at meetings and activities by direct reference to women or by use of the feminine ending *(in)* on words like *Genossin* and *Arbeiterin*. Obviously, such signals can be read in two ways. On the one hand, readers could note that those events and meeting reports that did include women were a minority of all meetings reported. On the other hand, the deliberate mention of female presence suggested an editorial and party cultural emphasis on inclusivity and outreach.

As Table 1 indicates, a small percentage of *Vorwärts* reports about nearly all categories of routine party activities – membership meetings and activities, as well as special events and campaigns organized by party chapters – included a specific reference to female participation. Overall, women were mentioned in about 15 percent of the events and activities reports in sampled issues of *Vorwärts*. Women were more common in articles about special events and public meetings, where they were mentioned in over 40 percent of the announcements and reports, but fewer in articles about routine party meetings (18 percent), organizing or electoral activities (9 percent), and union activities (12 percent). Women, then, were not equally visible in all categories of activism, and the papers' shifting and varied coverage of different types of activities meant that the place for women in the papers' representation of militancy also shifted over time.

5. Organizing and Attending Meetings

The "Versammlungen" (Meetings) sections of *Vorwärts* often offered clues about the kinds of members who had attended or were expected to attend various sorts of meetings. Readers could learn, for example, that a thousand people turned out at a Berlin meeting of *Handlungsgehilfen und -*

gehilfinnen (male and female shop assistants), where they listened to a one and one-half-hour talk, participated in a debate, and elected a governing board.[20] Or that the socialist electoral association of Lichtenberg held an open meeting on the question of rents and housing policy that was "extraordinarily well attended by men and women."[21] Berlin area chapter announcements also frequently signaled which events were appropriate for women. A 1907 section included the following:

> – *1st electoral district. Sunday, 6 March at 6:00 in the evening in the Arminghall ... Versammlung mit Frauen [meeting with women]; sociable get-together and dance. Requesting a large number of participants.*
>
> – *Alt-Glienicke Electoral Association. Membership meeting. Duty of all Genossen to appear punctually ....*
>
> – *Waidmannslust. Electoral Association membership meeting. Widow Bergmann's inn. It is the duty of every single Genosse to appear.*[22]

What was the logic behind this pattern of discrimination in announcements? Locals themselves no doubt varied in the seriousness of their commitment to recruiting women, but, of course, there were legal constraints as well. From the very moment of the party's re-legalization, members engaged in a series of legal battles, one of which was precisely over the issue of which sorts of meetings women (and minors) would be allowed to attend.[23] Laws of association in effect in many German states, particularly Prussia, explicitly banned women and youth from belonging to political organizations and attending their meetings. It was to avoid the consequences of this law that the socialist women's organization was set up separately from the SPD. But the legal restrictions also held implications for methods available for organizing women. Activities that could be advertised as educational public events rather than political meetings made female attendance permissible and helped socialists to organize women despite legal constraints.

One early campaign – the 1891 effort against high tariffs – demonstrated this sort of strategy. The July 1891 issue of *Vorwärts* recounted progress in a popular campaign opposing the grain tariff increases. In this campaign, the party used an important political issue as the basis of a grass-roots mobilization effort it literally took to the streets. The campaign involved public meetings, demonstrations, and door-to-door signature-gathering drives. *Vorwärts* carried reports of seven meetings in different cities, and two explicitly mentioned that the meetings were "attended by many women." An additional longer notice on a meeting in Strassburg noted that it attracted six hundred *Genossen und Genossinnen* and even *Bauernmädchen* (peasant girls), who showed their support for lower tariffs with bouquets.[24]

If the latter commentary presents women in a decorative role, other campaign reports suggested that women participated in debates and at public meetings where there were votes on resolutions protesting the tariff. Reports of signature gathering on protest petitions, apparently including women's signatures, presented these as crucial to the campaign. In other words, this early organizing effort of the newly legal party used public events to include women in pseudo-electoral processes despite their official exclusion from the suffrage and from political organizations. And the newspaper's reconstruction employed language ambiguous enough to suggest the party's encouragement of female expressions of citizenship without blatantly crossing the line into illegality.

Other public educational and mobilizing efforts lent themselves to female outreach as well. For example, a public meeting in 1906 in Treptow-Baumschulenweg discussed conscription. The announcement noted that since "the theme is important for mothers, it is a duty for women in both localities to appear in large numbers. Men are also reminded of their duty to appear."[25] But, if women were well represented as participants in these kinds of activities, it is also clear that public meetings were a relatively small proportion of the total number of activities reported in *Vorwärts,* and their proportion diminished over time.

In *Gleichheit* announcements or reports of public meetings or speeches by local speakers or national speakers on tour accounted for a persistent and substantial proportion of all organizing activities. (See Table 2.) For example, the first issue of 1892 listed twenty-four separate events under the rubric of "public meetings" *(öffentliche Versammlungen).* These included "the first public women's meeting ever held" in the small town of Nedersen, a "well attended" meeting of the *Hilfsarbeiter* and *-arbeiterinnen* in the Leipzig publishing industry who listened to a talk on "Women and the Shortening of the Workday," and a speech by *Genosse* August Bebel on "The Social Position of Women in the Present Day" delivered to a crowd of 1,200 Berliners.[26] In an issue just two months later, the list of activities was even more formidable. Between 30 January and 26 February 1892, according to a summary article, twenty-five separate public meetings were held in addition to nineteen meetings of organizations that were exclusively or partly run by the socialist women's movement – including, for example, the Tabak*arbeiter und -arbeiterinnen* (male and female tobacco workers), the Allgemeine *Arbeiterinnen* Berlin und Umgegend (the General Association of Female Workers of Berlin and the Surrounding Area), and the Verein der in der Glasindustrie-beschäftigte *Personen* (Association of Persons Employed in the Glass Industry) (emphases added to underscore the gender-inclusive language). Reports of the twenty-five public meetings listed the names of twenty-three different speakers on topics ranging from "Miners Strike" and "The

Benefits of Unions" through more general political topics such as "Women and Socialism" or "Proletarian Women and Militarism." Six of the twenty-three speakers were listed as *Genossinnen* and the rest *Genossen*. At the organizational membership meetings listed, topics of discussion again varied, but of fifteen listed speakers, an even higher proportion – nine – included women among the speakers.[27]

The emphasis on public meetings and informational speeches as vehicles for organization was more pronounced and persistent in the pages of *Die Gleichheit* and continued even while they diminished in the reporting in *Vorwärts* as other kinds of activities – especially union activities and meetings of electoral associations and other party membership organizations – took precedence. While such meetings remained important in *Gleichheit*'s reporting of organization building, they took on a different form as they increasingly centered around speaking tours of prominent party leaders rather than completely local events. (More on this below.)

With the growth and organizational development of the socialist movement, a growing proportion of the activities reported in the papers came to center on party-affiliated organization membership meetings. This category included not only the electoral associations (*Wahlvereine*) that were at the heart of socialist electoral organizing, but also a whole range of socialist affiliated cultural, consumer, and leisure organizations.[28] In both papers such meetings were among the most frequently reported activities. In actual practice they were no doubt more numerous than the articles would suggest because, as the party developed, such meetings were deemed routine, not newsworthy, items and were advertised rather than covered.

Attendance at membership meetings, important as such activities were, proved problematic for *Genossinnen* because it made them immediately susceptible to legal harassment. *Die Gleichheit* in 1892, for example, reported that the Munich Educational Association for Women and Girls was encountering difficulties because according to an especially strict interpretation of the law of association, all their public meetings were forbidden as "political."[29] (Still, the report went on, the group did manage to sponsor a talk and a dance that yielded a profit of 50 marks.) Fifteen years later, shortly before the new, 1908 Imperial Law on Association liberalized practices, another *Gleichheit* report, entitled "The authorities in battle against proletarian women," noted another form of police harassment of women's educational activities. The Elberfeld group was charged with violations of the association law. Its chair, *Genossin* Voigt, was fined, and the police insisted that she had to pay because she had been charged with a similar offense in 1894 and obviously had not repented![30]

Legal pursuits such as those noted by these two locals were a recurrent feature of partisan life. Fighting court battles and risking fines and imprisonments were mainstays of socialist press portrayals of party heroism, especially in the early years following re-legalization. If for *Genossen* such risks were incurred through editorial and press work, for *Genossinnen* the simple act of attending a meeting brought the risk of arrest and the associated opportunity for heroism.

6. Electoral Activities

Regarding specifically electoral activities, socialists found room to toy with the definition of what constituted forbidden political activities. Even before the law was changed in 1908, many women were reportedly beginning to get involved to some degree in socialist electoral work. Obviously, women could not vote or run for office, but the legal code did not categorically exclude the blatantly political act of electioneering. Could *Genossinnen* distribute campaign literature, for example, along with *Genossen*? Apparently so – at least sometimes.

Playing with the boundaries set by legal constraints on female political activity seems to have been as deliberate a part of socialist organizing strategy as playing with the limits of politically acceptable statements in the press or female attendance at certain kinds of meetings. In an illustrative exchange in *Die Gleichheit* in 1901, the middle-class radical Anita Augspurg defended herself against charges that she had claimed that bourgeois women had a relatively tougher time organizing around elections than socialist women did. In her defense, she admitted that socialist women, like all women, were victims of the legal prohibition on female political activity. But, she continued, socialist *men* were more cooperative in conducting their electoral business through "*öffentliche Volksversammlungen*" (public meetings), which were far more accessible to women than the "*Vereinsversammlungen*" (organizational or membership meetings) at which bourgeois parties handled their affairs. Hence, socialist women were not categorically excluded from party electoral work.[31]

The exchange between Augspurg and others on this issue pointed to further ambiguities in the law. Apparently women could involve themselves in some *Wahlverein* (electoral association) activities without clearly transgressing the law. The relevant practical distinction seems to have been between work for specific elections and long-term, organization-building activities with a goal of political agitation. The former was apparently sometimes permitted to women, the latter not.

Variations in *Vorwärts*' calls to electoral action may have been in part at least a product of this legal ambiguity. For example, a 1901 announcement directed toward Charlottenburg activists made it clear that women were included: "7:30 Sunday. Leaflet distribution. *Genossen und Gen-*

ossinnen are requested to turn out early and in large numbers."[32] Two months later, a list of similar announcements was directed exclusively at men. Of the nine calls for electoral activism, only *Genossen* are mentioned, and with a directness that seems deliberate. "Friedrichsfelde. Sunday 8:00 AM. Leaflet distribution at which every *Parteigenosse* should appear. Extraordinary help will be needed." Or, even clearer: "Pankow leaflet distribution. *Parteigenossen* are asked to appear to a man *(Mann für Mann)* at Hoffmann's."[33]

Attendance at routine *Wahlkreisverein* meetings was also tricky, but various subterfuges show up in announcements indicating a desire to get around the ban on women. Thus, two months after the previous announcement, also pertaining to the Berlin area, readers of *Vorwärts* could find out that at the coming Charlottenburg *Wahlverein* meeting, party leader August Bebel would be speaking and "the gallery would be reserved for women." The Steglitz-Friedenau *Wahlverein* announced that for its coming meeting, "Guests, including women, are welcome."[34]

Despite the ambiguity, inviting women could be, of course, an invitation to the closing down of a meeting, and until 1908 the involvement of women in electoral activities remained a source of contention with the police. For example, *Die Gleichheit* in 1907 ran a report on "Police Chicanery in the Election Campaign." At a recent meeting of a *Wahlkreisverein* in the Rheinland many women (happily) turned out. But after the meeting began, the police showed up and ordered the women to leave. When they refused (as was their right) the meeting was closed down.[35]

Given the lack of voting rights and such harassment, it is clear why organizing men electorally brought more immediate pay-offs to the party. Under these circumstances, it is interesting to note the evidence that women were being brought at all into electoral organizing before 1908. *Die Gleichheit* increased its emphasis on this dimension of female militancy in the last election cycle before the law was changed. The paper not only reported on but documented the cooperation of the *Genossinnen* in electoral campaigns in Bavaria where "in contrast with the last elections, many women attended meetings and helped out in election work." Their tasks included leaflet distributions, clerical duties, and the transport and distribution of ballots among the polling places. Women were also reportedly involved in electoral work in three Dresden electoral districts. "On the day before the election 120 to 130 *Genossinnen* came to the headquarters to help distribute leaflets. Their work brought harsh words from some recipients, but also a good reception by working-class women." In Frankfurt twenty thousand copies of a leaflet entitled "What Should Women Do about the Coming Reichstag Election?" were distributed. "The zeal of *Genossinnen* to get them into every corner of every proletarian district had the result of bringing to meetings women who had never before attended a meeting." In the Oberpfalz, *Genossen* and *Genossinnen* worked together on electoral activities. All the chores women did, especially in the suburbs, brought praise "despite the novelty of women as electoral workers."[36]

A last notice in the section on "Cooperation of Social Democratic Women in the Electoral Campaign" called attention not only to the high participation of women in the campaign, but also the task of documenting it for the enlightenment of the party's male leadership. The article reported that *Genossin* Baader had sent around four hundred questionnaires to *Vertrauenspersonen* and had already received one hundred and twenty back, providing evidence of some two thousand *Genossinnen* who participated in electoral work.[37] These reports suggest that electoral work was not categorically impossible for *Genossinnen*, although the percentage of women reportedly engaged in such activities remained low. (In the tables, electoral work is included in the category of Party Activities.)

7. Union Activities

Reports on union activities showed perhaps the most significant gender differences in grass-roots militant profiles. Both papers devoted a substantial proportion of their coverage to union work, but such coverage played a much greater role in *Vorwärts* than in *Die Gleichheit* (see Table 3). Moreover, there are marked differences in the tone and language of labor organizing reports in the two papers; in this arena more than any other, *Die Gleichheit* is far more insistent in its inclusion of women than *Vorwärts* and more directly suggestive of the tensions between male and female comrades.

Die Gleichheit left readers with the impression that women were a major presence in the labor force and in union efforts. For example, in one issue from 1906, the editors informed readers that:

> *– the increase in the cigarette tax had forced layoffs of half the workforce in Dresden (there were now four thousand unemployed, mainly* Arbeiterinnen*) while in Berlin cigarette workers were on shortened time;*
>
> *– in the textile industry, in a range of different localities, the ten-hour day movement was making progress;*
>
> *– a labor movement in the embroidery industry was building momentum;* and
>
> *– in the bookbinding industry in Berlin workers were raising the issue of whether or not the union was negotiating in good faith for* Arbeiterinnen*. Their raise was supposed to come in November (the same as for* Gehilfen*) but now was postponed until January.*[38]

When *Die Gleichheit* reported on women in the labor movement, it sometimes even used the occasion to editorialize and educate its readers about misogynist undercurrents in labor organizations. For example, an 1896 issue of the paper reported on the victory of the (male and female) workers of the Stuttgart book publishing industry. Not only did it explicitly use the terms "*Buchdrucker und Buchdruckerinnen*," it also noted that sometimes employers exploited differences between men and women employees. In this case, they failed, and "*Buchdruckerinnen* refused to become *Streikbrecherinnen*."[39] The section on *Gewerkschaftliche Arbeiterinnenorganisationen* (Union Women's Organizations), included at the turn of the century in the "Notizentheil" section edited by Lily Braun and Klara Zetkin, routinely included commentary as clearly directed to male as to female labor organizers. For example, one 1901 issue included the following notices:

> – *five thousand leaflets were distributed to Arbeiterinnen at the Brush, Paintbrush, Pencil, and Comb factory in Nuremberg by the Deutscher Holzarbeiterverband. The Wood Workers Union should also try to hold a meeting in which a woman is the speaker, which would support the leafletting effort.*
>
> – *the Verband der Schneider und Schneiderinnen [Union of Male and Female Tailors] is working with much effort to organize Arbeiter und Arbeiterinnen in ready-made clothing. It is especially necessary for them to organize wives and daughters involved in home work!*[40]

Activity reports of *Die Gleichheit* might also chide male comrades for their failure to support female militancy. For example, in 1906, the paper reported on a speaking tour of *Genossin* Kaehler who spoke on the subject of "The Struggle for Existence of the Westphalian *Tabakarbeiter-und arbeiterinnen*." At most of the meetings, women and girls comprised "nearly half" of the audience. The only exception, the reporter noted, was Herford, where the meeting left much to be desired. There, the men had left their wives home. "Maybe next time," the correspondent noted, "they'll bring them. The speaker for the most part berated the workers for not having brought along their female family members ... especially important in Herford, where women work as homeworkers in the wash branch for pitifully low wages." In contrast to the sorry event in Herford, however, the other tour stops were successful. One audience elected a woman *Vertrauensperson* and at that meeting eighteen new readers were won for *Die Gleichheit*. At another of these meetings, there were over 1,500 people in attendance.[41]

But *Die Gleichheit*'s coverage of women in union activities also revealed some defensiveness about women's roles and a retreat from the earlier focus in reporting exclusively on women's activities. By the first decade of the twentieth century, *Die Gleichheit* was increasing its reporting on union activities that did not explicitly involve female participation, the only category in which the paper did this. For example, a 1906 issue included under the "Gewerkschaftliche Rundschau" (Union Panorama) rubric the following notices:

– unions were active in electoral work, distributing leaflets, etc.;

– a wage movement is beginning in the Berlin woodworking industry;

– textile workers in Thuringia met with success in their contract negotiations;

– the Union of German Restaurant and Hotel Helpers [Gastwirtschaftsgehilfen] has grown from four to six thousand in the past year. Among the new members are two locals of female members in Munich und Nuremberg, of which the former alone has eight hundred members. This makes it clear that the organization of women Gastwirtsgehilfen is not as impossible as many have heretofore presumed. And the Gastwirtsgehilfenverband, which after many delays finally turned to organizing women, seems to have fared not too badly at it; and

– the Metallarbeiterzeitung *[official organ of the metal workers union] now has a circulation of 343,600!*[42]

Even if an increasing proportion (by 1910 as many as half of the labor articles in the sampled issues) discussed union activities without any particular mention of women in contrast to earlier reporting policies, *Gleichheit*'s coverage of union women was still far broader and less problematic from the point of view of female readers than that of *Vorwärts*.

The union movement played a larger role in organizing news in *Vorwärts*; in fact, by the late 1890s, this category of activities dominated the meeting and activity reports that made it into the paper (see Table 1). But in contrast to their apparent efforts to emphasize, no doubt even inflate, the role of female participation in some categories of activities, the *Vorwärts*' union activity reports were masculinist in tone and content. The problem of insensitivity to language in this arena contrasts with the greater inclusivity of other categories of coverage. Sometimes the paper covered female union participation in a tone that can only be described as patronizing. For example, in 1892 the paper reported that typefounders, mechanics, and female workers confronted a new set of work rules with a work stoppage. "For the first time *weibliche Arbeiter* (female workers) fought at the side of the *Gehilfe* (helpers) for their rights."[43] Other times, the gendering took the form of simply reprinting masculinist announcements from unions. For example, in 1902 the paper published an appeal from the Diamond Polishers Union of Hanau under the title "Diamond Workers in Amsterdam." The article reported on three thousand Amsterdam diamond workers who had been locked out:

These very workers have shown shining solidarity towards their German brothers … help us to pay the debt of honor we owe our brothers in Amsterdam. May every organized Arbeiter, every organization offer a contribution so that we can show our brothers in Amsterdam that German Arbeiter will not dishonor the example they showed us in 1897, but instead know how to fulfill the duties of solidarity.[44]

And even when women were mentioned in labor coverage, it was not always in the spirit of inclusion. In a 1906 issue four of eleven labor movement items mentioned women; two of them, however, were pejorative. The first article, "They Call It Protection of Willing Workers," reported that in the context of a construction workers strike, a day laborer was arrested for telling a female worker (*Arbeiterin*) who was not participating in the strike that "if you continue to work, you will be a strikebreaker." The following item in the paper, a report without editorial comment on a conflict in a leather factory, mentioned that the issue entailed reducing the number of *Mädchen* (girls) who were doing skilled work.[45]

8. Change over Time: Professionalization, Legalization, Grass-Roots Organizing, and Gender

How did the institutional development of the socialist movement affect the portraits of militants? Tables 1 and 2 suggest parallel trends over time in the total numbers of reports of grass-roots activities per issue in the two papers, and also in the proportions of women reported as participants in *Vorwärts*. All three trendlines start out high in the spurt of activities immediately following legalization, drop downward (more precipitously in *Die Gleichheit* and countered somewhat by rising union activity reports in *Vorwärts*) through the turn of the century, and rise again in the first decade of the twentieth century. Still these are not strong trends; by and large, the two papers display similarities and persistence over time in the representations of what constituted the stuff of militancy. The routines of grass-roots militancy were not represented as starkly different for men and women, despite the different legal situations of men and women in political organizations, even if relative levels of representation of *Genossinnen* varied across categories of activity. And these routines were well institutionalized and fairly stable throughout the period studied. The only really clear changes over time in the pattern of activities reported are the gradual diminution of reports of legal and police encounters, and, more noticeable still, the increasing domination of the activities reported in *Die Gleichheit* by the figure of the *Genossin* on organized speaking tours.

It is worth looking at the changing role of the speaking tour in some detail since it suggests an organizational shift with implications for the nature of grass-roots involvement of *Genossinnen*. If the separate engagements of these traveling speakers are counted individually they comprise the majority of all activities reported in the issues sampled for the first decade of the twentieth century. (See Table 2.) Even though the technique of recruitment centering on public meetings that featured a speaker was established during the period when most other sorts of activities were prohibited to women, the reliance on such events, and their professionalization around a core of *Genossinnen* willing and able to take on intensive tours, persisted even after the change in law opened other political activities to women. For example, the "Aus der Bewegung" section of a 1907 issue suggests a remarkably high level of what might be termed "professional" movement activity:

> *– the General Committee of Unions organized a series of meetings in Westphalia. The undersigned reporter [M. Backwitz] lectured on "The Evils of Home Work" in fourteen different localities; "lectures were well attended ..."*
>
> *– the undersigned [M. Jeetze] lectured for the Consumers Union in sixteen localities, every one well attended; normally "spoke for 1 1/4 hours ..."*[46]

This "professionalization" (not to mention bureaucratization) of the *Genossin*'s portrait in *Die Gleichheit* provides a contrast to the kinds of public meetings described earlier as typical of the 1890s. Ironically, such professionalization attests both to the benefits and the costs of organizational development. That the socialist women's movement could recruit, train, and subsidize speakers for this level of lecture activity offers evidence of remarkable organizational maturity. At the same time, however, in contrast with the more localized and spontaneous public meetings reported on in the 1890s, these later events bear the marks of both routine and top-down organization. Like the men's movement, the socialist women's movement was successful enough on the eve of World War I to be experiencing some of the less desirable symptoms of institutionalization, and these symptoms showed up in press portrayals of party activism.

A final word is needed on the impact of the changing legal status of women by the last years sampled, 1911 to 1912. In neither paper is there a dramatic shift in the portrayal of men's and women's activities in the movement by these later years. The legal changes certainly opened up new opportunities for organizing women, a view that was reflected in the optimistic tone of some of the 1911 to 1912 organizing reports. *Die Gleichheit* in 1910 pointed out some of the new possibilities:

> *– Agnes Fahrenwald visited twenty-six locations in Mecklenburg, where she spoke on "Women and Politics." The article, with a tone of confidence, listed all the places Fahrenwald had visited and proudly noted that she had helped recruit over six hundred new weibliche Mitglieder (female members). The meetings, "many of which were filled to overflowing," also brought many new readers to Die Gleichheit and to the Mecklenburg Volkszeitung. "For the first time, the meeting in Warin was chaired by a young Genossin."*
>
> *– in a report on the situation in Mecklenburg, Die Gleichheit noted that only one female comrade was present among the forty-four delegates from thirty localities at the first party congress that women were able to attend. But reflecting that same sense of confidence for the future, the paper noted that Genossin Zietz spoke up and that "... organizing work is ongoing."*[47]

If legalization brought new potential, it also, of course, brought new risks as the justification for a separate organization for women now disappeared. The new situation of the *Genossin* and its implications for organizing women were fought out in the pages of *Die Gleichheit* even as they were in local women's chapter meetings, especially around issues like the holding of a separate socialist women's conference. The change in the law removed some of the constraints shaping the somewhat different strategies for organizing men and women (a very major one – namely, the lack of women's suffrage – persisted, of course). These changes left *Genossinnen* on the eve of World War I with both new concerns about and new possibilities for the future of female socialist militancy. But for all the apparent tensions and frustrations around the role of the *Genossin*, it is nevertheless clear that the imagining of this role and the establishment of some practices to embody it were among the most significant and innovative accomplishments of the previous two decades of socialist organizing.

Even if the *Genossin* played a marginal role in *Vorwärts* that contrasted with her centrality in *Die Gleichheit*, both papers documented the arrival on the historical stage of the female activist. The *Genossin*'s ambiguous legal position lent an aura of heroism to activities like attending membership meetings or engaging in electoral work, even as legal harassment made socialist publishing heroic for socialist men. Other activities like public speaking or recruiting co-workers or distributing leaflets took the courage to overcome personal insecurities and to defy constraints imposed by gender stereotypes. But by World War I all of these activities had become routine, familiar, and imaginable to both men and women. The very banality of these activities of everyday organizing should not blind us either to their importance to the new model of organizing that the socialist movement developed or to the ways in which such activities helped to alter the gendering of popular political activism. Indeed, the resurfacing of less routine and more violent forms of protest at the end of World War I, and the accompanying masculinization of images of militancy that was noticeable during the Weimar era,[48] only underscore the historical interrelationship among forms of organization, gender identities, and the practices and images of political activism.

Table 1 Distribution by Year and Category of Militant Activities Reported on in Sampled Issues of *Vorwärts.*
(Proportion of articles mentioning female participation in parentheses.)

Years	Legal, Police Battles	Member-ship Meetings	Union Events	Party Activities	Public Meetings/ Events	Speaking Tours (Stops)	Obitu-aries	Women's Org. Events	*Total*
1891-1892	46 (.09)	88 (.11)	95 (.17)	4 (0)	18 (.39)	1 (0)	6 (0)	0 (0)	*258* *(.14)*
1896-1897	32 (.06)	36 (.03)	126 (.08)	5 (.20)	7 (.57)	1 (0)	4 (.25)	2 (100)	*213* *(.10)*
1901-1902	10 (.10)	65 (.17)	81 (.04)	10 (.10)	4 (.50)	1 (100)	3 (0)	3 (100)	*177* *(.12)*
1906-1907	18 (.11)	73 (.32)	107 (.18)	18 (.06)	3 (.67)	0 (0)	3 (0)	0 (100)	*222* *(.21)*
1911-1912	11 (.09)	90 (.19)	68 (.12)	19 (.11)	3 (0)	0 (0)	2 (0)	2 (100)	*195* *(.15)*
Total	*117* *(.09)*	*352* *(.18)*	*477* *(.12)*	*56* *(.09)*	*35* *(.43)*	*3* *(.33)*	*18* *(.06)*	*7* *(100)*	*1065* *(.15)*

Table 2 Distribution of Year and Category of Militant Activities Reported on in Sampled Issues of *Die Gleicheit.*
(All articles in all categories mentioned female participation except for the category Union Activities. In that case, proportion mentioning women is in parentheses.)

Years	Legal, Police Battles	Member-ship Meetings	Union Events	Party Activities	Public Meetings/ Events	Speaking Tours (Stops)*	Obituaries	*Total*
1891-1892	3	39	13	2	39	0	0	*96*
1896-1897	2	5	4	3	3	1 (9)	0	*18*
1901-1902	0	6	5	0	0	5(48)	0	*16*
1906-1907	4	12	18 (.61)	7	18	5(66)	1	*65 (.89)*
1911-1912	0	10	34 (.50)	3	3	7(73)	0	*57 (.70)*
Total	*9*	*76*	*74 (.68)*	*15*	*59*	*18(196)*	*1*	*252 (.90)*

Table 3 Distribution by Category of Militant Activities in Sampled Issues of *Vorwärts* and *Die Gleichheit*, 1891 to 1912.
(Proportions in each category in parentheses.)

	Legal, Police Battles	Member-ship Meetings	Union Events	Party Activities	Public Meetings/ Events	Speaking Tours	Obitu-aries	*Total*
Vorwaerts	117 (.11)	352 (.33)	477 (.45)	56 (.05)	35 (.03)	3 (0)	18 (.02)	*1058*
Die Gleichheit	9 (.04)	76 (.30)	74 (.29)	15 (.06)	59 (.23)	18 (.07)	1 (0)	*252*

Notes

1. For discussions of the impact of the outlaw period on the long-term development of German socialism, see Guenther Roth, *The Social Democrats in Imperial Germany: A Study in Working Class Isolation and National Integration* (Totowa, NJ, 1963), and Vernon Lidtke, *The Outlawed Party: Social Democracy in Germany, 1878-1890* (Princeton, 1966). For discussions of the continued legal harassment even after the party was re-legalized, see Alex Hall, "By Other Means: The Legal Struggle Against the SPD in Wilhelmine Germany, 1890-1900," *Historical Journal* 17:2 (1974): 365-86, and idem, *Scandal, Sensation and Social Democracy: The SPD-Press and Wilhelmine Germany, 1890-1914* (Cambridge, Mass., 1977), especially Chapters 2 and 3. Richard Evans, "Proletarian Mentalities: Pub Conversations in Hamburg," in idem, *Proletarians and Politics* (New York, 1990), 124-91, includes a discussion of police surveillance of the SPD in Hamburg.
2. Analysis of the changing forms and repertoires of collective protest in Europe that frames this account is shaped by the work of Charles Tilly. See, for example, *From Mobilization to Revolution* (Reading, Mass., 1978); *The Contentious French* (Cambridge, Mass., 1986); and "Contentious Repertoires in Britain, 1758-1834," *Social Science History* 17:2 (1993): 253-80. For an early application of collective action theory in the German historical context, see Louise Charles, and Richard Tilly, *The Rebellious Century* (Cambridge, Mass., 1975), and the discussion of subsequent historiography in Richard J. Evans, "The Crowd in German History," in idem, *Proletarians*, 28-47. For a discussion of the historical literature on changes in the processes of mobilization for electoral and other political purposes in Imperial Germany, see David Blackbourn and Geoff Eley, *The Peculiarities of German History: Bourgeois Politics and Society in Nineteenth-Century Germany* (Oxford, 1984).
3. There is an analysis of the role of SPD publications in recruitment into the socialist movement in Jürgen Loreck, *Wie man früher Sozialdemokrat wurde* (Bonn-Bad Godesberg, 1977).
4. Julius Bruhn, *"Es klingt im Sturm ein altes Lied!" Aus der Jugendzeit der Sozialdemokratie* (Berlin, 1921), 15.
5. There is a more extended discussion of this argument in my book, *Taking the Hard Road: Life Course in French and German Workers' Autobiographies of the Industrial Era* (Chapel Hill, NC, 1995), especially 153-80.
6. Historians have analyzed both the role of women in popular collective action and the role of gender in revolutionary iconography. See for example, Harriet B. Applewhite and Darlene Gay Levy, "Women, Democracy, and Revolution in Paris, 1789-1794," in *French Women and the Age of Enlightenment*, ed. Samia Spencer (Bloomington, Ind., 1984), 64-79; Temma Kaplan, "Female Consciousness and Collective Action: The Barcelona Case, 1910-1918," *Signs* 7:3 (1982): 545-66, on women in popular collective action. On representations of gender in European political protest, see Eric Hobsbawm, "Man and Woman in Socialist Iconography," *History Workshop Journal* 6 (1978): 121-38; Lynn Hunt, *The Family Romance of the French Revolution* (Berkeley, 1992); and Eric D. Weitz, "The Heroic Man and the Ever-Changing Woman: Gender and Politics in European Communism," in *Gender and Class in Modern Europe*, ed. Laura Frader and Sonya Rose (Ithaca, NY, 1996). On women in utopian socialism, where gender analysis played a somewhat different role, see Barbara Taylor, *Eve and the New Jerusalem: Socialism and Feminism in the Nineteenth Century* (New York, 1983), and Claire Goldberg Moses, *French Feminism in the Nineteenth Century* (Albany, NY, 1984).

7. Adelheid Popp, *Die Jugendgeschichte einer Arbeiterin: Von ihr selbst erzählt* (Munich, 1909), 60.
8. From the title of Ottilie Baader's memoir, *Ein steiniger Weg: Lebenserinnerungen einer Sozialisten* (Berlin, 1921).
9. For discussions of the role of women in the German socialist movement, see Werner Thönessen, *The Emancipation of Women: The Rise and Decline of the Women's Movement in German Social Democracy, 1863-1933* (London, 1973); Jean Quataert, *Reluctant Feminists in German Social Democracy, 1885-1917* (Princeton, 1979); Sabine Richebächer, *Uns fehlt nur eine Kleinigkeit: Deutsche proletarische Frauenbewegung, 1890-1914* (Frankfurt am Main, 1982); Heinz Niggemann, *Emanzipation zwischen Sozialismus und Feminismus* (Wuppertal, 1981); Ute Frevert, "Women Workers, Workers' Wives and Social Democracy in Imperial Germany," in *Bernstein to Brandt: A Short History of German Social Democracy*, ed. Roger Fletcher (London, 1987), 34-44; and Richard J. Evans, "Socialist Women and Political Radicalism," in idem, *Proletarians*, 93-123.
10. The exceptions tend to be studies that examine the history of socialism and affiliated organizations through local materials or cases studies. See, for example, Heinz Niggemann, *Emanzipation*; Adelheid von Saldern, *Auf dem Wege zum Arbeiter-Reformismus: Parteialltag in sozialdemokratischer Provinz Göttingen (1870-1920)* (Frankfurt am Main, 1984); Mary Nolan, *Social Democracy and Society: Working-Class Radicalism in Düsseldorf, 1890-1920* (Cambridge, Mass., 1981); Eric D. Weitz, *Creating German Communism, 1890-1990: From Popular Protests to Socialist State* (Princeton, 1997); Vernon Lidtke, *The Alternative Culture: Socialist Labor in Imperial Germany* (New York, 1985). For a summary history of class relations and the workers' movement in Imperial Germany, as well as comprehensive coverage of the historical literature, see Gerhard A. Ritter and Klaus Tenfelde, *Arbeiter im Deutschen Kaiserreich, 1871 bis 1914* (Berlin, 1992).
11. The newspapers were part of a broader movement culture that, of course, also framed the images circulated in the press. There have been a number of important historical studies of the political culture created by central European socialism including Lidtke, *Alternative Culture*; Niggemann, *Emanzipation*; Dieter Langewiesche, "The Impact of the German Labor Movement on Workers' Culture," *Journal of Modern History* 59:3 (1987): 506-23; and Helmut Gruber, *Red Vienna: Experiment in Working-Class Culture* (New York, 1991). On the press itself, see Hall, *Scandal*.
12. *Vorwärts*, 1 July 1891.
13. Ibid., 8 January 1897.
14. Ibid., 1 November 1906.
15. These sections originally were bylined by Lily Braun and Klara Zetkin, but the byline disappeared with Braun's marginalization by the socialist women's movement.
16. *Die Gleicheit*, 14 November 1906.
17. The sample drawn for the systematic analysis of the newspaper representations of activism consisted of ten daily issues per yearly sample (July through June), one year of every five for *Vorwärts*. I read all sections under the organizing rubrics listed and recorded the nature of the event announced or reported on and any indication of whom the participants were. In *Gleichheit*, I read one biweekly issue per quarter for the same years as the *Vorwärts* sample. These were both nationally distributed papers. It is very likely that results could be quite different, and varied, in local socialist newspapers.
18. *Die Gleichheit*, 16 September 1896.

19. Ibid.
20. *Vorwärts*, 28 April 1892.
21. Ibid., 16 July 1901.
22. Ibid., 1 March 1907.
23. For a summary of the pertinent laws, see Niggemann, *Emanzipation*, 18-22.
24. *Vorwärts*, 1 July 1891.
25. Ibid., 1 July 1906.
26. *Die Gleichheit*, 11 January 1892.
27. Ibid., 8 March 1892.
28. For a history of the whole range of party-affiliated social, cultural, and consumer organizations, see Lidtke, *Alternative Culture*.
29. *Die Gleichheit*, 8 March 1892.
30. Ibid., 23 January 1907.
31. Ibid., 13 March 1901.
32. *Vorwärts*, 1 November 1901.
33. Ibid., 22 March 1902.
34. Ibid., 15 May 1902.
35. *Die Gleicheit*, 23 January 1907.
36. All of the above quotes from ibid., 6 March 1907.
37. Ibid.
38. Ibid., 14 November 1906.
39. Ibid., 16 September 1896.
40. Ibid., 22 May 1901.
41. Ibid., 14 November 1906.
42. Ibid., 23 January 1907.
43. *Vorwärts*, 15 May 1892.
44. Ibid., 22 March 1902.
45. Ibid., 1 July 1906.
46. *Die Gleichheit*, 23 January 1907.
47. Ibid., 28 March 1910.
48. For interesting discussions of related developments, see Weitz, "Heroic Man," and Eve Rosenhaft, "Working-Class Life and Working-Class Politics: Communists, Nazis and the State in the Battle for the Streets, Berlin 1928-1932," in *Social Change and Political Development in Weimar Germany*, ed. Richard Bessel and E.J. Feuchtwanger (London, 1981), 207-40, and idem, "Women, Gender and the Limits of Political History in the Age of 'Mass' Politics," in *Elections, Mass Politics, and Social Change in Modern Germany: New Perspectives*, ed. Larry Eugene Jones and James Retallack (Cambridge, Mass., 1992), 149-73.

Chapter 6

THE SOCIAL DEMOCRATIC ELECTORATE IN IMPERIAL GERMANY

Jonathan Sperber

Central to the realm of activities carried out by the Social Democratic Party in Imperial Germany and to the political self-identity of its members was election campaigning, particularly for the democratically elected Reichstag. There are a host of reasons for the party's focus on elections, ranging from Ferdinand Lassalle's belief in universal manhood suffrage as the key to the solution of the social problem, to the peculiar circumstances of the Anti-Socialist Law from 1878 to 1890, when the party was illegal but its candidacies were not. Most important, though, was the significance of electioneering for the party's agitation. By campaigning in elections with a democratic suffrage, the Social Democrats could hope to reach a broad public – as was certainly true in the 1870s, when the party (before 1875 two parties) consisted of a handful of self-sacrificing adherents among a largely indifferent or hostile population; it was also true of the ever larger, ever more publicly present, and ever more bureaucratically organized SPD of Wilhelmine Germany. The central unit of party organization after 1890 was the constituency association *(Wahlkreisverein)*; party agitation and the activities of party activists centered around the general elections to the Reichstag, with preparations for them beginning as much as two years in advance.[1]

All this election campaigning should not be taken to imply a principled commitment to the German parliament as an institution, or to parliamentary democracy as a form of government. Opinions within the

Notes for this chapter begin on page 191.

party were divided on both the theoretical desirability of a parliamentary regime and the practical gains to be made by participating in the work of the Reichstag, a body with little power, either institutionally or constitutionally. Yet these mixed opinions about parliamentarianism in general and the German national parliament in particular did not extend to elections to it. For the Social Democrats, the Reichstag elections were their great opportunity to demonstrate and expand upon their public presence, the "review of the troops (*Heerschau*)," when they could show friends and enemies alike the extent of their movement and its public support.[2]

Two examples, from the first and last peacetime decades of the Kaiserreich, demonstrate quite effectively the broad consensus among Social Democrats about the agitational virtues of election campaigning. In 1876, *Vorwärts* defended the frequent absences of social democratic Reichstag deputies, by noting that they had more important things to do than participate in parliamentary debate and voting – namely, to speak in Reichstag election campaigns. Some thirty years later, in the general elections of 1907, the party was threatened with the loss of its Kiel constituency. To defend the seat of incumbent deputy Carl Legien, chairman of the free trade union federation and a leading figure on the SPD's right wing, the party rushed in a whole group of prominent outside speakers, including Rosa Luxemburg and Georg Ledebour, two prominent and intransigent figures on its extreme left.[3]

The idea of the Reichstag elections as a *Heerschau* is, in many ways, as useful to historians as it was to party activists, because these elections, held under universal manhood suffrage, with a (semi) secret ballot, provide us with an opportunity to explore the nature of, growth in, and limits to the popular support – understood in the broadest possible sense – of the social democratic movement in Imperial Germany. The largest change in voting patterns in the general elections of the Empire was the growth in the social democratic vote, from 2 percent of votes cast in 1871, to almost 35 percent in 1912; thus, a study of social democratic voters offers information about the nature of the entire pre-1914 German electorate. This is certainly the point behind the best known and most influential theory of voting behavior in Imperial Germany, Rainer Lepsius's concept of "sociomoral milieus."

Lepsius's argument is that these milieus, an interleaved combination of social structure, organizational life, and religious and regional traditions, determined voting behavior, and that political parties in the Kaiserreich were largely the expression of the milieus supporting them. Lepsius asserts that three such milieus were the product of pre-industrial German society and existed at the introduction of universal manhood suffrage in 1867 to 1871: the urban/middle-class/Protestant milieu, associated with the liberal parties; the rural/Protestant one, associated with the conservatives;

and a Catholic milieu, closely tied to the Center party. With the growth of urbanization and industrialization there developed a large group of the German population, urban, working class, and nominally Protestant, outside any of the existing milieus. Lepsius believes that they were at first non-voters, because the act of voting, in his thesis, resulted from belonging to a milieu. These individuals were then organized and won over by the Social Democrats, recruited, in effect, into a new milieu, providing a social basis for the party but also setting the boundaries of its support.[4]

These ideas are part of a broader scholarly consensus on the nature of the social democratic electorate in Imperial Germany, containing three main features. The first point, on which there is perhaps the most disagreement, is that the growth of the social democratic vote over the four peacetime decades of the Kaiserreich was primarily the result of the mobilization of previous non-voters. Some authors, such as the late Werner Conze, see the SPD electorate as stemming just about entirely from previous non-voters. Others, among them Gerhard A. Ritter and Karl Rohe, agree that previous non-voters were important but suggest that voters switching from other parties also helped account for the Social Democrats' increasing vote totals. Scholars are much closer to unanimity on the second point: namely, that the composition of different levels of the social democratic movement was quite similar: that is, SPD party membership and SPD voters were alike in being largely urban, blue-collar, and nominally Protestant. The final point, following from the previous two, is that by the last general elections in the Kaiserreich, the SPD had about reached the limits of its support. With turnout at 85 percent of eligible voters in 1907 and 1912, the reservoir of non-voters had been exhausted. Having successfully mobilized a very large percentage of its Protestant, working-class following, and unable to gain much support from Catholics, the urban middle class, or farmers, the SPD had, electorally, nowhere to go.[5]

These three main points have formed the basis for the bulk of the scholarship on the social democratic electorate, with just a few authors of locally oriented works expressing any disagreement. Indeed, as a number of the studies cited in the previous note show, these three points were one of the few areas of agreement between historians of the former East and West Germany in discussions of the pre-1914 labor movement, a field of scholarly research not exactly characterized by common views on different sides of the intra-German border. Yet this scholarly consensus is based on a very thin empirical footing, as a result of the scant material available for study.

Judgments about the SPD's electorate involve statements about social and confessional groups, about the voting behavior of Catholics, for instance, or agricultural laborers. However, because the Reichstag elections took place under a secret ballot and before the advent of public opinion polling, we do not know how such groups voted. What we know about are the votes cast in a given area, be it a precinct, a Reichstag constituency, or a Prussian province, what is called, in the jargon of electoral analysis, "ecologically aggregated data." It is possible to make such geographical units the basis of a study of the SPD's electorate, or that of any other party, but the amount of information possible to obtain in this way is limited, and generally does not offer answers to questions such as those posed by Lepsius in his theory of sociomoral milieus.[6]

What we would like to do is to take this ecologically aggregated data and use it to develop estimates of the votes of individuals grouped by factors such as class, confession, or previous voting choice. Doing so involves the statistical method – actually, a family of methods – known as ecological inference. This is a procedure fraught with risks (the celebrated, if often exaggerated, "ecological fallacy"), sometimes yielding logically impossible results, and requiring a number of untestable assumptions. Nonetheless, the risks can be avoided, the impossible results adjusted, and the assumptions made plausible. Such methods have been applied to study past elections in a number of different locales; for Germany, the best known example is Jürgen Falter's work on the rise of the Nazi Party at the end of the Weimar Republic.[7]

As part of a study of voters and elections in Imperial Germany, I have developed three groups of estimates of voting behavior from the published, constituency-level Reichstag election returns. All these estimates are based on the first round of the general elections, carried out in all 397 Reichstag constituencies, not on the runoffs, occurring to a different extent and in different constituencies from election to election.[8] First, for every pair of general elections, from 1871/74 to 1907/12, I have estimated how voters at the first election voted in the second. With these estimates, I can trace the movements of voters from one party (including the "parties" of the new and non-voters) to another, thus, making it possible to ascertain the sources of a party's growing – or declining – vote totals.[9] Second, for every single general election, from 1871 to 1912, I have developed estimates of how members of different religious confessions voted.[10] Finally, for the general elections in Wilhelmine Germany, from 1890 to 1912, I have obtained estimates of voting by confession and social class – e.g., how Catholic workers or Protestant farmers voted. Unlike the two other groups of estimates, which can be calculated directly from the voting returns, these require the use of census data, and of the four occupational and industrial censuses taken in the Kaiserreich, only those of 1895 and 1907 are detailed and extensive enough for use in electoral analysis. Their predecessors in 1875 and 1882 are inadequate, so, regrettably, I have found it impossible to develop estimates of voting by class and confession for the first two decades of the history of the Empire.[11]

In this essay, I will use some of the results of this ecological analysis to consider the dominant view of the social democratic electorate in Germany before World War I. This essay will focus on three main questions. An obvious place to start is with the growth of the social democratic electorate. Did the party's vote increase as a result of the mobilization of previous non-voters, or did voters from other parties play a role, and if so, to what extent? Implicit in this question, and the scholarly literature it confronts, is the assumption that voters, once won over to the Social Democrats, stayed with them. There is no reason to assume, a priori, that this was so. Indeed, a political party's ability to retain its clientele is at least as important for its electoral success as attracting new voters. Consequently, this analysis must be two-sided, asking not just where the social democratic voters came from but also where they went. In other words, it must assess the flow of voters to and from the Social Democratic Party. Naturally, this and other questions might require a chronologically differentiated answer, since social democratic voters might have had different political backgrounds and different future loyalties at different times in the history of the Empire.

The second main focus of my investigation will be the class and confession of social democratic voters. Quite simply, what proportion of Catholic voters cast their ballot for the SPD; what proportion of Protestants? How many voters from the ranks of Protestant blue-collar workers or the Catholic middle class were supporters of the Social Democrats? Here, the issue is the heart of the scholarly consensus: the assertion that social democratic voters, like SPD party members, were overwhelmingly urban, Protestant, blue-collar workers.

Finally, I would like to consider some of the broader implications of the results of the analysis of voting patterns. The central point is the notion that the SPD had exhausted its reservoir of voters by 1912. From the estimates, one could see what proportion of different social and confessional groups did in fact vote for the SPD and whether some of them were completely accounted for. It would also be of interest to compare the pre-1914 social democratic electorate with the labor voters of the Weimar Republic, as Jürgen Falter has described them, or with the SPD vote after 1945 as revealed by survey research. Falter's work is particularly relevant to this issue, largely because of his celebrated description of the Nazis as the "first German people's party."[12] At the peak of their success in free elections, the balloting of July 1932, the Nazis received about 38 percent of the votes cast, not all that different from the 35 percent of votes going to the SPD at the general elections twenty years previously. It is fair to wonder whether the pre-war Social Democratic Party might have had some of the traits of a people's party as well.

Let me begin the analysis with a very simple chart showing the growth of the social democratic vote at general elections from 1871 to 1912.

Unlike the usual versions, that give this vote as a percentage of all votes cast, or, less commonly, as a percentage of all eligible voters, Figure 1 has two parameters. The dashed line shows the proportion of eligible voters who had the opportunity to vote for the Social Democrats, which is the percentage of all eligible voters residing in constituencies in which Social Democrats stood for office.[13] The solid line gives the percentage of eligible voters in those constituencies who voted for the Social Democrats.

Figure 1 Social Democratic Potential and Vote

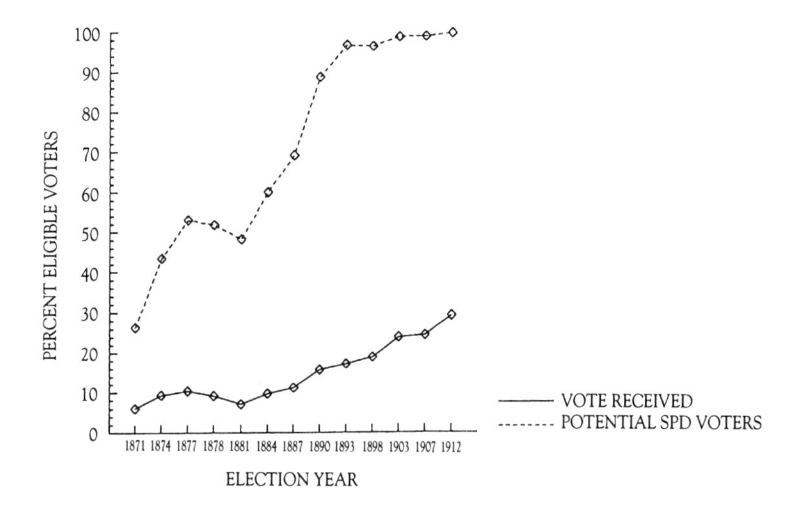

The dashed line shows the rapid growth of social democratic candidacies in the early years of the German Empire, peaking in 1877, the first general election following the unification of the two social democratic parties at the Gotha Congress of 1875, when some 53 percent of the entire electorate had a social democratic candidate to vote for. The reach of social democratic candidacies declined somewhat over the next two elections, a result of the increasingly intense persecution to which the party was subjected just before and after the passage of the Anti-Socialist Law. But as the government went over to the era of the so-called "mild practice," mitigating the worst effects of the law, and the party adapted to police persecution and learned to operate effectively under conditions of illegality, the number of candidacies increased sharply. They took their biggest jump between 1887, when about 69 percent of the electorate could vote for a Social Democrat, and the general elections of 1890, held after the Reichstag had refused to renew the Anti-Socialist Law, making it a dead letter and allowing the party to engage in an unprecedented, extensive election campaign. As a result, 89 percent of German voters had the opportunity to turn in a social democratic ballot.[14] Operating legally from the 1893 general elections onward, if still subject, of course, to all sorts of official harassment and chicanery, the SPD achieved essentially blanket coverage of the electorate.

Turning to the solid line – the percentage of eligible voters supporting the Social Democrats in those constituencies where the party put up candidates for office – what is striking is its steadiness over the elections in Bismarckian Germany, from 1871 to 1887. Excepting the very first elections of 1871, when the Social Democrats were not yet fully organized, and the elections of 1881, at the very peak of official persecution under the Anti-Socialist Law, the party received a fairly constant 10 percent of the eligible voters in constituencies where it put up candidates, the figures ranging from a low of 9.3 percent in 1878 to a high of 11.3 percent in 1887. The social democratic vote in Bismarckian Germany, in other words, largely moved up and down with the range of the party's candidacies, which were in turn determined by the extent of party organization and by changes in government policy towards (that is, the extent of persecution of) the labor movement.

The 1890 elections not only represented a new high for social democratic candidacies, they also presented a change in the amount of support obtained by each candidate. For the first time the Social Democrats broke through the 10 percent barrier, receiving the votes of almost 16 percent of the eligible voters in those constituencies where they put up candidates. The party vote totals moved upwards throughout Wilhelmine Germany, the SPD receiving the support of a greater percentage of eligible voters at each general election, but since the party's candidacies encompassed almost the entire electorate, the growth in the SPD's vote could only have been the result of enlisting a greater proportion of eligible voters per candidacy.[15] We might sum up these results by saying that the increase in social democratic votes before 1890 was extensive, primarily the result of adding more candidacies, while from 1890 onward the party experienced an intensive growth in its vote, a result of increasing its support in those constituencies where it had candidates.

These considerations suggest that the 1890 elections might have marked something of a turning point in the sources of the social democratic electorate and the ecological analysis confirms this. Table 1 gives the vote at the previous general election of social democratic voters, averaged across several groups of general elections from 1874 to 1912. For the readers' understanding, I need to make three points about this table that will also apply to the other results of my analysis. First, the Social Democrats were unusual in fielding such a wide range of candidacies; most of the other individual political parties ran many fewer candidates. For technical reasons involved in carrying out the regressions, it was necessary to combine the many political parties of Imperial Germany together into five party groups: 1) the conservatives, including the Conservatives, the Free Conservatives, and the post-1887 parties of the extreme right, the Anti-Semites and the Agrarian League; 2) the liberals, including the National Liberals and the various left-liberal and bourgeois-democratic parties; 3) the parties of the religious, regional, and national minorities, the Center, the French, Polish, Danish, and Lithuanian nationalists, the Hanoverians and other particularists, and, after 1890, the Bavarian Peasant League; 4) the Social Democrats, including both social democratic parties before their unification in 1875; and 5) the non-voters, also including the very small percentage of voters who cast scattered or invalid ballots.

Secondly, I need to say something about changes in the electorate from election to election. Between any one general election and the next, some voters died or left the country, while, at the same time, young men were reaching voting age; some voters left their constituencies and others moved into them. Unfortunately, there is no way of tracking this fluctuation, a problem with all kinds of ecological studies of voting across more than one election. All that can be done is to note the increase in the total number of eligible voters. Particularly in Wilhelmine Germany, when general elections were held every five years and the voting age population was increasing, this net increase could reach 8 or 9 percent of the electorate. The increase was not evenly distributed across the country, with the number of eligible voters in urban and industrial areas growing more rapidly than the national average, while those in rural areas grew more slowly or even declined absolutely in size. I call this increase in voters from the previous general election as a percentage of eligible voters "net new voters." These are not actual individuals (as would be, for instance, the voters for the conservative parties at the previous election) but a measure of the turnover in the electorate arising from natural causes and from migration, particularly from rural to urban areas. Between 1877 and 1881, however, the electorate hardly increased at all, so for the election pairs 1877/78 and 1878/81 there is no figure for net new voters.

Finally, I should say something about the grouping of elections together. Although I have calculated figures on voter movements, via the regression estimates briefly discussed in footnote nine, for every single pair of elections, from 1871/74 to 1907/12, giving them all individually would take up too much space and disguise longer term trends in a welter of details. Hence, for the purposes of this essay, I have combined several election pairs together. In the first column of Table 1, for instance, the figure on the percentage of previous liberal voters choosing the Social Democrats was obtained by taking the average of the percentage of 1874 social democratic voters who had voted for one of the liberal parties in

1871 (as calculated from the regression equations, comparing the 1871 and 1874 elections) and the percentage of 1877 social democratic voters who had chosen one of the liberal parties in 1874 (as calculated from the regression equations, comparing the 1874 and 1877 elections). I have generally aggregated the elections pairs by decade, making an exception for the election pairs 1877/78 and 1878/81, which were a little different from other succeeding elections, because the electorate did not grow in size from one general election to the next.

Table 1 Previous Voting of Social Democratic Voters

	GENERAL ELECTION PAIRS				
VOTE AT PREVIOUS ELECTIONS	1871/74-1874/77	1877/78-1878/81	1881/84-1884/87	1887/90-1893/98	1898/1903-1907/12
CONSERVATIVES	0%	2%	2%	7%	4%
LIBERALS	5	7	6	16	6
MINORITY PARTIES	0	2	1	4	3
SOCIAL DEMOCRATS	31	66	46	59	64
NON-VOTERS	44	23	31	7	11
NET NEW VOTERS	19	—	15	7	12
TOTAL	99	100	101	100	100

In Bismarckian Germany, the Social Democrats certainly were to a great extent the party of the previous non-voters, who comprised the largest or second-largest group in the social democratic electorate. At each election before 1890, there were more social democratic voters who had not voted in the previous election than there were voters switching from all the other parties plus the net new voters taken together. But, conforming to the idea noted above of a shift from extensive to intensive growth in the social democratic electorate around 1890, the importance of previous non-voters for the SPD declined drastically in the Wilhelmine Era. Particularly in the decade of the 1890s, voters switching from other parties to the Social Democrats substantially outnumbered previous non-voters among the social democratic electorate. Indeed, if we just take the elections of 1890, the year of the Social Democrats' great leap forward when their share of votes cast almost doubled over the previous general election three years earlier, we find that just 7 percent of the social democratic electorate that year consisted of previous non-voters, as against 40 percent who switched to the Social

Democrats from another party. Previous non-voters did make up a somewhat larger part of the social democratic electorate in the German Empire's three twentieth-century general elections, yet here as well, these voters no longer possessed the significance that they had had for the party several decades earlier.

Another way to approach this issue would be to focus on the non-voters, asking how they voted in subsequent elections. Table 2 does this. As with Table 1, the columns give the averages of several election pairs, but in this case the percentages were calculated in the opposite direction. In the first column, for instance, the figure for the Social Democrats is the average of the percentage of the non-voters in the election of 1871 who voted for the Social Democrats in 1874, the percentage of the 1874 non-voters who chose the Social Democrats in 1877, and the percentage of 1877 non-voters who cast their ballots for the Social Democrats in 1878. Note that such a calculation excludes net new voters, since it only deals with people who were eligible to vote in a previous election, albeit had not done so. Consequently, there is no need to consider the 1877/78 and 1878/81 elections separately in this case, so that the election pairs can be grouped by decade.

Table 2 Non-Voters and Their Subsequent Choices

	GENERAL ELECTION PAIRS			
VOTE AT SUBSEQUENT ELECTIONS	1871/74-1877/78	1878/81-1884/87	1887/90-1893/98	1898/1903-1907/12
CONSERVATIVES	7%	8%	6%	5%
LIBERALS	12	12	3	9
MINORITY PARTIES	6	8	9	9
SOCIAL DEMOCRATS	5	4	4	13
NON-VOTERS	70	68	77	64
TOTAL	100	100	99	100

If previous non-voters were not crucial to the Social Democrats, the converse is also true: the Social Democrats were not the special choice of the previous non-voters. Compared with the other parties, the Social Democrats did quite poorly among the non-voters, in last or next to last place among them, until the twentieth century. Even then, previous non-voters (an ever smaller portion of the electorate) preferred the other parties to the SPD by a margin of almost two to one. These results should not be entirely surprising, since the general elections with by far the largest increases in turnout, when the most previous non-voters were mobilized to vote, those of 1887 and 1907, were victories for the parties of the right.

In contrast, voter turnout in 1890, the Social Democrats' *anno mirabilis*, actually declined from the levels of the previous general election.

We can pose still another relevant question by asking about the subsequent voting of social democratic voters. Table 3 gives the results, the figures in it calculated the same way as in Table 2.

Table 3 Subsequent Votes of Social Democratic Voters

	GENERAL ELECTION PAIRS			
VOTE AT NEXT GENERAL ELECTION	1871/74-1877/78	1878/81-1884/87	1887/90-1893/98	1898/1903-1907/12
CONSERVATIVES	4%	5%	6%	2%
LIBERALS	18	12	8	12
MINORITY PARTIES	0	0	1	1
SOCIAL DEMOCRATS	55	71	77	81
NON-VOTERS	22	11	8	4
TOTAL	99	99	100	100

The party's hold over its voters was far from absolute, between 15 and 20 percent of them defecting to other parties – most commonly, the liberals – from any one general election to the next. The proportion of social democratic voters leaving for other parties did go down a bit in Wilhelmine Germany as compared with the two previous decades, but remained fairly substantial through 1912. In contrast, the proportion of social democratic voters departing the SPD for the ranks of the non-voters declined throughout the history of the Imperial Germany, with the sharpest drop coming in the 1880s. The growth of the SPD's electorate, thus, can be attributed to the non-voters, but in a negative way. One of the secrets of the party's success was its growing ability to turn out the vote, to keep its supporters from becoming non-voters by bringing them to the polls. Although it was clearly easier to do this after 1890, when the party was no longer illegal, this mobilization process, as the figures suggest, had begun under the Anti-Socialist Law. Before the 1887 elections, for instance, the Hamburg Social Democrats completed the heroic task of copying the city-state's entire Reichstag electoral register, containing over 120,000 entries, so that party supporters could be ensured they were properly recorded and eligible to vote.[16]

If the regression estimates given in Tables 1 through 3 are even vaguely accurate, then the scholarly consensus on the Social Democrats as the party of the previous non-voters is simply not correct. In Bismarckian Germany, to be sure, a large proportion of the social democratic vote came from previous non-voters, but before 1887 men who did not cast their ballot made up between 40 and 50 percent of those eligible to do so, the single largest group in the electorate. They were a reservoir of potential voters for all the political parties, not just the Social Democrats. While attracting previous non-voters was one of the reasons that the SPD's vote totals steadily increased in Wilhelmine Germany, winning voters over from the other parties was a much more important cause of the Social Democrats' electoral success after 1890. The increasing turnover in the electorate, both geographical in the sense of voters moving from rural to urban areas, and natural, in that more conservative older voters died and more left-wing, younger ones reached voting age, also contributed to the party's advances at the ballot box.

The movement of voters from other sources to the Social Democrats was not a one-way street. Particularly in the 1870s, the nascent, struggling party had difficulty hanging on to its voters, getting them to vote from election to election. Persecution by the authorities clearly played a role here, but probably more important was the party's primitive organizational structure and meager resources in both finances and agitators. As they improved – and official prohibition could not keep them from doing so – the Social Democrats were able to mobilize their regular clientele ever more efficiently from one election to the next.

These results suggest, however, that the social democratic electorate also included a fairly sizable group of swing voters.[17] In Bismarckian Germany, these were mostly voters who swung away from the Social Democrats to other parties, typically the liberals. After 1890, the SPD began to attract voters from other parties in large numbers, above all the liberals, and, after 1900, to lose voters to the liberal parties once more. Throughout the Kaiserreich there was, thus, a constant stream of voters moving back and forth between the social democratic and liberal political parties. In Wilhelmine Germany, the SPD began gaining voters from the conservative and minority parties. There were fewer of them than former liberals among the SPD electorate, but unlike the case with the liberals, the voter flow from these parties to the SPD was primarily one way: once voters switched to the SPD from the conservatives and the minority parties, they were much less likely to go back. We might conclude from these results that for at least some voters there was not an insuperable mental barrier between the Social Democrats and the liberals; the possibility of switching from one party to another and back was not to be excluded. The change involved in switching allegiances from the Conservatives, the Center, or the Polish nationalists to the SPD clearly involved a greater effort and commitment: it was neither lightly taken nor easily revoked.

The confessional composition of the social democratic electorate is both more easily expressed and can be calculated more simply. Before presenting the results, I need to note one point. Figures are only given for Catholic and Protestant voters. There were far too few others – Jews, Mennonites, those of no religion and so on – for the procedures of ecological regression based on the 397 Reichstag constituencies to yield reliable estimates. A study of their voting behavior would require working with precinct-level data in individual constituencies where such groups were present in large numbers; for this essay, they have been included with the Protestants. This noted, Figure 2 gives the percentage of eligible Protestant and Catholic voters who cast their ballots for the Social Democrats.

Figure 2 Social Democratic Vote by Confession

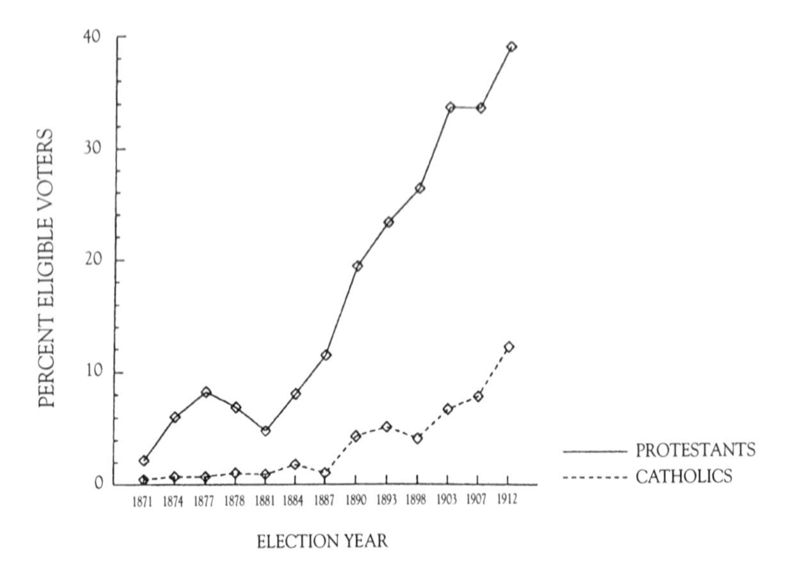

There is not much need to belabor the point. In all the general elections of Imperial Germany, Protestants were much stronger supporters of the Social Democrats than were Catholics. At no election before 1890 did as many as 2 percent of eligible Catholic voters cast their ballots for the Social Democrats. To be sure, the SPD had greater success among Catholic voters in Wilhelmine Germany, and the gap between the confessions closed a bit. The ratio of the percentage of eligible Protestant voters supporting the SPD to the percentage of eligible Catholic voters doing so declined from the six or eight to one it had been in Bismarckian Germany to about four to one after 1890. Still, the Social Democrats remained a Protestant party as the confessionally differentiated support for them at the last pre-war general elections in 1912 testifies. About 12 percent of eligible Catholics cast their ballots for the SPD, while 40 percent of their Protestant counterparts – 44 percent of Protestants actually voting – did. In other words, at the same time that Catholic support for the SPD finally reached double digits, the Social Democrats had almost become the majority party of German Protestants.

In this case, statistical analysis fully confirms the conventional wisdom and I would not quarrel with the standard explanation for this state of affairs. Many of the Protestants who supported the Social Democrats were Protestants in name only. The SPD was the party of the de-christianized, the party of the non-churchgoers, and the influence of organized religion had declined much more greatly among Protestants than among Catholics. Clergy and pious laymen of both Christian confessions denounced the Social Democrats in no uncertain terms, but there were fewer Protestants prepared to listen to them.[18]

Understanding the role of confession in determining the SPD electorate is a necessary precondition to studying the social class of social democratic voters, because class preferences in voting behavior among Germans were, and are, mediated by confession. The working class vote in, say, 1912 was an average of two quite different figures: the vote of Catholic workers and that of Protestant workers. For technical reasons, the voting choices of different social classes need to be calculated separately for each confession; even putting such technical considerations aside, it is more than a little illuminating to see how social, occupational, and confessional criteria interacted to create the social democratic electorate.

Before presenting some of the results, I need to make a few points about the limitations of the procedure. The single largest one is the relatively limited number of social groupings – once again for technical reasons – I could use. The practical maximum, in fact, was three and the three that I chose were 1) farmers, everyone gainfully employed in agriculture, including proprietors, tenants, managers, and laborers; 2) the middle class, composed of independent businessmen and craftsmen, salaried employees, civil servants, professionals, and rentiers; and 3) the working class, that is wage laborers in industry, crafts, commerce, and transportation and day laborers outside of agriculture. For each of these three groups, the percentage of social democratic voters has been calculated separately for the two confessions, thus, giving six results altogether: percentage of Protestant farmers supporting the SPD, percentage of Catholic farmers, and so on.

By this point, most readers will no doubt have raised a storm of objections to this whole procedure, so let me try to disarm in advance at least two interrelated criticisms that might emerge. First, it could be objected that these categories are far too broad, that they are not real social classes. Calculating the voting preferences of such a broadly defined middle class hides the real class issue – the attitudes of a tiny but wealthy and powerful capitalist bourgeoisie. Similarly, Junker landowners are lost in a broad sea of small proprietors and agricultural laborers.

One simple response to this objection is that calculating the voting choices of a small elite, numbering 5 percent or less of the population, is impossible with the methodology of ecological regression, at least from the nationwide data being used here. (Such small elite groups cannot be found in most broad-based contemporary public opinion polling, either.)[19] More important, though, we are dealing with elections held under a democratic franchise in which political parties had to have a mass base of support, extending well beyond the ruling class, in order to be successful. The dominant scholarly opinion about the Social Democrats is that their electoral base was limited not just because they could not get votes from the 5 to 10 percent of the wealthy and powerful in Germany society, but because they were unable to gain the support of a wider range of middle- and lower-class groups: farm laborers, smallholding farmers, master craftsmen, small shopkeepers, salaried employees, and lower-level civil servants. Such groups make up the vast majority of the first two categories in this study.

The reader might wonder, though, why it was necessary to stop at three categories, especially since comparable sorts of statistical studies of the Weimar Republic by Jürgen Falter and Thomas Childers employ a broader array of social groups, differentiating salaried employees from independent businessmen, for instance, rentiers and pensioners from those exercising an occupation, or workers in crafts from workers in industrial enterprises. The problem here is that the number of categories (since the explanatory categories act in the regressions as the independent variables) one can employ depends on the number of geographically aggregated units (the number of observations in the regressions) one has to work with. For the Weimar Republic, the geographical units making up the published census returns, from which one can ascertain class structure, and the geographical units making up the published election returns, giving the vote, are similar and easily comparable. Falter and Childers have between two and eight hundred aggregated units for their regressions, thus, permitting them to work with a larger number of categories. Unfortunately, the boundaries of the census and the election units in the Kaiserreich were quite dissimilar: they have to be grouped together to form geographically similar units, leaving me with just seventy-seven (from the 1895 census) or seventy-eight units (from the 1907 census) with which to work. Even using three categories is pushing the limits of what is feasible.

Having, thus, explained and defended this choice of social groups, a final point about their relative size is also necessary. The voting age under the Imperial constitution was twenty-five, but most people left school and entered the labor force at the age of fourteen or fifteen. Because the census returns include detailed breakdowns of the population by class and age, it is possible to eliminate underage individuals.[20] Age and class were related: 40 percent of male blue-collar workers were under twenty-five and hence ineligible to vote, while over 95 percent of the owners of farms and businesses, on the other hand, were of voting age. Non-agricultural workers, some 60 percent of the labor force, were just a minority of the Reichstag electorate: about a third according to the 1895 census and some 40 percent in 1907.[21] Protestant workers, in the standard interpretation the core constituency of the SPD, were just 24 percent of the electorate according to the census of 1907.

Let us begin with figures on the support for the SPD, broken down by confession and social group, at the party's pre-war high point, in the general elections of 1912. Each cell of Table 4 gives the percentage of eligible voters (not the percentage of votes cast) in the respective social and/or confessional group supporting the SPD.

Table 4 Percentage of Eligible Voters in Each Confessional and Social Group Choosing the SPD in 1912

SOCIAL GROUP	CONFESSION		
	PROTESTANT	CATHOLIC	ALL
FARMERS	8%	0%	5%
MIDDLE CLASS	45%	13%	35%
WORKERS	54%	22%	42%
ALL	39%	12%	29%

A greater proportion of Protestant, urban (more precisely, non-agricultural) workers did vote for the SPD than did members of any other social group, but almost as great a proportion of the Protestant middle class cast social democratic ballots. The most important determinant of SPD voting was occupation: the percentage of voters working outside of agriculture and voting for the Social Democrats outnumbered the percentage of farmers doing so by about seven-and-a-half to one. Confession was in second place, the ratio of the proportion of Protestant voters supporting the party to the proportion of Catholic voters being greater than three to one. Class was last, blue-collar workers' support for the party outnumbering the non-agricultural middle class by just 1.2 to 1. Class did make more of a difference among Catholics, with Catholic blue-collar workers being almost twice as likely to vote for the SPD than the Catholic middle class, but the difference between these social groups was much smaller for Protestant voters.

If these estimates are even approximately right, then they tell very powerfully against the scholarly consensus on the pre-1914 social democratic electorate. This actually ought not to be too surprising, when we remember that because the voting age was twenty-five, just 24 percent of eligible voters were Protestant blue-collar workers. Even if all of them had turned out to vote and had unanimously voted for the SPD, they would not have sufficed to make up the 29 percent of eligible voters who chose the party in 1912. If we assume that between 30 and 45 percent of these Protestant workers did not vote for the SPD, but were either non-voters or supported candidates of other parties (and about that many Protestant workers did not vote for one of the labor parties at most elections in the Weimar and Federal Republics), then at least 40 percent of the SPD's vote most have come from outside its core constituency.[22]

The 1912 elections were not a unique exception in this regard. Table 5 gives the proportion of different social and confessional groups voting for the SPD in Wilhelmine elections, the figures averaged by decade. As with the previous table, the entries in each cell are the percentage of eligible voters belonging to a social or confessional group choosing the SPD.

Table 5 Percentage of Eligible Voters in Each Social and Confessional Group Choosing the SPD in Wilhelmine Elections of the 1890s and 1900s

SOCIAL GROUP	CONFESSION					
	PROTESTANT		CATHOLIC		ALL	
	1890-1898	1903-1912	1890-1898	1903-1912	1890-1898	1903-1912
FARMERS	5%	6%	1%	0%	3%	4%
MIDDLE CLASS	24%	43%	6%	9%	19%	33%
WORKERS	40%	48%	8%	16%	29%	36%
ALL	23%	36%	5%	9%	16%	26%

At no general election in Wilhelmine Germany were the Social Democrats exclusively, or even very heavily, a party of blue-collar workers. Instead, they consistently drew support from a wide range of non-farm voters. Among these voters, the most important change between the 1890s and the three twentieth-century general elections of the Empire was determined by the intersection of class and confession. Protestant, blue-collar voters voted for the party in large numbers early on and their levels of support did not increase all that much after 1900. Although a substantial number of Protestant, middle-class voters cast their ballots for the SPD in the 1890s, the proportion who did so lagged behind that of working-class voters; after 1900, middle-class, Protestant support for the SPD increased substantially. For Catholic voters, the trend went in the opposite direction. About the same modest percentage of eligible middle-class and blue-collar Catholic voters cast their ballots for the SPD in the 1890s, but after the turn of the century Catholic workers increasingly outpaced their middle class counterparts in support for the Social Democrats.

In other words, it was members of the Protestant middle-class who accounted for the large majority of the non-working-class portion of the social democratic electorate. These voters were also responsible for a good deal of the increase in the SPD's voting totals during the Wilhelmine era. It would be interesting to know something more about who they were. Certainly, some of them were proletarianized master craftsmen, nominally independent, but really under the sway of merchant capitalists. The successes of the social democratic ticket in elections of the employers' representatives to the industrial conciliation courts – among other places, in Frankfurt and Nuremberg – suggests this. The middle-class group best represented in the SPD's membership, retailers and tavernkeepers with a working-class clientele, was presumably also a prominent part of the party's middle-class electorate.[23]

There is also a problem in the interpretation of the census figures. About 15 percent of the eligible middle-class voters were rentiers, and the census included in their ranks not just individuals living off their capital, but also recipients of pensions from the government social insurance system, and unfortunately the published returns do not distinguish between these two groups. Although old-age pensioners in Imperial Germany were few and far between, there was a rapidly growing number of recipients of disability pensions, so some of the "middle-class" rentiers voting for the SPD were really sick and injured workers.[24]

Still and all, there must have been a substantial group of Protestant businessmen, salaried employees, civil servants, and professionals who cast their ballots for the SPD. Careful local studies, generally not considered by proponents of the scholarly consensus on the social democratic electorate, have identified such middle-class SPD voters in Hamburg, Frankfurt, and Ludwigshafen.[25] Historians themselves have often noted that the Social Democrats presented themselves to the voters – from their first experiences with the Reichstag elections in the 1870s onwards – not as a workers' party but as a people's party, trying to rally a broad popular cross-section of the population against the regime. [26] Contemporaries knew about the cross-class nature of the social democratic electorate, the most famous example being the study of the sociologist Robert Blank. In 1905, he wrote that with regard to the SPD's "social composition … [it is] a great coalition party, in which the democratic elements of various social classes strive for liberty, equality and social progress."[27]

Although there have been a number of criticisms of Blank's analysis of the social democratic electorate, these criticisms did not touch the core of his argument, which was basically correct.[28]

Perhaps it is more accurate to say that Blank's assertions were correct for the urban society of Wilhelmine Germany, for the SPD found little support among the farming population. Although it is often forgotten, the party had made an enormous effort to win over farmers in the 1890s, with some signs of success early in the decade. Deciding on the appropriate ways to approach farmers and choosing the right issues to gain their votes was the single most important, perhaps the dominant question for the party during those years, passionately debated by members at all levels, from the leadership to the rank and file. Much of what would later be known as the revisionism controversy was about, or at least stemmed from, the debate on the relationship of the SPD to the agrarian population.[29]

In the end, the party had little to show for its effort, and the inability to gain any substantial degree of support from small-holding farmers or agricultural laborers represented the SPD's one major electoral defeat in Imperial Germany, a defeat with decisive consequences. It would permanently limit the party's appeal in a society where, for all its rapid urbanization and industrialization, a third of the population still earned a living in agricultural pursuits. Other socialist parties of the early-twentieth century, while never as successful at the ballot box as the SPD, were nonetheless able to recruit voters and members from the ranks of farmers and agricultural or forest laborers – in France, for instance, or Italy, Sweden, and even Oklahoma.

The reasons for the party's lack of success are many and complex, but the one to emphasize here is the central role in Wilhelmine politics of the linked question of farm prices and the cost of living. The outcome of the agrarian debate in the 1890s was that the SPD made itself unambiguously into a party of cheap food and, thus, low farm prices. As Hans-Georg Lehmann has convincingly demonstrated, this was largely a result of the spontaneous and angry intervention of the party's ordinary members in these discussions. The emphasis on this issue was a constant theme of the party's agitation from the late-nineteenth century to World War I – reaching its high point in the great, nationwide petition drive against the increase in agricultural tariffs of 1902 and the party's highly successful campaign in the general elections of the following year. While such an emphasis on food prices had a powerful appeal for Protestant middle-class urban consumers, and helped pry Catholic workers away from the Center, it meant abandoning the farming population to the agricultural special interest groups, the Agrarian League and the Christian Peasant Leagues, with their calls for higher farm prices via protective tariffs and their close ties to the Conservative, Center, and National Liberal parties. Precisely those issues that enabled the SPD to gain urban voters outside its core constituency alienated those Germans who earned their living producing food.[30]

All these regression analyses demonstrate the broad and diverse character of the social democratic electorate. SPD voters included long-term party loyalists, previous non-voters, new entrants into the electorate and, after 1890, former supporters of all the major political parties. The party's voters were disproportionately Protestant, although the representation of Catholics among them was increasing, particularly in the decade before the World War I. Finally, the social democratic electorate included large numbers of workers and members of the middle class, at least from the non-agricultural population. Besides contradicting most studies of the SPD in Imperial Germany, these findings also raise questions about the long-term electoral development of the party in the course of the twentieth century.

One point is whether the party had reached the limits of its support before 1914. If we define limits as the overwhelming majority of a social and confessional group, such as the 90 percent of Catholic farmers who have voted for the CDU/CSU at the Bundestag elections of the last forty years, then we would have to say the Wilhelmine SPD was very far from its limits. If we take into account future developments in the twentieth century, the situation is more complex. Comparisons of pre-1914 general elections with those in the Weimar and Federal Republics are complicated by a number of factors: the territorial changes of 1918, 1949, and 1990; a lowered voting age; the replacement of single-member constituencies with electoral systems based on proportional representation; and, most of all, the introduction of women's suffrage. Still, it is possible to sketch out some general developments, using as a basis for comparison Jürgen Falter's estimates of voting in the Weimar Republic based on ecological regression, and the polling data available for elections in the Federal Republic from 1953 onwards.

Falter has estimated that the proportion of Protestant workers voting for one of the labor parties – the SPD, USPD, or KPD – in the general elections of the Weimar Republic was generally in the 45 to 50 percent range, topping this figure, at close to 60 percent, only in 1920 – and probably in 1919 as well, although he has not analyzed the returns for that year. Table 4 gives the proportion of blue-collar workers supporting the SPD in 1912 as 54 percent, but because Falter includes agricultural laborers with other blue-collar workers, as I do not, his figures are not completely comparable to those in this paper. If one assumes, however, that all the Protestant farmers who voted for the SPD in 1912 were agricultural laborers (probably an exaggerated assumption, but useful to provide a rough basis for comparison), then about 47 percent of workers – by Falter's definition – supported the SPD that year. In other words, working-class Protestant support for the labor parties in the Weimar Republic only significantly exceeded pre-war working-class Protestant support for the SPD in the republic's two earliest, most revolutionary elections.

In the Federal Republic, on the other hand, Protestant working-class support for the SPD has been more substantial, ranging from 60 to 75 percent of votes cast, and this in a West Germany without such one-time strongholds of the labor movement as Saxony or Thuringia. In this case, we can compare the figures directly with my calculations, since the polling data from which these results are taken includes the very small number of agricultural laborers with other farmers.[31] In comparison to the 54 percent of Protestant workers voting for the SPD in 1912, or perhaps as a better comparison, the average of 48 percent of Protestant workers in the three general elections of 1903, 1907, and 1912, we can see a definite step forward for the party. Contrary to the scholarly consensus about the SPD in Imperial Germany, and to much of the sociological and historical literature on the decline of class consciousness in late-capitalist societies, the SPD has achieved by far its best results with (nominally) Protestant workers in recent decades.

The Protestant middle class presents a different story. Falter's figures on the proportion of Protestant white-collar workers and civil servants – the portion of the middle class he finds most sympathetic to the labor movement – voting for the labor parties throughout the Weimar Republic are in the 25 to 35 percent range, much less than was middle-class support for the SPD in the decade before World War I. Discussing the reasons for such a change go beyond the scope of this essay, but I would suggest that if the issue of high food prices, and the tax and tariff controversies surrounding it, played a major role in bringing Protestant middle-class voters to the SPD before 1914, the decline in significance of this issue was important in moving such voters away from the parties of the labor movement. Economic issues of comparable moment in the Weimar Republic, such as dealing with the great inflation, the post-1924 demands of creditors for the revaluation of their obligations, or the controversies over the salaries of the civil service, were not the sort that would attract middle-class voters to the SPD or KPD.

Once again, the social definitions in post-1945 polling data are much closer to the ones I have used in my ecological analysis. The polling results show that through the mid-1960s, middle-class Protestants cast their ballots for the SPD at levels 15 to 20 percentage points lower than their predecessors between 1903 and 1912. It was only in the SPD's two great election victories of 1969 and 1972 that middle-class Protestant support for the party reached the levels of the late Wilhelmine Era.[32] In other words, by 1912 the SPD had truly reached the historical limits of its support from this key group in its constituency.

The Social Democrats' support among the Catholic electorate, although still at modest levels in 1912 – just 12 percent – had been growing steadily for the previous two decades. These increases continued in the Weimar Republic, with between 15 and 20 percent of Catholics supporting one of the parties of the labor movement. Since, as is well known, female Catholic voters were much stronger supporters of the Center than were their male co-religionists, the increase in male Catholic support for the labor movement after World War I was more pronounced. This trend has continued in the Federal Republic, with the SPD receiving between 25 and 39 percent of the votes cast by Catholic voters. The high point, once again, was in 1972. This has meant that Catholics have been between one-half to two-thirds as likely to vote for the SPD as Protestants, compared to just one-third as likely in 1912. Although the SPD has remained to this day a predominantly Protestant party, the gap in voting support between the confessions narrowed after 1945.[33]

This brief long-term survey of the social democratic electorate does not entirely support the assertion found in much of the scholarly literature that the SPD went from being a workers' party to a people's party in the course of the twentieth century. The SPD was not a workers' party before World War I; the 1912 elections, in fact, seem to have marked a high point of Protestant middle-class support, at least for the next five decades. One important reason for the SPD's successes in the Federal Republic has been its ability to attract an ever greater share of the votes of its classical core constituency, urban Protestant workers. The massive support for the SPD that historians attribute to this group in the nineteenth century seems to have emerged only in the second half of the twentieth.

The social composition of SPD membership has taken a quite different course. Although there are no national membership statistics for the period before World War I, local figures have generally shown that blue-collar workers constituted over 90 percent of dues paying members. In localities where statistics for both the Kaiserreich and the Weimar Republic exist, they reveal a substantial increase in middle-class membership, to between 20 and 30 percent of party members. A nationwide survey of 1930 gave a membership that was about 58 percent workers, 20 percent various middle-class social groups, and 22 percent pensioners and housewives. Since the 1970s, about half the SPD's membership has consisted of middle-class social groups, and 30 percent blue-collar workers (down from 40 percent in the 1950s), with most of the remainder housewives and pensioners.[34]

These diverging trends between the SPD's membership and the party's electorate are less paradoxical than one might think, if we remember the position of the party in Wilhelmine Germany. The public act of joining – and joining was a public act, as membership lists had to be turned over to the police – meant signaling one's commitment to a political organization that, if not illegal, was the target of much hostility and persecution from the state and the most powerful groups in society. Blue-collar workers might do so, since the party and the affiliated organizations of the labor movement, particularly the unions and the consumer cooperatives, offered them prospects for a better life that could more than outweigh any disapproval of the authorities and the ruling class. But for civil servants, who could lose their jobs if they joined the party, salaried employees who were not organized into trade unions, businessmen and professionals facing loss of customers and a social boycott, the risks of membership far outweighed the benefits. The secret ballot, on the other hand, offered an opportunity to support the party, or to express one's discontent with the general state of affairs, without anybody having to know about it. The end of the Empire meant an end to the legal discrimination against the SPD, and at least the possibility of a gradual decline of prejudices against it, allowing middle-class individuals to join the party in greater numbers. At the same time, the switch to a republican form of government put the SPD in a position of political responsibility as it had not been before 1914, encouraging middle-class protest voters to select another political party to register that protest. The shift in economic issues around which a protest vote might be based, from food prices to the effects of inflation and its aftermath, only encouraged such a change in middle-class protest voting. We might say that before World War I, the middle class was underrepresented in the SPD's membership as compared with its electorate; between 1920 and the first decades of the Federal Republic, it was about equally represented in both categories; and in the last quarter-century it has been overrepresented in party membership as compared to the party electorate. These changing relationships suggest that historians ought to understand voting for a party and joining a party as two separate acts, not necessarily engaged in by the same groups of people, and should be careful to avoid drawing inferences about one from the other.

These observations, comparing the Empire with the Weimar and Federal Republics, leave out a period of German history when the government was violently hostile to the labor movement and the least that happened to the SPD was that it was outlawed. The Nazi regime is long thought to have resulted from a movement of the middle class, but as Jürgen Falter has demonstrated in a number of studies, the NSDAP's voters came in substantial numbers from all confessions and all social groups. Falter has gone on to assert that such a representation had been previously unknown, that the Nazis were, thus, the "first German people's party."[35] If we compare the Nazi electorate at the party's high point of support, the general elections of July 1932, with the SPD electorate of 1912, we might find some reason to question that assertion.

According to Falter, of the 31 percent of eligible German voters who cast their ballots for the Nazis, 83 percent were Protestants and 17 percent Catholics. The confessional breakdown of the 29 percent of eligible German voters who chose the SPD in 1912 was almost identical: 85 percent Protestant and 15 percent Catholic. The electorate of both parties was, thus, predominantly Protestant, with disproportionately low support from the Catholic population. In that sense, one often neglected by historians and social scientists fixated on class as a determinant of voting behavior, neither party was entirely a people's party, although they both did better than most parties outside of the Center in attracting Catholic votes.

Falter gives the social composition of the Nazi electorate as 39 percent workers, 19 percent civil servants and salaried employees, and 41 percent independent businessmen and farmers. Once again, my figures are based on a somewhat different social categorization; they show that 4 percent of the SPD voters in 1912 were farmers, 41 percent belonged to the urban middle class, and 54 percent were workers. The Nazis were strongest in the countryside and the small towns; Falter himself notes that a large number of the workers who voted for the Nazis were farm laborers. Given the nature of German society at the time, the social category "independent businessmen and farmers" contained a higher percentage of people in the agrarian sector than did either workers or the white-collar middle class. Consequently, this suggests the real difference between the two groups: the SPD was weakest among the farming population, while the Nazis were much stronger there. The SPD was strongest among the urban working class; the Nazis were weaker there, although not as weak as the SPD among farmers. Both parties had support in the urban middle class. SPD supporters in their ranks were more likely to live in big cities, Nazi supporters in small towns.

Both parties attracted a comparable amount of support from the electorate; neither was limited to one social or confessional group.[36] This comparison reinforces some points previously made here about the Wilhelmine SPD. Capping decades of organization and agitation, surviving government persecution and the open hostility of the wealthy and the powerful, it had attracted a large segment of the electorate, from diverse social, confessional, and political backgrounds. If not including large numbers of all groups – and the party's weakness with the agrarian population does stand out – it nonetheless had some voters from all groups and significant numbers from most. Rather than the Nazis, it was the SPD of the early-twentieth century that was the first German people's party.

NOTES

1. On these points, see Volker Eichler, *Sozialistische Arbeiterbewegung in Frankfurt am Main 1878-1897* (Frankfurt am Main, 1983), 79-84, 112; Rainer Paetau, *Konfrontation oder Kooperation: Arbeiterbewegung und bürgerliche Gesellschaft im ländlichen Schleswig-Holstein und in der Industriestadt Kiel zwischen 1900 und 1925* (Neumünster, 1988), 68; Adelheid von Saldern, *Auf dem Wege zum Arbeiter-Reformismus: Parteialltag in sozialdemokratischer Provinz Göttingen (1870-1920)* (Frankfurt, 1984), 56-58, 81; Wolfgang Schmierer, *Von der Arbeiterbildung zur Arbeiterpolitik: Die Anfänge der Arbeiterbewegung in Württemberg 1862/63-1878* (Hanover, 1970), 170-71, 182-83.
2. On German Social Democrats and parliamentarianism, see the very useful study of Elfi Pracht, *Parlamentarismus und deutsche Sozialdemokratie 1867-1914* (Pfaffenweiler, 1990), esp. 189-90, for the idea of the *Heerschau.*
3. Ibid., 119-20, and Paetau, *Konfrontation oder Kooperation*, 181. Similarly on the 1912 elections, Dieter Groh, *Negative Integration und revolutionärer Attentismus: Die deutsche Sozialdemokratie am Vorabend des Ersten Weltkrieges* (Frankfurt am Main 1973), 273.
4. M. Rainer Lepsius, "Parteisystem und Sozialstruktur: Zum Problem der Demokratisiserung der deutschen Gesellschaft," in *Die deutschen Parteien vor 1918*, ed. Gerhard Albert Ritter (Cologne, 1973), 56-80.
5. Examples of this consensus include Werner Conze, "Politische Willensbildung im deutschen Kaiserreich als Forschungsaufgabe historischer Wahlsoziologie," in *Vom Staat des Ancien Regimes zum modernen Parteistaat*, ed. Helmut Berding (Munich and Vienna, 1978), 331-47, here 342-43; Gerhard A. Ritter, "Die Sozialdemokratie im Deutschen Kaiserreich in sozialgeschichtlicher Perspektive," *Historische Zeitschrift* 249 (1989): 295-362; Dieter Fricke, *Handbuch zur Geschichte der Deutschen Arbeiterbewegung 1869 bis 1917*, 2 vols. (Berlin, 1987), 2: 718-44, esp. 743-44; Adelheid von Saldern, "Wer ging in die SPD? Zur Analyse der Parteimitgliedschaft in wilhelminischer Zeit," in *Der Aufstieg der deutschen Arbeiterbewegung: Sozialdemokratie und Freie Gewerkschaften im Parteiensystem und Sozialmilieu des Kaiserreiches*, ed. Gerhard A. Ritter (Munich, 1990), 161-83, esp. 164; Karl Rohe, *Wahlen und Wählertraditionen in Deutschland* (Frankfurt, 1992), 102-4; Groh, *Negative Integration*, 278-89; W. L. Guttsman, *The German Social Democratic Party, 1875-1933: From Ghetto to Government* (London, 1981), 87-112; Stanley Suvall, *Electoral Politics in Wilhelmine Germany* (Chapel Hill, NC, 1985), 80-84.
6. An example of such a study taking geographic ("ecological") units as its basis of analysis is Peter Steinbach, "Die Entwicklung der deutschen Sozialdemokratie im Kaiserreich im Spiegel der historischen Wahlforschung," in *Der Aufstieg der deutschen Arbeiterbewegung*, 1-37.
7. Two good introductions to the practice of ecological inference are J. Morgan Kousser, "Ecological Regression and the Analysis of Past Politics," *Journal of Interdisciplinary History* 4 (1973): 237-62, and Laura Irwin Langbein and Allan Lichtman, *Ecological Inference* (Beverly Hills and London, 1978). An important, although technically advanced work on the topic is Søren Risbjerg Thomsen, *Danish Elections, 1920-1979: A Logit Approach to Ecological Analysis and Inference* (Århus, 1987). The main results of Falter's research can be found in Jürgen Falter, *Hitlers Wähler* (Munich, 1990), and Jürgen Falter and Reinhard Zintl, "The Economic Crisis of the 1930s and the Nazi Vote," *Journal of Interdisciplinary History* 19 (1988-89): 55-85. An important methodological contribution of Falter

and his coworkers specifying the assumptions necessary for the validity of ecological regression is Jan-Bernd Lohmoeller, Jürgen Falter, Andreas Link, and Johann de Rijke, "Unemployment and the Rise of National Socialism: Contradicting Results from Different Regional Aggregations," in *Measuring the Unmeasurable*, ed. Peter Nijkamp, Helga Leitner, and Neil Wrigley (Dordrecht, Boston, and Lancaster, 1985), 357-70, esp. 365.

8. A convenient listing of the whereabouts of the published returns is in Gerhard A. Ritter and Merith Niehuss, eds., *Wahlgeschichtliches Arbeitsbuch: Materialien zur Statistik des Kaiserreichs 1871-1918* (Munich, 1980), 183-84. Unless otherwise stated, all figures and tables in this essay are from my calculations on these official statistics.
9. These estimates are based on non-linear, logistic regressions, which in this case give more reliable estimates than linear ones. (On this issue, cf. Thomsen, *Danish Elections*, 15-38.) Impossible results were adjusted using the proportional iterative fitting procedure described in Lohmoeller, Falter, Link, and de Rijke, "Unemployment and the Rise of National Socialism," 367-68.
10. Estimates are based on weighted linear regression, which yielded results virtually identical to those of logistic regression. Impossible results were adjusted using the above mentioned fitting procedure.
11. Technical difficulties are greatest for this group of regressions as well. There are serious problems of collinearity among the independent variables that invalidate the results of ordinary regression, whether linear or non-linear. I had to use ridge regression, a special procedure that alleviates the effect of collinearity, and to calculate the estimates of social groups for each confession separately. Impossible results were then fit against the estimates obtained in the previous group of regressions on the vote for the confessional groups as a whole. On ridge regression, see John Neter, William Wasserman, and Michael H. Kutner, *Applied Linear Regression Models*, 2nd ed. (Homewood, IL and Boston, 1989), 412-18. Special and heartfelt thanks to Professor Paul Speckman, Department of Statistics, and Dr. Linda Okamura, Campus Computing, of the University of Missouri, Columbia, for assistance with the ridge regressions.
12. Jürgen Falter, "War die NSDAP die erste deutsche Volkspartei?" in *Nationalsozialismus und Modernisierung*, ed. Michael Prinz and Rainer Zittelmann (Darmstadt, 1991), 21-47. There is an English translation of this essay, "The First German Volkspartei: The Social Foundations of the NSDAP," in *Elections, Parties and Political Traditions: Social Foundations of German Parties and Party Systems, 1867-1987*, ed. Karl Rohe (New York, Oxford, and Munich, 1990), 53-81.
13. The proportion is calculated from the official statistics requiring a minimum of 26 votes per constituency before a party's candidate would be listed, and not placed under the rubric of "scattered." Particularly at the first few elections, this rule was not strictly observed, so this procedure tends to underestimate, slightly, the extent of social democratic candidacies during the 1870s.
14. On these points, see in lieu of many other studies that might be cited, Eichler, *Sozialistische Arbeiterbewegung in Frankfurt am Main*, 26-224. A good overview of the 1890 campaign is in Wilfried Henze, "Die politische Massenarbeit der Sozialistischen Arbeiterpartei Deutschlands in Vorbereitung der Reichstagswahl 1890," *Beiträge zur Geschichte der Arbeiterbewegung* 27 (1985): 29-49.
15. Admittedly, this growth almost came to a stop in the general elections of 1907, when SPD votes were 24.6 percent of eligible voters in constituencies where the party put up candidates, as against 24.0 percent in 1903.

16. Helga Kutz-Bauer, *Arbeiterschaft: Arbeiterbewegung und bürgerlicher Staat in der Zeit der Großen Depression: Eine regional- und sozialgeschichtliche Studie zur Geschichte der Arbeiterbewegung im Großraum Hamburg 1873 bis 1890* (Bonn, 1988), 120.
17. The following comments refer to changes in voting between the first round of two subsequent general elections. Going from the first to the run-off round of one general election was a different matter. When their party was no longer in contention, voters could and did switch to parties they would never have supported in the first round.
18. On secularization, confession, and politics, see Vernon Lidtke, "Social Class and Secularisation in Imperial Germany: The Working Classes," *Leo Baeck Institute Yearbook* 25 (1980): 21-48.
19. One might be able to do it in a smaller-scale study, say of an individual city or rural area, based on precinct level voting returns, where elite groups might make up a larger proportion of the population under consideration.
20. The census returns allow the elimination of the two other large groups of ineligibles – women and active duty soldiers.
21. For a typical set of figures on the composition of the German labor force, see Guttsman, *The German Social Democratic Party*, 86.
22. For voting of Protestant workers (admittedly, defined somewhat differently, in different electoral systems, with a different age limit for voting, with women having the vote, and in a territorially different Germany), Falter and Zintl, "The Economic Crisis of the 1930s," 74-76; and Karl Schmitt, *Konfession und Wahlverhalten in der Bundesrepublik Deutschland* (Berlin, 1989), 315.
23. Heinrich Hirschfelder, *Die Bayerische Sozialdemokratie 1864-1914*, 1 vol. in 2 (Erlangen, 1979), 582; Eichler, *Sozialistische Arbeiterbewegung in Frankfurt*, 354-55; Saldern, "Wer ging in die SPD?" 166-67.
24. On recipients of social insurance pensions before 1914, see Volker Hentschel, *Geschichte der deutschen Sozialpolitik 1880-1980* (Frankfurt am Main, 1983), 24.
25. See Eichler, *Sozialistische Arbeiterbewegung in Frankfurt am Main*, 223-24; Kutz-Bauer, *Arbeiterschaft, Arbeiterbewegung und bürgerlicher Staat*, 162-64; and Rolf Weidner, *Wahlen und soziale Strukturen in Ludwigshafen am Rhein* (Ludwigshafen, 1984), 632-36. Another ecological analysis of the SPD's 1912 vote, using census data from 1925, has also concluded that there was a substantial Protestant and middle-class component to the party's electorate. Jürgen Winkler, "Die soziale Basis der sozialistischen Parteien in Deutschland vom Ende des Kaiserreichs bis zur Mitte der Weimarer Republik 1912-1924," *Archiv für Sozialgeschichte* 19 (1989): 137-71.
26. On this point, cf. Hirschfelder, *Die Bayerische Sozialdemokratie*, 258-60; Hans-Georg Aschoff, *Welfische Bewegung und politischer Katholizismus 1866-1918: Die Deutschhannoversche Partei und das Zentrum in der Provinz Hannover während des Kaiserreiches* (Düsseldorf, 1987), 186; Jörg Schadt, *Die Sozialdemokratische Partei in Baden: Von den Anfängen bis zur Jahrhundertwende (1868-1900)* (Hanover, 1971), 56-57.
27. Robert Blank, "Die soziale Zusammensetzung der sozialdemokratischen Wählerschaft Deutschlands," *Archiv für Sozialwissenschaft und Sozialpolitik* 20 (1905): 507-53. Two historians agreeing with his assertions are Jochen Lorek, *Wie man früher Sozialdemokrat wurde* (Bonn-Bad Godesberg, 1977), 88-90; and Geoff Eley, "Joining Two Histories: The SPD and the German Working Class, 1860-1914," in idem, *From Unification to Nazism: Reinterpreting the German Past* (Boston, 1989), 171-99, esp. 187.

28. A criticism of this argument, that is actually no criticism at all, is in Dieter Fricke, *Handbuch zur Geschichte der deutschen Arbeiterbewegung*, 742-43. To be taken more seriously are the remarks by Ritter, *Die Arbeiterbewegung im Wilhelminischen Reich*, 77-78, but the main point of Ritter's criticism, that a larger number of Catholic workers, and, hence, a smaller number of members of the Protestant middle class, voted for the SPD than Blank thought, is not confirmed by the regression estimates on Catholic support for the SPD.
29. On the SPD's agrarian agitation and the party debate on how to approach the farmers, there are two good studies: Hans Georg Lehmann, *Die Agrarfrage in der Theorie und Praxis der deutschen und internationalen Sozialdemokratie* (Tübingen, 1970), and Helmut Hesselbarth, *Revolutionäre Sozialdemokraten: Opportunisten und die Bauern am Vorabend des Imperialismus* (Berlin, 1968).
30. Lehmann, *Die Agrarfrage*, 175-90; Willi Breunig, *Soziale Verhältnisse der Arbeiterschaft und sozialistische Arbeiterbewegung in Ludwigshafen am Rhein 1869-1919* (Ludwigshafen, 1976), 236, 309; Bernd Liebert, *Politische Wahlen in Wiesbaden im Kaiserreich (1867-1918)* (Wiesbaden, 1988), 225-26; Brett Fairbairn, "Interpreting Wilhelmine Elections: National Issues, Fairness Issues and Electoral Mobilization," in *Elections, Mass Politics, and Social Change in Modern Germany: New Perspectives*, ed. Larry Eugene Jones and James Retallack (Cambridge, Mass. and New York, 1992), 17-48, esp. 36-39; Mary Nolan, *Social Democracy and Society: Working-Class Radicalism in Düsseldorf 1890-1920* (Cambridge, Mass. and New York, 1981), 157-64, 214; and especially the psychologically acute observations of Adelheid von Saldern, *Auf dem Wege zum Arbeiter-Reformismus*, 62-63, 76-77, 81-83, 89.
31. Polling data and definition of social categories from Schmitt, *Konfession und Wahlverhalten*, 113, 315.
32. Figures calculated from Schmitt, *Konfession und Wahlverhalten*, 315, by averaging the two categories *Selbständige* and *Angestellte + Beamte*. (The polling data gives SPD support as a percentage of votes cast – not of eligible voters – so to be comparable with my estimates the figures need to be reduced by the 10 to 15 percent of the electorate that does not vote in the Bundestag elections.) Since 1972, middle-class support for the SPD has declined again, but many of the middle-class voters leaving the SPD have chosen the Greens, thus, staying on the left side of the political spectrum.
33. Figures from ibid., 313-14; see also Gerard Braunthal, *The German Social Democrats since 1969: A Party in Power and Opposition*, 2nd ed. (Boulder, CO, 1994), 220-21. For much of the 1950s and 1960s, Catholic workers were about twice as likely to support the SPD as the Catholic middle class, just as had been the case in 1912, but since then the gap in SPD support between different Catholic, non-agricultural social groups has declined. Schmitt, *Konfession und Wahlverhalten*, 316.
34. Saldern, "Wer ging zur SPD?," 164-65; Richard Hunt, *German Social Democracy, 1918-1933* (New Haven, Conn. and London, 1964), 103-5; Peter Lösche and Franz Walter, "Auf dem Weg zur Volkspartei? Die Weimarer Sozialdemokratie," *Archiv für Sozialgeschichte* 29 (1989): 75-136, esp. 86-87; Braunthal, *The German Social Democrats*, 74-75.
35. Falter, "War die NSDAP die erste deutsche Volkspartei?," 41-44.
36. In one sense, the Nazis had a broader base in the electorate than the pre-war SPD, since they could receive the support of women, and of men aged twenty to twenty-five, who could not vote in the Kaiserreich.

Chapter 7

LATENT REFORMISM AND SOCIALIST UTOPIA

The SPD in Göttingen, 1890 to 1920

Adelheid von Saldern

1. Introduction

Historical research that focuses on the everyday life and social milieu of people at the local level changes substantially our understanding and interpretation of events. We begin to see people not merely as objects of great developments. Instead, we come to recognize the overarching importance of their subjective characters, which both express and shape the contours of daily life. From the local and subjective perspectives we find that people acquire reality in their own way. Their perceptions and experiences are frequently shattered by "objective categories" and often are not in line with the ordering system of scholarly research. Their appropriation of social realities does not necessarily follow the rules of an apparently rational procedure. Instead, interpretations of social reality may be mixed in people's minds in an individual and contradictory manner.[1] Often people cut themselves off from new observations that appear threatening and make them feel insecure. "The unknown is reduced to the supposed known, whose familiarity is merely assumed."[2]

The importance of the local and subjective perspectives is only underscored by the fact that the entire intellectual enterprise of " … grasping society as a whole, [of] conceptualizing its underlying principles of unity

Notes for this chapter begin on page 215.

... has passed into crisis."[3] At the same time, research into the world of everyday life illuminates workers (or members of other subordinate social groups) as independent thinking and acting subjects, a central aspect of their lives woefully neglected in most scholarly analyses.

To be sure, the effort to explicate the subjective lives of ordinary workers is a particularly difficult enterprise because they generally did not leave behind written records, and oral history is possible only for the more recent period. These difficulties only heighten the importance of investigating the *locality*, the only terrain in which it becomes possible to grasp the world of daily life and individual subjectivities. It is also primarily at the local level that one of the great cultural achievements of ordinary workers took place: their construction of the labor movement, notably the Social Democratic Party (SPD).[4] Yet even studies on the labor movement have generally neglected the ways of thinking and interpretive patterns of rank and file party members. A great deal has been written about the SPD leaders in the Imperial period – August Bebel, Karl Kautsky, Eduard Bernstein, and Rosa Luxemburg – but very little about the thousands upon thousands of unknown party members.[5] At best we read about the local party's official statements and activities, but there is almost nothing on those who constituted the party base. To uncover their lives, to illuminate the thoughts and views and practices of everyday people, vastly enriches our understanding of social democracy – and of daily life in general – in the nineteenth and twentieth centuries.

Hence, it was a unique discovery when the minutes of the SPD membership meetings in Göttingen from 1899 to 1911 were accidentally found in a storage room. The minutes permit a rough reconstruction of the discussions among the members. The texts are not immediately clear and easily understandable. There are many allusions; moreover, the speeches and discussions were only written down in indirect speech, in a very short form, and in bad German. Associations, illegible words, abbreviations, and the frequent usage of "etc." increase the difficulties of interpretation.[6] Fortunately for the historian, the internal meetings were observed by the police, who also left a record of the events. Their minutes were eventually written in a clearer and more legible form. Despite methodological problems, these two very different types of sources will be used together in the following article to reconstruct the ideas and attitudes of Göttingen Social Democrats in the context of their social milieu.[7] We will see how ordinary party members perceived politics and culture in general and party politics in particular, how they dealt with class and gender, and how certain elements of their milieu promoted the emergence of working-class reformism.[8]

"Reformism" is, however, a notoriously imprecise and politically charged term. Here I will use it not in a pejorative sense, but to describe a strategy that trusted in political and social reforms as the means of changing society. I will also use it as a term for an historical process that in Germany depended, above all, on the idea of the social welfare state, on the belief that out of the experience[9] of intense social conflict between workers, on the one hand, and the representatives of state and society, on the other, the state itself could ameliorate the harsh conditions of industrial life and aid in the transformation to a more just society.

"Radicalism" is no less a problematic term, and I use it also in a descriptive sense. The opposite of reformism, radicalism signifies offensive and aggressive attitudes and actions that often entail the deliberate violation of the rules of law and order. Radicalism involves a political strategy directed toward the fundamental transformation of society, often through revolution.

Reformism and radicalism are both nourished by two different roots, a social one and a political one. "Social reformism" and "social radicalism" signify that the specific orientation – reformism or radicalism – is closely entwined with the socio-cultural position of the individual or group in society.[10] Social reformism, for example, had its best chance for success in a local milieu in which the working class had not completely dissolved its ties to the local society and the local church, where workers were, at least in part, integrated into local society. "Social radicalism," in contrast, arose most often where workers, for many reasons, were *not* integrated but lived as "outcasts" among the established milieu, as did, for example, the migrants in the Ruhr region who stemmed from the eastern provinces. In this sense the origins of social reformism and social radicalism are to be found less in different mentalities and views of the world than in different situations and milieus.[11] While social reformism involved a political practice limited to legally permissible actions, social radicalism easily led to spontaneous, radical, illegal, and aggressive actions against "the oppressors."[12]

"Political reformism" and "political radicalism" mean something quite different. Both were less rooted in a particular local milieu. They entailed, instead, more intellectualized and more formally politicized systems of thought about long-term political goals and strategies.[13] This is clearly the realm in which the conflict among the different wings of the SPD during the Kaiserreich played out. The revisionist-reformist wing around Eduard Bernstein was diametrically opposed to the radical wing of Rosa Luxemburg and Karl Liebknecht. Party unity was preserved temporarily by Karl Kautsky's "in-between" position until the SPD finally split apart in 1917, first in the reformist Majority Social Democratic Party (*Mehrheitssozialdemokratische Partei Deutschlands*, or MSPD) and the leftist and pacifist Independent Social Democratic Party (*Unabhängige Sozialdemokratische Partei Deutschlands*, or USPD), followed by the foundation of the Communist Party (*Kommunistische Partei Deutschlands*, or KPD) in December 1918.[14]

The question to be raised, however, is whether using the analytical coordinates of the more formalized conflict between political reformism and political radicalism offers much insight into the social democratic world at the local level. This is especially the case given the fact that uniformity and centralization have lost their character as positive norms – in historiography as in so much else. Certainly, the notion that a less developed region – like Göttingen – will necessarily follow the same path as more highly developed areas has proven to be an utter chimera.[15] Rather than posit a standard model, we should ask about the *particular* possibilities and difficulties that a party faces in the province. What Aristide R. Zolberg wrote about nations is also true for localities: "If the advent of industrial capitalism … necessarily fostered the emergence of a working class, it did not of itself determine the dynamics of its development and its resulting structure. Viewed from this perspective, the process of working-class formation appears as the gradual crystallization of a limited array of patterns out of a broad spectrum of possibilities."[16]

2. Working-Class Life in Göttingen

In 1907, about one-half of the German population lived in middle-sized towns like Göttingen, in smaller towns, or in the countryside. Working-class life in a middle-sized or small town was not better than in a big city, and workers faced no less serious problems.[17]

In 1900, Göttingen was a city of around thirty thousand inhabitants, among them many students, members of the educated bourgeoisie (*Bildungsbürgertum*), and soldiers. The city experienced industrialization, but not as early or as intensively as the major industrial regions of the Ruhr or Saxony. Alongside older branches like textiles and tobacco, the "new industries" of the 1890s, especially electrical and precision engineering, led a surge of economic development in the town. The new industrial sectors were often connected to research institutes at Göttingen's old and prestigious university.

Economic development resulted in intensified urbanization, though, again, at a more leisurely pace in comparison with the more concentrated industrial regions of Germany. From 1890 to 1910 the population increased from 22,000 to 33,500. Many migrants came from the agricultural surroundings, from which workers commuted daily into the city to work. Others came from more remote villages and only returned to their homes on the weekend.

Most of the working-class people were quite poor. In 1892/93 14,533 inhabitants (65 percent of the population) earned less than nine hundred marks a year, a percentage that remained fairly constant until 1914. Precision mechanics constituted a small upper stratum, while most members of the working class, employed in handicrafts or in small firms, were badly paid compared to other regions, even though prices were quite high. Göttingen was said to be the most expensive city in the region of the former Kingdom of Hanover, partly as a consequence of the local taxes on such basic food items as alcohol, flour, meat, and beer. To increase their income the workers' wives had to earn some "supplementary" money, or the family had to take in lodgers. A segment of workers also had small allotments for subsistence gardening. And while the housing situation was a bit better than many other cities, workers' flats were unhealthy and deficient even according to the standards of the time.[18]

Unlike many other industrial areas, Göttingen had no mines. But the conditions of labor were hard. Workshops and factories were not well electrified and were poorly ventilated. Since the 1890s a ten-hour work day (except Sunday) and a two-hour break at noon were customary. Many of the workers were skilled but had few prospects of becoming independent artisans, and wages and working conditions in the small shops were often worse than in the factories. Schooling for workers' children was of average quality, perhaps even better than in other Prussian towns. Young people who were not apprenticed had to keep a work diary (*Arbeitsbuch*) issued by the police so that it was easier to check on them.[19]

Job possibilities existed for young girls and women, but these invariably were poorly paid and offered few prospects for the future. Many girls worked in households as maids or in restaurants and in shops. The large number of university students – uniformly male – and soldiers in Göttingen led to a high rate of illegitimate births. The Protestant church, meanwhile, continued to maintain its hold on the vast majority of the population.

In sum, at the turn of the century Göttingen, the city of the well-known university, was anything but a sleepy town. Certainly, work and life were still stamped by handicraft rather than factory production. The core of the workers were dependent "respectables" who formed a dense social network, while the commuters, the unskilled, and the migrating poor existed more or less at the fringes of this network.

3. Göttingen Social Democrats and Their View of State and Society

The Göttingen Social Democratic Party was founded in 1891, just after Bismarck's Anti-Socialist Law had lapsed. The number of party members reached 256 in 1910, a third of whom were women. Most of the male members were craft workers who labored in small shops presided over by petty-bourgeois employers.[20] Only a few members were independent artisans or shopkeepers, but they held influential positions in the party. Notable among them were the party leaders Wilhelm Stegen and Fritz Wedemeyer.[21]

Although the Göttingen Social Democrats did not concern themselves with the capitalist system as a whole, they were well aware of specific features of capitalism, such as workers' separation from their means of labor and the exploitative system of dependent wage labor. "The suppression of a class leads to class struggle" was a favored slogan. This point of view was due, first, to the decline of the older world of self-employed handicraft workers and, second, to a feeling of injustice which was based on the idea of "moral economy."[22] The sense of exploitation was also manifest in the widespread feeling that the upper "ten thousand" lived in luxury at the expense of those who actually labored. Master shoemaker Lange expressed this view at one of the meetings of the Göttingen Social Democrats: The capitalists "wanted only to suck dry the blood of workers. This must be changed. Wages have to be raised and the work day shortened."[23] Even the charity given by "them" to poor workers was not seen as a gift but as a chance of getting back a little bit of what basically belonged to workers: unemployment, bad housing, high taxes, the "proletarian illness" of tuberculosis, very long working hours, and high food prices – all the realities of daily existence frightened the Social Democrats, whose fear of starvation remained ever present.

Without citing "great theories" like Marxism, Göttingen Social Democrats understood concrete events as class-related.[24] They did not trust the ability of the Wilhelmine state to carry through important social reforms.[25] Indeed, they focused much of their attention on the Reich government in Berlin, which did, after all, produce the decisions that had grave ramifications for daily life, such as protective tariffs that raised the price of food.[26] The local and the regional, in contrast, were regarded as secondary concerns, a sentiment accentuated by the Social Democrats' desire to distance themselves from the seemingly "backward" former kingdom of Hanover, which became a Prussian province after 1866.[27] Social Democrats did, after all, accept the German national state as it had been founded in 1870 to 1871. They criticized not its existence, but many of its particular features: the constitution, the perceived lack of civil liberties, social inequities, and the Emperor with his rigid opposition to social democracy. Political scandals, such as the "Tippelskirch case," provided much grist for the social democratic mill of contemplation concerning the state administration.[28] The popularity of a scandal was presumably based on the narrative (suspense) components – such as a subject and a concrete plot – which characterized in general every scandal story.[29] These narrative (suspensive) components presumably made discussions easier for the members.[30]

The Göttingen Social Democrats were convinced that laws and judicial practice did not give workers and the workers' movement the same rights as other classes and organizations.[31] They accused the government of violating the constitution and analyzed cases of "class justice" and the brutal deployment of the police and military against strikers. Furthermore, they criticized both colonial policy and militarism. In their view, the veterans organizations (*Kriegervereine*) in Göttingen and elsewhere represented (petty) bourgeois military culture and authoritarian politics,[32] yet also provided competition to the social democratic workers' clubs. The Göttingen Social Democrats could not understand why these bourgeois clubs succeeded among many workers. "They want to be workers' associations .... In reality they are nothing more than tools in the fist of officials and employers." On other occasions the question was, how could workers forget that they were "wage slaves"?

In sum, although terms like "exploitation" and "wage slaves" stemmed from the arsenal of the Marxist critique of capitalism, the complaints in Göttingen were based less on the principles and basic patterns of the system and more on the concrete examples of the abuse of power, mismanagement, and injustice.[33] This sort of criticism was sometimes combined with a utopian hope, the rather ill-defined "ultimate goal" (*Endziel*).[34] In somewhat uneasy fashion, utopian hopes were entwined with the more prevalent pattern of "party realism." On very rare occasions, however, "great goals" were at least vaguely described, and they included "the freedom of the people" or "the rise of the workers," "the liberation from the chains of capital," "the end of wage labor," or "heaven on earth." As one of the minutes recorded: "Stegen called again for more active agitation and requested that each and every member keep in view the party's glorious goal *(schöne Ziel)*, its desire to make 'the world a kingdom of heaven for all, a realm that expresses all that is most human in men.'"[35]

The hopes that capitalism and the welfare state would in the long run improve living conditions constituted the soil for the flowering of political reformism. In Göttingen, however, Social Democrats had little basis for such hopes. Hence, political reformism remained undeveloped and the "ultimate goal" retained a profound resonance.

4. "Kampf" (Struggle) as a Path to New Society

The term *Kampf* (struggle) was central to the world view of Göttingen Social Democrats. *Kampf* meant, first of all, an institutionalized, legitimized struggle, namely the election campaigns for the Reichstag. These elections were the strongest challenge for the Göttingen SPD, the preeminent moment when they sought to mobilize and also move beyond the proletarian milieu to create a *Volkspartei* (people's party) by attracting middle-class votes, especially those of self-employed artisans and shopkeepers. In the view of Göttingen Social Democrats, electoral campaigns afforded the opportunity of " … enlightening the people, which brings us step by step further and closer to our goals …. The struggle conducted unceasingly against us has this advantage: We continually win new supporters because the people attain enlightenment through struggle …. Therefore we have every reason to look optimistically to the future."[36]

Although the number of the Göttingen social democratic voters was relatively impressive, they always failed to win a seat in the Reichstag.[37] To their intense disappointment, the educated bourgeoisie, highly represented in this university city, remained resistant to the siren song of socialism. Indeed, so disappointed were they that they predicted the emergence of a revolutionary situation in Germany not because of the activism of the working class, but because of the hostility and political backwardness of the bourgeoisie.[38] Yet like the centrist leader Karl Kautsky, the Göttingen Social Democrats did not dissociate elections and revolution.[39] The idea was that the SPD would one day gain the majority in an election and come into power. The ruling classes were expected to attempt to prevent the Social Democrats' legitimate takeover of power through a *coup d'etat*, which, in turn, would initiate a reaction on the part of the workers leading to revolution.[40] Hence, revolution would result from the unjust and irresponsible deeds of the ruling class.

At central party congresses the Göttingen Social Democrats tended to ally with the middle and right wings of the SPD.[41] Moreover, in the course of time the concept of revolution waned in significance and elections actually became the center of inner party life in Göttingen. Elections meant agitation and organization anchored in the everyday life of the party – since elections demanded a great deal of effort, especially in a provincial town. Brochures and other propaganda material had to be distributed not only among the people in the city, but also in the surrounding villages and small towns.

Alongside elections, strikes served as the central element of *Kampf*. But Rosa Luxemburg's belief in economic strikes as a "volcanic source" of revolution was not widely held among Göttingen Social Democrats. Many of them feared that Luxemburg's strategy of promoting mass strikes would lead to bloodshed. As a leading Social Democrat stated: "Here in Germany we don't want to run into bayonets or in front of cannon barrels. We want everything resolved correctly and properly."[42] Indeed, strikes in Göttingen were anything but clarion calls of revolution. Most occurred in regulated forms and ended in compromise with the employers. The striking workers wanted "only" to receive what other workers had already, namely, the elimination of the economic backwardness and the accompanying low wages of the province.[43]

Thus, workers believed in a "moral economy" marked by "just" wages, which, in their minds, made strikes a legitimate weapon of struggle. Under certain circumstances this attitude could have led to radicalism, a development that in Göttingen was, however, hindered by the courts of arbitration *(Einigungsgerichte)* and local wage committees *(Ortstarifämter)*, both of which were promoted by the mayor and the municipal officials. These new bodies, composed of equal numbers of employer and employee representatives and presided over by a leading municipal official, were responsible for negotiations and arbitration, and often led to formal labor contracts – still a rare occurrence in many other regions and industries of Germany.[44] In the view of workers, strikes and negotiations constituted the two, inextricably linked arms of industrial conflict. In the Göttingen world, wage strikes could not become a "volcanic source" because they were already channeled by corporatism and regulations. Indeed, for all of its "backwardness," Göttingen had a strikingly modern system of industrial relations by the turn of the twentieth century, a pattern that strengthened the tendency toward reformism.[45] In many ways, the industrial system outpaced Göttingen politics, in which a restrictive municipal voting law and a ban on street demonstrations deprived the SPD of influence. Because of the lack of local political power, Social Democrats directed their attention to the national level – in marked distinction from other reformist SPD groups, which tended to concentrate on the locality.[46]

5. Organization as Politics

Göttingen Social Democrats, like those elsewhere in Germany, devoted the greatest part of their energies toward developing the party organization itself. This was not merely "organizational fetishism," for in their view, substantive political and social change, the movement toward the new society, would only come about when workers had built successfully a powerful, popular political party.

Yet the beginnings of the working-class movement in Göttingen were anything but glorious. A number of efforts had been made to establish workers' associations in the Revolution of 1848 and again in the late 1850s. None of these had much success, nor did the attempt in the 1870s to establish a branch of Ferdinand Lassalle's General German Workers Association (ADAV). So little resonance did these efforts have that Göttingen Social Democrats had no knowledge or memory of them. Indeed, in their "social logic" they had little need for a collective memory of their unsuccessful socialist forebears. Instead, they looked to the future, to the transformative capacities of the central state and the national party and to the ever-growing links between German social democracy and the international workers' movement.[47]

The real history of social democracy began, then, after 1890 and especially after 1900 – at least in the view of local party activists. However tenuous the beginnings, they understood the development of the local organization as an absolute necessity if the SPD were ever to gain the desired majority in the Reichstag. The organization could not be strong enough, hence, they willingly listened to every bit of well-meaning advice and support, even when it meant a decline in local autonomy in favor of provincial centralization. As one activist expressed the point: "Should the proletariat one day assume leadership, then it is first necessary that the working class be brought to a higher level by its organization."[48] Indeed, the provincial party organization in Hanover considered the weakness of the Göttingen local a prime opportunity to extend its help and simultaneously gain influence.[49] As a result of this situation, the SPD in Göttingen was urged to increase the members' dues in order to contribute more to the regional party center in Hanover, which itself was increasingly taxed by its efforts to assume greater responsibility for agitation and organization in the entire region.[50]

Their somewhat precarious situation resulted in a certain level of insecurity among the Göttingen Social Democrats. They lacked the confidence in their own abilities that would have allowed them to follow their own path – if such a thing existed – and resist the increasing assertiveness of the provincial organization, which spared no occasion to remind the Göttingen group how really dependent they were on the support from Hanover. Committed to strengthening the party organization at all costs, the Göttingen Social Democrats voluntarily incorporated themselves into the regional party, which, under the domination of the revisionist and reformist wings, promised to guide Göttingen social democracy to success.

As the Göttingen SPD became increasingly subject to directives from beyond the city limits, it also became involved in three great national and even transnational movements: May Day, the campaign for free and equal suffrage, and anti-war agitation.

In Göttingen, May Day was not a day marked by walkouts from the factory and by street demonstrations.[51] In contrast to some centers of the social democratic movement, the Göttingen SPD did not even attempt to obtain the right to demonstrate in public. As a consequence May Day was celebrated in a legal way, that is during the evening hours in a meeting room or on Sunday, if possible combined with a day trip and a ball. The protests against the inequitable Prussian three-class voting system were carried out in the same manner. Meeting not in the streets but in the relative safety of rooms and halls, Göttingen Social Democrats listened attentively to a speaker – generally sent by the Hanover party organization – and invariably passed a resolution that condemned the existing electoral system. The entire procedure was relatively formal and "civilized."

The same characteristics of orderliness and formalism also marked the pre-1914 protest meetings against armaments and war. The basically pacifistic mood of the Göttingen Social Democrats concerned a war of aggression, not a war of national defense. In 1914 the government merely had to define credibly the start of World War I as a necessary measure of national defense in order to neutralize or to gain the support of the local Social Democrats. By joining the national consensus in favor of war, Göttingen Social Democrats, like their comrades elsewhere in Germany, demonstrated that they formulated their positions based upon a rather simple and clear conception of society, classes, and the decision-making process – a mode of operation that failed to capture the complexities and ambiguities of modern developments.

The collaboration with the trade unions only strengthened the tendency towards social reformism within the party. But these characteristics did seem to have a positive effect on the membership rolls. After some initial hesitancies, union members began to enter the ranks of social democracy in Göttingen in increasing numbers.[52] Furthermore, the party and the unions worked together on a number of campaigns: the Committee for Young People, the library, the Committee for Education, the Legal Aid Bureau, and the May Day celebration.

In most towns and cities, a variety of workers' organizations – sports associations, theater groups, choirs, hiking clubs, and many others – were linked to the SPD. They helped create the dense network of communications and social relations that characterized the German labor movement and that provided the main bridge between the realm of formal politics and the culture of daily life.[53] Labor movement organizations in this broad sense – party, unions, and social, cultural, and sports associations – thereby strengthened the so-called "secondary" or "negative" integration of Social Democrats into Imperial German society.[54] Yet in Göttingen and other provincial towns, few of these ancillary labor associations existed. A workers' gym club and a singing club, a cooperative, and the Legal Aid Bureau had been established, but that was a rather poor showing compared to other SPD locals.[55] Nor did the Göttingen SPD have its own local newspaper. If Göttingen workers had created a denser web of organizations, no doubt the level of social democracy's "negative integration" into the local society and polity would have been still greater.

6. "Bildung und Kultur" (Education and Culture) as Politics

Göttingen Social Democrats – following party leader Wilhelm Liebknecht's claim that knowledge is power (*"Wissen ist Macht"*) – considered education a means of improving the life circumstances of individuals and of changing society. They demanded, therefore, the democratization of education and culture, of school and university, and believed in workers' permanent desire for self-education and the positive effects of enlightenment. Stegen, the local SPD leader, argued that education consisted of three parts – scientific, physical, and artistic – all of which were essential to develop the full human capabilities of individuals.[56]

In sharp contrast to most other social democratic organizations, the Göttingen local did not emphasize the German classics. The SPD did not sponsor Schiller festivals, for example, and claimed that a classics education in arts was insufficient among workers in a provincial town like Göttingen.[57] Naturalistic plays, which depicted the real-life situation of common people, were regarded as more appropriate. The Committee for Education did, though, organize cultural events in which Social Democrats laid claim to the Enlightenment and classical cultural heritage.[58]

History and science were accorded more importance than the literary classics of German culture. For Social Democrats, with their eminently nineteenth-century, linear conception of progress, history provided the key to understanding politics and society and the evolutionary rise of their own party.[59] Their interest in Charles Darwin and his theory of evolution strengthened their belief in the linear course of historical development and legitimized their rejection of the biblical explanation of the genesis of the world.[60] The commitment to science and technology also reflected the workers' own desire for competence in these fields. In Stegen's words: "Social democracy is a party of culture and wants to see the lower classes participate in the achievements of art and science .... Just as our pioneers Lassalle and Liebknecht committed their life's efforts to the uplifting of workers, so we also should strive to bring ourselves to a higher intellectual level by reading good books – for which our library offers the best opportunity – and by listening to educational lectures. In this way we will be able to participate in the achievements of art and science."[61]

From 1914 on there are records of the books acquired by the library. Some of the books dealt with contemporary social issues and with social movements or other historical topics. Among the specifically socialist authors were Franz Mehring, Prosper Lissagaray, Friedrich Engels, Eduard Bernstein, Paul Louis, and Karl Kautsky. Books on science and technology, for example Specht's *Entwicklungsgeschichte der Welt* (*The History of the Development of the World*) or Nimführ's *Die Luftfahrt* (*Air Travel*), and tales and descriptions of the mores and customs of other countries, such as Nansen's *Eskimoleben (Eskimo Life)* and Lagerlöf's *Herenhofsaga*, were also well represented. However, the library was actually not often used by members. Apparently, workers preferred to receive information and knowledge via oral communication and evidently had problems coping with the written language.

For all of their commitment to science, rationalism, and the theory of evolution, Göttingen Social Democrats had extremely ambiguous attitudes towards church and religion – so far as it is possible to determine them. They rejected the church as an institution that presented odd stories on the genesis of the world and as a supporter of the hated Wilhelmine system, yet they "were not completely alienated from the church,"[62] as some clergymen commented. This ambiguity was legitimized by the general party tendency to regard religion as a "private matter."

All of the activities of the Göttingen SPD were subject to strict police surveillance. The party continually protested these activities, but to no avail. Gradually Social Democrats became accustomed to surveillance, and even learned to use creatively the incessant police presence as a means of informing municipal officials about their complaints and criticisms.

Order and discipline were never exclusively values imposed on the local SPD by the strict regulations of the local, state, and national governments. Order constituted a basic value and pattern of the party's culture. For Social Democrats in Göttingen and elsewhere, progress – social progress as well as the SPD's advance to majority status – could only be achieved through an ever more disciplined party.[63] One example may illustrate what order meant concretely: The Social Democrats wrote special regulations for their library in which strict rules for the handling of the book-lending system were established – as if there were not only a cupboard of books but a normal-sized library with many readers. Certainly the regulations resulted from the financial sacrifice every purchased book meant for them and from the highly symbolic value of the library. Yet the detailed rules demonstrate the way internal party life could be taken over by existing norms of order and regulation.

The same can be said concerning such values as dignity, decency, morality, and honor – all terms of immense importance in the cultural world of social democracy. Social Democrats wanted the workers to become aware of their dignity and were extremely sensitive when they were made to feel like second-class citizens. They rejected, for example, the one-sided familiar "you" (*Du*) which employers once used when talking to workers during a strike. They also protested against the long waiting queues during public vaccinations as well as the rude tone toward workers in the hospital. To be respected as a full human being was an important matter for them and language was often considered a demonstration of how they were seen by "the others." The emphasis on respecting human dignity shows that social democracy and trade unionism were movements committed to changing not only political and economic conditions, but also the patterns of everyday culture.[64]

This sensitivity toward manners was also directed toward the SPD's own members. Party festivals and meetings were to be performed with dignity – especially the May Day celebration, which should lift up and "ennoble" the participants and should offer a sparkling contrast to the normal, everyday grey and ugly world that enveloped workers.[65] Dignity also meant moderation especially with respect to alcohol as well as the rejection of the "craving for pleasure." Party policy was considered a serious matter and only "moderate pleasures" were suitable. May Day again served as a model – drinking, singing, dancing, and chatting, but in disciplined and moderate forms. Social Democrats expected enhanced power and reputation by disciplining their own physical urges and cultivating "respectability." They attached great importance to the socio-cultural distinctions between "proper, respectable" workers and the "others," even when the others constituted the rank and file of their own party. In fact, "respectable" behavior was leading, step by step, to the informal social – not political – acceptance of Social Democrats by the municipal officials and the police. The party members as well as many workers outside the party became socially respected and integrated as workers and inhabitants into Göttingen society – they were seen as "disciplined," hence "respectable," people, though still not as equal citizens nor as politicians who represented a distinctive constituency.

Until 1909 the members met in a pub located in the center of the city, a working-class neighborhood with old and poorly equipped houses. The "library" – really a cupboard of books and SPD periodicals – created the "right" party atmosphere. Usually, pub owners were pressured by the police and boycotted by soldiers and students if they granted meeting space to the SPD. So party members were grateful to find at least one pub owner who was willing to lease them space. In this pub, usually fifteen to twenty members met regularly twice a month, later once a month. Step-by-step the members learned how to handle the formal rules for associations and the discipline that was necessary for regular procedures during the meetings. They sought to impress the ever-present two policemen with their "professionalism" and formal correctness.

During the meetings, especially in the first years, the members often read some articles aloud. Most of these stemmed from the *Neue Zeit*, the periodical written by the Kautsky group, and *Vorwärts*, the official party newspaper. After some years the readings became rarer; instead, some of the members gave extemporaneous speeches that, in general, did not follow the principle of "exemplary learning."[66] Their talks were often characterized by a *tour d'horizon* method in which many matters were only briefly mentioned. It seems as if nobody wanted to be regarded as "provincial," as if the Göttingen Social Democrats derived a sense of security from the fact that they were part of a much larger world and an international movement. For example, a weekly political report touched on Russia, Austria, Belgium, England (the Boer War), the USA, Martinique, and German Polish policy, as well as the salaries for parliamentary deputies and the instability of the German government.[67] In another example, Stegen gave quite a long talk. As recorded in the minutes: "Comrade Stegen mentioned at first the peace manifesto that the Russian czar had announced a few years ago, then began to speak about the horrors that have occurred in Russia, the Russo-Japanese War, and the Herero uprising. Moving on to the domestic situation, Stegen spoke about the alleged Königsburg Geheimbund (Secret League) and touched on the theme of anarchism and social democracy and the struggle in the Reichstag. The speaker warned the gathering about the Bund der Landwirte (Agrarian League) and the struggle of the doctors and the sickness funds."[68] *Tour d'horizon* lectures can be seen – in some ways – as a form of counter-narrative that might have had, nonetheless, a similar effect as more standard, "learned" narratives: they stabilized the basic pattern of knowledge and interpretation of the world.

Most discussions arose when matters of organization and agitation or concrete decisions were concerned. To dare to enter into discussions, the Göttingen Social Democrats had to have the sense that they were competent in and directly affected by the matter at hand. In contrast, almost no discussion arose when they listened to a lecture on general political topics or when meetings were opened to the general public. Normally, time was not even allotted on the schedule for discussions. The lecturer generally spoke for two hours and in the end implored the audience to join the party.

A remarkable means of communication within the party was the "question box" from which the party leader pulled inquiries and answered them publicly. The questions ranged from political to everyday life topics. Some examples, dutifully recorded in the minutes, are:

What is the meaning of the May Day celebration?
Did the Göttingen SPD send a wreath for [Wilhelm] Liebknecht?
Why is coal so expensive?
Is it necessary to accept billeting?
What is the value of a human being?
What is solidarity?
What should the party think about the issue of parliamentary allowances for the Reichstag?

Two answers might illustrate the manner in which the questions were handled. To the question on the value of a human being the party leader responded in his own tried and true – that is, notably indirect and vague – fashion:

> *... One of our French colleagues says that the upper ten thousand have to be regarded as ballast, and when one of the property owners does something and one of the workers does the same thing, the property owner would not see it as the same; furthermore, the previous slaves were compared to the contemporary workers, etc.*[69]

In response to the question about the high price of coal, the leader pointed to industrial syndicates and cartels which were, it was claimed, inherent to the capitalist system; these organizations would increase the prices to such an extent that only socialization of the industry could provide the solution. The respondent also provided practical information by informing workers that cheaper coal could be bought at the Göttingen station.[70]

It is difficult to find out why, after 1902, this system of communication and information ceased. Perhaps the party found the question box too "simple" and, thus, harmful to the party's reputation. It is striking that in the following years daily life problems and conflicts were not discussed as much as in the previous period. This development was, however, not a consequence of any pressure from above, because the question box communication system had seldom been used from the outset and no cries of protest were raised against its elimination.

7. Gender and Party Life

Not until 1908 and the revision of the Reich association law were women allowed to be members of a political party. Most of the women who then joined the SPD in Göttingen were the wives of male members. Once they began to attend meetings, the hierarchical gender relations that characterized the SPD became quite apparent. Women remained an alien element within the party, as small details demonstrate: A woman, for example, was not addressed as "comrade" *(Genossin)* as was the case with a man *(Genosse)*, but as Mrs. or Miss or as "comrade Mrs." *(Genossin Frau)*. Social respect was mixed with social distance, as the following minutes also show: "Comrade Mrs. Peyer raised complaints about the immorality that reigns in our meeting pub, and requested that there be an immediate discussion about the location of our meetings. Comrade Precht proposed a resolution to table the issue and leave the matter to the Executive. Precht's resolution was accepted."[71]

As was the case elsewhere in the party, the hierarchical, gendered division of work and spheres never was a subject of discussion among the Göttingen SPD. As a consequence Social Democrats fostered a limited conception of politics. Hence, it is not surprising that women preferred "women only" meetings where topics were discussed that were customarily considered "female concerns," such as schools, education, insurance for women, the double burden of gainfully employed women, birth control, cooperatives, and the bourgeois women's movement. These subjects combined the individual interests of women with a much broader understanding of politics than prevailed among the men. Hence, it is also not coincidental that such meetings were quite successful ("*schöne Erfolge*") even in the period shortly before World War I, when the Göttingen Social Democratic Party as a whole was already stagnating. The ambiguity of these "women only" evenings is, however, also evident: the hierarchical understanding of gender corresponded to the segregation and subordination of women and "their" topics from what was seen as the "serious" political subjects presented at the official meetings of the Göttingen party members.

Moreover, male party members were insensitive toward the situation of women and frequently expressed prejudices against them. Ignoring the real situation of working-class women, male Social Democrats reproached them for their "craving for pleasure" *(Vergnügungssucht)* which allegedly led the men to spend more hours on leisure time activities than at party meetings. Although modern, commercialized mass culture was rare in the pre-war period, the basic problem already existed: the forced dichotomy drawn by Social Democrats between a "serious" political party and people's longings for "superficial" pleasures.

Men also expressed disdain when women complained about the *Volkswille*, the regional party newspaper. The male comrades felt that the women's discontent lay in their lack of interest in theoretical problems and their irrational desire to read local news such as gossip.[72] Little did these men realize that such subjects often comprised a serious aspect of women's daily lives and social networks.

In sum, male Social Democrats viewed women as both potentially useful supporters of the party, especially as voters, and as a "social disturbance" that disrupted the traditionally homogenous male-centered party life. Gender relations in the party were strongly hierarchical and "women's issues" were marginalized.

8. Conclusion and Prospects

The following remarks deal with the possibilities and limits of generalizations drawn from the case study of Göttingen.

1. *The complexity of political views:* This study of the Göttingen SPD has focused on the relationship between the social world and political

views. The socio-cultural as well as the economic status of workers in the town shaped their political views. A clear classification in the sense of "political reformism" or "political radicalism" is not possible. Both analytical categories are too undifferentiated and too one-sided. Göttingen Social Democrats displayed a vague and ambiguous mix of political views, which ever so slowly evolved in the period between 1890 and 1914. The main conclusion to be drawn from this study is an awareness that our analytical categories are nothing more than rough constructions that do not adequately capture the complex reality of life.

2. *Bourgeois cultural dominance:* In pre-war times it was extremely difficult to establish a social democratic milieu in a provincial town like Göttingen. Union halls, newspapers, and the cultural and social network of clubs and organizations – "from the cradle to the grave" – were lacking or relatively weakly developed. An indication of the underdeveloped provincial milieu – compared to the social democratic milieus in big cities – was the overwhelming cultural power of the bourgeoisie, which presumably hindered workers from voting for the Left. It is not surprising that many more people voted for the Social Democratic Party in secret elections than admitted to supporting the party in public.[73] Presumably they were afraid of repression and they did not dare risk a full break with their accustomed surroundings and everyday culture. This is an observation applicable not only for provincial areas, but also for the Ruhr region.[74]

3. *Regional party organization:* In the Wilhelmine period the regional party organization (and the regional union center) continually enhanced its powers in relation to local groups. Seen from today's point of view, the SPD developed an avoidable surplus of hierarchy, regulation, uniformity, and discipline. These trends included the local party and led to a highly problematic separation of party life from many arenas of everyday life, especially women's affairs. This trend characterized not only Göttingen and Hanover, but was widespread throughout the pre-war SPD.

4. *Lacking experiences in citizenship:* Moreover, the continuing efforts of the Göttingen Social Democrats to escape from their provincial situation were, to a certain extent, problematic as they did not learn from their own experience, from their local situation and local affairs. This pattern derived from the absence of any experience in citizenship. Because of the restrictive suffrage the Göttingen Social Democrats could not learn to take responsibility for local matters into their own hands. They were also too weak to demonstrate effectively and aggressively against the representatives in the city hall. They hoped to be able to change the local situation through higher levels of the state, which had to be "conquered" first. This idea was typical for the SPD, especially in Prussia, while the SPD in southern Germany had more opportunities to exercise political influence on local matters.

5. *Latent reformism:* It would be a misunderstanding to regard the "road to reformism," which the Göttingen Social Democrats were about to "take," as only a result of the "right-wing" Hanover regional party and its "right-wing" newspaper, the *Volkswille*.[75] That is only one side of the coin; the other side must be seen in the peculiarities of a provincial town where capitalism was in part embedded in a petty-bourgeois pattern, bourgeois cultural hegemony reigned supreme, and the plebeian-proletarian counter-public sphere remained quite limited and strictly observed by the police. Among Social Democrats these circumstances led to the recognition that no type of radicalism had a chance to succeed. Radicalism remained limited to words and phrases, yet given the lack of experience in citizenship, a fully formed reformism also could not emerge. Political reformism in the Göttingen SPD remained undeveloped, hidden in a wrapping of socialist idealism, verbal radicalism, and predictions that revolution lay on the horizon. The Social Democrats' anger about the lack of reforms was too intense and prevented the clear-cut adoption of political reformism. As soon as some progress with respect to social reforms had been made, they were neutralized – in the eyes of the Göttingen Social Democrats – by the fact that workers were regarded and treated only as inhabitants and not as citizens with equal political rights.[76] Without full citizenship political reformism had no real chance. In the Wilhelmine period the political reformism of the Göttingen SPD never lost its latent character, its status as a desired alternative if state and society were willing to alter their relations with working-class people in general and social democracy in particular.[77] Correspondingly the Göttingen SPD was more critical of the Wilhelmine state in particular than the bourgeois state (in the sense of Marx) in general.

6. *Social reformism:* Although the Göttingen Social Democrats were not politically accepted as citizens by local bourgeois society and municipal officials, they were, however, socially accepted. They were not considered outsiders or "the roughs," but good, reliable workers and artisans who had not completely broken with the church.[78] They were, in short, "respectable," a situation that basically favored – according to Rohe – social reformism and that accorded with the general pattern of social democracy in Wilhelmine Germany.

7. *Socialist embourgeoisement:* Such a constellation does not mean, however, the *embourgeoisement* of Social Democrats. The sense of dignity, order, respectability, and morals, as well as the demand to participate in high culture, were certainly "bourgeois" characteristics, yet they were also bound to a socialist context. The combination of *embourgeoisement* as attitude and socialism as social utopia is a characteristic feature of Social Democrats in the late *Kaiserreich* in Göttingen and elsewhere. Of course, this combination was basically a contradiction in itself, but it typified the

"in between" situation of the SPD, which continued into the Weimar Republic. By the 1920s, however, socialism as social utopia became conceived increasingly in terms of the working class rather than the whole society. "Cultural socialism" *(Kultursozialismus)* became the favored term and meant establishing socialist values and administrative experience as a precondition for the full socialist order of the future. While the ties between *embourgeoisement* and socialism became looser in the 1920s, they were finally dissolved only after 1949 in the Federal Republic.[79]

8. *Reformism after 1914:* During World War I living conditions deteriorated rapidly. The war radicalized many workers in Germany, but relatively few in Göttingen. In Göttingen the inhabitants remained quiescent, although the problems with getting sufficient food increased considerably. The queues in front of the shops, which elsewhere led to unrest, were nonexistent or, if they occurred, were kept under surveillance by officials in Göttingen.[80] The relative calm of Göttingen workers might be seen as a consequence of the attitude of the municipal officials. They convinced workers that they were doing everything in their power to improve living conditions. Another reason for the calm may be the well-developed subsistence economy among workers, which was more widespread in Göttingen than in big cities. Moreover, the Social Democratic Party continued to cultivate its tradition of discipline and believed in the Berlin party's interpretation of the war as a defensive one that required the maintenance of the domestic truce *(Burgfrieden)*. For this the party was "rewarded" by the military authorities and the police: They only harassed the very small group of the left wing organized in the USPD which split from the SPD in 1917. In sum, the Göttingen situation was different from that of many big cities and industrial regions where political and social radicalism grew rapidly during the war.

9. *November Revolution:* During the November Revolution of 1918, the MSPD in Göttingen participated in and eventually dominated the local workers and soldiers council. Ignoring the high expectations of many workers for more basic democracy and fundamental reform, the Göttingen MSPD cooperated in a relatively uncritical manner with the representatives of the bourgeoisie and with the established municipal officials. It believed in the ability and willingness of at least segments of these groups to change their minds and to learn from the very new situation. In this respect Göttingen mirrored what was happening in the Reich and the attitudes and policies of the MSPD at the national level. Inexperienced and completely trusting in the "correct politics" of the Berlin party center, the Göttingen MSPD pursued a policy that ultimately deprived it of power as the municipal officials and the new bourgeois militia (*Einwohnerwehr*) asserted themselves[81] – a development that angered and embittered many workers. Thus, in 1919-20, a new round of social and political radicalism emerged among

Göttingen workers and trade unionists. Much of this dissatisfaction was voiced by workers who had migrated to the city during or right after the war and become radicalized at the end of 1918 when they recognized that their hopes for a fundamental change in the society and economy did not have any chance of realization.[82] Social and political radicalism could not, however, dominate the entire working-class movement in Göttingen, and the USPD was only temporarily successful, the Communist Party even less so. Instead, political reformism developed subsequently in Göttingen under the new political system of the Weimar Republic and came to characterize the local MSPD. Men and women received the equitable suffrage and full citizenship for which they had long struggled.[83] The manifold hopes connected with these political reforms would not, however, be fulfilled.

I cordially thank Gisela Johnson and Eric Weitz for helping to translate this article as well as Inge Marßolek and Jutta Schwarzkopf for criticism and advice.

Notes

1. See Alf Lüdtke, "Was ist und wer treibt Alltagsgeschichte," in *Alltagsgeschichte: Zur Rekonstruktion historischer Erfahrungen und Lebensweisen*, ed. idem, (Frankfurt am Main, 1989), 9-48.
2. Thomas Leithäuser, et al., *Entwurf zu einer Empirie des Alltagsbewußtseins* (Frankfurt am Main, 1977), 47, 63-64. Compare also Pierre Bourdieu's concept of "habitus" in *Entwurf einer Theorie der Praxis auf der ethnologischen Grundlage der kabylischen Gesellschaft* (Frankfurt am Main, 1979), 183.
3. Nicholas B. Dirks, Geoff Eley, and Sherry B. Ortner, "Introduction," in *Culture/Power/History: A Reader in Contemporary Social Theory*, ed. idem (Princeton, 1994), 27.
4. In general, see Gerhard A. Ritter, ed., *Der Aufstieg der deutschen Arbeiterbewegung: Sozialdemokratie und Freie Gewerkschaften im Parteiensystem und Sozialmilieu des Kaiserreichs* (Munich, 1990). A good example of a local study is Karl Heinrich Pohl, *Die Münchener Arbeiterbewegung: Sozialdemokratische Partei, Freie Gewerkschaften, Staat und Gesellschaft in München 1890-1914* (Munich, 1992). On the concept of "culture" in the sense I am using it here, see Raymond Williams, *Gesellschaftstheorie als Begriffsgeschichte: Studien zur historischen Semantik von "Kultur"* (Munich, 1972), 392.
5. For a recent study of party intellectuals, see Stanley Pierson, *Marxist Intellectuals and the Working-Class Mentality in Germany, 1887-1912* (Cambridge, Mass., 1993). The book reconstructs the intellectual disputes within the party, but does not examine the working-class mentality "at the bottom."
6. Furthermore, the members' body gestures and the atmosphere cannot be reconstructed.

7. The methodological problems, inherent to the minutes, result from the knowledge that the police's particular views on the world and society differed fundamentally from those of Social Democrats. Discourse analyses in historiography have increased the awareness that the interpretation of the minutes, as of other historical texts, is only a "social construction." However, this social construction of the Göttingen SPD would never have been possible had I not also studied sources on the social living conditions of workers, and the relations between workers and the municipal officials and the bourgeoisie. Both types of sources have been analyzed in Adelheid von Saldern, *Vom Einwohner zum Bürger: Emanzipation der städtischen Unterschicht 1890-1920: Eine sozial- und kommunalhistorische Untersuchung* (Berlin, 1973), and idem., *Auf dem Weg zum Arbeiter-Reformismus: Parteialltag in sozialdemokratischer Provinz (Göttingen 1870-1920)* (Frankfurt am Main, 1984).
8. The issue of focusing more intensivly on politics and the state in working-class historiography is debated in several articles in *International Labor and Working-Class History* 46 (Fall 1994): 7-93.
9. In general, see Edward P. Thompson, *The Making of the English Working Class*, 2nd edition (Harmondsworth, 1968), who interpreted the making of the working class as an experienced relationship between the classes.
10. Karl Rohe, "Die Ruhrgebietssozialdemokratie im Wilhelminischen Kaiserreich und ihr politischer und kultureller Kontext," in Ritter, *Aufstieg der deutschen Arbeiterbewegung*, 317-45.
11. Rohe, "Ruhrgebietssozialdemokratie," 336. Examples for workers' radicalism are Düsseldorf, Penzberg, and Hamborn. See Mary Nolan, *Social Democracy and Society: Working-Class Radicalism in Düsseldorf, 1890-1920* (Cambridge, Mass., 1981); Klaus Tenfelde, *Radikalisierung und Widerstand in Penzberg, Oberbayern 1900-1945*, 2nd ed. (Munich, 1981); and Erhard Lucas, *Zwei Formen von Radikalismus in der deutschen Arbeiterbewegung* (Frankfurt am Main, 1976). Lucas's book could be misunderstood because he "only" wrote on two different forms of radicalism and totally neglected reformism. More important therefore are Rohe's considerations. A comparison can be found in Adelheid von Saldern, "Arbeiterradikalismus – Arbeiterreformismus: Zum politischen Profil der sozialdemokratischen Parteibasis im Deutschen Kaiserreich," *IWK* 20:4 (1984): 483-98.
12. Social radicalism can evolve into social reformism and vice versa. Social radicalism can also lead to political radicalism.
13. Rohe, "Ruhrgebietssozialdemokratie," 336-37. The influence of individuals could have played a role here.
14. On Kautsky, see Jürgen Rojahn et al., eds., *Marxismus und Demokratie: Karl Kautskys Bedeutung in der Geschichte der sozialistischen Arbeiterbewegung* (Frankfurt am Main, 1992).
15. The assumption of the "same path" was part of the older modernization theories. See e.g., W. W. Rostow, *The Stages of Economic Growth: A Non-Communist Manifesto*, 3rd ed. (Cambridge, Mass., 1990).
16. Aristide R. Zolberg, "How Many Exceptionalisms?" in *Working-Class Formation: Nineteenth-Century Patterns in Western Europe and the United States*, ed. Ira Katznelson and Aristide R. Zolberg (Princeton, 1986), 400-1.
17. For the following, see von Saldern, *Einwohner*, 67-85, and *Arbeiter-Reformismus*, 23-41.
18. See Fritz Wever, *Die Wohnungsverhältnisse in Göttingen* (Göttingen, 1891).
19. The beginning and termination of all employment was written in the "work diary" (*Arbeitsbuch*), which workers were required to present when seeking employment.

20. See Gerhard A. Ritter, *Die Sozialdemokratie im Deutschen Kaiserreich in sozialgeschichtlicher Perspektive* (Munich, 1989), and Adelheid von Saldern, "Wer ging in die SPD? Zur Analyse der Parteimitgliedschaft in wilhelminischer Zeit," in Ritter, *Aufstieg der Arbeiterbewegung*, 161-83. In the Göttingen SPD there were no precision engineers, railroad workers, or female textile workers. The precision engineers did not need the party, the railroad workers were kept under strict observation, and the textile workers lived in the surrounding villages.
21. Before the turn of the century there was a rapid turnover among the local party leaders. Wilhelm Stegen, a Lutheran, was born in 1862. He and his Catholic wife Luise Lothmann had three children who were baptized Lutheran. Stegen ran a small shoemaker workshop in the center of Göttingen. He headed the party from 1898 to 1909. Afterwards he lost influence and died in 1935. Fritz Wedemeyer (also Lutheran) was born in 1863; he learned carpentry, then worked in a brush factory. After 1910 he became a storekeeper in the association for the cheaper purchase and selling of coal (*Kohleneinkaufsverein*). In the last pre-war years he ran a cigar shop that belonged to a relative of his. From 1909 to 1912 Wedemeyer was the head of the Göttingen SPD, representing the reformist wing of the party.
22. On the notion of injustice, see Barrington Moore, *Injustice: The Social Bases of Obedience and Revolt* (White Plains, NY, 1978). On the concept of "moral economy," see Edward Thompson, "The Moral Economy of the English Crowd in the Late Eighteenth Century," *Past and Present* 50 (1971): 76-131.
23. Police minutes, 21 March 1903.
24. Compare Ossip K. Flechtheim, "Die Anpassung der SPD: 1914, 1933 und 1959," in *Politologie und Soziologie*, ed. Jürgen Fijalkowski (Cologne, 1965), 185.
25. At the turn of the century the most important social reforms were the following: improvements in the social security and the work protection laws (the latter especially for women and young people), the introduction of commercial courts (Gewerbe- und Kaufmannsgerichte), and the declaration of Sunday as a non-working day (in general). Moreover, reforms at the local level should also be mentioned, notably the introduction of commissions to supervise housing conditions and the labor exchanges. For local reforms in general, see George Steinmetz, *Regulating the Social: The Welfare State and Local Politics in Imperial Germany* (Princeton, 1993), 207.
26. See also Eric D. Weitz, "State Power, Class Fragmentation, and the Shaping of German Communist Politics, 1890-1933," *Journal of Modern History* 62:2 (1990): 262-70.
27. This is different from American workers. See David Montgomery, *Citizen Workers: The Experience of Workers in the United States with Democracy and the Free Market in the Nineteenth Century* (Cambridge, Mass., 1993).
28. The manager of the garment office (*Bekleidungsamt*) for the German colonial army in Southwest Africa was accused of having received a credit from the Tippelskirch company, which was the main supplier of such goods. The suspicion of corruption was strengthened by the fact that the Prussian minister of agriculture and his wife had business connections with Tippelskirch.
29. See in general Axel Hall, *Scandal, Sensation and Social Democracy: The SPD Press and Wilhelmine Germany, 1890-1914* (Cambridge, Mass., 1977).
30. In general, narratives have a "central character or subject and a delimited cast of dramatis personae." They also have a plot. For the impact of narratives on social science, see George Steinmetz, "Reflections on the Role of Social Narratives in

Working-Class Formation: Narrative Theory in the Social Sciences," *Social Science History* 16:3 (1992): 489-516.

31. For this and the following remarks, see, among other sources, SPD minutes, 15 February 1902.
32. SPD minutes, 17 January 1903.
33. This was also the opinion of the SPD in Berlin. See Hans-Christoph Schröder, *Sozialismus und Imperialismus: Die Auseinandersetzung der deutschen Sozialdemokratie mit dem Imperialismusproblem und der "Weltpolitk" vor 1914* (Ph.D. diss., Universität Köln, 1966), 183.
34. Compare Friedhelm Boll, *Frieden ohne Revolution? Friedenssstrategien der deutschen Sozialdemokratie vom Erfurter Programm 1891 bis zur Revolution 1918* (Bonn, 1980), 58, and Lucian Hölscher, *Weltgericht oder Revolution: Protestantische und sozialistische Zukunftsvorstellungen im deutschen Kaiserreich* (Stuttgart, 1989), 398. Hölscher unfortunately mentions the idea of the "ultimate goal" after 1890 only very briefly.
35. Police minutes, 7 January 1906.
36. Police minutes, 17 February 1906.
37. In 1898, the SPD received 30 percent of the votes in Göttingen; in 1903, 40.5 percent; in 1907, 36 percent; and in 1912, 37.5 percent. The percentages in the constituency (*Wahlkreis*) were respectively 29, 32, 28, and 33 percent. In the two run-offs of 1903 and 1912, the SPD received 39 and 49 percent of the votes respectively in their constituency.
38. This special type of expectation (*Attentismus*) means waiting for the revolution without having an offensive revolutionary strategy. See Dieter Groh, *Negative Integration und revolutionärer Attentismus: Die deutsche Sozialdemokratie am Vorabend des Ersten Weltkrieges* (Frankfurt am Main, 1973). See also SPD minutes, 21 February 1909.
39. Erich Matthias, "Kautsky und der Kautskyanismus: Die Funktion der Ideologie in der deutschen Sozialdemokratie vor dem ersten Weltkriege," in *Marxismus-Studien*, ed. Iring Fetscher (Tübingen, 1957), 190.
40. This concept was based on thoughts of Friedrich Engels that he recorded shortly before he died.
41. Compare Karl-Heinz Klär, *Der Zusammenbruch der Zweiten Internationale* (Frankfurt am Main, 1981), 51. Recent studies have called into question the standard tripartite division of the pre-war SPD into right, center, and left, personified by Bernstein, Kautsky, and Luxemburg. See Rojahn, *Marxismus*; Pierson, *Marxist Intellectuals*; and Helga Grebing, "Abwehr gegen rechts und links: Zentrismus - ein aussagekräftiger Begriff?" in Rojahn, *Marxismus*, 147.
42. Police minutes, 21 October 1905.
43. In general there is a tendency in the historiography to regard living conditions of the workers as improved over the course of the Kaiserreich. The living conditions were, however, not improved enough to be considered "appropriate." Moreover, social mobility and civil rights were very restricted so that many workers rightly regarded themselves as underprivileged and deprived of rights. See Gerhard A. Ritter and Klaus Tenfelde, *Arbeiter im Deutschen Kaiserreich 1871 bis 1914* (Bonn, 1992), 790.
44. The thesis of corporatism as proto-corporatism is stated in George Steinmetz, *Regulating the Social*, esp. 188-215. The combination of proto-corporatism and non-democratization of the political arena characterized many local constellations in the Wilhelmine period.

45. See Friedhelm Boll, *Arbeitskämpfe und Gewerkschaften in Deutschland, England und Frankreich: Ihre Entwicklung vom 19. zum 20. Jahrhundert* (Bonn, 1992), 627-9.
46. Reformist social democratic local policy could often be found in southern cities of Germany. See Adelheid von Saldern, "Die Gemeinde in Theorie und Praxis der deutschen Arbeiterorganisationen 1863-1920: Ein Überblick," *IWK* 12:3 (1976): 295-352, esp. 316-18.

    In the province Hanover the right to vote belonged only to "citizens," a status that depended on the payment of a relatively high sum which normally could not be raised by workers. Only 5 to 10 percent of the inhabitants of Göttingen were citizens, though by 1914 the figure had increased to 20 percent.
47. The sense of solidarity, accorded great political and cultural value, was expressed both verbally and by collections of money from workers nationally and worldwide.
48. Police minutes, 7 January 1906.
49. The basic pattern of the entire SPD organization can be characterized as a polycentric one: the party was based, to a considerable extent, on the regional party centers and not so much on the Berlin headquarters of the national party. Compare Adelheid von Saldern, "Parteizentren und Parteiprovinzen: Zentralisierungs- und Hierarchisierungstendenzen innerhalb der Wilhelminischen SPD," *IWK* 28:1 (1992): 1-21. For the extension of the regional party center of Hanover, see Friedhelm Boll, *Massenbewegungen in Niedersachsen 1906-1920: Eine sozialgeschichtliche Untersuchung zu den unterschiedlichen Entwicklungstypen Braunschweig und Hannover* (Bonn, 1981), 104.
50. The membership fee was increased from 20 (1906) to 40 Pfennige (1910).
51. In general, see Inge Marßolek, ed., *100 Jahre Zukunft: Zur Geschichte des 1. Mai* (Frankfurt am Main, 1989).
52. These unionists were called *Lokalisten*. See in general Dirk H. Müller, "Probleme gewerkschaftlicher Organisation und Perspektiven im Rahmen eines arbeitsteiligen Organisationskonzeptes," *IWK* 15:4 (1979): 569-80. *Lokalisten* could be found especially among construction workers and bricklayers.
53. See Ritter and Tenfelde, *Arbeiter*, 798.
54. The increasing relevance of social milieus as an analytic concept for historiography is based first on the recognition that this concept is more complex and therefore more realistic than the economically oriented concept of class, and second on the assumption that social milieus are relevant for political attitude and, thus, connect everyday life with political culture. See M. Rainer Lepsius, "Parteisystem und Sozialstruktur: Zum Problem der Demokratisierung der deutschen Gesellschaft," in *Die deutschen Parteien vor 1918*, ed. Gerhard A. Ritter (Cologne, 1973), 56-81.
55. For the workers' cultural movement, see Vernon L. Lidtke, *The Alternative Culture: Socialist Labor in Imperial Germany* (New York, 1985).
56. Police minutes, 3 December 1904.
57. Martin Rector, "Wozu der Arbeiter die bürgerliche Kultur braucht: Anmerkungen zur Schiller-Feier der SPD von 1905," in *Arbeiterbewegung und kulturelle Identität*, ed. Peter Eric Stüdemann and Martin Rector (Frankfurt am Main, 1983), 74-102.
58. The *Bildungsausschuß* offered for example a recorded concert of Richard Wagner's "Parzifal."
59. The socialists the Göttingen SPD honored most were Ferdinand Lassalle und Wilhelm Liebknecht – much more than Karl Marx and Friedrich Engels. Liebknecht especially impressed them because of his "love of mankind" (*Menschenliebe*).

60. How far elements of Darwinist thought, especially social Darwinism, were attractive to the social democratic rank and file is still an open question.
61. SPD minutes, 15 June 1910.
62. Cited in von Saldern, *Arbeiterreformismus*, 159.
63. This has been seen as "Prussianization" of the party.
64. Compare Ritter and Tenfelde, *Arbeiter*, 791.
65. In general see Brigitte Emig, *Die Veredelung des Arbeiters: Sozialdemokratie als Kulturbewegung* (Frankfurt am Main, 1980).
66. Oskar Negt, *Soziologische Phantasie und exemplarisches Lernen: Zur Theorie und Praxis der Arbeiterbildung* (Frankfurt am Main, 1971). Exemplary learning means to take an event as an example to be analyzed in order to extract the basic problems of the society.
67. Police and SPD minutes, 17 June 1902.
68. SPD minutes, 5 March 1904.
69. SPD minutes, 20 January 1900. The minutes changed from direct to indirect speech and often the content was only vaguely indicated. Unfortunately, the answer to the question about solidarity is lacking.
70. SPD minutes, 15 September 1900. The demand for socialization of the coal industry did not necessarily mean a fundamental opposition to the whole system of capitalism. It could be limited to leading branches of the primary sector.
71. SPD minutes, 15 February 1910.
72. Compare *Volkswille* 162 (15 July 1914).
73. In Göttingen in 1907, as in other party provinces, the SPD could only count 4 percent of the voters as members. In 1913 the percentage rose to 13.2.
74. For the Ruhr region compare Rohe, "Ruhrgebietssozialdemokratie," 331.
75. Compare in general Ritter, *Sozialdemokratie im Deutschen Kaiserreich*, 29-31.
76. See von Saldern, *Einwohner*.
77. See Ritter and Tenfelde, *Arbeiter*, 791.
78. A similar result was presented by Rohe for the Ruhr in "Ruhrgebietssozialdemokratie," 334-36.
79. This statement merely expresses the factual situation of the Göttingen SPD. It is not meant to support a new *Sonderweg* thesis, a notion that the entire German working-class movement really wanted to become a reformist, non-socialist *Volkspartei* (people's party) and was only prevented from embarking upon this "normal" path by the authoritarianism and rigidity of the Kaiserreich and the crises that enveloped the Weimar Republic. See, for example, Klaus Tenfelde, "Die politische Rolle der deutschen Arbeiterbewegung," paper presented at the 18th International Congress of Historical Science, Montreal, 27 August – 3 September 1995. The idea of socialism as espoused by Social Democrats and later Communists as well was never merely a reaction to political repression and other negative circumstances. Seen from a historical perspective, socialism was the most important utopia of the nineteenth and early-twentieth centuries.
80. Compare Boll, *Massenbewegungen*.
81. In general, see Hans-Joachim Bieber, *Bürgertum in der Revolution: Bürgerräte und Bürgerstreiks in Deutschland 1918-1920* (Hamburg, 1992).
82. In the election to the Constitutional Assembly in January 1919 the USPD received 143 votes, in the Reichstag election in June 1920 2,500 votes. In the course of 1919 the number of members increased to 450. In January 1919, out of a sample of fifty-two members of the USPD, nineteen were unskilled workers, thirteen metalworkers, nine messengers and the like, and eleven businessmen (*Kaufleute*) and low or middle white-collar workers. Some differences can be

seen with the MSPD membership in that unskilled workers had some greater preference for the USPD. For more information see von Saldern, *Einwohner*, 396-99.

83. In the new local town council, democratically elected in March 1919, the MSPD had the most votes. In the following years the Göttingen MSPD was, however, influenced from "outside" once more. This time it was not the Hanover party organization, but an academic, Professor Leonard Nelson and his International Youth Association (*Internationaler Jugendbund*, later *Internationaler Sozialistischer Kampfbund*). For the Nelson group and soon for the local SPD the main focus was the struggle against the influence of the church on school and society. This created problems with the national party, which had formed a coalition with the Center Party in Prussia. The Berlin center of the SPD finally decided against the Göttingen local and forbade double membership in the party and in the *Internationaler Jugendbund*. As a consequence the Göttingen SPD was reconstructed and in 1925 the old pre-war reformist Wedemeyer came to head the party again. Meanwhile, the Göttingen SPD faced a new political enemy. The party was confronted with the Nazis and other *Völkische* who very early established a stronghold of National Socialism in Göttingen.

Chapter 8

A Social Republic?

Social Democrats, Communists, and the Weimar Welfare State, 1919 to 1933

David F. Crew

1. Introduction

In Wilhelmine Germany (1890 to 1918), the Social Democratic Party (SPD) viewed the state as an instrument for the domination of the ruling classes and for the maintenance of capitalism. But even before the end of the nineteenth century, some Social Democrats were prepared to concede that the German state need not serve the ruling class alone. As political life in Europe became more democratized, as workers were enfranchised and as their numbers and organized strength grew, it seemed possible that the state might be transformed, through the electoral process, into a means of popular emancipation. This did not mean that the laws of capitalist social and economic development could be suspended altogether by the political power of working-class voters, even in a republic based on universal suffrage. But the working class, or, more broadly, the "people" (in Eduard Bernstein's revisionist formulation of the problem) could use the state to begin constructing elements of socialism within the existing capitalist economy. Democratization of the German state, therefore, constituted an important step in the transition to socialism because it enabled the working class directly to influence economic and social developments.[1]

Notes for this chapter begin on page 242.

It was with these understandings of the possibilities, as well as the limits, of parliamentary democracy that Social Democrats participated in the construction of the Weimar Republic (1919 to 1933). Historians have tended either to focus on the inability of the SPD to carry through a "true" socialist revolution in 1918 to 1919, or on its failure to nurture the popular democratic impulses exhibited in the revolutionary *Rätebewegung* (council movement).[2] However, these assessments of "failure" ignore the real sense of progress and possibility that pervaded social democratic political rhetoric in the early years of Weimar. To the Independent Socialists and the Communists, the Weimar Republic may have been a "betrayal" of the "revolutionary" German working class by its "opportunist" Majority Social Democratic Party leaders. But to Social Democrats, Weimar represented a new political opportunity.[3] The Republic provided the political space in which the organized working class might begin to lay the foundations of a future socialist political economy. Weimar Social Democrats regarded the expanded responsibility and activity of the state in such areas as industrial relations, welfare, and housing as one of the most important achievements of the Weimar period. In 1921, a German Social Democrat proclaimed that "we are witnessing the gradual coming into being of the welfare state, of the 'social state.'"[4] Weimar Social Democrats expected their contribution to this "welfare state" to be rewarded with working-class votes. But the Weimar welfare system soon become a bitterly contested terrain where Social Democrats and Communists battled one another for the support of the German working class.

2. Social Democracy, Welfare, and the Local State

Until recently, discussions of Weimar's welfare state have focused primarily on labor legislation, public housing, and the introduction of unemployment insurance in 1927.[5] But the 1920s also witnessed a massive expansion of state responsibilities, under the umbrella of the 1922 Youth Welfare Law and the 1924 National Welfare Decree, for a heterogeneous collection of often newly constituted welfare clients – ranging from single mothers, illegitimate children, and delinquent youths to all those whose lives had been damaged by the war and the inflation.[6] Contemporaries described this complex of means-tested support and educational "therapies," which supplanted both the Wilhelmine poor law and private welfare activities, as *Wohlfahrtspflege* or *Fürsorge*. During two major periods of crisis in Weimar's history – the inflation (1918 to 1924) and the Depression (1929 to 1933) – this new state welfare system became the primary means of public assistance for millions of Germans.[7]

The poor law system and the practice of bourgeois philanthropy under the Wilhelmine Empire had filled Social Democrats with anger and disdain. Wilhelmine charity and the poor law stigmatized the recipients and deprived them not only of their dignity but of many of their political and civil rights as well.[8] The SPD did not develop a coherent, alternative welfare program but socialists did insist that state welfare must replace private charity because only a public welfare system "could gain an overview of the entire population and register everyone who is in need of care."[9] Private welfare activities were, by contrast, far too fragmented. Moreover, the provision of welfare should be made more democratic and less discriminatory; benefits were to be received by all German citizens as a right and were not to be tainted by the stigma associated with the poor law. "In the Weimar constitution of 11 August 1919," Detlev Peukert observes, "the 'social state' received legal guarantees."[10] Yet the German Revolution did not produce a state monopoly of welfare activities, as socialists hoped. Responding to the political pressure exerted by the religious welfare interests (the Catholic *Caritas* and the Protestant *Innere Mission*), the 1924 National Welfare Decree ensured that the Weimar welfare state would be a hybrid formation combining public with private agencies and activities.

Marxism taught German Social Democrats that poverty and other social problems were symptoms of much deeper contradictions in capitalist society that would disappear only when capitalism was overthrown. But social democratic welfare experts saw that in a Germany whose population had suffered long years of war, mass hunger, and hyperinflation, welfare would necessarily assume a much larger economic and social function, hence, play a more significant political role than it had done in the years before 1914.[11] Socialists could not afford to neglect this field of work, especially when the religious welfare organizations continued to exercise such an important influence over welfare clients. In 1919, the socialist labor movement formed its own voluntary association, the *Arbeiterwohlfahrt* (Workers' Welfare). This new socialist organization was not to imitate or compete with the existing private welfare organizations, but rather to lobby persistently for the expansion of state welfare and to recruit working-class men and women to serve in this important branch of public administration.

The SPD's immediate goal was actively to contest the hegemony of "bourgeois" welfare interests and ideology by constructing a visible socialist "presence" in local welfare systems. Even where local political circumstances made it impossible for Social Democrats to play a prominent role, the party must still attempt to act as the "tribune of the people," a critical voice speaking for welfare clients.[12] Social Democrats could attempt to influence the administration of local welfare systems through voluntary work in the committees of the welfare office by supplying social work volunteers and by providing professional social administrators and social workers. By 1930, some 60 percent of all local *Arbeiterwohlfahrt* committees were, indeed, represented in local welfare systems. But the *Caritasverband* and the *Innere Mission* continued to exercise considerably greater influence.[13]

It was particularly difficult to introduce Social Democrats into the ranks of the paid, professional social work staff. In Prussia, for example, only about six hundred of the 3,606 female and 204 male social workers in the field were connected to the SPD by 1929.[14] Women were restricted primarily to social work in families and the neighborhoods. Very few socialist men and even fewer socialist women managed to gain higher-level administrative positions.[15]

Although the national state created the legal framework for the public welfare system in the Weimar Republic, the major responsibility for welfare activities was assumed by local government. In most parts of Germany, urban governments in the Wilhelmine period had been elected on the basis of extremely restrictive, often quite discriminatory suffrage systems that usually prevented Social Democrats from becoming a significant presence in town councils. The democratization of local government after 1918 allowed Social Democrats, Communists, and German women to penetrate this once exclusively middle-class, male, liberal preserve. But the strength of the Social Democrats in local government and their ability, consequently, to influence local welfare systems, varied considerably.[16] In 1929, the SPD newspaper in Stuttgart reported that "welfare activities are still exercised to a very considerable extent by … the charitable-religious associations, which receive large amounts of financial support from the city."[17] In the SPD "fortress" of Hamburg, in contrast, Social Democrats played a major role in the administration of local welfare services. Social democratic senators were responsible for the Hamburg Welfare Department, the Youth Office, and the Public Health Office.[18] Socialists were active at all levels of the welfare bureaucracy. There were socialists among the professional social workers, women such as Hanna Stolten, founder of a group for SPD welfare professionals.[19] And the majority of the volunteers who helped to administer the welfare system at its lowest levels in the neighborhoods and who had direct, day-to-day contact with welfare clients were drawn from the social democratic working class. By 1928, no fewer than 1,463 of the 2,221 volunteer welfare workers *(ehrenamtliche Pfleger)* in Hamburg were members of the *Arbeiterwohlfahrt*.[20]

Social democratic welfare experts argued that the achievements gained by the painstaking and persistent daily efforts *(Kleinarbeit)* of social democratic city councillors, welfare officers, social workers, and volunteers in local welfare systems would pay off at the polls.[21] But the fundamental political and economic contradictions of the "local state" in the Weimar Republic put the SPD in an unenviable political position.[22] Weimar local governments were squeezed between their responsibilities for the implementation of nationally decreed welfare policies and their dwindling capacity to finance these social programs. Welfare was often the largest single item in municipal budgets. Consequently, the SPD became the target of simultaneous attacks from both the Left and the Right. While the Communists viciously ridiculed social democratic claims that the social institutions of the Republic were already a step towards "socialism," the bourgeois parties savaged the Social Democrats for "reckless" welfare spending.[23] The "democratization" of urban government in the 1920s also generated:

> *a crisis of ideology .... The modern forms of urban self-government in Germany were concessions wrung by the urban bourgeoisie from the absolutist state in the early-nineteenth-century. In the 1920s the actual democratization of local government placed before sections of the bourgeoisie the prospect of losing control of institutions that they had created, and by the end of the decade it was clear that the price of maintaining control locally was abandonment not only of the principle of civic democracy, but even of local autonomy.*[24]

3. Gendering the Public Sphere: Women, Welfare, and the Local State

Marxist theory had traditionally seen wage labor as the road to female emancipation. But in the early 1920s, socialist women suggested that Marxist orthodoxy should be revised to reflect the fact that it was the family, not the workplace, that acted as the primary instance of politicization for most working-class women. Women "produced" human beings *(Menschenökonomie)*, not commodities. Their reproductive labor in the household assigned them the spheres of public policy that most directly affected the working-class family. According to the tenets of this "sex-specific strategy of emancipation," socialist women's political activity was a form of "organized motherhood," a natural outgrowth of women's informal social networks and a kind of mutual female self-help. While this new "emancipatory strategy" recognized and affirmed the importance of the reproductive sphere in the lives of most working-class women, it did not challenge and, indeed, often simply reinforced the existing sexual division of labor in both the private and public spheres. And this sexual division of political life also reproduced traditional masculine stereotypes concerning the inferiority and incapacity of women. The double burden of domestic/reproductive labor and waged work made it very difficult for many women to be politically active. Even committed SPD males were seldom prepared to assume a share of domestic labor. Most men continued to believe that politics was "men's business," and women were largely excluded from the leadership ranks and segregated into predominantly female "ghettos," such as the *Arbeiterwohlfahrt*.[25] In the mid-1920s, however, younger women, trained in the more radical egalitarianism of the youth movement, along with some of the older women on the left wing of the social democratic movement, began to demand a fundamental transformation of gender relations. They formulated a new theory of the "particular class position of women" which addressed women's dual identities as members of both a class and of a gender. Although this new approach enjoyed some success in Hamburg, it did not triumph at the national level. Weimar social democracy continued to be largely a "men's movement" representing "male" interests. Women were viewed and treated as second-class citizens whose votes were important to the party but whose gendered needs deserved no special consideration.[26]

The *Arbeiterwohlfahrt* was supposed to draw previously uncommitted working-class women into the socialist political orbit. But Christiane Eifert has concluded that the *Arbeiterwohlfahrt's* attempts to politicize women were successful only in the sense of winning new members for the SPD.[27] This increase in female participation in the social democratic sub-culture did not translate into a proportionate increase in the representation of women in local government. In 1926, for example, only 295 women were to be found among the 6,773 social democratic city councillors nationwide.[28] Many male activists refused to regard welfare work as political. At the founding of the organization in 1919, Marie Juchacz had insisted that the *Arbeiterwohlfahrt* must not become purely a woman's organization. But men were more likely to be involved in the *Arbeiterwohlfahrt* when the organization was able to construct a significant presence in the male public sphere of state institutions and party or trade union politics. More men had leadership positions, for example, in the Essen *Arbeiterwohlfahrt* than in some other local branches because welfare work provided important political contacts with large numbers of unemployed workers.[29] In localities where the *Arbeiterwohlfahrt* did not exert any real influence over the public welfare system, the overwhelming majority of the active members were female. The few women who were able to combine a political office, even in local government, with continued activity in the *Arbeiterwohlfahrt* generally had no, or only grown, children and were, perhaps, also able to profit from the political contacts of their husbands, fathers, or brothers with the local trade union or party organizations.[30] The strategy of attempting to politicize women through socialist welfare work appears to have segregated them within the broader political culture of the SPD.[31]

Social Democrats expected their welfare work to win them new voters, especially among the newly enfranchised female electorate. In 1929, for example, just before an important municipal election, Emma Woytinsky, a female activist in the Düsseldorf SPD, attempted to persuade her female readers of all that the party had accomplished for them.

> *The working-class woman is energetically supported by a local government that is sympathetic to the working class, not only in her most material worries, but also in her family life. If a needy woman is ill and requires help in the household, then the community nursing aide [Gemeindepflegerin] comes into her house. The municipality, acting as the guardian for an illegitimate child, presses its claims for support and carries through the necessary ... proceedings [against the father]. Nursery schools, daycare centers, and kindergartens are set up by the municipality so as to relieve the mothers of some of their burden.*[32]

Social democratic welfare experts claimed that motherhood was a "profession" which required training in "psychological studies and knowledge of biological interrelationships" that working-class women lacked.[33] "Rationalization" and "modernization" campaigns attempted to transmit "scientific" knowledge of child psychology, household management, health, and welfare to ordinary wives and mothers.[34] The representation of motherhood as a profession was certainly used to claim improvements in the status and material conditions of wives and mothers. But social democratic attempts to "rationalize" and "modernize" reproductive behavior, child rearing, and domestic labor also produced, as Karen Hagemann puts it, a "therapeutic siege" of the working-class family that required working-class women to conform to the dictates of a "knowledge" whose benefits were often far from obvious.

> *Most working-class women were skeptical about the recommendations made by "modern infant care." The behavior proposed to them was foreign. It contradicted their human feelings, made greater demands on their labor power and their nerves, and, in addition, cost more money .... They experienced the social worker's home visits as a burdensome form of surveillance .... The reduction of work that family planning and birth control had achieved was again increased by the enhanced demands of (modern) child care.*[35]

4. Socialist Social Work?

Working within the Weimar welfare system, Social Democrats were not able to pursue independent socialist welfare policies.[36] They did, however, hope to import a class-conscious perspective into the welfare state and to give its everyday practices a democratic inflection.[37] But social democratic welfare experts warned that participation in Weimar's welfare system might also cause socialists to lose sight of the class perspective that distinguished them from their "bourgeois" counterparts. In the case files of the bourgeois social worker, the prescription of various measures for the individual client counted as a successful "treatment" of a case.[38] Bourgeois social workers might sincerely believe that they were helping to build a "people's community" (*Volksgemeinschaft*). But socialists should not succumb to these illusions. Although welfare might help certain individuals, it could not contribute to the transformation of society so long as the condition of the working class as a whole remained unchanged. Socialists must seek to connect their efforts to the larger movement of proletarian self-help embodied in trade unions, youth organizations, worker educational associations, and sports clubs.[39]

Even so, socialists engaged in welfare work might be forced into the unwelcome role of defenders of the existing social order against "its dissatisfied, grumbling victims."[40] If welfare clients did not understand "the deeper social and economic causes of their suffering, but rather directed their anger against the individual welfare official with whom they had to deal," even socialist welfare officers might feel compelled to justify their decisions by citing laws and regulations with which, in their hearts, they did not agree.[41] These were the moments when the socialist welfare worker must display "class solidarity" with the unhappy welfare client:

> *When, for example, an unemployed man, embittered by his exclusion from the process of production and by the inadequate public assistance [he receives] … slams his fist down on the table and threatens "to make short work of the welfare office," then a socialist welfare officer must not dismiss him with harsh words as an "insolent disturber of the peace." Instead, with friendly objectivity, the socialist official must make clear to the client that the way he is acting will get him nowhere, that the official can only implement the existing regulations, and that these laws are made by the elected representatives of the whole people. If the welfare client wants to change things … then he should exercise his right to vote and participate actively in political life.*[42]

The socialist welfare worker must act neither as a "policeman" nor as a "patronizing schoolmaster." The claim to this type of tutelary power over welfare clients rested on the belief – unfortunately still shared by some socialist workers – that many welfare clients' problems were the result of their own "unwillingness to work, inability to manage money, dissipation, weakness of character, or a general lack of will."[43]

But cultivating a more "class-conscious" attitude did not solve the dilemma of the socialist who participated in the disciplinary power that was inseparable from modern welfare practices. Even the class-conscious welfare worker had to follow the officially prescribed rules for the construction of a case file.[44] The "knowledge" presented in a case file was produced by a "disciplinary microtactic," a form of "the gaze" identified by Foucault as an indispensable technique of "power/knowledge" that allowed welfare administrators to know, and to control, the clients with whom they had to deal.[45] This kind of:

> *individualizing visibility ... aimed at exhaustive, detailed observation of individuals, their habits and histories. Foucault claims that this visibility succeeded in constituting the individual for the first time as a "case," simultaneously a new object of inquiry and a new target of power.*[46]

"Scientific" social work modeled itself on medical diagnosis. In the construction of their case files, Weimar welfare officials were guided by the assumption that their "clients" were incapable of correctly assessing their own problems and needs. One welfare expert insisted that,

> *[t]he client generally comes to the welfare office lacking any understanding of the conditions which have caused his problems, but only with symptoms that suggest a "social illness." ... [T]he client turns to the welfare office primarily as a source of money, not as a source of "social treatment."*[47]

What clients had to say about their own lives was distinctly less important than the way that the welfare officials read this evidence and created a "case history" from it. But it was not only the client's spoken words that were expropriated by the social worker to construct a "social diagnosis" and to prescribe the necessary "treatment."[48] In 1932, a social work manual even suggested that "body language" should be read for the clues it could provide about the client's problems: "[T]he investigation of the influence of the client's personality can include gestures, speech, even handwriting."[49]

5. The Communist Critique

In communist eyes, the Social Democrats had betrayed the German working-class during the Revolution by settling for a merely "bourgeois" republic whose trappings of formal democracy did not hide the capitalist interests it served. The Social Democrats' loyal support of this "capitalist state" drew unrelenting criticism from German Communists. During the Depression, this critique was distilled into a single epithet, "social fascism." Nowhere were the Social Democrats more vulnerable to this political assault than on the terrain of the welfare state. As Eve Rosenhaft observes,

> *social democracy was the pillar of the Weimar system, its representatives in important regions like Prussia most visible to the working class as administrators and dispensers of state services – or, as they all too often appeared, withholders of services and dispensers of police justice.*[50]

The Communists offered an alternative public sphere for the circulation of discourses critical of social democratic welfare policies and practices. Communist city councillors intervened in debates on the local welfare budget, criticizing what they deemed to be abuses, often by describing in detail the treatment received by individual welfare clients. Communists regularly proposed increases in welfare benefits that both their socialist and non-socialist counterparts found totally unrealistic.[51] Communists used city council debates to present unfavorable comparisons between the Weimar welfare system and the achievements of Soviet Russia.[52] The KPD took politics from the city council chamber to the streets in the form of hunger marches and demonstrations of the unemployed. But communists also tried to bring voices from the street into parliamentary debates. In 1926, for example, in the middle of a discussion of Düsseldorf's welfare budget, a communist city councillor pointed to the presence in the visitors' gallery of delegates from the local Committee of the Unemployed and suggested that they be allowed to give a report of their grievances and demands.[53]

Communists ridiculed "social democratic leaders [who] use every key in the scale to praise the social institutions created after the Revolution."[54] Communists charged that Social Democrats could not hide the fact that "welfare clients, who were the victims of capitalist methods of exploitation, were actually worse off now than they had been under the Wilhelmine regime." Disputing the Social Democrats' claim about the Weimar system that "not only the name has changed [from Wilhelmine Germany] … but something more essential, the spirit,"[55] Hamburg Communists charged that:

> *[t]he old spirit of the Allgemeine Armenanstalt [Hamburg's pre-war poor law system] has very quickly broken through again and "Saint Bureaucracy" – men who go by the book and apparently lack all social feeling – is also at work.*[56]

Irritated by these charges, Social Democrats insisted that:

> *in Russia, despite the communist monopoly of power, social institutions are utterly inadequate. In Germany social institutions are constantly being expanded, improved and refined by the permanent, responsible cooperation of the representatives of the working class.*[57]

But the Communists continued to press their attack, portraying social workers and welfare officials as "spies," "snoopers," and "informers."[58] In 1930, for instance, the Cologne communist newspaper described the local welfare system as:

> *[a] monstrous apparatus of officials, "social workers," and spies, which is set upon the welfare clients, not to determine their needs and to relieve their misery, but to proceed against them with the basest means, to gather as much material as possible, so as to reduce the size of the army of clients receiving assistance …. The*

> *social workers are no more than criminal police, permanently assisted by an army of informers.*[59]

The Communists' target in Cologne was the dominant Catholic Center Party. Yet although Social Democrats did not play a powerful role in Cologne's welfare system, they were not allowed to escape unscathed. The "social reformist" Herta Kraus, one of the few Social Democratic women to hold a higher level administrative position, also earned communist abuse for her "collaboration" with the Catholic director of the city's welfare office.[60]

The KPD mocked social democratic pronouncements about the "protection of motherhood." Communists insisted that a massive housing crisis, widespread unemployment, and the legal restriction of birth control and abortion made it impossible for the majority of working-class women to achieve the "modernization" and "rationalization" of family life that Social Democrats desired. At a meeting of the Red Women's and Girls Union in Berlin-Wedding in 1926, one woman observed that poorer working-class mothers, living in overcrowded urban tenements, found the advice offered by child welfare "experts" to be simply absurd:

> *Light, air, and sun? I should probably just tie a strip of cloth around my infant's belly and hang him out the window; otherwise, there is precious little light, air, and sun for us proles!*[61]

At a conference of communist women in 1928, a speaker urged that municipal elections be used to expose the hypocrisy of the:

> *bourgeois parties, especially the Catholic Center and the SPD, who certainly know how to talk about their compassion for women, but do absolutely nothing to combat housing problems and hunger wages, the shameful paragraph 218 [against abortion], and legal discrimination against women. We have to focus women's attention very specifically upon the social policies of the cities and the towns.*[62]

According to the Communists, German workers had little to show for the constitutional promises to "maintain, protect, and promote the purity, health, and social position of the family as a task of the state and the municipalities."[63] The "state lets proletarian families live in holes-in-the-wall, condemns proletarian children to a life of hunger, and sends proletarian women to jail if they try to ward off starvation with an abortion."[64]

6. Counter-Narratives: Welfare Clients' Letters to the Hamburger Volkszeitung

To reinforce their assault upon the Social Democrats, German Communists encouraged ordinary welfare clients to speak out against the Weimar welfare state. In Hamburg, the communist newspaper, the *Hamburger Volkszeitung*, used a network of workers, non-communist as well as communist, to report on everyday life in the factories and the neighborhoods. This "worker correspondents" movement generated a stream of letters detailing clients' experiences in the welfare system.[65] With the publication of their letters, welfare clients were able to satisfy some important needs, foremost of which was the chance to tell their own story, rather than having that story told for them by the welfare authorities. The normal administration of welfare made it extremely difficult for the client's own story to be heard. Welfare authorities claimed the exclusive right to construct the case file narrative. Clients might provide the "raw material" for the story of their own lives, in combination with the testimony provided by neighbors, friends, relatives, or employers, but it was the social worker and the welfare official who constructed an officially acceptable narrative from these details.

The *Hamburger Volkszeitung* tried to show how the individual stories sent to it by readers should be read from a class perspective. But the readers' letters could not simply be subordinated to this political agenda. Indeed, the editor's comments were sometimes awkwardly at odds with the text itself in which the readers usually presented "melodramatic" accounts of their experiences of daily life in the Weimar welfare system.[66] Patrice Petro has observed that "melodrama was an important representational mode in Weimar" and that the popularity of melodrama can be explained by its ability to address:

> *the real, the ordinary, and the private life .... Yet, in contrast to realism, melodrama seeks excessively to expose and draw out the implications of everyday existence ... it is a melodramatic convention to use characters as types so as to stage a drama of ethical conflict and violent contrast, where characters are denied any illusion of depth, interiority, or psychological complexity. The very unambiguous social and psychic function assigned to characters in melodrama, thus, allows them to be instantly recognizable to spectators and deployed in such a way as "to reveal the essential conflicts at work – moments of symbolic conflict which fully articulate the terms of the drama."*[67]

As a genre melodrama appears to have been particularly appealing to women.[68] Many readers' letters were, indeed, sent by or described the dilemmas and grievances of women. Yet even when men were the authors of these letters they often assumed what might be described as the female voice and the female subject position in a melodramatic narrative.

Melodramatic representation gave welfare clients the satisfaction of inflicting rhetorical revenge upon welfare officials, who were usually cited openly by name.[69] By being held up to public ridicule, specific welfare officials could perhaps also be made to feel personally exposed and vulnerable to popular outrage which might even take the form of physical violence.[70] But the fixation of these little melodramas upon specific villains and victims could very easily lead to the conclusion that the problems of the Weimar welfare state were located in the personalities of the people who administered it, rather than in the system itself – clearly not the message that the Communists intended to convey.[71] The personal, however, might become political when the welfare officers who had allegedly engaged in abuses of their office could be identified as members or supporters of the SPD. The *Hamburger Volkszeitung* claimed in 1929, for instance, that "the Social Democrats, who are to be found everywhere in the district welfare offices, torment the poor women who are welfare clients."[72]

7. Organizing Welfare Clients

It was not only in print that Communists tried to give voice to welfare clients' grievances. The KPD also constructed a wide range of alternative organizations which claimed to speak for welfare clients: International Workers Aid, International League of Victims of the War and of Labor, Red Welfare, oppositional tenants' associations, even a League for Healthy, Non-Compulsory Motherhood. The Working Group for Social Policy Organizations (ARSO), founded in 1927, published the journal *Proletarische Sozialpolitik* and acted as an umbrella organization and coordinating instance for all of the various social policy activities carried on in the KPD orbit.[73]

The most important organizations at the local level were the Committees of the Unemployed.[74] Members of these committees did not have to be card-carrying communists, but they did have to be "revolutionary" workers. The regional committees were supposed to organize local meetings at the unemployment offices and labor exchanges. Smaller groups would, in turn, attempt to establish direct contact with the unemployed wherever they were to be found – in the welfare offices, soup kitchens, and warming rooms.

The Depression gave new life to Hamburg's regional Committee of the Unemployed, which had originally been set up in October 1926. The chairman of the Hamburg Committee, Anton Becker, a communist deputy in the Hamburg Parliament, edited a newspaper, *Der Arbeitslose*, specifically for the unemployed. *Der Arbeitslose* publicized alleged abuses in the welfare system, informed welfare clients of their rights, and encouraged them to engage in a variety of often quite original, if not markedly successful, forms of protest, resistance, or simply collective self-assertion. In its second November 1931 issue, for example, *Der Arbeitslose* advised the individual Committees of the Unemployed "to map out, quite concretely and systematically," the neighborhoods and sections of streets in order to call tenants' meetings and to organize rent, gas, and light strikes.[75] Other actions were to be organized to force a reduction in the frequency of the burdensome daily ritual of "signing on" at the labor exchange or welfare office. A publication commission was to distribute specialized newspapers or extra editions aimed specifically at the unemployed.[76]

Der Arbeitslose urged the Committees of the Unemployed to make a special effort to reach women of all political persuasions, including even National Socialists and those with no party affiliation. Women's Commissions were to gather information concerning daily conflicts with the welfare bureaucracy and the abuses to which welfare clients were subjected. Indeed, *Der Arbeitslose* made a point of describing in great detail individual cases in which women were alleged to have been harassed by welfare officials.[77] Because the responsibility of meeting the rent on time fell heavily on women, the women's commissions were also to organize campaigns to make local government pay the rents of the unemployed. "As an answer to the theft of benefits," *Der Arbeitslose* advised, "housewives must be won over to the idea of engaging in mass refusal to pay rents."[78] As an example of the kind of work that needed to be done, the same article cited a Women's Commission in Hamburg that had organized a rent strike to stop evictions of its members. And in Uhlenhorst, a Committee of the Unemployed claimed to have interceded with the district welfare office to prevent an eviction.[79]

The KPD clearly attempted to take politics right into the sites at which the welfare state was administered on a daily basis.[80] Having to process literally hundreds of individual cases each day, especially during crisis periods, the larger urban welfare offices depended upon the passive submission by welfare clients to the slow-grinding administrative machinery of the welfare system, which required them to endure protracted periods of waiting in welfare office lines. Yet these same lines could subvert the official need for quiet, order, and discipline because they provided the opportunity to construct an informal "counter-public," which permitted communication and the formation of (at least temporary) solidarities among welfare clients.[81] The KPD recognized the political possibilities presented by the long lines of increasingly desperate and impatient welfare clients at the welfare office. In 1929, for example, the SPD welfare senator for Hamburg, Paul Neumann, complained:

> *We have repeatedly observed that the daily business of the welfare district offices proceeds smoothly when people do not stand constantly in front of the gates and doors, handing out every possible type of leaflet and flyer, trying to encourage dissatisfaction among the unemployed.... It is sad to think that we must protect the welfare district offices with security police.... But it is just not acceptable to have instances of bodily injuries and damage to property almost every week.*[82]

The Communists tried to politicize other institutional sites in the welfare system. In Cologne, certain city councillors "maintain a constant presence ... in the barracks for the homeless so that they can collect complaints."[83] In 1932, a Cologne welfare official warned that difficulties were to be expected if a family was evicted from a municipal shelter even though the husband had failed to make any contribution to the rent for the past nine months. The Communists had threatened "not to tolerate the eviction." But the director of the welfare office insisted that the welfare authorities could not submit to this threat "otherwise, the city will lose all its authority."[84] In 1932, a proposed increase in the price of the food served at one of Hamburg's district soup kitchens set off a riot.[85] A social democratic observer claimed that to provoke the people who ate at this kitchen, communists had thrown fish heads into the food, which they then displayed in the front window of the *Volkszeitung's* editorial office with a sign that read: "Unemployed workers, take a look; this is the kind of rubbish that the SPD Senator Neumann dares to set in front of you!"[86]

While the KPD had followed its constituency from the factory to the labor exchange and the welfare office, the party failed to develop an adequate understanding of the differences between industrial conflicts and confrontations with state agencies. Instead, the KPD obstinately imposed "mechanical analogies with industrial struggles" on conflicts within the welfare system.[87] In October 1930, for example, some of Hamburg's welfare clients who were required to perform work in return for the public assistance they received went on strike. These "obligatory laborers" (*Pflichtarbeiter*) complained that they received only seventy five Pfennige per day, an unfair wage, especially when compared to the regular municipal employees. They demanded either the abolition of "obligatory labor" or the payment of the standard wage *(Tariflohn)*.[88] Both the bourgeois and socialist press thought the strike was meaningless, indeed silly, because the welfare office was not a normal employer. It had no particular interest in seeing that the strikers returned to work. Indeed, it had every right simply to cut off their welfare support.[89] The rapid collapse of the walkout cautioned communists against staging another "strike" of Hamburg's relief workers.[90] Welfare clients were encouraged, instead, to engage in "passive resistance" at the job sites. But this tactic proved equally ineffective; the welfare department simply fired these welfare clients for insufficient productivity and the Labor Court upheld this decision.[91]

8. Welfare as a Contested Political Terrain

The KPD was not the only party attempting to attract welfare clients and the unemployed during the Depression. Donna Harsch observes that

"Social Democrats in Saxony, Bavaria, the Rhineland, the Ruhr, and Hamburg began to imitate communist methods of organizing the unemployed."[92] In 1931, *Der Klassenkampf*, published by left-wing Social Democrats in Saxony, drew attention to the importance of the "street politics" created by mass unemployment:

> *Everywhere, there are ... gatherings on the streets and squares of the cities where the unemployed engage in discussions with each other. Certainly, the Communists are involved in a large number of these street discussions, but how many of the unorganized, how many of our own party comrades also have a need to go into the streets, to speak and to listen .... The street is organizing itself and the SPD must direct and lead this organization in the best interests of the proletarian class struggle.*[93]

If they were successful, these attempts would "deny the Communists the material for senseless putsch attempts."[94]

In Hamburg, Social Democrats were clearly at work in the local Committees of the Unemployed. Karl Ulrich, a social democratic member of the Hamburg parliament, warned in a flyer entitled "To All the Unemployed" that "KPD policy is senseless .... Germany is not Russia" and Hitler was just waiting to be put on the throne by the German bourgeoisie as their "savior against Bolshevism." The Social Democrats, by contrast, were pressing for "demands which are not just phrases but are realistic enough to be achieved." These included 2 kilograms of bread per week, weekly allowances of meat, 20 measures of coal, and an increase in support payments.[95] Another flyer, printed all in red, insisted that "the Communists are trapped in a dead end street" and that many KPD supporters were turning to the Nazis. Because the Communists had lost heavily in the last election they were now calling for "direct action" which could only hurt the unemployed. The SPD Association of the Unemployed in Hamburg-Neustadt preferred to support the far more constructive responses of the Social Democrats to the Depression, namely "economic planning and immediate job creation."[96]

Social Democrats also tried to mobilize women against the Nazi threat. In 1932, the author of an article in the SPD welfare journal, *Arbeiterwohlfahrt*, urged that a "comprehensive and intense" campaign be launched to enlighten women about the role that Nazism envisaged for them in the Third Reich. Women should be shown that Weimar's infant and child welfare programs, care for pregnant women, health insurance system, youth welfare, indeed, the entire welfare system, would be destroyed if the Nazis came to power. In meetings, women should be asked:

> *Do you want the sickly and weak children, who are the dearest to you, to be killed by the state? Do you want your old, grey husbands and parents also to be killed? Do you want the executioner to make yearly inspections to wrench away*

> *your dear "life burdens"? ... If so, then decide for the Third Reich and if you happen to be one of these "life burdens" then you will have signed your own death warrant!*[97]

But the Nazis also began to target the unemployed and other welfare clients in their search for the votes that would bring them to power.[98] Reporting from Hesse in 1932, the Social Democrat Anton Dey observed that the Nazis "now distinguish themselves from the most radical Communists only by the fact that their demands ... are even more unrestrained."[99] In Hamburg the Nazi press publicized the grievances of welfare clients in a language which could scarcely be distinguished from that habitually employed by communist newspapers. And like the communist press, the Hamburg Nazi newspaper published letters from disgruntled readers in a clear attempt to dispute the communist claim to speak as the "tribune of the people."[100]

The responses of welfare clients to these competing political voices could be both volatile and inconsistent. Adolf G., an invalided pensioner and long-time welfare client in Stuttgart, joined just about any organization that he thought might lend some support to his very personal war with the unfeeling welfare bureaucrats:

> *I am not a member of any party ... but I joined the tenants' union, the International League of the Victims of the War and of Labor ... the League of Child-Rich Families ... but everyone of them has let me down .... [L]eft all alone, in dire distress, not knowing how or where to turn, I sent an article to the S.A.Z [the KPD newspaper in Stuttgart] which they published.*[101]

From an ideological standpoint, these political involvements were contradictory – the International League, for example, was communist, whereas, the League of Child-Rich Families was politically conservative. Yet each of these organizations attempted to speak for a different element of the official identity Alfred G. was trying to construct – war victim, father of a "child-rich family," and evicted tenant.[102]

A welfare official in Esslingen claimed that the politics of another long-term welfare client, the "war victim" Emil N., were motivated solely by his belief that the official's political prejudices were the source of the "bad treatment" Emil N. claimed to have received.

> *... seeking revenge, he first attempted to set the International League, a left-wing organization of "war victims," upon me. When that failed, he became a member of the Württemberg League of Front Soldiers, politically the exact opposite of the first organization, in an attempt to win them over against me.*[103]

These may have been extreme examples. Nonetheless, the experiences, interests, and identities of welfare clients clearly did not lead them in a single or a coherent political direction. Attracted to the radical rhetoric of the Communists, welfare clients might soon abandon them for the Nazis or even the Social Democrats when they found that the "victories" the KPD claimed were largely rhetorical.[104] For many welfare clients, various forms of self-help, ranging from illegal street-trading to the falsification of welfare records, may have been more attractive and more important strategies for survival than formal political commitments.[105]

Neither Social Democrats nor Communists were able to provide welfare clients with a collective political identity that could bridge the divisions among them created by the welfare state's tendency to differentiate, label, and categorize increasing numbers of sub-groups, each receiving different forms of welfare treatment and benefits.[106] Welfare clients often spoke of themselves as victims – of the war, the inflation, and the Depression – who were competing with each other for scarce and shrinking welfare benefits: "[I]t was necessary to prove that one's needs were more pressing, one's predicament was more dire, one's sacrifice was far greater than anyone else's."[107] But it was hard to reconcile this rhetoric of victimization with a Marxist language of class. Social Democrats and Communists also had trouble recognizing and responding to the needs of welfare clients, especially of women, which could not be expressed in the class categories provided by Marxist theory. Both the SPD and the KPD tried to reach out to women by engaging with "women's issues."[108] Yet in both of the left-wing parties, the actual interests of women were consistently subordinated to the ostensible interests of the working class.

9. The Backlash Against the Welfare State, 1929 to 1933

During the Depression the national government shifted the primary burden of unemployment relief to the local state. By the beginning of 1933, the national unemployment insurance system paid benefits to only 0.9 million out of the total of 6.1 million officially unemployed.[109] This new burden of "administratively decreed" misery forced local welfare authorities to slash support drastically and reduce eligibility.[110] A social democratic city councillor in Frankfurt claimed that the German welfare system had in fact returned to the "alms economy" of the pre-war years.[111] Marie Juchacz agreed: "[T]he spirit of the old poor law has staged a triumphal re-entry."[112]

The frontal assault upon the welfare state and welfare clients during the Depression was powered by ideological as well as financial motives. The SPD Reichstag deputy Louise Schroeder warned that "we now confront the greatest danger because the men who rule Germany reject the 'welfare state' not just out of economic necessity, but on principle."[113]

Religious welfare organizations, meanwhile, demanded the re-privatization of welfare activities so as to free the charitable energies necessary for Germany's recovery from the "mechanistic" and "bureaucratic" straitjacket imposed by the state welfare system. "Social democracy" and the "welfare state" became virtually synonymous terms of abuse in the vocabulary of the religious welfare interests, who argued that state welfare threatened to secularize and "bureaucratize" all welfare practices, leaving no room for the traditionally important spiritual and religious dimensions.[114] To its critics, state welfare also appeared to be undermining individual self-reliance and family members' sense of responsibility for one another.[115]

In 1931, Hans Stichler, writing in the Catholic welfare journal *Caritas*, argued that a new connection had to be forged between "the state, the *Volk*, and social welfare." Stichler believed that Germany had raised "a belief in the holiness of state administration" above the "spirit of welfare." Public welfare activity always risked "the danger of becoming petrified in bureaucratic forms." The public welfare system must now allow "the largest possible room *(Lebensraum)*" to the private welfare organizations, "which live from and with the *Volk*."[116] But in concrete practice, this resolution of the problem, however appealing, ran into real difficulties, namely the private welfare interests' own limited resources and the magnitude of the social problems generated by the Great Depression.

A second solution was to transform the nature of the state that had made itself responsible for the welfare of the German nation. If Germany could become a truly popular state, a *Volksstaat*, then the "welfare state" could perhaps begin to become a "people's community" (*Volksgemeinschaft*). But the transition to this "new state" required the removal of what the enemies of "Marxism" regarded as its pernicious influence upon German public life.[117] This was what Nazism promised.[118] Hamburg Nazis vowed, for instance, that as soon as they gained power, they would rid the city's welfare system of "Marxist mismanagement."[119] In July 1933, the new Nazi senator responsible for the Hamburg welfare system announced the end of "the old system, which had allowed liberalism and its Bolshevik brother, Marxism, to infiltrate public life, [and which had] relieved the individual of all responsibilities to the race (*Volk*)." He also warned that the welfare department "must no longer be politicized and used to win followers."[120]

After 1933, the balance of power between welfare authorities and their clients shifted radically in favor of the former. The director of the Hamburg welfare department was pleased to report in 1934 that:

in the National Socialist state the officials can once again administer welfare with the necessary authority; they can reject the unworthy, use coercion against

> *the "asocial," get rid of the welfare cheats. They can do all of this because standing behind them is a strong state power. The time is passed when the welfare district offices were hot-beds of the worst kinds of disturbances, when police protection was necessary, when the welfare officers had to make their decisions under pressure from the masses. The days are gone when communist elements wreaked their terror, officials were spat upon, bombarded with inkwells and chairs.*[121]

By brutally silencing the Social Democrats and the Communists, Hitler's seizure of power cleared the way to a radical, racist redefinition of the welfare state. The Nazis were well aware of the relationship between their racist social policies and the changed political context after 1933:

> *The governments of the period of the System [Weimar] … did not utilize the findings of genetics and criminal biology as a basis for a sound welfare and penal policy. As a result of their liberal attitude they constantly perceived only the "rights of the individual" and were more concerned with his protection from state intervention than with the general good. In National Socialism the individual counts for nothing when the community is at stake.*[122]

The Nazis reduced complex social problems to simplistic biological formulae. On the ruins of Weimar's contested "social republic" Nazism erected a "racial state" which made the "racially inferior," the "genetically deficient," and other "community aliens" the victims of forced sterilization, "euthanasia," and extermination.[123]

Notes

1. See Lucio Coletti, "Bernstein and the Marxism of the Second International," in idem , *From Rousseau to Lenin: Studies in Ideology and Society* (London, 1972), 45-108, and Barry Hindess, *Parliamentary Democracy and Socialist Politics* (London, 1983).
2. See Barrington Moore, *Injustice: The Social Bases of Obedience and Revolt* (White Plains, NY, 1978); Brian Peterson, "Workers' Councils in Germany, 1918-19," New German Critique 4:4 (1975): 113-24; and Reinhard Rürup, "Problems of the German Revolution," *Journal of Contemporary History* 3:4 (1968): 109-26.
3. See, for example, Adelheid von Saldern, "'Nur ein Wetterleuchten': Zu den historischen Komponenten des 'Novembergeistes' von 1918/19," in *Von der Arbeiterbewegung zum modernen Sozialstaat: Festschrift für Gerhard A. Ritter zum 65. Geburtstag*, ed. Jürgen Kocka, Hans-Jürgen Puhle, and Klaus Tenfelde (Munich, 1994), 93-113.

4. Comments of Louis Korell, the head of the SPD welfare association (*Arbeiterwohlfahrt*) in Hamburg and member of the city-state's welfare administration, *Hamburger Echo*, evening ed., 28 November 1921. On this issue generally, see David Crew, "German Socialism and Democracy, 1890-1933," in *Social and Political Structures in West Germany: From Authoritarianism to Postindustrial Democracy*, ed. Ursula Hoffmann-Lange (Boulder, CO, 1991), 105-23.
5. See in particular Werner Abelshauser, ed., *Die Weimarer Republik als Wohlfahrtsstaat: Zum Verhältnis von Wirtschafts- und Sozialpolitik in der Industriegesellschaft, Vierteljahrschrift für Sozial-und Wirtschaftsgeschichte*, Beihefte Nr. 81 (Stuttgart, 1987), and Wolfgang J. Mommsen and Wolfgang Mock, eds., *The Emergence of the Welfare State in Britain and Germany, 1850-1950* (London, 1981).
6. Hedwig Wachenheim, *Republik und Wohlfahrtspflege: Eine Rededisposition von Hedwig Wachenheim* (Berlin, 1927), 8.
7. See, for example, Greg A. Egighian, "The Politics of Victimization: Social Pensioners and the German Social State in the Inflation of 1914-1924," *Central European History* 26:4 (1993): 375-405, esp. 391ff.; Heidrun Homburg, "Vom Arbeitslosen zum Zwangsarbeiter: Arbeitslosenpolitik und Fraktionierung der Arbeiterschaft in Deutschland 1930-1933 am Beispiel der Wohlfahrtserwerbslosen und der kommunalen Wohlfahrtshilfe," *Archiv für Sozialgeschichte* 25 (1985): 251-98; and idem, "Massenarbeitslosigkeit in Deutschland 1930-1933: Unterstützung und politische Verwaltung der Arbeitslosen," *SOWI* 14:3 (1985): 215. Rather than being consigned to a residual status, "means-tested" forms of relief actually expanded during the Weimar years, even invading the administration of unemployment benefits. See Karl Christian Führer, "Unterstützung und Lebensstandard der Arbeitslosen 1918-1927," in *Arbeiter im 20. Jahrhundert*, ed. Klaus Tenfelde (Stuttgart, 1991), 277-79.
8. Christoph Sachße and Florian Tennstedt, *Geschichte der Armenfürsorge in Deutschland*, vol. 2: *Fürsorge und Wohlfahrtspflege 1871 bis 1929* (Stuttgart, 1988), 15-45.
9. Wachenheim, *Republik und Wohlfahrtspflege*, 8.
10. Detlev J.K. Peukert, "Wohlfahrtsstaat und Lebenswelt," in *Bürgerliche Gesellschaft in Deutschland: Historische Einblicke, Fragen, Perspektiven*, ed. Lutz Niethammer, et al. (Frankfurt am Main, 1990), 348.
11. See, for example, Karin Hartewig, *Das unberechenbare Jahrzehnt: Bergarbeiter und ihre Familien im Ruhrgebiet* (Munich, 1993).
12. See, for example, "Was muß der Werktätige zum 17. November wissen?" "50 000 Kölner Arme hungern ...," and "Der Januskopf des Zentrums," *Rheinische Zeitung*, 9 October 1929, 24 October 1929, and 16 November 1929.
13. See Christiane Eifert, *Frauenpolitik und Wohlfahrtspflege: Zur Geschichte der sozialdemokratischen "Arbeiterwohlfahrt"* (Frankfurt am Main, 1993), 54, 56.
14. Ibid., 63.
15. See Annemarie Hermberg, "Die soziologische Bedeutung der öffentlichen und freien Wohlfahrtspflege," *Arbeiterwohlfahrt* 4 (15 August 1929): 491, and Dr. Michel, "Die soziale Ausgestaltung der Fürsorge und die Arbeiterwohlfahrt," *Arbeiterwohlfahrt* 3 (1 November 1928): 641-51.
16. See Eifert, *Frauenpolitik und Wohlfahrtspflege*, 56, 62, and Marie Juchacz and Johanna Heymann, *Die Arbeiterwohlfahrt: Voraussetzungen und Entwicklung* (Berlin, 1925).
17. "Schul- und Fürsorgewesen," *Schwäbische Tagewacht*, 17 October 1929: 6.
18. In the Hamburg parliament the SPD constituted the largest group until the summer of 1932, when the number of Nazi delegates slightly surpassed those of the

SPD. The proportion of KPD delegates fluctuated from around 14 to 22 percent. Typically, an elected political official assumed overall responsibility for each of the welfare departments, but a professional bureaucrat acted as the administrative director. See Ursula Büttner, *Politische Gerechtigkeit und sozialer Geist: Hamburg zur Zeit der Weimarer Republik* (Hamburg, 1985), 288-89.

19. See Hanna Stolten, "Die Fachgruppe der sozialistischen Fürsorgerinnen, Hamburg," *Arbeiterwohlfahrt* 6 (1931): 27, and "Bericht der Hamburger Fachgruppe," *Arbeiterwohlfahrt* 8 (1933): 184. See also Staatsarchiv Hamburg (hereafter StAHH), Handschrift 1685.
20. Paul Neumann, "Aufbau und Leistungen der staatlichen Wohlfahrtspflege in Hamburg," *Arbeiterwohlfahrt* 3 (1 August 1928): 455.
21. See for example "Aufbauarbeit in Hamburg," *Volk und Zeit*, Sondernummer 45 (1927), reproduced in Axel Schildt, "Als Arbeiterpartei im Senat: Vorsichtige Reformen, sozialistische Propaganda und Verteidigung der Republik. Die Hamburger SPD 1924-1933," in *"Wir sind die Kraft": Arbeiterbewegung in Hamburg von den Anfängen bis 1945. Katalogbuch zu Ausstellungen des Museums für hamburgische Geschichte*, ed. Ulrich Bauche et al. (Hamburg, 1988), 178.
22. See Jeremy Leaman, "The Gemeinden as Agents of Fiscal and Social Policy in the Twentieth Century," in *The State and Social Change in Germany, 1880-1980*, ed. W.R. Lee and Eve Rosenhaft (New York, 1990), 260.
23. Paul Neumann, *Rußland ein Vorbild? Eine vergleichende Darstellung russischer und hamburgischer Sozialpolitik* (Hamburg, n.d.); Otto Thiel, "Sozialpolitik und kommunale Wohlfahrtspflege" and F.D. von Hansemann, "Wir und die Sozialdemokraten," both in *Kommunalpolitik und Deutsche Volkspartei*, ed. Gustav Wittig (Berlin, 1929), 92, 102. See also Ben Lieberman, "Luxury or Public Investment? Productivity and Planning for Weimar Recovery," *Central European History* 26:2 (1993): 195-214.
24. Eve Rosenhaft, "Communisms and Communities: Britain and Germany between the Wars," *The Historical Journal* 26:1 (1983): 232. See also Volker Wunderich, *Arbeiterbewegung und Selbstverwaltung: KPD und Kommunalpolitik in der Weimarer Republik. Mit dem Beispiel Solingen* (Wuppertal, 1980).
25. See Karen Hagemann, *Frauenalltag und Männerpolitik: Alltagsleben und gesellschaftliches Handeln von Arbeiterfrauen in der Weimarer Republik* (Bonn, 1990).
26. Eifert, *Frauenpolitik und Wohlfahrtspflege*, 127.
27. Ibid., 129-30.
28. Ibid., 65.
29. Jens Geier, *"Praktischer Sozialismus oder Mildtätigkeit?" Die Geschichte der Arbeiterwohlfahrt Essen 1919-1933* (Essen, 1989), 125.
30. Eifert, *Frauenpolitik und Wohlfahrtspflege*, 129-30.
31. Ibid., 66. Women active in local welfare systems were sometimes also put forward as SPD candidates for elected municipal office. For examples, see "1. Amtliches Ergebnis der Bürgerschaftswahl am 9. Oktober 1927 auf Grund der Niederschriften des Wahlvorstandes," *Aus Hamburgs Verwaltung und Wirtschaft* (Hamburg, 1927), 227, and "Unsere Kölner Stadtverordnetenliste: Auf der außerordentlichen Generalversammlung der Kölner SPD beschlossen," *Rheinische Zeitung*, 16 October 1929. The views of social democratic women on the relationship between welfare work and women's involvement in municipal politics differed considerably. See Anna Blos, "Frauen im Gemeinderat," *Die Arbeitende Frau: Beilage der Rheinischen Zeitung*, 6 February 1923; Elisabeth Kirschmann-Rohl, "Die Frauen in der Gemeinde," *Kommunale Rundschau:*

Monatsbeilage der Rheinischen Zeitung 2 (13 February 1923); and Adelheid Torhorst, "Die Frau in der Kommunalpolitik," *Die Gemeinde* 5:3 (1 February 1928): 104.

32. Emma Woytinsky, "Arbeiterin und Gemeinde: Was jede Frau wissen sollte," *Rheinische Zeitung*, 15 November 1929.
33. Henny Schumacher, *Die proletarische Frau und ihre Erziehungs-Aufgabe* (Berlin, 1929), 21, and Hagemann, *Frauenalltag und Männerpolitik*, 99-132. The social democratic discourse on motherhood reflected fundamental socialist beliefs in enlightenment, rationalism, and progress. On non-socialist, bourgeois discourses of maternalism, see Seth Koven and Sonya Michel, "Mother Worlds," in *Mothers of a New World: Maternalist Politics and the Origins of Welfare States*, ed. idem (London, 1993), 1-42.
34. Hagemannn, *Frauenalltag und Männerpolitik*, 99-132, 220-305. See also "Hauswirtschaftliche Ausstellung: Rationalisierung im Haushalt," *Hamburgischer Correspondent*, 10 October 1927, in StAHH Staatliche Pressestelle 3241, and "Erhaltung von Altwohnungen," *Soziale Nachrichten aus den Ämtern und der freien Wohlfahrtspflege der Stadt Köln* (1929), 1-4.
35. Hagemann, *Frauenalltag und Männerpolitik*, 213.
36. The SPD and the *Arbeiterwohlfahrt* did, however, manage to introduce "progressive" welfare reforms in some local authorities where they had a particularly strong influence. On Berlin, see, for example, Elizabeth Harvey, *Youth Welfare and Social Democracy in Weimar Germany: The Work of Walter Friedlander* (Oak Villa, Scotland, 1987).
37. Christoph Sachßse, *Mütterlichkeit als Beruf: Sozialarbeit, Sozialreform und Frauenbewegung 1871-1929* (Frankfurt am Main, 1986), 181; Hedwig Wachenheim, "Ausbildung zur Wohlfahrtspflege," *Die Neue Zeit* 39:2 (1921): 303.
38. Paula Kurgass, "Die sozialistische Fürsorgerin: Gegen die Isolierung der Wohlfahrtspflege," *Arbeiterwohlfahrt* 1 (1 December 1926): 134.
39. Ibid., 133-36.
40. Clara Henriques, "Psychologische Schwierigkeiten und Möglichkeiten sozialistischer Wohlfahrtsarbeit," *Arbeiterwohlfahrt* 2 (1 August 1927): 454-455.
41. Ibid., 454-56.
42. Ibid., 455-56.
43. Ibid., 457. See also Hanna Stolten, "Etwas vom Fürsorgedienst im Selbstgespräch," *Jugend und Volkswohl* 4 (1928): 9-11.
44. See, for example, "Wie sollen gute Berichte aussehen," in Hanna Hellinger, *Das Kleine Lehrbuch: Ratgeber für unsere Helfer in der öffentlichen Wohlfahrtspflege*, vol. 2, ed. Hauptausschuß für Arbeiterwohlfahrt (n.p., n.d.), 38-40.
45. See Michel Foucault, *Power/Knowledge: Selected Interviews and Other Writings, 1972-1977*, ed. Colin Gordon (New York, 1980), and Nancy Fraser, "Foucault on Modern Power: Empirical Insights and Normative Confusions," in idem, *Unruly Practices: Power, Discourse, and Gender in Contemporary Social Theory* (Minneapolis, MN, 1989), 22.
46. Fraser, "Foucault on Modern Power," 23.
47. Siddy Wronsky und Prof. Dr. Kronfeld, *Sozialtherapie und Psychotherapie in den Methoden der Fürsorge* (Berlin, 1932), 32. On Siddy Wronsky, see Walter Tetzlaff, *2000 Kurzbiographien Bedeutender Deutscher Juden des 20. Jahrhunderts* (Lindenhorst, 1982), 364, and Eifert, *Frauenpolitik und Wohlfahrtspflege*, 33, 39, 41, 106, 112, 116ff.
48. Siddy Wronsky, "Behandlungsmethoden in der Fürsorge," *Jugend und Volkswohl* 6 (January/February 1931): 202-03.

49. Siddy Wronsky, *Methoden der Fürsorge* (Berlin, 1930), 16. This kind of intensive case work was only realistic, if at all, in periods of relative economic and social stability when the absolute numbers of cases assigned to each social worker were relatively small. See, for example, Hanna Dunkel, "Familienfürsorge," *Jugend und Volkswohl* 3 (1927): 189, a review of Marie Baum, *Familienfürsorge: Eine Studie* (Karlsruhe, 1927); StAHH, Sozialbehörde (hereafter SB) I/VG/25/11/1/1926-35, 6 January 1930, and SB I/VG/25/11/1/1926-35, 9 July 1930; and Stadtarchiv Düsseldorf (hereafter StAD) III/4060, 15 October 1931.
50. Rosenhaft, "Communisms and Communities," 229.
51. See Beatrix Herlemann, *Kommunalpolitik der KPD im Ruhrgebiet 1924-1933* (Wuppertal, 1977), 90-112.
52. See, for example, *Stenographische Verhandlungs-Berichte der Stadtverordneten-Versammlung zu Düsseldorf* Nr. 4, Sitzung vom 16 March 1929, 116; "Kommunistische Kampfforderungen zu den Kommunalwahlen am Mittelrhein," *Sozialistische Republik*, 9 November 1929: 2; and Peter Stahl, "Wohlfahrtsamt – Gesundheitsfürsorge – Arbeitszentrale," *Sozialistische Republik*, 28 August 1926.
53. *Stenographische Verhandlungs-Berichte der Stadtverordneten-Versammlung zu Düsseldorf*, Nr. 1, Sitzung vom 29 Januar 1926, 16.
54. "Der Segen der 'sozialen Einrichtungen,'" *Hamburger Volkszeitung*, 17 July 1923.
55. Paul Neumann, "Von Armenpflege zur sozialen Fürsorge," *Hamburger Echo* 32 (1 February 1928).
56. *Hamburger Volkszeitung*, 19 July 1923.
57. Neumann, *Rußland ein Vorbild?* 4. Neumann's brochure set off a round of rhetorical counter-attacks from the Communists. See "Material fur die heutige 'Arso' Konferenz in Hamburg: Die Hetzbrochüre des Senators Neumann," *Hamburger Volkszeitung*, Beilage, 22 May 1930, and "SPD-Senator Neumanns 'soziales' Hamburg: Wohlfahrtspraxis treibt zum Selbstmord" (Arbeiterkorrespondenz 709), *Hamburger Volkszeitung*, 5 April 1932, StAHH Pressestelle I-IV/3186.
58. "Spitzel des Wohlfahrtsamtes," *Hamburger Volkszeitung*, 13 August 1926.
59. "Rund um die Stempelkarte," *Sozialistische Republik* 277 (11 December 1930): 2.
60. "Dr. Schwering hereingefallen!" *Sozialistische Republik* 146 (23 June 1928): 2.
61. Lene Overlach, "Licht, Luft und Sonne: Frauen und Reichsgesundheitswoche," *Hamburger Volkszeitung*, 7 April 1926.
62. "Die Frauenkonferenz glänzend verlaufen," *Sozialistische Republik* 160 (10 July 1928): 2.
63. "Was leistet die Hamburger Bürgerschaft für die proletarischen Frauen," *Hamburger Volkszeitung*, 13 June 1923. See also the repeated communist attacks upon Mother's Day, as in "Zum Muttertag" and "Muttertag," *Hamburger Volkszeitung*, 4 and 12 May 1928.
64. "Was leistet die Hamburger Bürgerschaft für die proletarischen Frauen," *Hamburger Volkszeitung*, 13 June 1923.
65. See Christa Hempel-Küter, *Die kommunistische Presse und die Arbeiterkorrespondentenbewegung in der Weimarer Republik* (Frankfurt am Main, 1989), 240-44.
66. The veracity of the reports carried in the *Hamburger Volkszeitung* were, indeed, frequently challenged, resulting in numerous court cases and fines. As a result, the editors increasingly demanded that worker correspondents supply supporting evidence or name witnesses who could confirm their claims. See ibid.
67. Patrice Petro, *Joyless Streets: Women and Melodramatic Representation in Weimar Germany* (Princeton, 1989), 26, 29-31. Her quote is from Peter Brooks, *The Melodramatic Imagination: Balzac, Henry James, Melodrama, and the Mode of Excess* (New Haven, Conn., 1976), 53.

68. See Eve Rosenhaft, "Women, Gender, and the Limits of Political History in the Age of 'Mass Politics,'" in *Elections, Mass Politics, and Social Change in Modern Germany: New Perspectives*, ed. Larry Eugene Jones and James Retallack (Cambridge, Mass., 1992), 164-65.
69. See Pierre Bourdieu, *Language and Symbolic Power* (Cambridge, Mass., 1991).
70. See David Crew, "Gewalt 'auf dem Amt': Wohlfahrtsbehörden und ihre Klienten in der Weimarer Republik," in *Physische Gewalt: Studien zur Geschichte der Neuzeit*, ed. Thomas Lindenberger and Alf Lüdtke (Frankfurt am Main, 1995), 213-37.
71. See Hayden White, "Historical Emplotment and the Problem of Truth," in *Probing the Limits of Representation: Nazism and the "Final Solution,"* ed. Saul Friedländer (Cambridge, Mass., 1992), 42-43.
72. *Hamburger Volkszeitung*, 23 January 1929.
73. Johanna Piper, *Die Frauenpolitik der KPD in Hamburg 1928 bis 1933* (Cologne, 1988), 70-71. The SPD also formed its own organizations aimed at different categories of welfare clients. See, for example, David F. Crew, "'Wohlfahrtsbrot ist bitteres Brot': The Elderly, the Disabled, and the Local Welfare Authorities in the Weimar Republic 1924-1933," *Archiv für Sozialgeschichte* 30 (1990): 226-33. See also W. Landeskriminalpolizeiamt, 26 Juni 1925, Württemburg Polizeipräsidium Stuttgart, Staatsarchiv Ludwigsburg (hereafter StALu), E 191-3928, and "Der kommunistische Gemeindevertreter gehört in die 'Arso,'" *Die Kommune* 10:23 (1 December 1930): 190.
74. See Eve Rosenhaft, *Beating the Fascists? The German Communists and Political Violence 1929-1933* (Cambridge, Mass., 1983); Anthony McElligott, "Mobilising the Unemployed: The KPD and the Unemployed Workers' Movement in Hamburg-Altona during the Weimar Republic," in *The German Unemployed: Experiences and Consequences of Mass Unemployment from the Weimar Republic to the Third Reich*, ed. Richard J. Evans and Dick Geary (New York, 1987), 228-60; and Werner Müller, *Lohnkampf, Massenstreik, Sowjetmacht: Ziele und Grenzen der "Revolutionären Gewerkschafts-Opposition" (RGO) in Deutschland 1928 bis 1933* (Cologne, 1988). Until 1929 to 1930 the majority of Hamburg KPD members were still employed, but the numbers of the unemployed increased dramatically during the course of the Depression. See Reinhard Müller, "'Rotes Arbeiter-Hamburg': Zur Politik der KPD 1924 to 1933," in Bauche, "*Wir sind die Kraft*," 241. Among new recruits to the party in Hamburg in October, 1932, 62.4 percent were unemployed and in some individual districts, such as St. Pauli, Neustadt, Altstadt, Barmbeck-Center, and Hammerbrook, the figures were as high as 72 to 77 percent. See McElligott, "Mobilising the Unemployed," 241-42.
75. "Organisatorische Richtlinien zum Ausbau der Erwerbslosenbewegung," *Der Arbeitslose* 46, 1. Beilage, Zweite Nov. Ausgabe (1931).
76. Ibid.
77. *Der Arbeitslose* 50, Wochen-Ausgabe (1931).
78. *Der Arbeitslose* 49, Wochen-Ausgabe, 1. Beilage (1931).
79. "So wird die Not der Armen gelindert: Einige Tatsachen, die Senator Neumann in der Bürgerschaft verschwieg" (Arbeiterkorrespondenz 2501), *Hamburger Volkszeitung*, 12/13 December 1931.
80. McElligott, "Organising the Unemployed," 233-34.
81. See "Ein Vormittag in der Wohlfahrtskreisstelle," *Wohlfahrtsblätter der Stadt Köln* 2/3 (May/June 1926): 9-10, and StAD III/4059, November/December 1923.
82. *Stenographische Berichte über die Sitzungen der Bürgerschaft* (Hamburg), 31. Sitzung (1929): 1158.

83. Herrn Beigeordneten Dr. Schwering, Stadtarchiv Köln (hereafter StAKö), 902/198/3/501-1052, 6 November 1930.
84. StAKö 902/198/4/501-596, 28 June 1932.
85. "Erwerbslosen-Ausschüße und ähnl. 1929-1933," StAHH SB I/VG/25/11/1/ 1926-35, 15 September 1932; StAHH I/VG/73/11.
86. "Erwerbslosen-Ausschüße und ähnl. 1929-1933," StAHH SB I/VG/73/11.
87. Ibid., 229.
88. "Bewegungen gegen die Unterstützungsarbeit (Sammelakte mit 5 Einzelakten) 1930-31," 9 August 1930, StAHH SB I/AW/00/93; *Hamburger Volkszeitung*, 14 October 1930.
89. StAHH SB I/AW/00/93; *Hamburger Anzeiger*, 15 April 1930; *Hamburger Echo*, 16 October 1930.
90. See, however, for the Ruhr industrial district, *Rechenschaftsbericht der Bezirksleitung Ruhrgebiet der KPD für die Jahre 1930-1932*, reprint of 1932 ed. (Wentorf bei Hamburg, 1975).
91. "Einstellung der Notstandsarbeiten-Entlassung der Notstandsarbeiter," *Hamburger Anzeiger* 197 (25 August 1931).
92. Donna Harsch, *German Social Democracy and the Rise of Nazism* (Chapel Hill, NC, 1993), 214-15.
93. Siegfried Wagner, "In den Betrieben – An den Stempelstellen," *Der Klassenkampf* 5:4 (1931): 116.
94. Ibid., 117.
95. "Erwerbslosen-Ausschüße und ähnl. 1929-1933," StAHH SB I/VG//73/11, n.d., and leaflet from Barmbeck-Zentrum, 19, 13 February 1933. See also StAHH Handschrift 1754.
96. "Erwerbslosen-Ausschüße und ähnl. 1929-1933," StAHH SB/I/VG/73/11.
97. Ibid., 194, 195, 197.
98. Walter Auerbach, "Was wollen die Nationalsozialisten in den Gemeinden," *Die Gemeinde* 8 (1931): 493-94.
99. Anton Dey, "Nationalsozialismus und Wohlfahrtspflege," *Die Gemeinde* 9 (1932): 410.
100. See for example "Und nochmals die Wohlfahrt …," "Ein Wohlfahrtserwerbsloser schreibt an Senator Neumann," and "'Der Senat genehmigt …' Unerhörte Provokation der Wohlfahrtserwerbslosen," *Hamburger Tageblatt*, 116 (19 May 1932), 194 (26 August 1932), and 174 (31 July 1932).
101. Letter from Adolf G., Cannstatt, to the I. Strafkammer Landgericht Stuttgart, Staatsanwaltschaft Stuttgart, 30 May 1927, StALu E/180/II/V/76.
102. "Schwäb. Bund zum Schutze der Kinderreichen Familie," StALu E191/4119.
103. An das verehrl. OA Esslingen; Beschwerdesache des Kriegsbeschädigten Emil N. gegen Geschaftsführer S. bei BFB-E, 24 February 1926, StALu F164/II/725/ Oberamt Esslingen.
104. Rosenhaft, "Communisms and Communities," 229.
105. See for example, "Maßnahmen gegen Schwarzarbeit 1931-1933," StAHH SB I/VG/24/32, and Pressestelle I-IV/3334.
106. Committees of the Unemployed voiced the grievances not only of the jobless, but also of pensioners and other welfare clients. See a petition sent by the Kampfausschuß der Sozialrentner to welfare district office XI (Hamburg), 13 February 1932, StAHH SB I/VG/73/11.
107. Egighian, "Politics of Victimization," 400-01.

108. Rosenhaft observes, however, that the KPD's efforts always "stopped short at the mechanical functions of 'reaching out' and 'mobilizing' [women] as one of a series of 'allied strata.'" See "Communisms and Communities," 228.
109. Adelheid von Saldern, "Kommunale Verarmung und Armut in den Kommunen während der Großen Krise (1929 bis 1933): Am Beispiel der Finanz-und Wohnungs(bau)politik," in *Soziale Bewegungen*, vol. 3: *Armut und Ausgrenzung* (Frankfurt am Main, 1987), 76.
110. See Wilhelm Polligkeit, "Not und Existenzminimum," *Soziale Praxis: Zentralblatt für Sozialpolitik und Wohlfahrtspflege* 41:27 (7 July 1932): 821, and "Die Berücksichtigung des Arbeitseinkommens in der Familiengemeinschaft bei Bemessung der Fürsorgeleistungen," *Nachrichtendienst des Deutschen Vereins für öffentliche und private Fürsorge* (1931): 354-58. For criticisms see Marie Baum, "Die Familie in Sozial-und Fürsorge-Politik der Gegenwart," *Soziale Politik* 41:27 (1932): 833-34.
111. Stadtrat Dr. Michel, "Probleme der kommunalen Wohlfahrtspflege um die Wende 1932/33," *Arbeiterwohlfahrt* 8 (1933): 5.
112. Marie Juchacz, "Absinken der Fürsorge," *Arbeiterwohlfahrt* 7 (1 November 1932): 642.
113. Louise Schroeder, "Gemeinden und Fürsorge," *Die Gemeinde*, 10:5/6 (1 and 2 March 1933): 221.
114. Ibid., 143-44.
115. See for example G. Vöhringer, the general secretary of the Deutschen Liga der freien Wohlfahrtspflege, "Sparmaßnahmen für das Gebiet der freien Wohlfahrtspflege," *Blätter der Zentralleitung für Wohltätigkeit in Württemberg* 80:1 (January 1927): 1, and "Tätigkeitsbericht des Bezirkswohlfahrtsamts Ehingen für das Rechnungsjahr 1929," StAL E191/4698.
116. Quotes, in order, from Hans Stichler, "Staat, Volk, Soziale Fürsorge," *Caritas* (1931): 454, 455, 457.
117. See, for example, Bertha Finck, "Zeitschriftenschau: Wohlfahrtspflege im neuen Staat," *Innere Mission* (1933): 143.
118. See D. Adolf Stahl, "Oeffentliche und freie Jugendwohlfahrtspflege im neuen Staat," *Innere Mission* (1933): 130; "Der Neue Geist in der Wohlfahrtspflege," *Schleswig-Holsteinische Wohlfahrtsblätter* 8:3 (May 1933): 34.
119. "Gegen die rote Herrschaft in der Wohlfahrtsbehörde," *Hamburger Tageblatt* 93 (20 April 1932).
120. "Die Wohlfahrtsbehörde im neuen Staat: Senator v. Allwörden vor den Beamten seiner Behörde," *Hamburger Fremdenblatt*, 28 July 1933.
121. Quoted in Wolfgang Ayass, *"Asoziale" im Nationalsozialismus* (Stuttgart, 1995), 120.
122. Official justification for the Community Aliens Law, quoted in Jeremy Noakes, "Social Outcasts in the Third Reich," in *Life in the Third Reich*, ed. Richard Bessel (Oxford, 1987), 95.
123. Michael Burleigh and Wolfgang Wippermann, *The Racial State: Germany 1933-1945* (Cambridge, Mass., 1991).

Chaper 9

THE IRON FRONT

Weimar Social Democracy between Tradition and Modernity

Donna Harsch

On 16 December 1931, Otto Wels, chairman of the SPD, announced the formation of an "Iron Front of all republicans." Embracing the Social Democratic Party (SPD), the paramilitary *Reichsbanner Schwarz-Rot-Gold*, two trade union federations (ADGB and AfA-Bund), and the Workers Sport Federation, this super-organization was to coordinate the social democratic effort to defend the Weimar Republic against its enemies on the Right, in particular, the NSDAP. Created in the midst of national crisis and social democratic demoralization, the Iron Front went on to a meteoric career, distinguished by an unexpected talent for rousing Social Democrats but capped by an equally unforeseen failure either to defend republican institutions or extend its appeal to a broader electorate. Its popular authority collapsed under the one-two blow of the unresisted national coup against the SPD-led Prussian regime on 20 July 1932 and SPD electoral losses on 31 July 1932.

The achievements of the *Eiserne Front* marked a potential turning-point in the fortunes of the late Weimar Republic, while its deficiencies encapsulated dilemmas that vexed the SPD throughout the period. Its fate should not, however, be interpreted as the ironic reversal of a fortuitous last chance by an unlucky relapse. Rather than the simple negation of "break" by "continuity," the Iron Front embodied a paradox within a

Notes for this chapter begin on page 270.

paradox. Its power and weakness flowed from the same source – a dynamic strategic fusion of the SPD's established programmatic *content* and social *composition* with new tactical, stylistic, and symbolic *forms*.

This hybrid strategy grew out of an unusual internal alliance. One group in this loose coalition was composed of rank-and-file activists and functionaries of the SPD Left – that is, of Social Democrats who most feared that the Weimar party had cut loose from its proletarian moorings and jettisoned too much of its Marxist ballast. Leaders of the *Reichsbanner* and intellectuals of a neo-rightist tendency in the SPD made up the other contingent. Like the SPD's established right wing, these new rightists were candid incrementalists who believed that social change would come about through reform, not revolution, and accepted, even embraced, cooperation between the SPD and Germany's pro-democratic bourgeois parties. Unlike the old Right, but like the Left, they were eager to activate the party ranks and turn the SPD away from parliament toward street politics.

The SPD Left and *Reichsbanner* Right collaborated in a concerted effort to convince the SPD Executive Committee to form the Iron Front. Standing at the pinnacle of the party's organizational hierarchy but in the middle of its political spectrum, the Executive Committee clung to a decidedly abstract Marxism while fixing its sights squarely on the parliamentary arena. Cooperation between the margins against this powerful center emerged spontaneously in 1931; only in early 1932 did the *Reichsbanner* activist and intellectual Carlo Mierendorff call explicitly for a "new revisionism" that would fuse the old Left and the new Right against the stodgy economic reformism and anxious legalism of the SPD's ruling bodies. Practicing what he preached, Mierendorff joined forces with the self-proclaimed revolutionary Marxist Sergei Chakhotin to develop a strategic design based on a modern psychology of mass persuasion. Their version of the Iron Front, like the original one, was initially resisted by SPD leaders, but taken up enthusiastically by the *Reichsbanner* and by SPD districts controlled by either leftists or neo-revisionists. Under pressure from *Reichsbanner* leaders, the SPD Executive decided suddenly in mid-June to allow a refurbished Iron Front – dubbed the "new-style" Iron Front – to orchestrate the crucial July Reichstag campaign.

The origins, character, and context of the Iron Front's fusion of custom and innovation are the subject of this chapter. The focus is on the role of *Reichsbanner* leaders in the creation of the Front and on iconoclastic intellectuals such as Mierendorff and Chakhotin in developing the new style. The aim is to understand how and why these reformers came to promote a radical change of form as the key to the revitalization of social democracy, while neglecting and even belittling the reform of program. Their insistence on a drastic, but technical, overhaul is striking because the right-wing boosters of the new style had made names for themselves as critics of the SPD's political orientation. Moreover, at the very moment that the new style was being designed, right-wing leaders of the ADGB put forward a revisionist, and methodologically modern, public works program for the Iron Front. The new-style strategists spurned this program despite its popular promise. Their critique of the rationalist assumptions behind interest-based politics, on the one hand, and their reading of the modern as the triumph of form over content, on the other, led them to adopt a strategy in which changes in method and symbolic expression displaced revisions in substance and argument.

1. The Reichsbanner and the Origins of the Iron Front

The stunning electoral gains of the NSDAP and the impressive rise of the Communist Party (KPD) vote in the Reichstag elections of September 1930 shocked Social Democrats. Accustomed to seeing theirs as the largest and most modern party in Germany, they were now confronted by two popular and undeniably non-traditional adversaries. While the reaction of party leaders was to implement a defensive parliamentary strategy to block the ascendancy of these parties, many social democrats began to search for an offensive alternative or, at least, addition to their Reichstag delegation's "toleration" of Chancellor Heinrich Brüning, whose drastic budget cuts and apparent indifference towards the unemployed were driving hordes of voters towards the extremist parties.

Naturally enough, the strategies and tactics of their radical rivals riveted Social Democrats' attention. Socialists of the Left wanted to emulate the class-struggle strategy of the undiluted *Klassenpartei*, the KPD. Though the SPD had, in fact, never followed a radical policy commensurate with the communist one, the Left believed that a pure *Klassenpolitik* would return the SPD to its traditional – its authentic – roots. Self-proclaimed modernizers in the *Reichsbanner* and ADGB, meanwhile, wanted to go after the NSDAP's socially-diverse electorate and even borrow some of its nationalist rhetoric. Concentration on the extremists' equivalent styles – their muscular, male youthfulness, rhetorical flourish, permanent mobilization, and striking street presence – aligned Social Democrats along a different axis, however. Party dissidents and *Reichsbanner* activists decried the bureaucratic routine and ossification of social democracy, while SPD and ADGB leaders denied that anything needed to be fixed.

The *Reichsbanner* was the only major social democratic association in which many leading cadres identified themselves with political *and* organizational modernization. For various reasons, the *Reichsbanner* had become the repository of the non-traditional in social democracy. As its youngest ancillary organization, the *Reichsbanner* was less bureaucratic than the SPD or ADGB. A child of the Republic, the *Reichsbanner* was also distinguished by its unadorned republicanism and inclusive socio-political composition, criteria imposed by the SPD Executive against protests from the party Left.[1]

Formally, the *Reichsbanner* was a multi-class, not a proletarian, defense league on whose board sat representatives of the Democratic and Center parties. Its huge base, however, was social democratic and working class; by 1930, 80 to 90 percent of its roughly three million members voted social democratic. Its only *real* middle-class participation came from the few bourgeois men of the "generation of 1914" who had joined the SPD after 1918. An unusual group of highly-educated veterans – such as Mierendorff, Theodor Haubach, Kurt Schumacher, and Julius Leber – became dedicated, if critical, Social Democrats. Although they did not agree on all issues, all of these men were of a new Right in the SPD, rebels against the yoke of party tradition, critics of Marxism and, above all, of the attenuation of ties between leaders and followers in the SPD.[2]

The issue that first drew attention to these Young Turks was their plea for the SPD to "turn to the nation." They urged it to advocate a non-chauvinistic German patriotism and to recognize the need for a well-trained, though reformed, *Reichswehr*. They also rejected class-struggle ideology and the Marxist theory of immiseration. They wanted the SPD to appeal to middle-class Germans assertively and directly by addressing them as autonomous social groups, rather than "proletarianizing layers." Last but not least, they challenged the Marxist assumption that human beings are primarily motivated by rational and material interests rather than moved by emotional and intangible attachments. Among other consequences, they argued, its misunderstanding of the psyche led the SPD to exaggerate the significance of program and underestimate the importance of leadership in political life.[3] It is obvious why the NSDAP would impress this group. Indeed, one might ask, what protected them from ideological adaptation to the National Opposition? For one thing, they were neither racist nor revanchist; for another, they were committed socialists. The *political* divide between them and National Socialism was their passionate republicanism. They criticized Marxism because its precepts, they believed, subverted the SPD's will to put itself forward as the party of the republican nation.

A dense web of organizational and personal ties joined, though also separated, the various neo-revisionists, but all of them were absolutely committed to the *Reichsbanner* as a republican defense league. In it, many of them enjoyed a national reputation, while still limited to a regional one in the party. After September 1930, they worked eagerly to infuse it with a militantly republican, activist spirit.

Also in reaction to the elections, moderate leftists began to join the previously-shunned *Reichsbanner* because it, unlike other social democratic organizations, confronted Nazis in the streets. Along with neo-revisionists, these leftists rebelled against *Reichsbanner* chairman Otto Hörsing, a belligerent opponent of "proletarian defense" and personal enemy of the SPD Left. They were convinced that Hörsing was "sabotag[ing] the *Reichsbanner's* power to strike" to "forestall an attack [from the far Right]." SPD leaders wanted to retain Hörsing, but agreed to his replacement in early December 1931 in order to avert open rebellion against him and the SPD.[4]

Karl Höltermann, who stepped up from vice-chairman to chairman, leaned towards the rebels, but was no radical paramilitarist. Rather, he was affiliated with neo-revisionists who understood militancy less as a military posture than an assertive street presence and disciplined attitude. They complained that social democracy would never effectively confront the Nazis unless its individual associations overcame their ingrained distrust of an overarching coordination of extraparliamentary activity.[5] Höltermann's ascendancy meant that a man of the new Right replaced one of the old, but leftist militants accepted him because of his activist perspective and openness to cooperation with the Left.

The collaboration that led to Hörsing's demise was repeated in the formation of the Iron Front which, not by accident, took place soon after Höltermann became chairman of the *Reichsbanner*. For months, SPD leaders had ignored pleas for a "defense cartel" or "proletarian general staff" from functionaries in the party and the *Reichsbanner*. As late as early December, they rebuffed Höltermann when he called publicly for an "Iron Front." Despite the snub, Höltermann doggedly gathered allies. He received solid support from the Berlin *Reichsbanner* and from the left-dominated Berlin SPD. In the end, several members of the SPD Central Committee and, most important, the Executive Board of the ADGB also joined in the chorus for a "command-center." Under pressure from this uniquely broad internal coalition, SPD chairman Otto Wels finally consented to the official christening of an overarching authority that was threatening to materialize from below.[6]

The political viewpoint of the "militant republicans," and the contours of their imagined Iron Front, can be gleaned from speeches delivered at mass *Reichsbanner* rallies in the days after Höltermann became chairman and before Wels called the Iron Front into being. *Reichsbanner* leaders harped on the imminent threat of a Nazi coup and attacked the Brüning regime for handling Nazi violence with kid-gloves while it pounded communist offenders with an iron fist. They vented the anger of social democratic audiences who "do everything for the Republic that does nothing for you .... The state oppresses us ... treats us like the enemy .... " They were ready to restrict the democratic rights of "anti-state organizations," calling on Brüning to ban not only the SA, but also the NSDAP.[7] Though speakers might disparage the actual Republic, their *republicanism* was conspicuous and pugnacious. At a huge rally on 2 December, the leader of Berlin's *Reichsbanner* called for "republican action," "forceful defense" of democracy, "ruthless republicans at the [state's] summit." He warned its enemies, "We'll fight and sacrifice for a better Germany, for the authentic Republic in which state power will truly rest with the people." Speakers referred often to "*das Volk*" and not once to the "proletariat." The clearest breach of SPD tradition, however, was the unequivocal call for a *Volksfront* of all the republican parties, of "productive citizens and workers."[8] Höltermann and his lieutenants and mentors foresaw a militantly republican, exclusively extraparliamentary popular front that would exert heavy pressure on the regime to repress the political Right.

Meanwhile, the Berlin SPD also pressed for the formation of the Iron Front. Judging from debates at its local assemblies, however, its ranks envisioned a different sort of "general staff" from what *Reichsbanner* leaders saw. They wanted to excavate and restore the original intent of social democracy's founders. Members demanded that the SPD end toleration and return to its roots as a *Klassenpartei*.[9] Assemblies applauded calls for a general strike and assertions that the SPD must "fight capitalism, stop buttressing the State" and "return to Karl Marx! Onward to the class struggle!"[10] Not only in Berlin but elsewhere, activists were ever more sympathetic to a united front with communists, rather than to a popular front with bourgeois republicans.[11]

Nonetheless, counter-currents slightly diverted the course of the leftward tow. One notes pleas to break with the SPD's established approach to propaganda and adopt *Nazi* methods and style. Such suggestions were not limited to technical adjustments, but also questioned ideals customarily upheld by left-oriented Social Democrats. The Berlin SPD set aside its aversion to "personality cults" and pressed the editor of *Vorwärts* "to feature leaders as prominently as do the Nazis."[12] Leftists had earlier insisted that rational discourse was the only effective means to win firm support. Now left-tending Berlin functionaries argued for hyper-charged rhetoric, for more presentation and less deliberation.[13]

Moreover, not class-struggle principles, but a sense of betrayal underlay party members' disavowals of the Republic. They were as infuriated as *Reichsbanner* leaders by Brüning's refusal to crack down on the National Socialists except with restrictions on *all* public activity. One man lamented, "We always say, if Hitler takes over, there'll be no freedom. What kind of freedom is it, when we can't carry the Republic's colors in public .... [W]e have open fascism .... There's nothing left to defend. (Storm of protest.) ... Shame on us that we fear such a character as Hitler. (Thunderous applause.) Fight Fascism, but under the red flag of socialism." In other cases, outrage against treachery provoked not anti-republican sentiment, but a determination to reclaim the Republic. At a gathering of a decidedly leftist temper, several members exhorted comrades to join the *Reichsbanner* in its struggle against the Nazis. They got as much applause as those who called for socialism.[14]

A yearning for "unity and determination" and for a militant, extra-parliamentary orientation pervaded these assemblies. Members were ready to forgive their leadership much, if it would only "go on the offensive." Even the angriest crowds cheered speakers who professed readiness to fight for the party should it only call them.[15] The mood at the base of the Berlin Reichsbanner was similar to that in the SPD.[16] Such views explain why the proclamation of the Iron Front so stirred Social Democrats. No doubt, many of the SPD's one million members assumed that their leaders had finally created a "proletarian general staff" to organize the workers' struggle against fascism.

A mutual desire to seize the initiative unified Social Democrats at the base, on the Left, and at the higher levels of the *Reichsbanner*, but they were divided over the question of whether to build a people's or proletarian front, a disagreement that reflected a deeper divergence about the centrality of class to the social democratic project. One also notes dissimilarities between the tactics of the Left and the ranks on the one side, and those of the *Reichsbanner* on the other. Berliners exploded in fury against toleration, while *Reichsbanner* leaders never once mentioned it, though they too were fed up with negative support of the Hunger Chancellor.[17] The December rallies were a central tactic in the *Reichsbanner's* campaign for the Iron Front. Clearly, its leaders had decided that by disregarding parliamentary strategy – the SPD's domain – and highlighting extraparliamentary mobilization – the *Reichsbanner's* terrain – they could demonstrate the intensity of the desire for action without alienating party leaders.

Yet they could also not afford to estrange the ranks; indeed, the whole point of the Iron Front was to activate them. Not surprisingly, the call for a *Volksfront* quietly dropped off the agenda. Ironically, the vision of a popular front was probably the main point of agreement between SPD and *Reichsbanner* leaders about the structure of the proposed front. The SPD Executive did not promote this idea, however. Proletarian, not populist, rhetoric saturated Otto Wels' inauguration speech and his later "summons" to mobilization.[18] Party leaders hoped the reluctantly created Iron Front would distract Social Democrats from toleration and, more difficult yet, convince them to campaign for the re-election of the SPD's old enemy President Paul von Hindenburg in March 1932. The need to rally the ranks for the Junker Field Marshal was a major hindrance to turning the Iron Front into an explicit *Volksfront*. In the very act of building a de facto cross-class coalition for Hindenburg, the SPD had to emphasize the proletarian loyalties and composition of the Iron Front. Yet it was not, of course, a united front because neither SPD nor KPD leaders had the slightest intention of cooperating with each other and the Iron Front remained open to other republican parties and organizations, though their affiliation, much less their active participation, was not pursued.[19]

Party leaders did impose their vision of the Iron Front as an electoral machine, rather than a purely extraparliamentary organization or, even less, a paramilitary defense front. When it came to important decisions, the Iron Front was a "front" only in so far as it acted as a cover for the SPD. According to Karl Höltermann, the "Iron Front combat machine" functioned separately as did the *Reichsbanner*, trade unions, and party; its claim to organizational unity boiled down to "common propaganda" and a "center for exchanging views."[20]

In practice, the Iron Front was not the "organization of a new kind" that its *Reichsbanner* promoters wanted nor the break with a defensive parliamentary course that its left-wing backers desired. Nevertheless, its militant rhetoric, proclamations of republican determination and proletarian unity, and frequent and colorful military-style processions and music-filled rallies thrilled social democratic workers who signed up in the "Iron Book" by the tens of thousands. Party members who had drifted out of activity began to attend meetings again. Social Democrats spiritedly took the campaign for Hindenburg into Nazi-dominated enclaves that had not witnessed a republican rally for years. This subjective revival despite dreadful objective conditions and continued toleration of Brüning did not go unremarked. Berlin's republican press noted the revitalization with awe, the conservative press and internal memoranda of the KPD and NSDAP with chagrin. Party, trade union, and *Reichsbanner* leaders were almost as surprised by the change of mood as outside observers.[21]

2. Renewing the New Front

As satisfaction over Hindenburg's victory and Hitler's defeat abated, the initial impulse behind the building of the Iron Front flagged. The ambiguities of its status and mission that initially allowed it to embody disparate dreams and serve different purposes now threatened to break it apart. Having accepted it as an electoral construction, Social Democrats in the SPD, ADGB, and *Reichsbanner* disagreed over how to devise a winning strategy for elections looming in Prussia, Bavaria, Hamburg, and other states. Motivated, in part, by the urgency of the situation, and in part by the Iron Front's mobilizing power, a tug-of-war over its future intensified in the spring of 1932.

Cautious SPD centrists and rightists who dominated its Prussian diet delegation kept control of the Prussian electoral campaign. During it, the Iron Front retreated behind the SPD. Minister-President Otto Braun, pessimistic and exhausted, soberly emphasized SPD accomplishments and dourly warned of disaster should the electorate not come to its senses. No program to address mass unemployment or economic misery was offered. The results of the polling on 24 April were devastating. The NSDAP skyrocketed from 8 to 167 seats; the SPD shrank to 94 from 137 seats. The pro-republican parties no longer commanded a majority in the Landtag.

Simultaneously, a programmatic battle was fought between rightist ADGB leaders on one side, and the SPD Executive and Left on the other. To broaden the base of the Iron Front, and strengthen trade unions devastated by unemployment, ADGB leaders wanted it to adopt a forceful economic policy. The ADGB board noted, "The Iron Front has fulfilled its politico-propagandistic tasks .... Now [it] must contribute to increasing economic confidence. Its soldiers must take up the propaganda for public works."[22] To this end, ADGB leaders promoted the Woytinsky-Tarnow-Baade Plan (WTB) "to overcome the crisis." WTB called for massive public projects financed by state credit, which would both create jobs directly and jump start private production by stimulating demand.

WTB's principal author was the ex-Menshevik Wladimir Woytinsky, head of the ADGB Statistics Bureau. His prescriptions broke with the social democratic interpretation of the Depression as a crisis of overproduction. They articulated a modern economic perspective based on the still rudimentary ideas of Keynes whose writings had convinced Woytinsky that, first, deflation, not inflation, was the demon to fear and, second, a bourgeois state could manipulate fiscal policy to conquer a capitalist crisis. The WTB plan faced stubborn opposition within leading circles of the SPD because its foundation was non-Marxist. Their distrust of it was also political, however. For months, Woytinsky had subjected Brüning's deflationary policies to withering analysis. In attacking the left-liberal-conservative consensus about the danger of inflation, Woytinsky's plan threatened to align social democracy with the "free money" advocates of the far Right and to sabotage its cooperation with Brüning.

A deeper current in the SPD resisted acceptance of any plan to save capitalism and pressed for the adoption of one to terminate it. Like the union leaders whose reformism they abjured, the left-leaning leadership of the AfA-Bund and the radical Left in the party agreed that the SPD needed an "action policy," but their candidate was an "immediate" program for socialism. Sympathy for the WTB plan existed among the ranks as well as among some leftists, but the mood in favor of a socialist agenda was much more pronounced. Lack of resonance below and opposition from above sealed the fate of WTB as a single-issue electoral strategy for the Iron Front.[23]

In opposition to the "Prussian strategy" and unrelated to the programmatic debate, a third approach emerged in March-April 1932. According to this interpretation, the purely formal changes carried out by the Iron Front could of themselves unify broad masses behind the Republic and social democracy if they were deepened into a revolution in technique led by an internal coalition of the militant in spirit. Its champions wanted Iron Front mobilizations to sizzle with fiery rhetoric and dazzle with displays of the massed, disciplined ranks. They were convinced that the NSDAP "owes its power of attraction not least to its methods: the metaphorical effect of its psychological technique, symbolically rich ceremonies, art of staging, and military construction."[24] The impetus to push the Iron Front further in this direction came, again, from Höltermann, his lieutenants, and SPD districts led by neo-revisionists, such as Hamburg, and the Left, such as Berlin.[25]

Carlo Mierendorff, in particular, dedicated himself to transforming the Iron Front into an activist movement that would revitalize the SPD in its wake. Toward this end, he wanted to build a deliberate alliance among ideologically-diverse militants. Aware that an irresistible tow was dragging Social Democrats to the left, Mierendorff hoped to channel this tide towards a mass republican course that could attract workers who had defected to the KPD and even "revolutionary elements" in the orbit of the NSDAP.[26] In the Left SPD journal, *Marxistische Tribüne für Politik und Wirtschaft*, he published a plea for the old Left to work with revisionists to create an "an active, radical ... anti-conservative" SPD. The Left diagnosed correctly, he wrote, that the SPD's paralysis was caused by its fear of alienating the bourgeois parties. Leftists also realized that parliamentary power rested less on governmental posts than on popular support, while the "right wing" held on stubbornly to ministerial positions whose very exercise undermined the SPD's mass base.[27]

His praise of the Left did not mean that he wanted an "orthodox renaissance." Far from it, he hoped the SPD would secure its still precarious willingness to assume authority in a bourgeois state. Though he agreed with the Left that "Germany's future will be decided by the extraparliamentary situation," he defined that "situation" not as class struggle but, significantly, as "public opinion."[28] In fact, he condemned the metamorphosis of the SPD into a "proletarian Economic Party" and attributed this evolution to its "trade-unionization."[29] Consistent with this view, he rejected the WTB plan and bluntly told trade union leaders to keep out of political decision-making, although he also advised the SPD to adopt a program for public works! Unlike the Left (or Center), Mierendorff did not repudiate WTB on doctrinal grounds. Rather, he distrusted its source – the "economistic" trade unions.[30]

Mierendorff's paradoxical call for a "new Left" guided by a "new revisionism" was intended to provoke traditionalists of the Left and Right by confronting them with an essentially unprogrammatic, though not apolitical, vision. The publication of this piece in the only remaining Left SPD journal suggests that its editor, at least, was interested in Mierendorff's desire to refurbish the SPD's leftist posture – "militant, confrontational, and risk-taking" – without returning to class-struggle politics. Mierendorff's conviction that a combative spirit constituted a primary political attribute was certainly not limited to him alone. Neo-revisionists were distinguished by their questioning of the assumption that rational action and argument about material interests comprised not just the stuff of political bargaining, but the substance of political identification. Mierendorff and his closest friend Theo Haubach had long insisted that effective use of militant images in film, assertive symbols such as the republican flag, and aggressive signals such as harassment of reactionary professors could forge support for the Republic by establishing its self-assurance and resolve.[31]

A personal preference for the evocative over the mundane was given grist by Hendrik de Man's *Psychology of Socialism* (1926). The Belgian socialist's brief against the psychological obtuseness of orthodox Marxism profoundly influenced the group of Social Democrats who founded the journal *Neue Blätter für den Sozialismus* in 1930. Following the September Reichstag elections, Haubach and Mierendorff coaxed this magazine of "cultural socialism" towards a political focus on the strengths and weaknesses of the SPD on one hand, and on those of its most dangerous enemy, the NSDAP, on the other. Ironically, as they became more political, Mierendorff and Haubach wrote less about domestic issues, such as the SPD's stand on national defense. Instead, their articles and memoranda for the "*Neue Blätter* circle" hammered home the message that the SPD should re-orient itself toward the extraparliamentary arena, attend to "staging" and "*Symbolik*" rather than argue endlessly about policies and terminology, and turn itself into a "militant party" to challenge the Nazi "military party."[32]

In spring 1932, Mierendorff found the ideal ally to help realize his double project for a new Left and a newer Iron Front. Sergei Chakhotin was, like Wladimir Woytinsky, an imaginative Russian who was markedly conversant with modern developments in his field. He was not, however, tainted by trade union ties or economistic tendencies. Chakhotin offered, instead, revolutionary credentials and a theoretical framework for a psychological reorientation of social democratic propaganda. Out of his experience as a "director of revolutionary propaganda" during the civil war and his later work with Pavlov, he had developed a psychology of mass politics.[33] Communist and Nazi agitation, he maintained, was guided (if unconsciously) by the Pavlovian principle of conditioned reflex. Propaganda informed by *Psychotechnik*, as he dubbed it, punctuates the power of a movement, not the strength of its enemies as SPD propaganda tended to do. It displays a few arresting symbols; speakers and posters use short, provocative words; supporters shout rhymed chants. The message is simple and uniform, the media elaborate and varied – posters, banners, graffiti, cabaret, "stimulating dialogues" between speaker and crowd.

Obsessed with logic and reason, Social Democrats slighted the emotional impulses that sway the masses, he argued authoritatively. "Our circles are still haunted," he protested, "by the fatal mistake of seeing economic wisdom as the primary substance of politics." In the short run, he contended, economic questions did not determine politics, a fact that explained Hitler's popularity despite his outrageous, contradictory promises. Not what the Führer said, but *how* he said it, was the "secret" of Nazi success. The SPD too must caste off the "ways and means of the 1890s" and become "modern and effective."[34]

Chakhotin's theories were astoundingly similar to the ideas of Mierendorff and Haubach. Yet it was his creative practice that first caught Mierendorff's attention. The walls of Heidelberg, where Chakhotin lived, were as defaced by swastikas as every other German town in 1932. Noticing that someone had canceled a swastika with a chalk slash, it occurred to him to turn the slash into a downward-slanting arrow and so make the message crystal clear. He convinced a group of young *Reichsbanner* members to strike through every *Hakenkreuz* in Heidelberg. "The effect was amazing," one man remembered, "The Nazis were shocked, all Heidelberg abuzz with the news."[35] Next, Chakhotin made the single arrow, three, and provided them with metaphorical meaning. The *Drei Pfeile* (three arrows) stood for "unity, activity, discipline" as well as party, trade unions, and *Reichsbanner*, the pillars of the Iron Front. Chakhotin suggested that members of the Iron Front greet each other with a raised fist and the salute "Freedom!"[36] These apparently token-signs irritated and flustered National Socialists as had no social democratic action in months.

Chakhotin's "symbol-system" immediately made sense to receptive Social Democrats. The *Drei Pfeile* evoked cherished cultural associations, the *Freiheitsgruß* fostered solidarity and reminded them of what they were protecting. As old as was the iconography of the *Drei Pfeile*, so new was their form. Their non-representational, geometric design simulated the abstract modernism of Kandinsky and minimalist constructivism of El Lissitzky.[37] The *Freiheitsgruß* mimicked a militant communist gesture and simultaneously reclaimed the ground of liberty, theatrically evoking the fire and fury of two great revolutions with a motion and a word that could be variously interpreted by different observers (or participants).

Chakhotin's system took Heidelberg by storm, but met with considerable skepticism at higher levels of the SPD. In February 1932, he sent party headquarters an explanation of his symbols and a propaganda plan for the presidential campaign that was laconically brushed aside. In mid-March, Mierendorff managed to get him appointed director of *Reichsbanner* propaganda; its local chapters directed members to use the three arrows. But the Reich command center of the Iron Front, dominated by the SPD, rejected them with the argument that the socialist movement had too many insignia as it was. Others objected that the methods were superficial and similar to Nazi tactics that Social Democrats had derided for years.[38]

Chakhotin and Mierendorff set out methodically to persuade leading Social Democrats of the worth of the new propaganda. To overcome resistance to its discomfiting spotlight on the irrational, they emphasized, first, the *scientific* foundations of the new methodology. In *Grundlagen und Formen politischer Propaganda*, they argued that empirical evidence – the World War, Russian Civil War, and Hitler's ascent – demonstrated the significance of propaganda to modern politics. They reassured their readers that the new "rational" methods of political struggle and "systematic" propaganda would "not haphazardly," but "consciously" awaken passion. Indeed, they explained, the "new propaganda is nothing but the application of the findings of the modern mass psychology of the scientific organization of work to the political struggle of the workers' movement."[39] The link between the new propaganda and modern psychology was outlined in detail in the table "The System of human drives and their exploitation for propagandistic goals." This chart, inspired by Freudian, Reichian, and Pavlovian notions, categorized impulses as either "survival drives" (for nourishment or power) or "reproductive drives" (maternal or erotic) and listed the psychological aims and technical means of eliciting each. Thus, the drive for power could be stimulated by the *Drei Pfeile*, marches, and "battles of the flags" in order either to intimidate or to encourage. The "elementary, negative" erotic drive would, for its part, make the opponent "laughable, contemptible" and could be aroused by caricatures, carnevalistic processions, and "[Ernst] Röhm" (i.e., reference to the homosexuality of the commander of the Nazi Stormtroopers).[40]

Anticipating that Social Democrats might not be ready for all the discoveries of modern science, the *Grundlagen* employed a second argumentative strategy: it invoked the authority of tradition. Its authors reminded Social Democrats that Lassalle and Marx were the first to mate "science and labor." The architects of the new propaganda "only resumed an old tradition." In fact, socialists had invented techniques that they *appeared* to be borrowing from communists and fascists. Socialists had, after all, raised "the red flag, worn the insignia of the red carnation and the uniform of red necktie, floppy hat, and Bebel beard, and addressed one another as comrade." Thus, "we are merely following old paths that were blazed by us." In this spirit, the authors suggested that the Iron Front resurrect the goddess of liberty, a figure customary to pre-war social democratic festivals. True to the new science of the "elementary, positive" erotic, she should be portrayed by a "pretty, tall maiden"; faithful to the oldest traditions of the Left, she should wear a red robe and red Phrygian cap and carry in her left hand a red "flag of freedom" (with the *Drei Pfeile*); fusing modern psychology and tradition in one grand gesture, she should brandish in her right hand a forward-pointing sword.[41]

More prosaically, the new-style strategists paraded the relatively better electoral returns in districts and states that had adopted the new methods to prove the efficacy of "technique" and "mass psychology." In Hamburg, for example, the *Drei Pfeile* and *Freiheitsgruß* had been systematically deployed. Karl Meitmann, chairman of the Hamburg SPD, provincial leader of the *Reichsbanner*, and neo-revisionist, was responsible for Hamburg's embrace of the new methods. In February Chakhotin had addressed two thousand SPD officials there who had eagerly executed his ideas.[42] Berlin too did well in the April polling, Theodor Haubach claimed, because of early, intense activity by the Iron Front.[43]

Chakhotin and Mierendorff made a test case of the diet elections in Hesse on 19 June. Mierendorff prevailed on officials in his home state's SPD to institute a plan of action that divided the campaign into four weeks of a steadily increasing tempo.[44] Insistent use of the three arrows to cross out the swastika as well as their display on flags and lapel buttons unleashed a "symbol war" with the Nazis.[45] In the city of Darmstadt, the *Freiheitsgruß* eclipsed the Hitler salute. Rallies, addressed by noticeably younger speakers than usual, appealed unabashedly to emotion. Communists were dumbfounded that "SPD proletarians were downright enthusiastic about the Iron Front" in Hesse despite the miserable economic situation.[46] The outcome was modest but thrilled Social Democrats. The SPD moved up from 21.4 percent the previous November to 23.1 percent. It did especially well in Darmstadt, where the NSDAP declined slightly, though it swept up 44 percent of the state-wide vote. The KPD lost about twenty-five thousand votes. Mierendorff attributed the success to "intensive systematic work with the new propaganda methods."[47]

Mierendorff neglected to mention that the Iron Front effort in Hesse was also characterized by calls for socialism and appeals to "proletarian solidarity."[48] He did admit, however, that the campaign had focused on workers and tried to scare the middle classes away from the Nazis, rather than attract them to social democracy.[49] Not only in Hesse did the designers of the "new style" adopt a class-based strategy. Chakhotin assumed that "class-conscious workers" were the troops of the Iron Front, "unschooled" workers its audience.[50] Haubach castigated the organizers of the Prussian campaign for not assailing "the collapsing capitalist system." He warned a crowd in Hanover, "We take note of anyone – whether businessman or civil servant – who sneers at the working class and the Republic."[51] The class-oriented language of the Iron Front's dedicated promoters was indicative of its propaganda in general. The Hamburg SPD, the sole party district firmly in neo-revisionist hands, concentrated on winning working-class votes in its Bürgerschaft campaign in April.[52]

This orientation was, in part, a concession to activists and leftists who wanted the SPD "to see itself as a workers' party," mobilize "the masses of the working-class," and win "communist workers" to the Republic.[53] A "new Left" could only be forged with the support of social democratic workers for whom "class" constituted the cornerstone of their political identity. Moreover, the entire SPD lurched to the left in the wake of Brüning's fall at the end of May. At the lower echelons of the SPD, socialist trade unions, and *Reichsbanner*, the leftward shift manifested itself in a greater willingness to cooperate with communists in defense of demonstrations and neighborhoods against the again unshackled SA. At the upper levels, SPD and ADGB leaders dusted off their socialist rhetoric.[54] In Chakhotin's case, however, class language was not opportunistic but reflected his (unorthodox) Marxist perspective. And one senses that Mierendorff, Haubach, and fellow neo-revisionists had also moved leftwards under the impact of endless Depression and ever more violent struggle against the NSDAP.

Whether persuaded by the principles of modern psychology or the proletarian tenor of the new-style campaign in Hesse, in early June Berlin's "command center" requested that the Reich command center adopt the *Drei Pfeile* as the official emblem of the Iron Front. Several days later, the ADGB national committee suggested that the Iron Front "finally shed its reserve" and embrace the symbol-system. Karl Höltermann again put acute pressure on party leaders. Suddenly the party council developed an interest in the ideas of Mierendorff and Chakhotin, summoning them to appear before it. Under pressure from the same coalition that had called for the formation of the Iron Front, on 14 June, the day before the Reichstag campaign began, the SPD Executive endorsed the use of the *Drei Pfeile* and *Freiheitsgruß*.[55]

The new-style Iron Front led the campaign. Social democratic propaganda material displayed the logo "Iron Front" more prominently than "SPD." District officials of the SPD received a campaign battle plan designed by Chakhotin. They were advised by the Executive Committee that "all comrades must be involved in the symbol war." The main slogan of the campaign, "Iron Front against Hitler-Barons," made clear whom social democracy opposed, rather than what it wanted; nonetheless, it cleverly associated the Nazis with the widely despised cabinet of aristocratic reactionaries. Each week of the month-long campaign was fought under a secondary slogan as well. During the first week, speakers, posters, and leaflets demanded to know if Germans preferred "Freedom or Barons?" *(Freiheit oder Freiherrn?)* Not every slogan expressed the socially ecumenical sentiments of radical democracy. The third week's slogan highlighted the failure of capitalism and lampooned Nazi collusion with a bankrupt system.[56] Yet this too was an attack with which millions of middle-class Germans could identify.

Other evidence too indicates that the campaign's orchestrators hoped to broaden the electoral base of the Iron Front. Leaflets handed out in rural areas addressed farmers, urban literature appealed to specific occupational groups.[57] In addition, they engaged in more subtle efforts to sway a wide swath of Germans by eliciting a potpourri of cognitive associations. A pamphlet provided sample scripts for "agitational speaking choruses" to perform in public squares and at demonstrations. Every exchange between speaker and chorus consisted of three words, thus, alluding to the three arrows. The content of the dialogues was distinctly non-partisan. A "positive" cluster – Peace, Freedom, Bread – simultaneously evoked the famed Bolshevik slogan and universally desirable conditions. A bundle of epithets – Prince, Hitler, Baron – enclosed Hitler in a cabal of royalty and nobility. The chorus chanted rhymed couplets whose rhetoric was social democratic (red, worker, freedom, peace, unity, discipline, activity) and combative ("our Iron Front will smash them"; "Smash Hitler!"). Yet the texts also incorporated Nazi language. Not only did the equivocal term "freedom" replace the disputed "Republic," but the "Password" was "Germany awake!" Workers (not proletarians) and "*das Volk*" were invoked.[58] The mingling of discourses from antithetical ideological traditions and with conflicting metaphorical meanings represented the ultimate stylistic amalgam of Left and Right, old and new. This practice, long habitual and, indeed, integral to National Socialism, assumed bizarre forms in July 1932. Thus, Karl Höltermann was saluted as "der Führer" at a massive "Freedom Day of the Iron Front," while young Nazis strutted the streets of Berlin decked out in red shirts.[59]

Scattered attempts to break into new social circles must be set against the general pitch and program of a campaign whose *political* radicalism was classically socialist. In a widely distributed pamphlet, a hypothetical Social Democrat countered the arguments of a "Communist" in stylized proletarian lingo. Concluding the dispute, he proclaimed, "31 July must become a day of honor for the Republic. The fronts are completely clear: class against class!"[60] Banner headlines trumpeted "socialism is the solution!" and called on followers to fall in behind the "red flag of socialism!"[61] Election supplements inveighed against the "system" and laid out a platform that included expropriation of coal mines and large landholdings. Calls for jobs and public works dotted campaign literature but did not stand out among the plethora of demands.[62] Alwin Brandes, left-leaning chairman of the metalworkers, asserted that the SPD, released from the "crippling burden of toleration," could now propagate a consistent socialist policy and so compete with the KPD. The party should deemphasize public works, briefly focused on in May, "because *Arbeitsbeschaffung* might raise doubts about the seriousness of socialism as our goal." Even Woytinsky suddenly detected the need for a "future" economic program.[63] Eager to put as much distance as possible between themselves and the reactionary Chancellor Franz von Papen, Social Democrats were determined to "hoist the red flag to the main mast."[64]

In general, functionaries took up the refurbished Iron Front with enthusiasm and fought a truly passionate electoral campaign of "unprecedented rigor and acrimony."[65] Hanover's *Reichsbanner* leaders exhorted members to "touch emotion, soul, and heart so reason can conquer."[66] Local officials reminded the ranks that the "contemporary spirit thinks in abstract symbols."[67] For their part, left-wing intellectuals discovered the worth of mass psychology and described the *Drei Pfeile* as symbols of "socialist logic and ethics." "The Leipzig working class adjusted quickly to the new methods of struggle," according to the *Leipziger Volkszeitung*, while Berlin "transformed" its propaganda by giving free reign to "feeling instead of insight."[68] The bourgeois republican press depicted Iron Front mobilizations in Berlin as larger and more imposing than any the capital had ever witnessed. The Nazi press made fun of the *Drei Pfeile*, but internal reports anxiously noted their popular impact and, even more, that of the "Hitler-Barons" slogan.[69]

Papen's coup against Otto Braun's regime in Prussia slammed into the social democratic campaign and broke its momentum. On 20 July 1932, the national government illegally deposed a cabinet led by a Social Democrat; martial law was proclaimed in Berlin and Brandenburg province. Rather than resist the *Staatsstreich*, the SPD decided to challenge the imposition of a Reich commissioner before the supreme court. Thousands of Social Democrats were bitterly disappointed by the decision not to fight and "to secure the election" instead. In the last days of the campaign Social Democrats began to attend communist events in noticeable numbers. Both police informers and Communists noted that *Reichsbanner* members, the backbone of the Iron Front, were especially numerous among the sudden converts to a proletarian front.[70]

On 31 July 1932, the SPD lost ten seats in the Reichstag and for the first time in two decades did not return as the largest delegation, an honor now enjoyed by the NSDAP. The KPD won twelve new seats and emerged as the third biggest delegation. Both NSDAP and KPD gained from the SPD's losses, while the NSDAP completed its spectacular demolition of the voting bases of the (Protestant) bourgeois parties. The coup in Prussia alone cannot explain an outcome that was so terrible for the SPD and for the Weimar Republic. Social Democrats could not and would not match the intensity and comprehensiveness of the radicals' assaults on the "Weimar system" if only because the SPD was intimately associated with the calumnied Republic by enemies and friends alike. Yet it seems likely that the SPD could have strengthened its electoral chances if the Iron Front had single-mindedly propagated the WTB plan to overcome mass unemployment. The NSDAP did not simply ride its popular wave to victory or rely on vicious attacks on its adversaries; it also made its own version of a public works program a central feature of its propaganda.[71] However one explains its failure to convert its value among Social Democrats into electoral gold, the election results destroyed the allure of the new-style Iron Front. In the fall, Mierendorff as well as various SPD and *Reichsbanner* functionaries continued to propagate the new style, but both the top leadership of the *Reichsbanner* and the social democratic ranks were disillusioned. Party members complained that the *Drei Pfeile* were "hollow" and had to be cajoled into wearing them.[72] Chakhotin dropped out of political activity, disgusted because the Iron Front had only half-heartedly and inadequately implemented his theories.[73]

In the six months between 31 July 1932 and the appointment of Hitler as chancellor of Germany, the accumulated ravages of the interminable economic crisis, erosion of the SPD's electoral base, and renewed proof of its political passivity precipitated a crisis of confidence in party leaders and their tortuous course of (in)activity. Disenchantment spread among the SPD's ranks and among leaders of the ADGB and *Reichsbanner*, undermining the solidarity of social democracy. On the one hand, having decided that the KPD's electoral challenge to the SPD now outranked the Nazi threat, the SPD's centrist leadership accelerated the rhetorical drift to the left that had become evident during the July Reichstag campaign. In December, it rejected the ambivalent political advances made by Weimar's last chancellor, General Kurt von Schleicher. On the other hand, both ADGB and *Reichsbanner* extended their own hesitant feelers towards the conservative regimes of Papen and Schleicher in an effort to build some sort of anti-Nazi bulwark, even if an authoritarian one. Meanwhile, the Left and neo-revisionists groped their way towards a common rejection of the Weimar Republic. In doing so, however, the Left reaffirmed its commitment to radical proletarian democracy, while Mierendorff and his co-thinkers speculated more openly about the prospects of a national, cross-class renewal of the Republic's foundations. Centrifugal tendencies revealed the increasingly discordant responses of different groups of Social Democrats to the obvious disorientation of the party Executive. Tragically, very few Social Democrats recognized the extreme danger of the political situation. The NSDAP's loss of two million votes in the Reichstag elections of 6 November 1932 and the subsequent internal squabbles among leading Nazis had convinced many political observers, including Social Democrats, that the Nazi threat had substantially abated. Only at the last moment did powerful Social Democrats in the party and ADGB realize that Hitler's accession to power loomed.[74]

3. Conclusion

The story of the Iron Front suggests that Weimar social democracy had a more complex relationship to modernity than has generally been recognized. Most party ideologues, it is true, reacted with intense suspicion to the economic modernism of WTB. ADGB leaders, however, were quite open to any plan that promised relief from mass unemployment. Moreover, despite philosophical commitment to a rational model of human motivation, leading Social Democrats of the Left and old Right, in the SPD and the ADGB, finally succumbed to the claims of modern psychology and aesthetics in a political climate that seemed impervious to logical arguments about interests and rights. The reaction to change by those who set the political course was highly ambivalent, but not hidebound. Nonetheless, the decision to risk change came very late and its implementation was short-lived. Ideological deterrents restricted the scope of change, while structural obstacles limited its depth. The Iron Front only superficially and temporarily overcame the ossification that afflicted social democracy. In December 1931, party leaders agreed to create a new organizational form and, in June 1932, to modify the Iron Front's style, but they did not accede to a redistribution of decision-making power among or within the various organizations in the Iron Front. The entrenched, and aging, bureaucracy of the SPD reacted with suspicion to demands for younger speakers and candidates and with hostility to the idea that the *Reichsbanner* should actually direct the Iron Front or that the trade unions could develop an economic program. Unfortunately, organizational jealousies were not confined to the top hierarchy of the SPD. Even at the height of enthusiasm for the Iron Front, functionaries at every level and in every branch of social democracy, whether *Reichsbanner*, ADGB, or Workers' Sport, zealously defended their organizational turf and resented the counsel of other Social Democrats.[75]

The dialectic between the modern and the traditional going on inside social democracy was not merely determined "from above" but was also influenced by the politico-cultural convictions of those at the lower echelons of a huge, long-lived, and multi-dimensional movement. The SPD was bureaucratic, but not completely bureaucratized. Its political success rested not only on the support of voters but on the active campaign work of thousands of members. Most of these members were still workers or workers' wives who wanted to hear the commitment of their party to the proletariat and to socialism reaffirmed, especially in the inhospitable political atmosphere of 1932. If they were to rejuvenate the SPD, "modernizing" intellectuals such as Mierendorff had to mobilize the very ranks who were most attached to its traditional class message.

Finally, dissident intellectuals who identified themselves with modernity interpreted its mandate in various ways. Chakhotin believed wholeheartedly, and the old Left perhaps more hesitantly, that a fusion of psychological and aesthetic modernism with radical Marxism could lay the basis for a renewed, recharged social democracy. For his part, Mierendorff and other neo-revisionists embraced psychological symbolism, but wanted to retain only the radical spirit of Marxism and harness that to a militant republicanism. The new-style Iron Front was a product of the interactions among these assorted organizational and individual players in the difficult circumstances of 1931 to 1932. Yet the particularly dramatic interplay between custom and innovation that plotted the short trajectory of the Iron Front was emblematic of the general interlocking of continuity and change that culturally enriched but politically immobilized social democracy during the Weimar Republic as a whole.

Notes

1. See Karl Rohe, *Das Reichsbanner Schwarz Rot Gold* (Düsseldorf, 1966).
2. For literature on the militant republicans, see Donna Harsch, *German Social Democracy and the Rise of Nazism* (Chapel Hill, NC, 1993), 24 nn. 57-60; 100 n. 104; 176 n. 44.
3. Ibid.
4. SAPMO-BA, DY 30 I2/705/23, Bl. 283.
5. Rohe, *Reichsbanner*, 392-93.
6. Harsch, *Social Democracy*, 169-70.
7. The first quote is from *Vorwärts* 565 (3 December 1931), the second from "Die Kundgebungen des Reichsbanners: Die Grossen gehören auf die Anklagebank," *Die Welt am Montag* 48 (30 November 1931).

8. *Vorwärts* 565 (3 December 1931). In practice, the Weimar SPD had participated in several people's fronts, whether as partners with bourgeois parties in ruling coalitions or as members of the *Reichsbanner's* national board. Cross-class cooperation was, however, hotly contested by the Left and even made many leading centrists uncomfortable. Social Democrats rarely conceptualized such collaborative efforts as a *people's* front, much less advertised it as such.
9. SAPMO-BA, DY 30 I2/705/23, Bl. 115, 233-34, 260. Also see "Rebellion in Berliner SPD," *Rote Fahne* 235 (21 December 1931). For similar views in other cities, see SAPMO-BA, DY 30 I2/705/23, Bl. 205, 254, 249.
10. SAPMO-BA, DY 30 I2/705/23, Bl. 266.
11. For such views in Leipzig, see SAPMO-BA, DY 30 I2/705/23, Bl. 170. For Berlin: I2/705/23, Bl. 207, 230, 260, 255, 246. Also see, "SPD und KPD einig," *Augsburger Abendzeitung*, 4 November 1931.
12. SAPMO-BA, DY 30 I2/705/23, Bl. 189, 206, 177, 115.
13. For the earlier attitude, see Harsch, *Social Democracy*, 142. For the new view, see Herbert Zech, "Demonstrationen – Ein Wort zu unserer politischen Technik," *Unser Weg* (hereafter *UW*), December 1931, 281-82.
14. SAPMO-BA, DY 30 I2/705/23, Bl. 266, 278.
15. SAPMO-BA, DY 30 I2/705/23, Bl. 170, 260, 203, 196-97, 278. Also see Werner Zorn, "Angreifen – die Parole für 1932," *UW*, January 1932, 7; Herbert Duwald, "Ausserparliamentarische Abwehr des Faschismus," *UW*, June 1931.
16. See, e.g., SAPMO-BA, DY 30 I2/704/23, Bl. 203, 277, 258-59.
17. Nordrhein-Westfälisches Staatsarchiv Münster (hereafter NWStAM), Bestand SPD und Reichsbanner, Nr. 9.
18. See Wels's speech, printed in ADGB, Vorstand, *Leipart und Breitscheid über die Notverordnung* (Berlin, 1931), 29-31; Wels et al., *Eiserne Front: Vier Aufrufe* (Berlin, 1932), 1-4.
19. Besides individual bourgeois republicans, only a few chapters of the liberal State Party joined the Iron Front.
20. Rohe, *Reichsbanner*, 414, 398-99.
21. "Die Republikaner im Sportpalast," *Berliner Tageblatt* (hereafter *BT*) 53 (1 February 1932); "Reise in den Wahlkampf," *BT* 114 (8 March 1932); "SPD Spiegel," *Deutsche Führerbriefe* 83 (25 October 1932); SAPMO-BA, DY 30 I2/4/7, Bl. 1-4; Niedersächsiches Hauptstaatsarchiv Hanover (hereafter NHStAH) Hann. 310I/B13; Harsch, *Social Democracy*, 173.
22. Documents 85 and 86, in *Die Gewerkschaften in der Endphase der Republik 1930-1933*, compiled by Peter Jahn, vol. 4: *Quellen zu Geschichte der deutschen Gewerkschaftsbewegung im 20. Jahrhundert*, ed. Hermann Weber, Klaus Schönhoven, and Klaus Tenfelde (Cologne, 1986), 550-52.
23. For a discussion of WTB, opposition to it, and the historical literature concerning the controversy, see Harsch, *Social Democracy*, 155-68.
24. Walther Pahl, "Was bedeutet die Eiserne Front?" *Sozialistische Monatshefte* (hereafter SM), 7 March 1932, 230.
25. Rohe, *Reichsbanner*, 404.
26. Fritz Borinski, "Die 'Neue Blätter für den Sozialismus': Ein Organ der jungen Generation von 1930 bis 1933," in August Rathmann, *Ein Arbeiterleben: Erinnerungen an Weimar und danach* (Wuppertal, 1983), 75-78.
27. "Aufbau der neuen Linken," *Marxistische Tribüne für Politik und Wirtschaft*, February 1932.
28. Mierendorff, "Die volle Wahrheit," SM, 9 May 1932, 399.

29. Ernst Fraenkel first used the epithet "proletarian Economic Party" in "Die politische Bedeutung des Arbeitsrechts," *Die Gesellschaft* (hereafter *DG*), January 1932, 46.
30. "Bedrohtes Deutschland," *SM*, 7 March 1932, 220-21. His disgust over the ADGB's explicit offensive against reparations, and implicit attack on the Versailles Treaty, fueled Mierendorff's opposition to union politicking (222). He argued in favor of public works at the annual meeting of the Darmstadt SPD (*Hessischer Volksfreund*, 17 February 1932).
31. Carlo Mierendorff, "Republik oder Monarchie?" *SM*, July 1926, 437-38; Carl Zuckmayer, *Carlo Mierendorff* (n.p., 1944); Walter Hammer, ed., *Theo Haubach zum Gedächtnis* (Frankfurt am Main, 1955).
32. Martin Martiny, "Die Entstehung und politische Bedeutung der 'Neue Blätter für den Sozialismus' und ihres Freundeskreises," *Vierteljahrshefte für Zeitgeschichte* 25:3 (1977): 373-419; Theodor Haubach, "Die militante Partei," *Neue Blätter für den Sozialismus* (hereafter *NB*), May 1930; Mierendorff, "Lehren der Niederlage," *NB*, November 1930; Walter Glenlow (Haubach), "Politik und Agitation," *NB*, December 1931. Also see Haubach, "Vom Gegner lernen!" *Das Reichsbanner*, 4 October 1930; Haubach, "Parole: Angriff," *Hamburger Echo*, 19 September 1930.
33. Sergei Tschachotin (Chakhotin), "Aktivierung der Arbeiterschaft," *NB*, March 1932, 149. The biographical note appended to this article implies that Chakhotin propagandized for the Bolsheviks. He actually worked for the White General Kornilov. He considered himself a Marxist, however, and in exile grew ever friendlier to the USSR. In 1932, he was a researcher at the Institute for Physics in Heidelberg. See Richard Albrecht, "Symbolkampf in Deutschland 1932: Sergej Tschachotin und der 'Symbolkrieg' der drei Pfeile gegen den Nationalsozialismus als Episode im Abwehrkampf der Arbeiterbewegung gegen Faschismus in Deutschland," *IWK* 22:4 (1986): 509-13.
34. Chakhotin, *The Rape of the Masses: The Psychology of Totalitarian Political Propaganda* (London, 1940), 94-95, 99-101, 121, 191; idem, "Die positive Seite unserer Niederlage," *Deutsche Republik* (hereafter *DR*), 24 May 1932, 1093; idem, "Lehren der Wahlkämpfe," *DR*, 31 May 1932, 1135; idem, "Die Technik der politischen Propaganda," *SM*, 9 May 1932, 425-31; Rohe, *Reichsbanner*, 404-5.
35. Albrecht, "Symbolkampf," 523.
36. Chakhotin, *Rape*, 103-6.
37. Albrecht, "Symbolkampf," 525. Chakhotin abhorred the "Kitsch" that marred social democratic propaganda under the false assumption that the "crude and artistically inferior" masses could not appreciate the "truly beautiful" (Tschachotin, "Lehren der Wahlkämpfe," 1136).
38. Harsch, *Social Democracy*, 178-79.
39. Sergei Tschachotin and Carlo Mierendorff, *Grundlagen und Formen politischer Propaganda* (Magdeburg, 1932), 1-5.
40. Ibid., 48.
41. Ibid., 37. Accompanying photographs showed that this suggestion had already been implemented locally, presumably in Darmstadt.
42. Friedrich-Wilhelm Witt, *Die Hamburger Sozialdemokratie in der Weimarer Republik* (Hanover, 1971), 131, 138, 143; *Hamburger Echo*, 15 January 1932; Chakhotin, *Rape*, 203.
43. Walter Glenlow (Haubach), "Geist und Technik des Preussenwahlkampfes," *NB*, May 1932, 233-39.
44. Chakhotin, *Rape*, 206.
45. K. Wiegner, "Mit Höltermann im Hessenwahlkampf," *RB*, 18 June 1932.

46. Chakhotin, *Rape*, 207, 209; *Das Freie Wort* (hereafter *FW*), 3 July 1932, 24-25; *HVF*, 11 and 18 June 1932. The communist view is expressed in BAK, R45 IV/21: Remscheid, 29 June 1932.
47. Mierendorff, "Die Freiheitspfeile siegen in Hessen," *NB*, July 1932, 386-87; Mierendorff, *Vorwärts* 287 (21 June 1932). See also Tschachotin, "Das Hessische Experiment," *DR*, 19 July 1932, 1355-58; Künkele, "Lehren der Hessenwahl," *FW*, 3 July 1932, 24-26.
48. See, e.g., Chakhotin, *Rape*, 206; *Hessischer Volksfreund*, 28 May 1932.
49. Mierendorff, "Die Hessenwahl," *Vorwärts* 287 (21 June 1932).
50. Tschachotin, "Aktivierung der Arbeiterschaft," *NB*, March 1932, 149. Despite his radical Marxism, all Chakhotin's articles appeared in revisionist social democratic journals.
51. *Hanover Volkswacht*, 23 February 1932; Walter Glenlow (Haubach), "Geist und Technik des Preussenwahlkampfes," *NB*, May 1932, 233-39.
52. Rohe, *Reichsbanner*, 402 n. 4; Witt, *Hamburger Sozialdemokratie*, 143.
53. First quote: NSDAP HA R. 93/F.1898: Sektionsversammlung, 10 May 1932; second and third quotes: *FW* 3 July 1932, 11, 13.
54. Harsch, *Social Democracy*, 189-90, 196-97.
55. Document 97 in *Gewerkschaften*, vol. 4, 593-95.
56. See NWStAM Bestand SPD und Reichsbanner/Nr.8: Mobilmachung für den Wahlkampf, Parteivorstand, 14 June 1932; NHStAH Hann.310II/C/25: Rundschreiben des Reichsbannergaues Hanover #16/1932, 17 June 1932; Hann.310II/A/38: Material für die Reichstagswahl 1932. Also see Chakhotin, *Rape*, 215-19.
57. NWStAM Bestand SPD und Reichsbanner/Nr.8: (SPD) Rundschreiben, Recklingshausen, 8 July 1932; NHStAH Hann.310II/A/38: Material für die Reichstagswahl 1932, Sonderflugblätter; Wolfram Pyta, *Gegen Hitler und für die Republik: Die Auseinandersetzung der deutschen Sozialdemokratie mit der NSDAP in der Weimarer Republik* (Düsseldorf, 1989), 397, 415-17, 433.
58. SPD Vorstand, ed., *Agitations Sprechchöre: Reichstagswahl 1932* (n.p., 1932).
59. "Freiheitstag der Eiserne Front," *Das Reichsbanner*, 16 July 1932; Decker, "Nach der Preussenwahl," *DG*, June 1932, 473.
60. SPD Vorstand, *An der Stempelstelle: Ein Wahlgespräch* (Berlin, 1932), 7.
61. *Vorwärts* 267 (9 June 1932); *Leipziger Volkszeitung*, 12 May and 2 June 1932.
62. *Betriebswacht*, May 1932 and July 1932, Flugblattsammlung 1932 (SPD), AsD.
63. Michael Schneider, *Das Arbeitsbeschaffungs-Programm des ADGB: Zur gewerkschaftlichen Politik in der Endphase der Weimarer Republik* (Bonn-Bad Godesberg, 1975), 97.
64. Wolfgang Zollitsch, "Einzelgewerkschaften und Arbeitsbeschaffung: Zum Handlungsspielraum der Arbeiterbewegung in der Spätphase der Weimarer Republik," *Geschichte und Gesellschaft* 8:1 (1982): 109. Quote from *FW*, 21 August 1932, 18.
65. NWStAM Bestand SPD und Reichsbanner/Nr.8: (SPD) Rundschreiben, Bezirk Westliches Westfalen, 13 June 1932 and 18 July 1932; (SPD) Rundschreiben, Recklingshausen, 13 July 1932; Lothar Frey, *Deutschland, wohin?* (Zurich, 1934), 12-13.
66. *Rheinische Zeitung*, 15 June 1932; NHStAH Hann.310II/C/25: Rundschreiben des Gauvorstandes Hanover des Reichsbanners, 7 May 1932.
67. *FW*, 10 July 1932, 13.
68. *Leipziger Volkszeitung*, 4 July 1932; Dietmar Klenke, *Die SPD-Linke in der Weimarer Republik* (Münster, 1983), 360; *FW*, 3 July 1932, 22-23; G.W., "Die Berliner Partei im Wahlkampf," *UW*, September 1932, 257-60.

69. "Idee gegen Uniform," *BT*, 5 July 1932; BAK R45 IV/28: [KPD] Bericht über die Durchführung der Reichstagswahl im Juli 1932 and Bericht über die Wahlkampagne Reichstagswahl 1932, Unterbezirk II (Dresden); NHStAH Hann.310I/B11/I: Bezirksleitung Goslar (NSDAP) [n.d.]; Ortsgruppe NSDAP Alfeld, 8 August 1932; Blankenburg/Harz, 10 August 1932.
70. See, e.g., BAK, R45IV/21: Bericht über die Versammlungstournee in den Bezirken Ruhrgebiet, Mittelrhein, Saargebiet u. Niederrhein vom 30.6. bis zum 30.7.32.
71. Harsch, *Social Democracy*, 190, 201.
72. *Vorwärts* 560 (28 November 1932); Mierendorff, "Die Bedeutung der neuen Propaganda," *NB*, October 1932; Richard Albrecht, *Der militante Sozialdemokrat: Carlo Mierendorff 1897-1943. Eine Biographie* (Berlin/Bonn, 1987), 99.
73. Chakhotin, *Rape*, 232.
74. For a detailed discussion of the complex developments summarized in this paragraph, see Harsch, *Social Democracy*, 203-38.
75. Harsch, *Social Democracy*, 175-77, 201.

Chapter 10

Communism and the Public Spheres of Weimar Germany

Eric D. Weitz

1.

The founding congress of the Communist Party of Germany (KPD) convened in the very last days of 1918. Germany was enveloped in revolution and the disorder of military and economic demobilization. Miners were on strike in the Ruhr. In cities and towns throughout the country, workers' and soldiers' councils watched over the endeavors of mayors and other officials of the old Imperial German bureaucracy. Demonstrations, often raucous affairs in front of a city hall, a factory owner's residence, or a military garrison, were daily occurrences. For the radicals who convened to form a new political party, the establishment of socialism seemed a matter of the burning present, not a long-term goal to be fulfilled in some distant, hazy future. Rosa Luxemburg, the fiery radical who provided the critical intellectual and political leadership for the nascent communist movement, articulated for the participants the heady optimism that prevailed amid the disorder and deprivation of the winter of 1918 to 1919:

> *Now, comrades, today we are experiencing the moment when we can say: We are again at Marx's side, under his banner. When we today declare in our program: the immediate task of the proletariat is nothing less than … to make socialism fact and reality, to eliminate capitalism root and branch, then we place ourselves on the same ground on which Marx and Engels stood in 1848 and from which they … never diverged.*[1]

Notes for this chapter begin on page 288.

For Luxemburg and her comrades, the creation of socialism seemed a matter only of its proclamation: an audacious political act by a party and a class prepared to seize the historical moment and do battle with the enemy, from factory owners and army officers to reform-minded trade unionists and social democratic politicians. Should the party and the proletariat fail to take action, then the historical prospects were frightful indeed – a descent into barbarism even worse than the mass slaughter of World War I, whose guns had been stilled only eight weeks previously.[2]

Yet the party that Luxemburg helped found was never a simple act of self-creation, a Jacobin thrust into the future, nor were the politics it pursued a matter only of ideological pronouncement. The KPD, founded in revolution, became one of the nation's major parties and a mass movement amid the murky and turbulent, but decidedly non-revolutionary, waters of Weimar Germany – and amid the explosive and conflictual experiences of Bolshevik Russia and the Soviet Union. The latter gave the KPD a model of revolutionary militancy, a connection to like-minded parties around the world, and an authoritarian orientation that would come to include some of the worst features of Stalinism. But Weimar was no less important in the shaping of German communism. Weimar provided the KPD with an open, wide-ranging political tableau, a set of hyperactive public spheres marked by loud and persistent conflicts over the most basic features of society. The KPD, in short, evolved historically within the vibrant and highly contested public spheres of the Weimar Republic; it was never simply the creature of its own founders and leaders or, later, of the Soviet Union.[3]

The public spheres that shaped German communism were varied, overlapping, and conflicting realms defined by class, gender, political orientation, and, very decisively, by the nature of Weimar's political and social economy.[4] The realms themselves evolved as all the varied forces – radical workers and conservative employers, reformist Social Democrats now ensconced in power and fascist military bands, working-class women and army officers, promoters of mass marketing and sexual reformers – engaged in battle, actual and virtual, over the contours of German society. For German communism, the ultimate result of its emergence within this active and lively – and very dangerous – matrix was the creation of a party and movement marked by a highly combative, intransigent, and masculinized political culture. These traits were not simply imposed from above by a party leadership that, under Soviet influence, adopted in the course of the 1920s an increasingly authoritarian mode of practice. The critical features of German communism can also be seen in the day-to-day practices of party members, both leaders and rank and file, at the base level. Examples drawn from the daily life and activities of Communists will illustrate the point, as will a more careful delineation of the salient characteristics of the Weimar public spheres.

2.

The democratic norms of the Republic, inscribed in the Weimar Constitution, can hardly be underestimated as a factor shaping the development of German communism.[5] To be sure, there were infractions and violations of democratic strictures. The state at various times banned the KPD or its affiliates like the Red Front Fighters League. The party was always subject to the most exacting police supervision, which kept all levels of the state well informed about the KPD's activities. State officials, including Social Democrats, worked in close cooperation with employers to remove Communists from the workplace. Nonetheless, the democratic norms of Weimar gave the KPD access to all the varied realms of public discourse. The KPD remained largely free to contest elections, publish its newspapers, and bring its supporters together in demonstrations and rallies – an almost unique history among communist parties in the moment of their emergence as mass movements. British and American communism, operating in an even broader democratic environment, only achieved pockets of popular support and never quite became mass parties on a national scale. The French party, a possible exception, made its initial breakthrough in the 1930s. But most European communist parties made their breakthroughs as popular armies in the resistance against Nazi occupation in World War II, and it took this experience for the French party to consolidate and expand the gains won in the 1930s. The combination of the harsh conditions of a national uprising and Soviet directives forced these communist parties to develop programs of reform, to articulate communism in national terms, and, in general, to seek support beyond the industrial working class. In sharp contrast, the KPD made its popular breakthrough within the structures of a democratic society. Ironically, the experience of democracy did not serve to foster a democratic political culture among German Communists or an interest in recruiting support beyond the ranks of the proletariat. Instead, the frustrations of competition in a democratic public sphere helped foster an intransigence and authoritarianism precisely because other political groups won and retained the loyalties of large segments of the proletariat, the class the KPD claimed as its own.[6]

The chronology itself is significant. The KPD emerged as a mass party in the most revolutionary period in Europe since 1848, a period marked by the Bolshevik Revolution and uprisings, mutinies, mass strikes, and demonstrations all across the continent. Radical workers and Communists sought the forcible overthrow of the existing regimes and the construction of alternate sources of power, the party and the workers' and soldiers' councils. In contrast, international communism defined World War II and its aftermath as *non-revolutionary* situations in which the cross-class and cross-political alliances of the Resistance would establish democratic-antifascist regimes and prepare a gradual transition to socialism. In the 1920s, however, German communists expressed a revolutionary confidence that grew out of the model of the Bolshevik Revolution and their own experiences of engagement in the embattled public spheres of the German Revolution of 1918 to 1920. The Russian events in particular provided them with a model of the violent seizure of power, the heroic myths of the storming of the Winter Palace and the rout of the White forces in the Civil War.

Violence came to have political meaning and a certain psychological allure for Soviet as well as German Communists, and found its expression in the day-to-day political and cultural practices of the KPD. Erich Mielke, the long-time Minister of State Security in the German Democratic Republic who was convicted some sixty years later for the 1931 slaying of two policemen, was not alone in his fondness for weaponry. Even the so-called "rightist" Heinrich Brandler packed a pistol. The memoirs of Erich Wollenberg, active in the military apparatus of the KPD, depict a conspiratorial life on the run, a life of secretive meetings with comrades, altercations with the police, and underground military exercises.[7] The paramilitary Red Front Fighters League became the standard bearer of party demonstrations by the late 1920s. The communist press of the 1920s was infused with depictions of heroic male proletarians, marching in disciplined military formation or manning the barricades, weapons in hand – the latter a 1920s reprise of a form of political conflict more suited to 1848 than the twentieth century. John Heartfield's many dramatic covers for the *Arbeiter-Illustrierte-Zeitung*, photos and photomontages of powerful male fists and arms, helped create an aesthetic of combative, male militancy.

In the democratic public spheres, the KPD competed especially with the SPD, the *Staatspartei* of the Weimar Republic. Nowhere else in Europe did a mass-based communist party face a mass-based social democratic party integrally identified with the state, which gave the communist-social democratic split special virulence in Germany. Even when the SPD functioned outside the Reich government, as it did from 1920 to 1928, and again from 1930 onwards, it retained power in numerous municipalities and federal states. Social democratic-led police forces in Prussia and Hamburg, for example, intent on maintaining order, faced Communists intent on fomenting civil disorder. Moreover, many better-paid, skilled workers moved into the new housing developments promoted especially by social democratic-led municipalities in the 1920s and adapted to the orderly, "respectable" life-style expected of the residents. Communists, in contrast, retained support among the less well-off, often unemployed men of the old working-class *Quartier* with its less regulated, more turbulent forms of social interaction.[8] Social fissures, thereby, reinforced the political conflicts between the two labor parties, creating the most barren soil imaginable for popular front-type politics.

Clearly, then, the hostility between the two labor parties was by no means merely imposed from above. Even KPD functionaries complained that the rank and file simply wrote off all Social Democrats as "bosses," and were convinced that "one can speak with SPD workers, but it's impossible to convince them."[9] In 1932, KPD activists in Eisleben (Prussian Saxony) were out plastering the town with party posters. They came across a group of SPD members doing the same, and proceeded to steal (and presumably destroy) the Social Democrats' materials and sent them running home with threats that something worse might befall them. When the Communists then encountered Nazis pasting up their posters, the two groups engaged in discussion and reached an agreement that they would not rip down one another's posters![10] To be sure, some instances of communist-social democratic cooperation developed toward the end of the Weimar Republic as the Nazi advance posed new and dangerous problems.[11] But probably more typical were the experiences in the Halle-Merseburg region, where the hostility between the SPD and KPD was so pronounced in the small industrial town of Zeitz and at the Leuna chemical plant that communist and socialist workers in the same enterprises used different train cars in their commute, ate in different sections of the company cafeteria, and changed their clothes in different dressing rooms.[12]

Hence, the public sphere of party politics in Germany, the *logic* of the nationally specific party system, had a fateful legacy for the German Left. In a sense, both Social Democrats and Communists paid dearly for the precocious development of their movements in Germany – the SPD as the *parti modèle* of the Second International and then the *Staatspartei* of the Weimar Republic, the KPD as the first mass-based communist party outside the Soviet Union and the standard bearer of the Third International in Western Europe.[13] The powerful position of both parties, at least in international comparison, and their deep rootedness in proletarian social life made the competition between the two all the more bitter and irreconcilable.

The Weimar public spheres in which the KPD became a mass party drew on patterns established well before World War I – patterns of mass mobilization by modern political parties, of working-class associational life, of a literate public, and many others.[14] But the public spheres became more intense and more openly contested in Weimar, and not just because Weimar was the era of "classical modernity."[15] In the Revolution of 1918 20 workers *created* the open and hyperactive public sphere of Weimar by their incessant strikes, demonstrations, campaign rallies, and armed rebellions. These forms of popular protest constituted the raw materials out of which the KPD manufactured its rhetorical and organizational program. These activities provided the sub-stratum of popular protest that the KPD sought continually to elevate and transform into a more clearly defined ideological and political struggle against the capitalist economy and republican polity of Weimar Germany. At the same time, the KPD sought to bring popular protest within the confines of the party's own ideology, strategy, and organization, an enterprise that proved far less successful, particularly in the second half of the Weimar Republic.[16] Many workers were unwilling to allow their actions to be politicized along communist lines, which lent a certain tenor of frustration and anger to the political culture of the KPD. Popular protests both stimulated and delimited the successes of the KPD; in both senses, the KPD's emergence as a mass party was inextricably bound up with the form and character of popular working-class protest.

However, the open and raucous public spheres created by workers in the course of the Revolution and the Weimar Republic did not go unchallenged. Driven together by common fears, real and imagined, of chaos and Bolshevism, the old forces of order – army officers and state officials, industrialists and agrarian capitalists – forged a tenuous, but no less real, coalition of order with Social Democrats and trade unionists.[17] The strategy they devised was neither easily imposed nor completely successful. Order had to be continually renegotiated and required the absorption of at least some of the demands raised in popular struggles. The constituent elements of the coalition fought bitterly over the substance and extent of democracy and social welfare. But together they sought ways to reconstitute order and discipline in society. They built a more efficient state security apparatus, rationalized production, extended both private and public social welfare, and sharply delimited the vibrant public spheres created in the Revolution and replaced them with corporatist and parliamentary modes of representation.

The KPD served as the primary bonding agent of the coalition. Against its continual efforts to foment unrest and to create a soviet Germany, the members of the coalition came together and developed their strategy of domestic containment. The very existence of the KPD as a mass-based party, the deep-seated, unrelentingly hostile opposition it engendered, decisively shaped the contours of the Weimar Republic's political and social economy and its public spheres. At the same time, the reconstruction of order profoundly shaped the nature of German communism. The discontent generated by military repression, economic rationalization, and insufficient social welfare produced continual popular support for the radical politics of the KPD. Perhaps most significantly, the reconstruction of order resulted in the spatial transformation of the public spheres. The superior firepower of the state drove the KPD from the battlefield, while rationalization coupled with the impact of the Great Depression drove the party from the workplace. Consequently, the streets came to serve as the KPD's primary space of political mobilization, which encouraged a politics of *display and spectacle*, a politics of ideological pronouncements and physical confrontations. The specific character of the reconstitution of authority thereby contributed decisively to the creation of a communist party with a particularly intransigent cast, a party almost instinctively hostile to compromise and the champion of an ethos of male physical prowess as the decisive revolutionary quality.

For labor parties, the workplace constituted one central communicative realm of the public sphere. In the Revolution of 1918 to 1920 and the succeeding few years, the workplace served as the site of the most intense forms of activism. Worker representatives patrolled the domain of the factory and the mine, mass meetings convened during working hours; and hated foremen and overseers found themselves unceremoniously run out of the workplace. In mass meetings workers articulated their demands and desires and chose representatives. Workers argued politics and threatened those who seemed to ally with the "enemy." But as part of the strategy of domestic containment, employers, with the active support of the state and trade unionists, sought drastically to limit the raucous public sphere that workers had created within the factories and mines. Employers fired radical workers, formed their own private security forces, and reestablished control of the workday. Where worker representatives had roamed at will, employers now prohibited mass meetings and allowed works councillors only the most limited access to the workers they were supposed to represent – and only in the company of managers. All of this was accomplished in close cooperation with state officials.

And yet employers could never completely close down the workplace as a site of communication and agitation. Even in the depths of Depression, workers argued politics inside the factories. At the large Leuna chemical works in Halle-Merseburg, labeled "Leuna Penitentiary" by Communists because of the harsh internal regime imposed by management, a party instructor reported workers saying that after the Prussian elections of 1932:

> *[workers] discussed from morning to night in the factory. In all units social democratic and Nazi workers talk with our comrade and the main theme is: what will the Communists in the Prussian Landtag do?*[18]

Yet for the most part, communists found themselves excluded from the workplace. Employers used the opportunities presented by rationalization and Depression to rid the factories and mines of radical workers and communists. The KPD lost access to the workplace, a most ironic situation for a party whose entire existence and identity was bound up with the proletariat. Instead, the streets became the major locus of communist politics.

Clearly, then, the public spheres of the Weimar period were not only constituted "from above," by the structures and norms of politics and economics. The public spheres were shaped by the contestation over order and discipline in German society, by intense, active popular protest and, in response, the strategy of domestic containment carried out by the coalition of order.

But active protest was not the only realm of popular engagement. The public spheres were also composed of partly autonomous associational life that had been an essential aspect of popular culture in Germany at least since the liberal nationalist efforts of the 1820s. Sports leagues, chess clubs, radio clubs, choirs, and many others – these were the creation as much of rank and file workers in the 1920s as of the labor parties. For many individuals, participation in the varied associations of the labor movement provided an outlet for their talents and interests, a place to develop their identities as human beings as well as workers or communists or socialists. Ludwig Turek, a member of the KPD since its founding, mentioned at the end of his autobiography, published in 1929, the organizations of which he and his wife were members in addition to the party: Red Aid, the Union of Popular Health, the Nudist League, the Union of German Book Printers, the Union of Graphical Workers, a consumer cooperative, and the Workers Gymnastic and Sports Association.[19] As was the case with popular protests, the party sought to bring these associations under more disciplined direction, but never with complete success.[20] To the chagrin of party leaders, communist workers all too often relished singing in workers' choirs, engaging in chess tournaments in the workers' chess association, and going on trips with the workers' bicycle league at the expense of "party work" in these associations. In Hamm, the Ruhr KPD in 1926 reported to the Central Committee, the comrades in the sports associations were too concerned about sports and not enough about politics. In Dortmund, a strong KPD group existed among the swimmers, while bicyclists in general were reformists. The Gelsenkirchen workers' sports federation had a strong KPD fraction, while in Essen a "hard struggle" had routed the reformists. The Friends of Nature, meanwhile, were too involved with rocks:

> *The Friends of Nature are a very special class of people who exist in a world of their own. Instead of carrying out party work in their organization they look for rocks and worry about other things.*[21]

In time, continued the report, it should be possible to convince even the Friends of Nature that they had to work in line with the direction of the party. Two working-class choir associations existed in the district, which caused the KPD no end of trouble, but the atheists set a record: their Free Thinker Movement *(Freidenkerbewegung)* had five different federations in the Ruhr, and Communists were represented in all of them![22] As ever, the leadership complained that comrades had failed to recognize the necessity of carrying party work into the associations and of the need to create a unified free-thinker organization.

The insufficiencies of party work and the Comintern's radical turn of the third period led the KPD leadership at the end of the 1920s to foment splits in virtually all of the broad-based working-class cultural associations.[23] Communists were now expected to enter separate communist-led sports, chess, free-thinker, and choir associations and federations. In this realm, as in many others, the KPD narrowed the scope of party work to a small, select group of party members; the party not only emerged in the public spheres, it also contributed to their narrowing over the course of the Weimar Republic. These developments complemented the KPD's growing isolation as a party of the unemployed, a party of a particular segment of the working class as opposed to a broad-based popular movement. Still, the public spheres of associational life were deeply inscribed with politics, which enabled the party to penetrate more deeply the social networks of proletarian life and placed the KPD firmly within the lineage of popular political movements in Germany.

The public spheres were also highly gendered. Women were, to be sure, involved in all the myriad forms of popular protests, in strikes and demonstrations and mass meetings.[24] But despite the KPD's promotion of women's emancipation, Communists, along with virtually every other political and social group, conceived of the workplace as a preeminently masculine sphere.[25] At the highpoint of the Revolution of 1918 to 1920, for example, workers launched a vibrant, broad-based effort to socialize the mines. At this moment, miners broke through the boundaries of politics and of representation, if in inchoate form. They sought to restructure their own workplace and industry through the establishment of workers' control. This signified an effort to create new institutional forms within which popular deliberation over politics and economics would occur – that is, a broadening of the public sphere in the fullest meaning of the term. The arena would be *inclusive*, involving workers, employees, and managers. But it would be an *exclusive* arena in terms of gender. Precisely because revolutionary efforts focused on reordering the *productive* sphere – understood by virtually all the participants in the socialization debate, from radical workers to owners, as a masculine sphere, even though the reality was far more complex – the efforts at socialization excluded from consideration the reproductive realm and the issues associated with it. The wave of consumer protests over goods shortages and inflated prices, which had begun during the war and continued during the crisis periods of the Republic, most often involved working women. Yet these protests were reduced to a problem of social order even by the Revolution's advocates. Communists, in turn, had an ambivalent attitude toward such actions.[26] Communists supported almost any effort of social disruption, but remained fixated on the workplace and the male proletariat. Women's protests could only be seen as of secondary significance. Communists and other radicals could envision the contours of a new society created out of strikes, but not out of crowds of women at the marketplace forcing merchants to reduce their prices. The socialization movement, the most broad-based radical effort of the revolutionary era, recreated, indeed, probably strengthened, the existing gender regime.

Developments in succeeding years only accentuated this trend. The high levels of unemployment in the second half of the Republic provided the KPD with a fruitful field of engagement. The party promoted the organization of the unemployed, which meant in essence the male proletariat, despite ritual paeans to the importance of organizing women. The gendered nature of the labor market had, in the first place, made the workplace and union organization inhospitable to women, so relatively few were eligible for unemployment benefits. Second, women were also discriminated against in the granting of unemployment benefits, so were less likely to appear at the places of mobilization. Third, in the deep economic crisis of the Depression years, the household burdens on women only increased, giving them less time for political activities. All of these factors ensured that, by the time of the Depression, the unemployed movement remained overwhelmingly male, which no doubt facilitated its incorporation into the KPD's masculinized political strategy of street battles and political violence.

There was another realm to the public sphere, new – at least in its full articulation – in the 1920s, and that was the realm of mass culture, which provided intense competition for the time, loyalties, and energies of younger workers especially. Film, radio, and the dance hall provided outlets for leisure time, such as it was. More than the SPD, the KPD at least recognized the potential of mass culture as a medium Communists could use. Its highly successful illustrated weekly, the *Arbeiter-Illustrierte-Zeitung*, openly imitated the style of the popular bourgeois magazines. Radical artists associated with the party like John Heartfield and, more tenuously, Hannah Höch, proved adept at inventing new media like photomontage that were disseminated through mass circulation periodicals. The party's promotion of the Bertolt Brecht film, *Kuhle Wampe*, indicated an awareness of the importance of cinema. In political campaigns, the KPD, by the end of the 1920s, began to recognize the value of modern forms of advertising. In the 1928 electoral campaign, for example, the district leadership in the Ruhr reflected an attentiveness to modern communications techniques when it advised:

> *The large colored posters were too complicated, too involved. In the future it is recommended … to put out one especially effective poster in various sizes and to hammer the masses in the skull. Bourgeois advertisements of each brand of cigarettes demonstrate the theoretical principle: one catch phrase as brief as possible, one clear illustration or dramatic, pictorially pointed scene. Then we will more sharply distinguish ourselves from the hodgepodge and confusion of the other parties.*[27]

Also important were the use of camouflaged autos, records, and, "above all else, electoral films, which had a stellar [impact] and were a great help in the electoral struggle."[28] Clearly, the KPD had learned to use the techniques of modern propaganda and advertisement. Along with the mass mobilization of the party rank and file, the intermittent articulation of the new woman and an emancipated sexuality, and the general evocation of a bright socialist future, they demonstrated the modernity of the KPD, one of the reasons for the party's attractiveness.

Still, if not quite as hostile to mass culture as the SPD, the KPD nonetheless found in it a difficult and elusive opponent. Communists also complained that youth were attracted by the diversions of cinema and spectator sports. While promoting images of the new woman, an enormous tension reigned in the party over gender issues. If generally supportive of Weimar sex reform, the party only intermittently granted women the right to control their own reproduction – bourgeois society lay at fault, but a proletarian state could claim to intervene in issues of reproduction and sexuality in general.[29] Men in the party showed very little sympathy for women's issues. In Essen, in 1927, party leaders ordered male comrades to attend a meeting about the party's work among women. The men were incensed and made complaint after complaint. They wanted to know why they had to be at a meeting devoted to "women's matters." At the same time, some of the women clearly wanted the women's section to remain their province. As the Central Committee's instructor reported:

> *The mistaken position of a number of male and female comrades concerning [party] work among women as a task solely for female comrades was expressed numerous times in this meeting. The leader of the women's section of the district leadership explained that she did not understand why the male comrades had been invited to a "women's meeting." At the beginning of the discussion there was a nasty mood among the women toward the men and vice versa, which led to numerous interruptions and sharp reproaches on both sides.*

The Central Committee's instructor managed, not very convincingly, to pull some positive observations out of the meeting:

At the beginning of the talk the male comrades showed no interest in the questions about party work among women, but in due course they became interested and became convinced of its importance.[30]

Yet in the discussion it became apparent that various party sections had had no involvement whatsoever with women's issues. At a meeting the next day in Cologne, the same kind of tone permeated the discussion. The men were "astonished and just about unwilling" to attend a meeting devoted to party work among women.[31]

3.

In both its construction of the first mass-based communist movement outside the Soviet Union and its drastic defeat at the hands of the Nazis, the KPD was very much a creation of Weimar society. It was, and always remained, a child of World War I; its maturation occurred within the public spheres of a Republic that was so deeply shaped by the war. The narrative of "Stalinization," long the dominant mode of explanation for the history of German communism from its founding to the collapse of the German Democratic Republic, is, then, deeply flawed, at best incomplete. Articulated, with great verve and empirical knowledge, by Hermann Weber, the Stalinization thesis found its way into most West German historiography, including Heinrich August Winkler's masterful trilogy on Weimar labor.[32] In the wake of the Revolution of 1989, the Stalinization thesis received a new lease on life by appraisals emanating from the former DDR, which were quick – too quick – to embrace a perspective castigated in the past and now held up as the explanation for every supposed deformation in the history of German communism.[33] In both its original articulation by Weber and the more recent, and even less compelling, reprise of the Stalinization perspective, the KPD, rooted originally in the social and political life of German labor, increasingly took on the character of its Soviet mentor. Practices developed out of backward, authoritarian Russian conditions were grafted onto German politics and society. The initial democratic impulses of the party, articulated most forcefully by Rosa Luxemburg, were increasingly replaced by the dictatorial methods characteristic of Lenin and Stalin. The authoritarian state socialism of the DDR marked the inevitable culmination of this process, the imposition on German soil of an alien form of politics.

Certainly, the Communist International and the Soviet Union had an immense impact on the KPD and its successor, the Socialist Unity Party (SED). But the Stalinization perspective almost inevitably directs the causative gaze eastward, away from German conditions and to the forces – of light or of darkness, depending on one's view – emanating from

Moscow. Yet Soviet power in and of itself could never create a mass-based party. The ideologies and strategies developed in Moscow had to be translated into practices and discourses that made sense to German workers. The significant question is how Bolshevik ideology and Soviet power interacted with the socio-political history of German labor and with the more general history of German society. Leaving aside ritual paeans concerning the need to ground German communism in its own historical context, West German historiography overwhelmingly interpreted the historical development of the KPD in the Weimar Republic and the SED in the German Democratic Republic as a process whose origins had to be located in Moscow. The historical development of the DDR was written out of German history in the twentieth century, only to find its way back – the prodigal son returning – in 1989 to 1990. If German Communists took to Stalinism with alacrity, if "[they] early on copied Soviet Stalinism with 'German thoroughness [*deutscher Gründlichkeit*],'" then this process needs to be explained with recourse to German as well as Russian/Soviet history.[34] "*Deutsche Gründlichkeit*," whatever its particular form, is not known to be a genetically inherited trait; it needs to be explained historically.

The crucial historical markers, as I have tried to explain here, consisted of the myriad, highly contested public spheres of Weimar Germany. Soviet influence served to sharpen, to intensify characteristics of German communism as it developed in the context of Weimar society. The "two camps mentality," with Social Democrats clearly in the "wrong" camp; an emphasis on a voluntaristic politics of engagement; an ethos of tough masculinity as the essential revolutionary quality; an abiding faith in revolution as the essential means of political progress – all that emanated both from Moscow and the social, ideological, and political formation of at least a segment of German workers and the German labor movement. Moreover, the public sphere of the streets of a democratic polity bred a politics of ideological pronouncements and harsh physical combat, which only intensified an ideological rigidity derived from both Luxemburg and Lenin, an understanding of politics as always directed *auf das Ganze*, at the totality. In the late 1920s this Luxemburgist-Leninist hybrid became increasingly subject to Stalin's particularly authoritarian interpretation of Leninism. Under Stalin the Soviets added a strong dose of direction from above and sought to create clear lines of authority coupled with disciplined and submissive parties. Soviet influence in the 1920s and 1930s certainly promoted an authoritarian mode of practice within the German party, and, of course, the other members of the Communist International. But the Soviets did not own the patent on the creation of a mass-based communist party with a particularly intransigent cast.

The Weimar public spheres were preeminently modern in character, and the tensions and contradictions of modernity, so evident in nearly every aspect of Weimar society,[35] also ran straight through the KPD. The party supported the right of single women to a sexual life and ridiculed bourgeois sexual conventions. At the same time, it only rarely and inconsistently articulated the right of women to control their own reproduction. Its youth and women's leagues were to be well-disciplined training camps for the class struggle, not the setting for an emancipatory and pluralistic culture. The KPD adapted its political tactics to the modern media, but castigated popular culture as a capitalist opiate that diverted workers from politics. But the party's complexion was modern enough that it helped inspire the fascist onslaught against every element of Weimar modernity except technology and eugenics. Against the fascist aestheticization of politics, against the emotional and sexualized appeal of the leader in particular, the KPD had very little to offer.

The tension-laden culture of Weimar communism was then carried into the drastically altered circumstances of the Third Reich, the Soviet occupation, and the foundation and development of the DDR. The party culture of the Weimar KPD helped foster the intransigence of the party-state, its opposition to cultural pluralism and experimentation, its fixation on class as the single-focal lens to view the world. The emergence of the KPD as a mass-based party in Weimar also gave the SED a usable past, one that could be carefully cultivated to lend legitimacy to the DDR, a past that was invented and constructed, to be sure, but not out of the blue sky. It was also a past that, ultimately, drastically curtailed the party's openness to new ideas and strategies and prepared the way for the utterly unexpected and complete collapse in 1989 to 1990.

Notes

Note: Some of the material in this chapter is drawn from my book, *Creating German Communism, 1890-1990: From Popular Protests to Socialist State*, © Princeton University Press, 1997.

1. Luxemburg quoted in *Der Gründungsparteitag der KPD: Protokoll und Materialien*, ed. Hermann Weber (Frankfurt am Main, 1969), 179.
2. "Socialism or descent into barbarism!" as the oft-cited slogan went. Luxemburg used it in the draft program for the Spartacus League, which was then adopted as the KPD's program at the founding congress. See "Was will der Spartakusbund?" in Rosa Luxemburg, *Gesammelte Werke*, vol. 4: *August 1914 bis Januar 1919*, 5th printing (Berlin, 1990), 441.

3. For a somewhat parallel argument, see Klaus-Michael Mallmann, *Kommunisten in der Weimarer Republik: Sozialgeschichte einer revolutionären Bewegung* (Darmstadt, 1996).
4. For effective, critical appropriations of Jürgen Habermas's concept of the public sphere, see Geoff Eley, "Nations, Publics, and Political Cultures: Placing Habermas in the Nineteenth Century," in *Habermas and the Public Sphere*, ed. Craig Calhoun (Cambridge, Mass., 1992), 289-339; and Belinda Davis, "Reconsidering Habermas, Gender, and the Public Sphere: The Case of Wilhelmine Germany," in *Society, Culture, and the State in Germany*, ed. Geoff Eley (Ann Arbor, Mich., 1996), 397-426.
5. Generally on the importance of democratic norms, see Geoff Eley's contribution in this volume, "Cultural Socialism, the Public Sphere, and the Mass Form."
6. For a comparative perspective, see Eric D. Weitz, *Popular Communism: Political Strategies and Social Histories in the Formation of the German, French, and Italian Communist Parties, 1919-1948*, Western Societies Program Occasional Paper no. 31 (Ithaca, NY, 1992).
7. Erich Wollenberg, Memoirs (typescript, n.d., Hoover Institution Archives).
8. See especially Adelheid von Saldern, *Häuserleben: Zur Geschichte von städtischen Arbeiterwohnens vom Kaiserreich bis heute* (Bonn, 1995), 119-92.
9. "Bericht für die Woche vom 11.-16. April [presumably 1932]," BAK, R45/IV/11/55.
10. "Bericht über den Bezirk Halle-Merseburg (2.-6. Mai 1932)," BAK R45/IV/11/112.
11. For some examples, see Donna Harsch, *German Social Democracy and the Rise of Nazism* (Chapel Hill, NC, 1993), 196-200; "Bericht von der Versammlungstour im Bezirk Halle-Merserburg vom 30.6.-2.7.32," BAK R45/IV/11/200-01.
12. "Politischer Bericht des Bezirke Halle-Merseburg für die Monate September und Oktober," 12 November 1926, SAPMO-BA, ZPA I/3/11/16/43-44.
13. On the SPD, see the classic articles by Annie Kriegel, "Le parti modèle (La Social-Démocratie allemande et la IIe Internationale)," in idem, *Le Pain et les Roses: Jalons pour une histoire des socialismes* (Paris, 1968), 159-73, and J.P. Nettl, "The German Social Democratic Party 1890-1914 as a Political Model," *Past and Present* 30 (1965): 65-96.
14. On mass mobilizations especially, see Larry Eugene Jones and James Retallack, eds., *Elections, Mass Politics, and Social Change in Modern Germany: New Perspectives* (Cambridge, Mass., 1992), and Eley, *Society, Culture, and the State in Germany*.
15. Detlev Peukert, *Die Weimarer Republik: Krisenjahre der Klassischen Moderne* (Frankfurt am Main, 1987).
16. Internal party reports are replete with complaints about the insufficiencies of party work in the factories and mines, in mass cultural organizations, among the unemployed, among women. For more detail, see Eric D. Weitz, *Creating German Communism, 1890-1990: From Popular Protests to Socialist State* (Princeton, 1997), and Mallmann, *Kommunisten in der Weimarer Republik*.
17. See Weitz, *Creating German Communism*, 100-31.
18. "Bericht über den Bezirk Halle-Merseburg (2.-6. Mai 1932)," BAK R45/IV/11/113-14.
19. Ludwig Turek, "Ein Prolet erzählt," in *Proletarische Lebensläufe: Autobiographische Dokumente zur Entstehung der Zweiten Kultur in Deutschland*, vol. 2, ed. Wolfgang Emmerich (Hamburg, 1975), 264-65.
20. In general on labor movement cultural organizations in the Weimar Republic, see Peter Lösche, ed., *Solidargemeinschaft und Milieu: Sozialistische Kultur- und*

Freizeitorganisationen in der Weimarer Republik, 4 vols. (Berlin, 1990-93); W.L. Guttsman, *Workers' Culture in Weimar Germany: Between Tradition and Commitment* (New York, 1990); and Hartmann Wunderer, *Arbeitervereine und Arbeiterparteien: Kultur- und Massenorganisationen in der Arbeiterbewegung (1890-1933)* (Frankfurt am Main, 1980).

21. Bezirksleitung Ruhrgebiet, "Bericht der Bezirksleitung," 9 December 1926, SAPMO-BA, ZPA I/3/18-19/11/200-02, quote 202.
22. Ibid., 202-03. See also "Bericht über den Bezirk Halle-Merseburg (2.-6. Mai 1932)," BAK R45/IV/11/113, in which members of the Red Sports League in Halle roundly attacked the party leadership and were in turn accused of being "opportunists" and adopting a line "hostile to the party."
23. See Guttsman, *Workers' Culture*, 97-106, and Wunderer, *Arbeitervereine und Arbeiterparteien*.
24. On women's involvement in protests and the reshaping of the public sphere in World War I and afterwards, see Davis, "Reconsidering Habermas, Gender, and the Public Sphere"; Karin Hartewig, *Das unberechenbare Jahrzehnt: Bergarbeiter und ihre Familien im Ruhrgebiet* (Munich, 1993); idem, "'Eine sogenannte Neutralität der Beamten gibt es nicht': Sozaler Protest, bürgerliche Gesellschaft und Polizei im Ruhrgebeit (1918-1924)," in *"Sicherheit" und "Wohlfahrt": Polizei, Gesellschaft und Herrschaft im 19. und 20. Jahrhundert*, ed. Alf Lüdtke (Frankfurt am Main, 1992), 297-322; Karen Hagemann, *Frauenalltag und Männerpolitik: Alltagsleben und gesellschaftliches Handeln von Arbeiterfrauen in der Weimarer Republik* (Bonn, 1990); and Ute Daniel, *Arbeiterfrauen in der Kriegsgesellschaft: Beruf, Familie und Politik im Ersten Weltkrieg* (Göttingen, 1989).
25. See Eric D. Weitz, "The Heroic Man and the Ever-Changing Woman: Gender and Politics in European Communism, 1917-1950," in *Gender and Class in Modern Europe*, ed. Laura Levine Frader and Sonya O. Rose (Ithaca, NY, 1996), 311-52.
26. See especially Silvia Kontos, *"Die Partei kämpft wie ein Mann": Frauenpolitik der KPD in der Weimarer Republik* (Frankfurt am Main, 1979).
27. [Bezirksleitung Ruhrgebiet], "Bericht über den Wahlkampf im Bezirk Ruhrgebiet," [1928], SAPMO-BA, ZPA I/3/18-19/13/124-25.
28. Ibid., 125.
29. See especially Atina Grossmann, *Reforming Sex: The German Movement for Birth Control and Abortion Reform, 1920-1950* (New York, 1995).
30. "Bericht über Parteiarbeiterkonferenzen zur Arbeit unter den Frauen," [April 1927], SAPMO-BA, ZPA I/3/18-19/35/1.
31. Ibid., 2.
32. Hermann Weber, *Die Wandlung des deutschen Kommunismus: Die Stalinisierung der KPD in der Weimarer Republik*, 2 vols. (Frankfurt am Main, 1969), as well as idem, *Kommunistische Bewegung und realsozialistischer Staat: Beiträge zum deutschen und internationalen Kommunismus. Hermann Weber zum 60. Geburtstag*, ed. Werner Müller (Cologne, 1988); idem, *Aufbau und Fall einer Diktatur: Kritischen Beiträge zur Geschichte der DDR* (Cologne, 1991). See also Heinrich August Winkler, *Von der Revolution zur Stabilisierung: Arbeiter und Arbeiterbewegung in der Weimarer Republik 1918 bis 1924* (Berlin, 1984); idem, *Der Schein der Normalität: Arbeiter und Arbeiterbewegung in der Weimarer Republik 1924 bis 1930* (Berlin, 1985); idem, *Der Weg in die Katastrophe: Arbeiter und Arbeiterbewegung in der Weimarer Republik 1930 bis 1933*, 2nd ed. (Bonn, 1990). For a refreshing departure from the standard mode of argument, see Mallmann, *Kommunisten in der Weimarer Republik*.

33. For views from the former DDR and other ex-socialist countries, see many of the contributions to a 1990 symposium on Luxemburg in *Beiträge zur Geschichte der Arbeiterbewegung* 33:4 (1991).
34. Hermann Weber, "Aufstieg und Niedergang des deutschen Kommunismus," *Aus Politik und Zeitgeschichte* B40/91 (27 September 1991): 25-39, quote 39.
35. Peukert's argument in *Weimarer Republik*.

Chapter 11

THE RISE AND FALL OF RED SAXONY

William Carl Mathews

Saxony well deserved its claim to be the model of German social democracy. If the seeds of democratic socialism were broadly strewn throughout Germany, they had been sown into very fertile soil in Saxony. As early as 1867 these seeds sprouted in the Vogtland of southwestern Saxony and flowered to become the brightest red rose of social democracy. For nearly half a century, this rose continued to bloom until, as if there were political seasons, it suddenly faltered in the wake of the hyperinflation of 1923. Although it struggled to recover much of its former glory, the coming of the Great Depression of 1929 further stunted its growth, turning it first towards communism and then, tragically, causing it to wither and "brown" under the impact of National Socialism.

Saxony provides one of the few opportunities to examine the development of a social democratic movement uncompromised by bourgeois coalition partners. Despite the schism among Social Democrats and communists that emerged after 1914, a community of socialist solidarity based on common class and cultural identities suppressed political rivalries enough on the Saxon Left to provide an electoral majority for socialist parties and socialist-communist coalition regimes until 1923 to 1924. This red majority and the political limits and possibilities it offered for socialist political strategies at the regional level of political engagement *(Landespolitik)* must be examined against the background of the political structure of both Saxony and the Weimar Republic. For if red Saxony should appear as a "missed opportunity" in German and Weimar history, the profound failure of red Saxony after 1924 illustrates the consequences

---

Notes for this chapter begin on page 308.

of attempting to implement radical reforms with a narrow base of political support, unstable coalitions, and a tenuous majority faced by a solid bloc of opposition in both Dresden and Berlin.

The brilliance of red Saxony came only in part from the densely organized and lively activity of local SPD party life. SPD members made up on average 1.5 percent of all German citizens in 1912; in Saxony they constituted 4 percent. Even more pronounced, however, was the density of participation in socialist cultural activities, ranging from sports clubs to movements for life style reform. During the Weimar Republic, Saxony made up about 8 percent of the Reich's population, but in terms of membership in socialist organizations, the Saxons weighed in at 14 percent of the SPD's members, 16.5 percent of free trade union members (ADGB), 19.5 percent of socialist soccer players and 40 percent of socialist sports facilities, 39 percent of socialist entrepreneurs, and 75 percent of health reformers.[1] This cultural milieu extended far beyond the more narrow political elite of party life with its mix of daily activities, contacts, and networks that reinforced social democratic identity and commitment and sustained them between elections.[2]

The emergence of this broader social democratic milieu reflected an ideal environment. As the pioneer land of German industrialization, Saxony had become the workshop of Germany before 1870. Transformed by the leading sectors and modes of production of the early Industrial Revolution – textiles and domestic manufacturing – Saxony was also a world of small and medium-sized enterprises that preserved the craft identity of the workers and presented them with superb economic and cultural opportunities for effective self-organization. Spread rather evenly across Saxony, small but densely populated industrial hamlets sprang up despite the virtual absence of large cities, except perhaps around Leipzig after 1914. Finally, as the land of the Lutheran Reformation, Saxony had both a homogeneous Protestant population, with virtually no significant concentrations of Catholics, and also the highest percentage of religious non-conformists in all of Germany. With the virtual absence of union-busting, large-scale heavy industry and no competition from the Catholic Center Party, Saxony provided a political environment that was especially conducive to the emergence of a powerful social democratic tradition. In 1903 the SPD reached its historic high water mark, sweeping twenty-two of twenty-three Reichstag seats and collecting nearly 60 percent of the votes and providing the state with its appellation, the "red kingdom of Saxony."[3]

World War I and the November Revolution of 1918 seemed, at least superficially, to confirm that the red Saxon model would continue to thrive. Although the large Leipzig party split off to join the Independent Social Democratic Party (USPD), and elsewhere small, rather marginal organizations of Independents formed in opposition to the majority, the SPD's overall organizational network remained fairly intact at the local level. Moreover, despite the split in social democracy after 1914, the cohesion of local party organizations within Saxon regions was strong enough to reproduce a clearly red majority in the elections to a Saxon constituent assembly (*Volkskammer*) in 1919. Throughout the Revolution and the Weimar period, the Communist Party (KPD) remained relatively harmless despite some significant support in Chemnitz-Zwickau.[4] A will to power by means of a practical socialism swelled from below to push USPD and the Majority SPD or MSPD back together in what was at first a hesitant, but then an increasingly fruitful pragmatic cooperation that led to reunification by 1922. This is not to say that red Saxony was not shaken by revolutionary radicalism and did not teeter at times on the brink of civil war in 1918 to 1919. Generally, however, practical wisdom and realism prevailed over ideological dogma and radicalism, and solidarity asserted itself over sectarianism and elitism within the working class until 1923.

Democracy is more effectively conducted on the basis of direct participation, consensus, and pragmatically oriented activism than on the basis of ideology and conformity to party hierarchy. In the sense that it both produces and reproduces concerted power, this approach to political organization is particularly effective and rewarding for its active members. It seems that the Saxon Social Democrats generally understood these lessons of grass-roots democratic organizing very well until they came into conflict with political realities coming from beyond Saxony after 1923. Then came the frustration, bitterness, and finally the crisis that irrevocably weakened red Saxony.[5]

In Leipzig, however, the Independents and the strong local trade union cartel based themselves on the council movement that grew out of the April 1917 general strike in the local munitions factories. But in Dresden the SPD, led by Georg Gradnauer and backed by the Chemnitz party, resisted the efforts of Richard Lipinski (USPD) to orchestrate the councils behind Leipzig leadership. The SPD inclined toward parliamentary elections, and then defeated and discredited KPD efforts to build a regime based on workers' councils *(Räterepublik)* through local seizures of power led by small vanguards in Dresden, Leipzig, and Zwickau. The narrow base of these efforts among the unemployed, the reliance on armed violence directed against the elected workers' councils (as well as deception and provocation employed as manipulative techniques polarized) the working class against communism.[6] The failure of KPD actions in 1919 led the Chemnitz communists toward the right wing of the KPD led by Paul Levi. In contrast, communists in Dresden and Leipzig were influenced by the Bremen Left and were hostile to both party organization and the trade unions. As a result of these problems, the KPD could never escape its own isolation within the socialist community. Even in Saxony, one of its most prominent districts, it could never successfully lay claim to an active revolutionary leadership of the Saxon working classes.[7]

Although it overshadowed the USPD in the voting to the Saxon constituent assembly, the SPD was embarrassed by the workers' protest strikes for socialization and the councils in the spring of 1919. Responsible for law, order, and the public welfare in despairing times of defeat, hunger, and unemployment, the Saxon SPD confronted force with force in an effort to stabilize the political and economic disturbances unleashed in the Revolution of November 1918. The low point came on 12 April when a crowd of disabled veterans in Dresden was whipped into a frenzy against the Saxon Minister of the Military, Gustav Neuring (SPD). Neuring, who hoped to avoid a repeat of the March confrontations between crowds and troops that had led to bloodshed, attempted, unarmed and unprotected, to negotiate with the crowd in an effort to calm them. For his effort, Neuring was brutally beaten, thrown off a bridge into the waters of the Elbe, and shot dead as he struggled ashore. As a result, support for the Reich Defense Minister Gustav Noske's harsh military measures against revolutionary radicalism was quite strong among the leaders in Noske's Chemnitz as well as in Neuring's Dresden.[8]

For the broader socialist milieu, however, the red majority of 57.9 percent, won in the elections to the Saxon constituent assembly on 2 February, was being squandered.[9] With the USPD in opposition over the issue of the councils, the SPD regime in Dresden had to rely on cooperation and toleration from the liberal bourgeois Democrats (DDP) to pass a constitution for the new Free State of Saxony. After all of the mass action was over, the mood swung to the right in late 1919 as a National Opposition formed around the stab-in-the-back legend (*Dolchstoßlegende*) and threw itself against the Treaty of Versailles, the November Revolution, and the Weimar Republic. With the USPD daily growing stronger in late 1919, many Saxon Social Democrats sensed that an opportunity to bring fundamental change was slipping away in Saxony as well as in the nation at large.

The Kapp-Lüttwitz Putsch in March 1920 helped pave the way for a rapprochement between the USPD and SPD and alerted the KPD to the danger of political isolation. Common interest in defeating the paramilitary coup and defending the Republic helped bring the parties behind the general strike. Cooperation among SPD, USPD, and KPD was successfully cemented in action against the Putsch in the Chemnitz area and produced a short-lived "united front" of the working classes.[10] While elsewhere the SPD suffered heavy losses in the June 1920 elections to the Reichstag, it fared better in Chemnitz by avoiding acrimony directed against class comrades on the Left and focusing instead on the need for solidarity against the danger from the Right; hence, the Chemnitz line called for unity of the working class as the key to a red majority and an active defense of the Revolution outside of parliament.[11] This Chemnitz line steadily gained the upper hand within both the Dresden and Leipzig party organizations in 1920, if not always among their leaders. The Dresden line, supported by Georg Gradnauer and Wilhelm Buck, leaned heavily on Noske's repressive military measures to secure stability and order in the Reich at the expense of the red majority in Saxony, forcing the SPD into a coalition with the liberal DDP at the cost of socialist and working-class identity. However much they resented the murder of Neuring, radicals as well as revisionists in the Dresden SPD wanted to initiate a practical socialism as a part of a sweeping democratization of the defunct monarchical state. A host of opportunities for reform at the level of urban government – especially municipal socialization and school reform – loomed as possibilities, but not in coalition with the DDP, which increasingly sought to rein in the SPD and after June 1920 pulled rightward towards the more nationalist and openly capitalistic German People's Party (DVP).[12] The opportunity to work through the institutions of a democratic state helped pull both the SPD and the USPD toward a reformism that counted among its major goals the purge of conservatives from the bureaucracy, a more consequential separation of church and state, a sweeping secularization and modernization of the schools and their pedagogy, and the democratic participation of parents, pupils, and teachers in school administration.[13]

Continual political acrimony among the labor parties found little support from the rank and file, who clearly recognized the potential benefits of cooperation. A new group of leaders emerged at the local and *Land* levels in the early 1920s, and for them too the positive prospects of labor unity loomed large.[14] And the Saxon USPD's vote against Moscow's conditions for joining the Third International meant that there was real common social democratic ground between SPD and USPD after all, along with the possibility of a democratic majority for red Saxony.[15]

The first regular elections to the Saxon Landtag in December 1920 produced a weakened socialist bloc compared to 1919, but still the red majority held just barely above 50 percent.[16] The Dresden line with the DDP was ruled out except in the form of a Great Coalition that included the much strengthened DVP, which as an organization representative of the capitalist class and sympathetic to the National Opposition was anathema to the SPD; a coalition with the bourgeois DDP was unthinkable for the Independents.[17] Everything hinged on the KPD, which held the swing vote in the Landtag. Although the KPD took a tough profile outwardly, it could not afford to bear the stigma of deserting the united front of the working classes, particularly in the aftermath of its own very embarrassing and contradictory policies during the Kapp Putsch.[18] To the amazement of the adherents of the Dresden line, the KPD tolerated the regime of Wilhelm Buck (SPD) and Richard Lipinski (USPD) for nearly two years and gave red Saxony its chance to unfold a socialist program at the state level without compromises forced through coalition with bourgeois parties.

The Buck-Lipinski regime, which initially appeared so fragile, was strengthened by its own programs as much as by the hostile opposition it encountered from the bourgeois parties. Conflicts between Leipzigers and Dresdeners soon dissolved into positive political administration and the pursuit of common objectives. Initially, for example, the SPD ministers feared that USPD desires to link up with similar socialist regimes in Thuringia and Braunschweig would bring on disaster through dilettantism. However, this cooperation among like-minded social democratic regimes in central Germany proved useful in forging a common position against Prussia, and, anyway, it proved to be largely inconsequential.[19] Reform legislation concerning local government, welfare policies, and democratization of state personnel, police, and schools fell largely to the USPD ministers Lipinski (Interior) and Fleissner (Culture). Despite criticism from his own staff, Lipinski found solid support from his cabinet colleagues for his rather cautious pace of reform. Lipinski's professionalization of the state police transformed it from a squad of veteran soldiers into a formally trained law-enforcement agency. He also established a special "political commissar" who mediated successfully between the police and workers in the often chaotic economic environment of the inflation, thus, keeping bloodshed in Saxony to a minimum.[20]

To the intense surprise of its opponents, the Saxon KPD remained remarkably passive throughout 1921 to 1922. The KPD, however, was dwarfed by the still-cohesive Saxon USPD. The KPD developed substantial members only in the Chemnitz-Zwickau area, but even there, much as had happened in Berlin, the KPD was overcome by the even larger SPD and its local networks of support from cultural organizations and the trade unions.[21] Elsewhere in Saxony, the Left USPD followed Richard Lipinski's course against Moscow and remained with the Independents, depriving the KPD of new recruits.

Revolutionary radicalism in Saxony was led by the KAPD during the "March Action" of 1921. Its activists exploded some bombs in a vain effort to provoke the workers into action. Max Hölz (KAPD) even rallied a Red Army into armed insurrection against the state security forces in the neighboring province of Prussian Saxony, but the Saxon KPD, led by Heinrich Brandler and Paul Böttcher, remained conspicuously passive during the "March Action" and could not be shaken from their support for united front tactics within red Saxony.[22]

Finally and most decisively, the Buck-Lipinski regime was saved by the openly anti-socialist strategy of the Saxon branch of the German People's Party (DVP). Sensing the weakness of the red regime, the DVP used its influence over the DDP, the Center, and the openly monarchist DNVP to forge an aggressive coalition of bourgeois parties *(Bürgerbloc)* that aimed at bringing the government down prematurely through a referendum launched almost immediately after the December 1920 elections.[23] Together with attacking the social democratic ministers as incompetent, this strategy galvanized the socialist camp against the reaction it saw forming out of monocled monarchists, anti-Republican paramilitary forces modeled on the Bavarian Orgesch, the Saxon League of Industrialists, weak-kneed liberals, and the religious Right.

These conditions spurred red Saxony into positive work and struggle for "practical socialism" at all levels, ranging from Republican festivals, school board elections, demonstrations against unemployment and an ever rising cost-of-living, to massive protests against the death-squad activities that left such prominent leaders of the Republic as Matthias Erzberger, Karl Gareis, and Walther Rathenau murdered in the streets in 1921 and 1922. There was a social democratic world to build and defend in Saxony. As late as 1923 the Saxon Social Democrats continued to attract new members at a time when the Reich party was itself stagnating and beginning to decline.

In November 1922, new elections were forced in Saxony when the KPD joined in a bourgeois resolution of no confidence against the government. Long anticipated by the Dresden line, the KPD's move aimed at testing its strength against the mounting political crisis in the Reich and in Saxony. The bourgeois referendum was on the verge of succeeding in forcing elections, and the KPD sensed a groundswell of radicalization among the masses intensified by the unrelenting development of fascism in Germany as well as a frustration on the left wing of the reunited SPD with the Reich tax compromise of 1922, mounting inflation, and the persistent reparation crisis. The debate over the Great Coalition at the SPD's Görlitz party congress offered further hope to the KPD that it could attract the left wing of the SPD. Finally, the KPD needed to consolidate its hold over renegade Independents, syndicalists, factory councils, and other splinter groups that had fallen out with the KPD in the past.

Certainly there was trouble brewing in the Saxon SPD, but it was directed more against the Berlin Executive and the party's Reichstag delegation than at the regime in Dresden. Local party groups were calling their Reichstag deputies for instructions from the grass roots against the tax compromise and against the posturing of Reich Chancellor Wirth's coalition toward the anti-labor DVP. The Saxons wanted to take the Chemnitz line onto the national level – forge a united front of the working class in sharp opposition to the bourgeoisie and go to new Reichstag elections to save the Republic with a red majority in Berlin.

While both the KPD and the bourgeois bloc sensed an easy score, the SPD appealed successfully to its grass roots in the Saxon Landtag elections on 5 November 1922. The result was a record high participation of 81.1 percent of the electorate, and it gave the party just over one million votes, improving on the combined SPD/USPD 1920 Landtag results by almost as many votes as the 266,835 ballots the KPD received. The red majority increased by 2 percent.[24] Although the KPD deputation in the Landtag grew to ten seats, that could mean little to an allegedly revolutionary party contemptuous of parliament. The KPD still held the swing vote and would still be responsible should the regime supported by the workers be brought down by a communist vote of no confidence and replaced by a reactionary bourgeois coalition. Despite sharp criticism from the Berlin Left within the KPD, Heinrich Brandler and Paul Böttcher nevertheless felt it necessary to stay the course of toleration after contenting themselves with some personal vengeance against Lipinski for his role in leading the USPD's opposition against Moscow at the Halle party congress in 1920.

The following year brought the dénouement of red Saxony under tenuous circumstances. The KPD's toleration was strictly conditional. Despite all efforts of the SPD's negotiating team, the 7-Committee, the KPD refused to accept formal participation in the regime. Many SPD deputies in the Landtag were wary of continuing under such conditions and would have preferred to try negotiations with the DDP, but they soldiered forward bound to serve the very clearly expressed general will of the Saxon party to hold to the red regime rather than opt for a coalition with any party that had supported the hated bourgeois referendum of 1920 to 1922. While the Left SPD hoped to realize the vision of the Chemnitz line and draw the KPD into the united front government, others hoped simply to win enough time from the KPD to complete the reform course for town government and schools while maintaining control of state power in Saxony in order to defend the Republic. The KPD, much like the tail that tried to wag the dog, hoped to challenge the red regime by defending working class interests, exposing the red regime's weaknesses, and ultimately rallying a workers' regime based on a revolutionary mass movement of the factory councils, proletarian defense organizations, and economic self-help organizations that formed out of the opposition against the SPD's parliamentary politics.

The events of Dr. Erich Zeigner's regime, brought together in March 1923 and tolerated by the KPD, are better known chapters of Saxon history.[25] By pursuing the illegal paramilitary organizations known as the Black Reichswehr, Zeigner came into open conflict with Reich Chancellor Wilhelm Cuno and the army. In the wake of the general social and economic unrest that swept the Reich in the spring and summer of 1923 due to accelerating currency depreciation, hyperinflation, and local shortages of food and capital, Zeigner was rendered particularly vulnerable to the persistent attacks of the Saxon League of Industrialists, especially after Cuno finally fell from power and Gustav Stresemann became Chancellor of a Great Coalition in the Reich. Stresemann, the former chair of the Saxon League of Industrialists and a frequent guest at their congresses, was ready to act on their demand that law and order be enforced in Saxony by means of a direct intervention by the army. Modeled on a similar *Reichsexekution* applied against Bavaria in 1919, such plans had long been discussed as the preferred solution of the bourgeoisie for a persistent red majority. Certainly both the KPD and SPD feared that Bavarian-style paramilitary politics would be imported by Stresemann in order to make red Saxony go brown. On the left, Zeigner felt pressure from both the KPD and his own party to combat the growth of fascism coming into Saxony over its borders, but Zeigner did not help himself by joining the Left SPD's broader attacks on the Great Coalition and by denouncing the SPD *Reichstagfraktion* and Executive in Berlin. It is also clear, however, that Zeigner's regime was not responsible for any special level of violence and unrest in Saxony. After all, the chaos of hyperinflation had already led to political violence in the Ruhr, Berlin, and Bavaria. Finally Saxony itself, especially in the Vogtland and Erzgebirge, experienced a wave of spontaneous unrest in the late summer that brought Zeigner's regime into conflict with the Reich.

By October the political situation had worsened. Martial law was declared after the end of the Ruhr struggle, while armed mutinies broke out in Kürstin and were threatening to boil over in Bavaria, as Stresemann's government lurched from crisis to crisis over stabilization measures. At this moment the KPD, now acting under belated direction from Moscow, launched its plan for a German Red October. Entering a Saxon "workers' government" that was about to be invaded by the bourgeoisie in Berlin, the KPD naively thought it could arm the proletariat for world revolution.

Eager to realize their own aims of roping the KPD into a political, but not a military, defense of the Free State and the Republic, Zeigner and the SPD's 7-Committee negotiated the entry of Brandler, Böttcher, and Fritz Heckert into the regime on 10 October. Following the summoning of a factory council congress in Chemnitz between 23 and 25 October, Brandler gave the KPD's planned signal for a general strike and armed insurrection despite the fact that KPD proposals were rejected overwhelmingly by the factory councils assembled in Chemnitz; countermanded by the KPD, the call to arms was followed only in distant Hamburg. It gave Stresemann reason to proceed with a *Reichsexekution* against the Saxon regime, which had resisted the military's exercise of martial law and whose KPD ministers had called for the overthrow of the

Republic. However, before Stresemann could complete the *Reichsexekution*, Zeigner dismissed Brandler and Böttcher from his government, thereby removing the cause given by Stresemann for using Article 48 powers. Ignoring the changed legal circumstances, the Reichswehr proceeded to occupy Dresden and, with military fanfare, removed Zeigner's government and tried to force a bourgeois regime upon the Landtag. Against the background of calls for a general strike against the Reichswehr, the SPD in Berlin brought Stresemann to a halt and forced him to reverse this unconstitutional and brutal bullying of the Saxon Landtag. On 29 October an SPD minority regime under Hermann Fellisch was formed in Dresden with the toleration of the DDP; the KPD refused to renew its toleration of a regime that would not defend the workers' interests with revolution and armed force.

With a vengeance the Reichswehr, often linking up with illegal paramilitary forces, proceeded to enforce brutal, arbitrary, and capricious martial law over Saxony. Targeted were the public servants, police, and school teachers of socialist persuasion, many of whom were summarily removed from their posts, often to the open glee of the non-socialist camp in Saxony. Also occupied were the cultural facilities of the socialist milieu, including sports complexes. In many places the homes of SPD officials were ransacked. As resentment mounted among the workers, protests formed and, as in Freiberg in the Erzgebirge, bloodshed followed.[26] Fellisch's government felt honor-bound to spare no effort to expose the Reichswehr's excesses and humiliate Defense Minister Otto Gessler (DDP). Not too unexpectedly, however, this strategy ended the toleration of the DDP, which toppled Fellisch on 14 December.[27]

The Saxon Social Democrats, thus, faced a question that was hardly new: Should they try once again to reach an accord with Brandler and Böttcher, or should they go in for a coalition with the DDP and, most likely, the DVP, or should they again put the matter to the voters? The SPD Executive had tried to narrow the choices for the Saxons by summoning the Party Council to Berlin. There it denounced any further political cooperation with a KPD that was clearly being orchestrated from Moscow against the Weimar Republic; furthermore, it tried to make the Landtag deputies subject to national party guidelines as well as those of the state party.[28]

Anticipating the end of its relationship with the DDP, the Saxons summoned an emergency state-level party congress on 1 December, that resulted in a bitter critique of the Berlin Executive's responsibility for the disastrous course of the Great Coalition; moreover, it refused to accept the Party Council's resolution as binding on its own by-laws. When the DDP brought the Fellisch government down, the 7-Committee once again followed the Saxon party congress instructions to seek out an arrangement of some sort with the KPD, oblivious to the fact that this option had been publicly vetoed by Böttcher.[29] Looking for new guidance from the Saxon party, still another congress was planned for 6 January 1924 to decide whether to proceed with negotiations for a coalition with the bourgeois parties as desired by Berlin, or to move for new and probably disastrous Saxon elections in the midst of the stabilization crisis of 1923 to 1924 and the party's own financial bankruptcy.

On the very eve of the Saxon party congress, Max Heldt and a majority of the SPD Landtag delegation, urged on by Wilhelm Dittmann from the Berlin Executive, negotiated a coalition with the DDP and DVP in Dresden in order to resolve the endemic coalition crisis in Dresden and to secure the interests of the national party in the wake of the stabilization crisis. For all intents and purposes, it was the end of red Saxony and marked the beginning of the "Saxon conflict" (*Sachsenstreit*) that lasted well into 1929, a conflict that pitted Saxon against Saxon as well as against the Reich within the SPD.

When the Saxon party congress met on 6 January 1924, it denounced Heldt's government and ordered the Landtag delegation to vote the government down. However, enough deputies refused to obey the Saxon party congress so that Heldt's regime survived. SPD national party congresses in 1924 and 1925 saw the Executive try to cover Heldt's actions and absolve the infamous twenty-three deputies who had supported him while simultaneously recognizing the ultimate authority of the Saxon party congress and executive over the Landtag delegation. After November 1924, consequently, formal expulsion proceedings were begun within Saxony against the so-called "twenty-three" for refusing to follow the explicit directions of a Saxon party congress to vote against the Heldt regime. The "twenty-three" remained undaunted, expecting the Berlin Executive to vindicate their defiance. Under relentless pressure from the Saxon party, Heldt and his followers were formally expelled from the SPD on 22 May 1926. On 6 June 1926 the expellees formed the "Old Social Democratic Party" (ASPD) in Saxony, nominally still based on the SPD's official Heidelberg program, while Heldt's regime held constitutionally slated elections on 31 October 1926.[30]

If one counts the ASPD along with the SPD and the KPD as part of red Saxony, then a socialist majority might theoretically have been possible in 1926. Politically, however, that was rendered nugatory by the SPD's political isolation within Saxony. The ASPD was disappointed to win only four seats and 4.2 percent of the vote in 1926, but it remained part of the Saxon regime until 1929, when its share of the vote, just 1.5 percent, merited only two seats, and it became irrelevant in a Landtag now sharply polarizing against the Left under the impact of bourgeois splinter parties, the arrival of the Nazis, and the coming of the Great Depression.[31]

For the SPD proper, as late as 1930 there still lingered the prospect that it could overcome the damage of 1923, but in fact the delicate balance of power in Saxony had shifted. The loss of control over the Dresden regime during the stabilization crisis of 1924 meant that much of the support for the party within the state apparatus was lost as a result of personnel cuts.[32] While there were still possibilities for the party to exert itself at the local level, fiscal support from Berlin and Dresden was now lacking for the pursuit of municipal socialism. East and West Saxony were able to continue their reform activities by borrowing until the coming of the Depression exposed their debt-ridden finances and limited their responses to the crisis of unemployment and falling revenues. In the Vogtland and the Erzgebirge, however, where the cultural milieu of the SPD was less deeply rooted, the SPD lost many of its old constituencies to communism and nazism.[33]

The idea of a red Saxon *Landespolitik* remained popular within the SPD until 1930. Now dominated by Leipzig leaders in alliance with the Left SPD in Dresden and Chemnitz, the party remained bitter over the inflation, which in its view had been used by the bourgeois reaction to destroy Zeigner's regime and shift politics at the Reich level to the Right.[34] It could, therefore, conceive only of maintaining the politics that had worked so well at the grass-roots level in 1919 to 1923, sensing that as soon as the *Sachsenstreit* was resolved the red majority would reassert itself through the solidarity of the working classes. Although the party did improve its position within Saxony up to 1929, it had in fact fallen into political isolation and become divorced from a changing reality. How could the red *Landespolitik* be coordinated with a hostile regime in Berlin and a lack of sympathy even from the national SPD?[35] Moreover, there was no sign that the KPD, now dominated by the ultra-Left in Berlin, could be brought back into a united front with the SPD and ADGB until late 1932. The possibility of reviving red Saxony had become increasingly remote, not to say ridiculous. The hope that opposition would expose the harshness of the reactionary bourgeoisie and revitalize the red majority backfired; the bourgeois regime built its politics after 1929 around eliminating the SPD from meaningful participation in Saxon politics. Only with the Nazis at the door in 1931 did the Saxon party start to consider the very distasteful need to defend the Republic in coalition with the liberal bourgeoisie. By that time, however, the SPD was isolated and virtually irrelevant in Saxon politics.

The broad socialist milieu also suffered real strategic damage in 1923 to 1924. Saxon enthusiasm for the Weimar Republic waned after the Reichswehr's intervention, particularly among the left wing of the SPD. The ADGB was crippled in Saxony after the inflation, losing almost half of its members in the stabilization crisis, and most of these never came back.[36] The KPD gained some support as a result of disappointment with the SPD, but the gains were marginal and meant little due to the KPD's isolation within Saxony.[37] The signs of a prolonged structural crisis in the textile industry and in the Erzgebirge had been veiled to some extent by the inflation pump.[38] Until 1928 to 1929, Saxon industry, especially fine manufacturing and metals, was still growing in the Leipzig and Dresden areas, but increasingly the Vogtland and especially the Erzgebirge were pulled into an abyss of desperate poverty.

The year 1923 revealed another strategic weakness, one Saxon Social Democrats in particular had difficulty confronting: the national question. As long as the party concentrated on domestic issues, it could do well, but when faced with real decisions on foreign-policy issues, the SPD looked weak on the issue of defending the nation. By 1918, the stinging defeat in World War I was already being lumped onto the SPD's shoulders and after 1923 the responsibility for breaking off the Ruhr struggle was attributed to the party. Under the influence of the so-called "National Bolshevik" Ernst Niekisch, the ASPD program came to express national and socialist elements, but historians must also realize that workers drifted to both the left and the right wings of the SPD over issues related to the Treaty of Versailles and the party's failure to develop a statesman-like sense of political responsibility.[39] The checkered and tarnished "Golden Age" of Weimar's middle years provided little substance for the SPD's hopes that a policy of peaceful revision and fulfillment of the Treaty would win votes. Cynical arguments in support of international revolution and war against the imperialist peace sprang from both Bolsheviks and National Bolsheviks and constantly tore away at the SPD's constituency throughout the Republic.[40] Given the SPD's problems with the national issue, the electoral landslide of the Nazis in 1930 was not at all extraordinary.

The triumph of the Chemnitz line also drove a more bitter wedge of class struggle through the modes of production than was perhaps necessary, advisable, or realistic. Saxony was utterly dependent on industry and commerce. The Leipzig Trade Fair was the pulse of the Saxon economy. Unless the competition from entrepreneurs and international firms could somehow be overcome, socialization of the means of production and exchange would remain a pipe dream in Saxony.[41]

Such economic realities may explain the strength of revisionist and reformist socialism in Saxony, which, with their concept of a "market socialism," could adapt to the Saxon mode of production; but they also demonstrate a fundamental weakness of red Saxony as its aging textile and domestic manufacturing industries began to stagnate. Not as dynamic in the new leading sectors of the "second industrial revolution" after 1895, the Vogtland and Erzgebirge needed either an economic plan to overcome structural problems and retrain the work force or better housing programs around Dresden and Leipzig to facilitate the mobility of labor.[42] Bringing new industries into Saxony was not impossible, so plans for such projects as the development of cheap and plentiful electrical energy based on the Saxon state coalfields around Hirschfelde and Böhlen were far-sighted.[43] However, the shift of power in the wake of the November Revolution brought higher wage levels to Saxony. The cultural improvements of practical socialism resulted in higher taxes and debts than elsewhere in the Reich by 1929.[44] Indeed, the sudden collapse of red Saxony after 1929 may be directly related to the SPD's often exclusive responsibility for high municipal debts, mounting local unemployment, and continuing welfare mandates in the midst of high taxes and falling revenues. One can hardly overlook the pits of poverty, hunger, and despair present among the Saxon working class and its children, but a realistic solution to these complex problems required conservation of a competitive economic base in the Free State. Certainly red Saxony had its work cut out for it trying to demonstrate positive achievements for its working-class constituents without freezing industry and commerce in a "cold socialization" of labor regulations, state controls, and taxation that threatened profit margins rather than private property. The task was not made any easier by the presence of the League of Saxon Industrialists, persistently one of the most outspokenly hostile forces arrayed against the Weimar Republic. At the same time, the Left often drew the line of class struggle too rigidly and rhetorically.[45]

Despite its hold over the working class until 1930, red Saxony had reached the limits of its power and influence much earlier in 1923 and was unable ever after to tip the balance of forces decisively in its favor. To grow, it needed to expand its influence into middle-class constituencies while simultaneously capturing even more of the working class. Middle-class voters came to count in various ways for around 40 percent of the SPD's vote nationally.[46] Indeed, the Saxon party's ability to function as a mass party *(Volkspartei)* and not merely as a party of the working class had made it viable throughout the 1920s. The expanding socialist cultural milieu helped win new middle class sources of support for the SPD, particularly from school teachers, public-sector workers, and lower-level officials. Ironically, this often meant that the more seasoned socialists, the workers, had to endure the radicalism of these bourgeois groups at a time when the workers increasingly wanted to end their isolation within Weimar politics. The refusal to collaborate with the DDP after 1920 hurt any effort to go further into the middle class and forced the DDP into more uncompromising reliance on the DVP; however, the united front of the Chemnitz line may have strengthened the pull of the SPD among the working classes and kept them from drifting into communism. If the Dresden line toward the DDP was unacceptable within the SPD and became even more unacceptable as the DVP emerged in 1920, it is also true that the Chemnitz line was fundamentally flawed in its assumption that a Moscow-oriented KPD would be forced to support red Saxony. Waiting for a return of the red majority meant giving up positions of power and, ultimately, influence. The so-called "balance of class power" well describes the Saxon dilemma, for the balance of power swung quickly against red Saxony once it lost its ability to protect its school teachers, public officials, public housing projects, and welfare networks from political retaliation.[47] Moreover, once the Nazis came to power, they quickly understood how to transform these networks into new sources of support for the NSDAP.[48]

The SPD also could not expand its press and communications media to compete with the bourgeois press, and increasingly this meant it could not relate its program to the non-SPD milieu, especially the intelligentsia. In intellectual isolation, it could not counter the arguments directed against it.

Women too became a difficult problem for the SPD. However much the SPD deserves credit for winning women civic rights of equality in the November Revolution, it proved less able than the parties of the religious Right and center in mobilizing women's support. The Saxon party and milieu seem to have done a better job in this regard than the national party, and certainly the SPD did a better job of it than the KPD. But the SPD increasingly realized that it had emancipated women only to see them vote against the Left. The explanation for this phenomenon is no doubt complex and almost certainly does not stem solely from alleged working-class male hostility directed against working women on the job during and after the demobilization of 1918 to 1919. It may well be that party life fell somewhere in the male sphere of cultural activity in Germany and that women preferred more direct engagement in the practical activities related to socialist politics and culture.[49]

There are also clear signs that the socialist milieu itself must account for its stagnation and decline after 1923. For example, the Saxon cultural milieu smacked of the extremism and eccentricity that George Orwell noted among British socialists in the 1930s. Up to a point at least, the utopian vision of the alternative life-style movements tended to be self-exclusive. Although this might have been quite feasible for individuals, collectively and politically it generated isolation, contempt, and hatred, particularly when it was connected to the bitter class and religious tensions of the interwar years.[50]

The "new man" of red Saxony probably could have survived Franz von Papen's "new state," but he could not survive the Nazi *Gleichschaltung*. Once in control of the state, the Brownshirts acted with a ruthless determination and an almost insider knowledge of the socialist party and its milieu to tear out the red rose by the roots after trampling on it.

The tough, cynical image of the communist revolutionary had little appeal, let alone much promise of success, in Saxony before 1933.[51] Revolutionary violence would have been the worst scenario for urban industrial Saxony, and there is evidence that the Saxon KPD understood the hopelessness of an armed uprising, even if Berlin and Moscow did not. But was there a democratic "third way" for Saxon socialism between east and west, between dictatorship of the proletariat and a coalition with the bourgeoisie? The persistence of the red majority suggests that there was a way in Saxony, but it was by no means an easy one to tread and required balance, vision, and moderation to master the external political and economic context of the Weimar Republic. The very admirable grass-roots democracy of the Saxons could generate activistic cadres, but no leaders arose within red Saxony to manage the balance between loyalty to the democratic ideals of the broader socialist movement and recognition of the harsh realities of power inside and outside Saxony.[52]

Notes

1. This essay is based largely on a session of the American Historical Association, "Social Democracy in Saxony 1890-1933: From 'Red' to Brown Hegemony." See William Carl Mathews, "The Impact of the Inflation on the SPD in Saxony," and Simone Lässig, "Social Democracy in Saxony, 1890-1914," American Historical Association, 170th Annual Meeting, Session 60 (27-30 December 1992), University Microfilms International, Reference #10485. More extensive references to, and discussion of secondary literature can be found there. The statistics are found in Franz Walter, "Sachsen – ein Stammland der Sozialdemokratie?," *Politische Vierteljahresschrift* 32:2 (1991): 212-14.
2. Franz Walter, Tobias Dürr, and Klaus Schmidtke, *Die SPD in Sachsen und Thüringen zwischen Hochburg und Diaspora: Untersuchungen auf lokaler Ebene vom Kaiserreich bis zur Gegenwart* (Bonn, 1993), 11-48.
3. Walter et al., *SPD in Sachsen und Thüringen*, 12; Walter, "Sachsen," 207-31; and especially Gerhard A. Ritter, "Das Wahlrecht und die Wählerschaft der Sozialdemokratie in Sachsen 1867-1918," in *Der Aufstieg der deutschen Arbeiterbewegung*, ed. idem (Munich, 1991), 49-101. See also James Retallack, "'What Is To Be Done?' The Red Specter, Franchise Questions, and the Crisis of Conservative Hegemony in Saxony, 1896-1909," *Central European History* 23:4 (1990): 271-312; idem, "Anti-Socialism and Electoral Politics in Regional Perspective: The Kingdom of Saxony," in *Elections, Mass Politics and Social Change in Modern Germany: New Perspectives*, ed. Larry Eugene Jones and James Retallack (Washington, DC, 1992), 49-91.
4. I have encountered few sources on the Saxon communist movements in the 1920s except for the year 1923. I explain this largely as a result of the fact that the

Saxon KPD remained oriented toward a mass mobilization of the workers that, in the end, produced none of the revolutionary legends of the Berlin KPD or Comintern. Saxon KPD leaders were hounded by the Stalinists, in Paul Böttcher's case until the mid-1950s. As such, the Saxon KPD was written out of history by SED historians.

5. I share much of the insight into the *Vertrauensleute* of W. G. Guttsman, *The German Social Democratic Party, 1875-1933: From Ghetto to Government* (London, 1981), 149-53. On the "gentle" side of the Social Democrats, as opposed to the cynical realism of the KPD and its resulting lack of popularity in Dresden, see the autobiography of the very well informed British wife of a school teacher and active SPD member, Madeleine Kent, *I Married a German* (New York and London, 1939), 111, 113. Kent emphasizes the limited appeal of the KPD's hard-line image, a point also made by SPD analysis: SPD Bezirksverband-Dresden, *Geschäfts-Bericht vom 1. April 1925 bis 31. März 1925* (Dresden, 1925), 3-4.
6. Ruth Fischer, *Stalin and German Communism: A Study in the Origins of the State Party* (Cambridge, Mass., 1948), 216-25, notes that the Chemnitz KPD was on the right wing of the KPD. According to Horst Dörrer, Wolfgang Marschner, and Fritz Kriegerhardt, *Die Novemberrevolution und die Gründung der KPD in Ostsachsen*, 32, the early Dresden KPD was influenced by the Bremen Left; a copy of Dörrer et al. can be found in the Saxon State Library in Dresden. Sigrid Koch-Baumgartner, *Aufstand der Avantgarde: Die Märzaktion der KPD 1921* (Frankfurt am Main, 1986), 50-63, has many insights into the state of the KPD in 1919-20. Relations within Saxony among SPD, USPD, and KPD are examined by Richard Lipinski, *Der Kampf um die Macht in Sachsen* (Leipzig, 1926), 53-56, a largely autobiographical account of the red Saxon experiment. See also Eberhard Kolb, *Die Arbeiterräte in der deutschen Innenpolitik 1918-1919* (Frankfurt am Main, 1978), 297-300, 315-16, 321-24. Because the KPD's actions were directed against the existing councils and against the USPD as well as the SPD and ADGB trade union activists elected to those councils, the radicals were utterly discredited within the organized working class; the KPD seems to have had a base only among organized construction workers around Chemnitz and among some opposition to the metalworkers union in Leipzig (DMV); otherwise, KPD influence was restricted to the unemployed, youth groups, and the very activistic anarcho-syndicalist groups that were influential among newly formed proletarians in the lignite mining areas.
7. See Max Seydewitz, *Es hat sich gelohnt zu leben: Lebenserinnerungen eines alten Arbeiterfunktionäres* (Berlin, 1976), 65-91. Seydewitz was a left SPD secretary from Chemnitz and later was prominent in the SED during the DDR. Heinrich Brandler, the chief Saxon KPD man and occasional chairman of the KPD in 1921 to 1923, expressed the limits of the KPD in Saxony in Isaac Deutscher, "Record of a Discussion with Heinrich Brandler," *New Left Review* 105 (1977): 48 ff. Koch-Baumgartner, *Aufstand der Avantgarde*, 445-47, presents KPD membership statistics from 1920 through 1923: the four Saxon districts had between forty and forty-five thousand members, nearly half of them in the Erzgebirge-Vogtland. The Saxon KPD hardly benefited from crossover USPD members after December 1920 and declined into early 1923.
8. Noske's policy of using the Free Corps to enforce law, order, and political stability in 1918 to 1919 is given a sharp critique from Hans Mommsen, *Die verspielte Freiheit: Der Weg der Republik vom Weimar in den Untergang 1918 bis 1933* (Berlin, 1990), 100. It was, I think, a more tragic situation: see William Carl Mathews, "The Economic Origins of the *Noskepolitik*," *Central European History* 27:1 (1994): 65-86.

9. Jürgen Falter, Thomas Lindenberger, and Siegfried Schumann, *Wahlen und Abstimmungen in der Weimarer Republik: Materialien zum Wahlverhalten 1919-1933* (Munich, 1986), 108.
10. The united front tactics are covered by Arnold Reisberg, *An die Quellen der Einheitsfrontpolitik: Der Kampf der KPD um die Aktionseinheit in Deutschland 1921 bis 1922*, 2 vols. (Berlin, 1971), but Reisberg stresses the role of the KPD and Comintern rather than local forces in Saxony and Chemnitz. Critically more demanding in her analysis of the KPD in 1920 to 1921 is Koch-Baumgartner, *Aufstand der Avantgarde*, 64-104, who points out the roles of Paul Levi and Heinrich Brandler in developing the tactics.
11. Susanne Miller, *Die Bürde der Macht: Die deutsche Sozialdemokratie 1918-1920* (Düsseldorf, 1978), 414. For an indispensable source on the Saxon Left, see Dietmar Klenke, *Die SPD-Linke in der Weimarer Republik: Eine Untersuchung zu den regionalen Grundlagen und zur politischen Praxis und Theoriebildung des linken Flügels der SPD in den Jahren 1922-1932*, 2 vols. (Münster, 1983), 366-446. The "Chemnitz line" is my characterization of it. The "Dresden line" was brought into focus as the grass roots turned against its leaders, "Sächische Angelegenheiten. Minierarbeit der 'Dresdner Richtung,'" *Dresdner Volkszeitung* (hereafter cited as DVZ) 9 (12 January 1921).
12. On Gustav Stresemann's Saxon background, see Donald Warren, *The Red Kingdom of Saxony: The Lobbying Grounds of Gustav Stresemann 1901-1909* (The Hague, 1964); Erich Heinz Schlottner, "Stresemann, der Kapp-Putsch and die Ereignisse in Mitteldeutschland und in Bayern im Herbst 1923: Ein Beitrag zur Geschichte der Weimarer Republik" (Ph.D. diss., Frankfurt am Main, 1948), is unintentionally less than flattering to the *Vernunftrepublikaner*. The Saxon SPD's perspective can be found in "Stresemann Partei," *DVZ* 242 (18 October 1920). On the DDP and DVP in Saxony, see Larry Eugene Jones, *German Liberalism and the Dissolution of the Weimar Party System, 1918-1933* (Chapel Hill, NC, 1988), 110.
13. See Lipinski, *Kampf um die Macht*, 19-23; Walter Fabian, *Klassenkampf in Sachsen: Ein Stück Geschichte* (Löbau, 1930), 74-92; Burkhard Poste, *Schulreform in Sachsen 1918-1923: Eine vergessene Tradition deutscher Schulgeschichte* (Frankfurt am Main, 1993), 35-179; and Klenke, *SPD-Linke*, 411-20, 834-46.
14. See Dietrich Orlow, *Weimar Prussia 1918-1925: The Unlikely Rock of Democracy* (Pittsburgh, PA, 1986), 32, 34-35; Lipinski, *Kampf um die Macht*, 19-23; Fabian, *Klassenkampf in Sachsen*, 74-92; Simone Lässig, "Politische Radikalität und junge Kunst – Zum Wirken von Otto Rühle in Dresden," *Dresdner Hefte* 25:1 (1991): 53-67.
15. Heinrich August Winkler, *Von der Revolution zur Stabilisierung: Arbeiter und Arbeiterbewegung in der Weimarer Republik 1918 bis 1924* (Berlin, 1984), 468-507, covers the events of the unification of the Left USPD with the KPD at Halle in December 1920. David Morgan, *The Socialist Left and the German Revolution: A History of the German Independent Social Democratic Party, 1917-1922* (Ithaca, NY, 1975), 377, shows that the Saxon USPD was conspicuous in its opposition to Moscow at the Halle party congress.
16. Falter et al., *Wahlen und Abstimmungen*, 108. See "Landtagwahl-Ergebnis," *DVZ* 265 (15 November 1920). The SPD thought it had picked up USPD votes particularly in Dresden, "Aus dem Parteileben: Funktionaere des 6. Kreis," *DVZ* 269 (20 November 1920).
17. Alfred Kastning, *Die deutsche Sozialdemokratie zwischen Koalition und Opposition 1919-1923* (Paderborn, 1970), 82-90, covers the USPD's way to coalition politics.

18. "Regiererungsbildung und Kommunisten," *DVZ* 273 (25 November 1920). The KPD declared little confidence in the regime but did not want to play into the hands of the DNVP in Saxony. See "Sächische Angelegenheiten: Über die Lebensdauer der neuen Regierung," *DVZ* 292 (17 December 1920). The Berlin KPD had opposed joining the SPD/USPD/ADGB general strike launched against the Kapp Putsch; the Chemnitz Communists, therefore, had to break party discipline when they followed Paul Levi's appeal to defend the Republic and oppose Kapp.
19. SStAD, Staatskanzlei, Nr. 109, St. Min. Braunschweig to St. Min. Saxony (10 October 1921), Bl. 1, and "Gesehen." (18 October 1921) Gesandtschaft Berlin, Nr. 362.
20. Fabian, *Klassenkampf in Sachsen*, 109-12; Lipinski, *Kampf um die Macht*, 31-33. The charges seem to be related to Lipinki's lack of formal education, especially in law.
21. In addition to n. 8 above, see Hans-Joachim Krusch, *Um die Einheitsfront und eine Arbeiterregierung: Zur Geschichte der Arbeiterbewegung im Bezirk Erzgebirge-Vogtland unter besonderer Berücksichtigung der Klassenkämpfe im Zwickau-Oelsnitzer Steinkohlrevier von Januar bis August 1923* (Berlin, 1966), 71-127, where the weaknesses and limits of KPD actions are noted. Often syndicalists initiated radical actions, forcing the KPD to follow; much of the KPD's use of united front tactics in 1923 was aimed at recovering the KAPD groups and syndicalists that had left the party in 1919.
22. Rudolf Luz, *KPD: Weimarer Staat und politische Einheit der Arbeiterbewegung in der Nachkriegskrise 1919-1922/23* (Konstanz, 1987), 412-28.
23. Letters from the only Center deputy in the Saxon Landtag, Paul Hesslein, "Sächische Politik," *Germania* (1 May 1922) and "Sächische Regierungsmethode," *Germania* (20 December 1922), in SStAD, Gesandtschaft Berlin, Nr. 362, Bl. 22 and 25, give a good insight into the politics of the referendum.
24. Falter et al., *Wahlen und Abstimmungen*, 108.
25. Donald B. Pryce, "The Reich Government versus Saxony, 1923: The Decision to Intervene," *Central European History* 10:2 (June 1977): 112-47, is a solid and detached study, but see Gerald D. Feldman, *The Great Disorder: Politics, Economics, and Society in the German Inflation, 1914-1924* (Oxford, 1993), 631-803, for the Saxon events against the background of the hyperinflation. Winkler, *Von der Revolution zur Stabilisierung*, 553-670, covers the events with reference to national developments and the SPD in Berlin as well as Dresden. Raimund Wagner, "Die 'Arbeiterregierung' in Sachsen im Jahre 1923" (Phil. Diss., Institut für Geschichtswissenschaft beim ZK der SED in Berlin, 1957), is a DDR version.
26. Winkler, *Von der Revolution zur Stabilisierung*, 655, reports twenty-three dead and thirty-one wounded along with four wounded soldiers in the Freiberg incident.
27. The Saxon government's perspective emerges in Zeigner to RK (29 October 1923) and Fellisch to Staatsgerichthof (6 November 1923) in SStAD, Nr. 363, Bl. 4 ff., 12 ff. Also in this file on the *Reichsexekution* are numerous complaints from Fellisch to Gradnauer, the Saxon official representative in Berlin, regarding use of Black Reichswehr forces and abuse of power.
28. "Beratung des Parteiausschusses," *Vorwärts* 555 (28 November 1923). The events between Saxony and Berlin are well summed up in Franz Osterroth and Dieter Schuster, *Chronik der deutschen Sozialdemokratie*, vol. 2 (Bonn, 1975), 133-39, which should also be consulted for the *Sachsenstreit*.
29. Lipinski, *Kampf*, 76.

30. On the formation of the ASPD, see SStAD, Gesandtschaft Berlin, Nr. 987, Bl. 47-48.
31. Falter et al., *Wahlunden und Abstimmungen*, 108. The ASPD soon drafted a new program, *Was will die Alte Sozialdemokratische Partei?* (Dresden, 1926); see also Jones, *German Liberalism*, 263-65, 363-65. The ASPD drew heavily from the Dresden and Leipzig areas.
32. See SPD-Landtagsfraktion, *Vier Jahre sächische Politik* (1926), 88.
33. William C. McNeil, *American Money and the Weimar Republic: Politics on the Eve of the Great Depression* (New York, 1986), 52, 238-45.
34. *Vier Jahre sächische Politik*, 19-20.
35. Orlow, *Weimar Prussia*, 188-217, notes there was a linkage of Reich coalition politics and the regime in Prussia as early as 1921. After 1924 the pressure of the DNVP was repeatedly exercised at the national level to try to force a change in the Prussian coalition; under these circumstances, there was hardly room for a Red Saxony alongside a *Bürgerbloc* in Berlin.
36. Heinrich Potthoff, *Freie Gewerkschaften 1918-1933: Der Allgemeine Deutsche Gewerkschaftsbund in der Weimarer Republik* (Düsseldorf, 1987), 350. From a high of 989,272 members in 1922, the Saxon ADGB fell to 534,638 in 1924 and to 674,486 in 1930. In 1931 it had 603,735 members.
37. August Thalheimer, *1923: Eine verpasste Revolution? Die deutsche Oktoberlegende und die wirkliche Geschichte von 1923* (Berlin, 1931), gives a critical analysis of the Saxon episode; the KPD lost much of its influence among the trade unions, especially the metalworkers and factory councils, as a result of the Red October. KPD, *Material der Kommunistischen Partei über die Sachsenpolitik: Zur Landtagwahl Herbst 1926*, 158, shows that there were only very brief gains for the KPD in 1923 to 1924 before the party slipped back to 1922 levels of performance. The KPD would win additional seats in 1926, but they meant nothing once the bourgeois coalition was in place and the SPD was in opposition.
38. Gerald D. Feldman, "Saxony, the Reich, and the Problem of Unemployment in the German Inflation," *Archiv für Sozialgeschichte* 27 (1987): 102-44.
39. See Benjamin Lapp, "A 'National' Socialism: The Old Socialist Party of Saxony, 1926-32," *Journal of Contemporary History* 30:2 (April 1995): 291-310.
40. See Conan Fischer, *The German Communists and the Rise of Nazism* (New York, 1991).
41. See the analysis of Rudolf Harnisch (SPD), Minister of Justice in 1920, "Das Nötigste zur wirtschaftlichen Rettung Deutschland," *DVZ* 203 (3 September 1920) and 206 (6 September 1920).
42. Frank B. Tipton, *Regional Variations in the Economic Development of Germany During the Nineteenth Century* (Middletown, Mass., 1976), 122-23.
43. Hellmut Kretzschmar, "Königreich und Land Sachsen," in *Geschichte der Deutschen Länder: Territorien-Ploetz* (Würzburg, 1971) 551, 557; also Fabian, *Klassenkampf in Sachsen*, 58.
44. The weight of the debt may not have been excessive before 1929 (see McNeil, *American Money*), but afterwards it was confining. Harold James, *The German Slump: Politics and Economics, 1924-1936* (Oxford, 1986), 80, 207.
45. Hermann Fellisch, the Minister of Economics, launched a class-conscious concept of economic policy of rhetorical bombast, as in "Die deutsche Wirtschaft und die Arbeiterklasse," *DVZ* 149 (29 June 1921). See also Gerald D. Feldman, "Bayern und Sachsen in der Hyperinflation 1922/23," *Historische Zeitschrift* 238 (1984): 569-609.

46. Peter Lösche and Franz Walter, *Die SPD: Klassenpartei – Volkspartei – Quotenpartei* (Darmstadt, 1992), 19. Ritter, "Das Wahlrecht und die Wählerschaft," 94-105, shows that in the 1909 Landtag election, the SPD received considerable votes beyond the working classes. One could suggest, therefore, a similar estimate for the SPD in Saxony.
47. See Richard Saage, "Das Dilemma der Sozialdemokratie in Deutschland und Österreich 1918 bis 1933" and " 'Gleichgewicht der Klassenkräfte' als Problem in Deutschland und Österreich zwischen den Weltkriegen," in *Rückkehr zum starken Staat?* (Frankfurt am Main, 1983), 61-135. The Saxons saw it in precisely these terms as well. See SStAD, Gesandtschaft Berlin, Nr. 362, Bl. 185, 187.
48. Kent, *I Married A German*, 66-67, 160-61, 165, 191, 195, 228.
49. Walter, *SPD in Sachsen und Thüringen*, 52-53, 40. The irony did not escape the East Saxon party, which noted that "to date only the bourgeoisie have benefitted from the right of women to vote": "Bezirkskonferenz der V.S.P.D. Ostsachsen," *DVZ* 148 (28 June 1923); Ute Frevert, *Women in German History: From Bourgeois Emancipation to Sexual Liberation* (New York, 1988), 149-217; Erhard Lucas, *Vom Scheitern der deutschen Arbeiterbewegung* (Basel, 1983), 45-71, makes insightful points based on studies in the Ruhr.
50. Kent, *I Married A German*, 112-13; George Orwell, *The Road to Wigan Pier* (New York, 1958), 216, 220.
51. Kent, *I Married A German*, 113.
52. Walter, *SPD in Sachsen und Thüringen*, 129-83.

Chapter 12

Cultural Socialism, the Public Sphere, and the Mass Form

Popular Culture and the Democratic Project, 1900 to 1934

Geoff Eley

1. Defining the Public Sphere: The Trouble with Habermas

The parties of the Left, and perhaps a majority of Left intellectuals for most of the time, have had enormous difficulties coming to terms with the commercially produced and distributed entertainment cultures of the twentieth century in their mass-mediated forms. More often than not, the Left have belittled, demonized, and disavowed the popularity of mass culture, as opposed to taking it as an important ground of democracy. The Left's history is replete with difficulty when it comes to popular culture, with suspicion and unease, with the sense that the people's availability for radical or oppositional politics (or for just politics *tout court*) was being undermined by the escapist and depoliticizing effects of the commercially provided enjoyments that have become increasingly dominant in twentieth-century social life (although the degree to which popular culture was more "indigenous" or self-made before the age of mechanical reproduction is a classic instance of wishful thinking, we might add, a romantic projection, a chimera of authenticity).

The strongest critique of mass culture has been associated perhaps with the Frankfurt School, a critique that has received a latter-day

Notes for this chapter begin on page 337.

reworking from Jürgen Habermas in *The Structural Transformation of the Public Sphere*, with its story of the public sphere's twentieth-century degeneration and decline.[1] Despite its virtues, there are many grounds on which Habermas's conception of the public sphere may be questioned. It works best, for instance, "as the organizing category of a specifically liberal view of the transition to the modern world and of the ideal bases on which political and intellectual life should be conducted." But it is also "an extremely idealized abstraction from the political cultures that actually took shape at the end of the eighteenth and start of the nineteenth century." "The public sphere in its classical … guise was partial and narrowly based … and was constituted from a field of conflict, contested meanings, and exclusion."[2] In its foundational period, the idea of the public sphere was constructed around a system of gendered meanings, whether in the formal intellectual discourse of politics, citizenship and rights, the institutional arenas of publicity, the associational universe of civic engagement and sociality, or the private sphere of domesticity and family. Moreover, to construct his ideal of liberal proceduralism and communicative rationality within a discretely circumscribed public sphere, Habermas effectively brackets major domains of popular democratic activity. His story of bourgeois emancipation, therefore, needs to be confronted with an important counter-story of popular politics, of social movements, of politics made in the streets, of taking politics out of doors. Habermas, one might say, needs to be confronted with the accumulated findings of social history, particularly the huge weight of research on plebeian cultures and popular publics of the late-eighteenth and early-nineteenth centuries, and especially the work of Edward Thompson.[3]

In other words, there was an element of conflict to the very possibility of the public sphere, to its constitutive conditions of emergence, which runs counter to the normative prioritizing of reasoned exchange Habermas puts at its center. The public sphere in this latter sense is an abstract desideratum, but a never-attainable ideal, whose pursuit might easily militate against an equally important priority, namely, recognizing the necessity of conflict and difference in the conduct of political life and as a principle of workable democratic arrangements. It makes more sense to see the public sphere plurally, as an arena of contested meanings, where different and opposing publics maneuvered for space, and from which certain "publics" might be excluded altogether (for instance: women, subordinate nationalities, popular classes like the urban poor, the working class, and the peasantry, or populations defined by ethnicity, by race, by sexual orientation, and so on). The contest of publics occurred in class-divided societies structured by inequality, so that questions of domination and subordination – power, in all its economic, social, cultural, and political dimensions – were also involved. Consequently, the public sphere could be a neutral context of rational political discourse only in a formal sense, because processes of hegemonic construction – the harnessing of public life to the priorities of one particular group, a social bloc ordered around the interests of dominant classes – were also at work. Moreover, such hegemonies had to be systematically worked at, whether consciously and programmatically, or increasingly as the "natural" and unreflected administration or reproduction of established ways.

This element of conflict – the fractured and contested character of the public sphere – was crucial to the constitutive moment of the public sphere's emergence, and also needs to be considered in later periods of its history, which Habermas presents increasingly as a story of degeneration and decline. From the last third of the nineteenth century, in Habermas's argument:

> *the growing contradictions of a capitalist society – the passage of competitive capitalism into monopoly or organized capitalism, the regulation of social conflicts by the state, and the fragmentation of the rational public into an arena of competing interests – serve to erode the independence of public opinion and undermine the legitimacy of its institutions. In the cultural sphere proper, from the arts to the press and the mass entertainment industry, the processes of commercialization and rationalization have increasingly targeted the individual consumer while eliminating the mediating contexts of reception and rational discussion, particularly in the new age of the electronic media. In this way the classic basis of the public sphere – a clear distinction between public good and private interest, the principled demarcation of state and society, and the constitutive role of a participant citizenry, defining public policy and its parameters through reasoned exchange, free of domination – disappears. The relations between state and society are reordered, to the advantage of the former and the detriment of a free political life.*[4]

It is in this vision of decline, of the impoverishment of a once vital and reason-affirming public life, that Habermas comes closest to the classical pessimism of his Frankfurt School forebears, "etching an unforgettable portrait of a degraded public life, in which the substance of liberal democracy is voided in a combination of plebiscitary manipulation and privatized apathy, as any collectivity of citizenry disintegrates."[5]

What I am suggesting, clearly, is that Habermas's framework needs to be recast in the light of other theory. Gramsci provides one source of the latter, and my commentary on the insufficiencies of Habermas's model presupposes a reading of Gramsci in this sense. Furthermore, the insistence on *rational* discourse, certainly in the social and gendered exclusiveness of its late eighteenth-century terms, was simultaneously a claim to *power* in Foucault's sense, and so to Gramsci, therefore, must also be added Foucault. Third, we also need the accumulated feminist critique of the last twenty years, which has compelled us to see the silences and suppressions around which the virtues of publicness, in both their founding forms and their later transmutations, were actually ordered. Last, in the specifically eighteenth-century context, Edward Thompson also has much to teach us. His social history scathingly challenges the sufficiency of older approaches focused on the limited public sphere of the eighteenth-century political nation. It forces us to consider the democracy "out of doors," whether via the opposition of "patrician society" and "plebeian culture," or the later confrontation between parliamentary government and the extra-parliamentary radicalism of the English Jacobins in the 1790s. A knowledge of Thompson's work makes the narrowness of Habermas's understanding of the public sphere abundantly clear: "Habermas's concentration on *Öffentlichkeit* as a specifically *bourgeois* category subsumes forms of popular democratic mobilization that were always already present as contending and subversive alternatives to the classical liberal organization of civil society in which Habermas's ideal of the public sphere is confined."[6]

2. Democratizing the Public Sphere in the 1920s

In this paper I want to explore the conditions of democracy of a later time, in the legally guaranteed public sphere of the Weimar Republic after 1918 to 1919. Here I am starting from Habermas's treatment of the public sphere's long-term impoverishment and decline, and I would like to consider some contexts of popular politics in the 1920s that do not easily fit with this jeremiad for the lost ideal of the rationally deliberating public. I want to consider a different way of reading the cultural history of the early-twentieth century in its political dimensions. I want to present some examples of cultural politics on the German Left, which suggest that Habermas's formally circumscribed understanding of the public sphere as a kind of magic circle of liberal proceduralism misidentifies the important sites of democratic innovation, and that a good way of conceptualizing public life's contested nature is via a Gramscian notion of counter-hegemonic potentials. First, I will offer a Gramscian reading of certain aspects of the Left's cultural politics, which allows us to answer Habermas's lament with a strong counter-story of popular democratic creativity. But second, I would like to destabilize my own optimistic counter-narrative of the latter with a critique of cultural socialism's collectivist ethic drawn from our own contemporary political sensibility, including the post-Foucaultian, recent feminist, and more emergent queer-theoretical recognitions of the socialist tradition's deficiencies. From our late twentieth-century vantage point, these once-attractive anticipatory socialisms now seem marked by forms of political normativity that look increasingly bleak.

But before we go any further, we need to say something about the overall context of the democratic project in post-1918 Europe, and in the first instance that means the constitutional question in the narrower sense. Here the transnational and European-wide context of democratization after 1917 to 1918 is key, and I would argue more generally that the democratic agenda has been set to a great extent beyond the reach of particular national histories through a series of big horizon-expanding and limit-setting European-wide conjunctures between the late-eighteenth century and the present. There have been arguably five such conjunctures, or transnational constitution-making moments of European history, through which the limits and possibilities for democracy were established for the following eras: a) 1776 to 1815, b) 1859 to 1871, c) 1914 to 1923, d) 1943 to 1949, and e) 1989 to 1992.[7] From our point of view, for instance, the 1860s established the legal-constitutional and institutional terrain of popular democratic politics for the next several decades, naturally with national variations and specificities, but also with a continental generality that proved remarkably stable and lasting until a fresh set of radicalized contestations over the forms and limits of the constitutional settlements began to dissolve its permanence between 1905 and 1914. Within this long period, popular democratic aspirations were articulated consistently within the liberal constitutionalist frameworks enduringly laid down in the 1860s, while political stability was predominantly secured *through* the available parliamentary forms.

Of course, the dominance of such a politics was never automatic, and was hedged constantly by the repressive and regulatory police and administrative actions of national and local states, by the authoritarian proclivities of employers, by the countervailing anti-democratic logics of much religious authority, by class inequalities in the access to political rights, and so on. The ability of socialist leaderships to ground their parliamentary-democratic strategies in the active consent of generalized working-class support also rested on complex and uncertain negotiations of the latter's everydayness, whose needs, pressures, and rhythms might remain extremely unmanageable and disruptive. Moreover, there were parts of Europe where the ground of parliamentary politics was far less secure or absent altogether (Spain, Italy, Russia) and popular politics took a different turn. Between the 1890s and 1914 the growth of syndicalist militancy across Europe also articulated a different model of popular democratic empowerment through direct-action and workplace forms. But syndicalist strength was usually localized in particular industrial and urban settings rather than graduating into a fully fledged national movement, and by its own formal inclinations in any case backed *away* from challenging power in the already constituted liberal state. Furthermore, the most successful instances of the general strike (outside the special case of the 1905 Russian Revolution), in Belgium and the Scandinavian countries, were linked not to the syndicalist panacea, but to the agitations for universal suffrage and the strengthening of the parliamentary constitution. In Germany the prevalence of the latter was certainly the case.

If the experience of the 1860s established a lasting set of parliamentary constitutional norms for European political life, the next transnational conjuncture of constitution-making, which reshaped these norms, came after World War I. Here I am concerned less with the insurrectionary revolutionary projects of the Bolsheviks and other extreme Lefts than with the reformist initiatives those challenges precipitated. For even where the revolutionary Left was at its weakest and socialist parties recorded only modest gains in postwar elections, this effect could clearly be seen – as in France (with a law on collective agreements, the eight-hour day, and an electoral reform between March and July 1919); in Belgium (the eight-hour day, a progressive tax reform, social insurance legislation, and an electoral reform during 1918 to 1921); and in the Netherlands (again, the eight-hour day, a forty-five hour week, social insurance legislation, public housing, corporative involvement of the trade unions in the new Ministry of Social Affairs, and votes for women during 1918 to 1920). Similar effects can be seen in Britain and Scandinavia. In Germany and Austria, and in the new successor states of East Central Europe, new republican sovereignties were constructed via processes of national-democratic revolution, accompanied by varying degrees of social reform. Finally, in most of the successor states and some others (Romania, Yugoslavia, Bulgaria, Greece, Czechoslovakia, Poland, the Baltic states, and Finland) there were major land reforms.

This was a major increment of reform. In a large part of Europe – essentially the pre-1914 central and north European "social democratic core," where socialist parties had won 20 percent or more of the popular vote in parliamentary elections (Austria, Germany, Switzerland, Czechoslovakia, and all the Scandinavian countries), together with France, the Low Countries, and Britain – the position of the Left had become much stronger than before. Yet this took a very specific form – that is, it was not so much a specifically socialist advance as it was a further strengthening of parliamentary democracy, the expansion of workers' rights under the law, further recognition of trade unions, growth of civil liberties or civil rights, and significant social legislation, which in some cases amounted to the beginnings of a welfare state. In particular, the enhancement of the public sphere – in parliamentary, publicistic, and cultural terms – was a major strategic gain, especially in countries where public freedoms had been cramped and harassed before 1914. This toughening of civil society through the enhancement of the public sphere was a vital dimension of democratization, and in the newly created sovereignties of East Central

Europe (including the new republican sovereignty of Weimar Germany) the legal constitution of the public sphere was also a vital process in the overall project of nation-forming.

Thus, we need to assert, as strongly as possible, the value of liberal legality and a strong formal constitution of a democratic kind as indispensable conditions of possibility for the kind of popular democratic potentials seemingly available to the German and Austrian Social Democrats in the 1920s. Without the protection of the law, the achievements of Red Vienna and of cultural socialism (the two cases to be discussed below) were unimaginable. This was apparent in both the demise of the republican constitutions in 1933 to 1934, which spelled the destruction of the socialist movements and their legal existence, and in the republics' original creation in 1918 to 1919, which had first brought the German and Austrian Socialists to positions of plausible or credible national leadership. In this sense, it was less the failure of the two parties to break through to genuinely socialist construction during the revolutions of 1918 to 1919, I would argue, than the new democratic capacities and legal resources which the liberalized constitutional frameworks made available that should focus our attention.

Legality was vital in a double sense. It certainly allowed the socialist movements to organize their own interior relations without fear of police harassment, political reprisals, or the state's hostile regulation. But it also gave the socialist movements access to wider social and political influence, to potential supporters beyond their own ranks, and to the resources of a wider public realm. Without this benefit of an expanded and legally protected national or society-wide public sphere, the socialists would remain confined within their own defensive and self-referential ghettoized subcultural space. Under the least promising situations, subcultural self-organization was possible, but without the access to a wider public domain such achievements lacked either the national-popular credibility of a plausible counter-hegemonic claim, or effective resistances against counter-revolutionary repression (if and when it came).[8]

Thus, subcultural vitality without the wider arena of a nationally organized and legally guaranteed public sphere, however impressive its defensive supports at a level of survival, could only secure the limited integrity of a subaltern public. Conversely, it was the impressive democratic gains of the post-1918 political settlements in Europe, with the redrawing of the social contract they entailed, and what I have called the considerable enhancement of the public sphere in some crucial enabling ways, that opened the way for elements of a counter-hegemonic challenge. This is how I would like to think of the Left's cultural politics in the 1920s, but at the same time the latter do not provide an undivided story. The plausibility of the cultural-socialist commitment to the mass form, which embodied the drive for prefigurative or anticipatory values between the wars, for a cultural politics that already imagined or performed the values of the future, has been severely compromised by two intervening histories of a more negative kind.

One of those histories is the extreme dourness and authoritarianism of official culture in the Stalinized societies of the state-socialist world, with their well-deserved reputation for collectivist uniformity, standardization, puritanical morality, and repressive disciplinary power, epitomized in the paramilitary conformities and boy-scout ethos of the Young Pioneers and other official youth cultures, in the regimentation and relentlessness of the official sporting culture, in the hostility to sexual dissidence, in the highly gendered languages of collectivist identification, and so on. Moreover, if our impression of cultural socialism's collectivist ideals is bound to be qualified by the regimented forms of their realization in the actually existing postwar socialist future, the second intervening history giving us pause for thought is that of the fascists. There are ways, after all, in which the aestheticization of politics under Fascist Italy and Nazi Germany consciously appropriated the mass forms developed by the socialist tradition during the previous fifty years. We do not need to go the route of a George Mosse and find Nazi forms and techniques of mass mobilization already inscribed in the essential logics of monumentality, mass ceremonial, and collectivist display per se in order to argue that cultural socialism and the fascist staging of the mass spectacle drew upon a common repertoire of techniques and forms (huge rallies and festivals, public displays of collective discipline and strength, the choreographed massed march, the mass gymnastic displays and mass choirs, the development of distinctive rituals and the elaboration of a distinctive political symbolic, and so on).[9] The importance of the nation and the ability to occupy the ground of patriotic identification were vital to this fascist creativity. The precise nature of the affinities this correspondence of forms implies between the Left and the fascists is one of the questions this paper will raise, but not answer.[10]

3. Little Moscows, Red Vienna, and Cultural Socialism

Using a Gramscian view of cultural struggle, I would like next to consider the existence within popular culture of significant resistances to the power of the dominant classes by showing how those oppositional resources could be organized into a series of counter-hegemonic potentials. For this purpose, I will look concretely at several successful instances of local socialism in Europe between the wars, in which local government, the delivery of services, and the provision of public goods allowed the possibility of a broader challenge to the dominant culture to be raised. These are:

1. "little Moscows" – a recurring transnational category of small, relatively homogeneous and usually single-industry and physically self-contained industrial communities, in which either Communists or left-wing Socialists established local hegemonies between the 1920s and World War II;
2. "Red Vienna" between 1918 and 1934, where the Austrian Social Democrats became the first such party to preside over a city of more than a million inhabitants, developing a long-term strategy to transform the entire infrastructure of a metropolis; and
3. the broader phenomenon of "cultural socialism" in Weimar Germany, which was less a physical location than a set of strategies for building a movement culture.

All these cases allow the question of a prefigurative politics – in which counter-hegemonic potentials were explicitly mobilized for the imagining of a different future – to be posed.

1. In his study of three British little Moscows – Vale of Leven and Lumphinnans in Scotland, Mardy in South Wales – Stuart Macintyre shows how local communists fashioned local solidarities into a countercultural challenge to existing authority by using combinations of industrial militancy and neighborhood solidarities to capture local government and establish significant bridgeheads to the courts and the educational system.[11] The resulting oppositional culture was grounded in a resilient popular morality that allowed legally constituted authority to be disregarded if it conflicted with elementary ideas of right and wrong, and provided ready materials for a vigorous kind of ethical socialism. But, of course, such ordinary morality had to be actively organized into a culture of contestation, and home-grown militants worked creatively inside the community's cultural practices to this end. Religion was a case in point, where communists both subverted the given authority (e.g., by devising their own rituals, like the "red funeral") and appropriated the language of populist and democratic Christianity for their own needs. Schooling was also a key site: the Left ran alternative institutions like the socialist Sunday School and its rival the Proletarian Sunday School, ran campaigns against corporal punishment, organized school children into Young Pioneers with red scarves and a news sheet, and called a public holiday for May Day. On a broader ideological front communists also contested prevailing forms of patriotic celebration, protesting Empire Day, refusing to stand for the national anthem and salute the Union Jack, and opposing the Jubilee and Coronation celebrations in 1935 and 1937. A key piece of this local picture was the extraordinarily popular branch of the Friends of the Soviet Union, through which positive images of an alternative society were affirmed.

It was in the area of the national symbolic, along an axis of anti-monarchism and pro-sovietism, that the cultural radicalism was most clear. At one level, the little Moscows showed the familiar texture of early twentieth-century working-class collective life – "the banners, the bands, the evening socials and sport, the youth groups, the Friends of the Soviet Union, and so on."[12] What was distinctive was the degree to which this everyday culture was articulated to an explicitly political identity. In the recognized genre of social histories of popular culture, this element of political meaning invariably recedes from discussion, leaving the field to a litany of conventionally "non-political" pursuits: brass bands and choirs; music halls, penny theaters, and free-and-easies; showmen, circuses, and fairs; pigeon-fancying, dog-racing, and prize fighting; football, cricket, and bowls; and so on. In the little Moscows, we can see how, under special local circumstances, the everyday working-class life-world – organized around basic values of community and cooperation, fellowship and mutuality, independence and disrespect for authority – could acquire politicized expression, so that the typical culture of laboring communities could be both organized for self-help and simultaneously fashioned into a weapon of contestation. In their proceduralism, these local arenas of popular empowerment corresponded to Habermas's ideal of the rationally constituted public sphere. In the face-to-face democracy of these working-class communities, the trade-union, cooperative, and other activities were all constituted on the sovereignty of the membership through the medium of the general meeting, with democracy lodged in a public arena of open and collective decision-making, at public meetings or in open air.

2. Red Vienna was the single most imposing showcase of municipal socialism in Europe between the wars. The Austrian Socialists were the first such party "to preside over a city with over a million inhabitants, and 'Red Vienna' was the first practical example of a long-term socialist strategy of reforming the entire infrastructure of a metropolis."[13] The centerpiece was the housing policy, which built 64,000 apartments between 1923 and 1933, mainly in the form of the large housing blocks, the famous *Wiener Höfe* which housed one-seventh of the city's population at a maximum of 5 percent of a worker's wage. The housing blocks were the framework for an ambitious project of "anticipatory socialism," deliberately constructed to express collectivist social ideals and an integrated idea of communal life. While the overall plans allowed for greenery and usable courtyards, the buildings also had interior space for cultural life – meeting places and club rooms, common baths and laundries, cooperative stores and restaurants, nurseries, playgrounds, and the general run of civic provision, from schools and libraries to parks, swimming areas, gymnasia, health facilities, and clinics. In effect, the usual infrastructure of

civic life was relocated to a physically demarcated socialist public sphere, which was further solidified by the twenty-one districts of party organization, with their lower subdivisions of electoral sections and house-cum-street associations, and the city-wide subcultural apparatus of clubs. The housing policy was also matched by a progressive educational reform (involving the common school, cooperative pedagogy, abolition of corporal punishment, lifelong learning) and innovative measures of health education and preventive care. The *Wiener Höfe* dramatically reshaped the landscape of the popular imagination, for symbolically, the housing blocks – the "worker palaces" or "red fortresses" – functioned as a physical counterpoint to the official architecture of monuments, palaces, and museums.

At the same time, there were limits to the Austrian Social Democrats' prefigurative vision. While the Vienna housing projects included provision for collective life and political culture, for instance, there was perhaps much less of an effort to create a participatory political ethic by turning management over to the tenants, as opposed to seeing the latter as the passive beneficiaries of a reforming but essentially paternalist municipal administration. Another side of the top-down quality of the provision was an understandable preference for standardization and the economies of scale, reinforced by the ideology of planning, which tended to foreclose alternative models (such as, for instance, the massive squatters movement on the outskirts of the city, which between 1918 and 1921 generated an impressive self-managing and cooperative housing association movement, but which by 1923 had been effectively squashed in favor of the building of the new superblocks). Finally, it could be argued, the hierarchical political frame of the housing culture produced effects that were essentially defensive and complacent, encouraging the illusion that capitalist power in the economy had somehow been by-passed by socialist command of leisure, and turning the old culture of socialism into a new culture of clientage, in which the ideal of the self-empowered worker-citizenry was traded for the administered consumption of services.

It is hard to take this too far. Red Vienna was still an imposing fortress of working-class solidarity. The Viennese working class was solidly within the fold of Austrian social democracy, either by joining or voting for the party or by belonging to its manifold clubs and associations, from Worker Choirs and Worker Sports, to Worker Stamp Collectors and Worker Rabbit Breeders. Moreover, aside from its electoral strength (reaching a peak of 42.3 per cent of the national vote in 1927) and municipal power, the party had its own militia after 1923, the *Schutzbund*, which at a peak of some eighty thousand national members was far stronger than the national army. Yet, ultimately, this internally cohesive class-political solidity was less significant than the indecision and passivity that allowed the movement to be destroyed between the crisis of July 1927 and the civil war of February

1934. The disastrous ease of the movement's suppression raises big questions about the political efficacy of the Austrian party's socialist culture in Gramsci's sense. In the 1926 Linz Program, Otto Bauer and other leaders had certainly evinced a continuing revolutionary intention. Given the upward trajectory of party support and the example of Red Vienna's anticipatory socialism, they expected in the natural course of things to come to power. In July 1931 at the opening of the Vienna Stadium, crowds of 240,000 watched a mass pageant of the movement's history performed by thousands from the party's cultural organizations, which climaxed with worker-actors toppling "a huge gilt idol-head representing capital from its scaffolding."[14] Yet the cultural energies and symbolic creativity concentrated in this event were never translated into the confrontational readiness necessary to convert the party's democratic legitimacy into real power.

3. At one level, of course, the Socialists' impressive subculture in Austria and Germany was a kind of displacement, because during 1919 to 1920 the socialist movements in these two countries found themselves shut out of national power, and were effectively cast back onto municipal and other local and intermediate arenas for their practical activity, so that the organizing of cultural life worked as a kind of compensation for the Socialists at a time when they were excluded from national governmental power. When we turn to cultural socialism in Weimar Germany, we can see this effect very well. Excluded from the possibilities of entering national coalition governments after summer 1920, yet firmly ensconced in Prussia and other states, and bunkered into the Weimar Republic's labor-corporative and welfare-statist arrangements, the SPD and trade unions found themselves practically integrated with the new parliamentary state. In this situation, "culture" acquired added import as a way of sustaining the movement's revolutionary élan and counteracting the so-called loss of utopia. As the party itself was properly focused on practical work, and needed to be free of grandiose ideological goals, it was argued, the task of propagating socialist values now fell to the cultural movement, which should become a "third pillar" of the movement as a whole, to be added to the party and trade unions. Specifically cultural organizations could cultivate the socialist ideal that would otherwise "be dirtied and trampled by the exigencies of politics." In fact, given the disappointments of the revolution, this was the best means of recovering radical momentum. Socialism became redefined as a prefigurative project. As one militant put it: "First of all, the picture of a new order has to be strongly anchored in the minds before it is possible to erect the building. And every political influence is pointless if the acquisition of education, knowledge, and culture does not take place at the same time." Or: "First the 'new human being,' and then the new socialist society."[15]

This is certainly reminiscent of Gramsci's language. It is not hard to be impressed by the scale of socialist cultural activity during the Weimar Republic.[16]

- *The Worker Sports and Gymnastics League grew from 169,000 members in 1912 to 770,000 in 1928.*
- *The Worker Singers grew from 192,000 to 440,000.*
- *The Worker Cyclists grew from 148,000 to 220,000.*
- *The Worker Athletes (boxers, wrestlers, weight lifters) grew from around 10,000 to 56,000.*
- *The "Nature Lovers" (ramblers, rock-climbers, skiers, canoeists) grew from some 10,000 to 79,000.*
- *There were also leagues for chess, sailing, angling, hunting, bowling, and gliding.*

All of these, no less than the directly educational and arts-oriented organizations of the SPD, propagated an alternative set of values, comprising collectivist and cooperative ideals of discipline and mutuality and a noncompetitive ethos of participation and collective endeavor, as opposed to winning, the star system, and an individualist cult of achievement. By the end of the 1920s, it is true, it was becoming harder to resist the pressure of younger members for conventional forms of competitive reward (trophies, medals, or at least certificates of merit), while in the commercial sector the modern spectacle of organized sport was creating a different set of expectations. Nonetheless, the deliberate cultivation of fellowship kept these influences reasonably at bay – by common socializing, by taking trips together, by sing-songs and the collective recitation of workers' poems, by providing contexts of sociality away from the crowded city (including the opportunities for sexual experimentation, one might add).

Two further aspects of this alternative culture may be mentioned. First, there was a notable upswing after 1918 in what we might call "lifestyle issues" – in natural and healthy living, exercise and fresh air, sensible nutrition (including abstinence from alcohol and tobacco), rational dress, preventive medicine, therapy and sex counseling – or "life reform" to use the German name. One new manifestation, given the liberalized public climate after 1918, was the Proletarian Nudist movement, and most impressively of all the variegated sex reform movement, which encompassed working-class birth control leagues, progressive doctors, women's groups, and socialist and communist welfare organizations. "Lay sex reform groups, with their illustrated journals filled with advice of sexual technique, contraception, eugenic hygiene, health, and the protection of mothers; their centers for the distribution of contraceptives; and their many therapeutic question-and-answer lectures, were an integral and crucial part of the working-class subculture of the Weimar Republic."[17] Finally, the changed climate that facilitated these developments was dramatically illustrated by the success of the Proletarian Freethinkers movement, with its demands for secularized rites of passage, abolition of religious instruction in schools, cremation, and leaving the church. From being a minority interest on the fringe of the SPD before 1914, this movement took off into mass status, reaching a peak of well over half a million members in the years between 1928 and 1932. From hovering around twenty thousand per annum before 1914, church resignations were averaging around two hundred thousand per annum in the last six years before 1933.[18]

Second, the socialist cultural movement tried to embody its collectivist ethic in new performance forms. Sport was one example, with the preference for team sports over individualistic ones, the mounting of mass gymnastic displays, and the experimentation with group forms such as swimming in formation, and with particular attention paid to the socializing of children and the involvement of family units. Music was another, and the massed choirs which graced most party festivals were held to symbolize the relationship between cultural emancipation, collective effort, and mass form: fifty thousand amateur musicians attended the first Workers' Song Festival in Hanover in 1928. The speaking chorus was a distinctive form of this type that the SPD developed. While present more loosely before 1914, and incorporated by the director Max Reinhardt into a theatrical production of the 1890s, it was developed by the poet Bruno Schönlank, the actor Adolf Johanneson, and the choreographer Martin Gleisner during the 1920s into a new literary and performance genre. As elements of dance and movement became integrated into the performances, the speaking choir became a classic case of the confluence between the labor movement and modernist influences from the arts, in this case from expressionist dance. By the 1920s it had become an established high point of SPD festivals and political events, as at the Magdeburg Party Congress in 1929, where Gleisner choreographed a two hundred-strong performance of *Flammende Zeit (Blazing Time)*, a composite of the movement's songs, poetry, and speech-choruses, to close the proceedings. Again, the form was meant to symbolize the proletariat's collective creativity and strength, and indeed was inseparable from the movement occasions on which such massed performances alone could take place.[19]

4. Problems with Popular Culture

On the face of it, the SPD's cultural socialism met Gramsci's criteria for a revolutionary cultural politics, one that was capable of mobilizing counter-hegemonic potentials, sharpening them into an oppositional challenge, organizing them into counter-publics, and converting the public sphere in the national or society-wide sense into a context of open rather than latent contestation through which power inequalities could be brought both subversively and productively into play as a basis for democratically transforming them, and for disrupting their naturalized reproduction. There was an impressive self-confidence to this cultural project. Far more than in the past, the SPD commanded the resources Gramsci defined as the double condition of an effective counter-hegemonic challenge, of seizing the moral-political initiative in a society: a) it disposed over an elaborate cultural apparatus, which included its own educational institutions, now expanded and strengthened by public recognition and the subsidized adult education systems of big SPD-run cities like Berlin, Hamburg, and Leipzig, and which managed the production of the movement's own cadres, its organic intellectuals, in Gramsci's notation; and b) under Weimar's liberalized legality, it now mobilized the sympathies of progressive intellectuals beyond its own ranks. Its movement culture sustained an ideal of emancipation, nourished the aspiration to large-scale social transformation, embodied the imagery of making a new human being, and kept a vision of the future alive. The SPD's Weimar histories permitted a far more effective challenge to the dominant culture's legitimacy than the subcultural ghettoization before 1914 had ever allowed.[20]

If that was the case, how then do we historicize the SPD's failure (and by extension the failure of the socialist tradition more generally), both in the shorter term of its collapse before fascism and in the longer term of its prosaic retreat from radical aspirations, its loss of utopia, its consigning of the latter to the museum, to the fantasy landscape of nostalgia, or a junkyard of exotic and superseded ambitions? I have several points to make here, as a basis for discussion, each of which is meant to re-connect to the Habermasian problematic of publicness and its possible forms of twentieth-century realization.

1. First, cultural socialism failed to escape the prevailing normativities regarding the place of women, and showed little interest in exploring the gendered dimensions of socialist consciousness. One simple measure was the weak presence of women in the cultural organizations. In a sizable city like Hanover, women were as much as 30.5 percent of the Worker Gymnasts (as against only 19 per cent of the rival non-socialist clubs), but in smaller working-class communities, where "traditional" working-class values were more securely in place, the situation was very different: in the labor movement's cultural and leisure organizations in "red Mössingen," a southwest German little Moscow, women were completely absent. More to the point, women never surfaced in leadership positions, and were assumed to belong in the movement's welfare organizations, where "feminine" virtues of caring and maternalism could prevail. Advocates of "anticipatory socialism" proved incapable of challenging assumptions

about men's and women's nature and their appropriate social place, whether directly in the official women's policies, or obliquely in the ideology of orderly domesticity that structured the model housing programs.[21]

This is an immensely ramified and complex subject, but one area of particular salience in the 1920s was the rationalization movement, which in its more developed versions amounted to a social program of totalizing ambition.[22] Though originating in certain strategies of business, the language of rationalization had also captured the common sense of the labor movement too, with its belief in the inevitability of technical progress and its commitment to industrial modernization and national economic competitiveness as the conditions of successful redistributive policies. Once even the trade unions and socialist cultural organizations saw themselves as promoting values conducive to the culture of productivity among the working class in this sense (sobriety, orderly family living, healthy lifestyles, the desire to get on in the world, self-motivated discipline, and so on), some sections of business began to withdraw from the older ambition to control their workforce politically through directly repressive means, opting instead for the virtues of a "depoliticized" and consensual acceptance of efficiency as a common societal goal to be pursued as a broad-gauged ideological strategy. In another sense, the interest in rationalization was also another aspect of the modernist temptation to planning and scientific regulation, which captured the imagination of left-tending intellectuals so powerfully in the 1920s.

This affected women in two powerful ways. First, it hardened the sex segregation of the labor market by concentrating skilled work as a male preserve and simultaneously accentuating the visibility of women as the unskilled, quite aside from the emphasis on rationalized domesticity it also encouraged. But second, these changes produced great anxieties about the resilience of the given social relations among women and men, particularly in the ascribed virtues of family life, as paid work was added to women's responsibilities in the home rather than replacing them. This situation encouraged grandiose speculations on the direction of cultural change. In his reflections on Fordism, Gramsci saw modernity as requiring a corresponding transformation of sexual culture, because "the new type of man demanded by the rationalization of production … cannot be developed until the sexual instinct has been suitably regulated and until it too has been rationalized":

> *It seems clear that the new industrialism wants monogamy: it wants the man as worker not to squander his nervous energies in the disorderly and stimulating pursuit of occasional sexual satisfaction. The employee who goes to work after a night of "excess" is no good for his work. The exaltation of passion cannot be reconciled with the timed movements of productive motions connected with the most perfect automatism.*[23]

This was a telling illustration of the Left's disablement on this issue, of its too-easy participation in a discourse not of its own making. Women, at least, were unlikely to benefit from an analysis that so clinically subordinated their own sexuality, so that the "wife waiting at home," as Peter Wollen says, becomes just another "permanent machine part."[24] If the sex reform discourse of the 1920s offered (however ambiguously) the promise of women's emancipation, that of rationalization showed how easily a new regime of regulation could take it back.[25]

The main source of a critique in the 1920s, sexology and the sex reform movement, did start to provide a context around the margins of existing left-wing and feminist organizations in which certain issues could be raised. On the one hand, this scientific discourse of sex did begin to authorize a new openness in the discussion of sexual pleasure, in which women were also allowed to be participants. While much of this took place outside a consciously political sphere (and many Socialists and feminists were relieved to keep it there), some voices did go further into a general politics of reproductive rights focused on birth control, abortion, and women's right to sexual self-determination. On the other hand, therefore, we can say that population politics, maternalism, and the growth of women's citizenship discourse were sometimes dramatically bringing sexual relations into political vision. But even the radicalism of Weimar sex reform was severely foreshortened. Its leadership and discourse were still generally male-centered. Despite the presence in Weimar Germany of important homosexual and lesbian subcultures, its outlook was axiomatically heterosexual. Its politics left many inequities of family life, from wife beating to child abuse, untouched. Its construction of the reproductive domain incorporated maternalist and eugenicist assumptions. Its scientific construction of sexual knowledge around naturalized notions of health and pleasure was no less centered on assumptions of male priority, which simultaneously hindered advocacy of the sexual autonomy of women.[26]

2. This brings us specifically to sex. Official socialist and communist discourses of sexuality were extremely conservative. We can see this clearly in Red Vienna, where the cultural grand design (of "creating a revolution of souls," as Otto Bauer called it) certainly incorporated the family and personal life, but where the ideas of women's place in particular showed (to say the least) a singular lack of imagination. The party's 1926 program did include public provision of birth control, for instance, but practically assimilated it into the natalist priorities of the city's thirty-six mothers' consultation clinics. Moreover, the party stopped short of genuine abortion reform, only partly because of the Austrian national culture's dominant Catholicism, and proceeded from eugenicist premises rather than

any developed recognition of women's reproductive rights. On the major censorship battles of the 1920s, the party fudged, defending freedom of expression legalistically on strictly constitutionalist grounds, rather than making any positive case for moral pluralism and sexual freedom. Sexuality was treated as a source of danger and disorder rather than pleasure and fulfillment. Whereas young people themselves might value the socialist youth organizations as a free space of experiment away from the parental eye (and the physical congestion of home and street), the party saw them quite differently, as a displaced context for realizing the ideals of moral respectability that were harder to attain in the rough conditions of much working-class domestic life. In socialist minds, sex education was to "prepare the young for the necessary subordination of their sex drive to the laws of socialist ethics."[27]

Of course, Red Vienna inevitably contained an unruly surplus of under-mastered radicalism. Beneath the strait-laced party morality, youthful working-class sexuality found its own expressions, and some dissidents tried to connect with this more radically, as in Wilhelm Reich's Sexual Consultation Clinics for Workers and Employees launched in 1929 and his general agitation against the workers' "sexual immiseration." But the party culture's main stress was on control and containment. Sexuality was to be "shaped and constrained" to produce an "*ordentliche* [orderly, decent, and respectable] family," which could lay the ghost of sexual decadence and promiscuity to rest and bring the party moral credit. Here there was no space for the sexual independence of women (or actually the sexual independence of anybody). Such thoughts were suppressed for the affective needs of the family. Measured against the latter, the sexual activity of the young was an unhealthy disturbance, comparable to smoking and drink, for which the "cold showering" of physical exercise – in the Workers' Association for Sports and Body Culture – was the recommended solution. In this sense, the party's attitude toward sex, particularly among its recognized experts (like Julius Tandler, "the medical Pope of social democracy" and head of the Vienna Public Welfare Office since 1920, or the educational and youth leader Otto Felix Kanitz), was austerely cramped and repressive. It "showed little concern for sex as a source of pleasure and as a normal and important part of everyday life." Instead, "sexuality was to be sublimated ... to make the workers' 'marriage' to the party possible."[28]

The power of this perspective in twentieth-century socialist movements – an ideal of controlled respectability, in which sex was to be marital, procreative, heterosexual, and clean – has been enormous. What I am saying here, clearly, is that there were major dimensions or domains of life, to do with gender, family, domesticity, sex, the body, where the socialist cultural politics of the interwar years was not exactly inactive, or inattentive, but where its assumptions and practices, and sometimes its programmatic ambitions, crystallized a regime of regulation that was extremely disciplinary, oriented to containment and control.

3. To a great extent, I would argue, this was connected to the tendency of cultural socialism to construct itself in opposition to a particular representation of the working-class everyday. It saw its purpose as "a putting aside of the everyday person," in which the workers' ennoblement could be counterposed to his (the working class was inevitably gendered male in this discourse) degradation in the labor and poverty of the present day. In practice, the cultural Socialists bracketed precisely those arenas (the workplace, the party-political structures, the family) where the putatively socialist culture would have to be most imaginatively and tenaciously pursued, if values were really to change.

This hallowing of culture, as we might call it, its dignification and separation from the everyday, was all the more fateful because the interwar years were precisely the period when popular culture was being transformed by the new technologies of mass entertainment and leisure, although, of course, the key developments had already started before 1914 – beginning with photography and continuing through film, the phonograph, and radio, as well as other essential features of twentieth-century life like the bicycle, the motor car, the telephone, the typewriter, and so on. On the whole, Socialists preferred to ignore the new media, neither recognizing the technical and formal possibilities nor validating the pleasures the mass working-class audience found in them. In fact, before 1914 socialist culture had always seen itself as rising above the general run of working-class behavior, stressing the virtues of self-improvement and sobriety over the disorderly realities of much actually existing working-class existence, with its negative imagery of drunkenness, gambling, undisciplined sexuality, violence, criminality, and unstable family life. Socialists drew a sharp moral-political line between their own self-educated respectability and the unenlightened and frequently apolitical roughness of the working-class poor.

Given such suspicions of actually existing popular culture, therefore, it was hardly surprising that Socialists saw film as just a new form of escapism, frivolity, and corruption in a still uneducated working class. As the Frankfurt left-socialist newspaper put it in 1919, in the midst of the German Revolution, lamenting the moral decline of working-class youth: "The path to the gambling dens of the big city begins in the dance halls and the cinemas .... Surrounded by superficial din and deadened in their souls, the misled section of the proletarian youth dances its way into depravity."[29] In the 1920s, the gap between the traditional socialist conception of cultural progress and the actual behavior of workers widened disconcertingly because, when faced with the opportunities of expanding leisure, workers turned only partially to the socialist cultural organizations but flocked in masses to the picture-palaces and dance-halls of the brashly commercialized new urban space. Most socialist commentators dug themselves more deeply into a hole of resentment and disdain. The movies were a capitalist trick, a medium of ideological manipulation "cleverly used to dope the workers," a form of "pseudo-culture," "whereby [workers'] attention is diverted from the class war and whereby their slave status is maintained." For the British Communist novelist Edward Upward, such entertainments were nothing "but hypocritical decorations concealing danger and misery, fraudulent as vulgar icing on a celebration cake rotten inside with maggots, sugary poison to drug you into contentment."[30] The film craze was seen as a symptom of working-class apathy, an expression of false consciousness. But more accurately, it was a symptom of the difficulty Socialists had in engaging with the everyday culture of the working class when this failed to correspond with the idealized representation of what the working class ought to be, and of their tendency in response to moralize, pronounce, discipline, and improve. This was all the more damaging for the Left's prospects because the cinema and the dance hall were especially exciting for women and the young (survey research suggested that half of film audiences were young people, and 75 percent of adults were women), a neglect which only reemphasized socialism's limiting and entrenched fixation on the self-improving skilled working man.

5. Conclusions

Now, if we get back to the more abstract question of the public sphere, and ask what this detailed argumentation tells us about the conditions and contexts of public life in the early twentieth century, there are a number of things to be said.

1. First, the histories I have been recounting make the point powerfully enough that the public sphere was an arena of contestation in which different and opposing publics maneuvered for space, in which access was unequally structured, and some meanings were more privileged than others, and where certain publics were excluded altogether. Moreover, the formation of often very vigorous counter-publics, even at their most utopianly oppositional, was not immune to these processes of privileging, marginalization, and suppression. If we examine the character of the main oppositional publics of these years, those organized by the Socialists and the Communists, then we find similar forms of hierarchy, silencing, and exclusion taking place.

2. In particular, socialism's relationship to the actually existing working class has been fraught with difficulty. Invariably, Socialists constructed this relationship via a particularly patronizing and moralizing kind of pedagogy, in a relation of improvement and discipline, in a posture (of course) that performed the Socialists' own desire for a reformed everydayness of their own, defined by uprightness (and uptightness), sexual sobriety, the purification of the body, and the policing of excess. Despite the enormous positivities the organized culture of the labor movement delivered for working people – the resources, skills, and solidarities necessary for fighting exploitation, the self-confidence and agency that collective organization produced, and the sense of possibility in a progressive future, an identity *as* workers, as the working class acting in history – this was a problem. This tendency of Socialists to place themselves into an exterior relationship to the working-class everyday identifies a key political neglect. The yearning for respectability, for modalities of public comportment that enacted the collectivist social ethic of the future, for a public culture of familialism, heteronormativity, healthy recreation, orderly fellowship, and pleasure in the mass, for a socialist public sphere whose redeployment of the national symbolic challenged the national-political hegemony of the bourgeoisie and imagined an upstanding socialist nation, a prefiguring of the democratic respectability the bourgeoisie asserted but could never provide – all of this positioned the socialist cultural movement in a relation of difficulty to the very popular constituencies it was seeking to represent. This disregard of the actually existing working-class everyday desensitized the socialist movement to the ambiguities and contradictions through which its intended supporters were trying to live their lives.

I should be clear about my meaning here. By the everyday I mean the place where the abstractions of domination and exploitation were directly encountered, processed into manageable meanings, and inscribed as the organizing sense of individual and collective lives. As such, "everydayness" can be produced in all manner of practical, informal, organized, and instituted ways. The everyday is no less a site of creativity and contestation than the more conventionally recognized public places where official politics takes place, even as the latter defines itself via processes of abstraction and separation from the everyday, via its boundedness, via constructing and instituting the boundary itself. This sense of the everyday is meant to subvert the conventional binaries of the personal and the political, the public and the private. The point is *not* to establish a new binary between the public sphere, politics, and ideology on the one hand, and "real experience" and the everyday on the other, but to show how it is precisely here, in the borderlands, and in the "production and reproduction of immediate life," that politics is also working busily away.

Moreover, I am not postulating the everyday as a realm of experience somehow anterior or more "authentic" than the organized culture of the socialist movement, as morally superior, or a source of legitimacy that is *ipso facto* more democratic. The point is rather that socialist movements were held in a complex field of different, tense, sometimes antagonistic, and at all events contradictory relations with the working-class and popular cultures for which they claimed in some unitary sense to speak, but which invariably confronted them as "other," as something unmanageable and unruly, as excess.[31]

3. This is why the new entertainment cultures were so important, because they were coming to occupy so thickly the human space of the everyday. To close, I want only to reiterate that Habermas's story of the public sphere's corruption and decline tends to disallow this domain of commercialized popular culture as a site of positive political importance. It is possible to argue, for instance, that it was precisely this private economy of desire, organized around family, sex, friendship, creation, and the body, that fascism proved so successful in mastering. Conversely, it was the domain of dreaming and pleasure, sexuality and recreation, that the Left was so bad at understanding. The interwar labor movements simply lacked the political languages for appealing to the new generations of young working women, for instance, the shopgirls, hairdressers, typists, assembly-line workers, and cleaners, and what the SPD's social policy expert, Marie Juchacz, called the "destructive" pleasures of "the young prettily dressed girls" who poured from the shops and businesses at the end of the day.[32] Instead, the SPD was busily constructing the familial sphere of maternalist citizenship and political dependency as the logical place of women's main identity.

Faced with the new leisure habits of young working-class people, Socialists tended all too easily to moralize, invoking traditional working-class values and the worthy pursuits of the socialist subculture against the frivolity of the new entertainments. This proved extraordinarily shortsighted. Fascism was not just the instrument of anti-democratic terror (although it was certainly that), but also harnessed needs and longings the Left neglected at its peril. If we are to ask how politics works through everyday life, therefore, it is to this area of enjoyment and pleasure that we must also look. If politics organizes at the intersections of public and personal life, colonizing our imaginations, shaping our needs, and inscribing our everyday transactions with its rules, then the same process can also describe a key space of resistance. And it is the forms of articulation between the context of the everyday and the formal spaces of the national political process that a fully democratic conception of publicness and the public sphere will have to address.

Notes

Special thanks are owed for the evolution of this essay to Lauren Berlant, Atina Grossmann, Michael Warner, Eric Weitz, and audiences at Cornell, Stony Brook, Princeton, Michigan, Southampton, and the German History Seminar at the University of London.

1. Jürgen Habermas, *The Structural Transformation of the Public Sphere: An Inquiry into a Category of Bourgeois Society* (Cambridge, Mass., 1989).
2. Geoff Eley, "Nations, Publics, and Political Cultures: Placing Habermas in the Nineteenth Century," in *Culture/Power/History: A Reader in Contemporary Social Theory*, ed. Nicholas B. Dirks, Geoff Eley, and Sherry B. Ortner (Princeton, 1993), 310.
3. I have explored this context of critique and relativization in another essay: Geoff Eley, "Edward Thompson, Social History, and Political Culture: The Making of a Working-Class Public, 1780-1850," in *E. P. Thompson: Critical Perspectives*, ed. Harvey J. Kaye and Keith McClelland (Oxford, 1990), 12-49. See also Günther Lottes, *Politische Aufklärung und plebejisches Publikum: Zur Theorie und Praxis des englischen Radikalismus im späten 18. Jahrhundert* (Munich, 1979).
4. Eley, "Nations, Publics, and Political Cultures," 301.
5. Perry Anderson and Peter Dews, in their interview with Habermas, "A Philosophico Political Profile," in *Autonomy and Solidarity: Interviews with Jürgen Habermas*, ed. Peter Dews (London, 1986), 178.
6. Eley, "Nations, Publics, and Political Cultures," 327.
7. I purposely, and perhaps provocatively, exclude 1848 from this sequence of constitution-making conjunctures because the revolutions of that year *failed*. By contrast with the five "moments" I have selected, 1848 produced no immediate restructuring of the European political landscape, certainly in the constitutionalized sense I am describing.
8. I have explored another aspect of this question, namely, the changing relationship of the labor movement to the intellectuals, in Geoff Eley, "Intellectuals and the German Labor Movement," in *Intellectuals and Public Life: Between Radicalism and Reform*, ed. Leon Fink, Stephen T. Leonard, and Donald P. Reid (Ithaca, NY, 1996).
9. See George L. Mosse, *The Nationalization of the Masses: Political Symbolism and Mass Movements in Germany from the Napoleonic Wars Through the Third Reich* (New York, 1975).
10. This question of the homologies between socialist and fascist forms of cultural politics is difficult and complex and cannot be addressed within the bounds of this paper. To find such similarities is certainly not in itself to indict the Left's pursuit of the mass form, or its celebration of the collectivist spectacle per se. But the forms of discipline, regulative control, regimentation, and conformity invariably entailed in such cultural practices are profoundly out of keeping with the radical-democratic sensibilities of the end of the twentieth century. The sublimation of personal desires, and the effacement, often the crude erasure, of individuality in socialist and communist collectivisms squeezed the space for experimentation and unconventional ways of living, especially of course for dissident sexualities and other reconstructions of personhood that breached the wholesomeness and decorums of the approved forms of collective life. Left-wing cultural politics did not *prepare* the way for fascism or produce a fascist mentality directly, nor did fascist appropriations of the mass form simply take socialist or communist practices over directly. The mutually hostile values involved remain fundamentally impor-

tant. The fascist mass spectacle entailed its own specificities, and theorizing an adequate framework for understanding these differences is an important task. But we do not need an Orwellian conflation of Left and Right in order to acknowledge the unsettling points of correspondence. In the meantime, see the following: Anson G. Rabinbach, "The Aesthetics of Production in the Third Reich," in *International Fascism: New Thoughts and New Approaches*, ed. George L. Mosse (London and Berverly Hills, 1979), 189-222; Wolfgang Emmerich, "'Massenfaschismus' und die Rolle des Äesthetischen: Faschismustheorie bei Ernst Bloch, Walter Benjamin, Bertolt Brecht," *Antifaschistische Literatur*, vol. 1, ed. Lutz Winkler (Kronberg, 1977), 223-90; Saul Friedländer, *Reflections on Nazism: An Essay on Kitsch and Death* (New York, 1984); Peter Reichel, *Der schöne Schein des Dritten Reiches: Faszination und Gewalt des Faschismus* (Munich, 1991); Brandon Taylor and Wilfried van der Will, eds., *The Nazification of Art: Art, Design, Music, Architecture, and Film in the Third Reich* (Winchester, 1990); Alice Yaeger Kaplan, *The Reproduction of Banality: Fascism, Literature, and French Intellectual Life* (Minneapolis, Minn., 1986), esp. 3-35; and Richard J. Golson, ed., *Fascism, Aesthetics, and Culture* (Hanover, 1992).

11. Stuart Macintyre, *Little Moscows: Communism and Working-Class Militancy in Interwar Britain* (London, 1980). I use Macintyre's British examples because the analysis is exceptionally rich. For a German example, see Hans-Joachim Althaus et al., *Da ist nirgends nichts gewesen außer hier: Das "rote Mössingen" im Generalstreik gegen Hitler. Geschichte eines schwäbischen Arbeiterdorfes* (Berlin, 1982). This village was notable for its general strike against the formation of the Hitler government on 31 January 1933, when, out of four thousand village inhabitants, some four to five hundred demonstrated in the streets and brought two of the largest factories to a halt, before being broken by a massive police invasion that resulted in eighty arrests.
12. Macintyre, *Little Moscows*, 173.
13. Anson G. Rabinbach, *The Crisis of Austrian Socialism: From Red Vienna to Civil War, 1927-1934* (Chicago, 1983), 27.
14. Helmut Gruber, "History of the Austrian Working Class: Unity of Scholarship and Practice," *International Labor and Working-Class History* 24 (Fall 1983), 50ff.
15. Dieter Langewiesche, "Working-Class Culture and Working-Class Politics in the Weimar Republic," in *Bernstein to Brandt: A Short History of German Social Democracy*, ed. Roger Fletcher (London, 1987), 106-8. The first quotation is from Valtin Hartig, director of the Leipzig Workers' Educational Institute, at the 1924 Leipzig Workers' Cultural Week; the second is from Erich Winkler on the same occasion. The third quotation at the very end of the paragraph is Langewiesche himself.
16. Membership figures and capsule descriptions of the workers' cultural and sporting movement may be found in Dieter Fricke, *Handbuch zur Geschichte der deutschen Arbeiterbewegung 1869 bis 1917*, vol. 2 (Berlin, 1987), 1022-42, and Horst Ueberhorst, *Frisch, Frei, Stark und Treu: Die Arbeitersportbewegung in Deutschland 1893-1933* (Düsseldorf, 1973), 111ff.
17. Atina Grossmann, "'Satisfaction is Domestic Happiness': Mass Working-Class Sex Reform Organization in the Weimar Republic," in *Towards the Holocaust: The Social and Economic Collapse of the Weimar Republic*, ed. Michael N. Dobkowski and Isidor Walliman (Westport, Conn., 1983), 266. Now see above all Atina Grossmann, *Reforming Sex: The German Movement for Birth Control and Abortion Reform, 1920-1950* (New York, 1995).

18. See Jochen-Christoph Kaiser, *Arbeiterbewegung und organisierte Religionskritik: Proletarische Freidenkerverbände in Kaiserreich und Weimarer Republik* (Stuttgart, 1981), 350ff.
19. For the speech-chorus, see Willfried van der Will and Rob Burns, "The Politics of Cultural Struggle: Intellectuals and the Labor Movement," in *The Weimar Dilemma: Intellectuals in the Weimar Republic*, ed. Anthony Phelan (Manchester, 1985), 184-86; Uwe Hornauer, *Laienspiel und Massenchor: Das Arbeitertheater der Kultursozialisten in der Weimarer Republik* (Cologne, 1985); and Jon Clark, *Bruno Schönlank und die Arbeitersprechchorbewegung der Weimarer Republik* (Cologne, 1984). See also Richard Bodek, "Red Song: Social Democratic Music and Radicalism at the End of the Weimar Republic," *Central European History* 28:2 (1995): 209-27.
20. I have developed this argument in detail in Eley, "Intellectuals and the German Labor Movement."
21. See Adelheid von Saldern, "Arbeiterkulturbewegung in Deutschland in der Zwischenkriegszeit," in *Arbeiterkulturen zwischen Alltag und Politik: Beiträge zum europäischen Vergleich in der Zwischenkriegszeit*, ed. Friedhelm Boll (Vienna, 1986), 40ff.; Althaus, et al., *Da ist nirgends nichts gwesen außer hier*, 204-21.
22. See above all Mary Nolan, *Visions of Modernity: American Business and the Modernization of Germany* (New York, 1994); Dagmar Reese, Eve Rosenhaft, Carola Sachse, and Tilla Siegel, eds., *Rationale Beziehungen? Geschlechterverhältnisse im Rationalisierungsprozess* (Frankfurt am Main, 1993), esp. Tilla Siegel, "Das ist nur rational: Ein Essay zur Logik der sozialen Rationalisierung," 363-96; Atina Grossmann, "Girlkultur or Thoroughly Rationalized Female: A New Woman in Weimar Germany?" in *Women in Culture and Politics: A Century of Change*, ed. Judith Friedlander, Blanche Cook, Alice Kessler-Harris, and Caroll Smith-Rosenberg (Bloomington, Ind., 1986), 62-80; and Charles S. Maier, "Between Taylorism and Technocracy: European Ideologies and the Vision of Industrial Productivity in the 1920s," in idem, *In Search of Stability: Explorations in Historical Political Economy* (Cambridge, Mass., 1987), 22-53.
23. Antonio Gramsci, "Americanism and Fordism," in *Selections from the Prison Notebooks of Antonio Gramsci*, ed. Quintin Hoare and Geoffrey Nowell Smith (London, 1971), 297, 304ff.
24. Peter Wollen, "Modern Times: Cinema/Americanism/The Robot," in idem, *Raiding the Icebox: Reflections on Twentieth-Century Culture* (Bloomington, Ind., 1993), 39.
25. Gramsci's construction of "rationalized" sexuality was definitely the sterner and more austere version, and it was possible to frame the modernist project of reconstituting personal life far more liberally. See Atina Grossmann's now-classic essay, "The New Woman and the Rationalization of Sexuality in Weimar Germany," in *Powers of Desire: The Politics of Sexuality*, ed. Ann Snitow, Christine Stansell, and Sharon Thompson (New York, 1983). "The justification for sexual freedom was its unsentimental rationality ... sexuality properly expressed could be tamed and made functional for the good society ... only when repressed was sexuality explosive and dangerous. Even Wilhelm Reich, the great apostle of sexual radicalism, contended that a liberated orgasmic (genital, heterosexual) sexuality would create a better socialized (disciplined) human being. The sexually satisfied comrade will be a better comrade, said the radical sex reformer; the sexually satisfied worker will be a better worker, said the bourgeois sex reformer. Both sought to rescue sexuality by taming, domesticating, and rationalizing." (166)
26. This paragraph is based on Grossmann, *Reforming Sex*, 46-136.

27. Helmut Gruber, *Red Vienna: Experiment in Working-Class Culture 1919-1934* (New York, 1991), 175. My account in this paragraph is based on Gruber's succinct discussion of sexuality, 155-79.
28. Ibid., 156, 175, 160. The phrase "cold showering" is taken from the earlier version of Gruber's analysis, "Sexuality in 'Red Vienna': Socialist Party Conceptions and Programs and Working-Class Life, 1920-1934," *International Labor and Working-Class History* 31 (1987), 50.
29. James Wickham, "Working-Class Movement and Working-Class Life: Frankfurt am Main during the Weimar Republic," *Social History* 8:3 (October 1983), 336.
30. The earlier quotations are from the British Marxist intellectuals Eden and Cedar Paul and a statement by the Llanelly Constituency Labour Party. See Stephen G. Jones, *The British Labour Movement and Film 1918-1939* (London, 1987), 53, 57.
31. I have explicated these arguments at some length in Geoff Eley, "Labor History, Social History, *Alltagsgeschichte*: Experience, Culture, and the Politics of the Everyday – A New Direction for German Social History?" *Journal of Modern History* 61:2 (1989), esp. 312-43. See also Alf Lüdtke, "Polymorphous Synchrony: German Industrial Workers and the Politics of Everyday Life," *International Review of Social History* 38 Supplement (1993): 39-84.
32. Quoted from the discussion at the SPD's 1927 Kiel Congress in Heinrich August Winkler, *Der Schein der Normalität: Arbeiter und Arbeiterbewegung in der Weimarer Republik 1924 bis 1930* (Berlin, 1985), 353-55.

Chapter 13

THE SOCIAL ORIGINS OF UNITY SENTIMENTS IN THE GERMAN SOCIALIST UNDERGROUND, 1933 TO 1936

Gerd-Rainer Horn

1.

West German resistance historiography has suffered from a variety of ills that have resulted in less-than-satisfactory overall assessments of the character and evolution of German anti-Nazi resistance. Francis R. Nicosia recently recalled the outsider status of any serious research on German resistance that took place in the first two decades of the Federal Republic: "In the 1950s and 1960s, surviving resisters were regarded by many in Germany as traitors, and accordingly resistance was not a popular topic among academics, publishers, educators and the public at large."[1] Once grudgingly accepted as a genre of historical studies, disproportionate attention has been placed up to the present day on the plots and subplots hatched by (mostly) elite last-minute resisters, exemplified by the ill-fated conspiracy forever linked to the events of 20 July 1944.[2]

Some prominent historians have gone beyond this limited focus on elite conspirators and have drawn attention to earlier manifestations of the anti-fascist will to act. Martin Broszat, for instance, locates the first wave of resistance at the very beginning of the Nazi regime in the early- to mid-1930s, a variety of resistance firmly based in the socialist and com-

Notes for this chapter begin on page 353.

munist milieus. And Broszat underscores that the Nazi regime was only able to consolidate its political and cultural hegemony *after* this working-class resistance was effectively crushed, in effect ascribing major importance to this first wave of anti-fascist activism within German borders.[3]

But even a historian as clear-sighted as Broszat perpetuates some long-standing myths. One of the supposed certitudes oft-repeated even by that branch of German resistance historiography that recognizes the relative strength of early working-class resistance is the affirmation of an *insurmountable* division between Social Democrats and Communists in the German underground, thus, rendering an internally divided Marxist David unable effectively to combat the Nazi Goliath. Martin Broszat is by no means the only researcher to think along those lines. Most observers of the early German underground appear to agree that – apart from dissent within the Protestant church – most underground action up to 1936 originated in Germany's organized working class but that this underground was *irreversibly* split and, thus, left an already mortally wounded agent ready to be crushed by the forces of Nazi law and order.

And, in fact, even a cursory glance at documents pertaining to the working-class underground in the early years of Nazi rule strongly suggests that the deeply seated animosities between Socialists and Communists, dating back to the traumatic experiences of the Weimar era, left underground activists with few effective ideological weapons to overcome this elemental rift. Indeed, until 1935 the German Communist Party (KPD) exile leadership belonged to that minority faction of the Communist International (Comintern) which held on to the invidious notion of social fascism, the idea that social democracy constituted one of the twin pillars of fascism. The German Social Democratic Party (SPD) leadership, for its part, effectively expelled in early 1935 the two tendencies within the socialists' ranks – the Revolutionary Socialists and New Beginning – that had worked most doggedly for unity within the working-class Left.[4] And in early 1936 the same SPD Executive ordered its affiliates to forego "common actions with communist representatives or organizations" in exile and the underground.[5]

Nevertheless, on the basis of a close reading of documents readily accessible in German archives, I would like to propose that this vision of a fundamentally fractured Marxist underground in the years of its greatest impact (1933 to 1936) is only partially vindicated by the evidence. Whereas indeed no national unity agreement was ever achieved, the archives yield a multitude of indications that, on a local level, unity, though not the norm, was frequently a fact of life and former political enemies worked side-by-side. Furthermore, whereas unity was never the rule throughout the working-class German underground, even on a local level, most active social democratic resisters in effect strongly advocated unity in action with members of the KPD. In doing so, members of the social democratic resistance forces clearly contravened the preferred mode of operation mandated by their exile leadership headquartered in Prague. At the heart of my argument lies my contention that the source of this dissension between Social Democrats in the underground and Social Democrats in Prague was located in the fundamentally changed social circumstances – compared to the Weimar years – determining the daily reality of underground activism under the Nazi boot.

My research centers on the social democratic underground, and most of the results apply first and foremost to this branch of the anti-Nazi resistance. But much of the evidence I will adduce points in the direction of a strong dynamic towards unity on the Left going far beyond the circle of committed Social Democrats. Many pieces of the puzzle strongly suggest the relative irrelevance of party-political divisions in the face of mortal danger for many German communists as well, and this tendency was already firmly in place long before the KPD leadership decided to comply with Comintern directives and blunt its anti-socialist edge in the course of 1935.

2.

Up until 1933 one of the most noticeable traits of German social democratic as well as communist politics was a deeply-felt mutual hatred and distrust.[6] But the collapse of German democracy led a substantial segment of the SPD membership to question – in a very thorough manner – the validity of the party's course in the run-up to January 1933, including the party's unrelenting anti-communist stance. With virtually no exceptions all participant-observers record a deep disillusionment within the ranks of the SPD as the true dimensions of the catastrophe became obvious in the weeks and months after Hitler was appointed Chancellor. For instance, in a detailed letter in mid-May 1933, the party functionary Fritz Blümel informed the SPD Executive of the mood then prevalent in Berlin which may stand for countless similar observations: "In the eyes of the workers the party has suffered such a tremendous loss of confidence in every respect that in all likelihood it will be impossible to rescue it. Let us take care to ensure the survival of the [social democratic] idea in new organizational forms, and let us see to it that the idea will regain respect through struggle."[7]

It only stood to reason that a similar mood of near-total disenchantment with their party's prior course would have affected the KPD as well. Many social democratic informants underscored this point in their reports on the first years of the German underground. In a July 1934 report on the Munich underground, Waldemar von Knoeringen informed the SPD Executive: "The overwhelming majority of socialist workers in Germany today reject both the Communist Party and its old leadership as well as the Social Democratic Party. They believe that both organizations have been overtaken by reality and can not reemerge. Already now there exist strong groups of workers in Munich, who still call themselves Communists, but who want nothing more to do with the old party."[8]

Johanna Kirchner probably captured the mood of more than just the Frankfurt underground when she reported that the political orientation of the Frankfurt activists "is based on the realization that *all* old proletarian organizations, regardless of their political coloration, are politically and organizationally finished as a result of the fascist surprise conquest. The new form and the new content of the German socialist labor movement will only reemerge out of the practice of illegal struggle against fascism."[9] Knoeringen, in his July 1934 report on Munich, noted the profound sentiment in favor of unity immediately after he had highlighted the skepticism of the Marxist underground vis-à-vis *all* pre-existing political parties:

> *These groups want a unified socialist class party of the proletariat. The comrades gave me examples of how workers reject communist leaflets as soon as they start up their old insults of the SPD. They do not want the continuation of the old tone, and they believe that the new era has created entirely different preconditions for class struggle. The divisions of yesteryear are cleared away; the methods of struggle have become uniform; the terrain is prepared for a united workers' movement. If the party hierarchies do not reach unity, then this will happen from below, all by itself, and organically. This development will simply ignore the remnants of the old parties.*[10]

Many reports on the daily practice of the German underground repeat the theme of social democratic-communist rapprochement. In the course of a conversation with an SPD functionary in Czechoslovakia, visiting Berlin Communists asserted that "in the circles of the Berlin working class, inasmuch as it is involved in illegal activity, cooperation among socialists of all former tendencies is aimed for and in many cases practiced."[11] And summarizing the reports by SPD members who had gathered in Paris in early 1936 in an ill-fated attempt to bring about anti-fascist unity at the leadership level, Rudolf Breitscheid remarked: "By the way, those comrades who entertain direct contacts with illegal activists in Germany ensured us that in very many locations Social Democrats and Communists work hand-in-hand."[12]

Gestapo reports confirm the movement towards unity among underground Social Democrats. For instance, in the ten months between October 1934 and August 1935 alone, informants related the establishment of socialist/communist united fronts in the state of Thuringia, Frankfurt am Main, Essen and Oberhausen, Cologne, Düsseldorf, Mainz and Groß-Gerau, Hamburg, Hanover, Zeitz, and Braunschweig.[13] Naturally, it remains difficult to judge the relative importance of such actually existing united fronts. And by virtue of inclusion in this list these efforts at united fronts were known to the Gestapo and were, therefore, mostly short-lived affairs with few long-term consequences. At the very least, however, their relative frequency suggests their less-than-exceptional nature.

Far more common than these actually existing united fronts was an atmosphere favoring close cooperation between KPD and SPD expressed by social democratic resisters in countless localities throughout Nazi Germany. Earlier on, I referred to the strong sentiment in favor of superseding the limitations of both party-political traditions by the construction of a new united organization of the Marxist underground. In subsequent sections of this essay, I will cite additional evidence for this grass-roots movement away from hatred and disunity towards tolerance and cooperation. Of course, the advocacy of unity is qualitatively distinct from unity itself, and I certainly do not wish to create a "countermyth" to the dominant myth of German resistance historiography, which sees working-class resistance as totally fractured. But I would like to suggest that the evolution of the social democratic underground – certainly its stated goals, if not everywhere its practice – conformed to very different patterns compared to the reality of the Weimar years and the expectations of its exile leadership. The fratricide of German Marxists helped seal the fate of the Weimar Republic. But, contrary to the impression created by subsequent historiography, at the grass-roots level the fratricide on the Left came to a relatively sudden halt in 1933 and began to reverse itself with remarkable ease.

From the vantage point of the social democratic underground, there existed two main obstacles to the actual construction of united fronts. One such encumbrance was the knowledge that local unity sentiment found no parallel expression in the upper reaches of the parties' hierarchies. Sealing unity at the grass-roots level, the argument went, would be doomed to failure as long as the upper hierarchy would not back up such cooperative moves. In South Nuremberg in early 1934, for instance, local Communists approached SPD activists in search of unity in action. But the response of the Social Democrats was to demand that Nuremberg Communists "shall first convince their [national] leadership to cease their stupid attacks on social democracy. Once the Communist high command has attained the same level of reasonableness and desire for unity as we have, then the Communists shall come to see us again, so that we may then perhaps consider real unity."[14] Less willing to assign blame unilaterally, a female underground activist from Unterbaden reasoned along roughly similar lines in a letter addressed to the SPD leadership abroad: "A further task for the comrades abroad shall be to establish contacts with the Communist leaders who are likewise exiled. All instances of ideological rapprochement and unity with Communists *within* Germany are practically worthless as long as the exiled leadership layer is unable to institute constructive agreements. In this respect the social democratic leadership can fulfill an important mission for the German proletariat."[15] In these and similar cases local unity was possible but preempted or delayed for lack of more general leadership support.

Frequently, local informants aired a slightly different complaint. In a number of instances local unity was rendered difficult and/or impossible for a variety of stated or unstated reasons, but underground Social Democrats utilized precisely this difficulty to achieve local unity as an argument strengthening their case for the necessity of a united front at the national (exile) leadership level. A national top-level agreement, they reasoned, would reduce and/or eliminate obstacles standing in the way of an effective local united front. Social Democrats in Weiden (Lower Bavaria), for instance, pressured the exile leadership for the negotiation of a top-level agreement with the KPD. In Weiden itself the social democratic underground had been unable to reach such an agreement with local Communists. "But the [SPD] Executive has more clever heads," they wrote, "it should be able to do the job."[16] Similarly in Upper Bavaria Waldemar von Knoeringen reported at the end of 1934: "The question of the united front with Communists is of no local importance anywhere in our region, but it is of utmost interest in regard to the international ramifications of the negotiations. Our comrades reject local negotiations with Communists but would welcome a more serious push in this direction on the part of the exiled leadership."[17]

In some cases, then, local unity was possible but avoided for lack of national parallels. In other cases local unity was impossible but activists nevertheless clamored for national support in order to facilitate the construction of local or regional united fronts. The second and perhaps the most common rationale for the lack of an effective local united front was the social democratic activists' perception of the Communists' greater proclivity towards risk-laden activities that could needlessly endanger activists. Report after report emanating from underground Social Democrats reiterates this point. "Now as ever the Communists are shunned. They are unreliable, for the most part politically untrained, and their ranks are teeming with spies."[18] "But [Social Democrats] are now as ever staunch opponents of the ongoing communist activities with their senseless methods of how to influence the masses, the strong infiltration of spies, etc."[19] And a report from a social democratic underground unit operating in Berlin captures the atmosphere better than most others:

> *Originally we had excellent relations, organized joint discussions, and even planned [jointly] to publish an internal newsletter which was to enable all revolutionaries to carry out theoretical debates. At the same time we were repeatedly forced to confront the lunatic tactics of the KPD. The Communists, who dispose of fabulous human resources, constantly endanger their people by distributing leaflets to everybody and their brother, by organizing demonstrations. In addition they constantly order strikes, orders, however, that are not even heeded by their own members and sympathizers.*[20]

Small wonder that actually existing united fronts were not the rule. But that many Social Democrats favored unity despite these uncongenial circumstances was a powerful indication of the changed mood of the German working-class underground after January 1933. What may account for this 180 degree turn compared to the SPD's (and KPD's) attitude prior to Hitler's victory?

The desperate situation of severely handicapped underground organizations facing the entire gamut of repressive measures unleashed by the brutal Hitler regime served as a powerful catalyst for unity moves. A December 1935 assembly of exiled Saarland Social Democrats pleaded for anti-fascist unity and argued that "one thing is certain: The communist will to topple Hitler is sincere! And that alone suffices to justify united action. Especially if one is willing not to be too discriminating in the search for auxiliary troops."[21] A report on the 1936 Silesian underground advocated unity and suggested that "one really should discontinue hate-mongering [vis-à-vis Communists] especially now, for we have been sufficiently punished, and the united front is now the only possibility to extricate ourselves from the morass."[22] The former head of the SPD Reichstag delegation, Rudolf Breitscheid, wrote to the Prague Executive: "Regardless of our programmatic orientation, we must endeavor to seek a common platform in all those questions in which we are in agreement regarding the fight against Nazism."[23] And a Gestapo report on the founding of a German underground united front in the Dutch city of Arnhem pointed to "the realization that the uncoordinated parallel efforts of untrained groups of people is doomed to failure" as the foremost reason for the construction of that particular alliance.[24]

A closely related catalyst for unity was the growing realization that the embattled and constantly decimated Marxist underground could only regain a measure of self-confidence if it could manage to concentrate *all* of its disparate elements into *one* fighting force. Arguing in favor of anti-fascist unity with his party colleague Paul Hertz, Emil Kirschmann cited this passage of an earlier letter by Hertz: "The most important conclusion I have drawn from the developments of the past three years is the conviction that the German working class may only regain its self-confidence, which it has lost under the Hitler regime, by means of a concentration of all socialist forces."[25] A report on the Saxon underground stressed the following observation:

> *The ideological situation remains unchanged. We were indeed able to recruit more helpers and fighters. But everyone agrees that many, very many of those who are at present standing aside from the struggle could be won for cooperation, if we could suggest a goal on which everything could be focused. They say that the concentration of all anti-fascist socialist forces must occur before we can [begin to] lead an energetic struggle against fascism.*[26]

In some cases, then, the necessity to search for allies after years of inbred enmity brought together former enemies. Oftentimes networks of sociability, sometimes dating back to Weimar democracy, smoothed the path towards cooperation. Earlier I cited the case of Nuremberg Social Democrats who had been approached by local Communists in search of unity. Characteristically, the contact person for the Nuremberg communist cell was a Social Democrat who had worked side-by-side with the Communists in the local workers' sports association up to January 1933.[27] More common yet were intimate ties based on identical employment patterns. When the Gestapo proudly proclaimed the snuffing out of a united front in Frankfurt am Main in October 1934, they noted that "in almost all instances" participating members had been white-collar employees "who were still 'organized' at the time of their arrest."[28] A united front among Düsseldorf tram workers was likewise based on occupational affinities.[29] A Gestapo report on efforts at united fronts in Berlin highlighted negotiations to this effect from Steglitz to Prenzlauer Berg, while emphasizing the role of the workforce in large enterprises as the vanguard of such moves.[30]

On occasion the presence of particularly respected representatives from either party at unity negotiations could have a positive impact on the outcome. The Essen united front succeeded at least in part because of the work done by the communist worker Hans Degel. Even the Gestapo agent reporting on this process felt obliged to characterize Hans Degel in the following, almost glowing terms: "He is an extraordinarily capable functionary of the KPD, who is well-known from the years before the national revolution [i.e., the Nazi conquest of power]."[31] And the united front in neighboring Oberhausen was likely in part the result of a favorable attitude by the social democratic "leader of the negotiations, an able former unionist," according to an internal communist report cited by the Gestapo.[32]

Likewise the local presence of some intermediary groups, oftentimes originating in earlier splits or expulsions from the SPD or KPD and at that moment leading separate organizational lives, may have eased the road to unity or prepared the ideological terrain for unity sentiments to gain ground. Many of these independent socialist or dissident communist groups had focused on the necessity of the united front for quite some time and tirelessly worked towards its realization. According to a May 1935 Gestapo report, pro-unity agitation on the part of members of the left socialist Socialist Workers Party (SAP) was in part responsible for the unusually early emergence of a viable united front in the industrial town of Zeitz (Prussian Saxony), which operated ever since the beginning of 1934.[33] Sometimes one or several of these *Zwischengruppen* were able to form a limited united front with just one of the two large parties, as was the case in Thuringia or Cologne.[34] Such a partial united front could then grow to encompass all Marxist parties, as happened in Hanover, where a united front composed of SPD, SAP, and the Communist Party Opposition (KPO) eventually attracted the remainder of the illegal KPD after a successful Gestapo crackdown on the latter.[35]

The sudden push towards unity was also related to a generational change as the SPD adjusted to life underground. The relevant primary and secondary literature is replete with information stressing the slide towards passivity on the part of many formerly leading individuals. A foe of the united front, Gustav Ferl, had this to say about the situation in Cologne: "In Cologne we have the misfortune that not a single one of the old functionaries participates in [underground] work." Instead, a former member of the SAP revitalized the party's work.[36] A report on Magdeburg stresses the "characteristic" fact "that the young generation was very willing to work and was glad no longer to remain politically passive. They declared, however, that they would have refused to cooperate if I would have suggested individuals from the old political leadership as their superiors [*Führer*]."[37]

While the information is insufficient to warrant any general conclusion about the age of active socialist resisters, it is only logical that the physical demands of underground work would tend to favor younger party comrades who were perhaps better able to withstand the rigors of such activity. But whether young, middle-aged, or old, active resisters were by definition more action-oriented than the average pre-1933 member of the SPD.

This newly found orientation towards active engagement with the enemy, spawned by the drastic circumstances of defeat, in turn facilitated a more favorable view of KPD activities. By all accounts, the KPD displayed the greatest amount of underground activity in the early years of illegality. As I indicate above, much of this activism could be self-defeating and/or counterproductive and could lead to alienation from potential allies unwilling to take unnecessary risks. But not every KPD local was engaged in the same caliber of activities, and most observers ascribe a certain aura of fascination and glory to this dynamic comportment of the KPD.

Rudolf Breitscheid at one point warned his party comrades in the Prague Executive that "the Communists have been able to mobilize broad bourgeois anti-fascist circles in France, England, America, etc. These people in turn regard the Communists ... as the sole, or certainly the most important, [anti-fascist] force, and I believe it necessary that Social Democrats – even if only in their capacity as individuals – begin to play a role in order to correct this impression."[38] What was true in foreign exile was doubly true in the underground. Social democratic resisters from Berlin-Köpenick gave this account of the first year in the underground:

> *After the first shockwave our instincts pushed us, like most workers, leftward, in the direction of the KPD. With a fairly reasonable attitude the KPD could have made major gains from the deep disappointments affecting wide circles of social democratic workers. But [the KPD] was unable to do so because it did not do justice to the deep and sincere longing for unity on the part of German workers, but instead increased its tedious and ludicrous recitation of stock phrases about social fascism, the victorious KPD, and similar nonsense.*[39]

And the following piece of advice by a moderate Social Democrat, Gustav Ferl, on the situation in Magdeburg perfectly combines the themes of the youthfulness of social democratic underground resisters, their radicalization and heightened activism, and their openness towards communist ideas: "The main thing is that we do not let the need for activity in the circles of our younger comrades dissipate. In addition we must not drive our young elements into the hands of the Communists."[40]

3.

What emerges, then, from the plethora of first- and second-hand accounts emanating from the underground – supported by Gestapo spy reports – is the presence of a definite pro-unitary mood among the active social democratic underground up to 1936. Given the haphazard survival of documentary evidence, it is impossible to judge with anything approaching statistical certainty the precise relationship of forces between supporters of a unitary course and detractors of such measures. The evidence, however, strongly suggests that in many regions of Nazi Germany, the surviving Marxist underground pulled closer together, or at least desired such an understanding, rather than continuing along the well-trodden path of fratricide and mutual exclusion that had facilitated the Nazi victory in the first place. And it would have been astounding if the disabling pre-1933 traditions had survived intact in one of the most momentous turning points in the history of the German (and European) workers' movements.

In the foregoing pages I have attempted to portray the atmosphere behind, and the reasons for, this strong desire for unity. The loss of social democratic (and communist) self-confidence; the desperate position of underground fighters facing a brutal and determined common enemy; the growing recognition of a common past as well as present spawned by ongoing or revitalized networks of sociability; contingent factors such as the presence of particularly well-respected and talented underground activists in one or both of the major two Marxist underground parties or the equally contingent presence of smaller splinter groups as catalysts for unity; the growing social weight of youthful activists; the greater reliance on activists willing to take risks – these and other social and political conditions determining the lived reality of anti-Nazi socialist resisters ensured that the mood favoring unity would not remain a transitory phenomenon associated with the initial shock effect of Nazi terrorism.

Two of the most powerful obstacles to the effective consummation of this quasi-instinctual reaction to the tragedy of German democracy were the leadership bodies of the two Marxist parties. Unlike most other continental European social democratic parties in the mid-1930s, the SPD remained a staunch opponent of efforts at united fronts throughout the period of illegality.[41] In parallel fashion, the KPD constituted one of the last bastions of opposition within the Comintern when the Communist International in the mid-1930s began to consider abandoning its habitual characterization of social democracy as a twin of fascism.[42]

Interestingly, there are many indications that the seemingly insurmountable barriers between SPD and KPD began to be lowered within Germany even before illegality forcibly removed many of the preconceptions that had kept their members at loggerheads. The construction of the social democratic Iron Front crucially revitalized social democratic spirits and gave the stagnant party a direly needed activist inflection for much of 1932 which opened up possibilities for cooperation. One of the most astute participant-observers of the fall of Weimar democracy, the one-time Menshevik and then Left socialist journalist Alexander Schifrin, later reflected on this development from his French exile:

> *At the high point of the crisis, just before the catastrophe, an explicitly anti-reformist majority existed within the German proletariat composed of the KPD and the left wing of the SPD. This anti-reformist majority, however, was rendered unable to act. One part was blocked by the apparatus and tradition of the SPD, the other undermined and disabled by the KPD. The push toward construction of unity spontaneously gripped the membership of both workers' parties.*[43]

As it was, unity was never established before it was too late, and even then actually existing united fronts were established haphazardly and never became the national norm. But all available evidence from the social democratic side suggests that advocates of unity carried the day within the active social democratic underground. That these sentiments did not translate into concrete achievements was at least as much due to established patterns of animosity fostered by both exile leaderships as it was a result of distinctive communist and social democratic practices in illegality. Yet the relative absence of concrete united fronts did not mean that Communists and Social Democrats formed two distinct battalions, fought completely separate battles, and, therefore, had as little in common in the underground as in the closing years of Weimar democracy.

German underground Communists were indeed more prone to expose themselves to needless risks than Social Democrats – that is one reason for the relative paucity of concrete alliances between the two groups. But, certainly in regard to the active resisters among Social Democrats, Martin Broszat's above-mentioned depiction of illegal socialist units and illegal communist units as ships passing in the night is a partially distorted mirror of the first phase of German underground reality.

4.

In a conference presentation on the role of proletarian resistance in Nazi Germany, Detlev Peukert noted the limits of the employment of memoirs and memory in the search for historical meanings of the past. In particular when concentrating on "the presentation of larger contexts" or "on the reconstruction of contemporaneous moods," Peukert urged extreme caution in the reconstruction of the past based on personal recollections. Characteristically, Peukert drew attention to cases of subconscious historical amnesia affecting recollections of the effects of Stalinism in the communist underground and, more importantly in this context, "memories of nowadays no longer acceptable cooperation with Communists" in the case of underground social democracy.[44] This essay was written to corroborate and substantiate this insight which was frequently aired by one of Germany's most talented historians, who never found the time specifically to affirm this important but generally overlooked aspect of life in the early days of the anti-Nazi underground.

Notes

1. Francis R. Nicosia, "Introduction: Resistance to National Socialism in the Work of Peter Hoffmann," in *Germans against Nazism: Noncompliance, Opposition, and Resistance in the Third Reich. Essays in Honour of Peter C. Hoffmann*, ed. Francis R. Nicosia and Lawrence D. Stokes (Leamington Spa, 1990), 5.
2. The doyen of this important branch of resistance studies remains Peter Hoffmann, whose most important works are *The History of the German Resistance 1933-1945* (Cambridge, Mass., 1977) and *German Resistance to Hitler* (Cambridge, Mass., 1988).
3. See, for instance, his succinct article, "A Social and Historical Typology of the German Opposition to Hitler," in *Contending With Hitler: Varieties of German Resistance in the Third Reich*, ed. David Clay Large (Cambridge, Mass., 1991), esp. 26-29.
4. The "Rundschreiben der Sopade (Prag)," 30 January 1935, announcing the severing of ties is perhaps most easily accessible in Erich Matthias, ed., *Mit dem Gesicht nach Deutschland* (Düsseldorf, 1968), 227-28.
5. SPD Executive order, "An die Grenzsekretäre und Vertrauensleute," 24 January 1936, AsD, Sopade, Mappe 8.
6. The most recent comprehensive study of the workers' movement in late Weimar Germany is Heinrich August Winkler, *Der Weg in die Katastrophe: Arbeiter und Arbeiterbewegung in der Weimarer Republik 1930 bis 1933* (Bonn, 1987). A recent informative work on the social democratic component is Donna Harsch, *German Social Democracy and the Rise of Nazism* (Chapel Hill, NC, 1993).
7. Fritz Blümel to Paul Hertz, 21 May 1933, pp. 4-5, AsD, Nachlaß Paul Hertz, Film XXX, "ba" h.
8. "Michel" [= Waldemar von Knoeringen], "Bericht Südböhmen-Südbayern," July 1934, p. 42, AsD, Sopade, Mappe 63. In this citation, as on occasion in other quotes, the term "socialist" denotes both Communists and Social Democrats, not the narrower definition of Social Democrats only.
9. Johanna Kirchner, "Bericht über illegale, politische Organisationen in unserem Bezirk," probably written during 1934, p. 1, AsD, Sopade, Mappe 61, emphasis in the original.
10. See n. 8 above.
11. E. Hahnewald [= Wilhelm Sander?], "Bericht über den Besuch des Naturfreundehauses 'Königshöhe' bei Reichenberg am 11., 12. und 13. August 1936," p. 1, AsD, Sopade, Mappe 107.
12. Rudolf Breitscheid, "Niederschrift über die Konferenz der Deutschen Volksfront," p. 3, Institut für Zeitgeschichte, Munich (hereafter IfZ), Nachlaß Wilhelm Hoegner, Bd. 2.
13. BAK, RSH, R 48/456, 2-3 (Thuringia); R 58/460, 14 (Frankfurt am Main); R 58/460, 63-65 (Essen and Oberhausen); R 58/460, 142 (Cologne); R 58/596, 9 (Düsseldorf); R 58/596, 68 (Mainz and Groß Gerau); R 58/596, 99a (Hamburg); R 58/596, 99b (Hanover); R 58/ 596, 116 (Zeitz); and R 58/596, 136-7 (Braunschweig). In the Mainz and Groß Gerau case it is conceivable, however, that a formerly social democratic organization may have been overtaken from within by Communists.
14. Hans Dill, "Tätigkeitsbericht," 6 February 1934, p. 2, AsD, Sopade, Mappe 31.
15. Letter signed by "Eine Genossin aus Unterbaden," written probably in September 1933, p. 4 (emphasis added), AsD, Sopade, Mappe 90.

16. Hans Dill to Hans Vogel, 23 May 1934, p. 4, AsD, Sopade, Mappe 31. The passage is a paraphrased summary of a report by a local informant given to Hans Dill informing the latter about the mood of the SPD underground. The German original of the cited phrase is: "Der Parteivorstand hat doch gescheitere Köpfe, der müßte es fertig bringen."
17. "Michel" [= Waldemar von Knoeringen], "Bericht (Schema C), Jahresbericht 1934, Organisationsbereich I, b," p. 12, AsD, Sopade, Mappe 64.
18. Gustav Ferl, untitled report, 17 August 1934, p. 1, AsD, Sopade, Mappe 37.
19. "Mündliche Ergänzungen des Genossen Pr. zu seinem Reisebericht," 28 June 1935, p. 2, AsD, Sopade, Mappe 91.
20. Copy of a report on social democratic underground units' operation in Berlin, 28 August 1933, p. 4, IISG, Sozialistische Arbeiter Internationale, Mappe 3520.
21. Collective letter to the SPD executive, 15 December 1935, p. 1, AsD, Paul Hertz, Film XXXII, "44."
22. Helmut (Hertel) [= Franz Bögler], "Lagebericht vom 18. Juni 1936," p. 5, AsD, Sopade, Mappe 21.
23. Breitscheid, "Niederschrift," p. 3.
24. BAK, RSH, R 58/596, 4. This report was dated 17 January 1935. One day later another Gestapo spy contradicted the earlier account of the meeting in Arnhem: see BAK, RSH, R 58/596, 6.
25. Emil Kirschmann to Paul Hertz, 5 February 1936, p. 2, AsD, Paul Hertz, Film XXXII, "44." In this and the following citation, the term "socialist" once again denotes both Social Democrats *and* Communists.
26. Otto Thiele, monthly report, 6 September 1934, p. 20, AsD, Sopade, Mappe 135.
27. Dill, "Tätigkeitsbericht," p. 2.
28. BAK, RSH, R 58/460, 14.
29. BAK, RSH, R 58/596, 9.
30. For May 1935, see BAK, RSH, R 58/596, 121-2. For August 1935, see BAK, RSH, R 58/596, 169a-169b.
31. BAK, RSH, R 58/460, 63.
32. BAK, RSH, R 58/460, 65.
33. BAK, RSH, R 58/460, 65.
34. BAK, RSH, R 58/456, 2 (for Thuringia); BA, RSH, R 58/460, 142 (for Cologne).
35. BAK, RSH, R 58/596, 99b.
36. Gustav Ferl, "Bericht an Sopade für März 1934," 5 April 1934, p. 1, AsD, Sopade, Mappe 37.
37. Report included in a letter by Gustav Ferl to Sopade, 17 August 1933, p. 2, AsD, Sopade, Mappe 37.
38. Rudolf Breitscheid to SPD Executive, 24 January 1936, p. 2, AsD, Sopade, Mappe 23.
39. Verbatim report included in Willi Lange, "Bericht vom 9.2.1934," AsD, Sopade, Mappe 96.
40. Gustav Ferl to Sopade, 17 August 1934, p. 4, AsD, Sopade, Mappe 37.
41. A concise and brief account of the political trajectory of the illegal SPD is Patrick von zur Mühlen, "Sozialdemokraten gegen Hitler," in *Widerstand und Verweigerung in Deutschland 1933 bis 1945*, ed. Richard Löwenthal and Patrik von zur Mühlen (Berlin, 1982), 57-75. For one of the earliest – and still one of the best – accounts of the inner turmoil of the SPD Executive-in-exile, see Lewis Edinger, *German Exile Politics* (Berkeley, 1956). In my dissertation, I draw attention to the seeming anomaly – when placed in a comparative context – of SPD attitudes towards working-class unity; see my "European Socialists

Respond to Fascism: The Drive Towards Unity, Radicalisation, and Strategic Innovation in Austria, Belgium, France, Germany, and Spain – 1933-1936," University of Michigan, 1992. A revised version of this study has been published as *European Socialists Respond to Fascism: Ideology, Activism and Contingency in the 1930s* (New York, 1996).

42. Hermann Weber furnishes a useful summary of the KPD's political itinerary in his "Die KPD in der Illegalität," in Löwenthal and von zur Mühlen, *Widerstand und Verweigerung*, 83-101. For a detailed study, see Horst Duhnke, *Die KPD von 1933 bis 1945* (Cologne, 1972).
43. Alexander Schifrin, "Revolutionäre Sozialdemokratie," *Zeitschrift für Sozialismus* 1: 3 (December 1933): 87.
44. Detlev Peukert, "Zur Rolle des Arbeiterwiderstands im 'Dritten Reich,'" in *Gegner des Nationalsozialismus*, ed. Christoph Kleßmann and Falk Pingel (Frankfurt, 1980), 76.

Chapter 14

Communist Resistance between Comintern Directives and Nazi Terror

Beatrix Herlemann

The last election of the Weimar Republic took place on 5 March 1933 under the dark shadow of Nazi Storm Trooper (SA) terror. A great proportion of the leading cadres of the Communist Party of Germany (KPD) had already been rounded up in the mass arrests that immediately followed the Reichstag fire. The party chairman, Ernst Thälmann, was among those who fell into the hands of the police at the beginning of March. Until his execution in the Buchenwald concentration camp in 1944, he would spend the remaining years of his life locked behind bars, deprived of any trace of due process. In the balloting, the KPD lost one million votes from the last general election held the preceding November. Nonetheless, 4.8 million voters – 12.3 percent of the electorate – cast their ballots for the Communist Party of Germany.

The KPD, founded at the very beginning of 1919 as a left-radical split-off from the Social Democratic Party (SPD), had undergone a structural transformation in the course of the Weimar Republic. From a party characterized internally by numerous factions and a great variety of opinions, it had become a strict, centrally led organization. Its hierarchically structured apparatus forcefully implemented the political directives of a leadership that ruled autocratically. As a section of the Communist International (Comintern), the KPD was not an independent actor, but a party whose

Notes for this chapter begin on page 370.

policies and strategies were subordinated to the interests of the communist international movement. As the Communist Party of the Soviet Union (CPSU) developed toward complete Stalinization, the KPD moved in parallel fashion. In Germany it followed without reservation the Comintern's political line – namely, the "social fascism" thesis, launched in 1928 to 1929, by which the KPD directed its entire force toward the fight against social democracy and enormously neglected the growing danger of National Socialism. The KPD sought to split the trade unions and all other organizations of the labor movement, which weakened the forces that fought to maintain the Weimar Republic. The strong stance against the hostile "brother" – social democracy – would run like a red thread through the entire history of the KPD. Only twice – in the context of the popular front policy of 1935 to 1936 and in the forced unification of the KPD and SPD in 1946 – did it retreat from this position, and then only for short periods and because of strategic considerations.

The immense wave of arrests in the spring of 1933 left the party, at first, virtually incapable of any action. Its rigid, centralized leadership style coupled with the elimination of inner party democracy – following the model of the CPSU – had gradually deprived the three hundred thousand members of their own initiative. The endless flow of detailed instructions and directives had served to create a following that found it exceedingly difficult to react independently to the new situation. To be sure, the rank and file had considered the possibility of a situation of illegality, and plans existed for going underground. Yet these were modeled on earlier persecutions like the period of the Anti-Socialist Law under Bismarck, the tsarist Okhrana, or the brief banning of the KPD by the Weimar Republic in 1923 to 1924. Nothing had prepared Communists for the brutal, overwhelming terror of a Nazi state driven by a limitless will to power, a state that completely disregarded all legal principles and sought to repress its political opponents to the point of physical annihilation.

When Hitler assumed power on 30 January 1933, the KPD issued a call for a general strike, but this was largely ignored. The party never seriously considered an armed uprising despite all the propaganda reports of supposedly numerous, hidden communist arms caches. The striking failure to understand the National Socialist danger, coupled with the overwhelming condemnation of social democracy, led to more than the KPD's demise. These positions also made an immense contribution to the devastating defeat of the German labor movement in general, once widely seen as the model for labor movements around the world.

With the Nazi seizure of power the labor movement suffered an unprecedented loss of those rights and resources for which workers and their representatives had struggled long and hard: publishing houses; educational institutions; labor halls; defense, sport, cultural, and welfare associations; and party and union treasuries. The broad membership had believed in the insurmountable power of their great organizations, a belief nourished by the KPD leadership as well as by the SPD and the unions. The utter destruction of all of the subcultural organizations and associations caused an immense shock. Yet because the German party was bound to the Comintern and the directives it issued, the KPD Politburo had for years no longer been oriented toward the realities of the situation in its own country but to the requirements of Soviet foreign policy.[1]

In the Comintern's estimation, National Socialism in power in no way signified the end of the KPD and all the socialist forces in Germany, but only a temporary setback. The KPD would, when necessary, lead the masses out of illegality to victory. This optimistic – though completely illusory – scenario may have helped the members maintain their allegiances and commitments, though thousands of them in the spring of 1933 already populated the first concentration camps in Dachau and Emsland and uncounted others suffered arbitrary torture at the hands of the SA. Indeed, prevailing estimates indicate that around one-third to one-half of the KPD's three hundred thousand members in 1932 endured continual or intermittent imprisonment at the hands of the Nazis. At the time, party members considered the life of a comrade well spent if he managed to carry out illegal party work for three months prior to arrest.[2]

Despite the intense repression suffered by German Communists, most maintained the belief that the Hitler regime would last only a short time. In the communist view, Hitler was only one of a parade of chancellors, each of whom served ever shorter terms, all of whom were fascists and were supported by social democracy. The KPD leadership understood these developments as confirmation of its position, trumpeted for years, that a revolutionary crisis was "ripening" which would ultimately bring the Communists to power in Germany.

The Politburo quickly found it necessary to move its activities abroad. The KPD established a Foreign Directorate (*Auslandsleitung*) in Paris in May 1933 with Wilhelm Pieck, Thälmann's representative, in charge. In the autumn Walter Ulbricht and the other leaders followed, as they could no longer maintain themselves underground in Berlin. In the emigration countries around Germany the KPD established border stations, as did the SPD, which were designed to provide multifarious support for the resistance within the country. These stations were the first address for comrades fleeing Germany, who were checked out, provided support by the local Red Aid, and sent on to their ultimate destinations. Activists in the German underground sought aid and advice, and picked up leaflets, newspapers, and pamphlets to smuggle into Germany. This literature instructed the rank and file in Germany about the current situation and raised the call for a popular struggle against Hitler. Through these border stations the renowned "Brown Book on the Reichstag Fire and Hitler Terror," compiled by the KPD and Comintern propaganda expert Willi Münzenberg, was also smuggled into the Third Reich.[3]

According to the directives of the émigré Politburo, a central Domestic Directorate (*Inlandsleitung*) in Berlin was supposed to lead resistance activities. Eight advisors (*Oberberater*) were to be responsible for the party's twenty-four districts. Despite the drastically altered conditions of illegality, the Politburo called on the members to maintain the central organization of the party from the top down to the most local level, now divided into cells of three to five men. Each party organization was also to maintain its three-headed leadership, with each of the functionaries responsible for politics, organization, or agitprop. Subject to the same directives, the affiliated organizations, such as the Communist Youth Organization, Red Aid, the Red Sports Leagues, and others, also attempted to maintain their organizations and their activism in the underground.

The daily reality of persecutions and denunciations exacted a high price from this rigid and inflexible organizational structure. The party found it increasingly difficult to replace arrested cadres. Those members ready and willing to engage in activism were decimated by tactics that had been appropriate for the Weimar Republic but led to huge losses under the extraordinary conditions of the Third Reich – mass distributions of leaflets; flying demonstrations, whereby Communists would gather with a loudspeaker, shout a few slogans or give short, impromptu speeches and then quickly move on to a new location; collections of membership fees. Yet the leadership needed public signs of the KPD's continued existence in order to challenge the Nazis' claims that they had destroyed the party and eliminated the "Bolshevik danger." And it also needed proof of an active underground resistance as support for its arguments in the discussions within the Comintern.

The Thirteenth Plenum of the Executive Committee of the Comintern (ECCI), meeting in December 1933, devoted intensive discussions to the issue of fascism in Germany. Wilhelm Pieck, yet again, presented the scenario of the KPD's rapidly rising influence among the working masses, the ascending revolutionary wave, and the intensifying inner contradictions of the fascist regime. Yet again he attacked "treasonous social democracy" and called for the foundation of independent, class-conscious trade unions, the party's policy, launched in 1929, of splitting the existing trade unions.

Herbert Wehner, the Politburo's technical secretary, had been active in the underground for a year in Berlin. Amid the greatest difficulties, he had sought to adapt illegal work to the altered conditions in Germany. In his memoirs published years later, he remarked:

> *At the ECCI plenum, the German Politburo members delivered speeches that were far removed from reality. They painted a rose-colored picture that included ludicrous boasts. These same speeches were printed in brochures and had to be distributed [illegally in Germany] by members who daily placed their lives in danger.*[4]

This unrealistic strategy changed only in 1934 to 1935 and only because of the alterations in Soviet foreign policy. When the Soviet Union entered the League of Nations, it established, at least for a while, somewhat less hostile contacts with the western powers. Nor could the Soviet Union any longer deny the reality of the consolidation of the National Socialist regime in Germany.

The first manifestation of the change in course took place in relation to the Saar. As mandated by the Versailles Treaty, a referendum was scheduled for 13 January 1935 by which the population would decide between a continuation of its administration by the League or union with Germany. The KPD at first raised the slogan, "For a red Saar in a Soviet Germany." It attacked the SPD as a "vassal" of France and the "bailiff" of imperialism because it called for a maintenance of the status quo. Yet after a critique by the ECCI presidium in July 1934, the KPD fully reversed course. It dropped its slogan – which Moscow had rightly disqualified as an inadmissible variant of the referendum – and shifted to a common campaign with Social Democrats and Catholics in favor of the status quo. The KPD, thereby, began to move in accord with the Comintern's new line in favor of the united front. The shift, however, came much too late and had no impact on the results, in which 90.8 percent of the Saar residents voted for union with Germany.[5]

The communist rank and file maintained its strict rejection of National Socialism. But the overwhelming vote in the Saar for Germany; the bloody liquidation of the SA leadership a half-year before, which found no opposition; Germany's violation of the Versailles Treaty with the institution of universal conscription in March 1935, also met without opposition; and, above all, the gradual decline of unemployment, even if only because of the armaments build-up – all this made clear to the Communists that the National Socialist regime would not fall to pieces on the basis of its own internal contradictions, as their leaders had predicted. The Nazis had solidified their domination and had become largely accepted by the population as well as by the governments of the other European countries. The Communists, in contrast, found themselves in isolation, hopelessly cut off from the oft-cited masses whom they presumed to conquer.

After a very painful learning process, whose effects had cascaded through the ranks in all regions of Germany, the remaining underground forces embarked on a retreat.[6] They ceased the production of printed material designed to inform and instruct the population as well as their own comrades and refused to distribute the ever greater volume of literature produced by the party émigrés abroad and smuggled into Germany.[7] What was the use of distributing to the German underground Stalin's speech to the Soviet Stakhanovite workers? Was it worthwhile to go to prison, to endanger health and life, to place one's family at risk, all for the completely unrealistic speeches of the party leaders? More and more illegal activists answered "No" to these questions and ceased their efforts to maintain the organizational structure in the underground. They concentrated instead on their own survival and kept up contacts with a few trusted comrades and discussed urgent matters only in the narrowest circles.

So when the Comintern met in Moscow in August 1935 for its Seventh – and last – Congress and launched the new and innovative policy of the popular front, it simply affirmed, belatedly, existing practice. This is even more true of the transference of the new Comintern line to German conditions at the KPD's conference in Moscow – called the "Brussels" conference to deceive the Nazis – held shortly after the Comintern Congress. The new policy signified a realistic recognition of the relative weaknesses of communist parties, which by themselves were not capable of fighting successfully the various forms of fascism that had emerged in a number of countries. With the popular front strategy, the Seventh Congress oriented the Comintern and the member parties toward the further development of cooperation among communist, socialist, and democratic parties that had been pioneered in France and Spain. The Comintern's general secretary, Georgi Dimitrov, promoted the tactic of the "Trojan horse," by which Communists were secretively to join enemy organizations with the intention of using them for their own goals – an idea that became the focus of intense discussion in the KPD.

Pieck's report to the party conference indicated the immense loss of personnel that the KPD had suffered. Of 422 leading cadres, 219 were in German imprisonment, 125 had been forced into exile, forty-one had left the party, and twenty-four had been murdered. A mere thirteen still worked in the German underground. The district leaderships, as in Hamburg, had been replaced seven times. The last domestic directorate in March 1935 had lasted only three short weeks before it was destroyed. Yet Pieck still tried to gloss over the failures and mistakes of the resistance leadership, a position that led to controversial discussions. The roughly two dozen delegates from within Germany and the emigration outside of the Soviet Union were not restrained in their criticisms, which led to new elections to the Politburo – a move the existing leadership would have gladly avoided.[8] Eight new members joined the Central Committee, which was reduced in number from twenty-seven members and twenty-three candidates to fifteen members and three candidates. The new members – Anton Ackermann, Walter Hähnel, Elli Schmidt, Herbert Wehner, and Weinrich Wiatrek, and as candidates Wilhelm Knöchel, Werner Kowalski, and Karl Mewis – all had been influenced by long periods of illegal work in the German underground. The narrow leadership circle of the Politburo was also recast. Palmiro Togliatti, one of the leading members of the Comintern, strongly admonished the German comrades by pointing out that a concrete analysis of the real situation in Germany was fundamental to the new concept of activism. The new line could not be accomplished with a mere change in slogans.

The next task was to disseminate the resolutions of the conference to party members within Germany, but also among the émigrés as reflected in the party slogan, "the emigration as a post of struggle." The conversion and extension of the border stations to border secretariats (*Abschnittsleitungen*) had to be completed quite rapidly. With extended powers, the secretariats were to be entrusted with responsibility for resistance groups in the adjacent regions of Germany. The secretariat in Prague had responsibility for Saxony, Central Germany, and Silesia; in Zurich for southern Germany; in Brussels for the middle Rhine region. The secretariat in Amsterdam was charged with responsibility for western and northwestern Germany, which included the relatively well-developed underground groups in the Ruhr and the Rhineland, the northern secretariat in Copenhagen for Schleswig-Holstein, Hamburg, and Mecklenburg. In Paris a Foreign Directorate was established as both the overall leadership arm – under the émigré Politburo, now ensconced mainly in Moscow – and with territorial responsibility for southwestern Germany.

The border secretariats were to maintain contact with communist resisters via instructors, who were to travel regularly into Germany but had only advisory and informational functions. The instructors were directed to give the illegal cadres a great range of independence. The massive transfer of printed materials from abroad was halted. This new, decentralized structure, decided upon in Moscow, marked a radical departure for the KPD. It signified the abandonment of the hierarchical organization with state *(Land)*, district, and subdistrict leaderships. Moreover, the ultra-Left slander against the SPD and the effort to forge independent, communist unions fell by the wayside, replaced by an interest in forging a popular front. Yet most of the underground groups, under the intense pressure of persecution, had already carried out these measures on their own initiative. In the relative freedom from party directives that resulted from quotidian life in the Third Reich, the vast majority of the illegals, again on their own initiative, decided against the tactic of the Trojan horse. They feared that they would only be discredited in the eyes of friends and colleagues who were not aware of the tactic. Sympathetic friends, uninformed about the motivations, would hardly have understood the grounds for individual Communists becoming active in National Socialist mass organizations. In addition, Nazi organizations left little room for initiative, so an opponent of the regime would find himself or herself discredited with friends and isolated from those Nazis whom he or she was attempting to influence. And to present oneself to outsiders as an advocate of National Socialism, and at the same time to try to convince others according to one's true beliefs without betraying oneself – that was a balancing act that few could accomplish.

Social Democrats also had little positive to say about the new communist tactics. To be sure, under the conditions of illegality the hostile brother parties had become somewhat friendlier. In discussions widespread agreement existed that the split between them had contributed in a major way to the common defeat they had suffered. Already in the summer of 1934 "Germany Reports" (*Deutschland-Berichte*), edited by the émigré SPD Executive, maintained: "The longing for unity of the working class in Germany is strong as never before."[9] Yet in the view of most Social Democrats, common practices could develop only slowly with increasing trust. The well known fact that Gestapo spies had penetrated communist groups made collaboration seem even less advisable. Only occasionally did communist attempts to forge agreements with Social Democrats in relation to mutual help, support for families of those arrested, exchange of written materials, etc., come to fruition, as in Berlin, Hildesheim, and Calbe an der Saale. The fate of these efforts at cooperation only confirmed the caution of Social Democrats. Repeatedly, Gestapo incursions into the ranks of the Communists led to arrests of their social democratic partners as well.[10] The Gestapo had also followed and evaluated the new impulses emanating from Moscow and the resolutions of the Comintern Congress. The KPD and Comintern intention to strengthen party activism in the workplace had already been deprived of one of its critical points of contact: the elections for worker delegates *(Vertrauensleute)* in the factories had gone badly for the Nazi German Labor Front (*Deutsche Arbeitsfront*, or DAF) in 1934 and 1935, so Hitler simply forbade further contests.[11]

In the emigration, the new strategy was initiated with greater initial success than in the German underground. In Paris a committee was founded to work toward a German popular front. Under the chairmanship of the widely admired author, Heinrich Mann, the committee included leading Social Democrats, Communists, representatives of socialist splinter groups, and bourgeois intellectuals. The participants sought to draw up a binding program that would unite the opposition against Hitler. Yet already in the summer of 1937 the committee had run aground, largely as a result of the activities of the Communists, especially

Walter Ulbricht, and the general impact of the Stalinist purges, which had begun in 1936. As the key KPD operative in Paris, Ulbricht raised senseless demands, defamed individual members of the committee, and launched the hunt against supposedly ever-present "Trotskyists" – tactics that alienated virtually all the other members of the committee.[12]

The KPD's actions in Paris were symptomatic of a wider trend – the Comintern leadership's retreat to the old, pre-1935 positions. The hope that a broad coalition strategy would contain Germany's aggressive designs had proven false. Moreover, the domestic German opposition was in no position to foster an effective antiwar sentiment among the population at large. As a result, Soviet strategic calculations gave more weight to other factors, a development that became abundantly clear in its ambivalent actions in the Spanish Civil War. Communists and socialists by the thousands, profoundly moved by the spirit of internationalism, came to the aid of the hard-pressed Spanish Republic. The Soviet Union, in contrast, dished out its arms supplies sparingly, though it exercised a decisive influence on Spanish domestic policies and helped strengthen Communists at the expense of socialists and anarchists, whom the Soviet secret police (GPU) – built up in the background – pursued with massive persecutions.

Officially, the Soviet Union joined the Western European non-intervention policy. The approximately five thousand German members of the International Brigades, most of them Communists, had little notion of Soviet policies. The Spanish situation offered them the opportunity, at long last, to fight against fascism with arms, not just with propaganda – and they paid a high price in blood. About two thousand of the German members of the International Brigades fell in Spain. Most of the survivors were evacuated across Spain's northern border in the spring of 1939, where they were interned in concentration camps. After the Nazi occupation of France, they were shipped to German concentration camps. A few of the leading cadres managed to flee to the Soviet Union. Those who then managed to survive the rigors of Dachau and Buchenwald became active after 1945 in the construction of the East German People's Police and National People's Army.

The new shift in policy was also evident in the leadership of the resistance within Germany. In February 1937 the ECCI called upon KPD representatives to move energetically against "defeatist elements" in their own ranks, those who saw little chance for successful mass activism in Germany. Under orders from the émigré leadership in Paris, the border secretariats sought once again to establish tighter, more disciplined contacts with the German underground. Women, apparently less endangered than men, played key roles in maintaining the links between the secretariats and resisters inside the country. Forty or fifty instructors traveled surreptitiously into Germany every few weeks. Yet they could not induce their contacts to undertake more aggressive actions. The instructor reports make clear that the united and popular fronts had not developed beyond initial efforts. Moreover, work among youth and efforts to enhance the knowledge of cadres had almost completely ceased.

The most obvious sign of the return to the pre-popular front strategy – the strategy that had been condemned in 1935 as the reasons for the KPD's immense losses in the first few years of the Nazi regime – was the party conference held in January 1939 near Paris (the so-called "Bern Conference"). Nearly all of the twenty-two exiled leaders were present, yet representatives of the German underground were not to be found – even though this conference also marked the twentieth anniversary of the founding of the KPD. The speakers displayed complete ignorance of the conditions in Germany. Despite the increasingly obvious danger of war and the strengthened vigilance of the Gestapo, party leaders called for enhanced organizational work as a step toward the creation of an active, mass resistance. Toward this end, they called for the renewed creation of party leaderships in the workplace, localities, and regions of Germany.

Only a handful of the loyal Communists in Germany were aware of the decisions of the 1935 Brussels Conference. The resolutions of the Bern Conference remained completely unknown. The efforts of the Paris directorate and the individual border secretariats to involve all available comrades in the drive to reactivate contacts in Germany had no success. Even veterans of the Spanish Civil War were to be sent into Germany to prepare party organizations for the event of war – all to no avail. Their slight chances of success were only further reduced by the German-Soviet Non-Aggression Pact of August 1939. The agreement, completely unexpected, confused and weakened what remained of the communist rank and file. The leadership's attempts to interpret the Hitler-Stalin Pact as an act of peace hardly proved convincing in view of the German attack on Poland, which came only two weeks afterwards, and the Soviet Union's silent toleration of, indeed, participation in, in the spoils of conquest. No more convincing was the KPD's claim that World War II was only an imperialist war for which the western democracies bore the blame. KPD supporters, disoriented by the Pact and trapped in the delirium of the Blitzkrieg, were left in a kind of waiting situation until the German attack on the Soviet Union in June 1941 brought a new kind of clarity to their political outlook. Up until this point, party life had just about ground to a standstill – as the Gestapo's monthly statistics of imprisonments and seizures of printed material under the rubric "Communism/Marxism" demonstrate.[13]

In December 1939 the German Politburo in conjunction with the ECCI in Moscow issued a "Political Platform" that envisioned the establishment of a new domestic party leadership in Germany – another sign of the return to the ignominious strategy that had been abandoned in

1935. When the war began, most of the border secretaries were immediately interned by the authorities of the various countries in which they resided. Deprived of their freedom of movement, the secretaries reached the obvious conclusion and dissolved their organizations. According to the Political Platform, the instructors, the single remaining means of contact between leadership and base, were to be sent back into Germany where they would prepare for the return of those Communists who would make up the new domestic leadership. But at the outset of the war the Nazis had imposed still more intensive internal security measures. As a result, only a few instructors, mostly from Scandinavia, managed to reach Germany, and they could not achieve what the party had already failed to accomplish in the first years of the Nazi dictatorship. The instructors were soon arrested and executed. Their fate demonstrated all too drastically the fantasies of the Political Platform, whose authors had anticipated a certain loosening of internal German conditions with the signing of the German-Soviet Non-Aggression Pact.

The functionaries designated to take over the domestic leadership had all been arrested in Scandinavia.[14] Wilhelm Knöchel was the only Central Committee member who successfully reached Germany. He crossed the Dutch-German border and established an organization centered in the Rhein-Ruhr region and in Berlin. Yet even he and his comrades had hardly any contacts with resistance groups established within Germany, which had become more active since the attack on the Soviet Union. The domestic groups emerged independently of party directives. The leading figures were mostly middle-level party functionaries, who in the first, "heroic phase" of the resistance had been arrested and had spent long years in prison and concentration camps. Most had been set free only in 1939/40. They had used contacts established in detention to build up, gradually and carefully, new networks, which would enable them to avoid past mistakes. Most of the groups also adopted defensive positions to protect themselves from exposure. The new tactics worked to the extent that significant opposition circles, fully isolated from one another, arose in industrial centers such as Berlin, Hamburg, Leipzig, Mannheim, and Magdeburg. The growing conviction that Germany would be defeated lent a new quality, a new determination, to the rejuvenated efforts to gather resistance forces. They began again to edit and distribute newspapers. Their works councils attempted individual acts of sabotage against armaments production. They promoted slowdowns in the factories and tried to establish contacts with the massive numbers of foreign forced laborers and prisoners of war.

A few of the groups with some hundreds of members, such as those under Robert Uhrig in Berlin, Georg Lechleiter in Mannheim, and Bernhard Bästlein in Hamburg, fell to the Gestapo as early as 1942.

Then too, the group around Herbert Baum, composed mostly of young Jews, was exposed by a spy shortly after its arson attack on an anti-Soviet exhibit in the Berlin Tiergarten – an action that passed virtually unnoticed by the public. The circle around Harro Schulze-Boysen, a first lieutenant in the Reich Air Force Ministry, and Arvid Harnack, a senior official (*Oberregierungsrat*) in the Reich Economics Ministry, was a special case. This group engaged in espionage for the Soviet Union alongside other resistance activities, but its members were also exposed and arrested in 1942.[15]

The organization created by Wilhelm Knöchel and his co-workers wrote and distributed hectographed newspapers – *Der Friedenskämpfer*, *Ruhr-Echo*, and *Freiheit* – , leaflets, small posters, and handbills. They called on the population to undertake actions designed to bring a quick end to the war. Yet Knöchel's group also fell into the hands of the Gestapo after only a year of secretive work. A Hitler Youth member had denounced to the Gestapo the activities of his conspiratorial father.[16]

Knöchel had established a radio connection to the Comintern through Amsterdam. With the destruction of his group, the last direct link was broken between the Politburo in Moscow and the German underground. Only the German-language broadcasts of Radio Moscow could have an influence on Communists inside Germany. But because the Nazis had imposed stiff penalties for listening to foreign broadcasts, the wider dissemination of foreign reports could cost an individual his or her life. The Soviets also sent agents into Germany by parachute. These were exiles who had been trained by the Red Army for informational tasks and who sought to establish contacts with illegal operatives in Germany. All of the participants, the parachutists and their domestic contacts, were caught and taken to the gallows.[17]

The members of the Berlin underground who had escaped the Gestapo net in 1942 were soon gathered together by Anton Saefkow, an experienced party functionary who finally in 1939 had been released from six years' detention. The new group was organized in a network of cells in numerous Berlin factories. The activists now included Social Democrats, trade unionists, former members of the worker sports associations of the Weimar Republic, and others who had not tended toward the KPD before 1933. A similar pattern prevailed in other regional resistance groups with which Saefkow established contact in 1943 to 1944. Along with Dr. Theodor Neubauer in Thuringia, Georg Schumann in Saxony (both members of the Reichstag before 1933 and imprisoned from 1933 to 1939), and Hermann Danz and Martin Schwantes in Magdeburg, Saefkow managed to establish in the autumn of 1943 a kind of Operative Leadership in Germany that sought to mobilize a broad resistance front throughout the country. Its theoretical positions delineating the character of Germany after the war diverged significantly from those adopted in the Soviet Union by the "National Committee for a Free Germany" (*Nationalkomitee "Freies Deutschland,"* or NKFD).[18] This body was established in July 1943 at Krasnogorsk upon Soviet initiative by exiled Communists and German prisoners of war in the Soviet Union. The NKFD called for a democratic Germany with strong nationalistic hues. In contrast, the resistance groups in Germany called for a socialist social order directed by a dictatorship of the proletariat. They did not align themselves with the position of "unity of the anti-fascist allies" but continued to speak of the "imperialist western powers." Nor did they envision the future leading role of the Soviet Union. Instead, they promoted a concept of an international order composed of fully equal socialist states.

The KPD's practical cooperation with non-communist forces took on a new dimension in the summer of 1944, when for the first time a large, anti-Hitler conspiratorial circle came into being with communist and social democratic members. But shortly after the encounter a spy let loose. The ensuing arrests, which took place before the 20 July 1944 assassination attempt on Hitler, completely destroyed the resistance organizations in Berlin, Saxony, Thuringia, and Magdeburg. A very high proportion of the hundreds arrested paid with their lives, including the entire leadership corps.[19]

The Communist resistance, both the reactivated one during the war as well as the broader movement in the first years of the National Socialist regime, along with the engagement of Communists in the emigration and those members, were daily threatened with death, in the concentration camps – all this is worth valuing as constituting an integral part of the all-too-weak opposition to National Socialism in Germany. Even when the KPD's own drastically mistaken policies made it partly responsible for the catastrophe of 1933, even if the struggle, at tremendous cost, in the underground remained without effect, even if the KPD ultimately was not in favor of a democratic alternative to Hitler – even in view of these factors, the Communists' unconditional will to take on a criminal regime deserves to be honored. And honored it has become, at long last and over tremendous political opposition, with the Memorial to the German Resistance in Berlin.[20]

Translated by Eric D. Weitz

Notes

1. See Hermann Weber, ed., *Die Generallinie: Rundschreiben des Zentralkomitees der KPD an die Bezirke 1929-1933* (Düsseldorf, 1981).
2. BAK, Kleine Erwerbungen 609/3, Rudolf Schlesinger.
3. See Beatrix Herlemann, *Die Emigration als Kampfposten: Die Anleitung des kommunistischen Widerstandes in Deutschland aus Frankreich, Belgien und den Niederlanden* (Königstein/Ts., 1982).
4. Herbert Wehner, *Zeugnis* (Cologne, 1982), 99-100.
5. Gerhard Paul, *"Deutsche Mutter – heim zu Dir!" Warum es mißlang, Hitler an der Saar zu schlagen. Der Saarkampf 1933-1935* (Cologne, 1984), and Klaus-Michael Mallmann and Gerhard Paul, *Das zersplitterte Nein: Saarländer gegen Hitler* (Bonn, 1989).
6. A very wide-ranging literature on resistance and persecution at the local and regional levels has appeared in the last twenty years. These works almost universally contain detailed chapters on the KPD at the local level. The initial impulse came from three research projects funded by the Friedrich-Ebert-Stiftung: Kurt Klotzbach, *Gegen den Nationalsozialismus: Widerstand und Verfolgung in Dortmund 1930-1945. Eine historisch-politische Studie* (Hanover, 1969); Hans-Josef Steinberg, *Widerstand und Verfolgung in Essen 1933-1945* (Hanover, 1969); and Kuno Bludau, *Gestapo geheim! Widerstand und Verfolgung in Duisburg 1933-1945* (Bonn, 1973). Detlev Peukert produced an exemplary monograph, *Die KPD im Widerstand: Verfolgung und Untergrundarbeit an Rhein und Ruhr 1933 bis 1945* (Wuppertal, 1980).
7. On the scope and content of the production of resistance literature, see Heinz Gittig, *Illegale antifaschistische Tarnschriften 1933-1945* (Leipzig, 1972); Peter Dohms, *Flugschriften in Gestapo-Akten: Nachweis und Analyse der Flugschriften in den Gestapo-Akten des Hauptstaatsarchives Düsseldorf* (Siegburg, 1977); and Jürgen Stroech, *Die illegale Presse: Ein Beitrag zur Geschichte und Bibliographie der illegalen antifaschistischen Presse 1933 bis 1939* (Leipzig, 1979). On the widespread retreat from illegal work see the works cited in n. 6. From the documentation of the numerous trials, it is clear that many of those who received and distributed illegal materials destroyed them without passing them on further. While these statements in part served as a means of self-defense before the court, Gestapo statistics demonstrate a sharp reduction in the volume of printed material that the authorities seized, confirming the change in view among the underground activists.
8. The only protocol of the conference available in Germany was in the party archive of the SED and was inaccessible to researchers until 1989. A selection of the speeches and comments, edited by Klaus Mammach, carefully excluded the critical elements of the discussion. Herbert Wehner's account, however, was more faithful to the record. See Klaus Mammach, ed., *Die Brüsseler Konferenz der KPD (3.-15. Oktober 1935)* (Berlin, 1975), and Wehner, *Zeugnis*, 148ff., including n. 4. Cf. also Peukert, *KPD im Widerstand.*
9. *Deutschland-Berichte der Sozialdemokratischen Partei Deutschlands (Sopade)*, reprint (Frankfurt am Main, 1980), vol. 1 (1934), 460.
10. See Frank Moraw, *Die Parole der "Einheit" und die Sozialdemokratie* (Bonn-Bad Godesberg, 1973), 38-42, 47-54; Hans-Dieter Schmid, "Einheitsfront von unten? Der organisierte Widerstand aus der Arbeiterschaft in Hildesheim 1933-1937," *Hildesheimer Jahrbuch* 63 (1992): 99-161; and for Calbe, BAK, Zwischenarchiv Dahlwitz-Hoppegarten, NJ 294/869/1278/10272.

11. Timothy W. Mason, *Sozialpolitik im Dritten Reich: Arbeiterklasse und Volksgemeinschaft* (Opladen, 1977), 206, and Wolfgang Zollitsch, "Die Vertrauensratswahlen von 1934 und 1935: Zum Stellenwert von Abstimmungen im 'Dritten Reich' am Beispiel Krupp," *Geschichte und Gesellschaft* 15:3 (1989): 361-81.
12. Ursula Langkau-Alex, *Volksfront für Deutschland?* (Frankfurt am Main, 1977), and idem, "Versuch und Scheitern der deutschen Volksfront," *Exil* 1 (1986): 19-37.
13. BAK, R58, Reichssicherheitshauptamt, passim.
14. Those arrested included Herbert Wehner, who soon afterwards left the KPD. In the postwar period he became one of the leading members of the SPD.
15. Luise Kraushaar, *Berliner Kommunisten im Kampf gegen den Faschismus 1936-1942: Robert Uhrig und Genossen* (Berlin, 1981); Erich Matthias and Hermann Weber, eds., *Widerstand gegen den Nationalsozialismus in Mannheim* (Mannheim, 1984); Konrad Kwiet, *Helmut Eschwege: Selbstbehauptung und Widerstand* (Hamburg, 1984); Hans Coppi, Jürgen Danyel, and Johannes Tuchel, *Die Rote Kapelle im Widerstand gegen den Nationalsozialismus* (Berlin, 1994).
16. Beatrix Herlemann, *Auf verlorenem Posten: Kommunistischer Widerstand im Zweiten Weltkrieg. Die Knöchel-Organisation* (Bonn, 1986).
17. Ibid., 76-78, and Günther Nollau and Ludwig Zindel, *Gestapo ruft Moskau: Sowjetische Fallschirmagenten im 2. Weltkrieg* (Munich, 1979).
18. The founding manifesto of the NKFD called for a sovereign, democratic German state after the fall of Hitler, which would guarantee individual rights and economic liberties while avoiding the weaknesses of the Weimar Republic. See Eva Bliembach, "Flugblattpropaganda des Nationalkomitees 'Freies Deutschland,'" in *Widerstand gegen den Nationalsozialismus*, ed. Peter Steinbach and Johannes Tuchel (Bonn, 1994), 488-94, and Alexander Fischer, entry on NKFD in *Lexikon des deutschen Widerstandes*, ed. Wolfgang Benz and Walter H. Pehle (Frankfurt am Main, 1994), 257-67.
19. See the scholarly articles on the individual groups in Benz and Pehle, *Lexikon des deutschen Widerstandes*, 190-91, 268, 288-92.
20. The Gedenk- und Bildungsstätte on Stauffenbergstraße at first concentrated only on the events of 20 July 1944. In the 1980s, a scholarly-based expansion of the exhibit was erected such that it now embraces the entire spectrum of the German Resistance. Writings, speeches, and academic conferences as well as popular exhibitions have been dedicated to the varied results and forms of the resistance against National Socialism.

Chapter 15

Rethinking Social Democracy, the State, and Europe

Rudolf Hilferding in Exile, 1933 to 1941

David E. Barclay

The years of repression and exile between 1933 and 1945 have long, and rightly, been regarded as a tragic caesura in the history of German social democracy. Although social democratic resistance to Nazi terror was both genuine and heroic, the fact remains that such opposition was largely ineffective, both within Germany and among the exiles who had left the country after 1933.[1] Still, for German socialists those twelve bitter years were marked by more than simply fruitless resistance, inner emigration, or bitter recrimination among various groups of exiles. Among other things, the catastrophe of 1933 inevitably encouraged many thoughtful Social Democrats to reflect critically upon the adequacy of the socialist project itself. In their effort to understand what had happened to them, to their movement, and to their values, they began to rethink the nature of Marxism, the essence of the modern state, the significance of organized modern terror in the context of modern dictatorship, and the appropriate roles of diplomacy and force in modern statecraft. Similarly, some Social Democrats began to think in critical and non-utopian ways about the contours of a new Europe after the destruction of fascism. Among those most deeply engaged with this process of reformulation and rethinking was Rudolf Hilferding, the Austrian-born physician turned economist who has almost universally been recognized as the SPD's foremost theoretician in this century.

Notes for this chapter begin on page 390.

This essay will trace Hilferding's efforts to make sense of the catastrophes of the 1930s. Hilferding's efforts will demonstrate that his reflections on these matters represented far more than an epilogue to his earlier, sometimes distinguished, and often controversial public career. Rather, his work in exile constituted an important and original chapter in his own extraordinary intellectual life: a life that was, however, savagely and prematurely cut short by the Vichy police and the Gestapo in 1941. In the final analysis, Hilferding's writings in exile did not directly affect the reconstructed SPD after 1945, but they do shed light on that party's evolution from *Klassenpartei* to *Volkspartei*, from the party of Erfurt to the party of Heidelberg and ultimately Bad Godesberg. This essay will explore the connections between Hilferding's ideas about the nature of the state in a "totalitarian" age, the future of Europe, and the prospects for those humanist and democratic values which had always underpinned his vision of socialism.[2] After reviewing his earlier life and career, it will consider his relationship to the rest of the exiled party leadership after 1933 and then turn to an evaluation of his activities in exile, especially his day-to-day political journalism.

1.

Rudolf Hilferding was an obvious target of Nazi thugs during the weeks and months that followed Hitler's accession to power on 30 January 1933, and on a couple of occasions he narrowly escaped potentially dangerous situations. On 23 March, he and his close associate Rudolf Breitscheid did not attend the notorious Reichstag session that approved the Enabling Act, and shortly thereafter both men went into exile along with other important party leaders. Hilferding first made his way to Denmark, and from there he proceeded to Saarbrücken, Paris, and, finally, Zurich, which remained his home for the next five years.[3] Although he maintained his contacts with the "Sopade," the newly established social democratic Executive Committee in exile, he chose not to live close to its headquarters in Czechoslovakia.[4] The distance between Hilferding and his old comrades was more than simply geographic. As a bourgeois, Jewish, Austrian intellectual, he had never been close to traditional SPD leaders like Otto Wels, and after his journey into exile he did not become an official member of the party's Prague Executive. Though he attended Sopade meetings and was still deeply involved with party journalism, his alienation and estrangement from much of the social democratic leadership steadily increased as the years passed. To all appearances, his earlier career as party intellectual and politician had been a failure, a series of blunders, errors, and miscalculations, culminating with the disaster of 1933.

Despite his "outsider" status, Hilferding had long been one of Europe's most influential socialists. Born into a white-collar Viennese family in 1877, he became attracted to socialism while still at school, and as a university student he became acquainted with an extraordinary array of exceptionally talented socialist intellectuals.[5] Although he studied medicine and worked as a practicing physician for a few years, his real interest lay in Marxist economics. By 1902 he had become a regular correspondent for *Neue Zeit*, one of the German Social Democrats' major journals, and in 1906 he moved to Berlin, where he taught at the SPD's party school before joining the editorial staff of *Vorwärts*, the party newspaper. Here he continued to enjoy the support of his fellow Austrian, Karl Kautsky, by far the most influential Marxist theorist in the Second International. In 1910 Hilferding's own reputation as a party intellectual and theoretician soared with the publication of *Finance Capital*, a work that is still rightly regarded as one of the most influential and original contributions to Marxist economics in this century.[6] This important analysis of modern financial structures and the development of monopoly capital was followed after the outbreak of World War I by further pathbreaking reflections on what Hilferding called "organized capitalism": that is, the development of centralized structures of planning and economic organization. These structures, in his view, helped to stabilize capitalist institutions and overcome the "anarchic" tendencies of the market. Thus, there was no guarantee that the war, itself a product of imperialist rivalries, would necessarily lead to the disappearance or the revolutionary transformation of world capitalism.[7]

How should socialists respond to this development? The answer, Hilferding suggested, was essentially *political*: the creation of a truly democratic socialism presupposed the democratic acquisition of state power by the working class itself. Only then could the contradictions of capitalist *Machtpolitik* be transcended, and the foundations laid for what Hilferding later called "economic democracy."[8] Accordingly, during the war years Hilferding rejected the politics of *Burgfrieden* and of class collaboration, and he criticized the reformist embrace of *Sozialpolitik* as a feeble substitute for real class – i.e., democratic political – struggle. Not surprisingly, he disagreed with the SPD's support for war credits in 1914, and in 1917 he joined the USPD. After the November Revolution, Hilferding edited the new party's newspaper, *Freiheit*, and continued to criticize the tepid caution of the majority party's leadership. His commitment to majoritarian and parliamentary democracy remained unbroken, and early on he rejected the violence and authoritarianism of the Bolsheviks. By 1922 he was back in the reunited SPD, where he quickly reemerged as one of the party's most prominent and visible spokespersons. After 1924 he edited *Die Gesellschaft*, the SPD's influential theoretical journal; he served as a member of the Reichstag; and on three occasions in the mid-1920s he was a keynote speaker at Social Democratic Party congresses. Hilferding played a crucial role in drafting the SPD's revised party program, which was adopted at the Heidelberg congress in 1925. More controversially, during the Weimar years he twice served as finance minister, first in the Gustav Stresemann cabinet during the hyperinflation crisis in 1923, and again in the cabinet of Hermann Müller in 1928 to 1929. On both occasions he had to resign under considerable political pressure. Most historians agree that, for all his intellectual acuity, Hilferding's career as a practical politician was less than successful.[9]

They also agree that, for all his putative radicalism, Hilferding shared considerable responsibility for the political failures of social democracy during the Weimar Republic. Even in his earlier writings, some scholars contend, Hilferding had begun to emphasize the relative autonomy of the state; he was never "economistic" in his views, nor was he reductionist or determinist. What ultimately mattered was who controlled the instruments of state power, and for what purposes. The modern state was not inevitably the instrument of finance capital, nor did it necessarily have to be violently transformed in the fashion of the Leninists. Indeed, by 1923 to 1924 Hilferding had come to the conclusion that the democratic state offered the working class the best possibilities for a permanent transformation of society and the gradual establishment of a genuine social democracy. Despite many missed opportunities after 1918, all was not lost. The war, followed by the establishment of a parliamentary republican system, had offered workers the chance ultimately to gain access to the levers of state power.[10] The state had become the "political instrument for the construction of socialism."[11] Therefore, one of the major tasks of social democracy after the stabilization crisis was both ideological and "educational": namely, to come up with a "functional explanation" of the development and character of the modern democratic state. In other words, as Harold James has described Hilferding's views, "Democracy represented an *opportunity* to extend the range of political rhetoric beyond class interests: it was through the assertion of general or national interests that the labor movement could increase its leverage over the political game" – and, thus, lay the foundations for "economic democracy."[12] Moreover, by emphasizing its commitment to parliamentary democracy, the SPD could ultimately make itself attractive to social groups beyond the working class. The one-time radical had become a parliamentary reformist and, in practice, an advocate of coalition arrangements with bourgeois parties and of the evolution of the SPD itself into a pluralistic *Volkspartei* in a pluralistic state.[13]

Hilferding's arguments helped to provide a theoretical justification for the SPD's participation in government between 1928 and 1930 – in which, as we have already noted, Hilferding served as finance minister. Unfortunately, Hilferding's assumptions about the potential of the democratic state in Germany were far too optimistic, as events after 1929 to 1930 clearly demonstrated.[14] Moreover, following his own resignation as finance minister in December 1929 and the collapse of Hermann Müller's government several months later, Hilferding vigorously supported his party's "toleration" of Heinrich Brüning's economic and fiscal policies. At the same time, as a rather orthodox economic thinker, he opposed innovative anti-deflationary proposals to alleviate the crisis, such as the work-creation proposals advanced in the "WTB Plan" of 1931.[15] As a result, he has often been roundly criticized for justifying the fatalism, passivity, and unimaginativeness of the established SPD leadership during the crisis years of the early 1930s: years that, it seemed, apparently demonstrated the inadequacy of his own theory of political pluralism and the democratic state.

In short, Rudolf Hilferding was an immensely complex man, at once influential and an outsider, at once a brilliantly acute and dangerously myopic observer of his own society and his own political movement. According to virtually all contemporary observers, he remained a bundle of contradictions. He was always a passionate, morally committed socialist. As a practical economist, however, he was in many ways resolutely liberal; in the words of one Social Democrat who knew Hilferding well, "Adam Smith and Ricardo would have enjoyed him." He was a bourgeois *bon vivant* who enjoyed good food and fine cigars. He got on well with conservative politicians like Heinrich Brüning and literati like Harry Graf Kessler, while within his own party he always seemed a bit out of place.[16] As one of his younger contemporaries said of him many years later, "He lives in my memory as a man of high intellectual gifts and an irreparable shortage of practicality and of the ability to act. He was not a political fighter. He was not a politician by temperament."[17]

2.

Reflecting in his new Swiss exile on his own circumstances and those of Germany itself, Hilferding continued to defend the SPD's policies in the years just before 1933 as "necessary and correct," and he insisted that an alternative policy would not have led to a different outcome. Just the same, the German working class itself had failed to stand up for democracy, for freedom, and for the Republic; and he was under no illusions about the magnitude of the defeat that democratic forces in Germany had just suffered. Because the National Socialists had seized control of the levers of state power, they were now in a position to consolidate their authority. Thus, Hilferding concluded, "I am rather pessimistic about the future. The whole matter can last for a long time."[18]

Hilferding's own straitened circumstances, both personally and within the party, exacerbated that pessimism. For months he was deeply depressed, and his financial situation was parlous. Instead of moving to Prague with the rest of the exiled leadership, he remained in Zurich, where he lived in a small hotel, personally isolated and frequently separated from his wife, who preferred to stay in Paris. In Zurich, Hilferding was visited by a fairly small circle of close friends, especially Oscar Meyer, an exiled liberal and a former member of the German Democratic Party.[19]

As a result, he remained a political outsider within the exile community, if not among other European socialists. For six years he served as a Sopade representative to the Labor and Socialist International, which gave him ample opportunity to travel and maintain his contacts with like-minded colleagues in Western Europe.[20] Among exiled German Social Democrats, however, only Wilhelm Hoegner (Bavarian Minister President after World War II) and, to a lesser extent, Rudolf Breitscheid and Paul Hertz saw him with any regularity.[21] Moreover, Hilferding's reputation within the party as a whole had been seriously weakened, as we have already noted, because of his own strong association with the SPD's failed policies after 1929 to 1930. As always, he was most effective as a theorist and a journalist, and in June 1933 he began to write regularly for *Neuer Vorwärts*, the party's newspaper in exile edited by Friedrich Stampfer. Here and elsewhere Hilferding wrote under the pseudonym "Dr. Richard Kern." He also became involved with efforts to create a new theoretical journal to succeed *Die Gesellschaft*.[22] Once again, though, he encountered the suspicion and resentment of several colleagues. The traumatic circumstances of defeat and exile had exacerbated massive discontent and unhappiness, both at home and in exile, with the existing leadership, and gave an impetus to critical members of the old party Left who believed that Hilferding's passivity had cost him his political credibility. Among them were two new members of the Sopade, the veteran leftists Heinrich Böchel and Siegfried Aufhäuser, "who demanded a complete break with the evolutionary socialist-democratic tradition."[23] Speaking at a meeting of the party Executive on 7 July 1933, Böchel contended that Hilferding should on no account edit the proposed theoretical journal, arguing that an "intellectual reorientation is necessary." Despite these reservations, Hilferding was named to edit the journal, the *Zeitschrift für Sozialismus*, with the respected Curt Geyer serving as editor for domestic affairs.[24]

Surprisingly, perhaps, Hilferding at first seemed to sympathize with his critics on the Left. Calling for a repudiation of the SPD's failed policies, he contended that radical, truly revolutionary "political action" had become necessary if German fascism were to be overthrown. The triumph of National Socialism was itself one particular expression of the general crisis of capitalism. Despite the revolutionary tenor of the age, the Hitler regime had succeeded in depoliticizing the German people while creating at the same time "a broad mass basis" to a much greater extent even than the Bolsheviks or the Italian Fascists. As a result, "The total state, as the Fascists and National Socialists describe their dictatorship, is characterized by the emergence of an absolute state power and its simultaneous, monstrous expansion."[25] In view of these new circumstances, Social Democrats would have to reformulate radically their ideas about the relationship of socialist political organizations to modern state absolutism. The first significant result of this reformulation was the Sopade's "Prague Manifesto."

Hilferding was the principal author of this statement, which was published in late January 1934 under the title "Struggle and Goal of Revolutionary Socialism."[26] He had not been satisfied with the Sopade's original draft, which had been prepared by Curt Geyer, Erich Rinner, and Friedrich Stampfer; the time had come, he said, to move beyond "declamations" and rhetoric.[27] The result was an apparently radical call for disciplined action by an organized, revolutionary elite to smash the fascist state and create a revolutionary dictatorship, at least on a temporary basis. Only a "total revolution" could displace the "total state" in Germany. And only if the labor movement again became an effective mass movement could it hope to reestablish democratic structures and institutions within the country. Barring a war, only revolutionary violence could topple the Nazi regime, and in the wake of such violence it would be necessary to avoid the mistakes of 1918. Thus, the Prague Manifesto called for such things as the establishment of a revolutionary tribunal, an effective purge of the civil service, the judiciary, and the military, and the genuine socialization of the means of production and exchange in the context of a rigorous system of economic planning. In a subsequent commentary on the Manifesto, Hilferding noted that Social Democrats had no choice but to resort to techniques of illegality and even armed struggle in their efforts to overthrow the regime. As a result, the party's leaders had opted for a "radical break with reformism ... in order to achieve the socialist transformation of society."[28]

Although critics on the socialist Left remained skeptical about the Sopade's apparent political shift, others regarded the Prague Manifesto as unprecedentedly "revolutionary"; and one recent scholar agrees with this assessment, describing the document as "the most radical program" in the history of social democracy.[29] In fact, though, the Prague Manifesto did not represent a fundamental break in Hilferding's own political and intellectual evolution. His rather short-lived espousal of revolutionary violence was itself conditioned by his perceptions of the nature and character of the modern state. The Prague Manifesto may have seemed quasi-Leninist in its affirmation of conspiratorial action by a trained revolutionary elite, but Hilferding believed that the brutal realities of the repressive Nazi state had made such methods unavoidable. For one thing, that state had become a kind of autonomous essence in itself. Moreover, the victory of National Socialism had not represented the triumph of a "small ruling clique," but was the result of an "active mass movement."[30] Accordingly, the anti-fascist struggle could not and did not represent a new variant of old-fashioned forms of class struggle. It was something different. Although certain bourgeois interests had thought that they would benefit from fascist rule in Germany, National Socialism represented a new and unprecedented form of barbarism. It was not simply an epiphenomenon of bourgeois society. Thus, the struggle against the total state would require the radical seizure and transformation of state power by the foes of Nazism.[31]

At no time, however, did Hilferding endorse Leninist ideas about the restructuring of German society *after* the violent destruction of the National Socialist regime. Indeed, his own notions about socialization and economic planning were quite consistent with the views he had espoused as an Independent Social Democrat after 1918. He also insisted that the struggle against fascism represented a higher form of struggle, higher even than old-fashioned class struggle: it represented a defense of civilization itself, of the universal and humane values that had developed over the course of centuries.[32] To be sure, he admitted that a post-Nazi revolutionary regime might well turn into a "*dictatorship against the working class*," as in the Soviet Union. But at this stage, at least, the seizure of state power and the destruction of fascism represented the most urgent and pressing task that German socialists faced. Everything else was secondary.[33]

Although the Prague Manifesto generated considerable discussion within the ranks of German exiles, its effects were nugatory, while its contributions to working-class unity or even to unity among the exiles themselves were derisory. The group around Aufhäuser and Böchel, who were finally expelled from the party in 1935, remained strongly critical of the document.[34] The Prague Manifesto had reflected an assumption that, sooner rather than later, the Nazi regime would lurch toward crisis as a result of its own contradictions and its own failures. At first Hilferding himself believed that the Nazis had not succeeded in overcoming Germany's economic crisis. The Nazi policy of militarization would, thus, lead to wild inflation, to a dismantling of the country's remaining social-welfare institutions, and to its international isolation. Such developments would work to the advantage of a revolutionary working-class movement.[35]

Hilferding and many of his colleagues continued to adhere to these notions throughout much of 1934.[36] After the Röhm Putsch of late June, Hilferding contended that the regime had failed on three critically important fronts. Its financial and economic policies were chaotic; diplomatically, Hitler had maneuvered himself into a position of "isolation and complete powerlessness"; and the brutality of the putsch itself had delivered a severe blow to the semi-religious "mystique" which had sustained the National Socialist leadership for a long time. This situation alone would not lead to a revolutionary crisis, but it demonstrated that the National Socialist state was dangerously exposed; certainly, it could accelerate the revolutionary seizure of state power.[37]

By the middle of 1935, however, it had become clear to Hilferding that these hopes were illusory and that the National Socialist regime was not going to be displaced in the near future. For one thing, economic conditions had begun to stabilize against the expectations both of "vulgar" economic liberals and of "vulgar" Marxists. This stabilization reflected the "extraordinary strengthening of state power, which has established its relative autonomy vis-à-vis society and its individual social classes and strata."[38] This critically important insight – that the power of the state had become independent and autonomous, and not necessarily a reflection of class or productive relationships – was, as we have seen, rooted in Hilferding's older ideas of organized capitalism and the evolution of the modern state; it now became the leitmotif of virtually all his writings in exile after 1935. In a world shaped by what he came to call "totalitarian state power," foreign policy, war, and diplomacy themselves had gained an autonomy that was far from merely superstructural in the sense of what Hilferding dismissed as "vulgar" Marxism. Indeed, everything else had become secondary to them. The National Socialist regime, Hilferding concluded, was placing its economy on a war footing and had consolidated its total control over the levers of state power. Thus, it faced no serious internal challenges, and to suggest otherwise was foolish.[39]

Well before his last theoretical writings of 1940, Hilferding had also concluded that the fascist regimes and the Soviet Union shared a number of structural similarities, although, like most social democratic commentators of the 1930s, he used the term "totalitarian" with a certain amount of conceptual imprecision.[40] In an important essay that appeared in late 1936, for example, Hilferding traced the history of the fascist regimes to the great-power competition that had preceded the world war. During that conflict the state had finally asserted its domination over the economy, and in virtually all the combatant nations "the last remnants of economic liberalism were submerged." This "acceptance of state omnipotence continued into the crises of the postwar period," especially in countries like Germany and Russia. Under dictatorships the state had penetrated and absorbed civil society into itself. Moreover, the foreign-policy aims of the totalitarian states were both simple and primitive: "The supreme goal of the totalitarian state apparatus is the maintenance and expansion of its power." Its economies had become primitive, and, thus, the expansionism of the dictators had little to do with the sophisticated finance-capital imperialism of the era before the world war. Rather, it represented a new kind of "primitive accumulation," analogous in some ways to the predatory expansionism of European states during the sixteenth and seventeenth centuries.[41]

At the same time that the fascist regimes were pursuing their own primitive state interests, Hilferding added, the Soviet Union was essentially doing the same thing. In sharp contrast to other socialists who argued that, for all their disappointments, the Soviet Union was still worth defending, Hilferding insisted that Stalin's state had long since abandoned any claim to speak for the international working class: "Communist ideology increasingly stood in the service of Russian power politics; Russian power was not in the service of the communist idea .... Russian power politics are derived from other motives than the interests of the labor movement, and thus they are shaped by other laws."[42] Of course, Hilferding's hostility to the Soviet Union was of long standing, while throughout the years of exile he continued to blame the KPD for the divisions within the German labor movement. Germany's Communists were agents of Moscow's own state interests; long before 1933 they had "become objective helpers of reaction," and as a result the "divided working class had become the prey of fascism."[43] Thus, he remained deeply skeptical about the utility of popular fronts, abjuring the possibility of fruitful collaboration either with the Soviet Union or with foreign Communists.[44]

Hilferding's skepticism regarding cooperation with the Communists was entirely consistent with his views on the "totalitarian" state, and, above all, his tendency to stress the functional, economic, and organizational similarities between the Soviet Union and the fascist powers. As William Smaldone has noted, Hilferding had begun to develop these ideas at least as early as 1935 to 1936: that is, at the height of popular front-style collaboration among anti-fascist forces in Europe.[45] By 1937, in fact, Hilferding was denouncing the Soviet regime as a "*Stalin-Faschismus*";[46] and in an important article published in November 1937, he tried to demonstrate, more clearly than in most of his previous writings, that Bolshevism and fascism were historically linked phenomena. Both were products of the world war, which had "destroyed the power of the state in the defeated countries, shaken the structure of society, and opened the way for determined, well-organized groups to seize power violently and to use violence to sustain themselves in power." In revolutionary Russia, the Bolsheviks had succeeded for the first time in separating the idea of socialism from the idea of freedom, and had created a new kind of "total state power" in which ordinary people had become "slaves of the state." It had created a new kind of despotism; and, although Hilferding speculated elsewhere (and privately) that Stalin personally might be "paranoid," he insisted that the phenomenon of Stalinism was the logical consequence of Leninism.[47] At the same time, Hilferding continued, the victory of the Bolsheviks had ensured that their ideology had become an "independent" factor in global politics, with special appeal to societies with "denatured democracies" in which the "drive for personal and political freedom had struck the most shallow roots." But just as Soviet-style Bolshevism had a powerful resonance among the oppressed masses in these societies, "the fascist-nationalist ideology has now placed itself in opposition to Bolshevik ideology. It has adopted the doctrine of the total state, the denial of democracy, and the rejection of intellectual and political freedom. In the cruelty of its methods it does not lag behind its prototype." In short, despite important differences in social composition and ideological appeal, Bolshevik and fascist ideologies ultimately pointed to similar outcomes: a new kind of "total state" based on a rejection of the democratic values that alone made the "struggle for social emancipation" possible.[48]

Unfortunately, the main defenders of democratic values – France and Britain – had become hopelessly enfeebled. Although Hilferding's articles between 1935 and 1939 sometimes expressed the desperate hope that Britain would finally realize that Hitler's Germany was boundlessly "predatory" and even preparing for "total war," for the most part he remained deeply pessimistic. France's response to the civil war in Spain clearly demonstrated, he said, that it had become a "second-rate power," while Britain's foreign policy was "completely aimless."[49] Only after the Sudeten crisis, Hilferding complained, had it finally become clear to the British that Germany's appetites were boundless, and that the Munich accords had represented not an end to the danger of war but rather a "beginning with no end."[50]

Moreover, he believed, it was an illusion to take the anti-communism of the fascist powers very seriously. Arrangements like the Anti-Comintern Pact were a sham; and, though the fascist states represented a "bloc of aggressors" that was aiming for a "new division of the world," their aggressive designs did not necessarily pose a threat to the Soviet Union.[51] According to Hilferding, it was, thus, entirely logical and consistent that the Soviet Union would conclude its notorious Non-Aggression Pact with Germany on 23 August 1939; and the coming of the war itself on 1 September was its equally logical outcome.[52] As he sarcastically put it in an article published the next day in *Neuer Vorwärts*, "Since discovering that Hitler is a worthy adversary, Stalin has succeeded in reducing foreign policy to the criminal level that has always characterized his domestic policy: *Par nobile fratrum*, what fine little brothers, *Parteigenosse* Stalin and *tovarish* Hitler! Which of these two is now the anti-Bolshevik, and which the anti-fascist?" Their alliance had demonstrated once and for all that there was little essential difference among the dictatorships: "There is no difference in outlook and morals among the dictators, and they will all end up in the same damnation, regardless of whether they are ruling in the name of a proletarian dictatorship or in the name of National Socialism. *Dictatorship means ruin, and whoever supports it is the enemy and must be treated accordingly*."[53] When he wrote those words, Hilferding was confident that, despite the failures of their pre-war appeasement policies, the military power of France and Britain would be sufficient to meet the challenge of a Germany that he believed was economically vulnerable and even ill-prepared for war. He would soon be tragically disabused of this illusion.

3.

Hilferding himself witnessed the outbreak of the war in Paris, where he had moved in early 1938. The Sopade had also relocated to Paris in early 1938 as a result of growing pressure from the Czech government, which had not wanted to offend the Germans. In the last few years of his life Hilferding, thus, became more active in party affairs than he had been for many years; as we have seen, he continued to write actively for the party press, and after the summer of 1938 he participated regularly in meetings of the party Executive.[54] When the war came, he remained in Paris and continued to take part in party affairs; indeed, he was relatively confident that the German war machine would soon sputter out. In the months before the war he had argued that German military spending had become an "insatiable Moloch" that would impoverish the country and leave it ill-prepared for war.[55] Even in late April 1940, Hilferding was confident that the Nazi invasion of Scandinavia would end in a disaster for the German war effort. Germany would be unable to maintain imports of Swedish iron ore, and, as a result, "Hitler's defeat is becoming clearer and clearer."[56] Only a few weeks later, German forces entered the Low Countries and then France itself. Hilferding was able to escape to the unoccupied zone in the south of the country; by August he had made his way to Marseille with his fellow German socialists Rudolf Breitscheid, Tony Breitscheid, and Erika Müller-Biermann (the daughter of Hermann Müller, Germany's last SPD Chancellor). Léon Blum, Heinrich Brüning, and others tried to arrange exit visas for the refugees. In September, however, the Vichy police forced Breitscheid and Hilferding to leave Marseille for Arles, where the two men continued to wait for exit visas or alternative means of escape.[57]

During that turbulent year of upheaval and despair, Rudolf Hilferding developed his last – and in many ways most important – reflections on the nature of the totalitarian state, on the future of democracy, and on the future of a Europe liberated from the demons of dictatorship. Two of the essays that he composed that year were subsequently published and have frequently been analyzed. The first, "State Capitalism or Totalitarian State Economy," was written at the invitation of his Russian friend, Boris Nikolaevskii, and originally appeared in April 1940 in the Menshevik exile journal *Sotsialisticheskii vestnik*. In it Hilferding responded to an argument that had been advanced by R. L. Worrall, who contended that the Soviet Union was not yet socialist, but had become a "state capitalist" economy. Hilferding vehemently rejected this view, insisting that, without a functioning market, it was absurd to speak of "state capitalism" in the Soviet context. It was also absurd to think that the functions of capitalist owners or managers had been assumed by Soviet bureaucrats. In fact, the Soviet Union was a "totalitarian state economy" dependent upon the whims and wishes of its ruling clique and especially Stalin himself. The Communist Party had been "an instrument in the hands of its leaders" from the very beginning, and by creating an "unlimited personal dictatorship" it anticipated the practice of fascist and national socialist movements as well: "In this way it created the first *totalitarian state*, even before this term had been invented." Thus, the Soviet experience demonstrated two things: first, the Bolshevik economic system could hardly be described as socialist, as socialism is inextricably bound up with democracy; and, second, that in modern times and especially in totalitarian societies, as Hilferding had argued for years, the state had assumed an autonomous and even dominant position relative to the economy.[58]

The latter argument figured prominently in another essay, "Das historische Problem," which Hilferding composed at Arles in September 1940. Published posthumously in 1954, it is essentially a fragment, the beginning of an unfinished revision of Hilferding's understanding of Marxism. In it Hilferding reflects on the role of violence and, indeed, of "subjective" or psychological factors throughout history. Violence was an independent variable, and one which often played a decisive role in human affairs. Moreover, Hilferding again insisted that the modern state had achieved a degree of autonomy which in turn necessitated a revision of Marxist notions of the historical process. Marxists, thus, had to rethink their ideas about causality, class, the class struggle, and the role of relations of production in history.[59] The essay was very much a product of the time and circumstances in which it was written, and its conclusions remain fragmentary and, as its critics have noted, contradictory. These critics also allege that Hilferding had failed, in this essay and elsewhere, to understand the truly dialectical qualities of Marx's own thinking, and especially the extent to which, in Marx's view, the class struggle was a political struggle and not simply determined by economic factors. Moreover, they continue, Hilferding's schematic interpretation of Marxism reflected a misunderstanding that was widespread among German Social Democrats.[60] These theoretical objections to Hilferding's ideas may or may not be true, and, in the present historical conjuncture at the end of the twentieth century, they are probably a bit anachronistic. More important is the fact that Hilferding's essay represents the culmination of a long-standing attempt to find a new basis for social democratic understandings of the modern state (especially the new phenomenon of the "totalitarian state"), the relationships between states, and the possibility of political action to maximize freedom and universal, humane values in a time in which these values were everywhere under attack.

These same concerns inform the third significant piece that Hilferding wrote in 1940. Composed at about the same time as his article for *Sotsialisticheskii vestnik*, it took the form of an oral presentation to the Sopade in late January 1940: that is, before the fall of France and before the traumas that so obviously shaped his reflections in "Das historische Problem." Although it has scarcely been noticed in the historical literature, it is of considerable interest, largely because of Hilferding's discussion of war aims and his speculations on the future of democracy and on the shape of Europe after the defeat of fascism.[61]

The Sopade had been discussing the likely shape and course of the war several months before its actual outbreak in September 1939, so his remarks of January 1940 represented an elaboration on ideas that he had been developing since at least April 1939.[62] His view regarding the fundamental aim of the war was quite simple: an Allied victory had to be achieved at all costs, especially now that the Soviet Union, "the other barbarian great power," had linked itself to Nazi Germany. The war represented quite simply a struggle on behalf of universal, humane values, and if Hitler were to win, "then the entire basis of the cultural development for which we have worked will no longer exist. We will then have to reckon with a setback of centuries."[63] Thus, the complete victory of the Allies was the necessary precondition for the democratic reconstruction of Europe after the war.

In contrast to other German and Austrian exiles, however, Hilferding was not convinced that a postwar European federation was desirable or even possible.[64] A federal state in Europe would inevitably require a powerful "central authority" *(Zentralgewalt)*. Where, in an individual country like Germany, a federal state would weaken the power of the central state, some sort of central body or structure would still have to be created at the continental level. A second problem, Hilferding noted, concerned the participants in such a federation. In its present form, Russia would necessarily have to be excluded, while Great Britain absolutely had to join; and, in any case, a postwar European federation would have to take account of the concrete military and economic interests of both Britain and France. He was skeptical that either country would (or should) sacrifice any of its vital interests for the sake of membership in a European federation.

The reorganization of Europe would, thus, have to take place within the context of a renewed and regenerated League of Nations. Despite its failures, which Hilferding largely attributed to the shortcomings of British policies, the old League had served a useful purpose, and a new League could be even more effective. But one should avoid the utopias and illusions of the period after World War I. Even a more vigorous League would not be an "absolute guarantee of peace."[65] The new League, he continued, should not be limited to Europe; Great Britain would want to incorporate its Empire and Commonwealth into the new body, and the active participation of the United States would also be critically necessary. Finally, a rejuvenated League of Nations and a federated Europe would inevitably require that their members surrender at least part of their sovereignty. A total Allied victory might make such an arrangement possible.

Throughout his remarks, Hilferding emphasized how important it was not to be led astray by idle or utopian speculation. A democratic reorganization of Europe, he stressed, could only take place within the context of concrete power relationships. Thus, he argued strongly against the idea of Allied disarmament after the war and admitted that, in this respect, his own ideas about militarism had changed. Social Democrats had earlier been convinced that "militarism is the same in all countries," but this view had been a mistake: "The institution in itself is not decisive, but rather the use that is made of it."[66] The situation in Europe and in the Far East would be dangerous for years to come, and general disarmament in postwar Europe would be foolish.

Economic cooperation would have to be one of the hallmarks of a democratic postwar order, though here too, Hilferding asserted, it was necessary to avoid exaggerated expectations. Such cooperation would have to be based on free trade, which he had long supported. Still, it would not be possible instantly to introduce full-scale free trade to Europe, or to create a European customs union *(Zollverein)*; years of protectionism had created distortions that could only gradually be eliminated. A new, cooperative European economic system would also have to address the question of raw materials and natural resources. Although Germany's raw materials had been entirely sufficient for its recovery after World War I, the raw-materials question had been a deeply emotional one, and future European leaders would have to take account of such matters.

Finally, a new Europe would have to address the problem of nationalism. From his vantage point in early 1940, Hilferding assumed that nationalism would remain a powerful force even in a defeated Germany. Still, a permanent peace could only be created if Europeans recognized that there was in fact no absolute right to national self-determination. Thus, Germany should not expect to keep Austria or the Sudetenland after the war was over. Indeed, Hilferding had noted on an earlier occasion that he had been opposed to *Anschluß* since 1919.[67] He agreed with his fellow Austrian socialist, Karl Renner, that individual peoples had a right to cultural autonomy, but they did not necessarily have a right to an independent state. In Central and Eastern Europe it would be impossible to create a stable postwar order on the basis of the "principle of nationality." A plethora of national states in those regions would lead only to instability and crisis. Accordingly, those parts of Europe would especially benefit from an effective postwar federation.

Obviously, Hilferding's comments reflect the conditions that existed shortly after the war's outbreak, and surely he can be forgiven for not having foreseen the course that the conflict would take and for not having prophesied the rapid decline of Europe's political influence after 1945. Moreover, he did not anticipate the Nazi attack on the Soviet Union, or the emergence of the Soviet Union and the United States as postwar superpowers. Still, his analysis is interesting for several reasons. Many Social Democrats had been speculating for a long time on the future of the German nation and its relationship to a democratic, post-Hitler European order.[68] Although Hilferding exaggerated the continuing influence and significance of France and especially Britain, his analysis of the prospects of a future "League of Nations" and of a European federal state were rather prescient – even as they hint at a kind of nostalgia for the Habsburg Monarchy of his own youth. His faith in postwar economic cooperation, his belief in the continued importance of a global security system, his cautious commitment to an effective federalism on the basis of a credible armed force and limitations on sovereignty, his doubts about the future role of the Soviet Union, and his skepticism about the right of national self-determination suggest that he had come a long way since 1910; in some respects his ideas anticipate some of the directions that social democratic foreign and economic policies were to take, especially after 1959.[69]

Hilferding himself was never able to witness or help to shape the lineaments of the postwar order. As we have already noted, in September 1940 Hilferding and Breitscheid were required to move from Marseille to Arles. The two men had never been truly close friends, and in Arles Hilferding reported that he was cut off from news of the outside world and that he was suffering from a "deep depression" and "almost a kind of solitary confinement psychosis."[70] A number of people had been attempting to rescue the two German socialists, but all their efforts – legal and illegal – to get them out of the country were in vain.[71] Finally, in late January 1941, it seemed that they might indeed be able to leave Vichy France. They were granted exit visas and were preparing to depart, when suddenly their visas were rescinded.[72] In early February they were arrested by Vichy police. The circumstances of Hilferding's subsequent death were rather mysterious; but the most thorough research suggests that, on the night of 10 February 1941, he took an overdose of poison and died two or three days later. Rudolf Breitscheid was sent to Berlin and thence to Buchenwald, where he met his death in August 1944.[73]

4.

It would be an idle exercise in counterfactual history to speculate on how Hilferding's views might have evolved had he survived the war. Although, as we have noted, the ideas that he had developed during his years in exile anticipated some of the directions that European Social Democrats took after 1945, they certainly had no influence on postwar debates and discussions. Nor is there any evidence that he prophesied those postwar sociological transformations of the working class (and, indeed, of Western European societies generally) that encouraged the SPD's transformation from a *Klassenpartei* into a *Volkspartei* anchored in a mixed, "social market economy." Certainly, though, his last writings of 1940 suggest that, as some scholars have emphasized, he had indeed distanced himself from the Marxism of his earlier years. But these writings do not represent a radical intellectual rupture or departure from his earlier notions; as we have seen, his post-1933 ideas about the modern state evolved logically from the positions that he had taken before 1933. Like Jacob Burckhardt before him, Hilferding had come to regard the modern state as an autonomous essence, and not simply as the expression of a particular set of class interests or as an epiphenomenon of systems and relationships of production. The state could achieve positive ends, or it could be perverted for monstrous purposes. Thus, vigorous institutional safeguards were necessary to limit the dangers inherent in uncontrolled state power. Parliamentary democracy and constitutional institutions consequently represented the *sine qua non* of socialism. Democracy and socialism were inevitably bound up with each other; and, as Klaus Voigt has put it, Hilferding remained convinced that democratic institutions alone could maintain "the cultural and spiritual unity" of Europe against the assault of the totalitarian dictators.[74] This understanding of democracy was deeply rooted in Germany's social democratic traditions, and it gained new life and new vigor in the postwar SPD. And so Hilferding, despite the tragedy of his life and the understandable limitations of his vision, does indeed represent a kind of intellectual bridge between the older party of August Bebel and Karl Kautsky and the newer party of Willy Brandt and Helmut Schmidt.

Notes

1. Richard Löwenthal, "Widerstand im totalen Staat," in *Widerstand und Verweigerung in Deutschland 1933 bis 1945*, ed. Richard Löwenthal and Patrik von zur Mühlen (Bonn, 1984), 13.
2. On Hilferding's contribution to the "totalitarianism" debate, see André Liebich, "Marxism and Totalitarianism: Rudolf Hilferding and the Mensheviks," *Dissent* 34: 2 (Spring 1987): 223-40. A fuller version of this essay, with endnotes, appeared in 1986 as Occasional Paper No. 217 of the Kennan Institute for Advanced Russian Studies, Washington, DC. See also Walter Laqueur, *The Dream That Failed: Reflections on the Soviet Union* (New York, 1994), 78-79; Abbott Gleason, *Totalitarianism: The Inner History of the Cold War* (New York, 1995), 47. On Hilferding's humanism and intellectual consistency, see Harold James, "Rudolf Hilferding and the Application of the Political Economy of the Second International," *The Historical Journal* 24: 4 (1981): 848-49.
3. Heinrich August Winkler, *Der Weg in die Katastrophe: Arbeiter und Arbeiterbewegung in der Weimarer Republik 1930 bis 1933*, 2nd ed. (Bonn, 1990), 878; Erich Matthias, "Die Sozialdemokratische Partei Deutschlands," in *Das Ende der Parteien 1933*, ed. Erich Matthias and Rudolf Morsey (Düsseldorf, 1960), 166-72, esp. 171 n. 23; Donna Harsch, *German Social Democracy and the Rise of Nazism* (Chapel Hill, NC, 1993), 347 n. 200; William Thomas Smaldone, "Rudolf Hilferding: The Tragedy of a German Social Democrat" (Ph.D. diss., State University of New York at Binghamton, 1990), 446-47, 464.
4. On the establishment of the Sopade, see most recently Marlis Buchholz and Bernd Rother, eds., *Der Parteivorstand der SPD im Exil: Protokolle der Sopade 1933-1940* (Bonn, 1995), xiii-xiv.
5. William Smaldone's dissertation, "Rudolf Hilferding: The Tragedy of a German Social Democrat," is thorough, though its central thesis – that Hilferding was tragically transformed from a young radical into an unimaginative supporter of the SPD's conservative oligarchy – is overdrawn. A revised version will be published in 1998. On Hilferding's intellectual development, see Wilfried Gottschalch, *Strukturveränderungen der Gesellschaft und politisches Handeln in der Lehre von Rudolf Hilferding* (Berlin, 1962); and Horst Klein, "Zu den Gesellschaftsideen Rudolf Hilferding's," *Beiträge zur Geschichte der Arbeiterbewegung* 33: 1 (1991): 25-36. See also Cora Stephan, ed., *Zwischen den Stühlen oder über die*

Unvereinbarkeit von Theorie und Praxis: Schriften Rudolf Hilferding's 1904 bis 1940 (Bonn, 1982); Minoru Kurata, "Rudolf Hilferding: Bibliographie seiner Schriften, Artikel und Briefe," *IWK* 10: 3 (1974): 327-46. See also the biographical surveys in Alexander Stein, *Rudolf Hilferding und die deutsche Arbeiterbewegung: Gedenkblätter* (Hamburg, 1946); Werner Blumenberg, *Kämpfer für die Freiheit* (Berlin, 1959), 141-47; *Biographisches Handbuch der deutschsprachigen Emigration nach 1933*, vol. 1: *Politik, Wirtschaft, Öffentliches Leben*, ed. Werner Röder and Herbert A. Strauss (Munich, 1980), 295-96; Walter Euchner, "Rudolf Hilferding (1877-1941): Kühne Dialektik und verzweifeltes Zaudern," in *Vor dem Vergessen bewahren: Lebenswege Weimarer Sozialdemokraten*, ed. Peter Lösche, Michael Scholing, and Franz Walter (Berlin, 1988), 170-92. F. Peter Wagner, *Rudolf Hilferding: Theory and Politics of Democratic Socialism* (Atlantic Highlands, NJ, 1996), appeared too late to be consulted in detail here.

6. Rudolf Hilferding, *Das Finanzkapital: Eine Studie über die jüngste Entwicklung des Kapitalismus* (Frankfurt am Main, 1968; orig. 1910).
7. Heinrich August Winkler, "Einleitende Bemerkungen zu Hilferding's Theorie des Organisierten Kapitalismus," in *Organisierter Kapitalismus: Voraussetzungen und Anfänge*, ed. Heinrich August Winkler (Göttingen, 1974), 9-18.
8. Rudolf Hilferding, "Probleme der Zeit" (1924), in Stephan, *Zwischen den Stühlen*, 170.
9. On Hilferding during the Weimar years, see Smaldone, "Hilferding," Chaps. vi and vii, and esp. Richard Breitman, *German Socialism and Weimar Democracy* (Chapel Hill, NC, 1981), Chap. vii, esp. 117-29.
10. Rudolf Hilferding, "Probleme der Zeit" (1924), in Stephan, *Zwischen den Stühlen*, 177; cf. Euchner, "Hilferding," 179-83.
11. Quoted in Stephan, *Zwischen den Stühlen*, 182.
12. James, "Hilferding," 857. See also Gottschalch, *Strukturveränderungen*, Chap. vi.
13. Rudolf Hilferding, "Die Aufgaben der Sozialdemokratie in der Republik" (1927), in Stephan, *Zwischen den Stühlen*, 214-36. Cf. Peter Lösche and Franz Walter, *Die SPD: Klassenpartei – Volkspartei – Quotenpartei: Zur Entwicklung der Sozialdemokratie von Weimar bis zur deutschen Vereinigung* (Darmstadt, 1992), 23.
14. Euchner, "Hilferding," 182-83.
15. Harsch, *German Social Democracy*, 159-65.
16. Hans Staudinger, interview with author, 12 September 1972, New York.
17. Erich Rinner, interview with author, 14 September 1972, New York.
18. Rudolf Hilferding to Karl Kautsky, 13 April 1933, IISG, Nachlaß Karl Kautsky, K DXII/660. Also discussed in Smaldone, "Hilferding," 465-69, and Winkler, "Endphase," 151-52.
19. Oscar Meyer to Alexander Stein, 7 November 1946, IISG, Nachlaß Alexander Stein, 35.13; Oscar Meyer, *Von Bismarck zu Hitler: Erinnerungen und Betrachtungen* (New York, 1944), 157, 202; Liebich, "Marxism," 238. See also Smaldone, "Hilferding," 493, 517-18.
20. Ibid., 480. One well-informed Nazi police official noted in 1941 that among the German exiles the "well-known Hilferding had the big connections." Beauftragter des Chefs der Sicherheitspolizei und des SD für Belgien und Frankreich, Dienststelle Paris to Reichssicherheitshauptamt Berlin, 24 June 1941, SAPMO-BA, ZPA, Sozialdemokratische Partei Deutschlands. Parteivorstand, II 145-56, Bl. 1-3.
21. Rudolf Breitscheid to Paul Hertz, 28 August 1933, and Hertz to Breitscheid, 5 August 1935, Hoover Institution on War, Revolution, and Peace, Stanford, California (hereafter: HIA), Nachlaß Paul Hertz (microfilm), Reel 41; Hertz to Karl

and Luise Kautsky, 22 July 1935 and 18 March 1937, IISG, Nachlaß Karl Kautsky, K D XII/483 and 523; Hertz to Breitscheid, 12 December 1935, and Breitscheid to Hertz, 28 March 1936, HIA, Nachlaß Paul Hertz (microfilm), Reel 41; Hilferding to Oscar Meyer, 4 February 1937, IISG, Nachlaß Alexander Stein, 37.6; Wilhelm Hoegner, *Der schwierige Außenseiter: Erinnerungen eines Abgeordneten, Emigranten und Ministerpräsidenten* (Munich, 1959), 149.

22. Smaldone, "Hilferding," 476, 480-81.
23. Lewis J. Edinger, *German Exile Politics: The Social Democratic Executive Committee in the Nazi Era* (Berkeley, 1956), 82; Gerd-Rainer Horn, "European Socialists Respond to Fascism: The Drive towards Unity, Radicalisation, and Strategic Innovation in Belgium, France, Germany, and Spain, 1933-1936" (Ph.D. diss., University of Michigan, 1992), 84-85.
24. "Protokoll der Parteivorstandssitzung am 7. Juli 1933" and "Protokoll der Parteivorstandssitzung am 4. August 1933," in Buchholz and Rother, *Parteivorstand*, 10-13, 14-15.
25. [Rudolf Hilferding,] "Die Zeit und die Aufgabe," *Zeitschrift für Sozialismus* (hereafter: *ZfS*) 1: 1 (Oct. 1933): 6, 5. Cf. the detailed discussion in Smaldone, "Hilferding," 496-501.
26. "Kampf und Ziel des revolutionären Sozialismus: Die Politik der Sozialdemokratischen Partei Deutschlands," *Neuer Vorwärts* (hereafter: *NV*) (28 January 1934) and *Sozialistische Aktion* (28 January 1934). The "Prague Manifesto" has also been reprinted, with commentary, in Erich Matthias and Werner Link, eds., *Mit dem Gesicht nach Deutschland: Eine Dokumentation über die sozialdemokratische Emigration. Aus dem Nachlaß von Friedrich Stampfer* (Düsseldorf, 1968), 215-25. See also Edinger, *Exile Politics*, 110-19; Gottschalch, *Strukturveränderungen*, 232-40; Smaldone, "Hilferding," 501-11.
27. Hilferding to "Klinger" (Curt Geyer), 10 January 1934, in Matthias and Link, eds., *Mit dem Gesicht*, 213; "Protokoll der Parteivorstandssitzung am 20. Januar 1934," in Buchholz and Rother, *Parteivorstand*, 32-33.
28. "Dr. Richard Kern" [Rudolf Hilferding], "Revolutionärer Sozialismus," *ZfS* 1: 5 (February 1934): 145.
29. Detlef Lehnert, "Vom Widerstand zur Neuordnung? Zukunftsperspektiven des demokratischen Sozialismus im Exil als Kontrastprogramm zur NS-Diktatur," in *Der Widerstand gegen den Nationalsozialismus: Die deutsche Gesellschaft und der Widerstand gegen Hitler*, ed. Jürgen Schmädeke and Peter Steinbach, 3rd ed. (Munich, 1994), 507; Smaldone, "Hilferding," 502.
30. Rudolf Hilferding, unpublished draft of Prague Manifesto, appendix to letter to Curt Geyer, 10 January 1934, AsD, PV-Emigration (Sopade), Mappe 54.
31. On the "total state," see William Smaldone, "Rudolf Hilferding and the Total State," *The Historian* 57: 1 (1994): 97-112, esp. 107-12.
32. Dieter Groh and Peter Brandt, *"Vaterlandslose Gesellen": Sozialdemokratie und Nation 1860-1990* (Munich, 1992), 213.
33. Hilferding, "Revolutionärer Sozialismus," 148.
34. Ursula Langkau-Alex, "Zwischen Tradition und neuem Bewußtsein: Die Sozialdemokraten im Exil," in *Die Erfahrung der Fremde: Kolloquium des Schwerpunktprogramms "Exilforschung" der Deutschen Forschungsgemeinschaft*, ed. Manfred Briegel and Wolfgang Frühwald (Weinheim, 1988), 68.
35. Hilferding, unpublished draft of Prague Manifesto, AsD, PV-Emigration, Mappe 54.
36. See "Dr. Richard Kern"'s 1934 articles on economic issues in *Neuer Vorwärts*: e.g., 4 and 25 February, 8 and 15 April, 20 and 27 May, and 8 July.

37. "Dr. Richard Kern" [Rudolf Hilferding], "Die deutsche Krise," *ZfS* 1: 11 (August 1934): 337-51.
38. "Dr. Richard Kern" [Rudolf Hilferding], "Das Wirtschaftsjahr 1935," *NV* (5 January 1936).
39. Hilferding to Stampfer, 28 August 1936, in Matthias and Link, *Mit dem Gesicht*, 282-85; cf. Euchner, "Hilferding," 187-88; Smaldone, "Hilferding," 515; Groh and Brandt, *Vaterlandslose Gesellen*, 220.
40. Liebich, "Marxism," 231-32; Gleason, *Totalitarianism*, 31-50.
41. "Dr. Richard Kern" [Rudolf Hilferding], "Grundlagen der auswärtigen Politik," *NV* (15 November 1936). Note some similar ideas in idem, "Das Ende der Völkerbundspolitik," *ZfS* 20: 20/21 (May/June 1935): 629. Smaldone, "Hilferding," 523, also quotes the *NV* article. I disagree with Smaldone's view (ibid., 524) that Hilferding had "jettisoned" many of his older ideas.
42. "Dr. Richard Kern" [Rudolf Hilferding], "Die Politik der Sowjetunion: Kommunistische Ideologie und machtpolitische Realität," *NV* (6 December 1936).
43. Hilferding, unpublished "Entwurf" of Prague Manifesto, AsD, PV-Emigration, Mappe 54.
44. "Protokoll der Parteivorstandssitzung am 26. April 1939," in Buchholz and Rother, *Parteivorstand*, 372.
45. Smaldone, "Hilferding," 521; Euchner, "Hilferding," 188.
46. Hilferding to Paul Hertz, 2 April 1937, quoted in ibid.
47. "Dr. Richard Kern" [Rudolf Hilferding], "Die Expansion der Diktatur," *NV* (21 November 1937); Hilferding to Meyer, 4 February 1937 (copy), IISG, Nachlaß Alexander Stein, 37.6.
48. Hilferding, "Expansion."
49. "Dr. Richard Kern" [Rudolf Hilferding], "Die Vorbereitung des totalen Krieges," *NV* (21 February 1937); Hilferding to Friedrich Stampfer, 28 August 1936, in Matthias and Link, *Mit dem Gesicht*, 284; Hilferding to Oscar Meyer, 16 June 1936 (copy), IISG, Nachlaß Alexander Stein, 37.6.
50. "Dr. Richard Kern" [Rudolf Hilferding], "An der Schwelle des Krieges," *NV* (9 July 1939). See also idem, "Ein neues Experiment," *NV* (19 March 1939); idem, "Auf dem Höhepunkt der Gefahr," *NV* (16 April 1939).
51. See "Dr. Richard Kern"'s articles on these matters in *NV*: 15 May, 16 October, and 20 November 1938, and 14 May 1939.
52. Smaldone, "Hilferding," 520.
53. "Dr. Richard Kern" [Rudolf Hilferding], "Der Kurs der russischen Außenpolitik," *NV* (2 September 1939).
54. Buchholz and Rother, *Parteivorstand*, xxv-xxvi.
55. "Dr. Richard Kern" [Rudolf Hilferding], "Der unersättliche Moloch," *NV* (23 July 1939); idem, "Der Raubcharakter des Systems," *NV* (26 March 1939).
56. "Dr. Richard Kern" [Rudolf Hilferding], "Hitlers Niederlage im Eisenkrieg," *NV* (28 April 1940); Oscar Meyer to Alexander Stein, 7 November 1946, IISG, Nachlaß Alexander Stein, 35.13.
57. Among various accounts, see esp. Hilferding to Oscar Meyer, 18 October 1940 (copy), IISG, Nachlaß Alexander Stein, 37.6; Peter Pistorius, "Rudolf Breitscheid 1874-1944: Ein biographischer Beitrag zur deutschen Parteiengeschichte" (Ph.D. diss., Universität zu Köln, 1970), 378-80; Smaldone, "Hilferding," 528-32.
58. Rudolf Hilferding, "Staatskapitalismus oder totalitäre Staatswirtschaft?," in Stephan, *Zwischen den Stühlen*, 293-94, 295. The essay was originally published in Russian, and in 1947 in English. Cf. Gottschalch, *Strukturveränderungen*, 242-44; Liebich, "Marxism," 238-40; Smaldone, "Hilferding," 524-28.

59. Rudolf Hilferding, "Das historische Problem," in Stephan, *Zwischen den Stühlen*, 297-328.
60. Gottschalch, *Strukturveränderungen*, 244-61; Smaldone, "Hilferding," 534-39.
61. To my knowledge, the only discussion of Hilferding's address is in Klaus Voigt, "Europäische Föderation und neuer Völkerbund: Die Diskussion im deutschen Exil zur Gestaltung der internationalen Beziehungen nach dem Krieg," in *Deutschland nach Hitler: Zukunftspläne im Exil und aus der Besatzungszeit 1939-1949*, ed. Thomas Koebner, Gert Sautermeister, and Sigrid Schneider (Opladen, 1987), 107, 108-9, 116, 118.
62. See his comments at *Parteivorstand* meetings of 19 April, 26 April, 5 July, 12 July, and 21 July 1939 in Buchholz and Rother, *Parteivorstand*, 366, 372, 391, 395, 399-401, and the analysis in ibid., xlvii-il. See also Albrecht Betz, "`Der Tag danach': Zur Auseinandersetzung um Deutschland nach Hitler im Pariser Sommer 1939," in Koebner et al., *Deutschland nach Hitler*, 39-48.
63. "Bemerkungen des Genossen Dr. Rudolf *Hilferding* über die Frage der Kriegsziele und über das Problem der Vereinigten Staaten von Europa (Vorstandssitzung vom 29. Januar 1940)," AsD, PV-Emigration, Mappe 3, Bl. 1. The complete minutes of this meeting have apparently not survived; the only other reference to it is a note in Erich Ollenhauer's pocket diary for 1940. Buchholz and Rother, *Parteivorstand*, lix.
64. The Sopade itself was skeptical about a European federal state; various exile groups to the Sopade's left, such as Neu Beginnen or the Sozialistische Arbeiterpartei (SAP), were much more enthusiastic. Voigt, "Föderation," 106-7, 109.
65. "Bemerkungen," Bl. 3.
66. Ibid., Bl. 4.
67. "Protokoll der Parteivorstandssitzung am 5. Juli 1939" and "Protokoll der Parteivorstandssitzung am 21. Juli 1939," in Buchholz and Rother, *Parteivorstand*, 391, 400.
68. For example, see Erich Matthias, *Sozialdemokratie und Nation: Ein Beitrag zur Ideengeschichte der sozialdemokratischen Emigration in der Prager Zeit des Parteivorstandes 1933-1938* (Stuttgart, 1952); Matthias and Link, *Mit dem Gesicht*; Willi Jasper, "Entwürfe einer neuen Demokratie für Deutschland: Ideenpolitische Aspekte der Exildiskussion 1933-1945: Ein Überblick," *Exilforschung: Ein internationales Jahrbuch*, 2 (1984): 271-98; Helga Grebing, "Was wird aus Deutschland nach dem Krieg? Perspektiven linkssozialistischer Emigration für den Neuaufbau Deutschlands nach dem Zusammenbruch der nationalsozialistischen Diktatur," *Exilforschung: Ein internationales Jahrbuch* 3 (1985): 43-58; Voigt, "Föderation," 104-22; Brandt and Groh, "*Vaterlandslose Gesellen*", chap. 18.
69. On parallels between Hilferding's views on European federalism and those of Willy Brandt, see Voigt, "Föderation," 116.
70. Hilferding to Oscar Meyer, 18 October and 30 November 1940 (copies), IISG, Nachlaß Alexander Stein, 37.6. Cf. Stein, *Hilferding*, 43.
71. See the dramatic account of these matters in Varian Fry, *Surrender on Demand* (New York, 1945), 22-23, 40, 50-51, 80, 93, 166-67.
72. Hilferding to Charles Joy, 5 February 1941, AsD, Verschiedene Originalbriefe und Dokumente, Nr. 42.
73. Masaaki Kurotaki, "Zur Todesursache Rudolf Hilferdings," *Miyagi-Gakuin Joshi-Daigaku Kenkyu-Rombunshu (Beiträge der Miyagi-Gakuin Frauenhochschule)*, no. 61 (20 December 1984): 15. My thanks to Dr. Christoph Stamm, Friedrich-Ebert-Stiftung, Bonn, for helping me gain access to this article. Smaldone, "Hilferding," 539-45, 555, also refers to Kurotaki's article. Cf. Curt Geyer to Erich Ollenhauer,

21 February 1941, and Geyer to "Erich" (Ollenhauer?) and "Hans" (Vogel?), 13 March 1941, AsD, PV-Emigration, Mappe 44; Fritz Heine to German Labor Delegation and Sopade, 27 March 1941, in Matthias and Link, *Mit dem Gesicht*, 493-502; the older article by Kurt Kersten, "Das Ende Breitscheids und Hilferding's," *Deutsche Rundschau* 84: 9 (1958): 843-54; and Willi Jasper, "`Sie waren selbständige Denker': Erinnerungen an die 'Affäre Breitscheid/Hilferding' und die sozialdemokratische Emigration von 1933 bis 1945. Ein Gespräch mit Fritz Heine," *Exilforschung: Ein internationales Jahrbuch* 3 (1985): 59-63. The most thorough and up-to-date analysis suggests that Hilferding died in the custody of Vichy police before he could be delivered to the Gestapo. See Stefan Appelius, *Fritz Heine – Emigration and Wiederaufbau der SPD* (Essen, to be published 1998). My thanks to Dr. Appelius for permission to see the manuscript of his chapter on "Der Fall Breitscheid/Hilferding."

74. Voigt, "Föderation," 118.

Chapter 16

ORDNUNGSMACHT AND MITBESTIMMUNG

The Postwar Labor Unions and the Politics of Reconstruction

Diethelm Prowe

When Erich Potthoff, head of the West German labor unions' think-tank *Wirtschaftswissenschaftliches Institut* (WWI) between 1946 and 1949, reflected back three decades later on the first postwar years of his union, he highlighted two observations: "The labor unions were an *Ordnungsmacht* at that time," and "they wanted to have a part in running the planned economy *(die Planwirtschaft mitmachen)*."[1] The prototypically German term *Ordnungsmacht*, "force for order," nicely mirrors the enduring authoritarian language and mentality of those years. But in an era marked by intense feelings of insecurity and chaos, it also proclaimed that the labor unions were an institution committed to restore order and security not only for its particular clientele of workers, but for society as a whole – "from a profound sense of civic responsibility," as Potthoff added.

The unions' notion of "planned economy" was quite vague, as the former WWI chief readily admitted, but they were clear about one thing: that they must play a leading part in this planning. Socialists, unionists, and other reformers had held as an orthodoxy for some time, prompted first by World War I and reinforced by the Depression, that only planned economies could cope with crisis times. The catastrophic conditions of the *Zusammenbruchgesellschaft* (collapsed society) lent this view new vital-

Notes for this chapter begin on page 415.

ity. Goods were so scarce and the material needs of the population so great that society could not afford the waste that, it was widely believed, market economies produce because they are driven solely by greed for profit *(Profitwirtschaft)*, whereas planned economies would meet the real needs of people *(Bedarfswirtschaft)*. Because in their own minds the unions were the only "natural" representatives of all powerless "victims" of the collapse, it was clear to labor leaders that the unions must claim full and leading participation in this economic planning; that is, their role as *Ordnungsmacht* in the planned economy was from the start inseparably linked with labor codetermination or *Mitbestimmung*.

Hans Böckler, the Cologne septuagenarian who rapidly rose to become the patriarchal leader of the postwar labor movement, expressed this confident claim to responsibility and codetermination with splendid robustness:

> *The Nazis have turned Germany into a pile of rubble; and the chaos, with which they threatened the world so often, has become a horrible reality for our country. People and state have fallen into an abyss from which they can rise only through superhuman efforts. This will require the concentrated strength and absolute commitment of all to a task of such magnitude and difficulty as has never been faced by any people before.*
>
> *In this undertaking workers will be the force, the ready reserve, the critical factor to make the reconstruction, as well as the great work of reparations, possible. Of course, not simply the workers per se, certainly not as an undirected crowd. Nor as a mass which, lacking any insight into what the real needs are, is simply commanded from above to work and perform. It takes more than that, it takes first of all a democratic organization, the old familiar labor union, to instill the kind of understanding and good will to achieve efficient production, which can certainly be attained no other way. No one knows this better than the workers themselves; but sensible entrepreneurs, too, will not fail to agree with this assertion.*[2]

What is strikingly missing from this statement is the traditional union agenda and labor-management confrontation. Instead the first head of the West German labor federation, *Deutscher Gewerkschaftsbund* (DGB), four weeks after capitulation justified the urgent need to reestablish labor unions exclusively with the necessity for *production*. He extended a hand of *cooperation* to business and showed a remarkable confidence that "sensible" entrepreneurs would grasp this hand of cooperation and accept the labor unions as equal partners. There was finally a notable *distrust of unorganized workers* because they might be misled by demagogues. Like a number of postwar labor leaders, Böckler showed his deep disillusionment over the vulnerability of many workers to Nazism as well as communism.[3]

Such leadership bravado and rush to responsibility for the whole society strikes us as curious today. Yet it was centrally characteristic for the postwar unions and fit well with the political culture of this period. After the Nazi catastrophe, the labor movement believed that it had a moral legitimation to claim leadership in the new Germany as the only part of the old system that had not collaborated with the Nazis. The seeming failure of capitalism in the Depression and the subsequent cooptation, if not outright collaboration, of industrialists, large landowners, and the military under Hitler had left a political vacuum that gave the representatives of labor not only the right, but a special responsibility of leadership. This, in fact, seemed so obvious that the majority of the population and even most industrialists would, so labor leaders believed, wish unions to take a leadership role. The later West German Chancellor Konrad Adenauer raged against this wide-spread acquiescence by industrialists in a letter to former lignite magnate Paul Silverberg in May 1947: "These claims for total power by the labor unions are scarcely resisted by business because so many leading people on that side have – even if only slightly – brown [i.e., Nazi] stains and are, thus, too scared to defend themselves."[4]

At the first union conference in the British Zone, Böckler put it this way: "Capitalism is in its last gasps. For the moment it is unable to act. The problems with which we as labor unions are struggling today are the food situation, housing construction, economic reconstruction, settling people, and especially social care for our fellow workers. Today we are held responsible by the population as a whole."[5] There was hardly room for traditional battles for wages in a controlled scarcity economy, where wages were fixed. In "poorhouse Germany," there was little to distribute. Hunger did indeed drive workers into mass demonstrations and strikes, but union leaders were most ambivalent toward such signs of radical activism during the "hunger years" of 1946 to 1948 because they feared social unrest ultimately meant that there would be less to distribute.[6] The defense of labor interests had become much more broadly defined. The battle had moved to both a more basic, existential level and the higher plane of building the new society. On the basic level, unions had to ensure that enough was produced to provide for workers and the whole population. But ultimately these gains would be empty if the new political and economic order were not a fair and democratic one, resistant to reactionaries and demagogues.

This posture of the labor federation has been much criticized by labor historians, most notably in the classic studies by Eberhard Schmidt and Theo Pirker.[7] They blame this policy for what they regard as the consummate failure of the postwar unions – the missed opportunity for a fundamental transformation that would empower workers and achieve equality in the economy and polity. They point to how little of the 1945 to 1948 union program was achieved: no plants were socialized; labor achieved no parity in economic institutions or corporations, with the sole exception of the coal and steel industries; and the Factory Constitution Law (*Betriebs-*

verfassungsgesetz) of 1952, governing the position of the elected workers' councils in the factories, permitted only meager labor participation. While these historians generally hold the anti-socialist bias of the Western Allies, especially the United States, responsible for the weak starting position of the unions, they argue that the union leaders' cardinal error was that they did not steer a course of tough confrontation.[8] Schmidt blames this primarily on the old functionaries from the Weimar years, people who naturally dominated the post-1945 leadership positions because they were intent, in his words, on a "restoration of the ideas and mentalities of the labor unions of the twenties," when they had always "preferred to preserve the economic peace" for fear of conflict."[9]

In contrast to these "orthodox" labor histories, recent studies, inspired by Charles Maier's comparative work on postwar reconstruction and represented by Volker Berghahn for Germany, have emphasized the unions' long-term success, which they see as rooted in the postwar years precisely because of labor's "productionist" and cooperative posture.[10] This view most sensibly judges the success of the unions by labor's long-range economic gains rather than by any ideological-revolutionary goals or the political power balance between business and labor.

Yet this perspective, too, regards the specific policies of the dominant labor factions of the late 1940s as wrong-headed. While Schmidt judges the unions' posture as too conciliatory, Berghahn deems it radical and unrealistic. Even though the latter's skepticism regarding the long-term viability of the unions' postwar socialization and economic democratization schemes is convincing, neither Schmidt and his co-thinkers nor Berghahn, I believe, focuses sharply enough on the unique economic conditions and political culture during this brief postwar period. The unions, in fact, adapted remarkably well to those conditions. It was not that a liberal corporatist minority, led by productionist veterans like Fritz Tarnow, was fighting against a more radical, unrealistic majority, as Berghahn argues, but rather that the bulk of the leadership, including Böckler, Tarnow, and Potthoff, responded pragmatically and responsibly to the needs of the collapsed society and achieved considerable – though not total – success both for the workers' real goals of reconstruction and for the position of the unions in the transitional postwar political-economic system. When the situation changed with the triumphant social market economy of the early 1950s, essentially the same leadership would once again adjust swiftly and effectively. The most strikingly symptomatic figure for this flexible and effective policy of the postwar unions was, thus, not the closet "liberal corporatist" Tarnow, for Tarnow had, in fact, still raved about a controlled economy near the end of the war: "The war economy has been the most splendid and final proof for the superiority of an economy guided and controlled according to plan over a competitive market economy.... The war economy is, in fact, largely the model for a socialist economy...."[11] A more appropriate ideal-type representative might be Ludwig Rosenberg, who – as will be discussed below – was the leading figure in designing the postwar economic democracy concept and who just as successfully later integrated the unions into Ludwig Erhard's social market system, ultimately as DGB chief from 1962 to 1969.

For the brief period of the immediate postwar years, the unions became a different kind of institution whose primary goal was to take the lead in building "the concentrated strength" for reconstruction with all who were willing to cooperate. They remained committed to their essential mission of working for the most basic interest of workers, namely the betterment of their lot. In the years of scarcity and political-economic chaos this meant making the economy more *productive* in order to provide the goods most needed by the population. These essentials defined the principal union goals: 1) to forge a strong, comprehensive, and centralized labor organization (*Einheitsgewerkschaft*) as a power base; 2) to build structures for labor codetermination in the planned economy to assure that it would become a productive *Bedarfswirtschaft* (economy to meet real human needs); and 3) to promote cooperation with "progressive" business leaders and democratic government to strengthen democracy and the reconstruction effort.

The idea of creating such a comprehensive labor union organization arose first as a reaction to the disastrous defeat of the labor movement in the waning years of the Weimar Republic at the hands of the reactionary Right and, ultimately, Hitler. Among the routed labor leaders it quickly became a given that labor's fatal weakness during the Weimar years had been its divisions and disunity along political and ideological lines as well as among organizational types of unions and parts of the labor market. Because post-1945 union leaders quite naturally recruited themselves from individuals who had held significant leadership positions in the Weimar years, these lessons were not lost. The twelve long years of pondering the bitter failure of Weimar in exile abroad or hiding out at home had strengthened the determination to end the bitter rivalries within the labor movement and among democratic forces generally – often against considerable political pressures.[12] Even though they did not quite attain the highly centralized and uniform union envisaged in exile, and the public service employees *(Beamte)* and other white-collar groups eventually split off, the strength and resilience of the *Einheitsgewerkschaft* commitment speaks to the depth and power of these feelings. For the same reasons the postwar unions insisted on partisan neutrality, but only and emphatically within the confines of democratic politics. This excluded radicals both on the Left, namely Communists, and on the Right. Because the largest pre-war unions that merged into the comprehensive post-war organization were the social democratic ADGB and the Christian unions, this meant in practice the integration of members of the two largest post-1945 German parties, the Social Democratic Party and the Christian Democratic Union (CDU) within the DGB. Fittingly, the head of the union was a Social Democrat (Böckler and successors) and the first deputy a Christian Democrat (Matthias Focher until 1956).

But the *Einheitsgewerkschaft* could not have maintained its strength from past fears alone. It was also remarkably suited to and shaped by the realities of massive destruction and poverty and the "superhuman effort" of reconstruction, as Böckler put it – inescapable for labor and for the rest of Germans, who all had to be workers in this gargantuan task. Thus, *Einheitsgewerkschaft* in the postwar years embraced a greater claim. It was to be an institution representing the real majority, who felt themselves "objects" of the economy, including workers of all types as well as consumers, housewives, refugees, and other victims of the war.

Such all-embracing organizations very much accorded with the political culture of the postwar years. The merging of the traditionally competing unions reflected the typical postwar longing for *synthesis* and rejection of ideologies, which the traumatic experience of the Nazi catastrophe and the looming Stalinist tyranny had taught them to hate. Demands for such a new, supra-ideological synthesis pervaded the pronouncements of all political groups of postwar Germany.[13] Ironically, the Nazi years had already accustomed Germans to an all-encompassing labor organization through the Labor Front, which had enjoyed considerable appeal among workers, not least because of its insistence on broad inclusiveness and equality between "workers of the hand and the mind." Thus, the *Einheitsgewerkschaft* won natural acceptance just as readily as the new Christian Democratic parties, which finally healed the centuries-old Catholic-Protestant split in the land of Luther.

The *Einheitsgewerkschaft* concept also fit well with the complex views postwar Germans held toward public control and authority. On one hand they sought salvation from desperate scarcities and social chaos by turning to controls and strong authority. There were regular calls for "commissars" with full powers to deal with every crisis situation. On the other hand, the Hitler catastrophe left Germans with a strong fear of too much state power and an aversion to the war economy with its labyrinthine bureaucracies. Strong public organizations with a broadly based membership and grass-roots presence, thus, became an appealing alternative to provide the needed planning and control, especially if they were not compromised by the Nazi disaster. Institutions like the churches and the unions' direct counterpart in much of the post-1945 economic planning discussions, the chambers of commerce and industry, held a great deal of attraction. The labor unions in particular could act as credible champions of quasi-democratic order and control. Undoubtedly this trust was strengthened because the unions' leader, Hans Böckler, was the very embodiment of the kind of reassuring patriarch characteristically appealing to postwar Germans. In this sense the *Einheitsgewerkschaft* was an ideal expression of postwar political culture, and it remained the most lasting union achievement and most important basis of union strength for the half-century to follow.

This reality of postwar German political culture contradicts the historical legends, most popular among younger scholars in the 1970s but still pervading the literature, that there was a strong revolutionary mood in the early postwar period and that the labor movement initially rose spontaneously from the grass roots in the factories. To be sure, the power vacuum left at the outset at the local level, which the military occupation could not fill instantaneously, spawned small-group initiatives, which were usually aimed at community self-help in two areas: driving out old Nazi bosses and maintaining basic local services. Sometimes these self-appointed committees were dominated by activists with more radical agendas or by Communists seeking to instrumentalize the wide-spread anti-Nazi resentments under the cloak of anti-fascism – hence the commonly used term "Antifa Committees," reminiscent of Comintern language.[14] Works councils *(Betriebsräte)*, the elected councils of workers' representatives that dated back to the early Weimar Republic, also reappeared in a number of factories, demanding the ouster of former Nazi bosses. But in spite of British and American insistence that labor unions be founded from the grass roots up, union organizations were by and large constituted from above by former leaders and their local representatives.[15] As early as the summer of 1945, a so-called Committee of Seven of top labor leaders from the former unions, including Böckler and the later North Rhine-Westphalian Minister President Karl Arnold, who had been a Christian union leader, were in contact with military government officials in the British Zone.[16]

Similarly, the Antifas were already yielding to the traditional local elites, which reasserted themselves through their established networks of power and their expertise, even before a military government prohibition against the committees went into effect.[17] The continuities of German political culture, which had long respected established patriarchal authority, formal titles earned through education, and advancement through the hierarchy, as well as technical expertise, worked against spontaneous, especially radical initiatives by unlegitimated groups. This is not to say that radical left groups such as the Antifas might not have been able to cling to or even expand their power after 1945, especially with outside support, if the Western Allies had not acted determinedly against more radical alternatives from the Left as well as from the Right.[18] As in 1933, both large sections of the elites and the general population were probably too fearful to stop a determined radical power drive. But in the atmosphere of profound insecurity most postwar Germans clearly wished for order, stability, and reconstruction under trusted patriarchal authority. The union leadership reflected this sentiment and the realistic fear that radical confrontation would impede reconstruction and once more lead to destructive polarization of society rather than to democratization.

The unions' drive for codetermination grew out of this same claim to cooperative leadership and responsibility that spawned the all-embracing *Einheitsgewerkschaft*. The proposals for the creation of a comprehensive union that exiled leaders in Britain brought with them to Germany in 1945 already insisted that the newly integrated unions would be "absolutely necessary elements of democratic management of the economy." The old elites' complicity in Hitler's seizure of power would make long-term democratization impossible without labor's "equal participation in the creation and application of economic and social legislation."[19] Exiled unionists around Fritz Tarnow in Sweden similarly demanded a leading "influence on the shaping of state economic policy."[20]

Nor did this claim seem out of place in postwar society. All political parties called for an equal role of capital and labor, and they proposed various corporatist structures of business-labor councils and chambers to master reconstruction together.[21] Economic democracy was a postwar assumption, not only in labor circles. Yet its concrete meaning was imprecise, and assumptions about what it would mean for the future economy varied widely. Returning labor leaders brought back no tangible plans, just notions that derived from traditions and the theoretical constructs that had surfaced during the extraordinarily lively and creative discourse on socialism in the Weimar years, for which there was no parallel in the still cityscapes of rubble after 1945. Instead, post-World War II schemes for economic democratization were essentially shaped and in most instances justified by the immediate practical need for order and reconstruction. Unfettered free market capitalism was regarded not only as unjust and undemocratic, but as chaotic; and reconstruction could only be accomplished through common, democratic planning and investment. Germans had moved, as Tarnow put it in 1947, "from a rhetorical-ideological socialism to a practical-constructive socialism of the present."[22]

Central to this "practical-constructive socialism" of reconstruction was the assumption, shared by postwar Germans generally, that the future Germany must have a planned economy. All economic democratization concepts were built on this premise. The unions' first priorities for economic democracy were, therefore, 1) the creation or reform of economic policy-making and enforcing institutions to assure democratic control of the planning process through equal labor participation *(überbetriebliche Mitbestimmung)* and 2) the socialization of basic industries. The latter, which remained a core demand through the 1950s, was critical for the postwar planned economy for two reasons: to gain control of the "command posts" of the planned economy and to raise productivity. The third main element of economic democracy was codetermination within individual corporations and factories *(betriebliche Mitbestimmung)*, which sought a voice for labor both in establishing working conditions at the plant and in economic management decisions.

The reality of the controlled economy placed *überbetriebliche Mitbestimmung*, the democratization of the economic policy-making and enforcing institutions, on the agenda of the postwar unions from the start. In contrast to the other two pillars of the economic democratization program, this issue was always primarily promoted by the union leadership rather than either by political parties or the factory floor organizations.[23] Concrete proposals surfaced as soon after the war as labor union activity was permitted. Like the rest of the post-1945 socialism debate, they built on models from the Weimar years,[24] but adapted them to the postwar mood for codetermination and cooperation and to the reality of the controlled economy. Two kinds of institutions initially dominated in this economy: administrative control agencies closely supervised by the occupation powers, and the regional chambers of commerce and industry, which had survived the collapse mostly intact. The chambers traditionally represented all industrial and commercial businesses in a region and were entrusted by the government with such public tasks as vocational training, security exchange, quality control, and standardization. After the collapse of German governmental structures they were the only institutions left with the expertise to administer local raw materials allocation, labor, and distribution. "The chambers of commerce and industry are ... practically in charge of all economic decision-making in their districts," Werner Hansen, head of the North Rhine-Westphalian union and one of the prime movers for economic democratization wrote in 1947.[25] They naturally became the first focus of economic democratization.

As early as November 1945 the former Christian labor unionist and later North Rhine-Westphalian Minister President Karl Arnold proposed the creation of a hierarchy of economic chambers with equal business-labor representation.[26] The plan proposed "to create an institution designed to overcome antagonisms through business-like deliberations, to clear up misunderstandings among interest groups, and to take effective measures for reconstruction." Cosigned by the aging head of the Düsseldorf chamber,[27] the proposal was expressly built on a broad coalition for order and reconstruction, including even the national-conservative North Rhine Province President Robert Lehr, who sympathized with pre-Nazi corporatist ideas.[28] While the draft was a bit of a hybrid of Weimar labor and national-conservative Christian conceptions, Böckler happily identified it as the unions' own proposal.[29] British Zone union experts developed it further and eventually turned it into a legislative draft for the state of Lower Saxony.[30] Similar demands surfaced in the American Zone.[31]

By January 1947, when postwar economic conditions reached their nadir, these efforts had matured into a full-blown economic democracy concept, which was widely circulated as the Rosenberg Memorandum. Drafted by the economic policy committee of the British Zone DGB under the leadership of Ludwig Rosenberg, this plan proposed the immediate practical integration of labor into all levels of an expected planned economy through the establishment of business-labor economic chambers, which would be empowered to administer the economic plans.[32] Ironically, the model law based on this concept was published shortly after George Marshall announced the Marshall Plan in June 1947, which forecast a European reconstruction in the American free-market style.[33] But the preface of this draft law, which became the basis of a series of bills introduced by Social Democrats at the behest of the unions in state legislatures between 1947 and 1949, placed it squarely into the anticipated planned economy:

> *In a free democratic state the people as a whole must not be denied the right to determine the planning and administration of the economy, nor should it be in the hands of a state bureaucracy alien to the economy .... This economic self-government can not be the task of just one group in the economy .... The labor unions ... demand a system of self-administration in which both of the major economic groups, business and workers, represent the economy together as equal partners.*[34]

Underlying this economic democracy conception in the planned economy was the idea that overall economic policy should be legislated in democratic parliaments, dominated by political parties. But "since it is practically impossible" for parliament "to watch over the exercise of its delegated power continuously," the enforcement of these policies needed to be overseen by new democratic institutions with parity labor representation.[35] In the union economic committee these principles were summarized as follows:

> *It is among the responsibilities of political parties to exercise legislative powers, in this case to determine the principles of economic policy .... It is among the responsibilities of the labor union to help bring about and secure political democracy through democracy in the economy. In practice this means party control wherever actual parliamentary political decisions are made ... labor union control wherever these basic decisions are interpreted and applied in practice.*[36]

At the time such an expectation of a permanent power position of the unions *inside* the system, safeguarding both increased production and just distribution, seemed hardly unrealistic. "Progressive" members of the industrial elites had, to a limited extent, already opened the most important institutions of resource allocation and distribution in the controlled economy to labor representatives. Several chambers of commerce and industry had invited local union leaders to join their management or councils;[37] in Braunschweig the union leader had even been coopted into the presidium.[38] More importantly, the economic administration of the British Zone and the economics ministries of the states in the three Western zones since mid-1946 had been establishing expert advisory committees, increasingly with parity business-labor representation.[39] Such direct labor representation continued to play a powerful role in the changing institutions of economic administration well past the currency reform.

In response to a recommendation by the responsible official in the British military government, the chambers of the British Zone even passed a resolution recommending the inclusion of labor representatives in chamber committees and the formation of regional business-labor committees to deal with economic policy issues.[40] In the weeks following the circulation of the Rosenberg Memorandum, a number of chambers in the Rhineland in both the British and French zones were going beyond that offer and advocating one-third-participation of labor in their organizations.[41] The 1947 draft law simply proposed to convert these diverse forms of union influence in the controlled economy into an enduring institutional framework of a permanent planned economy, in which the cumbersome state bureaucracy would be replaced by institutions of economic democracy.

Ironically, the very recognition of the unions as established players in the controlled economy began colliding with their efforts to institutionalize this role permanently. The unions tried to play *Ordnungsmacht* in two different ways. The Rosenberg initiative for basic structural reform overlapped in early 1947 with efforts by other union leaders, led by Böckler, Albin Karl of Hanover, and others including Potthoff, to expand immediate practical influence of the unions on critical economic decisions in the severe scarcity of the *Hungerwinter*.[42] This led to a very interesting agreement between the chambers and labor unions of the British Zone in Wuppertal in February 1947 – reminiscent, in mini-format, of the Stinnes-Legien Agreement that had spawned the Central Industry-Labor Commission (*Zentralarbeitsgemeinschaft*) in 1918.[43] It established so-called Economic Committees (*Wirtschaftsausschüsse*) with equal representation of the chambers and labor unions throughout the British Zone, which generally met monthly over the next two years to discuss major economic problems and policies in the chamber districts. The central leaderships also met several more times.

Advocates of the Wuppertal Agreement and similar initiatives hoped that these ideas would prepare the ground for basic structural reforms.

Others, including Rosenberg, warned that such cooperative agreements would reduce the pressure for real change.[44] Later historians have generally sympathized with the latter view and accused labor leaders of lack of courage or clear strategy.[45] While the chambers clearly hoped that the Wuppertal committees would prevent full labor participation in the chambers themselves,[46] it is too easy to accuse labor leaders of simply being guilty of weakness or stupidity. In the scarcity years, workers had desperate immediate needs; and demands from below were intense. The hunger marches and strikes of the time were motivated far more often by such needs than by the struggle for "economic democracy," even on the factory level.[47] Urgent problems at the local level necessitated a great deal of labor-business cooperation and even led to some genuine friendships between union and chamber leaders. Several union-chamber committees on the pattern of the Wuppertal Agreement had already started working spontaneously.[48] Government administrators actively supported both forms of union involvement. Thus, the official responsible for economic organizations in the British Zone's Central Economic Administration attended and, with his agency, strongly promoted the Wuppertal Agreement. Yet he also, at the request of Rosenberg, prepared the July 1947 economic chamber law draft published by the unions.[49]

In the autumn of 1948, during the critical months of rapidly rising prices and unemployment following the currency reform, the unions even pursued three different paths simultaneously. To deal with the immediate price crisis, they formed Action Committees with the local chambers to force price rollbacks – in the tradition of the Wuppertal committees.[50] In the parliaments – with greatest success in the North Rhine-Westphalian Landtag – they promoted legislation on the Rosenberg draft model with the support of the SPD and a smaller number of CDU representatives.[51] Finally, on 12 November 1948, they raised their fist in the first strike initiated by a central labor union leadership in postwar Germany.[52] The two main goals of the one-day general strike were still those of the *Ordnungsmacht*. One was an emphatic reassertion of the unions' right to codetermination. But the second, "economic" demand – to stop the massive decline of purchasing power for the average German, caused by the continuing wage freeze at a time of rapidly rising prices – went beyond traditional economic interest representation. It was the unions' claim to the right to codetermine the basic direction of economic policy.

They reiterated this claim in May 1950, soon after the establishment of the West German DGB, in a programmatic document ambitiously called "Draft Law … for the Restructuring of the German Economy."[53] But by then the issue of a planned economy had faded. The DGB no longer asked to build a new order or to create order out of chaos, but called for the democratization of existing structures. In the case of the chambers, it only demanded additional business-labor chambers to take over the primary enforcement functions of the old chambers. Calls for an advisory Federal Economic Council and labor representation in chambers of commerce and industry as well as for handicrafts and agriculture have continued to this day, but in the context of an increasingly marginal campaign for labor codetermination in economic institutions generally.

Socialization – the other priority for the democratic planned economy envisaged by the unions – remained curiously static in postwar DGB programs. Socialization was far more successful at rousing the emotions of hungry, dispirited postwar Germans than chambers and councils; and it caught the public's attention and the imagination of later historians to a much greater extent. "The individual worker expected miracles from socialization and the participation of the union in the management of the company," Rosenberg remarked in 1949.[54] The demand to transfer "key industries" to public ownership rang through all union congresses and programs from the first postwar meetings to the end of the Adenauer era in 1963. Yet, in contrast to their pursuit of codetermination, the union leadership did not take the lead in the formulation of concepts, submission of bills, negotiations, or confrontations for socialization, except for regular public proclamations and rallies. The philosophical development and the legislative struggle were driven by the political parties, primarily the SPD. Thus, the major innovative schemes of the post-1945 period – most notably the Hessian drafts of Harald Koch, the Hamburg Plan, and the Berlin bill – stemmed from party or independent socialist intellectuals.[55] The unions' socialization plans consistently called for public ownership of all mining, iron and steel, chemical, and energy-producing corporations; banks, essential transportation, and utilities were added in the later programs.[56] Mindful of the Nazi and Stalinist abuse of state power, nationalization – i.e., direct state ownership – was to be avoided whenever possible; individual firms were to operate as autonomously as was feasible.

The centrality of production and *Bedarfswirtschaft* can be clearly heard as the typical union justification for public ownership: only through socialization "will it be possible to guide the production of basic industries, to adapt the capacities of these industries to the economic needs and utilize them accordingly, to execute the distribution of the critical basic resources to meet the needs of the economy most effectively" by eliminating "the political abuse of positions of economic power" by private owners.[57] These were the arguments of planners in a scarcity economy, not revolutionaries or ideological visionaries.[58]

The pragmatic focus on production and order also meant that socialization never took on the critical importance for the postwar unions' day-to-day work that it later occupied in the minds of the historians who proclaimed the unions' failure.[59] The union leadership's relatively quick endorsement of the Marshall Plan in June 1948, which in fact set aside socialization as a realistic goal, is testimony to the same sense of priority of production and the material welfare of the masses of workers – a sense that most of the latter undoubtedly shared. Rosenberg similarly identified as the only realistic goals of socialization in 1949: "1) that the workers keep their jobs, 2) that the industry is subsidized and remains viable, 3) that we furthermore try to improve the situation of the individual worker."[60]

Moreover, with the growing despair of the *Hungerwinter* and the rising communist threat in the Cold War, labor leaders increasingly feared the radicalization that could be fueled so easily by demagogues exploiting the emotional appeal of socialization as a "miracle cure." Eager to preserve order, production, and the tender beginnings of democracy, union leaders, therefore, tread very cautiously on this issue. It was never *Selbstzweck*, a goal for its own sake. The unions' investment in socialization remained always carefully limited. The success of the postwar unions is, thus, better measured by their attainment of the pragmatic and real goals of economic recovery and political democracy than by the realization of socialization or the planned economy. A young government official close to the unions later recalled Böckler's determination to nurture the young democracy: when delegates at the 1947 Bielefeld congress, upset at the food situation, tried to shout down Food Administrator Schlange-Schöningen, Böckler intervened with the words, "This state is our state!" and admonished them to hear *their* food minister.[61]

The third major plank in the postwar union program, codetermination within individual companies, has become most closely associated with the post-1945 labor unions because this is where they achieved their greatest long-term success with the introduction of (near-) parity labor representation on supervisory boards, first in the iron and steel industries in the British Zone (1947), then in West German coal, iron, and steel industries (1951), and finally in all corporations with at least two thousand employees (1976). In the popular mind it is this *Mitbestimmung* that has stood for the remarkable labor-management peace of *Modell Deutschland*.

Yet in the early postwar years this was not as central an issue for the union leadership as was the participation in the institutions of the planned economy and the great task of reconstruction generally. Like socialization, factory-level codetermination potentially clashed with the more fundamental principles of *Ordnungsmacht* and the maximization of production. While the unions genuinely believed in worker participation at all levels of the economy, the egotistic pursuit of self-interest on the company or plant level *(Betriebsegoismus)* by powerful works councils potentially endangered not only the leadership of the unions, but also the "superhuman effort" of reconstruction for the good of the whole population.

Thus, North Rhine-Westphalian DGB-chief Werner Hansen noted in 1948: "Economic democracy, which the unions want because they know that there can be no peaceful reconstruction without it, can by and large not rely on organizations within the factory."[62] Clearly Hansen did not deem the works councils qualified to codetermine economic policy, and they could not be depended upon to keep "politically unscrupulous elements," i.e., social radicals and particularly Communists, in check. Such views obviously clashed with the ambitions of the more activist councils. There was, thus, an uneasy relationship between the unions and works councils from the start. At the March 1946 conference in Hanover, the DGB (British Zone) took up the scattered demands of works councils for "responsible participation and codetermination in production and profit distribution" in their firms, and this became a regular plank in subsequent programs.[63] But in the face of Allied Control Council Decree #22 of April 1946, which restricted the role of elected factory-level councils to issues of the work place only, the unions remained initially passive. Not until almost a year later did they issue a model agreement for the role of works councils, after the first postwar strike in Hanover had demonstrated the potential explosiveness of this unresolved issue. Still, the hopes that this model would facilitate labor-management negotiations in individual companies, achieve a reasonable level of works council participation in production decisions, and preserve much-needed social peace were not fulfilled. Several more work stoppages followed, in which the codetermination issue blended with the deep frustrations over food shortages.[64]

Yet these confrontations demonstrated a common interest that reconnected this part of the quest for economic democracy with the unions' central postwar mission of co-managing the new democratic order – namely that there "can be no peaceful reconstruction without it [company-level *Mitbestimmung*]," as Hansen put it. And in this case the unions' expectation that "progressive entrepreneurs" would understand and cooperate from necessity, actually worked. Right in the midst of the labor unrest of late 1946, the British-appointed head of the iron-steel trusteeship agency and former finance director of *Vereinigte Stahlwerke*, Heinrich Dinkelbach, with British assent offered the unions in December 1946 the furthest-going participation to date: parity on the company boards of directors. He even linked his proposal to "the sense of a true economic democracy."[65] After long, frustrating talks with industry representatives had failed, here was Dinkelbach suddenly, after consultation with such heavyweights of the iron and steel industry as Karl Jarres, chairman of the board at Klöckner, and Hermann Reusch, CEO at Gute-Hoffnungs-Hütte, conceding codetermination as easily and naturally as Böckler and his colleagues had expected when they had pronounced the old capitalist system dead.

The unions were delighted and saw their strategy confirmed. Not only did labor gain significant industrial codetermination, but the final arrangement hammered out in the following weeks also conformed to the *Ordnungsmacht*/planned economy conception of the unions. Contrary to the earlier insistence of the companies and the expectations of the works councils, the labor participation was not limited to workers from within the firms, but the unions clearly dominated the labor representation on the company boards and within management. Of the five labor representatives on the board, two were appointed by the unions (one DGB and one the metalworkers union, IG Metall), two by the works council, and one by the government (in addition there were five management members and one neutral member). Because the DGB could exert significant influence on the works-council and government appointments, and it also nominated the *Arbeitsdirektor* (Labor Director) on the three-person top management team, it could be satisfied that its overall goals in the planned economy would prevail over narrow *Betriebsegoismus* on the labor side. These representatives would be union specialists with extensive training and expertise, which was critical for men like Böckler, Rosenberg, and Hansen. "To educate the democratic expert and to give him to our people, that is the great task of the unions," Rosenberg declared.[66]

Interestingly, it was the British military government controller who insisted on the dominant role of the unions in the labor representation precisely in order to keep parochial interests from interfering with the needs of reconstruction. The codetermination agreement was, thus, ultimately the fruit of an unusual convergence of interests, in which all sides sought the support of the unions for different reasons. The works councils expected aid from their brethren in the labor movement for internal company goals. The British needed union backing to assure the social peace required for reconstruction and to restrain the works councils, which they deemed too parochial and vulnerable to communist influence. Dinkelbach sought labor cooperation to safeguard the industries and raise productivity. Even the industrialists briefly hoped to use union support against Dinkelbach's massive restructuring and the much-feared socialization by offering limited labor participation in letters initiated by the iron and steel manufacturing association and signed by Jarres and Reusch.[67] This constellation shows the unusual power position the unions transitionally enjoyed due to the unsettled situation of the postwar years, in which all players were juggling in an atmosphere of constant insecurity.

Following the completion of the iron and steel codetermination in the spring of 1947, company-level *Mitbestimmung* again faded as an issue. In its place came the rapidly proliferating participation of union representatives in advisory councils in the agencies of the declining controlled economy of 1948 to 1949. In sheer numbers of expert committees for all branches of the economy and the individual states (*Fachausschüsse, Länderausschüsse*, and even *Länderfachausschüsse)* labor participation in the economy had now reached its peak.[68] In fact, union reports on these committees tell a story of increasingly frenetic activity in rapidly multiplying expert commissions that visibly led to growing exhaustion and exasperation – as though it had been planned by conspiring industrialists and government officials as a final coup against the very idea of economic democracy. The frustration grew among labor representatives that they were equal neither in numbers nor in influence.

It was not until the controlled economy had been replaced by a free market system administered by a pro-business government that company-level codetermination moved center stage again in the DGB's strategy. At that point the postwar paradigm of a planned economy had collapsed and with it the unions' postwar dream of *Ordnungsmacht*. Faced with the shambles of the planned-economy vision, the unions now turned back to the goal of labor participation for the sake of democratization as such or, as Ludwig Rosenberg expressed it in an influential pamphlet, to raise the worker "from subject to citizen of the economy,"[69] independent of the particular form of the economy. The unions continued to apply this principle to institutions such as chambers of commerce and industry and handicrafts, but the image of the oppressed subject held most meaning for the worker in big industry. Company-level *Mitbestimmung*, after all, was not dependent as such on the special conditions of the postwar controlled economy. It, therefore, remained in the DGB program well past 1950 and celebrated remarkable triumphs in the free market economy of the 1950s and 1970s.

When in his inaugural address Chancellor Adenauer announced fresh legislation on management-labor relations, thereby reopening the issue of codetermination in the iron and steel industries, the DGB responded with its draft for restructuring the German economy, in which it placed the intra-company codetermination at the beginning.[70] In the ensuing months Böckler and his associates once more banked first on the readiness of "progressive entrepreneurs" to accept their democratization plans. They were encouraged by the head of the employers' association, Walter Raymond, to believe that the employers were ready to cooperate, while Böckler in turn once more demonstrated his productionist conviction by assuring Raymond that codetermination must "never be established in a way that hurts production."[71]

Now, however, two camps among the business organizations encouraged the unions in two different directions – each at the expense of the other. The employers were ready to concede labor participation in the chambers of commerce and industry while the chambers intimated that labor participation should occur in the companies and through an advisory council on the federal level. When the representatives of the unions and employers' association met in Hattenheim and Maria Laach between January and July 1950, the employers, thus, tried to fend off company-level codetermination by making generous offers for labor parity in new chambers endowed with all the official functions of the traditional chambers.[72] Naturally this led to storms of fury among the chambers.[73] Moreover, the "progressive entrepreneurs" failed to materialize on the issue of company-level codetermination, while industrialists and the government coalition began to push for the abolition of even the iron-steel *Mitbestimmung*.

It was at this point that the unions were forced to abandon the substance of their *Ordnungsmacht* posture in order to salvage at least the *Mitbestimmung* they enjoyed in the iron-steel industry. They resorted to the direct confrontation they had eschewed as postwar *Ordnungsmacht*. They threatened a strike. It seemed that the DGB had finally discovered the strategy that had brought them – quite unintentionally – Dinkelbach's original concession because he and the British had been impressed with the *Hungerwinter* strikes. Now that the twin disasters of the collapsed society – impending hunger and radicalization – no longer loomed and the *Ordnungsmacht* of the unions had ceased, Böckler readied the unions for a strike, and it was Adenauer who blinked as the one responsible for the (no longer "superhuman") effort of reconstruction. It seemed to work. A codetermination law was enacted in May 1951, providing parity labor representation on the supervisory boards and a work director from labor in the management of the coal as well as iron and steel industries.

A triumphant Böckler proclaimed that the unions' drive for economic democracy was now on track. Yet this vision turned out to be a chimera. As Horst Thum has shown, the *Mitbestimmung* law owed its passage once again to a unique convergence of forces. Critical in this case was Adenauer's need for union support in his struggle for the acceptance of the Schuman Plan. The unions were momentarily empowered in Adenauer's tug-of-war with Ruhr industrialists, parliament, and the Americans.[74] For that moment the unions could act once more as an *Ordnungsmacht* for Adenauer's western integration, just as they had acted to stabilize the Ruhr production in 1947 and collected their reward. But their defeat in the *Betriebsverfassungsgesetz* (factory constitution law) of July 1952, which granted only one-third labor representation with limited union influence in the supervisory councils in other industries, demonstrated the swift decline of the unions' power since the immediate postwar years, as did their surprisingly decisive defeat in the May 1953 elections to the social insurance councils.[75] The unions' role as cooperative *Ordnungsmacht* in the service of the "superhuman effort" of reconstruction had become all but irrelevant. Whatever its failures for the unions' specific economic democracy goals, this strategy had been critical in promoting a recovery that had been as vital to workers as to anyone. But this role had now ceased; and the prestige and often very significant influence of the unions which had accompanied this role had been much diminished.

The shock of this turnabout caused an internal crisis in the DGB. The late Böckler's successor, Christian Fette, and most of his leadership team were voted out in October 1952. Yet the positive pragmatism that the unions had demonstrated in the face of the catastrophic crisis in the postwar years let them rapidly adapt to the changing conditions of the early 1950s as well. While a number of the old economic restructuring concepts remained in the program, the focus now returned to wage strategies – ironically propagated by the most doctrinaire socialization advocate, Viktor Agartz, as an "expansive wage policy."

Yet this necessary and painful policy reversal did not mean the unions had failed *in* the postwar years. The institution they built fit the postwar political culture very well, and their critical role in postwar reconstruction left them with a foundation of respect and a level of participation and political-economic clout in the free market economy that is not only remarkable in comparison to its previous history, but also in an international comparison as the German economy achieved high wage levels *with* high productivity. Perhaps this has not been healthy for the German economy in the long run, but the 1982 Kohl *Wende* never became a Thatcher or Reagan Reaction. While President Reagan and British Prime Minister Margaret Thatcher staged bitter showdowns with key labor unions, (West) German Chancellor Helmut Kohl included the unions in the roundtable discussions among the heads of government, business, and labor unions, initiated by his predecessors in the late 1960s (the so-called *Konzertierte Aktion*) to deal with difficult social-economic situations.

Notes

1. Personal interview, 19 April 1980.
2. Dated 3 June 1945 and quoted in Michael Fichter, *Einheit und Organisation: Der Deutsche Gewerkschaftsbund im Aufbau 1945 bis 1949* (Cologne, 1990), 130.
3. Cf., e.g., the Bavarian Social Democrat Wilhelm Hoegner, the only Social Democratic prime minister of Bavaria since 1920, Peter Kritzer, *Wilhelm Hoegner: Politische Biographie eines bayerischen Sozialdemokraten* (Munich, 1979), 151.
4. Konrad Adenauer to Dr. Paul Silverberg, 30 May 1947, Stiftung Bundeskanzler-Adenauer-Haus (hereafter StBKAH): 07.03.
5. *Protokoll der ersten Gewerkschaftskonferenz der britischen Zone vom 12. bis 14.* März *1946 im Katholischen Vereinshaus in Hannover-Linden* (Hannover, 1946; hereafter 1. Gewerkschaftskonferenz BBZ), 18.
6. Cf. Christoph Kleßmann and Peter Friedemann, *Streiks und Hungermärsche im Ruhrgebiet 1946-1948* (Frankfurt am Main, 1977), 37-65, 75; Gloria Müller.

Mitbestimmung in der Nachkriegszeit: Britische Besatzungsmacht, Unternehmer. Gewerkschaften (Dusseldorf, 1987), 288-93; Eberhard Schmidt, *Die verhinderte Neuordnung 1945-1952: Zur Auseinandersetzung um die Demokratisierung der Wirtschaft in den westlichen Besatzungszonen und in der Bundesrepublik Deutschland* (Frankfurt am Main, 1970), 101; Siegfried Mielke, "Die Neugrundung der Gewerkschaften in den westlichen Besatzungszonen 1945-1949," in *Geschichte der Gewerkschaften in der Bundesrepublik Deutschland: Von den Anfängen bis heute*, ed. Hans-Otto Hemmer and Kurt Thomas Schmitz (Cologne, 1990), 75.

7. Schmidt, *Verhinderte Neuordnung*, esp. 98-103; Theo Pirker, *Die blinde Macht: Die Gewerkschaftsbewegung in Westdeutschland 1945-55*, vol. 1 (Munich, 1960), 117-18. Cf. also Walther L. Bernecker, "Die Neugrundung der Gewerkschaften in den Westzonen 1945-1949," in *Vorgeschichte der Bundesrepublik Deutschland: Zwischen Kapitulation und Grundgesetz*, ed. Josef Becker, Theo Stammen, and Peter Waldmann (Munich, 1979), 281-87; Christoph Kleßmann, "Betriebsrate und Gewerkschaften in Deutschland 1945-1952," in *Politische Weichenstellungen im Nachkriegsdeutschland 1945-1953*, ed. Heinrich August Winkler (Göttingen, 1979), 44-73.
8. For the most balanced and detailed treatment of U.S. policy, see Michael Fichter, *Besatzungsmacht und Gewerkschaften: Zur Entwicklung und Anwendung der US-Gewerkschaftspolitik in Deutschland 1944-1948* (Opladen, 1982).
9. Schmidt, *Verhinderte Neuordnung*, 100-1.
10. Charles S. Maier, "The Politics of Productivity: Foundations of American International Economic Policy after World War II," and "The Two Postwar Eras and the Conditions for Stability in Twentieth-Century Western Europe," in idem, *In Search of Stability: Explorations in Historical Political Economy* (Cambridge, Mass., 1987), 121-84; Volker R. Berghahn, "America and the Shaping of West Germany's Social Compact," paper presented at American Historical Association annual meeting, 1995; more generally idem, *The Americanization of West German Industry, 1945-1973* (New York, 1986), 203-30. Cf. recent research on U.S.-German labor relations by Michael Fichter, "HICOG and the Unions in West Germany: A Study of HICOG's Labor Policy toward the Deutscher Gewerkschaftsbund, 1949-1952," in *America's Policy Toward Germany. 1945-1955*, ed. Jeffry Diefendorf, Axel Frohn, and Hermann-Josef Rupieper (Cambridge, Mass., 1992), 257-80; and Hermann-Josef Rupieper, *Die Wurzeln der westdeutschen Demokratie: Der amerikanische Beitrag 1945-1952* (Opladen, 1993), 251-76.
11. Fritz Tarnow, "Gedanken über sozialistische Ökonomie nach dem Kriege," manuscript, 16 August 1943, AsD, SOPADE/180.
12. Cf. Wolfgang Schroeder, *Katholizismus und Einheitsgewerkschaft: Der* Streit um den DGB und der Niedergang des Sozialkatholizismus in der *Bundesrepublik Deutschland bis 1960* (Bonn, 1992), 71-125, 269-84.
13. Cf. Ossip K. Flechtheim, stressing hopes for a "*synthesis* of economic and social systems," in "Der Dritte Weg in der deutschen Parteipolitik nach 1945," *Aus Politik und Zeitgeschichte* 23/B25 (1973): 3. For Christian Democrats/Center Party, Rainer Barzel: "synthesis of individual and community," in *Die geistigen Grundlagen der politischen Parteien* (Bonn, 1947), 107. For Social Democrats: Waldemar von Knoeringen: "Democratic socialism is for us the *synthesis* of freedom and order," in "Die Stunde des Sozialismus ist da! Eine grundsätzliche Auseinandersetzung mit der CSU," *Das Volk* 2/5 (early December 1947): 4. For liberals, Heinz Wilhelm Beutler: "synthesis between the private economy and community interests, which will help overcome the opposition between labor and capital, between socialism and individualism," in "Aufbau einer neuen Wirtschaft," report of 1. Delegiertenkonferenz der FDP-Nordrhein, Cologne, 28 April 1956, Friedrich-Naumann-Stiftung, Politisches Archiv: 987; also the liberal Franz Blücher: "to build a bridge between the two extreme economic systems between which the battle is raging," in "Aufsatz für die erste Nummer der *Hannoverschen Neuesten Nachrichten*," 1 July 1946,

BAK, Nachlaß (hereafter NL) Blücher 154. And for the labor unions, Georg Berger: "We see ... in socialization a living *synthesis* of the economy and the state," *Die Sozialisierung der Bergbauwirtschaft. Stellungnahme des Industrieverbandes Bergbau auf seiner Bochumer Zonenkonferenz am 29.1.1947 nach einem Vortrag von Dr. Georg Berger, Bochum* (Bochum, 1947), 15.

14. Hartmut Pietsch, *Militärregierung, Bürokratie und Sozialisierung: Zur Entwicklung des politischen Systems des Ruhrgebietes 1945 bis 1948* (Duisburg, 1978), 68-70; cf. Lutz Niethammer, Ulrich Borsdorf, and Peter Brandt, eds., *Arbeiterinitiative 1945: Antifaschistische Ausschüsse und Reorganisation der Arbeiterbewegung in Deutschland* (Wuppertal, 1976).
15. Siegfried Mielke, "Der Wiederaufbau der Gewerkschaften: Legenden und Wirklichkeit," in Winkler, *Politische Weichenstellungen*, 79-80, 87; generally, Mielke, "Die Neugründung," 28-41.
16. Peter Hüttenberger, *Nordrhein-Westfalen und die Entstehung seiner parlamentarischen Demokratie* (Siegburg, 1973), 31-32.
17. Niethammer, Borsdorf, and Brandt, *Arbeiterinitiative*, 690-91, 709-11; Michael Fichter, "The Labor Movement in Stuttgart, 1945-1949," paper presented at the German Studies Association annual meeting, 1987, 5.
18. Cf. Wolfgang Rudzio, "Die ausgebliebene Sozialisierung an Rhein und Ruhr: Zur Sozialisierungspolitik von Labour-Regierung und SPD 1945-1948," *Archiv für Sozialgeschichte* 18 (1978): 1-39; Rolf Steininger, "Reform und Realität: Vom Scheitern britischer Sozialisierungspolitik an Rhein und Ruhr," *Geschichte im Westen* 3 (1988): 35-45; Horst Lademacher, "Die britische Sozialisierungspolitik im Rhein-Ruhr-Raum 1945-1948," in *Die Deutschlandpolitik Großbritanniens und die britische Zone, 1945-1949*, ed. Claus Scharf and Hans-Jürgen Schröder (Wiesbaden, 1979), 51-92; Dörte Winkler, "Die amerikanische Sozialisierungspolitik in Deutschland 1945-1948," in Winkler, *Politische Weichenstellungen*, 88-110; and Daniel E. Rogers, "Transforming the German Party System: The United States and the Origins of Political Moderation, 1945-1949," *Journal of Modern History* 65:3 (September 1993): 512-41.
19. "Die neue deutsche Gewerkschaftsbewegung. Programmvorschläge für einen einheitlichen deutschen Gewerkschaftsbund" (ed. by exiled German labor unionists in Great Britain, London, 1945), reprinted in *Historische Entwicklung der Mitbestimmung nach 1945* (Quellensammlung für das gleichnamige Seminar am Lehrstuhl für Sozial- und Wirtschaftsgeschichte, Prof. Dr. D. Petzina; Bochum, October 1979), 15.
20. "Gedanken über den Wiederaufbau freier, unabhängiger Gewerkschaften in Deutschland," manuscript, March 1943, AsD, SOPADE/164.
21. Cf. Diethelm Prowe, "Economic Democracy in Post-World War II Germany: Corporatist Crisis Response, 1945-1948," *Journal of Modern History* 57:2 (September 1985): 451-82.
22. Fritz Tarnow, "Referat auf dem Bundestag des Freien Gewerkschaftsbundes Hessen," Frankfurt, 11 October 1947, Archiv beim DGB-Bundesvorstand (hereafter DGB): Protokolle des FGB Hessen, 1946, 1947.
23. This was also confirmed by a union leader of the time who personally did not favor the business-labor chambers: Personal interview Willy Gottmann, 23 April 1980.
24. Fritz Naphtali, ed., *Wirtschaftsdemokratie* (Berlin, 1928); reprinted as *Wirtschaftsdemokratie: Ihr Wesen, Weg und Ziel* (Cologne, 1977).
25. Werner Hansen to Walter Fliess, 27 March 1947, DGB, Gewerkschaftliches Zonensekretariat (hereafter GZ) 1947/1.
26. "Antrag an den Herrn Oberpräsidenten der Nord-Rheinprovinz über die paritätische Ausgestaltung (Besetzung) der Industrie- und Handelskammern, Handwerkskammern und Landwirtschaftskammern, sowie über die Bildung einer Provinzwirtschaftskammer für den vorläufigen Bezirk der Nord-Rheinprovinz," 10 November 1945, DGB, NL Böckler 5.

27. Karl Arnold to Robert Lehr, 15 November 1945, Archiv der Vereinigung der Industrie- und Handelskammern des Landes Nordrhein-Westfalen (hereafter VIHK-NRW): Protokolle der Präsidialkonferenzen, Präsidialsitzung, 15 January 1946, 4; Detlev Hüwel, *Karl Arnold: Eine politische Biographie* (Wuppertal, 1980), 145.
28. Summary of a meeting of Oberpräsident Robert Lehr with business and labor representatives, 6 November 1945, DGB, Hansen V. For Lehr's corporatist ideas cf. Robert Lehr, "Über Sinn, Ziele und Organisation deutscher Staats- und Wirtschaftsführung," manuscript, January/February 1942, Stadtsarchiv Düsseldorf: NL 27 Lehr/50.
29. "Protokoll über die gemeinsame Sitzung der Abeitgeber- und Arbeitnehmervertreter," 25 January 1946, 3, DGB, Hansen LII.
30. Erich Potthoff, "Anmerkungen zu dem Antrag von Arnhold [sic] über die Bildung einer Provinzialwirtschaftskammer," 3 March 1946, DGB, Hansen X; Birgit Pollmann, *Reformansätze in Niedersachsen* (Hanover, 1977), 83-84.
31. See "Stenographisches Protokoll von der im Auftrag der Militärregierung einberufenen Arbeitnehmervertretungen der Privatwirtschaft, der Verwaltungen und der Behörden," 20 November 1945, 8, BAK, NL Richter/3.
32. "Wirtschaftsdemokratie: Vorschlag zum Aufbau einer wirtschaftlichen Selbstverwaltung," (duplicated typescript, 1947) DGB, GZ 1947/1. Eberhard Bömcke, a *Zentralamt für Wirtschaft* official who was closely involved with the project, testified that Rosenberg wrote the memorandum largely himself: Personal interview with Eberhard Bömcke, 24 June 1980.
33. Bundesvorstand des Deutschen Gewerkschaftsbundes, *Wirtschaftskammer-Gesetz: Entwurf eines Gesetzes über die Errichtung und Aufgaben von Wirtschaftskammern* (Bielefeld, 1947).
34. Ibid, preface.
35. "Wirtschaftsdemokratie," 3.
36. Wirtschaftspolitischer Ausschuß der Gewerkschaften in der Britischen Zone, meeting of 8-9 November 1946, DGB, GZ 1946/1.
37. Minutes of Präsidialsitzung der Industrie- und Handelskammern Nordrhein, 31 July 1945, 4, VIHK-NRW; memo Bernhard Hilgermann, 19 November 1946, Rheinisch-Westfälisches Wirtschaftsarchiv (hereafter RWW), 1/186/3.
38. "Bericht über die in Braunschweig bisher geleistete Arbeit der Gewerkschaften," DGB: Gottfurcht 11.
39. Diethelm Prowe, "Foundations of West German Democracy: Corporatist Patterns in the Post-1945 Democratization Process," in *Coping with the Past: Germany and Austria after 1945*, ed. Kathy Harms, Lutz R. Reuter, and Volker Dürr (Madison, Wisc., 1990), 109-17.
40. British Military Government, Economic Sub-Commission, German Organisation Branch 775/65 (Wolfgang Friedmann), 27 November 1946; "Entschließung des Vorstandes der Vereinigung der Industrie- und Handelskammern in der britischen Besatzungszone," 4 December 1946, Archiv der Industrie- und Handelskammer Düsseldorf, 110-40/2.
41. "Protokoll der linksrheinischen Kammern," 10 January, 14 February 1947, RWW, 1/189/1; Bernhard Hilgermann to Josef Löns, ca. February 1947, RWW, 1/186/3.
42. Also Wilhelm Peterson, Hamburg I.G. Metall chief and member of the *Zentralamt für Wirtschaft* advisory committee, *Deutscher Wirtschaftsrat*, and Oskar Schulze, who was a main force behind the economic chamber bill in Bremen.
43. "Grundsätze für die Bildung, Aufgaben und Arbeitsweise von Wirtschaftsausschüssen," 18 February 1947, text and minutes of the meetings, WWA, K5-115/2/7.
44. Rosenberg to Gewerkschaft Aachen, 22 February 1947, DGB, GZ 1947/1.
45. Cf. esp. Schmidt, *Verhinderte Neuordnung*; Pirker, *Blinde Macht*; Pollmann, *Reformansätze*; Ullrich Schneider, "Wirtschaftsausschüsse als Mittel praktizierter Wirtschaftsdemokratie?," in *Idee und Pragmatik in der politischen Entscheidung:*

Alfred Kubel zum 75. Geburtstag, ed. Bernd Rebe, Klaus Lompe, and Rudolf von Thadden (Bonn, 1984), 317-32.

46. There were many such comments, e.g., Hans-Joachim Fricke, "Kammern und Gewerkschaften," *Niedersächsische Wirtschaft* 2/7 (10 April 1947): 1.
47. Kleßmann and Friedemann, *Streiks*, 35-54.
48. Vereinigung der Industrie- und Handelskammern der Britischen Besatzungszone, meeting of 18 February 1947, WWA, K5-115/2/7.
49. Interview Bömcke, 24 June 1980 and phone conversation, 2 July 1980; cf. also minutes of Wuppertal meetings, WWA, K5-115/2/7.
50. Union resolution: "Entschließung der Bundesbeiratssitzung vom 1. September 1948 zum Lohn- und Preisproblem," DGB, GR/Sept. 1948. Chamber response: VIHK-NRW, 30 September 1948, 3. Action Committee meetings, actions: Wilhelm Pawlik (DGB) to IHK Essen, 18 September 1948; reports on meetings in Essen on 23 September 1948, 11 October 1948, 29 October 1948, 21 December 1948, 9 January 1949, RWW, 28/102/2. Evaluation: DGB Bezirk Nordmark, *Rundschreiben* #62/48/II (5 November 1948), DGB, *Rundschreiben* Nordmark 1947-1948; DGB Bezirk Nordrhein-Westfalen, *Rundschreiben* #52/48 (5 November 1948), DGB, Hansen XII; *Der Bund*, 3/3 (29 January 1949): 1.
51. Diethelm Prowe, "Unternehmer, Gewerkschaften und Staat in der Kammerneuordnung in der britischen Besatzungszone bis 1950," in *Wirtschaftspolitik im britischen Besatzungsgebiet 1945 bis 1949*, ed. Dietmar Petzina and Walter Euchner (Düsseldorf, 1984), 243-48.
52. Gerhard Beier, *Der Demonstrations- und Generalstreik vom 12. November 1948 im Zusammenhang mit der parlamentarischen Entwicklung Westdeutschlands* (Frankfurt am Main, 1975).
53. *Gesetzesvorschlag des Deutschen Gewerkschaftsbundes für das Gebiet der Bundesrepublik Deutschland zur Neuordnung der deutschen Wirtschaft* (Düsseldorf, 22 May 1950), 9-26, 35-46.
54. Ludwig Rosenberg, "Die Praxis der Wirtschaftsdemokratie," speech of September 24, 1949, in AsD, NL Rosenberg/4, 9.
55. Cf. Heinz-Dietrich Ortlieb, "Der gegenwärtige Stand der Sozialisierungsdebatte in Deutschland," in *Untersuchungen zur sozialistischen Gestaltung der Wirtschaftsordnung*, ed. Walter Weddigen (Berlin, 1950), 189-287; Heinrich Zank, "Systeme der Sozialisierung," *Das Sozialistische Jahrhundert* II/7,8 (February 1948): 103-7; Norbert Konegen and Gerhard Kracht, eds., *Sozialismus und Sozialisierung* (Kronberg/Ts., 1975), 18; *Handwörterbuch der Sozialwissenschaften* (Stuttgart, 1952-66), 464-469: entry "Sozialisierung: (II) Geschichte (1) Deutschland," (written by Heinz-Dietrich Ortlieb and Gerhard Stavenhagen); Diethelm Prowe, "Socialism as Crisis Response: Socialization and the Escape from Poverty and Power in Post-World War II Germany," *German Studies Review* 15:1 (1992): 65-85.
56. "Die wirtschaftliche Neuordnung der Grundstoffindustrien: Grundsätze des Deutschen Gewerkschaftsbundes (DGB)," DGB (BBZ) Congress, Bielefeld, 22-25 April 1947, Nordrhein-Westfälisches Hauptstaatsarchiv Düsseldorf (hereafter HStAD), RWN 105/1; Deutscher Gewerkschafts-Bund, "Wirtschaftspolitische Grundsätze des Deutschen Gewerkschafts-Bundes," *Kongreß zur Gründung eines Gewerkschaftsbundes für das Gebiet der Bundesrepublik Deutschland, München, 12. bis 14. Oktober 1949*, DGB, BBZ Oct. 49.
57. Ibid., 4-5.
58. See, for example, Wirtschaftswissenschaftliches Institut der Gewerkschaften (Britische Zone), Gewerkschaftliches Zonensekretariat, "Argumente zur Sozialisierung. Eine Stellungnahme der Gewerkschaften zu den üblichen Einwendungen gegen die Sozialisierung" (Bielefeld, 11 April 1947), BAK, NL Blücher 383, 13, 6, 11, 4 respectively.

59. Ute Schmidt and Tilman Fichter, *Der erzwungene Kapitalismus: Klassenkämpfe in den Westzonen 1945-1948* (Berlin, 1971), 29-30. For a contemporary statement, cf. Ortlieb, "Sozialisierungsdebatte," 202-5.
60. Rosenberg, "Die Praxis," 10.
61. Interview Bömcke, 24 June 1980.
62. Werner Hansen, "Gewerkschaften und Betriebsräte," 6 May 1948, HStAD, RWN 249/39 (NL Hansen).
63. 1. Gewerkschaftskonferenz BBZ, 56; on early works council actions, see Müller, *Mitbestimmung*, 57-68.
64. Cf. ibid., 288-93.
65. Ibid. 129-43, quote 137.
66. Rosenberg, "Die Praxis," 8 (quote), 10; cf. training workshops conducted for advisory committee representatives: DGB-Nordrhein-Westfalen, Rundschreiben #197/50 (29 September 1950), and #205/50 (11 October 1950), DGB, Rundschreiben 1950.
67. Letters Karl Jarres (Klöckner-Werke A.G.) and Hermann Reusch and Ernst Hilbert (Gute-Hoffnungs-Hütte) to Einheitsgewerkschaft Köln, 18 January 1947, StBKAH, 07.14. Wilhelm Salewski, executive director of the iron and steel manufacturing association, told the author that these letters had been initiated by him and the association to prevent further radicalization and socialization: Personal interview, 18 December 1979.
68. For the general information below: Eberhard Bömcke, "Die wirtschaftliche Selbstverwaltung. Ihr Anteil an den staatlichen Aufgaben," *Wirtschaftsverwaltung* 1:6 (August 1948), 10-13; Verwaltungsamt für Wirtschaft des Vereinigten Wirtschaftsgebietes, "An alle Hauptabteilungen," Minden, 25 February 1947, DGB, Gewerkschaftsrat (hereafter GR): Allgemein I; Verwaltung für Wirtschaft des Vereinigten Wirtschaftsgebietes, "Richtlinien für die Bildung von Länder-, Fach, und Länderfachausschüssen bei der Verwaltung für Wirtschaft," 6 May 1948, DGB: GR April, May 1948; minutes and agendas, BAK, Z4 and Z8, and DGB: GR 1947-49; *Bundesgesetzblatt* 1950, 5 (20 January 1950).
69. Ludwig Rosenberg, *Vom Wirtschaftsuntertan zum Wirtschaftsbürger* (Cologne, 1948).
70. Cf. n. 54 above.
71. Raymond notes on discussion with Böckler, 15 November 1949, Gabriele Müller-List, ed., *Montanmitbestimmung: Das Gesetz über die Mitbestimmung der Arbeitnehmer in den Aufsichtsräten und Vorständen der Unternehmen des Bergbaus und der Eisen und Stahl erzeugenden Industrie vom 21. Mai 1951* (Düsseldorf, 1981), 7. Cf. also Berghahn, *Americanization*, 220-26.
72. Minutes of the DGB and employers' associations in Hattenheim, 9-10 January 1950 and 30-31 March 1950, and in Maria Laach, 5-6 July 1950, WWA, K5-100/2/21-V. The documents are reprinted in Müller-List, 11 ff.
73. Minutes of the meeting of DIHT Hauptausschuß, 13 April 1950, WWA, K5 100/2/2V.
74. Horst Thum, *Mitbestimmung in der Montanindustrie: Der Mythos vom Sieg der Gewerkschaften* (Stuttgart, 1982), especially 98-105; Thomas Allan Schwartz, *America's Germany: John J. McCloy and the Federal Republic of Germany* (Cambridge, Mass., 1991), 189-93, 196.
75. Kleßmann, "Betriebsräte," 44, 69; Werner Müller, "Die Gründung des DGB, der Kampf um die Mitbestimmung, programmatisches Scheitern und der Übergang zum gewerkschaftlichen Pragmatismus," in Hemmer and Schmitz, *Geschichte der Gewerkschaften*, 123-27; on the elections, Hockerts, *Sozialpolitische Entscheidungen*, 145-46.

Chapter 17

THE SOVIETS, THE GERMAN LEFT, AND THE PROBLEM OF "SECTARIANISM" IN THE EASTERN ZONE, 1945 TO 1949

Norman Naimark

The many shades of meaning in the idea of the "Left" have deprived the term of much of its historical validity.[1] Even when one ties the term to a concrete place – eastern Germany; a fixed time – the period of the Soviet occupation government, 1945 to 1949; and a relatively small group of anti-fascists, notions of the left spill all over the political spectrum, incorporating anarchists, trade unionists, communists of various sorts, Social Democrats (also of various sorts), and even Christian socialists from the supposedly middle-class party of the Christian Democratic Union (CDU). This chaotic intermingling of leftist groups in postwar Germany was nothing new to the German or European experience. One only has to think about the German Revolution of 1918 to 1919 or the Spanish Civil War to capture the diversity on the Left before World War II. What was new in Germany (and in most of Eastern Europe) after the war was the ability of the Soviet occupiers to circumscribe the political space for the Left by force and to collapse diverse leftists into mass ruling parties.

The Soviets also exploited their monopoly on the press and publishing to impose analytical categories that transformed chaos into order, spontaneity into rigidity, and experimentation into learning by rote. One

Notes for this chapter begin on page 438.

of the most powerful of these categories was that of "sectarianism," which was used by the Soviets and by German Communists who had spent the war years in Moscow to brand leftists who sought to use the defeat of fascism as the starting point for the socialist revolution in occupied Germany. German Left Communists had always been a problem for the Soviets and the Comintern. In his *"Left-Wing" Communism – An Infantile Disorder* (1920), Lenin laid the groundwork for the Soviet view of German "sectarians" by railing against their inability to compromise with other political forces and to work through parliament to attain power, and – paraphrasing Engels – for their tendency to substitute impatience for theory.[2] In subsequent years, the Luxemburgist mix of revolutionary purity and democratic ideals often earned the Soviet appellation of sectarianism.[3] But unlike Trotskyism, which Stalinist Russia categorized as nothing more than a front for the reactionary Right, the Luxemburgism of the German party remained in Soviet conceptions a "disorder" of the Left. The deviations of Tito and the Yugoslav comrades were initially characterized as sectarianism after the first meeting of the Cominform in Szklarska Poreba in September 1947; however, when the Yugoslavs were expelled from the Cominform in the summer of 1948, one of the accusations was that of Trotskyism, meaning the Yugoslav party had joined the bourgeois "enemy."

Like so much else in the historiography of postwar Eastern Europe, the Cold War created the terms for historical debate about political developments in eastern Germany. From the Soviet (and East German) side, the Red Army "liberated" eastern Germany, helped the German Communists and Social Democrats create the "anti-fascist democratic" bloc and then join together in the Socialist Unity Party (SED), insuring the future of communism in Germany. For western historians, before and after 1989, the Soviets "occupied" eastern Germany, eviscerated the Left by the forced union *(Zwangsvereinigung)* of Communists and Social Democrats, insuring Moscow's domination of the East. In *both* historiographies, organized Communists in the KPD, SPD, and the SED are considered to be the Left. Those whom the Soviets called sectarians are barely mentioned. The idea of this essay, then, is to look at both the reality and the discourse of "sectarianism" in the East. By doing so, I am not developing a counterfactual subplot that a "third way" was possible in the Soviet occupied zone or that Germany could have experienced a serious revolutionary upheaval had there been no Four-Power occupation.[4] Instead, I want to look at these so-called sectarian groups and the threat of sectarianism as they influenced the way the Soviets conducted their political business in the East.

Two notes of caution are appropriate at the outset. First of all, as I have indicated earlier, there were no real sectarians – only those in Soviet (and

German communist) parlance who deigned to place their interpretations of communist scripture – usually of a more revolutionary complexion – above those of Moscow's local representatives. Second, there were considerable articulated and unarticulated differences in the theoretical outlook of Communists in the KPD and later SED. Luxemburgism remained influential in both parties; German Communists who returned from exile in Mexico or had been interned in concentration camps had their own conceptions of the socialist future; and even among those German Communists who spent the war years in Moscow there were muted differences about the appropriate pace of the revolution. Even today, one could argue, the "infantile disease" of leftism continues to influence German communism in the Party of Democratic Socialism (PDS) and newly formed KPD.

1. The Soviets and "Stunde Null"

As a result of Georgi Dimitrov's planning on behalf of the Central Committee of the Communist Party of the Soviet Union (CPSU), three groups of KPD activists accompanied the Soviet armies into Germany in the spring of 1945. The "Ulbricht Group" joined the First Belorussion Front on 27 April and entered Berlin while the fighting was still going on.[5] Anton Ackermann's group linked up with the First Ukrainian Front on 1 May and moved with the Soviet armies into still-smoldering Dresden. Gustav Sobottka's group was attached to the Second Belorussian Front on 6 May and operated in Mecklenburg and the Baltic towns of Schwerin and Rostock. The KPD supported the creation of an anti-fascist democratic order, justifying this by pointing to pre-war KPD programs and to the activities of the German Communists in Moscow on behalf of the National Committee for "Free Germany" (NKFD), the anti-fascist organization of German prisoners of war in the Soviet Union. But the future of the NKFD depended on hopes for an end to the war through a German popular uprising, an army coup, or a negotiated peace. With the Nazis' unconditional surrender in May 1945, the NKFD was disbanded and its members, depending on their political profiles, were gradually integrated into the state and security apparatus of the eastern zone. The Communists were also asked to become administrators, at least in the short-run. Long years in the Soviet Union had convinced the leading members of the KPD that careful attention to the Soviets' political and international needs paid organizational and personal dividends. Few were better schooled in this lesson than Walter Ulbricht, and it was Ulbricht who oversaw the creation of a new German administration.

In the days following the Nazi surrender, local administrations were put in the hands of seventy German Communist emigrants from Moscow, as well as some three hundred former German prisoners of war in the USSR, most of whom had been associated with the NKFD and had attended anti-fascist schools. The 7th Section of GlavPURKKA (the Main Political Administration of the Red Army) was nominally in charge of the operation. The military brought in additional Soviet political workers who knew German and could be entrusted to organize propaganda among the population. The 7th Section sent out German-speaking propagandists on trucks mounted with loudspeakers to go from town to town announcing the new Soviet policies for Germany. They also published the first German-language newspapers.[6] The 7th Section and the German anti-fascists had their work cut out for them. The Germans were in a terrible state: panicked, depressed, and helpless. Only gradually did they emerge from hiding, having found out that the Soviets at least would not let them starve or ship them all off to Siberia, as Nazi propaganda had led many of them to believe. Still, the population was wary and scared, a problem that was exacerbated by continuing assaults on German men and women by Soviet soldiers. In the first six weeks of the occupation, suicides were quite common, including mass suicides by whole families or groups.[7] Even after the plague of suicides and assaults abated, the Soviets and their German helpmates faced hostility and suspicion among the population. Especially in the villages, but also in the cities, many Germans still pictured the Russians through the lenses of Nazi propaganda. Exhausted, apathetic, and hostile to the Russians, Germans looked to their futures with a combination of indifference and fear.

This generally bleak picture of "zero-hour" (*Stunde null*), as the Germans call the first weeks and months of the occupation, would not be complete without an understanding of the tremendous upswing of political activity within the remnants of the German Left in general and among German Communists in particular. Significant numbers of German Communists, previously interned in jails and concentration camps or hiding in the underground, erupted into political action toward the very end of the war. These Communists cared no less for the Soviet Union than did their comrades who had spent the war years in Moscow, but they were generally less adept at adjusting to the Kremlin's shifting political demands. Their views at the end of the war were remarkably consistent, given the lack of any central underground communist organization: the collapse of fascism and the victory of the Soviet Union made possible the creation of the socialist Germany for which they had fought so long and sacrificed so much. Many of these Communist groups suffered from what their critics (and later East German historians) called sectarianism.[8] In other words, they wanted to set up soviets (workers' councils), fight the counterrevolution, and – with the onset of the Soviet military occupation – begin the process of creating a "Soviet Germany."[9] In this way, there would be no need to ally themselves with other emerging parties because a highly centralized KPD, modeled on the Bolshevik party and the Red Army, would suffice to bring about the success of the revolution. Some groups even demanded weapons from the Soviet commandants to seize town halls and defend the barricades.

Especially during the first few weeks of the occupation, when instructions to the Soviet commandants were extremely vague and each commandant acted largely autonomously, the so-called sectarians dominated the emerging German political landscape.[10] Their radicalism had been hardened by years in the underground and in Nazi jails and camps. They rejected out of hand any idea of returning to a Weimar-style bourgeois democracy, which they held accountable for Hitler's rise to power. In their view, the only legitimate alternative to the restoration of Weimar was socialist revolution. Especially in the first days and weeks of the occupation, these views were shared by a remarkably large number of veterans of both the KPD and SPD.

Even Walter Ulbricht, Moscow's chief factotum in the German party, was unable to control these Communists and was criticized by his Soviet overlords for being badly out of touch with the situation.[11] Moreover, there was little agreement about tactics within and among the three German initiative groups. As a result of this chaotic approach to politics in the first period of the occupation, the reinvigorated Communist Left was allowed to indulge in fantasies about a new German Bolshevik revolution. Some local Communists began the collectivization of agriculture; others, waving red flags and singing the Internationale, set up Soviets of Workers and Peasants Deputies. In some districts of Berlin, party headquarters were decorated with red banners, and automobiles requisitioned by the Communists were painted with the hammer and sickle. In a variety of towns, streets were renamed after such German communist heroes as Rosa Luxemburg, Ernst Thälmann, and Karl Liebknecht; pictures of Stalin and Thälmann were carried as religious icons by KPD "revolutionaries."[12] Even when told by Soviet commandants that they were not allowed to establish "Soviet power" or the "dictatorship of the proletariat," the Communists answered: "Okay, fine, we won't call it Soviet power, but it will be Soviet power in any case, it can't be anything else."[13]

Usually, however, the Soviet commandants did not even bother to try to reign in the leftists. In Pirna (Saxony), the Communists changed the day of rest from Sunday to Friday and insisted that citizens greet each other with the KPD slogan "*Rot Front*" (Red Front) instead of "Good Day." Until 17 May, all of the Soviet zone of Germany was on Moscow time; soon, too, the leftists argued, Poland and Germany would also be Soviet republics. The first number of the Coswig (Anhalt) newspaper

Rote Fahne, published on 8 May 1945, recalled the sufferings and death of Ernst Thälmann in Buchenwald and ended with the call for "the building of a "Leninist-Marxist state. Hail to Moscow *(Heil Moskau)*." The third number of *Rote Fahne*, published on 16 May, indicated that the Communists controlled the economic and social life of the town. Schools were reopened by the "workers' state"; the local commandants issued their orders through the communist-dominated soviet.[14]

In several other towns KPD leaders called themselves "commissars," insisted that red flags and banners decorate the towns, and renamed streets and plazas. Inspired by the Greek and Yugoslav revolutions, the Eisleben Communists tried to seize local enterprises and drive off manufacturers and entrepreneurs. They were compelled initially by the American occupation forces to abandon their revolutionary pretensions, including the desire to erect in the center of town a statue of Lenin, which they had managed to conceal during the war. As a result, the Eisleben Communists eagerly awaited the arrival of Soviet troops, who according to Allied agreement would occupy the town at the beginning of July. Although they allowed the group to erect the Lenin statue, the Soviets proved no more receptive to revolutionary rhetoric and actions than were the Americans.[15]

Anton Ackermann expressed his frustration to the Soviet Central Committee about the Communists in Meissen, who had seized control of the local government before the Soviets entered town.

> *The mayor was the first commissar of the city, his deputy was a commissar for industry – for supplies [there was] a commissar, for trade a commissar, for finances a commissar, for the rebuilding of the destroyed city a commissar, for the socialization of industries a commissar, as head of a factory a commissar. In general, Soviet power in anarchist light.*[16]

The first Soviet reports on these activities reflected a kind of patronizing amusement regarding these "Reds." They also indicated that measures were taken to correct these KPD "errors and blunders."[17] More often than not, however, the commandants themselves contributed to the problem, either ignoring the leftists or condoning their activity. In Meissen, for example, high-level political instructors from the 7th Section were brought in to deal with the commandants about the unacceptability of the red commissar government. Soviet policy in Germany was motivated by Stalin's desire to reach a Four-Power agreement that would guarantee the payment of reparations and would satisfy Soviet security interests in the demilitarization and denazification of the entire country. The Soviets were not in the least interested in supporting revolutionary activity in Germany; in Moscow's view this would inevitably alienate the western powers and disrupt the creation of an Allied Control Authority.

Like his Soviet mentors, Ulbricht also had no love for the "sectarians," the "ultraradicals" *(Überradikale)*, as he frequently called them. In particular, the many supposedly sectarian groups in Berlin annoyed him to no end. In his view, they got in the way of the Zone's new administration and unnecessarily scared off the German bourgeoisie.[18] For Ulbricht, the sooner the sectarian KPD of the Weimar period was renewed by an influx of fresh, more pliable young recruits, the better.[19] Ulbricht sought to build a bureaucratized and hierarchical party on the Soviet model. He was interested in fostering efficient organization and exerting control – not in erecting barricades or forming workers' councils.

Ulbricht and the Moscow German Communists also were averse to another variety of underground German Communists in this period: those who wanted to abandon normal party activity for anti-fascist fronts, a tactic that many had learned initially from the NKFD broadcasts from the Soviet Union to Germany in 1944 to 1945. Several communist groups echoed the NKFD's call for the establishment of a "bloc of fighting democracy," which would join all anti-fascist organizations, parties, groups, and individuals in the struggle for a socialist democratic republic.[20] These Communists called for the dissolution of the KPD and the formation of new political unions as the way out of the traumatic errors of the past because, in their view, disunity had made possible the tragic Nazi seizure of power. Often, both KPD and SPD activists in the countryside and towns – at the grass roots, one can say with some confidence – found a variety of ways to merge their parties and actions, sometimes even joining with local Soviet commandants sympathetic to the general "united front" approach. In Koethen (Saxony), Communists and Social Democrats spontaneously merged their efforts in a "Socialist Workers Party," which NKVD General Serov characterized as suffering from "petit-bourgeois radicalism."[21] Fritz Koehn recalled that after he was liberated from prison in Treptow, he and his comrades thought that within a few months Communists and Social Democrats would form a large workers' party, the dictatorship of the proletariat would be introduced, and "we would not need any more middle-class people."[22] With the Soviet occupation, anti-fascist groups emerged from the underground, or were newly formed, with the clear agenda of uniting the former enemies of the Left, the Communists, and Social Democrats, and repairing the terrible rift that had made possible, from most socialists' point of view, the rise of fascism.

2. In Moscow

Soviet and German political leaders could look with some sense of accomplishment at the first month of the Soviet occupation. After the capitulation itself, resistance was minimal and Nazism seemed largely quiescent. Municipal administrations had been revived, and the infrastructures of the bigger cities had returned, if not to normality, at least to the level where water, electricity, and sewage disposal could be counted on. Food and medical services reached broad cross-sections of the population. The first newspapers were being printed by the military authorities, and the first cinema houses and even theaters were being reopened. Though gratified in general by the upsurge in political activity on the German Left, both the Moscow KPD leaders and the Soviets were concerned about the ideological chaos they perceived among German socialists. Serious political work among the German population, in their view, could be undertaken only with a unified approach to the problems of ideology. As a result, the leaders of the initiative groups, Anton Ackermann, Walter Ulbricht, and Gustav Sobottka, were recalled to Moscow at the beginning of June to consult with the Soviet leadership about the formation of political parties and trade unions authorized by a Soviet directive of 26 May 1945.

The first meeting between the initiative group leaders and the Soviet leadership – Stalin, Molotov, and Zhdanov – took place on 4 June 1945. Wilhelm Pieck was also there, and it is to his sketchy notes that we owe our knowledge of the discussions. The primary issue at hand was the intention of the Soviets to legalize the KPD as "the *party of labor* (workers, farmers, intellectuals)," whose goal would be "the completion of the bourgeois-democratic revolution." In other words, the KPD was to be a mass party, interested in democratic transformations. At this meeting, the Soviets and Germans also named a nine-member Politburo and a five-member Secretariat for the new KPD. In accord with Ulbricht's inclinations in particular, the Soviets endorsed the elimination of the anti-fascist groups: in Pieck's notes, "*the formation of anti-fascist committees* also is not useful, because the danger exists that they will have independent power next to that of the city and local government."[23] In a meeting with Dimitrov and Paniushkin of the Soviet Central Committee on 7 June, Ulbricht also warned of the dangers of "dual power" – reminiscent of the early stages of the Russian revolution – if the "Antifas" (anti-fascist committees) were allowed to continue.[24]

During the 7 June meeting, Dimitrov and Paniushkin also expressed a great deal of interest in the mood of the Germans and the possibilities for their reeducation. Both Ackermann and Ulbricht responded that the most difficult problem was to get the Germans to accept "responsibility for the crimes which were committed by the Hitlerites." Given the way the Germans responded to the problem of war guilt, Ackermann added, one would think 90 percent of them had been in the resistance.[25] Typically, Ulbricht attacked both the Social Democrats and Communists for their problems in accepting responsibility for the past. According to

Ulbricht, socialists protested the Soviet dismantling of German factories with the argument that the new democratic Germany could be trusted to embark on a path of friendship with Russia. Ulbricht reported that he rejected these protests in sharp and uncompromising terms with the argument that there was no guarantee that fascism would not rear its ugly head again in Germany.[26] Ulbricht was characteristically much more generous towards the Social Democrats and the bourgeois politicians than he was towards the "sectarians" and "anti-fascist committees," because the latter interfered with efficient administration. Ulbricht noted, for example, that getting Social Democrats and "the Catholics" (former Center Party members) to join local administrations increased the authority of the government institutions and of the Red Army. Ulbricht concluded that Germany did not need any new experiments or foolishness regarding the socialization of property. "Red Front" greetings scared away the average citizens. The primary tasks at the moment were to combine patient work in the local administrations with massive reeducation of the population through the newly formed political parties.[27]

Following up on the Moscow consultations, the Soviets and the KPD leadership disbanded at least two hundred anti-fascist committees from all over the Soviet zone. Ulbricht was pleased; already a month earlier he had written to Dimitrov: "I've had just about enough of these Antifas."[28] Like Ulbricht, SMAD (the Soviet Military Administration in Germany) was more interested at the moment in administration than in politics. There was a shortage of capable and reliable bureaucrats to occupy positions in town and village government. With their diverse political, educational, and cultural initiatives, the anti-fascist groups disrupted the flow of personnel into the German administrations. Protests by the anti-fascist committee members, some KPD activists, and even by some Soviet officers against breaking up the antifas were answered with the admonition by Zhukov and Ulbricht that the best of the anti-fascists should leave the work of politics and ideology to the parties and join the administrations and local governments instead.

The Soviet military government also closed down the anti-fascist groups because it wanted German leftists to participate in the political life of the parties it was about to legalize. According to Order no. 2 (10 June 1945), anti-fascist political parties, trade unions, and other professional and social organizations were allowed to carry on activities if they registered with and were found acceptable by SMAD. Many of the German anti-fascist activists, especially the Communists, were taken by surprise by the broad range of political options offered by the Soviets; others, however, were upset and disappointed by their banishment. On 11 June, the KPD issued its program, the one written by Ackermann in Moscow; the SPD announced its program and existence on June 15; and the Christian

Democrats and the Liberal Democrats (LDP) followed soon after. By setting up the SPD and the non-socialist parties so quickly, and then joining them in an anti-fascist bloc, SMAD preempted those Communists who advocated the establishment of Soviet power and the crushing of the bourgeoisie. The "sectarians" found as little sympathy within SMAD as they had among the Moscow KPD leadership. In setting up both the KPD and the SPD, SMAD also indicated that there would be no amalgamated workers' party to seize control of the administrations.[29]

3. "Unity of Action"

Soviet and East German historical literature noted with great satisfaction that by issuing Order no. 2, the Soviets were the first of the Allied occupation governments to allow political activities in their zone. But for large numbers of German anti-fascists, the beginning of the political parties and the operation of the anti-fascist democratic bloc meant the end of active politics. Especially in Berlin, many communist groups refused to join the reconstituted KPD because they considered its program a step backward from the pre-war program. SMAD's Order no. 2 did not simply create political parties; it gave the Soviets the opportunity to monitor, check, and control all political activities in their zone of occupation. Very quickly, the excitement and the initiatives of the first weeks after liberation faded into the mandates of bureaucratic politics. As many of the so-called "activists of the first hour" later testified, there was nothing later to match the exhilaration of the period *before* the foundation of the political parties.[30]

At the same time, the KPD leadership could take great satisfaction in its new status as a mass political party, even if the ideological level of the new recruits remained questionable. Most of the new members of the KPD were workers with non-Nazi backgrounds, recruited initially by SMAD and the KPD leadership to take leading positions in the administrations and local governments, as well as to assume important new posts as people's judges, policemen, and school teachers. Many of them were exuberant, hard-working, and dedicated to the new Germany. Some KPD reports indicate that the recruits were useful to the party in outflanking the numerous inflexible "sectarians" from the pre-1933 party. But other reports suggest that the new recruits created more problems than they solved. There were too many dishonest "adventurers," admitted Franz Dahlem, including "criminals [and] lawbreakers." Hermann Matern put the problem even more strongly: "Many dirty elements have placed themselves at the head of our ranks."[31]

Still, the KPD leadership complained much more about continuing sectarian tendencies in the party than about problems with careerists and criminals. Primary among them was the idea that socialism was imminent and that the Red Army guaranteed its establishment in Germany. Talking to a group of former Breslau anti-fascists in Dresden at the end of July 1945, Hermann Matern expressed the frustration of the KPD leaders on this issue:

> *To talk of the dictatorship of the proletariat today is utterly absurd and anyone who comes to us with such nonsense has either not understood the situation or is an enemy. I think that we understand each other. It is imperative that one says this in such a hard and sober way, because we live in hard times.*[32]

Maria Rentmeister, a leading KPD women's activist, reported that in mid-July in Halle many party members had not even bothered to read the 11 June KPD program, believing it to be nothing but a smokescreen; instead, "sectarian tendencies were everywhere."[33] In Weimar, Georg Schneider tried to rein in the KPD leftists by arguing that they were only helping the fascists with their communist extremism:"Every word about socialization in Germany is [pure] radicalism, is … petit-bourgeois chatter."[34] Berlin remained a severe problem in this regard, where report after report on local KPD groups spoke of the ubiquitous "sectarians." In Wedding and a number of other "red" districts, the KPD leadership could think of no other solution to the dominance of the "sectarian"" than changing the local leadership.[35]

In addition to continuing to bring up the problems of rape and dismantling – subjects which drove the leadership to distraction – the KPD "ultraradicals" simply did not accept the party's line on how to deal with former Nazis. The KPD leadership advocated working with the "small Nazis," the so-called "Pgs" (nominal party members), while at the same time strenuously insisting that the entire German nation was responsible for the Nazi crimes. The issue of general German guilt was often met with "icy silence" by KPD audiences, especially those of KPD workers, while attacks on Nazis, all Nazis, roused great enthusiasm.[36] In Bernau, the local party group cut rations to former Nazis, demanding that they "should work more and eat less." In Oranienburg, Nazis and even family members of former Nazis were not allowed to live in their houses and apartments.[37] The Soviet political officers noted, however, that the KPD leadership was getting nowhere with the issue of general German guilt and recommended that the KPD follow the successful example of the SPD and worry more about the future than dwell on the past.[38]

4. The SED

The story of the unification of the SPD and KPD into the Socialist Unity Party (SED) in April 1946 has been told often enough and well enough not to require recounting here.[39] For our purposes, it is important to note that the party was born with severe defects. Not only did it preempt political developments in the west and, therefore, undermine, as many predicted, any program for the unity of Germany, it also created an enormous problem in Berlin. The majority of the Berlin SPD did not join the SED, which the Soviets understood would be a serious handicap for the party. The Soviets were annoyed, as well, that some 10 percent of Berlin's *KPD* – even in the traditional communist districts of Wedding and Neukölln – did not join the SED, complaining that the new party was deviationist and "opportunistic."[40]

While the SED formally announced that it was a Marxist party, Ulbricht, Pieck, Matern, Koenen, and others did not give up their adherence to Leninism or their dedication to the Soviet style of government. Even their Soviet "friends" gently chided the former KPD chiefs for continuing to meet separately from the former SPD leaders and to talk and think of the SED's history in terms of the KPD.[41] This happened on the level of everyday activities as well. The situation in Schwerin, described by one SED member, was not untypical: "The SPD and KPD live under one roof – in a legal marriage, but inside [the house] they prefer to live separately."[42]

The party also continued to suffer from divisions on the Left. Charged with sectarianism in the early days, the Left increasingly was branded with the more dangerous appellation of Trotskyism. Berlin remained a serious problem in this regard. In fact, Hermann Matern told a visiting Soviet commission that so-called ultra-leftists in Berlin were more threatening to the Berlin SED than the Schumacherite Right. Many of the ultra-leftists did not want to join the SED in the first place, and those who did quickly sank into apathy and indifference. Those who did not join, some 10 percent of the total Berlin KPD, gravitated to "left factional groups of a Trotskyist sort." According to Matern, they existed in ten of the twelve districts of Berlin and concentrated their efforts on denouncing the Soviet Union as an imperialist power.[43] Trotskyist groups were also reported to have influence in Leipzig and Dresden, though in Saxony as a whole the SED leadership seemed most concerned with the so-called Brandlerists, followers of Heinrich Brandler, the communist dissident from the Weimar period. In fact, the large and influential Saxon SED was rent by all kinds of divisions. According to Fritz Grosse, there were "Muscovites, Spaniards, Buchenwalders, Sachsenhauseners, Mauthauseners, Waldheimers, and Auschwitzers – [there were] groups of the National Committee [NKFD], front school veterans, and old underground [activists], and also English emigrants."[44] Whichever group it came from, the criticism from the Left was mostly the same. The Soviet Union was not a socialist country but represented state capitalism.

Rather than liberating the German proletariat, the Soviets enslaved German workers anew by removing factories and equipment and, through their opposition to the Marshall Plan, condemned the German masses to hunger and unemployment.[45]

5. The Party of the New Type

At the Second Congress of the SED in September 1947, the party reiterated its commitment to Marxism. Grotewohl added that the "accomplishments of Leninism" should also be closely studied, but in no way mechanically applied to the conditions of Germany. In the months following the Congress, which coincided with the inaugural meeting of the Cominform at Szklarska Poreba, the tone of SED and SMAD pronouncements hardened noticeably. In December 1947, for example, Soviet political officer Colonel Sergei Tiul'panov expressed his displeasure with the flaccid qualities of the SED's ideological production. The party leaders needed, he said, to adopt a clear, unambiguous Marxist-Leninist stance and to accept the necessity of establishing the dictatorship of the proletariat in Germany. Still, Tiul'panov hedged, as did Grotewohl at the Second Congress; the dictatorship could take different forms in different countries, the Soviet colonel stated, leaving room for continuing rhetoric about the "German road to socialism."[46] But from the Soviet point of view, the SED did not act resolutely enough to bring its ranks into line with a pro-Soviet program. The party tolerated too many opponents on the Left, mostly "sectarians" from the former ranks of the KPD, and on the Right, the so-called "Schumacherites," unreconstructed former Social Democrats. The SED was particularly vulnerable to attacks from the Left on the USSR using "falsified Marxism-Leninism." "Only after our intervention," reported Lt. Colonel Blestkin, did the SED "begin to take measures to exclude several of them ['opponents of unity'] from the party."[47]

SMAD political officers were particularly disturbed by the situation in Thuringia, where they feared that the leftist and rightist criticisms of the Soviet Union would merge into a common anti-Soviet program, one which asserted that Lenin's policies followed Marxist traditions, but Stalin's had created an imperialist USSR. Here, a small group of leftists, led by the union leader Karl Schmidt, sought to "invigorate" socialism by "reviving" Lenin's policies. Schmidt and his comrades argued that the Soviets had abandoned Leninism through their policies regarding the Oder-Neisse (a clear violations of Lenin's "peace without indemnities") and dismantling, which left the working class in such terrible straits. The Soviets were upset that while Schmidt had been removed as head of the food-processing union, he continued to hold his positions in the party apparatus.[48]

During the course of 1948 and early 1949, SED leaders and their Soviet mentors increasingly called for a tightening of the ranks. Dissident socialists within the SED became the primary targets for party discipline. Ernst Braun, head of the Weimar city party committee, was chided both for being the captive of "social democratic traditions" *and* of being "not free of leftist *(levatskii)* tendencies" – and because he had criticized the participation of many former Nazis in the anti-fascist bloc and in city government.[49] The SED education specialist, Dr. Elchlepp, was disciplined by Ulbricht when he suggested that all school policies in the eastern zone should be based on the Marxist-Leninist principles of dialectical materialism.[50] Indeed, one of the fundamental characteristics of the so-called "party of the new type" was that no one could get things quite right except for the leadership. If local leaders talked about peace, unity, and democracy, they were accused of "hushing up the essential class nature of the party," thus, encouraging the ultra-leftist KPO (Communist Party Opposition), "opportunists," and sectarians to accuse the SED of "reformism." If they spoke too much about the class struggle or dialectical materialism, attacked Nazis or the special stores (HOs) developed for the elite, or impugned the special privileges introduced for intelligentsia recruits, they were accused of ultra-leftism and even Trotskyism.[51]

In a speech to the higher police school in Berlin (August 1948), Ulbricht emphasized that the "party of the new type" above all meant recognizing that the Soviet experience served as a model for the working class in every country of the world, Germany included. This model already dominated one-sixth of the world, and more was to come.

> *The close relationship with the Soviet Union is the basic precondition for the victory of the working class in Germany, and without the Soviet Union behind us, without the comradely, brotherly help of the Soviet Union, we cannot win, we cannot come to power.*

Ulbricht added, as well, that every institution in the zone needed to search the Soviet experience for lessons on how to organize and develop. For the police, for example, this meant establishing close relations with the officers and soldiers of the Soviet occupation army. From the Russians, the German police could learn the important lessons of how to win, how to beat the reactionaries.[52]

With the go-ahead from the Soviets to mobilize the party on a new basis, if not to create a new socialist society in eastern Germany, the SED held its First Party Conference from 25 to 29 January 1949. With great fanfare, the SED institutionalized "the party of the new type" that had been in the making at the latest since the early fall of 1948. Parity between the SPD and KPD, which had been a fiction for at least a year, if not longer, was now formally abandoned, and the percentage of former SPD leaders in the SED hierarchy rapidly diminished in the months that followed.[53] The Sovietization of the party was also institutionalized by the party conference. In addition to the various changes approved in Moscow – the creation of the Politburo, the Small Secretariat, party candidacy, and so on – the SED introduced democratic centralism as the reigning principle of party organization. Factions or groups within the SED were strictly forbidden; there would be no opportunity from the Left or Right to challenge Politburo orthodoxy. The SED also invigorated the Personnel Policy section of the party, which, like its powerful Cadres department (of the Central Committee) cousin in Moscow, would be at the heart of creating the emerging East German *nomenklatura*.[54] In sum, the First Party Congress marked the end of the unity party in practice and in theory. The new SED, already in the making by late 1948, became a mass German communist party of the Soviet type.

But even the new SED could not simply proclaim an end to criticism from the Right and Left and go about its agenda of communizing the zone. The SED, like the CPSU(b) of the 1920s to which the Soviets often compared it, developed its totalitarian style in contests with the opposition. Even the greater attachment to Marxism-Leninism fostered by the SED did not harness the leftist enthusiasms of many party members. In 1949, especially, a number of left SED members simply could not understand the perpetuation of the myth that a deal could be made to unify bourgeois western Germany with the socialist east. As Bernhard Koenen of Saxony-Anhalt stated the problem:

> *A part of the earlier members of the KPD see in our contemporary policies a rejection of internationalism. They would like to cease the struggle for the unity of Germany, the success of which, in their opinion, is impossible in any case, and together with the Russians, carry on a clear Soviet line!*[55]

While Koenen did not call his opponents on the unity question sectarians, Colonel General Russkikh of the Soviet Military Administration did, and he urged the SED to fight against these opponents of the National Front policy. But the resistance in the party was determined; numerous local SED groups felt deeply that "the National Front of Germany had already once led to fascism and they would not go along with 'such nonsense.'"[56]

Despite the continuing pressure on its critics from the Left, the SED unremittingly complained in 1949 about the ubiquitous opposition of "sectarians," "ultra-leftists," and "Trotskyists" – in the unions, the city administrations, and the evening schools. The party felt so vulnerable to leftist attacks that it charged the Higher Party School with formulating a "systematic argument" against the Trotskyists.[57] KPO sympathizers in Weimar continued to cause the party trouble by applying Leninism to the conditions of Stalinist Soviet Russia. Party Control Commission reports hammered at the sectarian and opportunistic tendencies that allegedly infused the Thuringian party and accused the leadership of being as guilty in this respect as the rank and file.[58] Even more critical was the situation in Berlin, where KPD groups in the western sectors, out of reach of Soviet and East German agents, influenced their SED cousins in the Russian zone. If anything, the ideological struggle for the "hearts and minds" of Communists in Berlin intensified in the late 1940s. At a Party Executive meeting of 4 October 1949, Ernst Hoffmann from Berlin denounced the persistent influence of "pure sectarian phenomena" on the life of the party. The Trotskyists, he added, posed a growing threat. For the first time since the founding of the SED, Hoffmann stated, the party leaders had to engage in fierce arguments against internal opponents, "where every comrade, who took part in them, was shaken to the core, and left the meetings upset and deeply shocked."[59]

Proclaiming itself a party of the new type in the Soviet mold did not spare the SED comrades from unrelenting advice from their Soviet "friends." In fact, if anything, Soviet officers took the new party line as an open invitation to instruct the Germans on the etiquette of being proper Marxist-Leninists. Not surprisingly, the Soviets found the SED lacking in many respects. They criticized the German party for not understanding the meaning of the dictatorship of the proletariat and for underestimating the importance of the struggle against revisionism. In particular, the Soviets hammered on the SED for harboring "Schumacherites" in its ranks, alleged agents and followers of the virulently anti-Soviet SPD leader in the west, Kurt Schumacher.[60] The Soviets chastised the SED for not sufficiently publicizing and discussing the Cominform resolutions on Yugoslavia, and for not understanding their meaning for the German party, no doubt an accurate claim. Soviet political officers seemed intent on getting local SED groups to proclaim out loud their fealty to the Soviet Union, as well as to the teachings of Marx and Lenin. The less ambiguous and more ritualistic the SED's proclamations in praise of Soviet communism, the more satisfied the Soviet observers were.[61] Local Soviet political officers also intervened more directly in the work of the "party of the new type," rewriting "imprecise" resolutions, showing the SED committee where to hang portraits of Luxemburg and Clara Zetkin for International Women's Day, or formulating the appropriate proclamations to be adopted by the SED for bringing in the harvest.[62]

The tasks of the SED at the beginning of the 1949 were delicate ones, and the persistent criticism from the Left did not make things any easier. The party leaders had at once to Bolshevize the German party while also appealing to Germans in the west to join the accommodationist National Front. They had to purge and discipline masses of party workers while coopting the LDP and CDU at home into continuing cooperation in the People's Congress movement. They had to satisfy the Soviets and earn entry into the Cominform while, at the same time, leading the movement for a united Germany. Wilhelm Pieck had these contradictions in mind when he stopped in Moscow for the 1 May 1949 celebrations on his way to a health resort near Sochi on the Black Sea. Pieck's notes from this visit indicate that the "Leonhard Affair" was very much on his mind at the time. Wolfgang Leonhard, a member of the Ulbricht initiative group fled "head over heels" from the eastern zone to Yugoslavia in March 1949.[63] Like other party veterans who were ready to use Marxism-Leninism as a tool for criticizing Soviet reality, Leonhard was condemned as a Trotskyist.[64] The fact that Leonhard taught at the "Karl Marx" Higher Party School before his defection created special problems for the SED because Leonhard had such widespread contacts among both the old and new generations of party leaders. The Party Control Commission was charged with reviewing the credentials of four thousand leading SED officials in order to ferret out others who might have shared Leonhard's supposed "Titoist-Trotskyite" heresy.[65]

In Pieck's view, the West German elections of August 1949 demonstrated the success of the massive anti-Soviet and anti-SED propaganda campaign conducted by the centers of western imperialism. But they also indicated that the time had come for the eastern zone to have its own German government.[66] There was no sense in putting off the critical step any longer. With the help of the SMAD's Political Advisor, Vladimir Semenov, the proper documents were prepared that would join the National Front to the People's Council and the other political parties. Problems in the SED – the "Party of the New Type" – were far from resolved in the zone and especially in Berlin. In the SED's view, sectarians continued to misunderstand and misstate the dimensions of the national question. But, as Pieck's notes affirmed, "Comrade St[alin]" provided the people of the eastern zone with wise advice on how to go about forming a German government by affirming the plan presented by the SED leaders.[67]

6. Conclusion

It is easier to trace the role of "sectarianism" and "sectarians" in the establishment of communist rule in the Soviet Zone of Occupation than to understand their meaning for the subsequent history of the German Democratic Republic. Conflicts within the German Left were submerged in, though hardly resolved by, the SED's efforts to build a new state. Within the party, there were still those who questioned the applicability in every instance of the Soviet model. There were others who called for a more determinedly revolutionary policy towards western Germany. Others wanted to push the transformation in the East in a more radical direction. In other words, the ultra-leftism of the immediate postwar period did not disappear altogether with the establishment of a socialist government. Moreover, some aspects of extreme leftist programs appealed to the leaders of the new state. During the occupation, Col. Tiul'panov was known to rebuff accusations that Ulbricht himself was a sectarian. Although he was clearly a master of the differences between tactics and strategy, Ulbricht nevertheless shared the "sectarians'" intolerance of diversity, dogmatic attachment to Soviet Leninism, and inability to compromise. Even Erich Honecker can be said to have carried forward "sectarian" traditions when he rejected Gorbachev's appeals to reform East German communism or be left behind by history. It should be no surprise that the PDS has been forced to deal with a substantial "sectarian" wing. The extreme Left was and continues to be part and parcel of the history of German communism.

Notes

1. Most of the material for this essay is taken from my book, *The Russians in Germany: A History of the Soviet Zone of Occupation, 1945-1949* (Cambridge, Mass., 1995).
2. V.I. Lenin, "*Left-Wing Communism – An Infantile Disorder*, in *Lenin: Selected Works*, vol. 3 (Moscow, 1967), 376-78.
3. For Luxemburgism on the German Left, see Eric D. Weitz, "'Rosa Luxemburg Belongs to Us!' German Communism and the Luxemburg Legacy," *Central European History* 27:1 (1994): 27-64.
4. For some of my reflections on these themes, see Norman M. Naimark, "Revolution and Counterrevolution in Eastern Europe," in *The Crisis of Socialism in Europe*, ed. Christiane Lemke and Gary Marks (Durham, NC, 1992), 61-83.
5. See the collection of German documents: *"Gruppe Ulbricht" in Berlin April bis Juni 1945: Von den Vorbereitungen im Sommer 1944 bis zur Wiedergründung der KPD im Juni 1945. Eine Dokumentation*, ed. Gerhard Keiderling (Berlin, 1993).
6. "Spravka o politicheskoi rabote sredi naseleniia Germanii," 5 July 1945, RTsKhIDNI, f. 17, op. 128, d. 791, l. 107.
7. Ibid., l. 107.
8. Günter Benser, *Die KPD im Jahre der Befreiung: Vorbereitung und Aufbau der legalen kommunistische Massenpartei* (Berlin, 1985), 189-90. Some Soviet com-

mandants were also criticized as sectarians. As a result, they were ordered by the political organs of SMAD to carry out policy strictly through the German administrations (and not through local committees or parties). N.I. Shishkov, "Sovetskaia voennaia administratsiia i pomoshch' SSSR narodam tsentral'noi i iugo-vostochnoi Evropy v 1944-45 godakh," *Voprosy istorii* 2 (1979): 16-29.

9. See, for example, SAPMO-BA, ZPA, EA 1845/2 (Rudolf Bühring), p. 386.
10. "Stenogramma soobshchenii t.t. Akkermana, Ul'brikhta i Sobotka o polozhenii v Germanii," 7 June 1945, RTsKhIDNI, f. 17, op. 128, d. 759, l. 9.
11. "Nekotorye fakty o rabote gruppy tov. Ul'brikhta v Berline," by Senior Lieutenant Fogeler, 8 June 1945, forwarded by 7th Section chief, M. Burtsev to Dimitrov, 14 June 1945, RTsKhIDNI, f. 17, op. 128, d. 39, l. 32.
12. See, for example, SAPMO-BA, ZPA, EA 1845/3 (Rudolf Bühring), p. 438, and RTsKhIDNI, f. 17, op. 125, d. 321, ll. 107-9.
13. "Stenogramma soobshchenii," 7 June 1945, RTsKhIDNI, f. 17, op. 128, d. 750, l. 7.
14. *Rote Fahne* 1 (8 May 1945), 3 (16 May 1945), SAPMO-BA, ZPA, NL 182/853, pp. 37, 38.
15. SAPMO-BA, ZPA, EA 0120/2 (Büchner), p. 7, and Benser, *KPD im Jahre der Befreiung*, 68, 87.
16. "Stenogramma soobshchenii," 7 June 1945, meeting, RTsKhIDNI, f. 17, op. 128, d. 750, l. 168.
17. "Spravka o politicheskoi rabote sredi naseleniia Germanii," 5 July 1945, RTsKhIDNI, f. 17, op. 128, d. 791, l. 109.
18. "Kurzer Bericht über die Arbeit der Berliner Parteiorganization der KPD," n.d., SAPMO-BA, ZPA, NL 182/852 (Ulbricht), p. 7.
19. Ulbricht to Pieck, 17 May 1945, SAPMO-BA, ZPA, NL 182/246 V, p. 6.
20. Horst Laschitza, *Kämpferische Demokratie gegen Faschismus: Die programmatische Vorbereitung auf die antifaschistisch-demokratische Umwälzung in Deutschland durch die Parteiführung der KPD* (Berlin, 1969), 199.
21. "Vertraulicher Bericht über die Bezirkskonferenz der Provinz Sachsen," 20 July 1945, SAPMO-BA, ZPA, NL 182/855 (Ulbricht), p. 33.
22. SAPMO-BA, ZPA, EA 0012 (Fritz Koehn), pp. 2-3.
23. SAPMO-BA, ZPA, NL 36/629 (W. Pieck), p. 62. These notes have been published in the *Frankfurter Allgemeine Zeitung*, 30 March 1990, with commentary by Manfred Wilke, and in *Utopie kreativ*, book 7 (March 1991): 103-5, with commentary by Rolf Badstübner.
24. "Stenogramma soobshchenii," 7 June 1945, RTsKhIDNI, f. 17, op. 128, d. 750, l. 177.
25. Ibid., l. 166.
26. Ibid., ll. 181, 185.
27. Ibid., ll. 178, 183-84.
28. Cited in Frank Moraw, *Die Parole der "Einheit" und die Sozialdemokratie* (Bonn, 1973), 93.
29. See Benser, *KPD im Jahre der Befreiung*, 87, and Wallrab von Buttlar, *Ziele und Zielkonflikte der sowjetischen Deutschlandpolitik 1945-1947* (Stuttgart, 1980), 40-41.
30. See, for example, Bernt von Kügelgen, *Die Nacht der Entscheidung: Autobiografie* (Berlin, 1978); Leon Nebenzahl, *Mein Leben begann von neuen: Erinnerungen an eine ungewöhnlichen Zeit* (Berlin, 1985); or Hans Rodenberg, *Protokoll eines Lebens: Erinnerungen und Bekenntnis* (Berlin, 1980). For other similar titles, see Marianne Lange, "Es hat sich gelohnt zu leben: Gedanken zur Memoirenliteratur in der DDR," *Weimarer Beiträge* 25:9 (1979): 42-87.
31. See, the report about the Thuringian district, fall 1945, SAPMO-BA, ZPA, NL 182/856 (Ulbricht), p. 111; "Stenographische Niederschrift über die Reichsber-

atung am 8. und 9. Januar 1946," SAPMO-BA, ZPA, I/2/2/17, p. 35; "Rede des Gen. Matern auf der Sekretär-Konferenz," 7 January 1946, SAPMO-BA, ZPA, NL 182/876, p. 70.

32. SAPMO-BA, ZPA, VG 127/7, p. 14.
33. SAPMO-BA, ZPA, EA 1213/1 (Maria Rentmeister), p. 107.
34. SAPMO-BA, ZPA, NL 182/856 (Ulbricht), p. 19.
35. "Kürzer Bericht über die Arbeit der Berliner Parteiorganization der KPD," July 1945, in ibid., p. 22.
36. "Bericht über öffentliche Versammlungen, 27. Juni-3. Juli 1945," SAPMO-BA, ZPA, NL 182/852 (Ulbricht), p. 33; Report by Waldemar Schmidt, in ibid., pp. 38-39.
37. SAPMO-BA, ZPA, NL 182/853 (Brandenburg).
38. Burtsev to Dimitrov, 16 August 1945, RTsKhIDNI, f. 17, op. 128, d. 39, l. 66.
39. The best account in English is still Henry Krisch, *German Politics under Soviet Occupation* (New York, 1974), 101-71. See also Dietrich Staritz, *Die Gründung der DDR* (Munich, 1984), 112-23.
40. "Stenogramma besedy s tov. Maternom," 25 September 1946, RTsKhIDNI, f. 17, op. 128, d. 151, l. 129.
41. Report of I. Filippov, Office of the Political Advisor to the Commander-in-chief of SMAD, 9 October 1946, RTsKhIDNI, f. 17, op. 128, d. 147, l. 116.
42. Ibid., l. 89.
43. "Stenogramma besedy s tov. Maternom," 25 September 1946, RTsKhIDNI, f. 17, op. 128, d. 151, ll. 9-10, 120.
44. Shikin to Zhdanov, 3 August 1946, RTsKhIDNI, f. 17, op. 128, d. 147, ll. 47, 80.
45. Tiul'panov, "Dokladnaia zapiska," 11 August 1947, RTsKhIDNI, f. 17, op. 128, d. 317, l. 33.
46. Tiul'panov to Baranov, "Dokladnaia zapiska o vnutripartiinom polozhenii v SEPG," 12 March 1948, RTsKhIDNI, f. 17, op. 128, d. 566, l. 56.
47. Blestkin to Tiul'panov, 10 February 1948, State Archives of the Russian Federation (hereafter GARF), f. 7184, op. l, d. 165, l. 159.
48. Kolesnichenko to Ponomarev, on the Thuringian parties, 29 November 1948, RTsKhIDNI, f. 17, op. 128, d. 572, l. 47.
49. Report of Lt. Col. Kirillov, Weimar, 3 February 1948, in GARF, f. 7184, op. l, d. 165, l. 64.
50. SAPMO-BA, ZPA, NL 182/927 (Ulbricht), pp. 125-26.
51. See, for example, Major Starodubov to Tiul'panov, 16 September 1949, GARF, f. 7184, op. l, d. 169, l. 25.
52. "Die Partei neuen Typus," speech of Walter Ulbricht at the Höhere Polizeischule Berlin, 27 August 1948, Abschrift, Hoover Institution Archives (hereafter HIA), Briegleb, box l, no. 46.
53. Hermann Weber writes that by March 1949, the Central Secretariat, which had never had full parity in any case, reduced the number of former SPD members to 10 percent. Weber, *Geschichte der DDR* (Munich, 1985), 178.
54. "Organization der Arbeit auf dem Gebiete der Personalpolitik," Beschluss des Politbüros, 8 March 1949, SAPMO-BA, ZPA, IV/2/4/5 (ZPKK), p. 9.
55. Bureau of Information SVAG, *Bulletin* 4 (4 February 1948), RTsKhIDNI, f. 17, op. 128, d. 577, l. 64.
56. "Zur Lage in der Partei," 18 August 1949, SAPMO-BA, IV/2/4/29 (ZPKK), p. 5.
57. SAPMO-BA, ZPA, IV/2/1/35 (Parteivorstand Protocol, 23-24 August 1949), pp. 13-14.
58. SAPMO-BA, ZPA, IV/2/4/1 (ZPKK), p. 14.

59. SAPMO-BA, ZPA, IV/2/1/36 (Parteivorstand Protocol, 4 October 1949), p. 51.
60. Tiul'panov to Ponomarev, "Dokladnaia zapiska," 17 September 1948, RTsKhIDNI, f. 17, op. 128, d. 71, ll. 88-94; Lt. Khabalov, Mühlhausen, "Donesenie," GARF, f. 7184, no. 1, d. 166, l. 18.
61. Major Shtykin, Gotha, to Lt. Col. Makarushin, 27 October 1948, GARF, f. 7184, op. 1, d. 166, l. 152.
62. Lt. Col. Makarushin to Tiul'panov, "O zemel'noi konferentsii SEPG v Tiuringii," 11 December 1948, GARF, f. 7184, op. 1, d. 66, l. 290; Major Bessonov, "Plan raboty otdeleniia informatsii," Kalau, GARF, f. 7077, op. 1, d. 241, l. 66.
63. Wolfgang Leonhard to Hermann Möhring, 6 January 1965, copy, HIA, Grabe, box 1.
64. SAPMO-BA, ZPA, NL 36/695 (Pieck), p. 85.
65. SAPMO-BA, ZPA, IV/2/4/1 (ZPKK), p. 21. The Party Control Commission questioned the reliability of 4 percent of those investigated or 344 SED members.
66. SAPMO-BA, ZPA, NL 36/695 (Pieck), p. 111.
67. Ibid., pp. 111, 115.

Chapter 18

PRONATALISM, NATIONBUILDING, AND SOCIALISM

Population Policy in the SBZ/DDR, 1945 to 1960

Atina Grossmann

And so once again today, paragraph 218 stands as the flashpoint [Brennpunkt] of all discussions in the states of the Soviet zone and Berlin. – Delegate to the Saxon Parliament, 18 June 1947[1]

No sooner had the Red Army finally conquered Berlin and the guns of World War II been stilled than the politics of reproduction and sexuality – especially abortion – instantly reemerged as pressing public issues for both Germans and occupiers. As the public sphere was reconstituted in the immediate aftermath of May 1945, doctors, health officials, the press, political parties, women's organizations, and church groups rehearsed the debates about abortion, birth control, fertility, and sexuality that had defined post-World War I and Great Depression discourse about social welfare and population policy. This time, familiar anxieties about the health and continued survival of the *Volk* were exacerbated by the physical devastation of warfare on German soil, occupation by four separate victorious powers, and the huge influx of German refugees from conquered eastern territories, concentration camp survivors, and other displaced persons.

Female experiences such as rape, abortion, childbirth, caring for malnourished and sick children, and grief over dying and dead children, as well as relations with occupiers and returning German soldiers and prisoners of war, became especially powerful markers of German victimization

Notes for this chapter begin on page 461.

and defeat as well as of the urgent need for healthy reconstruction. In the midst of a ruined physical, political, and moral landscape, and in the absence of a legitimate national past or clear national boundaries, calls for reconstruction of the "ethic of healthy and natural motherliness," family, and marriage were ubiquitous.[2] Equally pervasive was consternation about low birth rates, infant and child mortality, hunger and disease, "surplus women," delinquent youth, and the "plagues" of venereal disease, tuberculosis, abortion, and prostitution.[3] In the much-repeated and diffuse litany of postwar German misery, women appeared in various guises: as the sturdy tidiers of the rubble of war *(Trümmerfrauen)*; as villains "who will give themselves for a piece of bread and not think of their husband and children ... risking the health of the entire *Volk* ... betraying their children";[4] and, along with their children, as war's foremost victims who had to cope with the lack of food and fuel, outbreaks of rickets and flu, the absence or incapacitation of their menfolk, and, most dramatically, widespread rape by their Soviet liberators/occupiers.

1. Rape and Abortion

Especially in the Soviet zone (SBZ), population policy was driven by a complex and contradictory mix of factors: the legacy of Weimar communist and socialist commitments to social hygiene and sexual reform, Stalin's (in)famous pledge to rebuild the nation – "Hitlers come and go but the German *Volk* remains" – while simultaneously dismantling German infrastructure as reparations for a war-torn Soviet Union, and, most immediately, the extreme chaos and violence of war's end in the east. Indeed, in many ways the story of population policy in the Soviet zone (and later German Democratic Republic) begins with the experience of mass rape.

Perhaps one out of every three of about one and one-half million women (63 percent of the population) in Berlin at the end of the war were raped – many but certainly not all during the notorious days of "mass rapes" from 24 April to 5 May 1945 as the Soviets finally secured the capital city. Some recent estimates suggest almost two million rapes altogether as the Red Army pounded westward.[5] Historian Norman Naimark concludes in his careful history of the SBZ that while it is "highly unlikely that historians will ever know how many German women were raped by Soviet soldiers in the months before and years after the capitulation," "rape became a part of the social history of the Soviet zone in ways unknown to the Western zones."[6]

Whatever the numbers, and they vary wildly, it is unquestionably the case that mass rapes of civilian German women signaled the end of the war and the defeat of Nazi Germany. They were an integral part of the final bitter battle for Berlin. Moreover, these rapes were instantly coded, both by German and occupation officials, as social health and population political problems that required medical intervention in the form of abortion and venereal disease treatment. The Nazi regime had been draconian in its approach to abortions of future "Aryans," but facing the Red Army's onslaught, it had sanctioned "extra-legal" abortions of "Slav" or "Mongol" fetuses. The regime's collapse and the Soviet victory then led to a virtual moratorium on paragraph 218 of the penal code (and its ancillary sections) which criminalized most voluntary abortions.[7]

Clearly defensive about the rapacious behavior of the Red Army "liberators," but far from imposing a total silence, German Communists and Soviet military administration (SMAD) officials found multiple means of handling and acknowledging the massive incidence of rape. In the immediate postwar years 1945 to 1947 they tried simultaneously to deny, minimize, justify, shift responsibility for, contain, and above all eliminate the consequences of rapes by Soviet soldiers. Most concretely, municipal and occupation authorities in Berlin recognized the urgency of the problem by suspending paragraph 218, thereby allowing medical abortions on social and ethical (rape) grounds. The Communist-dominated Berlin *Magistrat* (City Council), formed on 20 May 1945, quickly set in place a policy to that effect, although not without grumbling on the part of some doctors and clear but irrelevant protest from Walter Ulbricht, the KPD (German Communist Party) leader flown in from Moscow on 1 May. "The gentlemen doctors should be reminded to exercise a bit of restraint in this matter," he laconically remarked; but the very statement shows how widespread the practice already was.[8]

Drawing on a mixed legacy of Weimar and National Socialist maternalist population policy and racial discourses, as well as occupation policy, women seeking (successfully) to terminate pregnancies told their stories by the thousands (and in highly specific terms) to medical commissions attached to district health offices. Moved by a complicated set of health, eugenic, racist, and humanitarian interests, physicians in Berlin authorized and performed abortions on grounds of rape – right up to the very last months of pregnancy – at an assembly line pace on women who wanted them. And as Dr. Anne-Marie Durand-Wever, soon to become the first president of the SBZ's women's federation, later reported, "they all wanted them."[9] Throughout 1945 and into 1946, these abortions, their dubious legality notwithstanding, were tolerated by all relevant authorities, including the *Amtsärzte* (municipal physicians) and the Protestant – although not the Catholic – church. Justified by extreme need (*Not*), they were relatively easily integrated into a continuing rhetorical commitment to pronatalism: the demographic reconstruction of a war-decimated German *Volk*.[10]

In tandem with the organization of medical abortions, high anxiety about venereal disease led SMAD and SBZ health officials (along with their counterparts in the western sectors) to institute harsh surveillance and treatment measures as well as popular "enlightenment" campaigns.[11] Venereal disease was decried as a threat to the health of the *Volk* and as a symbol of general moral degradation, especially among women who had learned to use their bodies as a means of negotiating the postwar chaos. But venereal disease was also widely attributed to rape by Soviet soldiers.[12] Order No. 030 by Marshall Zhukov, Supreme Commander SMAD, on 12 February 1946 and Order No. 273 on 11 December 1947 aimed to "combat venereal disease among the German population in the SBZ" by regular police raids and compulsory internal examinations of all women aged sixteen to forty-five working in public establishments, including hair salons, bathing facilities, public toilets, and cinemas, bars, cafes, and restaurants. Men aged 16 to 55 in similar situations were also affected; Soviets were exempted, much to the outrage of Germans who were reminded of Nazi policing of sexuality and procreation, and who pointed out the arbitrariness and limited efficacy of such measures.[13]

Beyond the public health response to mass rape, KPD and SMAD officials also deployed a wide range of rhetorical and political strategies. They freely admitted violations, excesses, abuses, unfortunate incidents (*Übergriffe*, *Auswüchse*) and vowed to get them under control (or to demand that the army do so). At the same time, however, they also trivialized rape, as an inevitable part of normal brutal warfare, as comparable to Allied excesses, and as understandable if not entirely excusable in view of the atrocities perpetrated on the Russians by the Germans.[14] Rapes figured prominently as public relations and political control problems because they provoked anti-Soviet sentiment, especially among women, youth, and dedicated anti-Nazis, precisely those groups considered most likely to support a new socialist and democratic peace-loving Germany.

2. Women and Mothers

Ironically, the Soviets, who had squandered much potential goodwill among a war-weary population by the marauding behavior of their troops, were eager – much more so than the western Allies – to present themselves as liberators rather than conquerors. Faced with a city in ruins and a beaten, demoralized population, the SMAD moved quickly and efficiently to organize municipal government, restore basic services, improve health conditions, and nurture a lively political and cultural life.[15] Already on 28 May 1945, the Magistrat ordered the reconstitution of the health insurance system. Women, and the social welfare and population policy issues traditionally associated with them, were central to this politics of rebuilding *Volk* and nation.

Women constituted the majority of Berlin's adult population and workforce and were highly visible as mothers struggling to nurse and feed their children, as wives mourning war casualties or awaiting the return of prisoners of war, as *Trümmerfrauen* clearing the rubble, and as sexual victims and villains in the tangled postwar web of rape, prostitution, and fraternization. They quickly became the focus of intense political interest and organization. In the postwar anti-fascist narrative, women were dually and centrally positioned: as culpable for Nazism and war because they had not sufficiently resisted male militarism, and as motherly carriers of hope for a peaceable future.

The first call for the establishment of women's councils (*Frauenausschüsse*) by the Berlin Magistrat on 23 August 1945 invoked this maternalist spirit and appealed to "the women and mothers of Berlin":

> *A new life must begin for us. Nazism and war have cruelly ravaged our Volk in our homeland (Heimat). In the millions our men and sons have fallen victim to these war criminals. Countless families stand stunned before the ruins of their homes.*

Acknowledging women's disproportionate burden of reconstruction in Germany's community of suffering, SBZ officials relinquished the rhetoric of class oppression for one more femininized and adequate to the distress of a defeated and humiliated nation: "Now every household is poor and so is the entire German *Volk*."[16]

Women's councils were given a mandate to promote democratic political education and organize relief efforts. Ostensibly non-partisan (*überparteilich*) and committed to overcoming the deadly splits within the working-class and women's movements that had – in the post-war communist version – contributed to the triumph of National Socialism, the women's councils attracted reemerging veterans of the Weimar women's movement as well as communist cadre. Primarily dedicated to pressing social welfare needs, the councils' "Action Save the Child" quickly produced – eventually for a small wage – over eighty thousand pieces of winter clothing in over 250 sewing circles (*Nähstuben*). Council activists also entered the fray on issues of abortion and birth control, vehemently protesting four-power occupation (*Kontrollrat*) plans to reinstitute the 1926 Weimar version of paragraph 218, which eased punishment but maintained the principle of abortion's illegality. The councils demanded not only the elimination of ruthless Nazi regulations but also the explicit legalization of socially necessary abortions (the "social indication"), long demanded by Weimar reformers. In another reprise of Weimar programs, they attacked Kontrollrat moves to require a doctor's prescription for contraceptives, and proposed instead to combat drastic shortages and the rampant spread of abortion and venereal diseases by contraceptive distribution in clinics and women's counseling centers.[17]

Within two years, the initially broad-based women's councils were coordinated into a central women's organization under communist control. Despite opposition from the majority of Social Democrats, the unpopular merging of the KPD and SPD in the eastern zone into one unified Socialist Unity Party (SED) was ratified in April 1946. In October 1946, the Communists' embarrassing loss to the SPD in Greater Berlin's first open elections was generally, if not explicitly, attributed to a majority female electorate remembering and responding to the actions of the Soviet "friends."[18] One month later, in November 1946, the Central Committee of the SED began to plan the subordination of some six thousand women's councils into one centralized organization. In March 1947 the SED overcame continuing protests by local activists and formed the Democratic Women's League of Germany (*Demokratischer Frauenbund Deutschlands*, or DFD).

Dr. Anne-Marie Durand-Wever, a bourgeois professional with no clear party affiliation and an untainted past as a seasoned women's and birth control rights advocate, agreed to serve as the DFD's first president. She precisely fit the "non-partisan" image the DFD was trying to project; the reliable SED cadre Käthe Kern took over as vice chair of what was to become essentially a mass organization of the SED. Appeals to unity were already strained by the departure of Christian Democratic women during the preparatory meetings, but Durand-Wever, like many women activists in both east and west, was still attracted to an organization that claimed to reject the political and class divisions of pre-Nazi feminism, while carrying on the tradition of the Weimar KPD women's delegate and conference movement.[19]

United "against war and militarism," the DFD characterized fascism as patriarchal domination and blamed the war, not the Nazi regime, for victimizing German women and children. This commitment to "peace" – in the west, the term was already being denounced as a codeword for communism – was consistent with the general politics of the Soviet zone which had come to define anti-fascism less by past actions than by willingness to support current KPD and occupation policies. A typical delegate at the DFD's founding "congress for peace" recounted her excavation of a bombed-out children's bunker:

> *their clothes ripped from their bodies, their eyes fixed and open … these children's eyes look at us so intently … as if they wanted to say, what have you done to us. Why have you mothers not prevented all this misfortune?*[20]

Finally, in November 1947 the SMAD ordered all remaining women's councils dissolved, reinforcing the general trend to unequivocal SED control of social, cultural and political policy. In the west, however, women's organizations began to exclude from their ranks Communists and those too closely associated with the DFD. The stage was set for the hardening Cold War division between east and west, rendered concrete in 1948 when currency reform in the west and the ensuing Soviet blockade and Anglo-American airlift sealed the division of Berlin and pointed toward the promulgation in 1949 of two separate German states.

3. Pronatalism and Abortion Reform

Key to the institutionalization of a central women's, social welfare, and population policy between 1945 and 1948 was the move from ad-hoc suspension of paragraph 218 to a more systematic abortion reform. Parallel and deeply connected – but without explicit reference – to the postwar rape experience of so many German women, the Weimar debate on abortion that had been abruptly silenced by the Nazi takeover quickly resumed. This was especially the case in the Soviet zone, where the SMAD took a much more aggressive role than the western Allies in structuring social and population policy. In addition, a considerable number of Communist and Social Democratic exiles as well as both Jewish and non-Jewish former inmates of Nazi jails and camps initially returned to the east, where they hoped to pursue in a "new and better" Germany their smashed Weimar visions for social health and welfare. The press was again filled with speakouts and interviews, women's conferences convened, students debated, and provincial parliaments argued about abrogating paragraph 218 and instituting new regulations.[21]

Postwar public speech in the Soviet zone for the most part, therefore, recirculated – in limited and refigured form – Weimar debates about reform and legalization. Remarkably, there was relatively little direct (or even indirect) reference to the immediate past of mass rape and Nazi racial policies, and only some fairly feeble attempts by conservative Christian opponents of abortion reform to invoke the Auschwitz or Nazi "euthanasia program" comparison when defining abortion as murder.[22] In familiar language, reform-minded physicians, journalists, and activists again asserted that women determined to terminate a pregnancy would do so no matter what the cost and noted the irrationality of unenforceable laws. They pointed to the social health consequences of botched abortions and unfit or unwanted offspring, the severity of the (temporary) crisis, and the necessity of contraception as an alternative to abortion, and made assurances that under happier circumstances women would certainly revert to their maternal roles. At the same time, the easily available Soviet model of recriminalization tied to pronatalist welfare measures cast its shadow on all discussions of postwar reform.

Some veterans of the Weimar Sex Reform movement played a major role in this process of appropriating and renovating pre-Nazi KPD proposals. They included former Communist Reichstag deputies Martha Arendsee and Helene Overlach, Dr. Friedrich Wolf, major protagonist in the 1931 campaign against paragraph 218, and Durand-Wever, the most prominent abortion reform advocate to have remained in Germany. Younger Sex Reform veterans Dr. Elfriede Paul – one of the few survivors of the Red Orchestra resistance group – and Dr. Barbara von Renthe-Fink, who had just become active in Weimar birth control organizations when the Nazis came to power, joined returning exiles in the Central Health Commission (*Zentralverwaltung für Gesundheitswesen*) led by Clara Zetkin's son, Dr. Maxim Zetkin.

In the immediate postwar years until 1948, health reformers, like women's activists, could still work together across the east/ west divide. It was in Berlin, jointly ruled by the four Allied powers, that social policies in the Soviet and western zones most clearly collided, overlapped, and influenced each other. Seeking direction for the reconstruction of health insurance clinics in both East and West Berlin, public health officials such as Ernst Schellenberg studied Weimar municipal guidelines for marriage and birth control counseling and old Health Insurance League yearbooks with their pioneering articles on maternal and birth counseling. They attempted to rebuild, on the Weimar Berlin social medicine model, centralized clinics *(Ambulatorien)* for prenatal and infant care and to treat tuberculosis, venereal disease, cancer, and mental disorders. They also aimed to resuscitate such Weimar initiatives as marriage and sex counseling centers, generous maternal protection, equality for working women, and legalization of socially necessary abortions.[23]

Friedrich's Wolf's anti-paragraph 218 drama *Cyankali*, which had inspired such passionate discussion and demonstrations in late Weimar, was restaged almost immediately. This time, as one reviewer noted, the entire *Volk* shared the working-class misery it portrayed.[24] Wolf himself returned from his Soviet exile, interjected himself into the "urgent" debate, and recycled his dramatic call: "a law that makes criminals of 800,000 women a year is no longer a law." In contrast to Weimar, however, even for the most committed reformers, including those few veterans of the Weimar campaigns who had stayed in or returned to Germany, the discussion now focused less on the abolition of paragraph 218 or permanent legalization and more on the limited, contingent, and transient conditions under which abortion could be justified in the name of *Volksgesundheit* and recovery. Even as the young SED labored mightily to convince its sometimes impatient cadre that the time was ripe, not for socialist revolution but rather for bourgeois democracy under SED leadership, Communists – as well as Social Democrats – expected that with socialism finally within reach, their longtime vision of happy healthy mothers who no longer required abortions would soon be fulfilled.[25]

On 8 December 1946 the illustrated women's magazine *Für Dich* (For You) published a front-page call for readers' views, modeled on the 1931 abortion speakout in the Berlin *Volkszeitung*.[26] One of the first responses, published a week later under a large photograph of a *Cyankali* performance, came from Durand-Wever. Specifically invoking memories of the Nazi years when her commitment to providing contraception almost led her into a Gestapo trap – "the suddenly opened purse clasp and the identity card of a Gestapo agent which fell to the floor saved me from accusation – others were less lucky" – Durand-Wever urgently reclaimed her Weimar slogan, "Don't Abort, Prevent!"[27] However, she had revised her corollary pre-1933 call for legalization of abortion. While acknowledging that, "there are cases in which an interruption must be performed,"[28] and surely also influenced by her experience with the necessary but "loathsome" late-stage abortions more recently performed on rape victims,[29] she was now more skeptical about even necessary legal abortions: "no woman's body, no woman's soul can endure such repeated operations."[30]

At the beginning of the postwar era, therefore, the abortion question was even more difficult to resolve than before. Communists (and Socialists) were now more explicit about the limits set on a woman's individual right to control her body. In the Soviet zone, a revamped motherhood-eugenics consensus emerged within the newly formed SED. Rejecting full decriminalization, it favored legalization of the social indication for abortion, in addition to medical, eugenic, and ethical (rape and incest) indication for abortion; it also championed extensive pronatalist measures, such as "adequate protection of mothers" and the "establishment of child care centers."[31]

In contrast to the demands of the Weimar KPD, the postwar goal was not "to abolish paragraph 218 but to make it superfluous."[32] In its memorable 1931 campaign, the KPD had touted the benefits of legalization for female health and fertility, and carried, albeit reluctantly, the banner "Your Body Belongs to You." After twelve years of National Socialism, a devastating war, the emigration of many of the most committed (generally Jewish) Weimar exponents of Sex Reform, and – very importantly, especially for the large numbers of returnees from Soviet exile now in positions of power – the 1936 Soviet retreat on legalized abortion, that old slogan was dismissed as anarchistic and individualistic. The terms of debate had shifted; the new goal was to construct a law that could reconcile the state's need for the preservation of the "biological and moral foundations for the continuation of the *Volk*" with its need for realistic (*lebensnah*) laws.[33] Only a few liberal bourgeois feminists, such as the former Democratic (now Liberal Democratic) party activist Katharina von Kardorff still insisted, as they had during Weimar, that paragraph 218 left women with "one leg in the grave and the other in the penitentiary."[34]

Defensively pleading with the SED Party leadership, female activists echoed Weimar assertions that nations unable to feed their children had no legitimacy in forcing their birth, but erased the earlier linked rhetoric of rights and bodily integrity. They insisted that calls for legal medical abortions were not individualistic demands for the right to control one's own body; rather, they were necessary expressions of collective social responsibility:

> *We do not believe in natural law, the law is a social category. And we grant to society the right to decide over the fate of mother and child; but under one condition: that the society guarantees at least a minimum of tolerable living conditions.*[35]

SBZ population policy envisioned a democratic and peaceful welfare state guided by, but not entirely beholden to, the Soviet model. Always keeping open the question of unification, Communists hoped that a new, healthy, and populous *Volk* would build a revitalized German nation. Adding a nationalist twist to maternalist Weimar KPD and SPD rhetoric about women's natural and only temporarily repressed wish for children, they affirmed that "Germany needs children if they can be raised under humane conditions so that they can become carriers of the new democratic life."[36] This "ethic of healthy and natural" motherhood was explicitly counterposed to the militarist (not the racial) intentions of National Socialist ideology.[37] Surely also impelled by fears about a population shift to the West, they avoided all but the most general references to Nazi racial policies and focused on the desperate need for healthy reproduction and reconstruction.

4. Legalization of Abortion

It was, however, precisely the postwar emergency conditions of destruction and deprivation which allowed the Soviet zone temporarily to recuperate the Weimar call for the abolition of paragraph 218 – and to fulfill it. The conflict between individual rights and collective welfare that had so bedeviled Weimar sex reformers was decided in favor of the latter, but in contrast to the western zones, it was defined as including – at least under the present unstable conditions – broad access to legal abortions. SED and SBZ officials who supported new liberalized laws were clearly prodded not only by press campaigns and female comrades, but also by SMAD Order No. 234 in October 1947 which called for the rapid reconstruction of German productivity and labor power, both to rebuild Germany and supply the Soviet Union with desperately needed goods. SMAD economic goals provided a major impetus for many welfare measures including marriage counseling, maternal and child care programs, and abortion reform.[38]

By the end of 1947, then, in the Soviet zone the long-time Sex Reform and Communist Party goal of abolishing paragraph 218 was achieved – briefly. New laws legalizing socially, medically, and ethically (on grounds of rape or incest) indicated abortions were promulgated in the separate state parliaments of the SBZ: in Saxony in June, Brandenburg and Mecklenburg in November, and Thuringia in December (only Saxony-Anhalt in February 1948 did not accept the social necessity indication). Commissions composed of doctors and lay representatives from trade unions and women's groups were charged with the task of approving – or denying – abortions. Paragraph 218 and the subsidiary paragraphs 219 and 220 of the criminal code that banned advertising of abortifacients and abortion services, were abolished. The 1935 amendment to the sterilization law sanctioning eugenic abortions, the 1943 law that sanctioned a possible death penalty for abortion, and the 1941 police ordinance that restricted access to contraceptives were also eliminated.[39] Additionally, and in dramatic contrast to states in the western zones which not only maintained paragraph 218, but in some cases limited themselves to suspending the Nazi genetic health courts, SMAD Order No. 6 of 8 January 1946 formally abrogated the Law for the Prevention of Hereditarily Diseased Offspring. In March 1947, the Berlin *Magistrat* had already officially confirmed the de facto rule that no punishment could be imposed or enforced on doctors who had performed abortions during the transition period: a decision obviously intended to protect doctors who had certified and performed the many abortions on women who reported having been raped. Fierce resistance by Christian Democratic (CDU) and some Liberal (LDP) delegates blocked the SED goal of uniform rules, but the Soviet zone nevertheless achieved what the Weimar Republic had failed to accomplish: the abolition of even the reformed 1926 version of paragraph 218. The SED paper *Neues Deutschland* proudly announced that "the deathknell [hour] of the quack" had sounded.[40]

Yet, by 1948, the sense of postwar social and health emergency had somewhat abated, and ambivalence about readily available abortion was becoming even more apparent. With the demise of the autonomous women's councils, the SED firmly in control of women's politics, and the Cold War in full swing, avid birth controller Durand-Wever resigned her DFD presidency in April 1948, ostensibly for health reasons. She had become increasingly isolated due to her "bourgeois stance" and her growing involvement in the "western-oriented" international planning movement.[41] Durand-Wever had always lived in West Berlin, crossing the border into the Soviet zone to do her political work. For some, like Elfriede Paul, the DDR remained the only place where "what had already been discussed in the 1920s could now be fulfilled,"[42] but many activists of the "first hour," including Renthe-Fink and Schellenberg joined Durand-Wever in the difficult decisions to commit to the west after 1948 when the city officially divided.[43]

Durand-Wever briefly continued to serve on the DFD's executive board and struggled to find a persuasive rhetoric equally suited to supporting safe legal abortions and calling for the reduction of abortion by making contraception more available. "A woman's health," she asserted at a meeting in September 1948 during the tense months of blockade and airlift, "was her most valuable possession … also the most valuable capital of the nation"; she warned that the "the entire economic plan will fail if women's health is ruined." For Durand-Wever, the obvious solution was the widespread use of contraception; it could protect women's health and fertility while allowing socially rational family limitation:

> *Prevention of pregnancy is an urgently necessary measure today because we are in the midst of reconstruction and because, if we want to raise healthy children, we must create healthy conditions.*[44]

Energized by a renewed correspondence with the American family planning champion Margaret Sanger and her first post-1933 birth control congress in Cheltenham, England, Durand-Wever urged her DFD comrades to support seminars for physicians on contraceptive techniques, such as had been successfully conducted in Berlin in the 1920s. She enthusiastically proselytized the benefits of contraception: "I can only say to you, we too know these methods and know how to use them … to help keep women healthy."[45] But the SED women in the DFD were painfully ambivalent, unsure about how to combine either abortion reform or widespread birth control use and education with their emphasis on producing and raising a new healthy generation for the new Germany. Durand-Wever's call was immediately challenged:

> *But for our doctors I would like to propose another special challenge. It does not matter how … doctors go on (sich auslassen) in articles, which are even available for public consumption, about what new methods are now used to interrupt pregnancies. What matters above all is that doctors should deal with the question of how our living children can be kept alive. That is much more important.*[46]

The entire postwar debate about abortion and birth control had been conducted tentatively and cautiously; it depended on the assumption that once conditions had normalized women would willingly bear children for family, state, and *Volk*. Political and rhetorical parameters had been set that would facilitate the abolition of the social indication only a few years later in 1950 by the newly installed German Democratic Republic. As in the Soviet Union in 1936, the discourse of social emergency and need that had so often been invoked to justify legalizing abortion and other Sex Reform measures was now deployed to justify recriminalization. As in the Soviet Union, the necessary conditions for the "healthy upbringing" of children – including the protection and equality of women – were now declared assured, and indeed promoted, by a variety of pronatalist benefits, such as baby bonuses for mothers of at least three children, expanded benefits especially for single working mothers, improved child care and prenatal and maternity facilities, as well as educational and training programs designed to outfit women for the double burden of full-time waged labor and childrearing.[47]

As in the Soviet Union in the 1930s, East German authorities argued that legalization had led to a veritable "abortion addiction; the more applications were granted, the more were submitted." It had failed either to promote the "will to children" or reduce the dangers of illegal abortions which continued at levels still described as "epidemic."[48] At the same time, the liberalized regulations – often misunderstood and variously applied – had failed to win the support of many physicians in the SBZ.[49] This was perhaps not surprising in the aftermath of the Third Reich; most of their progressive anti-paragraph 218, pre-Nazi colleagues were dead or in exile, and due to the acute shortage of medical personnel, caused also by the flight west by doctors fearing Soviet retribution, physicians had been specifically exempted from the sometimes harsh denazification regimen to which other professionals (such as teachers and government bureaucrats) had been subjected. Renewed restrictions on abortion were, therefore, welcomed by two groups often at odds, the SED leadership and the medical profession.

5. Recriminalization

On 27 September 1950, paragraph 11 of the Law for the Protection of Mother and Children and for the Rights of Women *(Gesetz über den Mutter-und Kinderschutz und die Rechte der Frau)* recriminalized abortion by abolishing the social indication. Henceforth commissions were only to approve abortions (*Schwangerschaftsabbrüche* as they were called) if there was clear evidence of serious medical danger for the woman or a severe hereditary disorder in either parent. Abortions were now generally illegal in both of the otherwise very different German states that had been officially established in 1949. Paragraph 11 – which had been added to the Women's Law almost at the last minute – provoked "very lively" protest from local SED and women's groups. Local party officials reported meetings that became so "impassioned and outraged that there was a tumult and a halt had to be called."[50] Some women workers attacked the law for expecting them to "bear children only for the state." "Why," they demanded, "do they want so many children – that would be like with Hitler."[51]

For their part, DFD and SED officials pointed rather plaintively to the positive measures incorporated in the law and tried to persuade disgruntled women "that we have after all, from the side of the state, done everything possible to facilitate birth." They contended that, "our *Volk* has to be renewed, not – like Hitler said it – in order to generate soldiers for war, but in order to ... assure its continuation in the future." And they hastened to add, "What is important is ... that a mother cannot be coerced to carry a child if her life and health or that of her child is on the line."[52]

The sudden recriminalization of abortion gave voice, therefore, to recent and still raw, if publicly muted, memories of coercive Nazi policies on motherhood. Following a logic established during the immediate postwar years (and which was in many ways common to east and west), the young DDR both appropriated and distanced itself from nationalist and *völkisch* language. The state's demand for babies was deplorable if made for militarist purposes but acceptable in the name of strengthening the *Volk*. Pronatalist policies denounced forced cannon fodder production, evaded discussion of Nazi racial hygiene, and insisted on the absolute necessity of stimulating *Geburtenfreudigkeit* (joy in birth) among German women.

But the rank and file were apparently not impressed, and Communists, especially women's activists within the DFD, were hard pressed to explain the party's turnaround.[53] Given years of selective pro- and antinatalist Nazi propaganda, followed by the mass rapes and social upheaval of war's end, as well as the SBZ's anti-paragraph 218 politics, the conviction that abortions were justified when socially or eugenically necessary was deeply ingrained in East German women. Women were likely to ask what a young dental technician asked in one of many press forums:

> *What use can it be for a state to have so many children, if they are malnourished and sick, only cost money, and may never be able to fulfill even the most average tasks expected of a human being?*[54]

Many also remembered the Weimar KPD's singular and resolute position against paragraph 218. Anne-Marie Durand-Wever submitted her final resignation to the DFD in 1950 as the organization struggled with the DDR's recriminalization of abortion. Even a disappointed Elfriede Paul conceded that:

> *the thought processes of the law ... were hard to follow – this must be said in all honesty – especially for those many women and men who had determinedly waged the decades-long struggle against paragraph 218.*[55]

Moreover, the vast social welfare network presumed by the new law was not in fact in place, and calls for widespread birth control availability had not been fulfilled. The DFD was reduced to occasionally intervening – apparently unsuccessfully – on applicants' behalf in the deliberations of commissions determining medical justifications as well as to urging members to recruit doctors from the West to staff counseling centers designed for the "protection" of mothers and children.[56] In vain, the DFD assured "our mothers and women" that they contributed to the "renewal and viability of our *Volk*" by their increased willingness to bear children, promising that besides the activities of official agencies women could count on all the members of the DFD for help and counseling.[57] Marriage and sex counseling was prescribed as an antidote to a renewed sense of "marriage crisis," fed by social workers' and doctors' oft-repeated stories about husbands who returned from war or imprisonment to find their wives with a newly acquired *Onkel*, or wives evacuated to the countryside who returned to find their spouses living with the *Bratkartoffelbraut* (fried potatoes bride) procured to care for the household in their absence.[58] On the one hand, newly tough and independent women faced with "dull, bitter and pessimistic" men were supposed "to learn that even where their marriages can no longer satisfy their sexual desires ... they have a ... duty towards their men and to mankind in general in helping to heal the terrible wounds of war in their own homes." On the other hand, divorces had to be negotiated for marriages that irretrievably had broken down.[59] But after twelve years of interventionist Nazi racial hygiene programs, women were as suspicious of state-provided sex and procreative advice as they were of the recriminalization of abortion by paragraph 11.

Functionary Käthe Kern sighed, "Especially in regard to paragraph 11, there is much ideological education to be done."[60] Clearly, SED women were not entirely comfortable with the compromises they forged. As Kern had earlier remarked with some resignation, "These are all very complicated questions. One cannot always do full justice to real life with paragraphs."[61] Yet a paragraph – now paragraph 11 and not paragraph 218 – exercised profound power over the reproductive lives of East German women in the 1950s and 1960s. It assumed – incorrectly as it turned out – that equality of the sexes and economic security obviated the need for broadly available legal abortion.

Paragraph 11 of the 1950 law and its ban on socially indicated abortions caused immense troubles of interpretation and enforcement. It also produced a lively correspondence between women citizens and the central Ministry of Health in which women energetically (and unsuccessfully) protested the denial of their requests for legal abortion by the local commissions entrusted with deciding the validity of medical, eugenic, or ethical indications.[62] Indeed, commissions and appeal commissions were overworked and often did not deliberate on a case until all deadlines for medically indicated abortions had passed. The contraceptives touted as alternatives to abortion were unreliable and in short supply, especially after the long hiatus in production and development during the Nazi years. Ironically, in some cases the pride of the young DDR in combating disease and providing decent treatment for diseases traditionally associated with poverty like tuberculosis mitigated against approving a medical indication. Moreover, doctors serving on the commissions were unpaid and mostly unenthusiastic about their task; professionals considered the lay members, especially those from the DFD, ill-qualified to make decisions about medical and eugenic necessity, and sometimes admonished them for being overly sympathetic to pleading women.

High anxiety about the law, its unpopularity, and fears about its possible effects on female health did mandate that (apparently) careful records on legal and illegal abortion be maintained. Local districts *(Bezirke)* kept detailed quarterly track of, and informed the central Ministry about, all applications for abortion, and how many were accepted or rejected (generally about half). They investigated whether abortions approved on medical or eugenic grounds *(schwere Erbkrankheiten)* proceeded without complication; they also checked on the progress of those pregnancies whose termination had been denied, documenting whether they were in fact carried to term, and how many of those babies were stillborn or premature. The files suggest great concern with continuing problems of infant mortality (especially among the premature for whom medical care was deemed woefully inadequate), as well as satisfaction with the fact that most women did complete pregnancies they had asked to terminate, rather than resorting to illegal (and presumably dangerous) abortions. However, at least in the first half decade after paragraph 11 had been included in the 1950 law for the protection of motherhood, the rate of illegal abortions continued to be high; from 1950 to 1955, estimates ranged from sixty-eight to one hundred thousand annually. Although numbers for both legal and illegal interruptions did steadily decline, it would seem that neither strategy – liberalizing access (until 1950) or restricting access (after 1950) – was truly able to combat the persistent German "abortion scourge" *(Abtreibungsseuche)*.[63]

Health officials continually tried to focus attention on the pronatalist and social welfare benefits of the *Mutterschutz* legislation, rather than its repressive aspects. This was especially important because abortion and population politics in general operated – like so much else in the DDR – in the context of anxious contact and competition with the supposed consumer and economic miracle state to its west (which, after all, also criminalized abortion). On the tenth anniversary of the law in 1960, DDR authorities proudly declared:

> *With the realization of the Law for the Protection of Mothers and Children and the Rights of Women we show the West German women that in our state women have a respected position in all areas of life and we also prove the superiority of our workers' and peasants' state over the reactionary clerical-military system of the Adenauer regime.*[64]

In the same year, however, the DDR hosted an International Planned Parenthood Federation (IPPF) regional meeting on abortion at the University of Rostock which brought together Weimar veterans Hans Lehfeldt from New York, Durand-Wever from West Berlin, and Hans Harmsen from Hamburg.[65] The DDR was not immune to the international trend towards population and birth control; it was clear that the ideological and pragmatic tide was turning. Frustrated and angry with decisions by local commissions, women, in petitions to the Ministry of Health, argued for their right to a legal abortion by exploiting the rhetoric of socialist citizenship and promises of social participation for women contained in the *Mutterschutz* law. Women did not accept the ruling logic that because the state had now provided (ostensibly) adequately for children, they should always bear them willingly. Women were convinced that, levels of state aid notwithstanding, if they did carry a pregnancy to term, they would inevitably be implicated in the child's care, to the detriment of their own lives as workers, citizens, and mothers. Indeed, once children were present, women *wanted* to mother them properly, as well as fulfill their other social and productive tasks; that was why they wanted to limit the number of children. The state proposed to resolve the problem of the (especially single) working mother by handing children over to institutionalized care. Health officials planned day and *Heim* (institutional) care for sick children so that mothers' work schedules would not be disrupted, but women were clearly suspicious and resistant. They were reluctant to be separated from their children (especially when they were ill) and they knew all too well the practical and emotional limits of state support (including the limited number of child care facilities actually available). Women clearly preferred not to bear children they felt they could not raise.

In 1965 standardized and liberalized "Instructions for the Enforcement of Article 11" were issued to the local commissions. In an implicit acknowledgment of defeat in limiting the demand for abortion, acceptable indications were broadened from the strictly medical and eugenic to include women under sixteen or over forty, those with more than five children, or whose average span between four births had been less than fifteen months after the last one. Rape, incest, or other criminal acts were explicitly reinstated as justifications for abortion; women who tried to self-abort were no longer deemed criminal; and, generally, a psychological as well as physical inability to bear a child was to be taken into consideration.[66] This shift represented a defensive response to the continuing and stubbornly high rate of illegal abortions and to women's lack of trust in the commissions. But; more positively, it was also perhaps a sanguine response to what had after all been a gratifyingly high birth rate after 1950 (according to official statistics, the birth rate jumped from 14.5/1000 in 1949 to 16.9 in 1951 to 17.5 by 1961).[67] Moreover, during the mid- to late-1960s, anti-abortion regulations were being liberalized in other Soviet-bloc nations and coming under attack in West Germany.

Despite the favorable demographic evidence and reports that the child care burden was cutting into women's labor force participation, trepidation about population quantity still blocked any formal or total abolition of paragraph 11. In contrast, however, to the West German model of "stay-at-home" mothers or part-time waged work, the DDR expected births, but not at the expense of female labor or civic participation.[68]

Eventually, after several years of steady loosening, the DDR's dual program of full labor force participation for women and pronatalist pressure, supported by extensive state welfare measures, would require the re-legalization of abortion. Re-legalization was officially promulgated in 1972, an action also influenced by the feminist campaigns against paragraph 218 in West Germany, which were of course no secret to television viewers in the east. The DDR's move in turn influenced the liberalization of abortion laws in the Federal Republic. Indeed, the easy availability of legal medical abortion – albeit under sometimes uncomfortable and humiliating conditions – became a benefit so much taken for granted by East Germans that they refused to relinquish it after the fall of the Wall in 1989, producing a major stumbling block to German unification. When formal unification came in October 1990, the two parts of Germany could not agree on a single standardized ruling, just as the various German states had not been able to agree after 1945. The tension between commitment to pronatalist policies and the provision of abortion for the truly "needy" remains an unresolved and highly contested issue in post-1989 German politics.

Notes

1. Frau Wenk, Liberal Democratic Party delegate to the Saxon Landtag, 18 June 1947, SAPMO-BA, Zentralkomitee (ZK) SED, IV/17/28, p. 109.
2. Richtlinien für Ehe-und-Sexualberatungsstellen, 17 September 1946, in SStAD, Landesregierung Sachsen, Ministerium für Arbeit und Sozialfürsorge 35/1, Nr. 1810 (Ministerium für Gesundheitswesen).
3. For West(ern) Germany, see Elizabeth Heineman, "The Hour of the Woman: Memories of Germany's 'Crisis Years' and West German National Identity," *American Historical Review* 101:2 (1996): 354-95.
4. First session of anti-fascist Women's Council, 21 March 1946, in SAPMO-BA, ZK SED IV/2/17/54 (Saxony); for discussion of social crisis and "depraved" women (*Verwilderung der Sitten, Verfall der Frau*), see also IV/2/17/55 (Berlin); and SStAD 35/1.
5. Helke Sander and Barbara Johr, eds., *Befreier und BeFreite: Krieg, Vergewaltigungen, Kinder* (Munich, 1992), 48, 54-55, 59; also Erich Kuby, *Die Russen in Berlin 1945* (Bern/Munich, 1965), 312-13.
6. Norman Naimark, *The Russians in Germany: A History of the Soviet Zone of Occupation, 1945-1949* (Cambridge, Mass., 1995), 133, 107.
7. For discussion of Nazi policies, see Atina Grossmann, *Reforming Sex: The German Movement for Birth Control and Abortion Reform, 1920-1950* (New York, 1995), 149-53.
8. SAPMO-BA, NL 182/246 (Walter Ulbricht papers), "Besprechung Gen. Ulbricht mit je 1 Genossen aus jedem Verwaltungsbezirk," Berlin, 20 May 1945, p. 47.
9. Dr. Anne-Marie Durand-Wever, "Mit den Augen einer Ärztin: Zur Kontroverse zwischen Prof. Nachtsheim und Dr. Volbracht," *Berliner Ärzteblatt* 83:14 (1970): Sonderdruck (n.p.n).
10. See Atina Grossmann, "A Question of Silence: The Rape of German Women by Occupation Soldiers," *October* 72 (1995): 43-63. See also LAB, Rep. 12, Acc. 902/5, Dienstbesprechungen der Amtsärzte 1945/46, and Ruth Andreas-Friedrich, *Schauplatz Berlin: Tagebuchaufzeichnungen 1945 bis 1948* (Frankfurt am Main, 1986), 93-96.
11. See for example the 1947 DEFA film, "Strassenbekanntschaft."
12. LAB, Rep 12, Acc. 902/5, Dienstbesprechungen der Amtsärzte 1945/46. The major focus of anxiety about venereal disease did not shift to prostitution and consensual sex until the arrival of U.S. troops in July 1945 and the clear failure of the short-lived and ill-fated ban on GI fraternization with German "furlines" (as soldierly parlance had it). See, for example (among myriad contemporary sources), Julian Bach Jr., *America's Germany: An Account of the Occupation* (New York, 1946), especially the chapter on "GIs between the Sheets," 71-83.
13. See, for example, complaints collected in SStAD 35/1, Nr. 1810.
14. See extensive discussion in Walter Ulbricht's papers. SAPMO-BA, NL 182, esp. file 856. See also W. Ulbricht to Marshall Zhukov, 31 May 1945, NL 182/246, p. 22, and Naimark's discussion in *Russians in Germany*, 69-140.
15. See Wolfgang Schivelbusch's engaging study of cultural politics, *Vor dem Vorhang: Das geistige Berlin 1945-1948* (Munich, 1995).
16. "Aufruf" of Magistrat for establishment of Zentrale Frauenauschüsse, 23 August 1945, in SAPMO-BA IV/2/17/55.
17. Abt. Frauenausschüsse to Deutsche Zentralverwaltung für das Gesundheitswesen in der Sowjetischen Besatzungszone, 22 August 1946, in SAPMO-BA, ZK der SED, IV/2/17/28.

18. See, for example, the relentless campaign against the SED in the (West) Berlin women's magazine *sie* in the months and weeks leading up to the election.
19. See Reingard Jäkl, "1945 – Eine politische Chance für Frauen?" in "*Ich bin meine eigene Frauenbewegung*": *Frauen-Ansichten aus der Geschichte der Großstadt* (Berlin, 1991), 268-97, and Corinne Bouillot and Elke Schüller, "'Eine machtvolle Frauenorganisation' oder 'Der Schwamm, der die Frauen aufsaugen soll': Ein deutsch-deutscher Vergleich der Frauenzusammenschlüsse der Nachkriegszeit," *Ariadne: Almanach des Archivs der deutschen Frauenbewegung* 27 (1995): 47-55. Käthe Kern, like many women functionaries, had "a long-term relationship" with an SED leader, the former Social Democrat Otto Grotewohl. See Naimark, *Russians in Germany*, 131.
20. *Protokoll des Deutschen Frauenkongress für den Frieden, Gründungskongress des Demokratischen Frauenbundes Deutschlands*, Berlin, 7-9 March 1947, pp. 32, 98. SAPMO-BA, DFD Archive (hereafter DFDA). For general discussion of antifascism as ideology and narrative, see the special issue of *New German Critique* 67 (1995). For a comparative perspective, see also Eric D. Weitz, "The Heroic Man and the Ever-Changing Woman: Gender and Politics in European Communism, 1917-1950," in *Gender and Class in Modern Europe*, ed. Laura L. Frader and Sonya O. Rose (Ithaca, NY, 1996), 311-52.
21. See the extensive collections of press clippings in SAPMO-BA, ZK SED IV/2/17/29. See also Grossmann, *Reforming Sex*, 189-202.
22. See, for example, Käthe Kern, SAPMO-BA, NL 145/50, p. 43.
23. See Grossmann, *Reforming Sex*, 199-201. See also Elfriede Paul, *Ein Sprechzimmer der Roten Kapelle*, ed. Vera Küchemeister (Berlin, 1981); Paul's papers in SAPMO-BA, NL 229; Peter Mitzscherling, "Auf dem Wege zu einer 'sozialistischen' Sozialpolitik? Die Anfänge der Sozialpolitik in der SBZ/DDR," in *Sozialpolitik nach 1945: Geschichte und Analysen*, ed. Reinhart Bartholomäi, Wolfgang Bodenbender, Hardon Henk, and Renate Hüttel (Bonn-Bad Godesberg, 1977), 94; Barbara von Renthe-Fink, "Aus der Nachkriegsgeschichte der Gesundheitspolitik in Berlin," in *Sozialpolitik nach 1945*, 69-70; idem, *So alt wie das Jahrhundert: Lebensbericht einer Berliner Ärztin* (Frankfurt am Main, 1982), 72; and LAB, Rep. 12/1641/271.
24. Walter Lennig, *Berliner Zeitung*, 3 March 1947, in SAPMO-BA, ZK SED IV/2/17/29, p. 63.
25. Dr. Friedrich Wolf, "Der Par. 218 und die soziale Indikation," *Neues Deutschland*, 17 December 1946, in SAPMO-BA, ZK SED IV/21/17/29. See also Paul Ronge and Friedrich Wolf, *Problem Par. 218* (Rudolstadt, n.d.[1946-47]).
26. *Für Dich* 1:17 (8 December 1946). See also the simultaneous discussion "For and against the social indication" in the SED paper *Neues Deutschland*, 30 November 1946, in SAPMO-BA, ZK SED IV/2/17/29.
27. *Für Dich* 1:18 (12 December 1946): 3.
28. Durand-Wever in DFD Bundesausschuß, 24 September 1948, SAPMO-BA, DFDA.
29. Durand-Wever used the terminology "loathsome" (*scheusslich*) in her unpublished diary, *Als die Russen kamen: Tagebuch einer Berliner Ärztin*; cited with kind permission of Dr. Madeleine Durand-Noll.
30. Anne-Marie Durand-Wever, *Bewusste Mutterschaft durch Geburtenregelung* (Rudolstadt, n.d [1946 or 1947]), 30. See also her other brochure, *Normale und Krankhafte Vorgänge im Frauenkörper: Schriften zur Ideologischen und Kulturellen Arbeiten der Frauenausschüssen* (Berlin/Leipzig, 1946).

31. Käthe Kern, "Was versteht man unter sozialer Indikation," Berlin, 19 December 1946, SAPMO-BA IV/2/17/28.
32. Notes in Käthe Kern's collected papers, SAPMO-BA, NL 145/50, p. 213.
33. *Für Dich* 1:18 (12 December 1946): 3.
34. *Kurier*, 13 December 1946, in SAPMO-BA, ZK SED IV/2/17/29. A few other dissenting voices pleading for women's right to decide, at least within the first trimester, appear in the letters column or in SED files. See the long letter from Anni König, a former nurse for the Weimar League of German Women Doctors, and from abortion rights advocate Dr. Hermine Heusler-Edenhuizen, in IV/2/17/29.
35. Abteilung Frauenausschüsse to SED Vorstand, 2 October 1946, SAPMO-BA, ZK SED IV/2/17/28.
36. Dr. Eva Kolmer, "Frauenschutzgesetz – nicht Par. 218," 29 January 1947, *Pressedienst*, SAPMO-BA, ZK SED IV/2/17/28. For similar statements, see Käthe Kern, collected papers, SAPMO-BA, NL 145 and her statement, 19 December 1946, in SAPMO-BA, ZK SED IV/2/17/28.
37. For example in Saxon marriage counseling guidelines, 17 September 1946, SStAD 35/1, Nr. 1810.
38. Kirsten Poutrus argues persuasively that the SMAD was also eager to expand the grounds for legal abortion to include the "social" indication in order to underplay the salience of the "ethical" grounds provided by Soviet soldiers' rapes of German women. See her "(K)eine Frauensache: Das Abtreibungsphänomen im sowjetisch besetzten Nachkriegsdeutschland (1945-1950)," in *Ohne Frauen ist kein Leben: Der Par. 218 und moderne Reproduktionstechnologien* (Berlin, 1994), 99.
39. Crimes justifying ethical indication had to be reported in two weeks and abortions after the first trimester had to be strictly medically indicated. Saxony-Anhalt's law in February 1948 stressed aid for women and newborns such as the provision of linens. See Kirsten Poutrus, "'Ein Staat, der seine Kinder nicht ernähren kann, hat nicht das Recht, ihre Geburt zu fordern': Abtreibung in der Nachkriegszeit 1945 bis 1950," in *Unter anderen Umständen: Zur Geschichte der Abtreibung*, ed. Gisela Staupe and Lisa Vieth for Deutsches Hygiene Museum Dresden (Berlin/Dresden, 1993), 73-85.
40. *Neues Deutschland*, 27 September 1947, in SAPMO-BA IV/2/17/29, p. 83.
41. Ill health was an unlikely claim given the campaign being waged against her. See letter from Maria Weiterer to Emmy Koenen (Demerius) referring to Durand-Wever, 20 June 1947; also Durand-Wever's statements in minutes of Vorstand meeting, 6 April 1948 and Arbeitsbesprechung, 14 April 1948, SAPMO-BA, DFDA.
42. In 1949 Paul became director of the central health insurance office in (East) Berlin where she worked closely with Martha Arendsee, former leader of the KPD social welfare organization, ARSO. She later established a birth control and marriage counseling clinic in Magdeburg directly modeled on her experiences with the Weimar *Bund für Mutterschutz*. See Paul, *Sprechzimmer*, and her papers in SAPMO-BA, NL 229.
43. On the painful transition from east to west in 1949 see von Renthe-Fink, *So alt*, 47-92. In 1960 she became an SPD health senator in West Berlin, and after her retirement, vice president of the (West) German Red Cross.
44. Durand-Wever, 24 September 1948, in SAPMO-BA, DFD Bundesvorstand 95, p. 292.
45. Ibid.

46. Frau Selbmann in DFD Bundesvorstand, 24 September 1948. SAPMO-BA, DFDA.
47. See the necessary conditions for recriminalization laid out by Chief Prosecutor Hilde Benjamin, *Mitteilungen der juristischen Arbeitskommission im Zentralen Frauenausschuß* 3 Folge, Juristische Grundlagen für die Diskussion über den Par. 218, Abt. Frauenausschüsse bei der Deutschen Verwaltung für Volksbildung in der SBZ, Berlin, 27 February 1947, in SAPMO-BA, DFDA. For a good summary, see *Ende der Selbstverständlichkeit? Die Abschaffung des Par. 218 in der DDR: Dokumente*, ed. Kirsten Thietz (Berlin, 1992).
48. See Dr. K.H. Mehlan, "Die Abortsituation in der DDR," in *Internationale Abortsituation. Kongress 5.-7. Mai 1960* (Leipzig, 1961), 52-63.
49. Numerous physicians also resisted elimination of the sterilization law, insisting on the respectable pre-Nazi history of eugenic sterilization. Moreover, they wanted to continue to report, as they had been ordered to in 1935, all suspicious miscarriages. See discussion in SStAD, Saxon Ministry for Work and Social Welfare 2144/290 (Health). There seems to have been a good deal of confusion, deliberate or not, about which regulations were in effect.
50. SED Landesverband Brandenburg to the ZK of the SED, Frauenabteilung, Potsdam, 26 October 1950, SAPMO-BA IV/2/17/30, p. 129.
51. Landesverband Brandenburg to ZK SED, Frauenabteilung, Potsdam, 18 October 1950, SAPMO-BA IV/2/17/30, p. 128.
52. Jenny Matern, Bundesvorstandssitzung, 11-12 June 1951, SAPMO-BA, DFDA.
53. See DFD Bundesvorstandssitzung, 11-12 June 1951, SAPMO-BA, DFDA. See also letters and discussion in SAPMO-BA, ZK SED IV/2/17/30.
54. *Die Frau von Heute* 8 (April 1947): 8.
55. Notes in Elfriede Paul Papers, SAPMO-BA, NL 229/13.
56. DFD Meeting, Berlin, 11-12 June 1951, SAPMO-BA, DFDA. See also reports in SAD 2145/29 and DFD Referentenmaterial in SAPMO-BA IV/2/17/28.
57. Rundschreiben Nr. 49/51, Berlin, 13 June 1951, pp. 4-5, SAPMO-BA, ZK SED Abt. Frauen IV/2/17/86.
58. For an *Onkel* story, see *Für Dich* 1:8 (October 1946): 4.
59. Stefanie Hirt, "Marriage Guidance in Berlin," *The International Journal of Sexology* (May 1949): 1-3.
60. Käthe Kern, DFD Bundesvorstandssitzung, 19-20 October 1950, SAPMO-BA, DFDA.
61. Notes for Women's Conference speech, 28 May 1947, in Kern papers, SAPMO-BA, NL 145/50, p. 125. As an example of the intense interest in the abortion issue among SED activists see the 35-page bibliography listing over eight hundred books, articles and dissertations: *Par. 218 StGB als rechtpolitisches Problem: Eine Literaturübersicht*, ed. Dr. Guenther Berg (Jena, 1947), included among Kern's papers.
62. See Ministry of Health files, BAP, DQ1/ 1686, 1647, 1676, and especially 6324. As Donna Harsch points out, clear and precise guidelines for the enforcement in practice of paragraph 11 were never issued. See Donna Harsch, "Society, the State, and Abortion in East Germany, 1950-1972," *American Historical Review* 102:1 (1997): 53-84. Interestingly, sterilizations, unlike abortions, were always decided on at the central Ministry of Health level.
63. The law did, however, have clear immediate effects. In 1950 the DDR recorded 311,000 births, 26,360 legal abortions, and circa 84,000 illegal abortions. In 1951, after passage of the law, the birth rate rose only modestly to 318,000, but the number of legal abortions dropped drastically to 5,037, the estimated num-

ber of criminal abortions to 68,000. See Mehlan, "Die Abortsituation in der DDR," 52-63. For estimates, see also Harsch, "Society, the State, and Abortion," 59-63.

64. Richtlinien zur Vorbereitungen des 10 Jahrestages des Gesetzes über den Mutter- und Kinderschutz und die Rechte der Frau vom 27 September 1950, BAP, DQ 1/ 5291.
65. See Mehlan, *Internationale Abortsituation.*
66. There is some confusion and inconsistency in the secondary sources about the exact scope of the 1965 regulations. See Harsch, "Society, the State, and Abortion," 62-68, and Katharina von Ankum, "Women and Re/Production in the DDR," *Women in German Yearbook* 9 (1993): 134.
67. *Statistisches Jahrbuch der Deutschen Demokratischen Republik* (Berlin, 1962), 38. For a similar point with somewhat different statistics, see Harsch, "Society, the State, and Abortion," 68-69.
68. For comparison, see Robert Moeller, *Protecting Motherhood: Women and the Family in the Politics of Postwar West Germany* (Berkeley and Los Angeles, 1993).

Chapter 19

German Social Democracy and European Unification, 1945 to 1955

Dietrich Orlow

The role of the Social Democratic Party of Germany (SPD) in the drive for a united Europe is something of a paradox. The SPD saw itself as leading Germany into a unified Europe. The continent would not fall back into a collection of warring nation states. Instead, the SPD and the other European socialist parties would establish supra-national institutions that would implement a Europe-wide democratic socialist society.[1]

The reality, of course, was rather different. Bourgeois politicians led the way in the actual construction of European unity. Among West Germany's political leaders, Konrad Adenauer, Walter Hallstein, and Karl Arnold certainly did more to advance the concrete reality of a united Europe than Kurt Schumacher or Erich Ollenhauer. Not surprisingly, their vision of a united Europe differed substantially from that of the Social Democrats. Their goal was not social democracy, but neo-liberalism and Christian democracy. The SPD quickly lost control of the European agenda, and instead of leading the way to a united Europe fought a bitter and continuous battle against the concrete proposals for supranational cooperation advanced by its political opponents. It was not until the mid-1950s that Germany's Social Democrats jumped on the (west) European bandwagon, which by then was firmly linked to Christian democratic and liberal concepts for unification.

Notes for this chapter begin on page 484.

There were a number of reasons for the SPD's paradoxical (and counter-productive) stand on European unity. To begin with, the Socialists set their sights too high, and in several respects. They hoped that success in Europe would compensate for their failure in West Germany. Konrad Adenauer and his political allies might be able to prevent the establishment of social democracy in Germany, but their domestic successes would soon be eclipsed by the creation of a social democratic Europe that would supersede the capitalist, Catholic-dominated nation states.[2]

The Social Democrats' hopes for the geographic expanse of a united Europe were also quickly disappointed. During the war enthusiastic Europeanists like Fritz Erler, the later deputy chairman of the SPD's Bundestag delegation, had anticipated a united Europe that stretched from Poland in the east to France in the west. (Spain and Portugal were to be exorcised as fascist states.) This new social democratic entity would simultaneously separate and form a bridge between the communist Soviet Union and the capitalist United States.[3]

The Cold War destroyed the illusion of a *Großeuropa* from Warsaw to Hendaye, and "European unity" soon meant a united Western Europe. However, even then the Socialists' visions proved overly ambitious. They continued to insist that at the very least "Europe" had to include both Great Britain and the Scandinavian countries. The SPD leaders were certainly disappointed by the Scandinavian countries' plans to remain aloof from Europe, but the Labour Party's decision to opt for a Little England policy was an especially hard blow. Not only did the German Social Democrats (like those in the other continental parties) see British membership in Europe as crucial for counteracting the Catholic and conservative orientation of continental Christian democracy, but the SPD leaders thought they had a special relationship with many prominent Labour politicians. After all, such German leaders as Erich Ollenhauer and Willi Eichler had spent the greater part of the war years in exile in London, where they maintained continuous contact with many Labour Party leaders.[4]

The British decision to remain outside Europe, disappointing as it was, in no way tempted the German Socialists to follow suit. They never doubted that Germany had to be an integral part of a united, western-oriented Europe. There were virtually no proponents of an east-west *Schaukelpolitik* (swing policy) among the SPD leaders. It should be emphasized, however, that when the Social Democrats spoke about Germany in Europe they assumed that the Germany in question was a reunited, sovereign country. They firmly rejected integrating West Germany alone into what in their view was a truncated Western Europe. Unfortunately for them, *Kleineuropa* turned out to be the only viable basis for European unification.[5]

The debate over the nature of a united Europe also confronted the SPD leaders with the question of the organizational road to European unity. They certainly wanted to mobilize popular support in favor of European unification, but they were divided on how the party should engage its resources in this effort. Some party leaders felt the SPD should work together with other democratic parties and organizations, while others argued the SPD should restrict its efforts to work *en famille*, that is to say, cooperate only with other socialist groups and the Socialist International. A few prominent Social Democrats, such as the mayor of Bremen, Wilhelm Kaisen (who was to remain a constant critic of his party's official policy on Europe), argued this debate was irrelevant and unnecessary. The cause of European unity was important enough for the SPD to affiliate itself with both the socialist *Mouvement Socialiste pour les États-Unis d'Europe* (MSEUE) and the multi-partisan United Europe Movement (UEM).[6]

The SPD's relationship to the UEM was particularly controversial. The UEM owed its organizational life to the charismatic, if short-lived, efforts of Winston Churchill. The British opposition leader's call for the political unification of Western Europe led to the creation of the UEM in May 1947. The organization in turn invited all supporters of the European unification movement to work together with the UEM to further the common goal. Kurt Schumacher and his associates at the *Büro Dr. Schumacher* decided to resist the siren call and keep the SPD at a distance from the UEM. The multi-partisan lobbying effort promoted only west European unity, and in 1947 many socialists were still dreaming of a continent-wide union. Even more important, the British Labour Party saw the UEM as little more than a political front for the British Conservatives, and rejected affiliation with it. In the interest of international socialist solidarity the continental social democratic parties, including the SPD, followed Labour's lead.[7]

Although Churchill himself soon lost interest in his brain child, the UEM quickly became the largest non-governmental lobbying effort for a united Europe, with national committees active in all of the west European countries. The UEM's high profile led a number of German Social Democrats to ask for a reevaluation of their party's official position; they felt the SPD should work together with the UEM. Both Fritz Erler and Carlo Schmid, at that time prominent SPD leaders in Württemberg, had been invited to attend the UEM's first major meeting on the continent, which was scheduled for May 1948 at The Hague, and both wanted to go. In 1948 they deferred to the wishes of the SPD's Executive and did not travel to The Hague, but in subsequent years not only Schmid and Erler, but a large number of prominent German Social Democrats worked actively, albeit unofficially, with the UEM's national and international committees.[8] Moreover, after the election of the first Bundestag and the establishment of the Council of Europe, social democratic parliamentarians routinely joined other European legislators to promote European unity in a variety of multi-partisan associations of parliamentarians.[9]

The divergence between theory and practice (a long-standing tradition in the SPD) became glaringly apparent in the battle between the old guard and its critics over the establishment of the embryonic European parliament, the Council of Europe. In principle, all factions in the party welcomed a European parliament, but they were sharply divided on this specific deliberative body. The reformers, who were led by the mayors of Bremen and Hamburg, Wilhelm Kaisen and Max Brauer, welcomed the Council as a forum in which the party could join forces with other democratic groups to advance the cause of European political unification. Working within the Council, they insisted, would in no way prevent the Social Democrats from attempting to further their specifically socialist agenda for the new Europe. In sharp contrast, Schumacher and his allies argued that the Council of Europe, which Churchill had envisioned as a democratic constitutional convention, would do nothing except to create the "Catholic, capitalist, and cartel-dominated" Europe of Konrad Adenauer's and Robert Schuman's design. For this reason the SPD should reject the Council's establishment, and refuse to participate in its work if it were established.[10]

On the surface Schumacher and his allies triumphed. By a large majority (350:11) the party's annual congress, held in May 1950 in Hamburg, passed a resolution condemning the Council in its present form. For good measure the party leader also insisted that Kaisen not be reelected to the SPD's Executive Committee.[11] It was, however, a pyrrhic victory. The Christian Democrats and their allies had the votes in the Bundestag needed for parliamentary approval of the legislation establishing the Council. Nor did Schumacher's wrath weaken the position of the reformers. Secure in their *Land* (federal state) basis, both Kaisen and Brauer retained their influence; Kaisen was reelected to the *Parteivorstand* at the next congress. Finally, the SPD did not actually boycott the Council of Europe after its establishment. Schumacher himself urged the SPD delegates selected by the Bundestag (at this time the members of the Council of Europe were selected by the national parliaments) to go to Strasbourg, and beginning with the quasi-parliament's initial meeting, the German social democratic delegates participated fully and enthusiastically in the Council's deliberations.[12]

The debate and subsequent action on the Council of Europe revealed the divisions within the party on "Europe," as well as the contradictions inherent in the SPD's official policy. While social democratic activists participated in the activities of a variety of "pro-Europe" organizations, they did so as individuals rather than as representatives of their party. The party leaders kept the party line "pure" by consistently refusing institutional affiliation with multi-partisan organizations. This situation did not change until the founding of Jean Monnet's *Comité d'Action pour l'Europe* in the early 1950s. After he left his post as head of the European Coal and Steel Community's (ECSC) High Commission, Monnet, the mastermind of France's postwar modernization program and one of the intellectual fathers of the Schuman Plan, created the Committee as a way of advancing functional cooperative agreements like the ECSC. Monnet was particularly anxious to secure the goodwill of the west European socialist leaders, and he succeeded in having the SPD break with its previous policy of refusing to become institutionally affiliated with multiparty organizations. Along with other continental socialist parties, the SPD became an active and enthusiastic member of Monnet's multi-partisan advocacy group.[13]

The SPD's institutional pat – from adamant rejection of multi-partisan European unity movements to enthusiastic endorsement of Monnet's Committee – in many ways paralleled the party's changing attitude on concrete projects for functional European cooperation. For most of the time under consideration here the SPD's reaction to west European unification was conditioned by its insistence that national reunification and the regaining of Germany's national sovereignty had to precede agreement on European cooperative ventures. Only a fully sovereign and reunited Germany could enter into any European compacts. As a result, the party rejected all projects which were limited to the integration of West Germany into Western Europe. According to the Social Democrats' official position, all such projects were designed to strengthen capitalism in Europe while making German reunification more difficult.[14]

Although the SPD maintained this oppositional stance until the mid-1950s, support for the party's hard-line policies on European integration steadily eroded as the negative consequences of the SPD's attitude became increasingly apparent. A growing number of critics pointed out that the SPD's obstructionism brought the party close to some unwanted political bedfellows, such as the East German and west European Communists, who also rejected West Germany's integration into the western alliance. Putting distance between the party and these undesirable allies required considerable skill in casuistic argumentation and allowed the Christian Democrats to put the SPD on the defensive. In addition, the critics noted that the party's opposition seemed to be based less on substantive objections to specific proposals than on a desire to maintain its intransigent opposition at any price. In other words, the SPD rejected west European unity because Konrad Adenauer and the CDU favored it.[15]

Schumacher and a majority of the party's leaders vehemently denied that only tactical considerations led them to reject the European vision of the Christian Democrats and Liberals. Rather, they insisted, it was the overall direction of the unity project that had gone terribly wrong. The derailing of true European unification began with the debate on the future of the Ruhr area, and accelerated with the Schuman Plan and the European Defense Community (EDC).

The SPD and its continental sister parties started with the conviction that economic cooperation was the cornerstone of a united and social democratic Europe. With its vast market the new, united Europe would bring efficiencies of scale and social justice reforms that could only be undertaken in a planned economy subject to democratic supranational control mechanisms. In short, an economically united Europe was the prerequisite for inaugurating the era of democratic socialism on the continent.[16]

In the immediate postwar era it was accepted as axiomatic by all concerned that the intense concentration of coal mining and steel production in the Ruhr Valley would play a key role in both German and west European economic recovery. Equally important, the German Social Democrats also agreed with Allied statesmen that ways had to be found to prevent the Ruhr from once again becoming the *Waffenschmiede* (arms forge) of a new Reich. The SPD's answer to what the French called the twin goals of *sécurité* and *charbon* was to institute public ownership of the coal mines and heavy industrial facilities of the Ruhr. Control by a democratically elected German government would ensure that the resources of Europe's industrial heartland would not be misused for evil purposes. The German Social Democrats accepted international control of the distribution of the Ruhr's products, but they vehemently rejected all schemes that envisioned a political separation of the Ruhr area from Germany, or the transfer of ownership of the area's economic resources to foreign proprietors. This included internationally supervised socialization measures, which some of the SPD's sister parties advocated.[17]

The SPD, of course, had no power to put its plans into effect without the permission of the Allied occupation authorities, specifically the British; Germany's industrial heartland lay entirely within the British zone of occupation. On this score the SPD was initially optimistic. The party's proposals showed considerable affinity with the nationalization projects that the Labour government had carried out in Great Britain, and for this reason the SPD expected the British to support the German Socialists' Ruhr proposals.[18]

The western Allies, however, had rather different priorities. While the Americans, the British, and the French disagreed on many aspects of the Ruhr's future, all three were determined to establish some sort of international control over the area.[19] This in itself did not yet preclude public ownership and control of the Ruhr resources, but by 1947 the Americans weighed in with decisions that essentially blocked major structural changes in the Ruhr. The U.S. authorities now gave priority consideration to the revival of the German economy, and, in the eyes of the Americans, that was a job best left in the hands of private entrepreneurs. With the Marshall Plan, the U. S. became firmly committed to supporting free enterprise in Western Europe, and at least for the foreseeable future there was to be no large-scale socialization or nationalization in the Ruhr area.[20]

The result was a series of Allied decisions in 1948 and 1949 that effectively blocked any implementation of the SPD's Ruhr plans. On 10 November 1948 the British promulgated Law Number 75. This ordinance confirmed that politically the Ruhr would remain part of Germany, specifically the *Land* North Rhine-Westphalia (a decision that ended French hopes for the separation of the area from Germany). At the same time, however, the Germans were prevented from implementing any of the socialization measures being considered by the North Rhine-Westphalian Landtag. Law Number 75 determined that structural changes could only be undertaken by a future German national government. Until such a government took office, ownership of the Ruhr factories and mines remained in private hands, subject to the controls already imposed by the British authorities.[21]

The next day, 11 November 1948, representatives of the western Allies met in London to work out a permanent solution to the Ruhr problem. After a month of tough negotiations, the three western powers agreed on a Ruhr Statute.[22] Its terms essentially confirmed the provisions of Law Number 75, but the agreement also established an International Ruhr Authority (IRA) that was to determine quotas for mining and steel manufacturing, and oversee the equitable distribution of the products of the Ruhr industry to both Germany and its western neighbors. Membership on the IRA included the three western occupation powers as well as Germans, although for the moment the IRA was limited to Allied representation. Until the formal establishment of a new German political entity (whose constitution was already being deliberated by the Parliamentary Council in Bonn), the occupation powers represented the Germans as well as themselves.[23]

The reaction of Europe's socialists to this novel experiment in supranational administration was mixed. Léon Blum, the grand old man of the French Socialist Party (SFIO), greeted the London decisions as the beginning of a new era of Franco-German rapprochement, and the party's general secretary, Guy Mollet, welcomed international control of the Ruhr as an important first step in the creation of an industrial Euro-region. He looked forward to the day when the iron fields and industrial facilities of Lorraine would be similarly deposited in the industrial bank of Europe.[24] The SPD had no such visions. It vehemently rejected the Ruhr Statute and the IRA,[25] inaugurating a series of obstructionist stands that continued for more than half a decade and increasingly isolated the German Social Democrats within the European unification movement and from its sister parties.

The SPD rejected the Ruhr Statute because it did not meet the party's minimum conditions for the future economic regime of the Ruhr: the area had to remain under exclusive German control, and the mines and heavy industrial plants had to become German public property. In the eyes of Kurt Schumacher and his associates, the IRA blocked the road to true European unity, prevented democracy from taking root in Germany, gave verisimilitude to the communist claim that the western Allies were exploiting Germany's resources for their exclusive benefit, and established the rule of foreign capitalists over German workers. With his usual habit of the *rhetorischer Kahlschlag* (no-holds-barred rhetoric), the party leader attacked the newly installed Adenauer government, which had accepted the Ruhr Statute as the best that could be obtained under the circumstances, for selling out Germany's national interest. It was the Ruhr Statute which occasioned Schumacher's infamous outburst in the Bundestag that Adenauer was the "Chancellor of the Allies." Almost as an anticlimax, the SPD demanded an immediate and thorough going renegotiation of the terms of the Statute. The result should be a "plan of higher socialist order."[26]

The party's official reaction, which Schumacher and other party leaders reiterated in an unending series of ever more strident speeches, was endorsed by most party activists, but a small group of insightful critics recognized even at this time that the party's stand was politically counterproductive. They questioned both the tone and the substance of the SPD's attack on the Ruhr Statute. Fritz Erler, Carlo Schmid, and the economics minister of North Rhine-Westphalia, Erik Nölting, were among those who were unhappy with the tone of the party's campaign.[27] In intraparty discussions they pointed out that Schumacher's Francophobic and demagogic appeals to German nationalism and his attacks on the personal integrity of the Federal Republic's governmental leaders served neither the causes of European unification and Franco-German rapprochement, nor were they helpful in creating a democratic consensus in the young West German Republic. Several of the SPD's popular *Landesfürsten* (state rulers) objected not only to the tone of the party's rhetoric but also to the substance of its opposition to the Ruhr Statute. They argued that in spite of its shortcomings, the Statute brought important concrete advantages. The Ruhr regime was a step on the road to European unification, it sharply curtailed the Allied program of dismantling German industrial facilities, and the IRA initiated Germany's reintegration into the family of nations.[28] Schumacher rejected all of these substantive considerations as irrelevant. The Ruhr Statute "exceeded [the party's] worst fears."[29]

In many ways the Ruhr Statute was the precursor of the Schuman Plan, formally the European Coal and Steel Community (ECSC). Like the Ruhr regime, the ECSC created a supranational administration for a specific economic activity; it made no effort to achieve full-scale political integration. But there were also significant differences between the IRA and the ECSC. The Federal Republic was now treated as an equal partner in the supra-national authority. Moreover, the Schuman Plan fulfilled the implicit European promise of the Ruhr Statute by extending the area subject to supra-national economic control to the heavy industrial regions of France, Italy, and the Benelux countries in addition to those of West Germany. Finally, the ECSC added a significant political and judicial dimension to the supra-national regime. Unlike the Ruhr Statute, the ECSC established a rudimentary legislature and a High Court of Justice with binding jurisdiction alongside the administrative institutions.

The ECSC was to become one of the major success stories on the path to European unification (even the Gaullists, who fiercely opposed the Schuman Plan when it was proposed, would later argue that it was very much in line with their leader's ideas for a united Europe),[30] and it is not surprising that a multitude of politicians rushed to claim authorship. All but forgotten in what would turn out to be a Christian Democratic triumph were the pioneering contributions of two Social Democrats, Carlo Schmid in Germany and André Philip in France, in preparing the way for the Schuman Plan. Shortly after the war both published proposals that contained the essence of what was to become the ECSC, although their writings and speeches elicited little response at the time.[31]

It is now generally agreed that if there was a father of the Schuman Plan, it was Karl Arnold, the Christian Democratic prime minister of North Rhine-Westphalia. It was he who publicly launched the idea of the ECSC in a New Year's Day address in 1949. As the chief executive of a West German *Land*, Arnold obviously lacked the prominence and influence to make European policy, but when another Christian Democrat, the French foreign minister Robert Schuman (who had in turn been influenced by Jean Monnet), formally proposed the ECSC on 9 May 1950, Europe's political leaders took immediate notice. Schuman's timing was not accidental. Growing international tensions (the Korean War was to begin in June 1950) had led the Americans to put pressure on Western Europe to increase its industrial output. This inevitably meant greater industrial strength for West Germany, and the Schuman Plan was initially designed to ensure that Germany's revitalized industrial power was permanently contained and subjected to supranational controls. To achieve this priority goal of *sécurité*, the French foreign minister was willing to agree that the heavy industries of France and other member nations of the ECSC be subjected to the same supranational authority.[32]

While Schuman's proposals undoubtedly reflected France's traditional fear of Germany's economic prowess, they were also a bold and daringly new initiative on the road to European unification. The success of the initiative was, however, by no means certain when the negotiations on the actual ECSC treaty began. Two major and unexpected obstacles quickly emerged. Schuman had assumed that Great Britain would become a charter member of the ECSC, but the British Labour government decided to remain outside the Community. In addition, spokesmen for France's heavy industry resolutely opposed the plan; they argued they needed protection from German competition.[33]

In view of the Social Democrats' avowed interest in the creation of a large-scale, cross-national market and supranational controls, it might have been expected that they would welcome the Schuman Plan and even claim credit for the idea. This was indeed true for the SPD's sister parties in what would become the ECSC member states. Although initially skeptical, most of Western Europe's socialists in time became some of the Schuman Plan's most enthusiastic supporters.

Not so the German Social Democrats. The ECSC might be supported by the West German labor unions and the other west European socialist parties, but the SPD maintained its thunderous "No!" The party stubbornly insisted that the Schuman Plan was detrimental to European unification and democratic socialism. The party's stand evolved over the course of several months. The German Social Democrats' first reaction was guardedly optimistic, but under the influence of Kurt Schumacher their cautious welcome turned to total rejection.[34] Some analysts pointed to the ever-present concern for gaining tactical advantages in Schumacher's political thinking as the primary motivation for his increasingly bitter attacks on the Schuman Plan. Because the Schuman Plan was a Christian Democratic proposal, the SPD would oppose it, as it opposed everything the CDU and Adenauer supported. Guy Mollet, the SFIO's general secretary, claimed that if the SPD had been in the government in West Germany, Schumacher and the party would have endorsed the ECSC.[35]

The SPD's leader advanced a number of substantive reasons for his opposition to the Schuman Plan. With the benefit of hindsight none sound very convincing, but all were rooted in the party leader's long-standing and deep-seated distrust of France, capitalism, and political conservatism. Most important, Schumacher claimed, was the ECSC's impact on the SPD's absolute political priority, German reunification. In addition, he claimed the ECSC represented a danger to German democracy. The SPD's leader was convinced the Schuman Plan would have negative consequences for Germany and German democracy in two respects. To begin with, by integrating West Germany into the little Europe of the Six, the ECSC would effectively solidify Germany's division. This in turn meant that political extremists in West Germany – Communists and neo-Nazis – could use the national issue in their campaigns against democracy in the young Republic. In his address to the party's *Soziale Arbeitsgemeinschaft* on 24 May 1951 Schumacher insisted, "I told the Americans privately, the Schuman Plan is the birth certificate of a new communist movement." According to Schumacher, only the SPD's drive against the ECSC served Germany's national and democratic interests. Even after the bitter campaign on the ECSC was over and the treaties had been ratified by the Bundestag and the Bundesrat, Schumacher insisted in discussions with representatives of the U.S. High Commissioner's office that only the SPD's opposition to the project had saved West German democracy.[36]

In addition, the party leader remained convinced that the Schuman Plan, like the Ruhr Statute, was primarily designed to keep Germany politically impotent while exploiting the country economically for the benefit of its neighbors, especially France. As evidence for this conclusion he cited, in addition to the continuing barriers to Germany regaining its full sovereignty, the planned status of the Saar. Under the Schuman Plan the Saarland, whose future the SPD's leader had decided was the *Gretchenfrage* of Franco-German relations, was to be treated as a separate political entity, economically tied to France. For Schumacher this was clear proof of French imperialism and neo-colonialism. Finally, Schumacher insisted, and here he was on firmer ground, that the ECSC would put an end to any realistic hopes for the socialization of Europe's coal and steel industry. Instead, it would lock in place a Europe that, in an alliteration which Schumacher repeated many times, would be "conservative, clerical, and dominated by cartels."[37]

Schumacher's convoluted reasoning allowed most party leaders as well as rank-and-file activists to live with the illusion that once the Schuman Plan had been defeated, the party and Germany would regain the initiative in foreign relations. When a member of the *Parteivorstand* asked what would actually happen if the ECSC failed, another answered blithely that the party and Germany would be free of all obligations for the next fifty years.[38] However, a significant and growing minority of party leaders was not convinced. These critics pointed to the negative consequences of isolation at home and abroad. The group of critics was not large, but it included some key men in the social democratic camp, including most socialist union leaders and some powerful *Landesfürsten*. Many of the names, like Kaisen, Brauer, and Reuter, were familiar from the debate on the Ruhr Statute, but this time at least some of the critics did not limit their opposition to the internal discussions of intra-party councils.

Spearheading the public criticism was Wilhelm Kaisen, the SPD's popular leader in Bremen. Convinced that the party's stand on the Schuman Plan would be disastrous for Bremen's and the Federal Republic's economic future, the mayor of West Germany's second largest seaport sent a long article critical of the Schumacher line to the SPD's official paper, *Vorwärts*. When the paper's editors, responding to pressure from the *Parteivorstand*, refused to print the piece, Kaisen turned to *Het Vrije Volk*, the newspaper of the Dutch Social Democratic Party, the *Partij van de Arbeid*. (The Dutch comrades were enthusiastic supporters of the Schuman Plan.) Schumacher and his allies were furious and insisted on punishing the mayor for his *parteischädigendes Verhalten* (behavior injurious to the party).[39] Other leaders, like Carlo Schmid, loyally supported the Schumacher line in public but lamented the party leader's "immoderate" tone in private.[40]

Significantly, while Schumacher kept control of the SPD's Executive and the party's official policy line, he was unable to prevent a spectacular and public split in the party's leadership ranks. The SPD's *Landesfürsten* openly defied the party leader on the ratification vote of the ECSC treaty. Subjected to the full impact of Schumacher's forceful charisma, the SPD's parliamentary delegation in the Bundestag voted unanimously against ratifying the ECSC treaty, but when it came up before the Bundesrat, the SPD-governed Länder joined the states with Christian Democratic cabinets to vote for ratification, thereby assuring West German parliamentary approval of the Schuman Plan.[41]

As far as the party itself was concerned, the SPD's vehement and demagogic rejection of the Schuman Plan had largely disastrous short-term, but, paradoxically, rather more fortunate long-term effects. In the short term the party was subjected to massive criticism from the socialist parties of the other ECSC member countries,[42] and, even more important, suffered a serious electoral setback at home. The SPD had had high hopes for the 1953 Bundestag election, but the disappointing results (the CDU/CSU obtained 45.2 percent of the popular vote, the SPD 28.8 percent) clearly showed that most West German voters were not convinced by the SPD's argument that rejection of the ECSC would improve the chances for national reunification. As Rolf Steininger has aptly put it, the party's stand on the Schuman Plan was a "*schwere Wunde*" (heavy wound) for the Social Democrats.[43]

From a longer perspective, however, the success of the ECSC paved the way for a fundamental change in the SPD's attitude toward European unification. Although the shift did not become official party policy until the mid-1950s, a new atmosphere could be sensed soon after Kurt Schumacher's death in August 1952. The party's parliamentary delegation in the Bundestag led the way, but the effort to escape isolation was also bolstered by changing attitudes in some of the regional organizations which had been particularly mistrustful of *kleineuropäische* proposals. Symptomatic of this evolution were developments in the party's organization in Rhineland-Palatinate. The SPD's district organization in this *Land*, which was a creation of the French occupation authorities, had always shared Schumacher's profound distrust of French motives. But then came the obvious benefits that the ECSC brought to Rhineland-Palatinate and the entire Rhineland. These benefits were instrumental in converting the SPD's regional leaders to supporters of functional European unification as well as reconciling them to the existence of the *Land* itself.[44]

While the SPD was traditionally interested in European economic unification, supra-national military cooperation was very much outside the party's purview. Traditionally, Europe's socialists, the SPD included, were suspicious of all military establishments and of military solutions to society's problems. The MSEUE expressed the Social Democrats' instinctive aversion to seeing the military as a positive force when it noted that any military pact ran the danger of substituting military solutions for political ones.[45]

At the same time, after 1945 there was the reality of the Cold War, increasing fears of Soviet aggression, and, as a consequence, American pressure for a greater military effort on the part of the west Europeans (including the Germans) to counter the threat of communism. After the outbreak of the Korean War, U.S. concerns focused on the Federal Republic; the Americans insisted there had to be a West German military contribution to the defense of the west.[46]

Ironically, in view of its subsequent position, the SPD had initially appeared to be sympathetic to such ideas. The party did not endorse pacifism, and it did not in principle reject a new German army. However, the SPD did insist that any German armed forces had to be under the control of a fully sovereign Federal Republic. Germans would participate in the defense of the west, but only on the basis of complete equality. Kurt Schumacher also linked Germany's military contribution to the party's constant priority goal of national reunification. Seemingly echoing John Foster Dulles's "rollback of communism" concept, Schumacher elaborated what he called a "forward defense strategy." In responding to overt Soviet aggression, the west should not limit its military measures to defensive operations, but mount a full-scale offensive which would reunify all of Germany, including the lands east of the Oder-Neisse line.[47]

It is unclear if Schumacher was naive or if his grandiose plans for an independent national army and a "forward defense" strategy were primarily designed to embarrass the Adenauer government for its ostensible lack of enthusiasm for German reunification. In any case, none of the western Allies were willing to endorse a German army along the lines envisioned by Schumacher and the SPD or to help the Germans regain the lands that were now administered by Poland. On the contrary, all Allied statesmen sought desperately for ways to integrate whatever German armed forces there might be into some sort of supra-national framework to prevent the establishment of a new Wehrmacht subject only to national German control.

The European Defense Community (EDC) was the brainchild of the French defense minister and Radical politician, René Pleven. It was designed to assuage French fears of a new German army while responding to American pressure for a German military contribution; in essence, the EDC was a Schuman Plan for the military. The member nations of the EDC would transfer all or a portion of their military forces to a joint European command; all of West Germany's new military establishment would be fully integrated into the EDC. Pleven was especially determined to prevent the reestablishment of a German general staff organization because the image of the *Generalstab* instantly evoked fears of renewed German militarism among the country's neighbors. Instead, the EDC would have a general staff composed of officers from all member countries, so that there would be no need for a separate German national general staff. Like Schuman, Pleven also fervently hoped for British membership in the EDC, but such hopes were again disappointed; Great Britain still decided to stay out of continental affairs. Membership in the EDC was limited to the same six nations that made up the ECSC.[48]

The EDC was controversial from its inception and it remained that way. For more than two years supporters and opponents in the intended member countries battled each other in the press and in parliament. Emotions and personal animosities ran high, and ideological affinities counted for little in the debate. The Socialist International and the socialist parties of the Six tried valiantly, but unsuccessfully, to arrive at a common response to the EDC. As Erwin Schöttle, one of the SPD's leaders in Württemberg, put it, "sometimes we have to recognize that other parties reach other conclusions."[49]

Throughout the debate, which continued unabated until the French National Assembly voted against ratification (or, more precisely, tabled a motion to ratify the draft treaty) in August 1954, the SPD's official position remained consistent: the EDC was not acceptable. As far as Kurt Schumacher and his close associates were concerned, Pleven's proposal contained no positive features. According to the SPD, the EDC limited German sovereignty, did not commit the west to a "forward defense" strategy, and solidified the division of Germany by creating yet another supra-national structure that bound West Germany to the confines of

Kleineuropa. And if that were not enough, the German Social Democrats, as they had during the debate on the Schuman Plan, once again raised the Saar question. The SPD claimed that because the EDC also treated the Saarland as an entity separate from Germany, the creation of the EDC would seal the fate of the Saar as a French protectorate. In place of the EDC the SPD proposed "*kollektive Sicherheit im größeren Rahmen*" (collective security in the larger frame), although the party did not indicate how this might be achieved.[50]

The SPD's stand on the EDC fit in well with the party's overall strategy of intransigent opposition against Adenauer and the CDU, but Schumacher and his allies were also convinced that opposition to the EDC would be popular with voters. Consequently, the party and especially Schumacher himself mounted a massive campaign to embarrass the Adenauer government and win the battle of public opinion. Schumacher gave full vent to his considerable demagogic talents. His claim that the EDC would "put German youth at the disposal of Allied generals" was one of his milder assertions. The party's Executive also decided to thrust the young Federal Republic into its first constitutional crisis over the EDC. The SPD brought suit against the EDC proposal in Germany's Constitutional Court, claiming the treaties needed to be ratified in the Bundestag by a two-thirds majority, not a simple plurality, because the terms of the agreements changed the provisions of the *Grundgesetz* (Basic Law) against a military establishment in West Germany.[51]

The party's campaign against the EDC polarized the German political scene, but it did not derail the ratification process in West Germany. The treaty easily passed the Bundestag with the votes of the CDU and its coalition partners. (The SPD's suit before the *Bundesverfassungsgericht*, Germany's high court, was rendered moot by the court's refusal to issue a ruling before the parliamentary ratification process had been completed, and by the decision of the federal president, Theodor Heuss, to delay submission of his required *amicus* brief.) Kurt Schumacher was not alive to see the results of the SPD's passionate opposition to the EDC but, although most of them did not say so, his successors were not very pleased with the situation into which their leader had led them. While the party's leaders had anticipated ratification by the Bundestag, they were severely disappointed that the SPD was unable to reap any political benefits from its stand; the expected positive response among voters never materialized. West German voters clearly did not see defeating the EDC as an issue of vital concern to them. At the same time, the campaign brought the Social Democrats several unwanted allies, including the East and West German Communists and the pacifist "*Ohne mich*" (Without Me) movement. On the international scene the results of the SPD's staunch opposition were at best mixed. True, the party accomplished its larger goal when the French parliament rejected the treaty, but the SPD's nationalistic rhetoric against the EDC also aroused deep resentments and disappointment among its sister parties. The German Social Democrats had reinforced their image as unreliable supporters of a united Europe.[52]

For this reason, some leaders within the party regarded the entire campaign as counter-productive. Again, a small number of critics voiced their concerns even in the heat of the campaign against the EDC. This time none went public (advocating a new military establishment was hardly a popular issue among the party's rank-and-file activists), and their efforts had little immediate effect on the party's official position, but from a larger perspective yet another campaign with no discernible positive results added to the cumulative effect that would lead to a fundamental policy shift in the mid-1950s.[53]

It was not altogether surprising, then, that the SPD's reaction to the EDC's alternative, West German membership in NATO, was far more moderate than its stand on the EDC had been. The SPD, now under the leadership of Erich Ollenhauer, continued to reject West German rearmament, but its opposition was a remarkably low-key performance.[54] A number of party leaders pointed out that the terms of German membership in NATO were a decided improvement over the EDC, since the thorny issue of West Germany's formal sovereignty had now been settled.[55] The party also did not persist in attempting to prevent the inevitable. The SPD accepted that ratification of the Paris Accords (which specified the terms of German membership in NATO) was a foregone conclusion and turned its attention instead to parliamentary control of the new army, the Bundeswehr.

In the course of the debate on the internal structure of the new West German armed forces, the Bundestag and the country experienced a foretaste of the new SPD of the 1960s. The key men here were Helmut Schmidt and especially Fritz Erler. They realized that the SPD's refusal to acknowledge the reality of the Bundeswehr would lead to a repeat of the animosities that had alienated the SPD and the Reichswehr in the Weimar Republic. But Erler and Schmidt were also determined to subject the Bundeswehr to parliamentary control so as to preclude that the German military would again form a "state within the state."

To achieve their goal, Erler and Schmidt pursued a dual-track strategy, working within the framework of the party Executive's Security Committee and the parliamentary committees of the Bundestag.[56] Schmidt, as chairman, and the other members of the Security Committee (Erler was also a member) used the deliberations of this committee to persuade the SPD's old guard on the party Executive and the general public that the Social Democrats should and would cooperate in creating a Bundeswehr that consisted of *Bürger in Uniform* (citizens in uniform), not members of a praetorian guard loyal primarily to itself. Simultaneously Erler, as deputy chairman of the SPD's Bundestag caucus, proved to be a master parliamentarian. Working together with far-seeing Christian Democrats, including Kurt Kiesinger, Erler succeeded in persuading the Bundestag to pass legislation that firmly subjected the Bundeswehr to parliamentary control. It was Erler, for example, who wrote the passage into the *Wehrdienstgesetz* (Military Services Law) requiring parliamentary approval for all officers with the rank of colonel or higher. Schmidt, Erler, and the reform wing of the party celebrated a noted milestone in the SPD's history when the 1958 Stuttgart party congress adopted a resolution expressing the party's "*ja zur Landesverteidigung*" (yes to defense of the country). The SPD's new attitude reached a climax of sorts when Helmut Schmidt, amid much media attention, briefly served in the Bundeswehr as a reserve officer.[57]

* * *

The party's quiet acceptance of the Federal Republic's membership in NATO marked the beginning of a dramatic change in its stand on European unification. That evolution continued with the Common Market and Euratom, both of which the SPD not only tolerated but endorsed. The Europeanists in the party had brought the SPD out of isolation and into the integrationist camp.[58]

The change came about as a result of a painful analysis of political reality on the part of the SPD's leaders. By the mid-1950s the SPD had to acknowledge that its European policies of the last decade had not been a success. Electoral defeats at home and isolation in the international socialist movement forced the party to give up a number of cherished illusions. Contrary to Schumacher's persistent conviction, the SPD was unable to dominate the Federal Republic's foreign policy agenda. The party could not convince either the West German voters or the western Allies that the SPD's priority goal of national reunification was a realistic alternative to the CDU's goal of integrating West Germany into Western Europe.

Facing this reality was a long process that stretched over more than a decade. Committed to continuing the legacy of the SPD's charismatic postwar leader, Schumacher's successors at first fought hard to continue his obstructionist line on Europe. Still, there is no doubt that the influence of the critics was steadily, if slowly, growing. Ironically, as the SPD's enthusiasm for a united Europe increased, that of its political rivals waned. By the mid-1950s it was the German Socialists, rather than the Christian Democrats, who were the model "Europeanists." This was a fortuitous development. The SPD's policy reversal gave the European unification movement a much needed boost, and, not incidentally, in time the party's political fortunes at home benefited as well.[59]

But had Schumacher's stand been right for the early postwar years, as the party leader and some later analysts contended? Did the SPD's strident nationalistic rhetoric and its intransigent opposition to west European integration keep the forces of the extreme Right and the extreme Left in West Germany from using the issue of "Europe" to destroy the Federal Republic's embryonic democracy?[60] Probably not. In retrospect, Schumacher's opponents within the party seem to have had the better arguments. The SPD's intransigent opposition to west European unification overestimated the strength of extremism in West Germany and underestimated the influence of the forces working for Franco-German rapprochement and genuine European cooperation in Germany's neighboring countries.[61] If the reformers in the party had had their way earlier, not only might "Europe" have come sooner, but the SPD might have been able to avoid the electoral disasters of the 1950s.

Notes

1. SPD, Bez. Hamburg, *Mitteilungsblatt*, 6 October 1945, and Carlo Schmid, *Erinnerungen* (Munich, 1979), 298-99.
2. Klaus von Schubert, *Wiederbewaffnung und Westintegration: Die innere militärische und außenpolitische Orientierung der Bundesrepublik, 1950-1952* (Stuttgart, 1970), 94; and Jean-Paul Cahn, "Le SPD et la Communauté Européenne de Défense," *Revue Allemagne* 19 (October-December 1987): 385.
3. Hartmut Soell, *Fritz Erler: Eine politische Biographie* (Berlin, 1976), I:85, 92, and 137; Willy Albrecht, "Einleitung," in Kurt Schumacher, *Reden, Schriften, Korrespondenzen, 1945-1952*, ed. Willy Albrecht (Bonn, 1985), 111; and Schmid, *Erinnerungen*, 296-97 and 417-18.
4. See the minutes of the meeting of the Comité Directeur of the French SFIO (hereafter: SFIO/CD), 13 September 1950 (Office Universitaire de Recherche Socialiste, Paris). See also Werner Röder, *Die deutschen sozialistischen Exilgruppen in Großbrittanien* (Hanover, 1968); and Geoffrey Warner, "Die britische Labour-Regierung und die Einheit Westeuropas," *Vierteljahrshefte für Zeitgeschichte* 28 (July 1980): 312-13.
5. SPD, Bez. Hamburg, "Die Aufgaben der sozialistischen Bewegung," *Referenten-Material* 1 (June 1946), in Forschungsstelle für die Geschichte des Nationalsozialismus in Hamburg; and Schmid, *Erinnerungen*, 427.
6. See the minutes of the meeting of the SPD's Parteivorstand (hereafter SPD/PV), 19 and 20 December 1947, Best. Vorstandsprotokolle, AsD; Kurt Thomas Schmitz, *Deutsche Einheit und Europäische Integration: Der sozialdemokratische Beitrag zur Außenpolitik der Bundesrepublik Deutschland* (Bonn, 1978), 68; and Rudolf Hrbek, "The German Social Democratic Party, I," in *Socialist Parties and the Question of Europe in the 1950s*, ed. Richard T. Griffith (Leiden, 1993), 71 n.

20. The MSEUE had been founded in 1947 by a group of French and British socialists. The founders were an eclectic group that included the French ex-Trotskyist Marcel Pivert, France's first postwar economics minister, André Philip, as well as some representatives from the left-wing British Independent Labour Party.

7. Walter Lipgens, *A History of European Integration* (Oxford, 1982), 333; and Wilfried Loth, *Der Weg nach Europa: Geschichte der Europäischen Integration, 1939-1957*, 2nd. ed. (Göttingen, 1991), 55.
8. Deutscher Rat der Europäischen Bewegung, "Hintergrund für die Presse," 9 June 1969, Best. Fritz Erler/118 (AsD); and the documentation in Best. Erler/111. See also, Schmid, *Erinnerungen*, 421-22; Soell, *Erler*, 1:135 and 566 n. 91; and Wilfried Loth, "Die Europabewegung in den Anfangsjahren der Bundesrepublik," in *Vom Marshallplan zur EWG: Die Eingliederung der Bundesrepublik Deutschland in die westliche Welt*, ed. Ludolf Herbst et al. (Munich, 1990), 69 and 74.
9. Erler to Ollenhauer, 9 December 1955, Best. Erich Ollenhauer (AdS); and Lipgens, *Integration*, 600.
10. SPD/PV/Parteiausschuss (hereafter PA), 22 and 23 January 1949. See also, Albrecht, "Einleitung," 199; Willy Brandt, *Erinnerungen* (Frankfurt am Main, 1989), 26; and Rudolf Hrbek, *Die SPD, Deutschland und Europa: Die Haltung der Sozialdemokratie zum Verhältnis von Deutschland-Politik und Westintegration 1945-1957* (Bonn, 1972), 86ff.
11. SPD/PV, 19 April 1950; Schmid, *Erinnerungen*, 474; and Friedrich Heine, *Dr. Kurt Schumacher* (Göttingen, 1969), 101-2.
12. SPD/PV, 24 June 1950; Erler to Brill, 7 March 1957, Best. Erler/171; and the documentation in Best. Erler/118, (AsD). See also, Albrecht, "Einleitung," 159ff.; and Schmitz, *Einheit*, 76.
13. See the documentation in Best. Ollenhauer/438-40. See also Brandt, *Erinnerungen*, 455; and Ernst Weisenfeld, *Welches Deutschland soll es sein? Frankreich und die deutsche Einheit seit 1945* (Munich, 1986), 108. On Monnet's committee, see François Duchene, *Jean Monnet* (New York, 1994), 284ff.
14. Schmitz, *Einheit*, 194-95; Schmid, *Erinnerungen*, 494-95; Kurt Klotzbach, *Der Weg zur Staatspartei: Programmatik, praktische Politik und Organisation der deutschen Sozialdemokratie 1945 bis 1965* (Bonn, 1982), 116; Hrbek, *SPD-Europa*, 89; and Ulrich Buczylowski, *Kurt Schumacher und die deutsche Frage: Sicherheitspolitik und strategische Offensivkonzeption vom August 1950 bis September 1951* (Stuttgart-Degerloch, 1973), 41.
15. SPD/PV, 20 and 21 January 1951; and Buczylowski, *Frage*, 41.
16. Ursula Rombek-Jaschinski, *Nordrhein-Westfalen, die Ruhr und Europa, 1945-1955* (Essen, 1990), 57.
17. See Heine to Markscheffel, 9 March 1946, Best. Kurt Schumacher/93 (AsD); SPD/PV, 28 and 29 May 1948; and the documentation in Best. Ollenhauer/452 and 453; Jean Laloy, "Entretien entre le Dr. Schumacher et M. Laloy," 16 February 1948, Bonn Ambassade, XP 65/XP 3/4 (Archive de l'Occupation française en Allemagne et Autriche, Colmar [hereafter AOFAA]). See also Wolfgang Rudzio, "Die ausgebliebene Sozialisierung an Rhein und Ruhr: Zur Sozialisierungspolitik von Labour-Regierung und SPD 1945-1948," *Archiv für Sozialgeschichte* 18 (1978): 9.
18. Rolf Steininger, "British Labour, Deutschland und die SPD, 1945/46," *IWK* 15:2 (1979): 194. Remarkably, some French statesmen had the same impression. See Vincent Auriol, *Journal du Septennat* (version intégrale), ed. Jean-Pierre Azéma (Paris, 1974), 1:79 (13 February 1947). But see also Lothar Kettenacker, "Großbritannien und die zukünftige Kontrolle Deutschlands," in *Die Britische*

Deutschland- und Besatzungspolitik, 1945-1949, ed. Josef Foschepoth and Rolf Steininger (Paderborn, 1985), 40.

19. Rombek, *Nordrhein-Westfalen*, 15-18; Rolf Steininger, "Großbritannien und die Ruhr," in *Zwischen Ruhrkontrolle und Mitbestimmung*, ed. Walter Först (Cologne, 1982), 11ff.; Raymond Poidevin, "Frankreich und die Ruhrfrage 1945-1951," *Historische Zeitschrift* 228:2 (1979): 317; and Rolf Steininger, ed., *Die Ruhrfrage 1945/46 und die Entstehung des Landes Nordrhein-Westfalen* (Düsseldorf, 1988), 672.
20. Rombek, *Nordrhein-Westfalen*, 56; Horst Lademacher, "Die britische Sozialisierungspolitik im Rhein-Ruhr-Raum," and Rolf Steininger, "Die Sozialisierung fand nicht statt," in Foschepoth and Steininger, *Britische Deutschlandpolitik*, 110-13, 143-44.
21. Frank Willis, *France, Germany, and the New Europe, 1945-1967*, 2nd ed. (Stanford, 1968), 63-64; and Steininger, "Sozialisierung," 146-47.
22. The French protested vehemently against Law no. 75. See Auriol, *Journal*, 2:695 n. 33; Poidevin, "Ruhrfrage," 326; and Willis, *France*, 65.
23. Steininger, *Ruhrfrage*, 215-16.
24. SFIO/CD, 23 November 1948; and Auriol, *Journal*, 2:585 (30 December 1948).
25. See the SPD's resolution of 7 January 1949 (and Carlo Schmid's annotations) opposing the Statute in Best. Schmid/1142 (AsD).
26. Schumacher to Edith Baade, 1 February 1949, in Schumacher, *Reden*, 626; and Schumacher's article, "Frankreich und die SPD," written for publication in the newspapers *Vorwärts* and *Freiheit* (Mainz), 25 February 1949, in Best. Ollenhauer/453 (AsD). See also Klotzbach, *Weg*, 154-58.
27. Claudia Nölting, *Erik Nölting* (Essen, 1989), 499-501.
28. SPD/PV, 21 and 22 January 1949.
29. Press release by the Sopade Informationsdienst, 7 January 1949, attached to ibid.
30. Pierre Maillard, *De Gaulle et L'Allemagne: Le rêve inachevé* (Paris, 1990), 98.
31. Carlo Schmid, "Das deutsch-französische Verhältnis und der Dritte Partner," *Die Wandlung* 2 (1947), cited in Lipgens, *Integration*, 655 n. 504; Raymond Poidevin, *Robert Schumans Deutschland- und Europapolitik zwischen Tradition und Neuorientierung* (Munich, 1976), 18; and Wilfried Loth, *Sozialismus und Internationalismus: Die französischen Sozialisten und die Nachkriegsordnung Europas, 1940-1950* (Stuttgart, 1977), 187, 369 n. 124, and 379 n. 32.
32. René Massigli, *Une comédie des erreurs, 1943-1956: Souvenirs et reflexions sur une étape de la construction européene* (Paris, 1978), 193-94; Georgette Elgey, *Histoire de la IVe République: La République des Illusions 1945-1951* (Paris, 1965), 1:443; Dietmar Petzina, "Von der Konfrontation zur Integration," in *Franzosen und Deutsche am Rhein 1789-1918-1945*, ed. Peter Hüttenberger and Hansgeorg Molitor (Essen, 1989), 177; and Oswald Post, "Karl Arnold," in *Treuhänder des deutschen Volkes – Die Ministerpräsidenten des westlichen Besatzungszonen nach den ersten freien Landtagswahlen: Politische Portraits*, ed. Walter Mühlhausen and Cornelia Regin (Melsungen, 1991), 262.
33. Loth, *Sozialismus*, 252. On the negotiations that led to the ECSC treaty, see Duchene, *Monnet*, 181ff.; and Renate Fritsch-Bournazel, "Die Wende in der französischen Nachkriegspolitik, 1945-1949," in *Die französische Deutschlandpolitik zwischen 1945 und 1949*, ed. Institut Français de Stuttgart (Tübingen, 1987), 25; Werner Bührer, "Die französische Ruhrpolitik und das Comeback der westdeutschen Industriellen 1945-1952," in Hüttenberger and Molitor, *Franzosen*, 42-43; and Raymond Poidevin, "La France devant le danger allemand (1944-1952)," in *Deutsche Frage und europäisches Gleichgewicht: Festschrift für Andreas Hillgruber*, ed. Klaus Hildebrand and Reiner Pommerin (Cologne, 1985), 256.

34. See SPD/PV, 19 May 1950; and Schumacher's address to the congress of the SPD's Palatinate district, 15 May 1950, in Best. Schumacher/153 (AsD). See also, Klotzbach, "SPD-Schumacher," 333-34; Albrecht, "Einleitung," 161ff; and Hrbek, *SPD*, 102ff.
35. SFIO/CD, 27 June 1951.
36. The speech is reprinted in, Schumacher, *Reden*, 809. See also Thomas A. Schwartz, *America's Germany: John J. McCloy and the Federal Republic of Germany* (Cambridge, Mass., 1991), 199.
37. Rolf Steininger, "Kurt Schumacher, die Sozialistische Internationale und die Ruhrfrage," in *Kurt Schumacher als deutscher und europäischer Sozialist*, ed. Willy Albrecht (Bonn, 1988), 83; and the press release of the SD-Pressedienst, 22 June 1951, Best. Schumacher/151 (AsD). Schumacher's famous alliteration can be found in the speech of 24 May 1951 cited in the previous note. See also, Schmid, *Erinnerungen*, 451-52; Susanne Miller, *Die SPD vor und nach Godesberg* (Bonn, 1974), 30-31; and Schmitz, *Einheit*, 78.
38. SPD/PV, PA, and KK, 8 and 9 September 1951.
39. SPD/PV, 30 March 1951.
40. Nölting, *Nölting*, 502; Hrbek, *SPD*, 125; Kurt Klotzbach, "Die deutsche Sozialdemokratie und der Schuman-Plan," in *Die Anfänge des Schuman-Plans*, ed. Klaus Schwabe (Baden-Baden, 1988), 343-44; Willy Brandt, *Links und frei – Mein Weg 1930-1950* (Hamburg, 1982), 448; and Schmid, *Erinnerungen*, 518.
41. On the Schumacher-Kaisen controversy, see Albrecht, "Einleitung," 160; and Renate Meyer-Braun, "'Rebell' Wilhelm Kaisen ... Briefwechsel zwischen Alfred Faust und Fritz Heine aus den Jahren 1950-1956," *Bremisches Jahrbuch* 67 (1989): 113-14.
42. See Socialist International, ed., "Minutes of the Frankfort Conference on the Schuman-Plan, 27-28 June 1951" (London, 1951), in Best. Schumacher/152 (AsD); and François G. Dreyfus, "Die SPD und die Deutsche Demokratische Republik 1949-1989," in *Deutschland und Europa nach dem 2. Weltkrieg*, ed. Heiner Timmermann (Saarbrücken-Scheidt, 1990), 511.
43. Steininger, "Kurt Schumacher," 82.
44. Schmid, *Erinnerungen*, 461; and Heinrich Küppers, *Staatsaufbau zwischen Bruch und Tradition: Geschichte des Landes Rheinland-Pfalz, 1946-1955* (Mainz, 1990), 177. On the success of the ECSC, see Willis, *France*, 221.
45. Loth, *Sozialismus*, 235.
46. Raymond Poidevin, "Die europapolitischen Initiativen Frankreichs des Jahres 1950 – aus einer Zwangslage geboren?" in Herbst, *Vom Marshallplan zur EWG*, 259-61.
47. Albrecht, "Einleitung," 169-71; and Buczylowski, *Schumacher*, 82ff. and 136-38.
48. See, Poidevin, "Initiativen 1950," 257; and Elgey, *République*, I:462ff. On the details of the negotiations, see Massigli, *Comédie*, 239ff.
49. SPD/PV, 18 September 1954; and "Resolution de la Conférence européenne d'IS," 28 February 1954, in Best. Erler/108 (AsD). See also Raymond Aron, "Esquisse historique d'une grande querelle idéologique," in *La querelle de la CED: Essai d'analyse sociologique*, ed. idem and Daniel Lerner (Paris, 1968), 9.
50. SPD/PV, 7 and 8 September 1951, and 29 July 1953; Schumacher, "Für ein starkes Europa – gegen nationalistischen Mißbrauch der Macht," 22 September 1951, in Best. Ollenhauer/420 (AsD); and the press release of the party's Politisch-Parlamentarischer Pressedienst, 7 January 1953. See also, Albrecht, "Einleitung," 174 and 180; and Buczylowski, *Schumacher*, 116.
51. See Schumacher's address to the SPD's *Soziale Arbeitsgemeinschaft*, 24 May 1951; and Schubert, *Wiederbewaffnung*, 119.

52. Quilliot, *SFIO*, 512-13. See also, Soell, *Erler*, I:441; and A. Mozer-Ebbinge and R. Cohen, eds., *Alfred Mozer: `Gastarbeider' in Europa* (Zutphen, 1980), 40.
53. See Max Brauer to M. Gironella (MSEUE), 25 July 1952, Best. Brauer, Div. Korr., 1949-1967 (For. Hbg.); Schmitz, *Einheit*, 106; Hermann-Josef Rupieper, *Der besetzte Verbündete: Die amerikanische Deutschlandpolitik 1949-1955* (Opladen, 1991), 115-16; and Beatrix W. Bouvier, *Zwischen Godesberg und Großer Koalition: Der Weg der SPD in die Regierungsverantwortung* (Bonn, 1990), 40.
54. SPD/PV, 10 and 11 December 1954; the documentation in Best. Ollenhauer/423 (AsD); and André François-Poncet to Ministère des Affaires Étrangères, 4 March 1955, Bonn Ambassade, XP 92/XP 3/4 (AOFAA).
55. Erler to Erich Bacher, 20 July 1956, in Best Erler/171 (AdS). See also Hrbek, *SPD*, 197ff.
56. See Schmidt to Castrup, 14 March 1966, Best. Erler/63; and the documentation in Bestand Ollenhauer/392 (AsD). On the relationship of the *Sicherheitsausschuß* and the PV, see Soell, *Erler*, 1:209-10.
57. On Erler's views of the SPD's Wehrpolitik, see his "Aktenvermerk," 17 July 1952, Best. Erler/426; Erler to Julius Deutsch, 20 July 1956, Best. Erler/171 (AsD); and the "Thesen zur Wehrpolitik für das Grundsatzprogramm der SPD," 3 July 1959, Best. Ollenhauer/388 (AsD). (The last document is unsigned, but there is little doubt about Erler's authorship.) See also Heino Kaack, *Geschichte und Struktur des deutschen Parteiensystems* (Opladen, 1971), 248-49. For Erler's frustration with the old guard's opposition to his views, see Erler to Ollenhauer, 8 December 1953, Best. Erler/66 I; and Erler to Franke and von Knoeringen, 21 March 1959, Best. Erler/67 II.
58. See H. Putzrath, "Kurzprotokoll: Sitzung [des] aussenpolitischen Ausschusses," 25 May 1955, in Best. Ollenhauer/442 (AsD). See also Hartmut Soell, "Die deutschlandpolitischen Konzeptionen der SPD-Opposition 1949-1961," in *Deutschlandpolitik der Nachkriegsjahre*, ed. Erich Kosthorst et al. (Paderborn, 1976), 60-61.
59. SPD/PV, 13 and 14 January 1956. See also Schmitz, *Einheit*, 196.
60. Heinrich August Winkler, "Kurt Schumacher und die nationale Frage," *Frankfurter Allgemeine Zeitung*, 31 October 1995.
61. See Brandt, *Erinnerungen*, 26; Miller, *SPD*, 17; and Marinus van der Goes van Naters, "Internationaal Socialisme," *Socialisme en Democratie* 9 (May 1952): 283-87.

Chapter 20

THE POLITICS OF CULTURE AND THE CULTURE OF EVERYDAY LIFE IN THE DDR IN THE 1950S

Anna-Sabine Ernst

1. Asserting Everyday Culture under a Dictatorship

Historical writing on the German Democratic Republic (DDR) up until 1989, whether by eastern or western authors, was characterized by an emphasis on the radical caesura after 1945 and a neglect of lines of continuity and tradition. Although the political system of party and state structures has been relatively well studied, broad segments of society remain in the dark. This is particularly true of everyday culture and ways of life. After the demise of the DDR, scholars became painfully aware of this deficiency: they lacked explanations not only for the state's forty-year-long stability but also for its – at first glance wholly contrary – rapid and surprising collapse. To be sure, historians' narrow-mindedness was not solely responsible for this restricted research perspective. More decisive were problems of methodological and theoretical approach and access to sources, which have, to some extent, still not been resolved today.

According to the theory of "totalitarianism" dominant until the early 1960s, studying the multifarious sub-areas of society could reveal nothing more than variations on political history anyway. Even from the perspective of the new research paradigms of "functional de-differentiation" (Meuschel) or "de-institutionalization" (Lepsius), "society" seems ready to disappear and, ultimately, to merge with the state.[1] This will remain

Notes for this chapter begin on page 502.

the case as long as the proponents of these paradigms persist in examining the DDR only in terms of bureaucracies and institutions. But how can we study from "below," from the perspective of everyday life, the history of a society controlled by the Socialist Unity Party (SED) state?

Sources presented, and continue to present, an additional problem. For those wishing to study everyday culture in the early DDR, the situation has improved only gradually since the demise of the SED-state. To be sure, previously secret studies and analyses from within the DDR have now become available, but they refer exclusively to the recent past. Sociological self-examination in the DDR did not even begin until the 1960s, and a more intensive study of lifestyles only in the late 1970s.[2] Cultural studies are also of little help here, as they were mainly interested in "high culture," while "everyday" and "mass culture" remained on the margins.[3] For the DDR's so-called "construction period," at least, we must for the time being make do with makeshifts such as literature, which thus far has been treated as a supposed "ersatz public sphere."[4] In order to write a history of everyday culture we also need basic social historical studies, but these are also still in their infancy.[5]

The present essay is an attempt to approach the "everyday culture" of the DDR in the 1950s through an examination of norms of behavior, so-called "good form." The main sources are advice literature in the form of etiquette books, often known in Germany as "Knigges" after the Enlightenment author of that name whose famous book can roughly be translated as "How to Get Along with People."[6] Other sources include the women's and fashion magazines that appeared in rapidly growing numbers from the mid-1950s on.[7] These texts document everyday life not so much as it was actually lived, but as it was imagined, and they must, thus, be conceived first of all as "patterns of interpretation" with which the various authors intervened pedagogically in the everyday praxis of popular cultural reproduction. Their primary task was to integrate societal groups into the social fabric by means of a codified "style." Because they responded at the same time to particular problem areas and – if only to a limited extent – to the needs of their readers, they may be read as snapshots of the new society's structuring process. First, however, we must examine the role played by the phenomena of everyday and mass culture in SED cultural policy planning.

2. Everyday Culture in SED Policy

The year 1945 did not mark a "zero hour" for KPD or SED cultural policy; instead, there were significant continuities with communist programs of the 1920s and 1930s. Although the new social order defined itself from the beginning as a counter-model to "bourgeois society," particularly against its reconstitution in the western part of Germany, the "bourgeois cultural legacy" was the main point of reference for its entire cultural policy.[8] The DDR claimed for itself the role of "trustee" and "executor," hence, the sole legitimate heir, of the "goods" and "treasures" of "bourgeois culture." As if bourgeois culture were a quarry, from which pieces could be removed at whim, only those elements deemed "progressive" were to be appropriated. German classicism was held in high esteem while modernism, including that part of the so-called "proletarian revolutionary legacy" that was modernist in style, fell victim to the verdict of decadence proclaimed by Georg Lukács, the Hungarian Marxist literary and cultural theorist.[9] The "cultural revolution" announced in 1957 was also ultimately limited to a mass appropriation of traditional "high culture." By gaining control of the state, it was believed, the party had secured the basis of socialism – including the elimination of the bourgeois privilege of education, the necessary precondition to the mass absorption of the aesthetics and values of high culture. The goal of a "cultivated nation," Walter Ulbricht proclaimed in 1960, required no revolutionary subject in the form of an organized, conscious class, but only a collection of individuals ennobled by education, individuals who, with an expenditure of "truly great, extraordinary effort," had taken upon themselves a laborious but in itself essentially unambiguous learning process.[10] It was, however, well worth the trouble, for whoever "expanded his educational horizons through the enjoyment of art … simply became a better human being, i.e., a better socialist."[11] The dominant notion seems to have been that culture could be directly functionalized for political ends. The cultural development of the DDR itself was conceived of primarily as an educational problem. Once ideological clarity had become rooted in the minds of the population, the "right" notions of art and the correct – i.e., "socialist" – way of life would follow of their own accord.

The reasons for the dominance of the "bourgeois legacy" are many. First, it permitted the authorities to emphasize and keep open the option of German unity to good propagandistic effect. With the advent of two German states in the late 1940s, the cultivation and preservation of cultural traditions was defined explicitly as a "national task." In this way the government also hoped to cement the domestic "alliance" with the indispensable middle-class strata. Second, in the Soviet Union itself an increasingly conservative, anti-modernist cultural policy, a sort of "Stalinist state classicism," had asserted itself. Third, and finally, we must also take account of the cultural models the leading minds of the KPD and SED had before them: the socialists of Imperial Germany had also been oriented primarily towards "bourgeois high culture" and, under the slogan "pure art for the people," had elevated a pedagogical popularization of art to a party program. They were absolutely opposed to the emerging institutions of commercial leisure, which they suspected of diverting workers' energies from the political struggle. In fact, talk of "movie mania" and the like documents the revolutionaries' lack of understanding of the consequences of modernization for people's everyday lives.[12] That this remoteness from mass culture largely continued after 1945, and became state policy, also explains why KPD and SED cultural policy was for a long time directed towards artistic culture, while everyday and mass culture remained underexposed. "Capitalism organized pubs for the worker. You organize life at the House of Culture," demanded Ulbricht in 1950. It was only logical that no pubs were to be attached to the new meeting places and venues for events.[13]

At the end of the 1950s, however, it was the "everyday front of culture" that moved to the center of cultural policy interest. How did this come about? On the one hand, it had become clear to the political leadership that the disappearance of capitalist relations of production had "not automatically spawned new socialist attitudes." Rather than leave everyday culture to continue on its own dangerous path, it was necessary, "in future, to treat the problems of socialist cultural policy within a broader context." It was no longer enough for the party leadership to concentrate its efforts, as it had been doing, on the political and cultural orientation of cultural producers. Instead, in future they must "guide and control all forms of art and cultural dissemination."[14] On the other hand, a significant sociohistorical transformation was in the offing: the definitive end of the postwar era. To be sure, housing remained tight, but the available national income had risen markedly with the end of reparations payments to the USSR. The last ration cards were abolished and working hours shortened.[15] An enormous spurt of modernization appeared to loom on the horizon, firing the imagination of planners – after all, in 1957 the Soviet "Sputnik" had also succeeded in overtaking its U.S. competitors in outer space. Readers of *Frau von Heute* were regaled with planners' visions for the household of the "not so distant future": according to these, the home would soon be fully mechanized, although some housework might still be performed as a "hobby." All work once done by the housewife would be performed in central kitchens and laundries; even shopping would no longer be necessary, for a system of pneumatic tubes would deliver goods directly to the home. Heating would come through the walls from a nuclear-powered district heating plant. The external walls, made of transparent synthetic materials, would ensure complete independence from the external environment. In addition to climate control, these walls would use electromagnetic fields to achieve varying colors and brightness in the rooms. The highlight: even the bed would be air conditioned, so that body temperature would automatically be kept constant during sleep.[16] The belief in progress and rationalization, too, was part of the SED's appropriation of the "bourgeois" heritage. The improvements in material conditions and modernization fantasies described above were reflected in official notions of culture. SED cultural functionaries recognized the need to elaborate "socialist cultural forms in all spheres of life, without exception."[17] They spoke of "mores and customs," "lifestyle" and "life culture," "the socialist way of life" and of a "socialist style of material culture."[18]

Does this mean that notions of culture had broadened? The positively inflationary use of the word "culture," which could be combined practically at will to form "clothing culture," "home culture," "work culture," "physical culture," "sales culture," or "shop window culture," cannot disguise the absence of theoretical concepts about the phenomena of modern mass culture, such as were developed by the Frankfurt School. Cultural policy institutions continued to orient themselves towards "artistic culture." Whether it was called "fashion" or "clothing culture," the way people dressed did not in itself belong to the field of what Pierre Bourdieu has called "legitimate culture." Ultimately it required the "higher consecration" of art. If fashion magazines like *Sybille* preferred to photograph models in museums, galleries or artists' studios, this was only evidence that a "legitimation transfer" continued to be necessary.[19] Even bad old "entertainment" had to be re-labeled as good "entertainment art" in order to enter the canon of that which state cultural policy deemed worthy of support.[20] The supposedly new phenomenon of "cultural work with the masses" was still consciously juxtaposed to "mass culture." Finally, the traditional mistrust that persisted after 1945 was increased by the necessity to keep up the defensive struggle against the west on the "everyday front of culture." Here jeans (referred to as "rivet trousers") or "boogie woogie," whose American origins made them seem not merely a cultural but also a political threat, were lurking everywhere.[21] For all this, the labored and permanent criticism of supposedly decadent western products, particularly fashion, only betrayed the lack of anything comparable to replace them, and the recognition that perhaps no other aspect of the bourgeois, capitalist way of life exercised such a great fascination and temptation. "Homegrown" products, such as the socialist Saxon variant of a "fashionable dance" called the "Lipsi" – the name testifies to its place of origin, Leipzig – which was created in 1958, had only limited appeal. This did not stop the party newspaper *Neues Deutschland* from praising it highly as a successful contribution to the "development of our own national dance music" which demonstrated "that it should not be difficult to overtake the west in the production of popular music as well." Although the melodies were influenced primarily by "German elements," the dance was "absolutely modern."[22]

3. Socialist Etiquette: New Wine in Recycled Bottles?

Not only did the literature on etiquette undergo a simultaneous renaissance in both German states in the second half of the 1950s, but the concrete elaboration of the East German compendia differed, surprisingly, scarcely at all from their West German counterparts.[23] In a society in which old class antagonisms had been abolished; the state-directed economy had brought many young people into positions of authority; thousands of individuals were traveling the path of upward social mobility, helped along by new criteria of competence, including political reliability and working-class or peasant social backgrounds; and female employment was rising rapidly and women's equality was the declared goal of state policy – given these dramatic transformations, one might have expected that the old rule of thumb of good form, "age before youth, ladies first, superiors before subordinates," would have become obsolete. Instead, seating arrangements were still organized according to a protocol in which academic titles, income, or position in the workplace or party hierarchy determined who was "worthy" or "respectable" enough to sit at the hostess's left.[24] Women's equality might be explicit state policy, and the "crane operator" might be celebrated in the media as a heroine of the growing female "working population," but after hours the old rules still applied: "A lady who asks a gentleman to dance is as ridiculous today as she was a thousand years ago."[25] In short, bourgeois rules of deportment had been adapted to the new society. Efforts to enforce them also reveal the cracks that appeared where old behaviors did not conform to new conditions.

DDR etiquette authors had no interest in making common cause with their West German counterparts, whom they regarded as simply taking advantage of their petty bourgeois clientele's yearning for social advancement. The audience these authors addressed encompassed the entire population of the "workers' and peasants' state." In the nascent socialist society, after all, everybody needed to learn new rules of proper behavior. "Good form" was posited as a prerequisite for interpersonal relations among civilized people. "Because the majority of Central Europeans behave this way, we should do the same. If people have been cutting potatoes with the edge of their forks for the past two hundred years, why should we suddenly decide to use knives?"[26] The DDR etiquette authors were by no means unworldly aesthetes or relics of bygone ages. Karl Kleinschmidt, the most prominent among them, was also an active proponent of the new socialist path. He was one of the few remaining clerics in the SED, a *Volkskammer* deputy, and vice-president of the *Kulturbund*. That the etiquette books themselves were considered politically significant is demonstrated by the fact that Kleinschmidt's book, *Don't Be Afraid of Good Manners: How to Get Along with People*, was commented upon by no less than Johannes R. Becher, poet, author of the DDR national anthem, and the minister of culture.[27]

In their books, the teachers of manners sometimes emphasized the "working class" as their target group. At any rate they claimed emancipatory aims for their writings:

> *The vast majority of the population has been excluded from the rules of good form and the opportunity to apply them, just as they have been excluded from the right to education. For the first time in German history, in the workers' and peasants' state, our DDR, the working population is setting the tone. It is now in a position to acquire those things that were withheld for so long: education, knowledge – including knowledge of the rules of good form, which help to determine how people live together.*[28]

The authors simply took for granted that the imagined reader needed to catch up. After all, in order to take a "leading role" in state and society, one needs cultural competence, including "good manners." "The working class of today requires confidence, superiority, and a command of all forms of societal and sociable interactions as well as a mastery of the production process."[29] All too obviously, however, many members of the working class refused to recognize this necessity. "Wild toasting" and "raucous laughter" at table or other violations of the rules, whether out of laziness, negligence, or ignorance, worried the etiquette experts. Their true bugbear, though, was the "proletcult," the deliberate flouting of "bourgeois" norms and rules of behavior, particularly by workers. Once a historical "necessity" for those with "awakening class consciousness," the act of visibly setting oneself apart from bourgeois manners was now considered completely "outmoded."[30]

Rules of etiquette were generally claimed as part of the "cultural legacy." It is no secret that the latter fell into progressive and reactionary segments. As the deportment experts admitted, even bourgeois "good manners," which had once corresponded to real class conditions, had degenerated to a "hollow shell" with the advent of imperialism.[31] In contrast to the arts, however, this verdict did not lead to the exclusion of certain rules or norms of behavior from that part of the legacy deemed "worthy of reception." In the arts, the accusation of "formalism" had been directed at the supposed emancipation of form from content, when – according to the principles of "socialist realism" – the two had to represent a unity. When it came to the rules of etiquette, however, the argument was the opposite one. While in the Federal Republic "good form" continued to mask social conflicts, the DDR was helping to realize Knigge's ideals, acting not merely as a trustee, but also as the executor of the bourgeois legacy. The appropriation of bourgeois modes of behavior was possible precisely because they had become divorced from their social origins and content. Kleinschmidt managed to express in his publications ideas that would have earned artists exclusion from their professional associations: there are "empty, meaningless, mere forms."[32] And the Party organ *Neues Deutschland* concurred: "Old forms can indeed be invested with new meaning. Forms intended to provide the appearance of harmony in the old world of embittered, individual combat can certainly express genuine harmony in a socially just order."[33] Here (in the DDR) for the first time, "politeness" became a true expression of respect and consideration among equals, because "inside" and "outside" – that is, morality and its behavioral expression – no longer contradicted one another.[34] The "heroic utopia of the cultural revolution," as Erhard John called it, seemed close to realization: "Man in socialist society, when it is in full bloom, will have neither the opportunity nor the desire to behave badly. He will not dissemble, or bow and scrape, or swindle, neither will he eat fish off a knife, or drink champagne out of red wine glasses, any more than he will rob or exploit others."[35] Given "socialist" relations of production and adequate material means, "external appearances" would gain in significance. "The person of solid morality is not only clean inside, but orderly and cultivated in his external self-presentation."[36] Good manners and tasteful dress appropriate to the occasion were elevated to proofs of moral integrity and the willingness to conform. They indicated, after all, whether a person "adapts to society or enjoys provoking others."[37]

Following the logic of this appropriation, the historical Freiherr von Knigge himself, the epitome of good form, was cast as a "radical democrat." To paraphrase one of the SED's favored slogans, the Kleinschmidt book and others just about proclaimed, "Learning from Knigge means learning Victory!"[38] Knigge belonged "to those German writers who had firmly supported the French Revolution and developed ever more radical opinions, not to those many proponents of liberal attitudes whose initial platonic love for the bourgeois revolution had changed to an anti-revolutionary stance. The book *Über den Umgang mit Menschen* was, thus, written by a revolutionary."[39]

The present generation could learn from Knigge how to tackle a problem that had reemerged under very different circumstances. A parallel was posited between the transition to socialism and Knigge's "nascent bourgeois society."[40] The corresponding verdict was that "his work contributed to making the bourgeois fit for polite society, and boosted his self-confidence vis-à-vis the feudal ruling class."[41]

The role of an established code of behavior in the process of post-revolutionary consolidation was construed thusly: in the proto-bourgeois revolutionary phase, there had been a sort of iconoclasm of manners. Having achieved influence and power, the bourgeoisie then "picked up many of the pictures it had stamped into the ground, rehung them and critically reappropriated them. They lifted the ragged cloak of politeness out of the dust, brushed it off, mended it and hung it around their own shoulders, adorned with bourgeois symbols."[42] Karl Kleinschmidt and his colleagues never tired of railing against "Jacobin boorishness" and iconoclasm in matters of deportment.[43] No wonder, since what they saw lurking behind them was mere "anarchy," which had been just as anathema to the leadership of the socialist labor movement as it had been to the bourgeoisie.[44] According to the DDR etiquette authors, attempts to develop specifically proletarian manners had been mired in the same sort of protest stance as had once immersed the rising bourgeoisie. "Proletarian protest behavior, the 'proletcult,' proves itself as rash and sterile as its proto-bourgeois predecessor." Just as unchivalrous conduct is not politeness, and impoliteness is not good manners, "rude behavior is not a proletarian attitude."[45] The struggle against the "proletcult," so well known from artistic debates, found its continuation here. In both cases, however, it served as a straw man for the party and probably exerted little real influence.[46] Stepping off the stage into the audience, the culprit now assumed the guise of the "shirt-sleeve proletarian," who went out for the evening in his work clothes, still not realizing that "dressing up is simply part of culture, particularly socialist culture."[47] Finally, the state's need for representation also entered the picture: "After ten years of the DDR, is it really necessary to go to the theater in a plaid jacket?"[48]

Whatever the motivations of individual etiquette authors may have been, the results of their pedagogical efforts corresponded to the party's renewed leadership concept.[49] The rules of good form also had economic significance: in the workplace they were redubbed "leadership style." Problems in the workplace were immense. The hierarchies of the state and party administrative bureaucracy fostered an authoritarian tone that often proved counterproductive, provoking insubordination instead of the desired effect. Walter Ulbricht himself took up this issue. Noting the "soulless bureaucratic behavior" he had observed, he remarked, "Surely this is not the way to attract people. Often with the best of intentions to serve our state and our cause, we thoughtlessly antagonize people by showing them too little respect … because we don't use the right tone, under the false assumption that politeness and good manners are inconsistent with socialism. Quite the contrary is the case. We must not take such matters too lightly."[50] What was needed now was "much tact, sensitivity, and human stature."[51] Outward "polish" in dealing with other people should replace those remnants of "Jacobin" crudity left over from the period of the struggle for political power. Apparently the political leadership had resolved to try clothing relations of subordination in more attractive garb.

It is, thus, no wonder that etiquette books devoted a separate chapter to this issue, which incidentally was one of the few topics not shared by their counterparts in the Federal Republic. "Today, workers and worker functionaries are respected people in the state. They wield power in our republic. Salaried employees, farmers, and the *Mittelstand* [artisans and shopkeepers] watch and learn from them. They must, thus, be models in life, work, behavior, good form, and also in dress. Functionaries in particular should be dressed well, appropriately and carefully, not negligently. Their apparel, too, should demonstrate taste and a healthy sense of the new era."[52]

The illustrative examples in the etiquette books address the often complicated workplace relations of the time: at the head of the factory was a senior laborer, who had been catapulted into a managerial position because of his political reliability. His subordinates were the highly qualified technical staff, often members of the "bourgeois" intelligentsia. As we know from other sources, the collaboration between these groups was anything but harmonious.[53] Political and professional hierarchies posed a threat of division and mutual obstruction. In such cases, "good form" was intended as a sort of cement that would bring together all levels of the plant hierarchy and prevent open confrontation.

It was in this spirit that Karl Kleinschmidt admonished his comrades to exercise "polite matter-of-factness," which had about as much to do with "appeasement … as a sledgehammer with partiality."[54] Etiquette authors unanimously rejected the universal use of the informal "*Du*" in the workplace. It was no longer appropriate "for everybody at the workplace from the director to the apprentice" to call each other "*Du*" indiscriminately. Now that the workers owned the means of production, the informal "*Du*" no longer served to express their class solidarity vis-à-vis the capitalists. Rather, it "smacked of pushy familiarity" and promoted "leveling mania." The time had come, instead, to "reprivatize" the use of "*Du*" and reserve it for special relationships. After all, "the order of a state-owned enterprise is a structured one; why should our social manners obscure this?"[55] In the end, the code of behavior that was propagated as socialist made sure that "high" and "low" kept to their accustomed places.

Although officially the renewed leadership concept was addressed simply and universally to the "DDR citizen," the measure was clearly tailored to the interests and needs of particular strata: the "intelligentsia" and the so-called "middle classes" (*Mittelschichten*).[56] As the SED Central Committee was informed in a Politburo study, members of the intelligentsia were always complaining about the "awkward, petty, and tactless behavior" of the state and Party organs and factory management. "The intelligentsia takes questions of tact, manners, and decent human relations particularly seriously, and violations of these frequently occasion dissatisfaction"[57] – and could even lead to their absconding from the country. Indeed, the intelligentsia's *Republikflucht* increased rapidly from the mid-

1950s onward. Like the reception of the cultural legacy in the arts, which the state expressly regarded as part of its "politics of alliances" with bourgeois forces, the propagation of traditional standards of behavior can also be interpreted as part of that "alliance bid," functionally, at least, if not intentionally. Despite all attempts to redefine the old forms by imparting to them a "socialist" content, middle-class groups could feel themselves confirmed in their demands. Their behavior and manners were regarded as collectively binding.

4. "See You Tonight at the House of Culture": Women and Socialist Etiquette

In her analysis of DDR illustrated magazines of the 1950s, Ina Merkel comes to a paradoxical conclusion on the subject of women in the workplace: the emancipatory element inherent in each photograph showing women penetrating male domains was marginalized in the form of representation itself. Individuality and self-confidence disappeared behind bent backs and bowed heads. Ina Merkel explains this phenomenon by noting that the drastic changes in women's lives "were only bearable if a minimum of feminine identity remained secure."[58] The articles and pictures were intended as advertisements for women's employment "by demonstrating how work and being a woman could be combined. The most important norm here was: nothing must be outwardly visible."[59] These results are of interest because the portrayal of women in etiquette books worked in a similar way to ignore the contradictions between the bourgeois image of woman and women's new role in the DDR.

The altered circumstances in which men and women in the DDR met in the workplace also attracted the attention of etiquette authors. They began by loudly propagating the work process as a "melting pot," "in which the traditional relations between the sexes are being recast."[60] In concrete terms, the focus was on maintaining the distance deemed necessary. "In the workplace woman is a colleague and equal – but still a woman."[61] Women in the workplace were, for example, faced with the problem of defending their privacy rights against men. Good form should mediate here, helping to maintain women's dignity. "To be sure, occupational life, with all its duties, is often somewhat rough and ready. But this must not simply be transferred to social intercourse."[62] If we are to believe the etiquette books, sexist assaults against women in the workplace were mainly of a verbal nature. Women were advised passively to resist dirty words and crude jokes on the part of their colleagues. "Woman should maintain her dignity in the workplace and close her ears rather than join in when male colleagues tell crude jokes."[63] If women remained reserved in the face of "familiarities or even dirty jokes, they were not being prudish, but rather using the simplest means of handling this sort of incorrigible men."[64] The authors called on men to stop separating private and public morality, to take seriously their role as protectors, and to think of women colleagues as members of their families. "Those colleagues who feel compelled to be impolite to female coworkers and tell off-color jokes should consider that they would certainly treat their own wives and daughters differently if they worked in the same firm. They should treat the wives and daughters of other citizens just as they would members of their own families, with respect and a willingness to help."[65]

In the DDR, balls and other dances were by no means intended to function as marriage markets, as they had in earlier societies. Precisely because of the high formalization of the invitation to dance, however, they did offer one of the few "proper" opportunities to make the acquaintance of members of the opposite sex. In the world of Knigges from both east and west, this was the almost exclusive province of men. "Equality does not apply when it comes to asking for a dance. This is (except for ladies' choice) a man's affair," remarked Karl Kleinschmidt in agreement with all of his fellow etiquette authors. "She" who violated the rules was digging her own social grave, because a woman who took the initiative here "is as ridiculous today as she was a thousand years ago."[66] Social change seems to have passed unnoticed, at least in this agreement to accord women object status in the choice of partners. But even with ladies' choice the pool of potential dance partners was limited. Even here, a "lady" was not free to make the "acquaintances" of her choice because she could "only ask the men who have already danced with her or whom she at least knows very well." At least the eligible gentlemen were then "obliged to accept the invitation … a gentlemen never refuses a lady." Once on the dance floor, though, the lady had to wait: "Conversation is always initiated by the gentleman, not by the lady."[67] Under these circumstances women needed particular skills and good old feminine wiles. The authors Schweickert and Hold advised that a man only ask a woman in the company of another gentleman to dance if the woman in question "has indicated her desire that another dancer compensate for the neglect by her companion. (Ladies can do this so subtly that only the gentleman with whom they wish to dance will notice!)"[68]

At least members of the agitprop group at the Institute for Teacher Training in Magdeburg felt that women's obligatory passivity contradicted their new social position. In order to remedy the situation it was agreed that the following procedure would apply within the institute: if a girl or young woman wished to dance with a particular man, she went to him and informed him of the fact simply and informally but also unobtrusively. The ritual then proceeded in the accustomed fashion. The man asked,

"May I have this dance?" The future teachers considered this solution particularly clever because it "demonstrated a different attitude towards woman," without – and this was emphasized several times – "making this different behavior visible."[69] The Magdeburg "reformers" considered the extension of "ladies' choice" beyond specially designated dances to be unsuitable, as this would have rendered visible the transformation of gender roles. To be sure, the denial of women's changing social position as such was not addressed in the etiquette literature. Rather, women's "sex-specific character"[70] was used self-evidently to justify the assignment of generally passive patterns of behavior. Here the authors take up, apparently seamlessly, a model developed within the educated bourgeoisie in the last third of the eighteenth century, although one of its historically constituent elements, the strict gender-specific separation of work and family life, was supposed to be abolished in the DDR, at least in theory.

Just as women's increasing employment outside the home was taken for granted, so was the persistent division of roles within the family. Women continued to be "specialists in 'human relations.'"[71] Thus, women also had "a special duty when it came to good manners. She set the tone that prevailed within the family." But not only there: the "workplace atmosphere" also depended upon her behavior. "She goes shopping and can provide a good example to the sales personnel with her quiet politeness. On public transportation she can correct inappropriate behavior in an even tone, and at parties, too, she manages to make the 'buoyant' mood conform to her dignity and grace."[72] Her taste was subject, as a matter of course, to "higher standards."[73] Tomaschewsky considered it a serious "offense" for a "housewife to be seen by her husband and children wearing an apron outside the kitchen in the afternoon and evening." Such a neglect of her appearance meant that "nobody really enjoys being with mother … feelings of love and respect gradually deaden and the inner cohesiveness of the family declines."[74]

5. Conclusion

The rules of etiquette, which appear anachronistic at first glance, were nevertheless consonant with DDR cultural and social policy. "Bourgeois" training in deportment served the interests of state functionaries who wanted to cement their own authority by creating disciplined behavioral norms. (As Foucault reminds us, such training was by no means system-specific.) Etiquette rules also served the functionaries' need for representation, which had not been fulfilled either by the "shirt-sleeve proletarian" or by the literary products of "worker-authors." The socialist system of values and morality did not represent an alternative to bourgeois society, which is why 1945 marks a political and social break much more than a cultural one. SED policy was highly contradictory, containing not only disciplinary but also emancipatory elements. Cultural policy offered, after all, opportunities for self-definition and self-realization, and that included the very large number of people incorporated into the administrative apparatus of the regime. The small circle of cognoscenti was to be expanded into a large one. Yet Bertolt Brecht's maxim that we should start with the "bad new" rather than the "good old" stood in diametrical opposition to the political leadership's concept of cultural policy. Instead, the SED perspective reduced proletarian culture and ways of life to their most impoverished form and then stamped them as a "non-culture" long since outgrown by the present level of civilization. At the same time, few concepts were available for thinking about the "masses" and "everyday culture," a problem that had already plagued the labor movement in the days of the Weimar Republic. Caught between the threat of an Americanization of everyday life, which they observed in the west, and the leveling tendencies of "proletarian behavior and attitudes born of necessity," a return to tried and true "solid bourgeois values" and prewar behavioral models seemed the only recourse.[75] Despite all the calls for a "socialist style," cultural and social policy had a rather conservative effect at the level of social interaction. Etiquette books and other "advice literature" doubtless belonged to the "channels of continuity" for bourgeois values and modes of behavior.

Translated by Pamela E. Selwyn

NOTES

1. According to this perspective, DDR society was characterized by weakly differentiated autonomous sub-systems, each of which functioned according to its own rationality. See Sigrid Meuschel, *Legitimation und Parteiherrschaft in der DDR* (Frankfurt, 1992), 306-12, and M. Rainer Lepsius, "Die Institutionenordnung als Rahmenbedingung der Sozialgeschichte der DDR," in *Sozialgeschichte der DDR*, ed. Hartmut Kaelble, Jürgen Kocka, and Hartmut Zwahr (Stuttgart, 1994), 17-30.
2. Among studies of ways of life, the works of Ingrid and Manfred Lötsch deserve particular mention. For detailed bibliographical references as well as on the development of sociology, see Horst Laatz, *Klassenstruktur und soziales Verhalten: Zur Entstehung der empirischen Sozialstrukturforschung in der DDR* (Cologne, 1990), and Peter Christian Ludz, "Soziologie als empirische Sozialforschung," in idem, ed., *Studien und Materialien zur Soziologie der DDR*, Sonderheft no. 8, *Kölner Zeitschrift für Soziologie und Sozialpsychologie* (1964), 327-75.

3. See the self-critical conclusions of East German specialists in cultural studies in *Informationen: Beilage zur Zeitschrift Unterhaltungskunst* 1 (1986), and from a western point of view, see Wolfgang Haible, *Schwierigkeiten mit der Massenkultur: Zur kulturtheoretischen Diskussion der Massenmedialen Unterhaltung in der DDR seit den siebziger Jahren* (Mainz, 1993).
4. An exemplary study is Irma Hanke, *Alltag und Politik: Eine Untersuchung zur erzählenden Gegenwartsliteratur in der DDR der 70er Jahre* (Opladen, 1987).
5. Kaelble, Kocka, Zwahr, *Sozialgeschichte der DDR*, provides an initial overview. For methodological and theoretical problems of a history of everyday culture and of social history, see Thomas Lindenberger, "Alltagsgeschichte und ihr möglicher Beitrag zu einer Gesellschaftsgeschichte der DDR," in *Die Grenzen der Diktatur*, ed. Richard Bessel and Ralph Jessen (Göttingen, 1996), 298-326.
6. The original edition, reprinted many times, is Adolf Freiherr von Knigge, *Über den Umgang mit Menschen* (Hanover, 1788).
7. Among the periodicals analyzed systematically are the women's magazine *Frau von Heute*, which began publication in 1946, the fashion magazine *Sibylle* (since 1957), and the thematically broad *Der gute Rat* (since 1955), which was also addressed to women. Of the more substantial etiquette books the following deserve particular mention: Walter Friedrich and Georg Kolbe, *Otto, benimm dich!* (Berlin, 1957); Karl Smolka, *Gutes Benehmen von A bis Z* (Berlin, 1957), which was reprinted for the tenth time in 1974; and the same author's *Junger Mann von heute* (Berlin, 1958) and *Benehmen ist nicht nur Glückssache* (Berlin, 1959); Karl Kleinschmidt, *Keine Angst vor guten Sitten* (Berlin, 1957); and Ulrich Schweickert and Bernd Hold, *Guten Tag Herr Knigge* (Leipzig, 1959), which had gone into fourteen editions by 1963 and twenty by 1969. For references to more out-of-the-way sources, e.g., on sex education, sports, or entertainment, see Anna-Sabine Ernst, "Erbe und Hypothek: (Alltags-) Kulturelle Leitbilder in der SBZ/DDR 1945-1961," in *Kultur und Kulturträger in der DDR: Analysen* (Berlin, 1993), 13-72.
8. For a detailed account with citations see Ernst, "Erbe," 16-30. On the politics of the cultural legacy, see also Wolfram Schlenker, *Das "kulturelle Erbe" in der DDR: Gesellschaftliche Entwicklung und Kulturpolitik 1945-1965* (Stuttgart, 1977).
9. Lukács's ideas had a strong influence on official cultural policy in the DDR, particularly his insistence that the norms derived from nineteenth-century realism should remain the yardstick of contemporary cultural production. See Schlenker, *Kulturelles Erbe*, 98-102.
10. Walter Ulbricht, "Programmatische Erklärung des Vorsitzenden des Staatsrates der D.D.R.," (Berlin, 1960), 53, from a speech given to the *Volkskammer* on 4 October 1960.
11. Alfred Kurella, "Der Sozialismus und die bürgerliche Kultur," *Einheit* 16:4 (1961): 634.
12. In the 1920s, faced with the breakthrough of mass culture, socialists had already conceived of themselves as the "custodians" of German bourgeois cultural traditions. See Horst Groschopp, "'Partei der planmäßigen Hebung Menschlicher Kultur': Anmerkungen zum Erbe sozialistischer Kulturkonzepte der deutschen Arbeiterbewegung in der DDR," *Mitteilungen aus der kulturwissenschaftlichen Forschung* (hereafter MKF) 30 (1992): 101-30, as well as Dietrich Mühlberg, "Modernisierungstendenzen in der proletarischen Lebensweise: Neuartige Ansprüche veränderter Menschen," *MKF* 30 (1992): 34-64.
13. Horst Groschopp, "Der singende Arbeiter im Klub der Werktätigen: Zur Geschichte der DDR-Kulturhäuser," *MKF* 33 (1993): 86-131, here 111ff.

14. From the minutes of the cultural conference of 1957, quoted in Elimar Schubbe, ed., *Dokumente zur Kunst- und Kulturpolitik der SED*, vol.1 (Stuttgart, 1972), 517.
15. On leisure, see Gerlinde Petzoldt, "'Freie Zeit – was nun?': Alltägliche Modernisierung in der Arbeitsgesellschaft DDR," *MKF* 33 (1993): 153-89.
16. The article consisted of extracts from the book *Unsere Welt von Morgen* (Berlin, 1958), which had already gone into a fourth edition by 1961.
17. Speech by Alfred Kurella at the Fifth Party Congress of the SED in 1958, quoted in *Zur sozialistischen Kulturrevolution: Dokumente*, vol.1 (Berlin, 1960), 402.
18. Quotes, in order, by Alfred Kurella and Walter Ulbricht at the Fifth Congress of the SED in 1958, in *Zur sozialistischen Kulturrevolution*, 405 and 372, respectively; Alexander Abusch, *Mit der Schöpferkraft des Volkes zu einem sozialistischen Kulturleben* (1958), quoted in Schubbe, *Dokumente* 1:521; and Horst Redeker, *Chemie gibt Schönheit* (Berlin, 1959), 12. Redeker was the director of the Institute of Applied Art in Berlin.
19. For a detailed account, see Anna-Sabine Ernst, "Mode im Sozialismus: Zur Etablierung eines 'sozialistischen' Stils in der frühen DDR," in *Lebensstile und Kulturmuster in sozialistischen Gesellschaften*, ed. Krisztina Mänicke-Gyöngyösi and Ralf Rytlewski (Cologne, 1990), 73-94, and idem, "Von der Bekleidungskultur zur Mode: Mode und soziale Differzierung in der DDR," in *Politische Kultur in der DDR*, ed. Landeszentrale für politische Bildung (Stuttgart, 1989), 158-79.
20. See Gabriele Stiller, "Pädagogismus versus Unterhaltung," in *Politische Kultur*, 147-57.
21. Here the SED was in accord with West German conservatives. To be sure, the latter supported Germany's political, economic, and military integration into the west. Ideologically, however, this support was overlaid with the notion of the Occident, and everyday morality and ways of life were supposed to take up seamlessly where the Weimar Republic had left off. This included educated bourgeois cultural anti-Americanism. See Kaspar Maase, "'Antiamerikanismus ist lächerlich, vor allem aber dumm': Amerikanisierung von unten, Arbeiterjugendkultur und kulturelle Hegemonie in der Bundesrepublik der 50er Jahre," *MKF* 33 (1993): 132-52.
22. Indeed, concessions had been made to contemporary tastes: the partner steps were loosened up with solo turns and open figures such as were common in rock 'n roll and boogie woogie. For more details see Ernst, "Erbe," 55-56.
23. In the Federal Republic of Germany etiquette books expressed a general atmosphere of social conservatism. On the social history of the genre and the background to its reception in the Federal Republic, see Ernst, "Erbe," 31-33.
24. Kleinschmidt, *Keine Angst*, 197-99, and Schweickert and Hold, *Guten Tag*, 65-66.
25. Kleinschmidt, *Keine Angst*, 233.
26. Smolka, *Gutes Benehmen*, 9.
27. For biographical information on Kleinschmidt, see Ernst, "Erbe," 32-33. Becher (1891-1958), who began as an Expressionist writer, had joined the KPD in 1919 and went into exile in Moscow during the Nazi period. He played an important role in the cultural policy of the Soviet Occupation Zone and was named minister of culture in 1954. His political influence, however, diminished from the mid-1950s onwards.
28. Smolka, *Gutes Benehmen*, 8.
29. Ulrich Franken, *Also dann bis heute abend im Kulturhaus: Gedanken über den Inhalt einer neuen, sozialistischen Geselligkeit* (Magdeburg, 1963), 59.
30. Kleinschmidt, *Keine Angst*, 47.
31. Ibid., 22.

32. Ibid., 33.
33. "Peter fand wenig Verteidiger," *Neues Deutschland*, 22 January 1959, supplement [no pagination]. This article was part of a larger series with reader comments on the subject of etiquette.
34. Schweickert and Hold, *Guten Tag*, 21, and Kleinschmidt, *Keine Angst*, 29.
35. Schweickert and Hold, *Guten Tag*, 8.
36. Smolka, *Gutes Benehmen*, 158.
37. Kleinschmidt, *Keine Angst*, 69.
38. The original, which dates from the summer of 1948, was the slogan, "Learning from the Soviet Union means learning Victory!"
39. Kleinschmidt, *Keine Angst*, 20.
40. Ibid., 25.
41. Friedrich and Kolbe, *Otto*, 5.
42. Kleinschmidt, *Keine Angst*, 43.
43. Ibid., 263.
44. Ibid., 191.
45. Ibid., 47, and Smolka, *Benehmen*, 157.
46. On the Soviet and international proletcult movement, see the article "Proletkult," in *Kritisches Wörterbuch des Marxismus*, vol. 6 (Berlin, 1986),1085-91.
47. "Festkleidung hebt die Stimmung," *Neues Deutschland*, 31 October 1959, supplement [unpaginated].
48. Ibid.
49. Kleinschmidt, a pastor and the son of a teacher, apparently sought to make his own personal style more widespread: "Before going into his office you automatically straightened your tie," reported one of his former colleagues. Interview in Berlin with Prof. Karl-Heinz Schulmeister, 5 December 1990.
50. Ulbricht, "Programmatische Erklärung," 57.
51. Ibid., 60.
52. Smolka, *Benehmen*, 249. The word *Mittelstand* is emphasized in the original.
53. See Peter Hübner, "Um Kopf und Kragen: Zur Geschichte der innerbetrieblichen Hierarchien im Konstitutioneprozeß der DDR-Gesellschaft," *MKF* 33 (1993): 210-32.
54. Kleinschmidt, *Keine Angst*, 163.
55. Kleinschmidt, *Keine Angst*, 109. After getting their factory back in the early 1990s, the doll manufacturing Steiner family, who under the DDR had been demoted to hired managers, summed up their feelings with a sense of satisfaction that makes past humiliations easy to imagine: "This people's own (*volkseigene*) fraternization, this 'Du' with which the porter addressed the company director, made no sense. All people are not equal." Martin Krüger, "Karriereknick: Ein Fabrikanten-Ehepaar zwischen VEB und Familienerbe," *Wochenpost* 25 (11 June 1992): 39.
56. At the Third Party Conference in 1956 it was decided that more attention should be devoted to the last group in the context of "the politics of alliances." See Kurt Lungwitz, *Über die Klassenstruktur der DDR* (Berlin, 1962), 10.
57. Politburo memorandum to Central Committee, 14 December 1960, on the situation of the intelligentsia, SAPMO-BA, ZPA IV 2/1/259/13-14. This called for new, "lively methods of working with the masses." In the Cottbus district, police "care" of members of the intelligentsia was now delegated to specially trained senior officers of the People's Police. In Suhl the district leadership of the SED went hunting with local doctors. See the compilation of reports by district secre-

taries on the situation of the intelligentsia, 11 April 1958, SAPMO-BA, ZPA IV 2/19/4.

58. Ina Merkel, "... *und Du, Frau an der Werkbank": Die DDR in den 50er Jahren* (Berlin, 1990), 43.
59. Ibid.
60. Kleinschmidt, *Keine Angst*, 111.
61. Irene Uhlmann, ed., *Die Frau: Kleine Enzyklopädie für die Frau* (Berlin, 1961), 680.
62. Smolka, *Benehmen*, 28.
63. Uhlmann, *Frau*, 680.
64. Smolka, *Benehmen*, 28.
65. Uhlmann, *Frau*, 680, and Smolka, *Benehmen*, 28.
66. Kleinschmidt, *Keine Angst*, 233.
67. Smolka, *Benehmen*, 311.
68. Schweickert and Hold, *Guten Tag*, 167.
69. Franken, *Also dann bis heute abend im Kulturhaus*, 32.
70. Karin Hausen uses this term to refer to a model that posited the existence of psychological sex-specific characteristics that corresponded to the physiological ones (active/passive). She locates the origins of this model in the educated strata of the late-eighteenth century. What was new in the definition of sex-specific characteristics was that the chosen principle of classification changed from a more particular to a universal one. Previously, statements about man or woman had primarily been statements about the person's estate, that is, about social positions and the virtues that corresponded to those positions. See Karin Hausen, "Family and Role-Division: The Polarisation of Sexual Stereotypes in the Nineteenth Century – An Aspect of the Dissociation of Work and Family Life," in *The German Family: Essays on the Social History of the Family in 19th- and 20th-century Germany*, ed. Richard J. Evans and W.R. Lee (London, 1981), 51-83. See also Ute Frevert, *Women in German History: From Bourgeois Emancipation to Sexual Liberation* (New York: 1989), 1-60.
71. Talcott Parsons, quoted in Hausen, "Polarisierung," 383.
72. Uhlmann, *Frau*, 675.
73. Kleinschmidt, *Keine Angst*, 90.
74. Karl-Heinz Tomaschewsky, "Die Erziehung zu gepflegten Lebensformen und kulturellen Gewohnheiten," *Pädagogik* 5 (1958): 388.
75. "The proletarian habitus, born of necessity, has largely given way to solid middle-class manners," noted a press report typical of the propagandistic optimism of those years. "Mode, Eleganz, Chic," *Leipziger Neueste Nachrichten*, 2 October 1959.

Chapter 21

Social Democratic Gender Policies, the Working-Class Milieu, and the Culture of Domesticity in West Germany in the 1950s and 1960s

Hanna Schissler

The Social Democratic Party (SPD) entered the postwar reconstruction period with immense moral authority. Many of Germany's other established groups had been severely compromised by their collaboration with the Nazis. The SPD, in contrast, could claim a stance of unbridled and untainted opposition to National Socialism, symbolized most effectively by party leader Kurt Schumacher, who had endured ten years in concentration camps. Many of the party's political goals, including socialization of major industries, were widely accepted even beyond the followers of socialist and communist ideas. The SPD seemed well-positioned to play the decisive domestic role in constructing the political and social order of postwar Germany.

In the shaping of Germany's political landscape, the female electorate was particularly important. World War II had taken an immense toll on male lives and tens of thousands of ex-soldiers languished in Allied prisoner of war camps. As a result of this demographic imbalance, about two-thirds of the electorate was female. For the SPD to fulfill its potential as the major force in the reconstruction of Germany, it had to pay attention

Notes for this chapter begin on page 526.

to women and their concerns and develop a convincing concept of women's place in society. Female support was all the more pressing because the division of Germany had deprived the SPD of some of its traditional strongholds in the central and eastern parts of the country, while the political weight in the west shifted toward the more Catholic Rhineland.

Yet the SPD generally failed to undertake efforts to mobilize women's support both in the immediate postwar period and the early years of the Federal Republic. As Eva Kolinsky has stated:

> *Despite repeated reminders from within its own ranks that women were in a majority and would decide Germany's political future, the SPD presented itself as the party whose democratic principles had been vindicated and whose policies needed no adjustments.*[1]

The reorganization of the SPD took place, as Helga Grebing has observed, in an astounding "theoretical vacuum," in a sort of *Selbstlauf* (running around in circles) in the attempt to reconstruct the old socialist milieu.[2]

To understand the SPD's glaring failure in relation to women requires first a brief historical overview of the party and its attitudes and policies toward the so-called "woman question" in the Kaiserreich and the Weimar Republic. I will then discuss the SPD's rather ambiguous understanding of women's equality even as it promoted the inclusion of the equal rights clause for men and women in the Basic Law (the constitution of the Federal Republic). Then I will proceed to describe the SPD's advocacy of the male family wage in the context of the West German culture of domesticity. I will end this chapter with an analysis of the SPD's rather belated recognition of the changing place of women in society and its even more belated adoption of an emancipatory program on issues of gender.

1.

Since its Erfurt program of 1891 the SPD was committed, at least theoretically, to women's legal, economic, and social equality. August Bebel's book, *Die Frau und der Sozialismus (Women and Socialism)* became a bestseller that had already gone into its thirty-fifth printing in 1903. Ever since the nineteenth century socialists had fought for women's liberation within the framework of the future socialist revolution. Far from denying women's disadvantaged position in society, socialists subsumed women's suppression under class conflict. Thus, the "woman question" had been persistently relegated to a "secondary contradiction" within the revolutionary struggle of the working class. Moreover, since the nineteenth century male workers had frequently been pitted against working women, because the grave pay inequality between male and female workers – women did not make more than one-third to one-half of men's wages – gave rise to male workers' fears about women's cheap competition on the labor market and women as strike breakers.[3] Already in the 1860s, Ferdinand Lassalle, the pioneer of the German socialist movement, demanded that women stay at home with their children. Lassalle and his followers advocated a male family wage, earnings sufficiently high that the male worker would be able to provide for a family, thus, making it unnecessary for women to seek employment outside the home – a position that would prove to be a double-edged sword. Arguments in favor of the male family wage underpinned workers' efforts to raise wages, but also served to strengthen patriarchal values within the working-class family and to support attempts to push women out of the labor force.

Yet social and economic developments during the last third of the nineteenth century had made it eminently clear that women's employment would not disappear and the ideal of men's wages that would be sufficient to feed a family belonged to the realm of utopia. The SPD, meanwhile, invited women to attend political meetings even though until 1908 the Reich Association Law banned female political involvement. After the law was reformed, the head of the party's women's bureau became a permanent member of the Executive. The SPD thereby recognized women's special concerns, but women's activities within the party remained relegated to special organizations, a pattern that prevailed until the late 1960s.[4]

"Proletarian antifeminism" was, then, a widespread phenomenon within both the working class generally and the organized labor movement in particular. It constituted a leitmotif of social democracy from the Kaiserreich all the way through the Weimar Republic, the Third Reich, and the reconstruction years, and on into the Federal Republic. The roots of this proletarian anti-feminism certainly were partly misogynist, but its main origins lay in the gender-segregated labor market that generated fears and insecurities and often fierce competition for jobs. After both world wars women were pushed out of their jobs to make room for demobilized soldiers and returning prisoners of war. Works councils, especially after World War I, functioned as powerful agents of these policies, which challenged women's very right to earn a living.[5]

During the Weimar years, the SPD had never been able to break through women's inclination to vote for the Catholic Center and the national conservative parties. As Renate Bridenthal has convincingly shown, these groups spoke to women's actual position as wives and mothers, participants in small family businesses *(mithelfende Familienangehörige)*, and temporary workers. The SPD, in contrast, mainly and in principle addressed the *working woman* and had little to say about women's actual position and the great variety of social roles in which they engaged. In essence, the party relegated the "woman question" to the distant future and the advent of socialism. When addressing women as voters, the SPD found itself in the peculiar position of first having to *transform* women into workers, thereby neglecting the thousands upon thousands of women who either were not industrial workers or who identified themselves primarily through their familial roles. The open or latent hostility of the union and party leadership toward women even in their own ranks did not help matters.[6] Nonetheless, the SPD provided the largest group of women parliamentarians in the Weimar legislatures (between 11 and 14 percent of the overall group), though none of these women made it to the level of state secretary.[7]

National Socialism had (inconsequentially and unsuccessfully) attempted to push women back into the domestic role. It nonetheless did manage to dequalify women professionally and to shift women's work back into domestic and agricultural forms of employment.[8] But the exigencies of total war led the Nazis, like their World War I predecessors, to mobilize and instrumentalize women for the production of a war economy. Once again women entered the factories in substantial numbers and maintained the home front. Social reality diverged from the radical separate spheres ideology espoused by the Nazis.

"Wars," Robert Moeller effectively maintains, "rupture boundaries that do not appear on maps – the boundaries between women and men."[9] In the postwar period these boundaries had to be redefined – because women's and men's lives had undergone substantial transformations in the twelve years of the Third Reich, because the Nazis' normative definition of women's role was no longer sustainable, and because women now were the majority of the adult population. The defeat of Nazi Germany and the experience of the "collapsed society"[10] meant that the viability and stability of any new system in Germany would rest on new (or renewed) social contracts. The positioning of almost all major groups within society had to be defined anew: the relationship between capital and labor, refugees and older residents, victims of National Socialism as well as (former) Nazis to the rest of society, and also women and men.

It makes sense, therefore, to describe the early years of the Federal Republic in terms of these new social contracts. The stipulation of legal equality between men and women was an important attempt to define anew social relations between the sexes. In many ways the fate of the country "lay in the hands of women," as politicians and occupiers never tired of repeating during the first years after the war. Many felt that women had in fact acquired at least tacit equality in the postwar period and now also deserved legal recognition of this situation. But surprisingly, the attempt to stipulate full legal equality between men and women met with unexpected resistance in the Parliamentary Council, which met in 1948 and 1949 to deliberate the new constitution for the Federal Republic, the Basic Law.

2.

The SPD group in the Parliamentary Council led the fight for the equal rights clause for women and men. On this issue, the SPD was led by Elisabeth Selbert, one of the four "mothers of the Basic Law" and the person who deserves the most credit for the eventual acceptance of the clause.[11] After meeting intense opposition in two readings in the Parliamentary Council, even within her own party, Selbert decided to go public. She mobilized the support of the women's groups that were quite active in the first years after the war.[12] Baskets full of protest notes arrived in Bonn and forced those who had opposed equal rights for women and men to admit that they had made a mistake. Carlo Schmid, one of the key people involved in the drafting of the Basic Law, suddenly spoke of the "ethical obligation" to acknowledge women's equality.[13] In the end, the simple words "men and women are equal" were incorporated into the Basic Law – probably one of the few moments in history when a legal principle was far more progressive than social reality.

Yet the meaning of equality between men and women remained heavily contested. Selbert herself had a clear vision that women's equal rights should extend into all social realms – marriage, family law, property rights, and the working world – and should include equal pay for equal work. But others had a far less clear-sighted and uncompromising vision. Käte Strobel, who in the 1970s would become minister for family and health, sought not only to acknowledge difference within equality, but actually wanted to build equality on the traditional female role. As she wrote in 1947:

> *For socialists legal equality for all is an unquestionable position .... Especially women with a socialist world view demand the equality of the sexes in all areas, with the exception of those that may require concern and consideration for women's bodies. We do not want a special position, which would be undemocratic. But we do demand that women be given the opportunity to prove their capabilities. We also know that equal rights means equal responsibilities and call upon all women to become conscious of and take in hand these rights and responsibilities. It is up to women to show that they possess the political maturity, reason, and intelligence to grow into these important tasks. The particularity of female nature, conditioned by her bodily and moral constitution, requires that we fulfill our roles as housewives and especially as mothers. Those roles cannot, under any circumstances, be neglected. Just the opposite. Social and moral recognition of these most basic and natural roles of women is also a demand for equality.*[14]

Strobel certainly advocated women's participation in public life and their claim to equal rights generally. But at the same time, she promoted a far more "traditional" view that women are different not just physiologically, but also psychologically from men, and that they still desire to be "women" who will continue to fulfill their duties as housewives and mothers.

Strobel sought in part to soothe the fears of those afraid of "leveling" or *Gleichmacherei*, a polemical and pejorative term signifying the erasure of differences between men and women. The word had been deployed since the nineteenth century against any attempt to improve women's political, legal, economic, and social situation, and was revived in the postwar discussion about women's place in society. But Strobel believed deeply that equality rested on women's "special role." In hindsight it is easy to dismiss Strobel's position as not demanding enough and as aiding in the construction of the culture of domesticity that saturated West German society in the 1950s. But in important ways her statement in 1947 reflected the concrete position of women right after the war: although women's position had been strengthened during the last years of the conflict and in the immediate postwar period, thus, giving legitimacy to women's claims for full equality, the irony was that their position had been strengthened in their *traditional* roles as mothers and housewives. In the immediate postwar period they not only performed men's work but, even more importantly, carried out the immediate survival work: women fed and clothed their children and kept their families together.[15] They organized their own and their families' survival after 1945 under conditions of extreme self-exploitation. For the collapsed public reproduction of industrial society they substituted their own (private) reproduction work.[16] Strobel's position reflected this reality even as she drew upon long-standing ideas in the German women's movement that built the claim for equality upon the ideology of separate spheres. In the context of the reconstruction years, it was neither unreasonable nor politically naive to argue for women's equality on the basis of their familial rather than their public roles.

The passage of the Basic Law obligated the Bundestag, the parliament of the new Federal Republic, to bring German civil law into accordance with the equal rights clause. Fierce discussions broke out on gender relations – though these were disguised as debates about women's and, in particular, mothers' roles in society and the family. The discourse on gender, women's place, and the very meaning of equality lasted for an entire decade. The divisions were so intense that the Bundestag failed to meet the 1953 deadline for legal reforms established by the Basic Law. In addition to adjusting civil law, the equality clause (article 3, paragraph 2) had also to be reconciled with other principles of the Basic Law. Women's claims for equality were greatly affected, in particular, by the special protection of the family as stipulated in article 6 – an important part of the social compromise between progressive forces within society as represented by the SPD and organized labor on the one hand and the Christian Democratic Union (CDU) and the churches on the other hand – and also by the freedom of contract between employers and workers.[17] Both provisions provided highly effective and widely used leverage to "tame" the consequences of equality enshrined in article 3, paragraph 2.[18] Not until 1957 did the Bundestag manage to pass the law on equality between men and women. The law was then modified by the *Bundesverfassungsgericht* (West Germany's supreme court) in 1959, which struck down a clause, supported by the CDU and the churches, that provided for the ultimate paternal (rather than joint) authority over the children.

In the decade-long conflict over gender equality, the SPD as a rule took more progressive positions than the CDU. Social Democrats frequently blocked the most retrograde measures promoted by the Catholic church and the CDU, such as a proposal to enshrine in law the husband's authority over the wife and the father's ultimate right to decide in cases of conflicts concerning the children.[19] Yet the SPD also remained mired in the theoretical ambiguity that had historically characterized its position towards women. "Throughout the 1950s," writes Eva Kolinsky, "the SPD remained uncertain whether it should target working or non-working women, and how this could best be done."[20] To be sure, the party advocated equal pay for equal work.[21] But at the same time, the overwhelmingly male-dominated SPD subscribed to policies that were firmly opposed to women with small children going out to work. As a result of *both* the socially restorative climate of the 1950s *and* the labor movement's own nineteenth-century traditions, the SPD and the unions pursued policies of increasing the male wage so that no mother would be forced by economic need to pursue paid employment and so that an entire family could be supported by the *pater familias*. Concretely, this approach resulted in substantial wage increases for men and measures to regulate working conditions for women, if and when they were mothers.[22] Women's social and economic equality was anything but a guiding principle in the formulation of these policies. The SPD in general lacked an understanding of the gender division of labor in industrialized societies and, as a consequence, failed to develop strategies that related to the changed position of women after the war (including the high number of single women and female-headed households) and that offered convincing concepts of equality between men and women.

Even while it promoted policies to enable workers' wives to stay home with their children, the SPD in practice did not quite know what actually to do with housewives or how to address them. "Socialist homemakers" or women workers – the SPD's approach to women remained deeply ambiguous. According to Eva Kolinsky:

> *The SPD wanted to keep options open; it aimed for the working woman while it hoped to appear as if it spoke for the ordinary housewife. It targeted working women at a time when work was not widely accepted as a positive goal in women's lives and it targeted blue-collar women while the growth of female employment occurred elsewhere. SPD women's politics at the time were out of phase with trends in the political culture.*[23]

This was already abundantly clear in the first Bundestag election. The SPD after 1945 had been preoccupied with the national question, with containing Communist influences, and with the issue of socializing the means of production. With these "big" matters on the agenda, the question of women's actual place in society seemed secondary. In fact and in rather unambiguous terms, Kurt Schumacher made women responsible for the SPD's loss of the 1949 election. He blamed women for being unpolitical, for not understanding the meaning of democracy, and basically for languishing as "misguided housewives" who were in dire need of political education:

> *This winter home heating fuel has been in short supply, factories have shut down, and unemployment has risen. Because women have stood aside from politics or have allowed themselves to be deceived by misleading words expressed shortly before election day, price-gougers and other swindlers have seen to a rapid rise in bread prices. Women should not allow themselves to be co-responsible for the misfortune of their people, their families, their own persons .... The excuse doesn't hold that they are so overburdened by the cares for the well-being and maintenance of the family, for husband and children, that they are no longer able to concern themselves with politics.*[24]

Schumacher expressed a sentiment, widespread in the SPD, of rage and disappointment that women in their majority had voted for the CDU. Many male Social Democrats must have had a sense of *déjà vu*: they remembered the Weimar Republic, when the first SPD government had granted women the vote only to discover that relatively few women rewarded the party with their votes. But Schumacher's fury also demonstrates that the SPD in 1949 had little inclination to investigate its own program as far as women and gender were concerned, and little insight into the possible reasons why women might not have voted for the SPD. Electoral defeat did not prompt any deeper reflections.

Social Democratic women, no less than men, could not visualize a concept of equality between the sexes that transcended the traditional submission of women's policies to the SPD's overall goals. Women in the SPD had internalized the reigning societal conception of women's place and colluded in their own subordination – in the party as well as in the overall society. In 1946, at one of the first postwar party meetings, Berty Mayer-Schreiber described her view of the role of women in the SPD:

It's now up to you, comrades, to give up your sense of complacency and bring along your wives and daughters. Have them educated in our circles, in our viewpoint .... Then we will prove ... that we are worthy of your trust. Then we will also be true comrades in marriage, and we socialist women will become the mothers and educators of everyone who wants what we struggle for – socialism.[25]

The tradition of male family wage policies fit neatly into the culture of domesticity within the Federal Republic to which the SPD subscribed together with basically all the other dominant social and political forces at the time. The housewife marriage was the ideal. The dominant forces considered the participation of women in the paid labor force a necessary evil for those who needed work to support themselves or their families. Women's economic and social position thus, tended, to be tied to their breadwinner-husbands, a position not only anchored in ideological assumptions but also inscribed into law. After the Bundestag passed the reforms needed to bring the civil laws in line with the Basic Law, the new paragraph 1356 of the Civil Code read: "Women have the right to gainful employment, to the extent that this is compatible with their responsibilities to marriage and the family."[26] At the SPD's initiative, this legal model of the housewife marriage was only replaced in 1975 by a new law that promoted the model of a true partnership within marriage, where the spouses could choose their respective roles in the family and in the working world. But until that point, one of the profound consequences of paragraph 1356 was that women's entitlement in the welfare state depended not on their own work as homemakers and mothers, or even as part-time workers, but on their mediated status as wives. Robert Moeller has pithily summarized women's place in the social contract of the early Federal Republic: "For many adult women, access to the social contract came not through the labor contract but rather through the marriage contract."[27]

3.

Yet it also needs to be stated that in the 1950s, for the first time, the housewife marriage actually became an historical possibility for a large segment of the population, including members of the working class. This new historical possibility arose out of the spectacular growth in economic productivity, the so-called *Wirtschaftswunder* (economic miracle). But the fact that women, if they chose to do so, had the option to be homemakers is only part of the story. In fact, economic growth pulled women in growing numbers into the labor market. The economy needed women's labor power, even when they were married to male breadwinners. The unfolding of the new consumer society sparked ever-expanding desires for material goods. And women themselves, especially when they were better educated, began to view work outside the home in terms of personal fulfillment.

But through the 1950s and 1960s, women's expanding role in the labor market coexisted in uneasy fashion with the nearly unquestioned dominance of the culture of domesticity. Indeed, the SPD's own unceasing efforts in favor of the male family wage merged quite neatly with the ideology that defined women in terms of marriage and maternity, that ideal of bourgeois gender relations. As one female union member remembered the period:

> *The goal of every good Social Democrat was to earn enough that his wife wouldn't have to work. That was the ideal .... My father was a real leftist, but he always told me: I have to earn enough that my wife can stay at home, enough that I can provide for my family.*[28]

Women also internalized the culture of domesticity and motherliness that saturated all of society. As one participant at the first Federal Women's Conference of the *Deutsche Gewerkschaftsbund*, the trade union federation, stated in 1952:

> *It is a matter of preparing young girls for their future profession as wives and mothers. The argument can not be formulated such that the worker comes before the woman. I believe that the educational project has to be directed primarily such that the woman comes first.*[29]

At the second conference in 1955, delegates advocated women's participation in the labor force in a defensive fashion, because some women were *compelled to work*, not because women had a right to work:

> *Because of the results of the war women are compelled to take care of themselves, their children, and, to some extent, the husbands who have been harmed by the war, as well as other family members. For this reason they must have the right to work.*[30]

As these quotes indicate, women by no means simply went along with men's definitions of women's place in the gender hierarchy. They were not only victims of the culture of domesticity; they were active agents of this process. Some female union members actively embraced domesticity by demanding that women leave the labor market and stay home with their children, as one participant stated at the third women's trade union conference in 1959:

> *We appreciate the fact that many women have to work because of the financial situation of their families. But not all of them have to! In some cases we have to have the courage to confront those women who are not absolutely forced to work. We have to advise them in general not to work .... Furthermore, we have*

to see to it that the father of the family is placed in a position on the earning scale that allows him truly to provide for his family, so that the contributions of wives are no longer necessary. (Applause) *We have to remember with reference to the right to work that it is not the rhythm of work which is the most important thing, but the rhythm of the life of our children!* (Applause)[31]

Women in the SPD and the unions embraced both: the family wage policies and the culture of domesticity and maternity.

Not only female activists advocated these positions. Within the working-class milieu women had been forcefully socialized into clear gender distinctions and into submission under a form of working-class patriarchy.[32] Women's own life stories provide the most insightful picture of this milieu and the circumstances in which women had to assert themselves. In the late 1960s, for example, the writer Erika Runge was in search of models of "achieved emancipation" in women's lives. She tells the stories of two young working-class women: "My mother, she's a housewife. Before, she was in, like, a factory, if I remember right."[33] The mother's previous role in the work world was somewhat blurred for the daughter. The mother was a *Hausfrau*, thus, fulfilling the role expectations that went hand in hand with higher male incomes.

Female socialization took on crude forms in working-class families. Gender roles were as clear as they were rigid within the working-class milieu.

And Sundays, then I had to make pretty much half of the meal, even more than half; my mother only did the meat, and I had to do the rest – soup, dumplings, and salad. My dad and my brothers would sit in the living room. Afterwards, my father usually did crossword puzzles … and my brother would listen to music and my younger brother would play.[34]

The older brother told his sister: "Yeah, that's what the housewife does, what a girl does. Some day you're gonna be a housewife, you gotta learn all of that now."[35] If the daughter sat down to write a letter, she immediately had to fear her father's interruption. "You can't just sit here and be lazy, you gotta help your mama."[36] For her own future this young woman wished:

More than anything, I want to be happy; I want my kids to get a good education – maybe better than mine – and I want a man who's not a playboy, who's a real father and husband.[37]

Although the young woman suffered from the discriminating role assignment within her family, she could not conceive of a different future for herself, but just of the self-fulfilling prophesy of her brother's remarks: "Some day you're gonna be a housewife, you gotta learn all of that now."

Another young woman described her family background: "I come from a pretty petit-bourgeois family. My father was a bricklayer foreman."[38] A classical working-class background was described in terms of the petite bourgeoisie. The father in this family behaved like the caricature of a bourgeois patriarch: "Okay, I'm the boss in this house. What I say goes."[39] The father obviously did not believe in education for girls:

> *But my father took the position that a girl doesn't need to go to school. She'll get married at nineteen or twenty anyway .... The main thing is that [girls] can take care of a household.*[40]

The mother, a housewife, acted as the agent to enforce morality. "I was obviously in the completely wrong circles, and the neighbors were already starting to be upset." Her daughter's coming home late triggered the mother to command: "This cannot go on. Tomorrow you will go to church. And just think: You're not yet twenty-one!"[41]

Twenty-one at that time was the legal age. This young girl had the good fortune to find a mentor among her teachers who tried to break the spell of imagining the "idyllic family life," where the husband goes out to work and comes home at night tired, expecting his wife to bring him the slippers and to keep the rambunctious children quiet. In the little town the teacher was labeled a Communist. He took part in the *Ostermärsche* (protest marches against rearmament), and his message, indeed, was quite subversive for the young woman as far as gender roles were concerned. His message appealed to her; the insights she got from him made her strive for education and she started to read compulsively, although both of her parents found that fairly unnecessary. Her wish to continue her education did not, however, materialize, and she left school after eight years. The work world was pretty rough, which (at age nineteen) "would have been a reason for me to get married or to consider marriage. But I didn't really want to. At that point I just didn't want to work."[42] Marriage functioned as an imagined escape from work – a common pattern among working-class women, and quite an understandable reaction given the kinds of jobs and the low pay available to women in the 1950s and 1960s. These stories show the impact of the ideology of the male breadwinner and female homemaker on women's (in this case daughters') lives and on the ways in which the gender division of labor played out in the working-class milieu.

Indeed, so powerful was the culture of domesticity that throughout the 1950s and 1960s most Germans contested married women's right to work. In a poll taken in 1963 by the *Allensbach Institut für Demoskopie*, Germany's major polling organization, 59 percent of those questioned were in favor of legally (!) forbidding mothers with children under the age of ten to work outside the home.[43] In the same year 90 percent of all women – whether they pursued paid employment or not, whether they were mothers or not – were of the opinion that mothers should not be working outside the home.[44] An effort by the governing CDU to incorporate such sentiments into the legal code by actually prohibiting women with small children from working outside the home met with clear and outspoken resistance from the SPD, which pointed out that such legislation was hardly in compliance with the Basic Law's equal rights clause for men and women. The SPD successfully blocked the initiative. But other than in such somewhat extreme situations, the SPD was virtually indistinguishable from the governing CDU when it came to the ways in which family roles and the division of labor between husband and wife were defined.[45]

Clearly, the culture of domesticity dominated German social life in the first two decades of the Federal Republic. A considerable number of women also embraced the roles of mothers and homemakers, and the SPD and the ruling CDU were almost indistinguishable on the questions of a hierarchical division of labor between men and women. No single explanation can account for the wide ranging social consensus on women's subordination.

First, women were extremely exhausted from the war and the impact of the hunger years. They longed for "normalization" and rest. For many this meant embracing the role of housewife again, as soon as this became possible. As mentioned before, women's strength in postwar Germany was built on their traditional domestic roles.

Second, women wanted to be left alone. They had been mobilized by the Nazis, virtually impressed into the war economy, and forced into backbreaking labor at home, on the streets, and in the factories as part of the effort to rebuild the collapsed postwar economy. Many turned away from politics, or they were pushed away by men who supposedly knew the location of "women's place."

Third, the model of "women's emancipation" in East Germany served as a tremendously powerful deterrent and promoted the anchoring of a different understanding of women's roles in the west.[46] The function of a convenient anti-communism can hardly be overestimated as a means of instilling the culture of domesticity in West Germany. The restorationist culture of domesticity and "normalization" in the young Federal Republic were to a considerable degree a consequence of the desire to move beyond the memories of the Nazi period and the war, and at the same time were also an expression of Cold War fears. As far as the latter is concerned, the situation in West Germany did not differ much from the circumstances in the United States that Elaine Tyler May has researched, with one critically important exception – people in West Germany saw much more clearly than Americans what "women's emancipation" in the east meant for women and their families.[47]

Herein also lie some of the reasons for the general consensus between the two major political parties on women's place in society. Both parties strove to distinguish the Federal Republic as sharply as possible from Nazism as well as from communism, as both regimes had instrumentalized the private sphere for public purposes – and in unique and all-encompassing ways. As a consequence, a heightened sensitivity to state intervention into family issues emerged within the Federal Republic. Whereas the CDU tried to make sure that its polices did not look too much like National Socialist policies (not always successfully),[48] the SPD needed to convince its voters that it had nothing in common with the Communists in East Germany and their "forced emancipation" of women and women's rigid integration into the labor force. The party needed to prove that it was different from the SED state. Hence, the implementation of the equal rights clause of the Basic Law fell victim to a minimalist consensus between CDU and SPD and the parties' mutual agreement on the need to avoid the instrumentalization of women as practiced by Germany's two "totalitarian regimes."[49]

4.

For two decades this consensus reigned nearly unchallenged. But in the meantime, German society underwent profound structural changes, not the least in areas relating directly to women. Belatedly and hesitantly, the SPD began to search for a more creative political response to the recast economic and social environment.

After 1945, the SPD had initially counted on the proletarianization of large parts of the population and the broadening of its constituency by default. Indeed, the downward mobility of the former middle class in the late 1940s seemed to confirm the expectation of a broad proletarianization of the population. But proletarianization proved, in fact, a temporary phenomenon. With the onset of economic recovery, the working population underwent decisive structural changes that no one would have been able to predict immediately after the war. Living conditions improved dramatically, a process that included, by the late 1950s, workers and their families.

Economic expansion also led to the absolute increase and a major shift in women's employment – despite the profound resonance of the culture of domesticity. Between 1950 and 1975 the rate of female employment increased from 47.4 percent to 54 percent.[50] Even more striking is the change in the internal structure of the female labor force. Between 1950 and 1985 the percentage of women working in agriculture declined from 34 percent to 7 percent, while the percentage of women's employment in the service sector rose from 12 percent to 32 percent, and the percentage in manufacturing industries remained stable at 25 percent.[51] Most notably, the share of *married* women with small children going out to work increased from 25 percent in 1950 to 42 percent in 1982, in spite of the never ending ideological war against working mothers and in spite of the fact that working mothers perceived their own immersion into the labor force as "neglect of their families."[52] Social reality transcended the ordained norms of "normal" behavior for women; a kind of silent revolution was underway, one that went widely unnoticed and that did not intentionally challenge dominant gender norms. In the long run, though, the silent revolution contributed decisively to the erosion of the consensus on gender that marked the Federal Republic's first two decades.

The gender inequities of the labor market created a backlog of grievances that helped to shatter the veneer of social and political stability in the late 1960s and 1970s. Certainly, the "economic miracle" led to a substantial rise in living standards. Male workers were the primary beneficiaries, and they experienced higher wages, full employment, a lasting reduction in working hours, and expanded and more generous social welfare policies.[53] These changes eventually amounted to what Josef Mooser has described as an historical break since the 1960s, a "spectacular, all-encompassing and social historically revolutionary" improvement in the living conditions of workers.[54]

Yet as Mooser has convincingly demonstrated, this process was dependent upon the making of a sub-class *(Unterschichtung)* of female and, later on, foreign workers. The existence of the sub-class enabled most male German workers to move up into the ranks of skilled workers.[55] Simultaneously, women workers were pushed into menial, unqualified jobs (as untrained workers), where they expanded in large numbers into the "pink ghetto" of low-paying office and sales positions. Married women frequently also went into part-time work. The labor market, in short, was heavily segregated along gender lines, more so than along the traditional "collar line" that separated manual labor from "clean" administrative work. The creation of the sub-class is best demonstrated by the movement of female wages: compared to men's wages, women's wages were pathetically low. During the 1950s female industrial wages were 45.7 percent lower and female white-collar wages were 43.7 percent lower than respective male wages.[56] In 1956 to 1957, 97 percent of female industrial workers and 48 percent of female white-collar workers earned less than the fictitious average income, whereas 83 percent of male industrial workers and 97 percent of male white-collar workers earned more than the average income.[57]

Nonetheless, the combination of increased male wages and expanded female participation in the labor market sufficed to carry most working-class families into the new consumer society of the 1950s and 1960s. The construction of a family home and the purchase of a family car now came within the horizons of regular workers – though often at the cost of extremely hard labor, excessive overtime, and women's double burden at home and on the job, along with the mutual help provided by the networks of family and friends.[58]

Clearly, women's increased participation in the labor market stood in sharp contrast to both the traditional patriarchal values of the working-class milieu and the gender norms of the Federal Republic. The number of workers' wives who pursued full-time employment rose from 32 percent in 1957 to 46 percent in 1969. Wives' full-time employment was even more common among white-collar workers. Both processes were perhaps the most visible sign of the "structural de-bourgeoisification" of white-collar workers and the "bourgeoisification" of the working class, the emergence of increasingly common living conditions among manual laborers and white-collar workers.[59] Many observers heralded this development as a sign of the success of the Federal Republic, its establishment of a stable, prosperous, and equitable society. Whether this is a permanent feature of postmodern societies or a more open-ended process whose goal is not only undetermined, but which can also be reversed, as the current downsizing of businesses on a large scale demonstrates, remains to be seen.[60] In any case, "*nivellierte Mittelstandsgesellschaft*" (leveled, midde-class society) was the term of choice adopted by contemporaries to describe this process. If read critically and stripped of its highly loaded ideological implications, "*nivellierte Mittelstandsgesellschaft*" is an important indicator of developments in West Germany that enabled workers (if they were male) to participate in the Federal Republic's wealth in spite of the heavy shift of income towards owners of capital, which Volker Berghahn has shown to have been a decisive element of the restructuring of the West German economy.[61] The increase in workers' family income (through raised male wages and women's additional income), together with conditions of full employment as well as the further expansion of the welfare state, constituted the material basis of the legendary social peace and harmony in West Germany during the 1950s and 1960s. The cake got bigger. Even the little pieces increased and everyone could nourish the feeling of being part of general improvements.

But as should have become clear by now, the price for the integration of the male skilled working class into the fabric of society was largely paid by women, and later on also by the foreign "guest workers." Women, if they were married to a male breadwinner, contributed to, as well as participated in, the historically unique increase in living standards, but they did so as second-class workers who were relegated to the pink ghetto of menial jobs or of low-paying jobs in the service sector, frequently on a part-time basis. As individuals women were left out of the overall social contract of wealth participation through increased wages and expanded social rights, a factor which was mirrored in the debates on equal pay that did not come to a rest during the 1950s and 1960s but were rendered largely invisible.[62] Because women, if they were married, participated in the overall social ascent of the working class, their own individual working conditions notwithstanding, it was easier systematically to overlook women's own severe disadvantage and the fact that they were linked to the wealth increase as well as to the entitlements of the welfare state basically through marriage. Considering the fact that women participated in the wealth increase "second hand," single women who were not protected by marriage were the stepchildren of economic growth. In the ways that they set women's wages, employers did not distinguish between women who provided an "additional" income to the male family wage and single women who had to fend for themselves and their children. Thus, miserly female wages hurt them in particular.[63]

5.

How did the SPD react to these structural changes within West German society? How did the party adjust, in particular, to the changed place of women in society?

The relative decline of blue-collar work, the expansion of the service sector, and the dissolution of the traditional working-class milieus eventually led the SPD in 1959 to modernize its political program at its party meeting in Bad Godesberg. In a society where blue- and white-collar workers approached one another in their concrete life circumstances, in an economy of steadily increasing (male) wages, the terminology of class struggle and workers' exploitation lost its defining power. Socialization of industries did not seem to be the solution, and the superiority of the West German model over the East German organization of the economy was obvious. Workers were on a journey of upward mobility and further integration into mainstream society, and the old slogans that had spoken to the experience of social exclusion and economic hardship lost their power. The SPD responded by becoming a modern *Volkspartei* (people's party) rather than an old *Klassenpartei* (class party). The party revoked its socialist world view and tried to appeal beyond manual laborers to other social groups, mainly white-collar workers, civil servants, and the progressive intelligentsia.

But as far as gender politics were concerned, the SPD still did very little. It remained trapped in its old conceptions and failed to address the question of gender hierarchies within the party as well as in society as a whole. The party's commitment to the protection of the family remained unchanged, including its promise to pursue a social policy that would allow mothers with small children to stay at home. In its program designed to turn the SPD into a modern party and leave socialist ballast behind, one could read the same old positions about women's essential maternal role:

> *Equality should not override attention to the psychological and biological particularities of women .... Housewife work must be recognized as professional work. Housewives and mothers need special help. Mothers with pre-school and school-age children should not be compelled to take a paying job because of economic necessity.*[64]

Yet as we have seen and in spite of the fabric of powerful social norms, the exclusive role of homemaker had never been the dominant reality, not even in the 1950s. Under the impact of the structural transformation of women's labor and the rise of the consumer society, the homemaker model also started to lose its normative power for women. Much more typical for women's life course was the "three-phase model": women pursued paid employment before they had children, usually as full-time workers, then stayed home to raise their children, then entered the labor force again after the children were no longer quite so dependent, frequently on a part-time basis. Even during the 1950s and 1960s female life courses showed considerable diversity, thus, defying a single social norm. Not only had the high number of single women with or without children always been forced to work, but married women as well, whether they had children or not, increasingly pursued paid employment. The imperatives of the consumer society continued to exert their influence, but gradually women's attitudes regarding paid employment had also changed. When Helge Pross published her study on the "silent majority" of West German housewives in 1974, it became patently obvious that the norm no longer was the exclusive homemaker, whether "socialist" or just plain "petit bourgeois," and that housewives had a massive inferiority complex toward "career" women.[65] It had become clear that women considered work no longer just a necessary evil or something that – should they actually enjoy it – needed to be hidden carefully in order not to be stigmatized as un-womanly or, worse, as a bad mother. These changes in women's attitudes toward paid employment also mirrored the educational revolution of the 1960s, when girls basically caught up on their educational deficit. Frequently they did better than their male peers in secondary education. Although this did not translate into better chances in the labor market on a broad scale, enhanced educational levels clearly increased women's demands for societal changes that would better accommodate women's needs and ambitions.

Through the 1950s, female membership in the SPD decreased and in the 1960s stagnated. At the party leadership level, however, women's representation had increased, though the male leadership made sure that female officials were mainly involved in mobilizing and recruiting women for party membership. Even women in the Executive were deprived of the opportunity of formulating policy goals. Women were integrated into the party and marginalized at the same time. In the 1960s a few women even made it to commission chairs, but this was not a sign that the SPD had seriously begun to develop a concept for female participation and comprehensive goals as far as women's place in society in general was concerned. These concessions were designed more to discipline women's demands from below.[66]

The new women's movement of the 1970s finally gave quite a number of women a voice to articulate their wish for social change and women's participation. The emergence of a cohort of better-educated young women with a strong commitment to their work outside the home also eventually influenced the SPD's attitudes regarding women's problems. Willy Brandt's chancellorship decisively started to change the SPD's image, giving it a more emancipatory outlook. At the threshold of the 1970s the party managed to change its image and move beyond the traditional dichotomy of working woman and homemaker. When Brandt became chancellor, the party finally succeeded in giving women the message that it would think seriously about ways women could combine their various activities. Brandt announced for his government in 1969 that "women should be helped more than to date to fulfill their equal role in the family, at work, in politics, and in society."[67] In 1972 women for the first time voted for the SPD in greater numbers than did men. The SPD had finally managed to be more in tune with what women really wanted – to combine family and work, and not be forced to choose between the two. The SPD profited from the emergence of a participatory political culture, in particular as far as women's involvement with the party was concerned. From 1965 to 1987 female membership in the SPD increased from 17.4 percent to 25.4 percent. Most of these women no longer came from the traditional socialist milieu.[68] With the Association of Social Democratic Women, a new generation of well-educated women started to push for real participation in formulating policy goals for the SPD. To show the successes and failures of these strategies goes beyond the scope of this chapter.

I wish to thank the editors of this volume, Eric D. Weitz and David E. Barclay, for their valuable advice which greatly helped me to improve this chapter.

Notes

1. Eva Kolinsky, "Political Culture Change and Party Organisation: The SPD and the Second 'Fräuleinwunder,'" in *Political Culture in France and Germany*, ed. John Gaffney and Eva Kolinsky (London, 1991), 212.
2. Helga Grebing, "Die Parteien," in *Die Geschichte der Bundesrepublik Deutschland*, vol 1: *Politik*, ed. Wolfgang Benz (Frankfurt am Main, 1989), 73, 76. She describes "the abstinence, hard to understand even in retrospect, in relation to the firm establishment of basic social rights and responsibilities" (80-81).
3. Laura Levine Frader, "Women in the Industrial Capitalist Economy"; Charles Sowerwine, "The Socialist Women's Movement from 1850 to 1940"; and Renate Bridenthal, "Something Old, Something New: Women between the Two World Wars," all in *Becoming Visible: Women in European History*, ed. Renate Bridenthal et al., 2nd ed. (Boston, 1987), 322, 401, 481.
4. Kolinsky, "Political Culture Change," 210.
5. Ute Daniel, "Women's Work in Industry and Family: Germany, 1914-1918," in *The Upheaval of War*, ed. Richard Wall and Jay Winter (Cambridge, Mass., 1988), 286, and Barbara Böttger, *Das Recht auf Gleichheit und Differenz: Elisabeth Selbert und der Kampf der Frauen um Art. 3 II Grundgesetz* (Münster, 1990), 78-79.
6. Bridenthal, "Something Old, Something New."
7. Kolinsky, "Political Culture Change," 211.
8. Ibid., 214.
9. Robert Moeller, *Protecting Motherhood: Women and the Family in the Politics of Postwar West Germany* (Berkeley and Los Angeles, 1993), 2.
10. The term *Zusammenbruchgesellschaft* was coined by Christoph Kleßmann, *Die doppelte Staatsgründung: Deutsche Geschichte 1945-1955*, 5th edition (Bonn, 1991), 37-65.
11. On the history of the equal rights clause, see Böttger, *Recht auf Gleichheit und Differenz*, 95-122, 191-214; Ines Reich-Hilweg, *Männer und Frauen sind gleichberechtigt* (Frankfurt, 1979); and Moeller, *Protecting Motherhood*, 38-75.
12. See Angela Vogel, "Frauen und Frauenbewegung," in *Die Geschichte der Bundesrepublik Deutschland*, vol. 3: *Gesellschaft*, ed. Wolfgang Benz (Frankfurt am Main, 1989), 162-97.
13. Böttger, *Recht auf Gleichheit und Differenz*, 166.
14. Käte Strobel, "Gleiche Rechte! Gleiche Pflichten!" in *Frauenbuch*, ed. Lisa Albrecht and Hanna Simon (Offenbach, 1947), 41-42.
15. Barbara Willenbacher, "Zerrüttung und Bewährung der Nachkriegs-Familie," in *Von Stalingrad zur Währungsreform: Zur Sozialgeschichte des Umbruchs in Deutschland*, ed. Martin Broszat et al. (München, 1989), 606-7.
16. Böttger, *Recht auf Gleichheit und Differenz*, 95-96; Willenbacher, "Zerrüttung und Bewährung"; Sibylle Meyer and Eva Schulze, *Wie wir das alles geschafft haben: Alleinstehende Frauen berichten über ihr Leben nach 1945*, 2nd ed. (Munich, 1985); Annette Kuhn and Doris Schubert, eds., *Frauen in der deutschen Nachkriegszeit*, 2 vols. (Düsseldorf, 1984 and 1986).
17. Hanna Schissler, "Women in West Germany from 1945 to the Present," in *From Bundesrepublik to Deutschland: German Politics after Unification*, ed. Michael G. Huelshoff et al. (Ann Arbor, Mich., 1993), 120, and Christine Homann-Dennhardt, "Gleichberechtigung via Rechtsnorm? Zur Frage eines Antidiskrim-

inierungsgesetzes in der Bundesrepublik," in *Frauensituation*, ed. Uta Gerhardt and Yvonne Schütze (Frankfurt am Main, 1988), 167.

18. This is meticulously documented in Moeller, *Protecting Motherhood*.
19. Ibid., 76-179.
20. Kolinsky, "Political Culture Change," 216.
21. "In the women's question and in general, the SPD viewed work as the pivotal point of societal reform. The target woman was the working woman, not the housewife." Kolinsky, "Political Culture Change," 217.
22. See Merith Niehuss, "Verhinderte Frauenarbeit? Arbeitsschutzmaßnahmen für Frauen in den 1950er Jahren," in *Von der Arbeiterbewegung zum modernen Sozialstaat: Festschrift für Gerhard A. Ritter* (Munich, 1994), 750-64. See also Moeller, *Protecting Motherhood*.
23. Kolinsky, "Political Culture Change," 218.
24. Quoted in Böttger, *Recht auf Gleichheit und Differenz*, 96.
25. *Protokoll des Parteitags der SPD (Westzonen)*, Hanover 9.-11.5. 1946, 122, quoted in Böttger, *Recht auf Gleichheit und Differenz*, 118.
26. Synopsis of the old and the new Civil Code in *Frauen in der Nachkriegszeit 1945-1963*, ed. Klaus-Jörg Ruhl (Munich, 1988), 191.
27. Moeller, *Protecting Motherhood*, 132.
28. Quoted in Sigrid Ingeborg Bachler, Karin Derichs-Kunstmann, and Mechthild Koppel, *"Da haben wir uns alle schrecklich geirrt …" Die Geschichte der gewerkschaftlichen Frauenarbeit im Deutschen Gewerkschaftsbund von 1945 bis 1960* (Pfaffenweiler, 1993), 148.
29. Quoted in Bachler, Derichs-Kunstmann, Koppel, *"Da haben wir uns alle schrecklich geirrt …"*, 163.
30. Antrag 137, Bundesfrauenkonferenz des Deutschen Gewerkschaftsbundes, 1955, quoted in ibid., 158.
31. Ibid.
32. See, for example, Anne-Katrin Einfeldt, "Zwischen alten Werten und neuen Chancen: Häusliche Arbeit von Bergarbeiterfrauen in den fünfziger Jahren," in *"Hinterher merkt man, daß es richtig war, daß es schiefgegangen ist": Nachkriegs-Erfahrungen im Ruhrgebiet*, ed. Lutz Niethammer (Bonn, 1983), 149-90.
33. Erika Runge, *Frauen: Versuche zur Emanzipation* (Frankfurt am Main, 1970), 7.
34. Ibid., 11.
35. Ibid.
36. Ibid., 12.
37. Ibid., 13.
38. Ibid., 14.
39. Ibid., 14.
40. Ibid., 18.
41. Ibid., 25.
42. Ibid., 28-30, quote 21.
43. Elisabeth Pfeil, *Die Berufstägigkeit von Müttern: Eine empirisch-soziologische Erhebung an 900 Müttern aus vollständigen Familien* (Tübingen, 1961), 35-36.
44. Margot Schmidt, "Im Vorzimmer: Arbeitsverhältnisse von Sekretärinnen und Sachberarbeiterinnen by Thyssen nach dem Krieg," in *"Hinterher merkt man"*, 206.
45. Moeller, *Protecting Motherhood*, 220.
46. See Ingrid Langer, "In letzter Konsequenz … Uranbergwerk! Die Gleichberechtigung in Grundgesetz und Bürgerlichem Gesetzbuch," in *Perlonzeit: Wie die Frauen ihr Wirtschaftswunder erlebten*, ed. Angela Delille and Andrea Grohn (Berlin, 1985).

47. Elaine Tyler May, *Homeward Bound: American Families in the Cold War Era* (New York, 1988).
48. Moeller, *Protecting Motherhood*, 109-41.
49. Ibid., 78, 138.
50. Adelheid zu Castell, "Die demographischen Konsequenzen des Ersten und Zweiten Weltkrieges für das Deutsche Reich, die Deutsche Demokratische Republik und die Bundesrepublik Deutschland," in *Zweiter Weltkrieg und sozialer Wandel*, ed. Waclaw Dlugoborski (Göttingen, 1981), table 10, 137.
51. Eva Kolinsky, *Women in Contemporary Germany: Life, Work, and Politics*, rev. ed. (Providence, RI, 1993), 160.
52. Statistisches Bundesamt, ed., *Datenreport: Zahlen und Fakten über die Bundesrepublik Deutschland* (Bonn, 1983), 84; Statistisches Bundesamt, ed., *Frauen in Familie, Beruf und Gesellschaft* (Stuttgart, 1987), 62-63; and Kolinsky, *Women*, 151-91.
53. See Josef Mooser, "Abschied von der 'Proletarität': Sozialstruktur und Lage der Arbeiterschaft in der Bundesrepublik in historischer Perspektive," in *Sozialgeschichte der Bundesrepublik Deutschland*, ed. Werner Conze and M. Rainer Lepsius (Stuttgart, 1983), 143-86.
54. Mooser, "Abschied," 162.
55. Josef Mooser, "Arbeiter, Angestellte und Frauen in der 'nivellierten Mittelstandsgesellschaft': Thesen," in *Modernisierung im Wiederaufbau: Die westdeutsche Gesellschaft der 50er Jahre*, ed. Axel Schildt and Arnold Sywottek (Bonn, 1993), 362-76.
56. Ute Frevert, *Women in German History: From Bourgeois Emancipation to Sexual Liberation* (Oxford, 1988), 277, 280. Although the wage differential between men and women decreased until the 1980s, female wages in industry were still 31.2 percent lower than men's wages in 1981. Between 1960 and 1980 the male-female wage differential in the lowest paying ranks in industry decreased from 31.2 to 20.6 percent, but in 1980 56.3 percent of the male workers were in the highest paid category, while only 5.4 percent of women reached that level.
57. Mooser, "Arbeiter, Angestellte und Frauen," 366.
58. Angela Vogel, "Familie," in *Geschichte der Bundesrepublik Deutschland* 3: *Gesellschaft*, 56-63.
59. Mooser, "Arbeiter, Angestellte und Frauen," 370-71.
60. Mooser, "Abschied," 186. See the critical comments on the concept of bourgeoisification of the working class in idem, *Arbeiterleben in Deutschland 1900-1970* (Frankfurt am Main, 1984), 229-36, and "Arbeiter, Angestellte und Frauen."
61. Volker R. Berghahn, *The Americanization of West German Industry, 1945-1973* (Leamington Spa, 1986). See also his *Modern Germany: Society, Economy, and Politics in the Twentieth Century*, 2nd ed. (New York, 1987), 197.
62. Mechthild Kopel, "Für das Recht der Frauen auf Arbeit: Ein Kampf gegen Windmühlenflügel in den Jahren 1945-1960," in *Da haben wir uns alle schrecklich geirrt ...*, 7-61.
63. Sibylle Meyer and Eva Schulze, "Von Wirtschaftswunder keine Spur: Die ökonomische und soziale Situation alleinstehender Frauen," in *Perlonzeit*, 92-98.
64. Gerda Hollunder, "Gleichberechtigung im Alltag? Die Rechte der Frauen in Ehe und Familie," in *Was haben die Parteien für die Frauen getan?* ed. Carola Stern (Hamburg, 1976), 23.
65. Helge Pross, *Die Wirklichkeit der Hausfrau* (Reinbek, 1976).
66. Kolinsky, "Political Culture Change," 218-22.

67. Quoted in ibid., 220 . See also Peter Lösche and Franz Walter, *Die SPD: Klassenpartei-Volkspartei-Quotenpartei. Zur Entwicklung der Sozialdemokratie von Weimar bis zur deutschen Vereinigung* (Darmstadt, 1992).
68. Kolinsky, "Political Culture Change," 223-5.

Chapter 22

IS THE SPD STILL A LABOR PARTY?

From "Community of Solidarity" to "Loosely Coupled Anarchy"

Peter Lösche

The likely disappearance of labor movements, of labor parties, and of the working class has been widely predicted for a long time. Indeed, such forecasts are almost as old as the labor movement itself. Although they were first used polemically and in the context of rivalries among various political factions and parties, they were later taken up analytically by historians and social scientists. Early on, for example, the possible disappearance of the labor movement surfaced as an issue in the debate between Eduard Bernstein and Karl Kautsky on the empirical basis of Marx's theory of crisis and revolution. This issue then received a somewhat different twist as a result of the conflict with the Bolsheviks and the new communist labor movement. The question had now become: What is the true labor movement, and who represents it?

In view of these long-term historical antecedents, it is not coincidental that, in a period marked by global economic crisis and by the decline of labor parties, a number of publications began to appear after the mid-1970s with titles like *Departure from the Proletariat*, *Whatever Happened to the Proletariat? A Historic Mission Unfulfilled*, or *The End of the Labor Movement*. What happened to the labor movement?, these authors ask. And to answer that question, another has to be posed: What is – or, rather, what was – the labor movement in the first place?[1]

Notes for this chapter begin on page 544.

The following remarks will not take up these exceedingly general questions. Rather, they will focus on the history of the SPD and its organizational network and on the possible end of the social democratic labor movement in Germany. To be sure, it would be tempting to undertake a comparative analysis and determine whether recent German developments have been "typical," or whether they represent a "separate road" or *Sonderweg* with their own specific conditions.[2] This discussion will also be chronologically limited to the period between Weimar and Bonn: that is, to that historical epoch in which "democratic parties of mass integration" evolved into "people's parties," "universal parties," "omnibus parties," or "catch-all parties."[3]

1. The Community of Solidarity

The social structure, the organizational network, and the program of the traditional SPD – that is, the party of the Wilhelmine state, the Weimar Republic, and the first decade after 1945 – all constituted parts of a unitary whole. German social democracy functioned both as a social movement and a political party, representing at once a life-style and a unique political culture with specific outlooks, values, mentalities, and patterns of behavior that distinguished Social Democrats from their larger environment. This traditional SPD can most precisely and usefully be categorized as a "community of solidarity" *(Solidargemeinschaft)*.[4] That community of solidarity was most obviously and clearly developed during the Weimar years, and was characterized by a number of distinctive features:

1. The community of solidarity constituted itself at the workplace and was composed of skilled workers. This fundamental social reality was as true for functionaries and dues-paying party members as it was for ordinary voters. Party intellectuals had to adapt themselves to this skilled-labor milieu for a simple reason. Within the social democratic community, upward mobility from worker to full-time party intellectual proceeded via the party's own editorial rooms, through party and workers' secretariats, and through educational activities with workers and party youth groups; it did not take place in state-sanctioned and state-supported academies of higher learning. Although the social democratic community of solidarity was constituted at the workplace, it embraced all areas of (skilled) working-class life, from residential patterns to leisure and education. Social democracy was, thus, not a party for all workers, but instead a party that was grounded in a particular proletarian milieu. Even today one can find remnants of this older milieu within the society of the Federal Republic and within the SPD itself. Indeed, its persistence has contributed to one of the many dilemmas faced by the recent SPD, an

extremely socially heterogeneous party that draws support at one end from conservative skilled workers and, at the other, Green-tinged new elements drawn from the educated upper-middle class.

2. A multifaceted and highly complex organizational network bound together the various areas of working-class life included in the community of solidarity. To be sure, the SPD's political focus on elections and parliamentary work remained paramount; at the same time, though, the organizational structure of the social democratic labor movement was also directed toward extraparliamentary work and toward the infusion of social democratic organizations and of social democratic consciousness into all areas of working-class experience. This organizational structure provided the institutional basis for that solidarity which was experienced and practiced in the arena of political struggle, at the workplace, and during leisure-time activities. Of course, Social Democrats always regarded their organizations as a protective bastion against a larger and threatening capitalist environment. But their function was more than simply defensive: social democratic organizations represented a socialist society in miniature, an anticipation of the future. Thus, social democratic organizational practice and reformist theories of socialism did not contradict each other, but in fact were bound up with each other.

3. This solidarity, as it was lived, practiced, and experienced, was absorbed into theoretical discussions among Social Democrats about the nature of socialism, and in the process it lent such discussions a connection to daily reality. Similarly, reformist theories of socialism could strike a receptive chord among social democratic workers because, among other things, working people were able to recognize their own organizational experience in such theories. Thus, for example, concrete social democratic ideas about organization as well as practical experience with organizational matters are clearly reflected in the concepts of "economic democracy" that Fritz Naphtali and Rudolf Hilferding advanced in the 1920s. These concepts were based on two central ideas: 1) the expansion, the continuous development, and the penetration of collective forms of economic organization into the rest of the economy; and 2) the democratization of capitalist society by the organized labor movement in the context of a long-term, cautious process.[5] Hilferding, Naphtali, and most social democratic functionaries believed that economic democracy would emerge as a result of the penetration of capitalist social, economic, and state structures by the organizations of the labor movement. Within the community of solidarity a collective feeling of "togetherness" manifested itself, among other things, in shared programmatic convictions which virtually assumed the character of natural law: the necessity of replacing capitalism with democratic socialism, and the necessity of defending democracy itself. The programmatic consensus which bound together

party members, officials, and the leadership was based on the belief that it was essential to socialize the means of production, to implement genuine human rights, and to defend parliamentary democracy. To be sure, the majority of party members and party officials tended to have an instrumental relationship to parliamentary democracy, which they regarded as the transitional stage on the road from monarchist-capitalist autocracy to socialism; it did not seem worth defending as a value in itself. And in the question of joining coalitions, which of course is of fundamental importance to a functioning parliamentary democracy, the Weimar SPD was split; while the party Left rejected coalitions with bourgeois parties as a matter of principle, moderates and adherents of the party Right were pragmatically willing to enter such coalitions, as in "red" Prussia under the leadership of Otto Braun.

The development of the social democratic community of solidarity during the Weimar Republic did not, of course, lead to a uniform, monotone organizational network extending throughout the entire Reich. The concept "community of solidarity" has to be understood in pluralistic terms, not in terms of uniformity or harmony. Two historical elements helped to shape this pluralistic community:

1. The social democratic organizational network was differentiated functionally and organizationally, and according to other criteria as well. Thus, for example, certain regions of the country were social democratic bastions, while others had to be regarded as part of a social democratic diaspora. The social democratic community of solidarity was composed of relatively autonomous cultural associations, consumers' and producers' cooperatives, political organizations, and other groups, which often enjoyed a local, decentralized, "grass-roots" authority.

2. Dissonance, disagreement, and competition often marked the relationships among social democratic organizations. Conflicts took place, while particularist interests were strongly represented and successfully defended. Similarly, factional activities, generational differences, and other conflicts within individual organizations were so numerous and so complex that they simply cannot be reduced to simple categories like "reformist-radical" or "Right-Left."[6]

2. Loosely Coupled Anarchy

The contemporary SPD stands in sharp contrast to the "community of solidarity" that typified the party during the Weimar years. The party's organizational practice, policies, program, and social composition all reflect a fundamental trend: by the mid-1990s the SPD was moving toward a condition which can be described as "loosely coupled anarchy." A similar process can be observed in Germany's other large party, the Christian Democratic Union (CDU), as well as elsewhere in Western Europe (for example, in the Labour Party in Great Britain or in the Parti Socialiste in France), the United States, Canada, Australia, and even to a certain extent in the African National Congress in South Africa. This development reflects a variety of general social changes.

What is meant by "loosely coupled anarchy"? Let us begin with a negative definition by describing what it is not. According to standard interpretations (or prejudices), the SPD represents a centralized, hierarchical organization in which party decisions proceed from the top down and in which inner-party democracy does not exist. Anyone who actually believes this argument has fallen into a trap laid by the renowned sociologist Robert Michels, who before World War I used the example of the SPD to illustrate an "iron law of oligarchy" that supposedly could be extended to all large organizations. According to Michels's view, the great political parties of the modern age were analogous to monstrous machines like the Prussian army, dominated by discipline and subordination, shaped by the language and terminology of military science, and controlled by powerful leaders at the top. In short: "Whoever speaks of organization is speaking of the tendency toward oligarchy."[7] This image has nothing to do with the organizational reality of the SPD, either in the past or in the present. To the contrary: these days, large political parties are essentially decentralized and fragmented service organizations in the political marketplace. To a certain extent these organizations are functional, but to an even greater extent they are dysfunctional. They are composed of "loosely connected fragments"; or, to use the terms of our own argument here, they represent a "loosely coupled anarchy." In the context of German social democracy, that anarchy can be described as follows:

1. The party is decentralized, fragmented, and flexible. Local party organizations of various kinds *(Ortsvereine, Kreisverbände, and Unterbezirke)* enjoy a high degree of autonomy, while organizations at the regional *(Bezirk)* or state *(Land)* level have their own, very considerable political weight. The party Executive *(Parteivorstand)* and the party Presidium do not stand at the summit of a centralized, pyramid-like structure; rather, they tend to function separately from the rest of the party. These three levels of the party – local, state, and federal – are almost unconnected to each other. Analytically, the party can be regarded as a great coalition composed of a variety of groups: local and regional party organizations; diverse interest groups organized into inner-party "caucuses" or *Arbeitsgemeinschaften* (e.g., women, senior citizens, and municipal politi-

cians, or groups like the Young Socialists and the Caucus for Workers' Issues); traditional party factions of Left, Right, and Center, named in some cases after the geographical locations where their supporters met for the first time (such as the "Frankfurt Circle" and the "Leverkusen Circle"); patronage machines; and ad hoc "citizens' initiatives" (*Bürgerinitiativen*) within the party. To these diverse groupings one has to add the party caucuses in the Bundestag, the legislatures at the state or *Land* level, and municipal legislative bodies, all of which can be distinctive political actors within the party. Indeed, about twenty-five thousand more or less firmly established political actors can be identified within the contemporary SPD. Thus, coalition-building necessarily plays a central role in decision-making processes within the party as a whole. In this respect German social democracy is becoming more and more like American political parties or like the decision-making process within Congress or within American state legislatures: coalition-building is the bottom line.

2. Compared to the 1950s and the 1960s, the social composition of voters, members, and officials of the SPD (and, indeed, of contemporary large parties in general) is extraordinarily heterogeneous. Skilled workers no longer dominate the party's structure. It can be characterized instead as a colorful mixture of workers with blue, white, and grey collars, of technicians and engineers, of university graduates, pastors, small entrepreneurs, and even a few farmers.

3. Programmatically and ideologically, the contemporary SPD is as colorfully diverse as its social structure. Although the party is informed by a vague ideological consensus, this consensus does not influence day-to-day political decisions.

4. The main goal of large political parties, including the SPD, is to gather votes and build an electoral coalition beyond the boundaries of class and confession in order to gain and maintain political power.

When we use the concept of "loosely coupled anarchy," it should, of course, be emphasized that we are not thinking of "anarchism" in the sense of bomb-throwing terrorists; rather, we are thinking of an organizational principle which can be applied to modern big parties – that is, a federation composed of federations of federations of local organizations.

Fragmentation, segmentation, decentralization, and functional differentiation are central to the organizational and political reality of the contemporary SPD. Indeed, in this connection one could well describe it as a "postmodern" political party. Its social diversity is mirrored in the various *interest groups* that are institutionalized within its structure. Moreover, a functional division of labor between inner-party decision-making and extra-party focus-group activities has been established among them. During the past two decades those interest groups that are organized into caucuses or *Arbeitsgemeinschaften* have won considerable weight within the SPD. Indeed, their influence has continued to grow, and their presence at party congresses, in party executive structures, and in party committees is stronger now than in the early 1990s. The *Arbeitsgemeinschaften* now have the right to issue motions and call for votes at party congresses; and in the future, party membership will no longer be a precondition for membership in an *Arbeitsgemeinschaft*. Thus, it is not coincidental that since the 1970s complaints have been raised that the SPD is degenerating into a loose collection of largely autonomous interest groups, while the *Arbeitsgemeinschaften* themselves are becoming transformed into substitute parties.

Within the contemporary SPD the individual *regional organizations (Gebietsverbände)* have also become largely autonomous. Local organizations and groups are rooted in their neighborhoods and are intimately connected with local associational life. Their primary interests are directed toward municipal issues, while their political perspective and political practice are overwhelmingly local in character. Even representatives to the Landtag or the Bundestag find, as the American politician "Tip" O'Neill famously said, that "all politics is local." Politicians are expected to perform a great deal of work at the constituency level, while political figures who focus exclusively on politics at the *Land* or federal level are susceptible to considerable local criticism. The SPD's political practice at the local level, thus, makes an exceptionally introverted, even autistic impression. The local party can react with increasing sensitivity to local and regional feelings and opinions, but sometimes at the expense of commitment to principles and party programs. Bonn and the party's grass roots are separated by a considerable gap. At the local level one repeatedly encounters feelings of alienation; it is quite obvious that the ordinary party member has hardly any influence over party decisions. Thus, it is not coincidental that, within the SPD, demands for American-style primary elections are becoming steadily more vehement. Indeed, in order to encourage more participation by individual party members (and even non-members), it has already become possible to nominate candidates for the Bundestag and the state parliaments in "primary"-style party referendums. After Björn Engholm's sudden resignation as party chair in June 1993, his successor, Rudolf Scharping, was essentially vaulted into office by a vote of the party membership. This internal referendum had a surprisingly positive mobilization effect, with 56 percent of party members participating. In fact, even today it would be possible to choose the SPD's candidate for chancellor by direct referendum. All that would be required is a change of the party's statutes. The possible consequences of such an arrangement, however, have not yet been seriously studied. It could well lead to the establishment of campaign organizations within the party in support of individual candidates, such as Gerhard Schröder, premier of Lower Saxony and a rival both of Scharping and of his successor, Oskar Lafontaine. A further fragmentation and segmentation of the SPD would be the result. The Democratic party in the United States is a negative example of where such trends could lead. In any event, these recent developments tend to confirm our argument that the SPD is well on its way to becoming a "loosely coupled anarchy."

At the local level it becomes especially clear that political parties are by no means exclusively, or even primarily, oriented toward the acquisition and exercise of power, despite Max Weber's well-known arguments to the contrary. In fact, the SPD is a social organization, an association in which some individuals try to confirm their own self-worth, "find themselves," and acquire a kind of emotional home for themselves. There is, thus, a great deal about the SPD which is amateurish, inefficient, and organizationally confusing, while its members often look to it for solidarity, a feeling of "clubbiness," and a sense of place or rootedness. Sometimes these tendencies lead to spontaneous improvisation, and at other times to endless, finely detailed labor on the texts of resolutions which then end up uselessly in the trash bin. Of course, clear divisions of responsibility, sharply focused political work, professionalism, and efficiency coexist with these confusing and inefficient tendencies, all of which simply demonstrates that the inner life of the party is contradictory and inconsistent.

And the party Executive at the top is by no means an oligarchical leadership structure. Represented within it are the various regional associations, factions, and interest groups, carefully balanced according to their respective weight and influence. The Executive holds these centrifugal forces together: it integrates the party, but it does not lead the party. And the "apparatus," the central party bureaucracy in Bonn's Erich Ollenhauer House (scheduled to move to Berlin's Willy Brandt House), is essentially a kind of service station which undertakes two major activities: inner-party communication as well as the preparation (and to a certain extent the implementation) of election campaigns.

The *programmatic positions* of the SPD are just as convoluted and as fragmented as the party organization, a phenomenon which again conforms to our description of the postmodern political party as a "loosely coupled anarchy." Among party members and party leaders one can encounter widely divergent opinions on just about every imaginable political issue. The 1990s, for example, witnessed debates on such things as changes in the law concerning political asylum; the use of electronic eavesdropping devices in the war against organized crime; German participation in UN military activities; the introduction of a European currency union; or possible limitations on the immigration rights of ethnic Germans from the former Soviet Union. Some points of conflict are splitting the party more and more.

Within the SPD, official party programs have lost their integrative force, while externally they have lost their effectiveness (if they ever had any) as public-relations or advertising instruments. But precisely for these reasons, some voices began to become even more vehement in their demands for a new program. For years the SPD was preoccupied with a debate on this matter, until finally the Berlin Program emerged in 1989. The famous Bad Godesberg Program of 1959, at that time a symbol of the SPD's modernization, hardly interested anybody by the mid-1960s, while in the 1970s only a few left-wing activists bothered to refer to it at all. The new Berlin Program of 1989 was modern, addressing a number of new social developments such as the environmentally responsible restructuring of the economy, women's emancipation, technological innovations, and postmaterialist concerns in general. There was only one problem. After the collapse of the postwar order in 1989 to 1990 the SPD's new program was in many respects, especially in the areas of social policy and domestic policy, *too* modern. The newly unified Germany witnessed the return of older social questions and of older, more positive attitudes concerning consumption and consumerism. The messages of postmaterialism were no longer reaching an attentive audience.[8] As a general rule, though, we can say that, in order to bridge divisions and differences among various groups of voters, the SPD's programmatic profile has become increasingly vague. Internally and externally, large parties like the SPD speak with many tongues and varied voices. Above all, they do not want to alienate prospective voters, and, thus, they often tend to avoid taking clear positions.

In short, a new vagueness, a new lack of clarity, has broken out in Germany's large political parties, including the SPD. Or, to use another metaphor, both the SPD and the CDU have come to resemble colorful patchwork quilts composed of a multiplicity of exceptionally diverse hues and materials of different sizes and cut in different ways. Their individual pieces are loosely linked to each other, at some places more tightly than at others. In the patchwork-quilt SPD we encounter traditional trade unionists and innovative Yuppies, people from the Saar and people from Hamburg, leftists and rightists, materialists and postmaterialists, feminists and traditionalists. Above all, though, the differences between the western and the eastern SPD are so great that they almost seem like separate parties. They are divided by their different histories, by the social composition of their members and functionaries, and by the political attitudes and socialization of their party members.[9]

Still, in its colors, composition, and contours, the SPD's patchwork quilt can not be confused with the CDU's. Thus, the SPD tends to be regarded as competent in the area of social policy and in the struggle against unemployment, while the CDU's strengths are considered to be in the areas of economic and foreign policy and in the struggle against crime. Within the SPD itself, coalition-building is essential and unavoidable. Anyone who wants to be personally or programmatically successful has to reach ad hoc or medium-term arrangements with other actors and organizations.

3. Why Did These Transformations Take Place?

What are the *causes* behind the transformations that have taken place within postmodern political parties, and the SPD in particular? They can be summarized under several headings:

1. Fundamental shifts have taken place in occupational structures and within the labor market during the twentieth century. They include the rapid shrinking of the secondary sector and the simultaneous expansion of the service sector. Increasing specialization and differentiation can be observed on the labor market, where we encounter not only white-collar employees and blue-collar workers but also a huge variety of engineers and specialists with "grey collars." On the whole, the social and political significance of the middle classes has increased.

2. The emergence of a complex and all-embracing welfare state has helped to ease class antagonisms and social conflicts, so that the old cleavage between capital and labor, which had earlier been reflected in the political-party system, became less significant in the 1970s and 1980s. To be sure, since that time, social antagonisms have increased in intensity, especially in the 1990s. The welfare state in the Federal Republic of Germany can hardly be paid for anymore, and it is destined to be restructured and reduced. Payments to welfare recipients and the unemployed are being reduced, while immense transfer payments to the new states of eastern Germany are putting considerable pressure on budgets. This new social fragmentation has not yet had clear party-political consequences, apart from growing public disenchantment with all political parties.

3. The increasing secularization of society has weakened tensions and conflicts between Germany's religious confessions, although religious attitudes and church affiliation still influence electoral behavior in important ways. For years the churches in eastern and in western Germany have been losing members. Many have left the church in order to avoid paying the church tax, which in Germany continues to be levied by the state and represents 10 percent of an individual's income tax. In the new states of eastern Germany, less than a third of the total population still belongs to a church.[10]

4. An educational revolution after the late 1960s contributed to an increase in social mobility within the Federal Republic. Today 40 percent of

the relevant age groups are attending a higher, pre-university school, while the number of university students recently exceeded two million for the first time. In 1960 to 1961, by contrast, only 247,000 students attended universities or related institutions in the former Federal Republic, a number which had risen by 1992 to 1993 to 1.7 million.[11] In connection with the educational revolution it should also be noted that the "Sixty-Eighters," the generation of radical students active in the "Anti-Parliamentary Opposition," tended to join the SPD at the beginning of the 1970s and now occupy the leading positions both at the middle levels and at the top of the party.

5. Also important are changing attitudes and patterns of political behavior which, according to sociologists, reflect an increasing emphasis on the individual and on individual values. This process of "individualization" leads not only to an atomization of society but also to new forms of sociability. People are turning less and less to traditional organizations like clubs, associations, parties, or trade unions. With the exception of the Greens (*Bündnis 90/Die Grünen*), all German political parties are losing members, but so too are trade unions and sports clubs. In 1976 the SPD had just over one million members, but at the end of 1995 that number had dropped to only 829,000.[12]

6. In recent years new challenges have emerged as a result of new social questions that have been taken up by the environmental movement, the women's movement, and the peace movement. To be sure, compared to the 1980s the new social movements have lost some of their energy, especially as older social questions concerning poverty and unemployment have reemerged. Still, activists devoted to postmaterialist causes have remained involved both with "citizens' initiatives" (*Bürgerinitiativen*) and with political parties, especially the SPD and the Greens. Moreover, the sharp discrepancy between postmaterialist saturation and new forms of poverty has contributed to current social cleavages within the Federal Republic.

7. Finally, the areas of economic and social policy now offer very little room for maneuvering. There is nothing left to distribute. Rather, budget deficits have to be reduced; and, in contrast to the 1950s and 1960s, budgets are no longer instruments for the establishment of political priorities. Thus, parties no longer offer political alternatives, but instead seem more and more powerless. One example will suffice to show how the SPD no longer has room to maneuver even in the struggle against unemployment, an area of social policy which in earlier times it could truly call its own. These days, the magic formula "innovation and investment" can no longer fulfill its old promise of creating new jobs. In the United States, for instance, key new industries like microelectronics have only been able to create a small number of new employment opportunities, while in older industries jobs are rapidly being lost.[13] Moreover, grand concepts or simple solutions

are no longer available in the arena of foreign policy. The clarity of the east-west conflict has been replaced by an exceedingly complex situation in which local and regional conflicts have come to assume greater significance.

4. What Is Holding the SPD Together?

What is holding the SPD together, despite those tendencies toward fragmentation and segmentation that are typical of "loosely coupled anarchy"? We can identify four factors:

1. The struggle for power remains important: or, to put it more precisely, participation in elections and in government in order to acquire as much patronage as possible at the local, state, and federal levels. Social democratic party machines continue to exist in some cities and in the boroughs of big cities; they are quite similar to the old urban machines that we know from American political history. At the same time, though, the SPD is encountering acute problems in attracting voters and controlling members in rapidly modernizing big cities with a large proportion of service and high-tech firms. Examples include Frankfurt am Main, Munich, Bremen, and Berlin.[14] In these locations the SPD is sharply divided, while younger, critical voters have been drifting toward the Greens. On the whole, though, we can still say that it is hard to exaggerate the importance of patronage in holding a party together, including the SPD.

2. Symbols – that is, the symbolic use of the party's program or its history – continues to play an integrative role. Thus, the Bad Godesberg program stands as a signal for modernization and innovation. August Bebel continues to be viewed as the universally respected forebear who helped to build the SPD into a mass party. The centennial of Kurt Schumacher's birth in 1995 witnessed attempts to portray as a hero the man who chaired the party between 1945 and 1952. For the eastern German SPD, however, certain symbols were appropriated by the Communist SED, such as the red flag, the "Comrade" mode of address, or May Day.

3. Until relatively recently, charismatic leaders like Willy Brandt or Helmut Schmidt were able to integrate their party. The new generation of party leaders – people like Oskar Lafontaine, Rudolf Scharping, Gerhard Schröder, or Heide Simonis – are not in a position to hold the party together through the force of their own personalities. Rather, they are absorbed by problems of coalition-building within the party; and, as a consequence of the SPD's structural problems, they come across as tacticians and not as strategists. Since Willy Brandt's resignation as party chair in the spring of 1987 the party has gone through a whole series of chairs and chancellor candidates, including Hans-Jochen Vogel, Johannes Rau,

Oskar Lafontaine, Rudolf Scharping, and Björn Engholm. None of these individuals was able to attain long-term or federal-level political stature. Premier Manfred Stolpe is very popular in his home state of Brandenburg, but because of his alleged connections to the "*Stasi*," the state security service of the former DDR, he is not a viable candidate for federal office.

4. Certain programmatic principles are rooted in the party's past and continue to bind it together in the present. These include such things as calls for the maintenance of basic rights, the emphasis on the social dimension of human rights, and the defense of parliamentary democracy.

5. Is the SPD a Labor Party?

The contemporary SPD is neither politically nor organizationally unified. It suffers from decentralization and fragmentation as well as from its dual role as a fighting political force organized to gain power and as a sociable association that offers self-fulfillment, a sense of belonging, and leisure-time opportunities to its members. Current discussions about organizational reform within the SPD are largely concerned with softening the effects of "loosely coupled anarchy," if not of eliminating it. "Loosely coupled anarchy" is a structural characteristic of the SPD and the other large party, the CDU; but it also demonstrates that, in contrast to Weimar, today's political parties in Germany have absorbed and in turn reflect the social structures of a pluralist democracy. Even when the big parties are still tied to particular interest groups – as the SPD is to the industrial unions in the German Trade Union Federation (DGB) – this does not significantly affect or weaken the relationship between "loosely coupled anarchy" and pluralist democracy.

In these remarks I have consciously overdrawn certain tendencies that manifest themselves in today's SPD. It was important to stress that the contemporary SPD is dealing with a structural problem that goes beyond marginal questions about the quality of individual leaders or the correctness of the party's positions regarding specific political issues. Although I have used certain concepts here that do not conform to the usual jargon of political science and can be regarded as a normative criticism of the SPD's organizational and political development, I have been concerned above all with the analysis of the structural transformation which has taken place since Weimar. Social Democrats themselves must understand this transformation analytically before they can proceed with necessary organizational reforms, such as an improvement of communications within the party.

The argument that the contemporary SPD can be understood in terms of a "loosely coupled anarchy" also helps us answer our opening question. Under Weimar, and until the middle of the 1950s, it remained a labor party. In terms of the social composition of its voters, members, and leaders, its political culture, its program, and its self-image, today's SPD is no longer a labor party. Naturally the party still includes voters who are skilled workers and who are organized into unions. But if the party wants to win majorities (if only to join a coalition government at the federal level), it has to appeal to the broadest possible range of voters. Within the party they extend from skilled workers to welfare recipients, the technical intelligentsia, Yuppies, and, above all, white-collar workers of all kinds in both the private and public sectors. In this effort, recollections of the SPD's past as a labor party can continue to be valuable and can even have an integrative effect within the party itself. For example, they can draw attention to certain principles such as the primacy of human rights, support for parliamentary democracy, and political engagement on behalf of the concerns of ordinary people.

Perhaps we can summarize this point in a single sentence. The SPD is no longer a labor party, but it remains a party in which workers are both members and functionaries, and within which organized union members can represent their interests through the Caucus for Workers' Issues (*Arbeitsgemeinschaft für Arbeitnehmerfragen*).

Translated by David E. Barclay

Notes

1. See Peter Lösche, *Das Ende der sozialdemokratischen Arbeiterbewegung? Zu Ehren von Henryk Skrzypczak* (Berlin, 1988).
2. For recent work on the SPD, see Siegfried Heimann, "Die Sozialdemokratie: Forschungsstand und offene Fragen," in *Stand und Perspektiven der Parteienforschung in Deutschland*, ed. Oskar Niedermayer and Richard Stöss (Opladen, 1993), 147-86; Peter Lösche and Franz Walter, *Die SPD: Klassenpartei – Volkspartei – Quotenpartei. Zur Entwicklung der Sozialdemokratie von Weimar bis zur deutschen Vereinigung* (Darmstadt, 1992). For an even more recent, if thematically exaggerated, argument, see Thomas Leif and Joachim Raschke, *Rudolf Scharping, die SPD und die Macht* (Reinbek bei Hamburg, 1994).
3. Sigmund Neumann, *Die Parteien der Weimarer Republik* (Stuttgart, 1965); Otto Kirchheimer, "Der Wandel des westeuropäischen Parteiensystems," *Politische Vierteljahresschrift* 6 (1965): 24-41.
4. This concept was coined by Peter Lösche and Michael Scholing, "Solidargemeinschaft im Widerstand: Eine Fallstudie über 'Blick in die Zeit,'" *IWK* 19 (1983): 517-61. It is more thoroughly developed and discussed in Peter Lösche and Franz Walter, "Organisationskultur der sozialdemokratischen Arbeiterbewe-

gung in der Weimarer Republik: Niedergang der Klassenkultur oder solidargemeinschaftlicher Höhepunkt?," *Geschichte und Gesellschaft* 15 (1989): 511-36; and in Peter Lösche and Franz Walter, "Auf dem Weg zur Volkspartei? Die Weimarer Sozialdemokratie," *Archiv für Sozialgeschichte* 29 (1989): 75-136.

5. Rudolf Hilferding, "Die Aufgaben der Sozialdemokratie in der Republik," in *Protokoll SPD-Parteitag Kiel 1927* (Berlin, 1927), 165-84; Fritz Naphtali, *Wirtschaftsdemokratie: Ihr Wesen, Weg und Ziel* (Berlin, 1928). See also Peter Lösche, "Über den Zusammenhang von reformistischen Sozialismustheorien und sozialdemokratischer Organisationspraxis in der Weimarer Republik: Einige Überlegungen," in *Reformsozialismus und Sozialdemokratie*, ed. Horst Heimann and Thomas Meyer (Berlin and Bonn, 1982), 13-32.
6. On these matters, see the studies of social democratic organizations in Peter Lösche, ed., *Solidargemeinschaft und Milieu: Sozialistische Kultur- und Freizeitorganisationen in der Weimarer Republik*, 4 vols. (Berlin and Bonn, 1990-93).
7. Robert Michels, *Zur Soziologie des Parteiwesens in der modernen Demokratie: Untersuchungen über die oligarchischen Tendenzen des Gruppenlebens* (Stuttgart, 1925), 25-26, 38, 40, 174, 261, 264.
8. Franz Walter, "Die SPD nach der deutschen Vereinigung – Partei in der Krise oder bereit zur Regierungsübernahme?" *Zeitschrift für Parlamentsfragen* 26 (1995), 86-87.
9. A few references to the specific development of the eastern German SPD will have to suffice here. Civil-rights activists in the DDR originally founded it in 1989 as the *Sozialdemokratische Partei* (SDP) without support from the West German party. At that time it was dominated by church ministers, but today engineers, physicians, and natural scientists determine its social structure. Apart from its emphasis on human and civil rights, the eastern German SPD incorporated elements of direct democracy into its program. At the same time, it is deeply skeptical about socialism of any kind, including the democratic socialism embraced by the western German SPD. In terms of organization and membership, the eastern German SPD represents an underdeveloped region. For years its membership has stagnated at around twenty-seven thousand, while the western German SPD has about eight hundred thousand members. The reasons behind the SPD's electoral failures in eastern Germany are superbly discussed in Franz Walter, Tobias Dürr, and Klaus Schmidtke, *Die SPD in Sachsen und Thüringen zwischen Hochburg und Diaspora: Untersuchungen auf lokaler Ebene vom Kaiserreich bis zur Gegenwart* (Bonn and Berlin, 1993).
10. Statistisches Bundesamt, ed., *Datenreport 1994: Zahlen und Fakten über die Bundesrepublik Deutschland* (Bonn, 1994), 170ff.
11. Ibid., 52, 62-63.
12. *Der Tagesspiegel* (Berlin), 9 November 1995.
13. Martin Baethge, "Übergang wohin? Zur Reinstitutionalisierung der Gesellschaft im Spannungsfeld von Innovativität und Sozialität," in *Im Zeichen des Umbruchs*, ed. Soziologisches Forschungsinstitut (Opladen, 1995), 33-48.
14. Walter, "Die SPD nach der deutschen Vereinigung," 102ff.

Chapter 23

GOOD-BYE TO ALL THAT

The Passing of German Communism and the Rise of a New New Left

Eric D. Weitz

In December 1989, just weeks after the Berlin Wall had been opened, the Socialist Unity Party (SED) met for what would be its last congress. The SED had been the unquestioned ruler of the German Democratic Republic (DDR) for forty years, beholden only to the Soviet Union. For most of its history it had known only two essential leaders, Walter Ulbricht and Erich Honecker. Now it was on its third prime minister in a matter of one month. The SED had claimed to embody "all that was progressive" in the history of the German people. Now the party leaders had to survey their shattered political landscape. Tens of thousands had fled to the west in the preceding months. The attitude of the remaining citizenry toward the party had turned into a cascade of resentment as revelations came to light about the luxurious lifestyle of the Politburo members and their closest allies, the web of domestic surveillance so extensive that it seemed to confirm the nightmarish vision of George Orwell in *1984*, the economic incompetence that had bankrupted the country.

The wreckage on the landscape lay densely packed, yet the reformers still had to convince the thousands upon thousands of loyal SED members that drastic changes were in order. With as much foreboding as enthusiasm, the SED, at long last, cast overboard the classic, Leninist features of the party, the politburo, central committee, and central control

Notes for this chapter begin on page 555.

commission. The new leader, Gregor Gysi, called for the abandonment of "Stalinism" and summoned from the grave the leftist heroes of the past – Karl Marx, August Bebel, Rosa Luxemburg, resistance fighters against the Third Reich – as witnesses to a new, reformed party. Gysi called for a "third way of a socialist character" defined by "radical democracy and a constitutional state, humanism, social justice, environmental protection, and the ... true equal status of women." The party should base itself upon "social democratic, socialist, non-Stalinist communist, anti-fascist, and pacifist traditions."[1] In an attempt to mollify the old guard, the congress did not abandon entirely the tarnished "SED," but gave the party the name of "Socialist Unity Party-Party of Democratic Socialism." The appellation was both unwieldy and politically inept, and the former SED soon became simply the PDS.

The SED's extraordinary congress evinced little of the euphoria of the other great founding congresses of German communism – 1918 to 1919, when Rosa Luxemburg proclaimed the future to be at hand, 1946, when the handshake between Otto Grotewohl of the SPD and Wilhelm Pieck of the KPD symbolized the labor party unity for which so many Socialists and Communists had yearned. Despite Gysi's enthusiasms, the forebodings were quite prescient. Over the winter of 1989 to 1990 the PDS's membership plummeted. In the elections of March 1990, the DDR populace did not even vote for social democracy, let alone revamped communism. It chose, instead, Christian democracy and Helmut Kohl's promise of immediate prosperity. A popular revolution followed quickly by the allure of the D-Mark accomplished what had eluded the Weimar police, the Nazis, U.S. troops, and West German-inspired isolation – the destruction of German communism.

Communism seemed finished, the final resolution of the epoch of high modernity. Yet in the elections of 1994, communism returned, at least in the former DDR, but also in a number of other former Soviet bloc states and, soon afterwards, in Italy. Local elections in 1995 and 1996 confirmed the PDS's new stature. Communism's obituaries, written with such profound joy in 1989 and 1990, suddenly seemed premature. In the 1994 Bundestag election, the PDS scored 19.8 percent of the vote in the "new federal states," though only 1 percent in the old West Germany.[2] The PDS became the beneficiary of a different kind of wreckage, the battered remains of Helmut Kohl's promise of immediate prosperity for all. The conditions in the five new federal states bespoke a different story, one of the inequities that inevitably accompanied the arrival of capitalism. Many people, particularly the young and educated, benefited from the new opportunities presented by unification, and economic expansion was evident all over the former DDR. But the deindustrialization Moloch devoured the antiquated factories of the DDR, leaving high unemployment in its wake. A reservoir of bitterness emerged, encouraged also by the dismantling of many of the DDR's vaunted social welfare programs, the imposition of a much harsher abortion law, and the litigation that engulfed thousands upon thousands of property owners, many of whom possessed simple houses or small plots of land.

Significantly, while over 90 percent of the PDS's membership in 1994 was composed of former SED members and a disproportionately high number were retirees, the party's supporters in the 1994 Bundestag election were, in contrast, much younger: 25 percent were between 18 and 34, 39 percent between 35 and 54. Moreover, in contrast to initial presumptions, the PDS support did not derive from the unemployed or the old working class, the "losers" in the unification process. A very large proportion of the PDS's electorate consisted of the technical and service middle class, those who were relatively well-educated and well-paid. Many of these people accept the realities of post-unification Germany, but resist the efforts to erase their identities in the DDR and resent the perceived arrogance of the westerners who direct the unification process.[3] As one electoral slogan and oft-quoted phrase had it, "my biography does not begin in 1989."[4]

Yet for all its successes in 1994 and afterward, the long-term prospects for the PDS and its counterparts in Poland, Hungary, and elsewhere seem dim indeed. Communism arose in Europe in the specific historical epoch of high modernity, which began around 1890 and lasted until about 1960. In this seventy-year period, one of the absolutely key markers was the rise of mass-based communist parties and communist-ruled states. More definitively, communist movements and states in Europe all arose amid the great crises – two world wars, the Depression, the rise of fascism – that engulfed the middle period of high modernity. Nowhere in Europe did a communist party break through to popular stature after World War II; with the exception of Yugoslavia, nowhere did communist states arise in Europe outside of the area conquered by the Red Army in World War II. The key features of the epoch of modernity and their relation to the rise of communism are worth delineating in greater detail, because they demonstrate the immense difficulties of turning a party like the PDS into an effective political vehicle in the contemporary, postmodern world.

Communism, like its socialist forebear, rested preeminently on a class-based view of the world. This understanding had its ideological roots, of course, in the utopian socialists, Marx, and Lassalle, and was propagated through the myriad practices of the labor parties, from the printed word (newspapers with titles like *Workers' Daily*) to associational life ("Worker Sports Association") to demonstrations and rallies and, later, to radio, television, and film. But class as an ideological and political construct was not created out of blue sky; it was intimately linked to the lived experience of workers. The language and ideology of class bestowed meaning on existence, on the often harrowing conditions of labor in factories and mines, on the discriminations workers faced in the public realm, on the miserable housing conditions so many workers endured. Moreover, the spatial dimensions of capitalist development emphasized the realities of class. While industrialization separated home and work, it did not sunder the links but refashioned them. As socialist and communist organizers understood, the realms of work, home, and neighborhood were tightly connected, even if a long tram ride separated the factory from the apartment. In short, communism emerged out of the realities of proletarian existence in the era of high modernity, which provided the substratum of experience that made some workers receptive to the language and ideology of class.

But communism emerged also amid the intense, traumatic crises of the first half of the twentieth century. It is difficult to imagine the Bolshevik Revolution, the German Revolution of 1918 to 1920, the formation of the KPD, and the establishment of the Communist International absent the disasters of World War I; impossible to imagine communist parties coming to power in Central and Eastern Europe and emerging as mass parties in parts of Southern and Western Europe absent the deadly experiences of World War II. The wars provided a basis for communism because they engendered material immiseration and national humiliations. Even more important, the total wars of the twentieth century required states to mobilize all the resources available. In something of a reverse image, the wars also led to mass counter-mobilizations, to struggles for peace and socialism in World War I, for national liberation and communism in World War II, on unprecedented scales. Total war created tight welds among proletarian, national, and, among Communists especially, international identities, which powered the upsurge of popular protests, from demonstrations and strikes to armed revolution and resistance, all across the continent. The repression and the magnetic appeal of National Socialism forestalled such mobilizations in Germany, but they did emerge in some fashion in the wake of defeat and had been powerfully present in the earlier period of World War I and the postwar demobilization. The counter-mobilizations opened up utopian vistas of socialism and peace; total war also lent to communist movements, the German included, a tenor of brutality, a belief in political violence as the means of social and political progress.

Communism always drew deeply from its socialist origins, even as it sharply contested social democratic parties. Communism served as a link between the two centuries of the modern era. It was rooted in nineteenth-century socialism, which had its own origins in classical bourgeois liberalism, but was also an expression of the even more conflictual, more violence-prone world of the twentieth century. Indeed, communism and fascism were the twin political expressions of the crisis-ridden world of "classical modernity," to use Detlev Peukert's evocative phrase.[5] Nowhere is this doubled expression clearer than in Germany, where both parties developed as mass-based, popular movements in the 1920s and early 1930s and contested for popular support, in many cases block by block, neighborhood by neighborhood. Both parties developed homologous forms of politics; both aestheticized politics through forceful, uncompromising rhetoric and demonstrations of massed men marching in tightly disciplined, military formation. National Socialism and its fascist allies around Europe became the victims of total war.[6] Communism, in contrast, triumphed – of a sort, because the founding of the DDR was, in reality, an expression of communism's weakness in Germany. Despite the optimism of KPD and SED leaders in the immediate postwar years, their great hopes and expectations that communism would come to power by the popular will, they were reduced in the end to establishing their system in a truncated state protected by the Red Army.

That power is, of course, now gone, along with all the communist-ruled systems in Europe. The revolutions that overthrew European communism in 1989 to 1991 were epoch-making events. They demonstrated that the conditions that gave rise to German and European communism have passed. As innumerable commentators have pointed out, the working class, both as a sociological entity and as a politically self-conscious group for whom class served as the preeminent form of identity, has been on the decline for decades. Workers remain; class identity, never exclusive in nature, now faces ever greater competition from ethnic, gender, and lifestyle identities. Moreover, the spatial dimensions of capitalism that had fostered the organization of the labor movement in the classic period have, in their more recent guise, undermined class identities.[7] Since World War II capitalist expansion has displaced the once-tight linkages between residency and workplace. Highways, automobiles, and urban renewal dispersed working-class populations; work itself is sometimes dispersed into cyberspace by computers and all over the globe by the hyperactive mobility of capital. Suburbia, exurbia, and the developing world are the sites of capitalist expansion, and none provides the social and cultural infrastructure for the classic labor movement that emerged in the developed world from 1840 through about the first half of the twentieth century.

Moreover, for all of their internationalist commitments and rhetoric, the socialist and communist parties emerged very much in particular national contexts. More accurately phrased, they were manifestations of transnational developments that received particular colorations in each national setting. The globalization of economic processes is a perhaps overworked, but nonetheless compelling, catch phrase these days. Socialist and communist parties and the labor movements associated with them were able to effect national legislation and contracts and, in the case of the SED and its counterparts in Eastern Europe, the ruling order of a defined territorial state. The efficacy of any national labor movement, even in its Christian and social democratic strongholds in northern Europe, is under attack by mobile capital and the emerging supranational political and economic structures like the European Union. The classic communist and socialist parties, with their preeminently national orientations – even within the confines of the Soviet bloc – would seem to be relics of the past, unable to promote working-class interests with the same efficacy as in the past.

And if the two world wars of the twentieth century promoted mass mobilizations that accentuated proletarian identities, their passing has likewise weakened the sense of class. Technology has rendered obsolete the mass engagements of the first half of the twentieth century. Modern wars are highly destructive but localized. They galvanize national and ethnic sentiments, as recent events in Bosnia and Chechnya confirm. It is hard to imagine a war within Europe that will be understood as imperial conquest or a consequence of rule by "the most reactionary wing of capital," a war that has to be answered with proletarian internationalism and revolutionary civil war.

Finally, since 1968, the locus of left-wing protest, west and east, has shifted to the new social movements. In West Germany, as in many other countries, feminist, peace, and environmental groups emerged out of the student movement. Their particularist concerns have forged, perhaps ironically, a broadened understanding of politics. In the DDR, citizens groups slowly emerged out of the "society of niches."[8] In the course of the 1980s, and rapidly and forcefully in 1989 to 1990, they articulated a humanistic Marxism notable for its desire to maintain the "solidaristic" aspects of DDR society alongside the institution of democratic practices throughout all the spheres of society. Although some West German leftist groups remained tied to classical Marxism and Marxism-Leninism with its emphasis on the proletariat, the new social movements, east and west, were more notable for ignoring the working class. With the SPD intimately tied to the establishment of West Germany and the SED the ruling party in the east, the classic labor parties no longer embodied the "Left."

Hence, culturally, socially, economically, and politically, the epoch that spawned the KPD and SED has passed. What, then, is left to their heir, the Party of Democratic Socialism? If it is to be successful, the PDS has to fulfill what Gysi, in fact, promised in 1989 – that the party would represent the multiple traditions of the democratic socialist Left. It is worth noting that the Left tradition, in Germany and elsewhere, always had multiple meanings.[9] The SPD, KPD, and SED each tried to establish its hegemony over the Left, rendering to the sidelines divergent voices both within and outside the party. But "Left" was never only what the SPD or SED said constituted the Left; multiplicity is not a postmodern invention. Opposition groups existed in all the parties. Syndicalist-oriented workers challenged the reformist and centralizing tendencies of the trade union movement. Feminism, or at least feminist concerns, were central to the utopian socialist movements of the mid-nineteenth century and constituted important, if often submerged, strains of the formal labor movement of the late nineteenth and twentieth centuries.[10]

The PDS, in short, will have to evolve into something far different from its immediate historical roots in the SED, will have to evolve toward multi-party, multi-group coalitions of the Left. And here recent developments within the PDS evince, at best, a mixed picture.[11] Reforming elements dominate the party, and they are striving to make the PDS a radical democratic socialist party that can govern in coalition with the SPD, the Greens, and other Left opposition groups. But the party is hampered by the SED backgrounds of the leadership and a membership that is composed overwhelmingly of former SED members. The continual recourse by some segments of the party to the political language of German communism, the talk of "class struggle," the attacks on the "pseudo-democracy" of the Federal Republic, the charge that the party leadership is promoting the "bourgeoisification" of the PDS – all this wins reassuring applause from some of the citizenry in the new federal states, but hardly enables the PDS to win new recruits, especially in the old states.[12] The fears of a deracinated communist party, of a "reformist" PDS, revive, in the last decade of the twentieth century, the language and political battles of the Second and Third Internationals from the 1890s into World War II. These attitudes hardly provide a formula for political success in the real, live postmodern world. Indeed, such attitudes will secure the PDS's status only as a regional opposition party for a very limited period of time. They may also revive that other beloved feature of Leninism, a party split, leaving the PDS to descend into the ranks as one more marginal, left-wing sect.

Marx asserted that the proletariat would find its true historical meaning when it abolished itself as a class. Things did not work out quite that way. The PDS, to find its meaning, will in effect have to abolish itself as a party. It will have to renounce more thoroughly the hegemonic claim on the meaning of "Left" that characterized all the socialist parties of the modern era, and must abandon as well its nostalgia for the DDR, however psychologically understandable that position is. Only in close working alliance with the array of opposition groups and social movements can the PDS move beyond a regional protest party and become a viable political force in the new world order of the postmodern Left. It can hardly serve as a workers' party when the classic era of labor representation is over. Much as Peter Lösche has argued for the SPD, but with a more radical turn, the PDS can nonetheless continue to be a party in which workers' interests are represented.[13] It can exercise the power of a tributary party, a party that, in alliance with the SPD, the Greens, and others, can extract wage gains out of elites as well as other social benefits for workers.[14]

The PDS is also positioned to promote those vibrant, democratic ideas that have arisen in the key moments of political breakdown in Germany but have always, in the end, failed. Like the workers' and soldiers' councils in 1918 to 1919, the Antifas in 1945 to 1946, and the citizens' groups in 1989 to 1990, the PDS can promote the notion of more wide-ranging democratization in which democratic practices are established through all the critical realms of society. In this vision, the Bundestag would no longer serve as the exclusive locus of democracy; alongside parliament, council-type institutions in the workplace, the bureaucracy, and the university would promote the ongoing participation of citizens.[15] Such plans are included in the PDS program. They are certainly far-fetched at the moment, but they have two advantages. The call for popular democracy would finally, irrevocably, move the PDS beyond its authoritarian legacy to reinvoke, in new circumstances, one of the most important political contributions of the Left, and could shake Germany (and other countries) out of the stagnation that seems to be gripping all the European party systems and states.

The PDS may or may not be capable of this kind of transformation. But one thing is certain. Both centuries of the modern era have had their "moments of madness" when popular protests and popular movements completely unexpectedly break through the confines of everyday politics.[16] At such moments, when the "political imaginary" moves down uncharted paths, there remains a storehouse of democratic ideas and practices to draw upon – the sometimes submerged traditions of the Left, communist and socialist, in Germany, which have had emancipatory and authoritarian elements.

Notes

1. Quotes in Gert-Joachim Glaeßner, "Vom 'realen Sozialismus' zur Selbstbestimmung: Ursachen und Konsequenzen der Systemkrise in der DDR," *Aus Politik und Zeitgeschichte* (hereafter APZ) B1-2/90 (5 January 1990): 13.
2. On the "super election year 1994," see *German Politics and Society* (hereafter GPS) 13:1 (1995), and on the PDS especially, the articles by Gerard Braunthal, "The Perspective from the Left," 36-49, and Laurence H. McFalls, "Political Culture, Partisan Strategies, and the PDS: Prospects for an East German Party," 50-61; and David R. Conradt et al., eds., *Germany's New Politics, German Studies Review* 1995 special issue, and especially Gerald R. Kleinfeld, "The Return of the PDS," 193-220.
3. For figures and analysis, see McFalls, "Political Culture," and Heinrich Bortfeldt, "Die Ostdeutschen und die PDS," *Deutschland Archiv* (hereafter DA) 27:12 (1994): 1283-84. For a somewhat different analysis of the same trend, see Russel J. Dalton and Wilhelm Bürklin, "The Two German Electorates: The Social Bases of the Vote in 1990 and 1994," *GPS* 13:1 (1995): 79-99. The presumably most complete analysis of the PDS, Gero Neugebauer and Richard Stöss, *Die PDS: Geschichte, Organisation, Wähler, Konkurrenten* (Opladen, 1996), was not yet available to me at the time of writing.
4. Quoted in McFalls, "Political Culture," 56.
5. See Detlev Peukert, *The Weimar Republic: The Crisis of Classical Modernity* (New York, 1992). In taking up his phrase, I am also criticizing his limited application of it to the Weimar period.
6. For an important statement on the specific historical character of fascism, see Diethelm Prowe, "'Classic' Fascism and the New Radical Right in Western Europe: Comparisons and Contrasts," *Contemporary European History* 3:3 (1994): 289-313.
7. For one important statement on understanding the spatiality of capitalism, see Eric Sheppard and Trevor J. Barnes, *The Capitalist Space Economy: Geographical Analysis after Ricardo, Marx, and Sfarra* (London, 1990).
8. The effective term coined by Günter Gaus, *Wo Deutschland liegt: Eine Ortsbestimmung* (Hamburg, 1983).
9. See Geoff Eley's fine essay, "Reviewing the Socialist Tradition," in *The Crisis of Socialism in Europe*, ed. Christiane Lemke and Gary Marks (Durham, NC, 1992), 21-60.
10. See, for example, Mary Jo Maynes, "*Genossen und Genossinnen*: Depictions of Gender, Militancy, and Organizing in the German Socialist Press, 1890 to 1914," in this volume; Harold Benenson, "Victorian Sexual Ideology and Marx's Theory of the Working Class," *International Labor and Working Class History* 25 (1984): 1-23; Atina Grossmann, "Abortion and Economic Crisis: The 1931 Campaign against Paragraph 218," in *When Biology Became Destiny: Women in Weimar and Nazi Germany*, ed. Renate Bridenthal, Atina Grossmann, and Marion Kaplan (New York, 1984), 66-86; Heinz Niggemann, *Emanzipation zwischen Sozialismus und Feminismus: Die sozialdemokratische Frauenbewegung im Kaiserreich* (Wuppertal, 1981).
11. Running commentary on PDS developments can be found in the monthly journal, *Deutschland Archiv*, albeit from a rather tendentious perspective.
12. For these quotes, see Heinrich Bortfeldt, "Pyrrhussieg der Reformer: 4. Parteitag der Reformer," *DA* 28:3 (1995): 228-32; idem, "Zurück zur SED?" *DA* 28:7 (1995): 678-80.

13. Peter Lösche, "Is the SPD Still a Labor Party? From 'Community of Solidarity' to 'Loosely Coupled Anarchy,'" in this volume.
14. I am adapting here Georges Lavau's characterization of the French Communist Party in the halcyon days of the Fifth Republic. See "Le Parti communiste dans le système français," in *Le Communisme en France*, Cahiers de la Fondation Nationale des Sciences Politiques no. 175 (Paris, 1969), 7-65.
15. For typically critical positions on the PDS's concept of democracy, see Armin Pfahl-Traughber, "Wandlung zur Demokratie? Die programmatische Entwicklung der PDS," *DA* 28:4 (1995): 359-69, and Giselher Schmidt, "Zwei rivalisierende Demokratie-Modelle: Ein Beitrag zum Verständnis der PDS," *DA* 28:8 (1995): 835-41.
16. See Aristide R. Zolberg, "Moments of Madness," *Politics and Society* 2 (1972): 183-207. For important reflections on cycles of protest, see Sidney Tarrow, *Power in Movement: Social Movements, Collective Action and Politics* (Cambridge, Mass., 1994), and Gerd-Rainer Horn, *European Socialists Respond to Fascism: Ideology, Activism and Contingency in the 1930s* (New York, 1996), 156-66.

Selective Bibliography

Abrams, Lynn. *Workers' Culture in Imperial Germany: Leisure and Recreation in the Rhineland and Westphalia*. London, 1992.

Angress, Werner. *Stillborn Revolution: The Communist Bid for Power in Germany*. Princeton, 1963.

Bahne, Siegfried. *Die KPD und das Ende von Weimar: Das Scheitern einer Politik 1932-1935*. Frankfurt am Main, 1976.

Barclay, David E. *Rudolf Wissell als Sozialpolitiker 1890-1933*. Berlin, 1984.

Benser, Günter. *Die KPD im Jahre der Befreiung*. Berlin, 1985.

Boll, Friedhelm. *Massenbewegungen in Niedersachsen 1906-1920: Eine sozialgeschichtliche Untersuchung zu den unterschiedlichen Entwicklungstypen Braunschweig und Hannover*. Bonn, 1981.

Bridenthal, Renate, and Claudia Koonz. "Beyond *Kinder, Küche, Kirche*: Weimar Women in Politics and Work." In *When Biology Became Destiny: Women in Weimar and Nazi Germany*, ed. Renate Bridenthal, Atina Grossmann, and Marion Kaplan, 33-65. New York, 1984.

Brüggemeier, Franz-Josef. *Leben vor Ort: Ruhrbergleute und Ruhrbergbau 1889-1919*. Munich, 1983.

Canning, Kathleen. "Gender and the Politics of Class Formation: Rethinking German Labor History." *American Historical Review* 97:3 (1992): 736-68.

______. *Languages of Labor and Gender: Female Factory Work in Germany, 1850-1914*. Ithaca, NY, 1996.

Crew, David F. "*Alltagsgeschichte*: A New Social History from Below?" *Central European History* 22:3/4 (1989): 394-407.

______. *Town in the Ruhr: A Social History of Bochum, 1860-1914*. New York, 1979.

Daniel, Ute. *Arbeiterfrauen in der Kriegsgesellschaft: Beruf, Familie und Politik im Ersten Weltkrieg*. Göttingen, 1989.

Domansky-Davidsohn, Elisabeth. "Der Grossbetrieb als Organisationsproblem des Deutschen Metallarbeiter-Verbandes vor dem Ersten Weltkrieg." In

Arbeiterbewegung und industrieller Wandel: Studien zu gewerkschaftlichen Organisationsproblemen im Reich und an der Ruhr, ed. Hans Mommsen, 95-116. Wuppertal, 1980.
Duhnke, Horst. *Die KPD von 1933 bis 1945*. Cologne, 1972.
Eley, Geoff. "Labor History, Social History, *Alltagsgeschichte*: Experience, Culture, and the Politics of the Everyday – A New Direction for German Social History?" *Journal of Modern History* 61:2 (1989): 297-343.
______. "Reviewing the Socialist Tradition." In *The Crisis of Socialism in Europe*, ed. Christiane Lemke and Gary Marks, 21-60. Durham, NC, 1992.
Engelhardt, Ulrich. *"Nur vereinigt sind wir stark": Die Anfänge der deutschen Gewerkschaftsbewegung 1862/63 bis 1869/70*, 2 vols. Stuttgart, 1977.
Evans, Richard J. *The Feminist Movement in Germany, 1894-1933*. London, 1976.
______. "Politics and the Family: Social Democracy and the Working-Class Family in Theory and Practice before 1914." In *The German Family*, ed. Richard J. Evans and W.R. Lee, 256-88. London, 1981.
______. *Proletarians and Politics: Socialism, Protest, and the Working Class in Germany before the First World War*. New York, 1991.
Evans, Richard J., ed. *The German Working Class, 1888-1933: The Politics of Everyday Life*. London, 1982.
Evans, Richard J., and Dick Geary, eds. *The German Unemployed: Experiences and Consequences of Mass Unemployment from the Weimar Republic to the Third Reich*. New York, 1987.
Falter, Jürgen, and Dirk Hänisch. "Die Anfälligkeit von Arbeitern gegenüber der NSDAP bei den Reichstagswahlen 1928-1933." *Archiv für Sozialgeschichte* 26 (1986): 179-216.
Feldman, Gerald D. *Army, Industry, and Labor in Germany, 1914-1918*. Princeton, 1966.
Fichter, Michael. *Einheit und Organisation: Der Deutsche Gewerkschaftsbund im Aufbau 1945 bis 1949*. Cologne, 1990.
Fischer, Conan J. *The German Communists and the Rise of Nazism*. New York, 1991.
Flechtheim, Ossip K. *Die KPD in der Weimarer Republik*. Hamburg: Junius, 1986, first published 1948.
Fletcher, Roger, ed. *Bernstein to Brandt: A Short History of German Social Democracy*. London, 1987.
Fricke, Dieter. *Handbuch zur Geschichte der deutschen Arbeiterbewegung 1869 bis 1917*, 2 vols. Berlin, 1987.
Geary, Dick. "Identifying Militancy: The Assessment of Working-Class Attitudes towards State and Society." In *The German Working Class 1888-1933: The Politics of Everyday Life*, ed. Richard J. Evans, 220-46. London, 1982.
Grebing, Helga. *Geschichte der deutschen Arbeiterbewegung: Ein Überblick*. Munich, 1966.
Groh, Dieter. *Negative Integration und revolutionärer Attentismus: Die deutsche Sozialdemokratie am Vorabend des Ersten Weltkrieges*. Frankfurt am Main, 1973.

______, and Peter Brandt. "*Vaterlandslose Gesellen*": *Sozialdemokratie und Nation 1860-1990*. Munich, 1992.

Grossmann, Atina. "The New Woman and the Rationalization of Sexuality in Weimar Germany." In *Powers of Desire: The Politics of Sexuality*, ed. Ann Snitow, Christine Stansell, and Sharon Thompson, 153-71. New York, 1983.

______. *Reforming Sex: The German Movement for Birth Control and Abortion Reform, 1920-1950*. New York, 1995.

Gruber, Helmut. *Red Vienna: Experiment in Working-Class Culture, 1919-1954*. New York, 1991.

Guttsman, W. L. *The German Social Democratic Party, 1875-1933: From Ghetto to Government*. London, 1981.

______. *Workers' Culture in Weimar Germany: Between Tradition and Commitment*. New York, 1990.

Hagemann, Karen. *Frauenalltag und Männerpolitik: Alltagsleben und gesellschaftliches Handeln von Arbeiterfrauen in der Weimarer Republik*. Bonn, 1990.

Harsch, Donna. *German Social Democracy and the Rise of Nazism*. Chapel Hill, NC, 1993.

Hartewig, Karin. *Das unberechenbare Jahrzehnt: Bergarbeiter und ihre Familien im Ruhrgebiet*. Munich, 1993.

Harvey, Elizabeth. *Youth and the Welfare State in Weimar Germany*. Oxford, 1993.

Hemmer, Hans-Otto, and Kurt Thomas Schmitz, eds. *Geschichte der Gewerkschaften in der Bundesrepublik Deutschland: Von den Anfängen bis heute*. Cologne, 1990.

Herbert, Ulrich. "Arbeiterschaft im 'Dritten Reich': Zwischenbilanz und offene Fragen." *Geschichte und Gesellschaft* 15:3 (1989): 320-60.

______. *A History of Foreign Labor in Germany, 1880-1980: Seasonal Workers/Forced Laborers/Guest Workers*. Ann Arbor, Mich., 1990.

Herlemann, Beatrix. *Die Emigration als Kampfposten: Die Anleitung des kommunistischen Widerstandes in Deutschland aus Frankreich, Belgien und den Niederlanden*. Königstein im Taunus, 1982.

______. *Kommunalpolitik der KPD im Ruhrgebeit 1924-1933*. Wuppertal, 1977.

Hickey, Stephen H.F. *Workers in Imperial Germany: The Miners of the Ruhr*. Oxford, 1985.

Homburg, Heidrun. "Anfänge des Taylorsystems in Deutschland vor dem Ersten Weltkrieg." *Geschichte und Gesellschaft* 4:2 (1978): 170-94.

______. *Rationalisierung und Industriearbeit: Arbeitsmarkt-Management-Arbeiterschaft im Siemens-Konzern Berlin 1900-1939*. Berlin: Haude und Spener, 1991.

Horn, Gerd-Rainer. *European Socialists Respond to Fascism: Ideology, Activism and Contingency in the 1930s*. New York, 1996.

Hunt, Richard N. *German Social Democracy, 1918-1933*. New Haven, Conn., 1964.

In den Fängen des NKWD: Deutsche Opfer des stalinistischen Terrors in der UdSSR. Ed. Institut für Geschichte der Arbeiterbewegung. Berlin, 1991.

Jessen, Ralph. "Die Gesellschaft im Staatssozialismus: Probleme einer Sozialgeschichte der DDR." *Geschichte und Gesellschaft* 21:1 (1995): 96-110.

Kaelble, Harmut, Jürgen Kocka, and Hartmut Zwahr, eds. *Sozialgeschichte der DDR*. Stuttgart, 1994.

Kleßmann, Christoph. "Betriebsparteigruppen und Einheitsgewerkschaft: Zur betrieblichen Arbeit der politischen Parteien in der Frühphase der westdeutschen Arbeiterbewegung 1948-1952." *Vierteljahrshefte für Zeitgeschichte* 31:2 (1983): 272-307.

______. "Betriebsräte und Gewerkschaften in Deutschland 1945-1952." In *Politische Weichenstellungen im Nachkriegsdeutschland 1945-1953*, ed. Heinrich August Winkler, 44-73. Göttingen, 1979.

Kluge, Ulrich. *Die deutsche Revolution 1918/1919: Staat, Politik und Gesellschaft zwischen Weltkrieg und Kapp-Putsch*. Frankfurt am Main, 1985.

Kocka, Jürgen. *Arbeitsverhältnisse und Arbeiterexistenzen: Grundlagen der Klassenbildung im 19. Jahrhundert*. Bonn, 1990.

______. *Facing Total War: German Society, 1914-1918*. Cambridge, Mass., 1984.

______. *Weder Stand noch Klasse: Unterschichten um 1800*. Bonn, 1990.

Kolb, Eberhard. *Die Arbeiterräte in der deutschen Innenpolitik*. Düsseldorf, 1962.

Kolb, Eberhard, ed. *Vom Kaiserreich zur Weimarer Republik*. Cologne, 1972.

Kontos, Silvia. *"Die Partei kämpft wie ein Mann": Frauenpolitik der KPD in der Weimarer Republik*. Frankfurt am Main, 1979.

Korff, Gottfried. "From Brotherly Handshake to Militant Clenched Fist: On Political Metaphors for the Worker's Hand." *International Labor and Working Class History* 42 (1992): 70-81.

Kruse, Wolfgang. *Krieg und nationale Integration: Eine Neuinterpretation des sozialdemokratischen Burgfriedensschlusses 1914/15*. Essen, 1993.

Langewiesche, Dieter. "The Impact of the German Labor Movement on Workers' Culture." *Journal of Modern History* 59:3 (1987): 506-23.

______. "Politik – Gesellschaft – Kultur: Zur Problematik von Arbeiterkultur und kulturellen Arbeiterorganisationen in Deutschland nach dem 1. Weltkrieg." *Archiv für Sozialgeschichte* 22 (1982): 359-402.

______. "Wanderungsbewegungen in der Hochindustrialiserungsperiode: Regionale, interstädtische und innerstädische Mobilität in Deutschland 1880-1914." *Vierteljahrschrift für Sozial- und Wirtschaftsgeschichte* 64:1 (1977): 1-40.

Leonhard, Wolfgang. *Child of the Revolution*. Chicago, 1958.

Lidtke, Vernon. *The Alternative Culture: Socialist Labor in Imperial Germany*. New York, 1985.

______. *The Outlawed Party: Social Democracy in Germany, 1878-1890*. Princeton, 1966.

Lösche, Peter, and Franz Walter. "Auf dem Weg zur Volkspartei? Die Weimarer Sozialdemokratie." *Archiv für Sozialgeschichte* 29 (1989): 75-136.

______. *Die SPD: Klassenpartei – Volkspartei – Quotenpartei. Zur Entwicklung der Sozialdemokratie von Weimar bis zur deutschen Vereinigung*. Darmstadt, 1992.
Lösche, Peter, ed. *Solidargemeinschaft und Milieu: Sozialistische Kultur- und Freizeitorganisationen in der Weimarer Republik*, 4 vols. Berlin, 1990-93.
Lucas, Erhard. *Märzrevolution 1920*, 3 vols. Frankfurt am Main, 1970-78.
______. *Zwei Formen von Radikalismus in der deutschen Arbeiterbewegung*. Frankfurt am Main, 1976.
Lüdtke, Alf. "Cash, Coffee-Breaks, Horseplay: Eigensinn and Politics among Factory Workers in Germany circa 1900." In *Confrontation, Class Consciousness and the Labor Process: Studies in Proletarian Class Formation*, ed. Michael Hanagen and Charles Stephenson, 65-95. New York, 1986.
______. *Eigen-Sinn: Fabrikalltag, Arbeitererfahrungen und Politik vom Kaiserreich bis in den Faschismus*. Hamburg, 1993.
______. "Organizational Order or Eigensinn? Workers' Privacy and Workers' Politics in Imperial Germany." In *Rites of Power: Symbolism, Ritual, and Politics since the Middle Ages*, ed. Sean Wilentz, 303-33. Philadelphia, 1985
Lüdtke, Alf, ed. *Alltagsgeschichte: Zur Rekonstruktion historischer Erfahrungen und Lebensweisen*. Frankfurt am Main, 1989.
Mai, Gunther, ed. *Arbeiterschaft in Deutschland 1914-1918: Studien zu Arbeitskampf und Arbeitsmarkt im Ersten Weltkrieg*. Düsseldorf, 1985.
______. "Die nationalsozialistische Betriebszellen-Organisation: Zum Verhältnis von Arbeiterschaft und Nationalsozialismus." *Vierteljahrshefte für Zeitgeschichte* 31:4 (1983): 573-613.
Maier, Charles S. *Dissolution: The Crisis of Communism and the End of East Germany*. Princeton, 1997.
Mallmann, Klaus-Michael. *Kommunisten in der Weimarer Republik: Sozialgeschichte einer revolutionären Bewegung*. Darmstadt, 1996.
Mason, Timothy. *Nazism, Fascism, and the Working Class: Essays by Tim Mason*, ed. Jane Caplan. Cambridge, Mass., 1995.
______. *Social Policy in the Third Reich: The Working Class and the National Community*. Providence, RI, 1993.
Maynes, Mary Jo. *Taking the Hard Road: Life Course in French and German Workers' Autobiographies in the Era of Industrialization*. Chapel Hill, NC, 1995.
Miller, Susanne. *Die Bürde der Macht: Die deutsche Sozialdemokratie 1918-1920*. Düsseldorf, 1978.
______. *Burgfrieden und Klassenkampf: Die deutsche Sozialdemokratie im Ersten Weltkrieg*. Düsseldorf, 1974.
Miller, Susanne, and Heinrich Potthoff. *A History of German Social Democracy from 1848 to the Present*. Leamington Spa, 1986.
Mommsen, Hans. *Arbeiterbewegung und nationale Frage*. Göttingen, 1979.
______. "Die Bergarbeiterbewegung an der Ruhr 1918-33." In *Arbeiterbewegung am Rhein und Ruhr: Beiträge zur Geschichte der Arbeiterbewegung in Rheinland-Westfalen*, ed. Jürgen Reulecke, 275-314. Wuppertal, 1974.

______. *From Weimar to Auschwitz*. Princeton, 1991.
______. *Die Sozialdemokratie und die Nationalitätenfrage im habsburgischen Vielvölkerstaat*. Vienna, 1963.
______. "Soziale und politische Konflikte an der Ruhr 1905 bis 1924." In *Arbeiterbewegung und industrieller Wandel: Studien zu gewerkschaftlichen Organisationsproblemen im Reich und an der Ruhr*, ed. idem, 62-86. Wuppertal, 1980.
Mommsen, Wolfgang J., and Hans-Gerhard Husung, eds. *The Development of Trade Unionism in Great Britain and Germany, 1880-1914*. London, 1985.
Morgan, David. *The Socialist Left and the German Revolution: A History of the German Independent Social Democratic Party, 1917-1922*. Ithaca, NY, 1975.
Moses, John Anthony. *Trade Unionism in Germany from Bismarck to Hitler, 1869-1933*. London, 1982.
Müller, Dirk H. *Gewerkschaftliche Versammlungsdemokratie und Arbeiterdelegierte vor 1918: Ein Beitrag zur Geschichte des Lokalismus, des Syndikalismu, und der entstehenden Rätebewegung*. Berlin, 1985.
Müller, Gloria. *Mitbestimmung in der Nachkriegszeit: Britische Besatzungsmacht, Unternehmer, Gewerkschaften*. Düsseldorf, 1987.
Na'aman, Shlomo. *Lassalle*. Hanover, 1970.
Naimark, Norman. *The Russians in Germany: A History of the Soviet Zone of Occupation, 1945-1949*. Cambridge, Mass., 1995.
Nettl, Peter. *Rosa Luxemburg*, abridged ed. Oxford, 1969.
Niethammer, Lutz. "Rekonstruktion und Desintegration: Zum Verständnis der deutschen Arbeiterbewegung zwischen Krieg und Kaltem Krieg." In *Politische Weichenstellungen im Nachkriegsdeutschland 1945-1953*, ed. Heinrich August Winkler, 26-43. Göttingen, 1979.
Niethammer, Lutz, and Alexander von Plato, eds. *Lebensgeschichte und Sozialkultur im Ruhrgebiet 1930 bis 1960*, 3 vols. Berlin, 1983-85.
Niethammer, Lutz, Alexander von Plato, and Dorothee Wierling. *Die Volkseigene Erfahrung: Eine Archäologie des Lebens in der Industrieprovinz der DDR*. Berlin, 1991.
Niethammer, Lutz, et al. *Arbeiterinitiative 1945: Antifaschistische Ausschüsse und Reorganisation der Arbeiterbewegung in Deutschland*. Wuppertal, 1976.
Niggemann, Heinz. *Emanzipation zwischen Sozialismus und Feminismus: Die sozialdemokratische Frauenbewegung im Kaiserreich*. Wuppertal, 1981.
Nolan, Mary. "Economic Crisis, State Policy, and Working-Class Formation in Germany, 1870-1900." In *Working-Class Formation: Nineteenth-Century Patterns in Western Europe and the United States*, ed. Ira Katznelson and Aristide R. Zolberg, 352-93. Princeton, 1986.
______. *Social Democracy and Society: Working-Class Radicalism in Düsseldorf, 1890-1920*. Cambridge, Mass., 1981.
Oertzen, Peter von. *Betriebsräte in der Novemberrevolution: Eine politikwissenschaftliche Untersuchung über Ideengehalt und Struktur der betrieblichen und wirtschaftslichen Arbeiterräte in der deutschen Revolution 1918/19*. Düsseldorf, 1963.
Offermann, Toni. *Arbeiterbewegung und liberales Bürgertum in Deutschland 1850-1863*. Bonn, 1979.

Orlow, Dietrich. *Weimar Prussia, 1925-1933: The Illusion of Strength.* Pittsburgh, 1991.

______. *Weimar Prussia, 1918-1925: The Unlikely Rock of Democracy.* Pittsburgh, 1986.

Peukert, Detlev J.K. *Die KPD im Widerstand: Verfolgung und Untergrundarbeit an Rhein und Ruhr, 1933 bis 1945.* Wuppertal, 1980.

Pierson, Stanley. *Marxist Intellectuals and the Working-Class Mentality in Germany, 1887-1912.* Cambridge, Mass., 1993.

Pohl, Karl Heinrich. *Die Münchener Arbeiterbewegung: Sozialdemokratische Partei, Freie Gewerkschaften, Staat und Gesellschaft in München 1890-1914.* Munich, 1992.

Potthoff, Heinrich. *Freie Gewerkschaften 1918-1933: Der Allgemeine Deutsche Gewerkschaftsbund in der Weimarer Republik.* Düsseldorf, 1987.

Prowe, Diethelm. "Socialism as Crisis Response: Socialization and the Escape from Poverty and Power in Post-World War II Germany." *German Studies Review* 15:1 (1992): 65-85.

Quataert, Jean. *Reluctant Feminists in German Social Democracy, 1885-1917.* Princeton, 1979.

______. "Workers' Reactions to Social Insurance: The Case of Homeweavers in the Saxon Oberlausitz in the Late Nineteenth Century." *Internationale wissenschaftliche Korrespondenz zur Geschichte der deutschen Arbeiterbewegung* 20:1 (1984): 17-35.

Reulecke, Jürgen, ed. *Arbeiterbewegung am Rhein und Ruhr: Beiträge zur Geschichte der Arbeiterbewegung in Rheinland-Westfalen.* Wuppertal, 1974.

Reulecke, Jürgen, and Wolfhard Weber, eds. *Fabrik, Familie, Feierabend: Beiträge zur Sozialgeschichte des Alltags im Industriezeitalter.* Wuppertal, 1978.

Ritter, Gerhard A. *Die Arbeiterbewegung im Wilhelminischen Reich: Die Sozialdemokratische Partei und die Freien Gewerkschaften 1890-1900.* Berlin, 1959.

______. "Workers' Culture in Imperial Germany: Problems and Points of Departure for Research." *Journal of Contemporary History* 13:2 (1978): 165-89.

Ritter, Gerhard A., and Klaus Tenfelde. *Arbeiter im Deutschen Kaiserreich 1871-1914.* Bonn, 1992.

Ritter, Gerhard A., with Elisabeth Müller-Luckner, eds. *Der Aufstieg der deutschen Arbeiterbewegung: Sozialdemokratie und Freie Gewerkschaften im Parteiensystem und Sozialmilieu des Kaiserreichs.* Munich, 1990.

Rohe, Karl. *Das Reichsbanner Schwarz Rot Gold.* Düsseldorf, 1966.

Rosenhaft, Eve. *Beating the Fascists? The German Communists and Political Violence, 1929-1933.* Cambridge, Mass., 1983.

Roth, Guenther. *The Social Democrats in Imperial Germany: A Study in Working Class Isolation and National Integration.* Totowa, NJ, 1963.

Roth, Ralf. *Gewerkschaftskartell und Sozialpolitik in Frankfurt am Main: Arbeiterbewegung vor dem Ersten Weltkrieg zwischen Restauration und liberaler Erneuerung.* Frankfurt am Main, 1991.

Rueschemeyer, Marilyn, and Christiane Lemke, eds. *The Quality of Life in the German Democratic Republic: Changes and Developments in a State Socialist Society*. Armonk, NY, 1989.

Rürup, Reinhard. "Problems of the German Revolution 1918-19." *Journal of Contemporary History* 3:4 (1968): 109-35.

Sachse, Carola. *Siemens, der Nationalsozialismus und die moderne Familie: Eine Untersuchung zur soziale Rationalisierung in Deutschland im 20. Jahrhundert*. Hamburg, 1990.

Sachse, Carola, et al. *Angst, Belohnung, Zucht und Ordnung: Herrschaftsmechanismen im Nationalsozialismus*. Opladen, 1982.

Saldern, Adelheid von. *Auf dem Wege zum Arbeiter-Reformismus: Parteialltag in sozialdemokratischer Provinz Göttingen (1870-1920)*. Frankfurt am Main 1984.

______. *Häuserleben: Zur Geschichte von städtischen Arbeiterwohnens vom Kaiserreich bis heute*. Bonn, 1995.

______. "The Workers' Movement and Cultural Patterns on Urban Housing Estates and in Rural Settlements in Germany and Austria during the 1920s." *Social History* 15:3 (1990): 333-54.

Saul, Klaus. *Staat, Industrie, Arbeiterbewegung im Kaiserreich: Zur Innen- und Aussenpolitik des Wilhelminischen Deutschland 1903-1914*. Düsseldorf, 1974.

Schiffmann, Dieter. *Von der Revolution zum Neunstundentag: Arbeit und Konflikt bei BASF 1918-1924*. Frankfurt am Main, 1983.

Schmidt, Eberhard. *Die verhinderte Neuordnung 1945-1952: Zur Auseinandersetzung um die Demokratisierung der Wirtschaft in den westlichen Besatzungszonen und in der Bundesrepublik Deutschland*. Frankfurt am Main, 1970,

Schneider, Michael. *Kleine Geschichte der Gewerkschaften: Ihre Entwicklung in Deutschland von den Anfängen bis heute*. Bonn, 1989.

Schönhoven, Klaus. *Expansion und Konzentration: Studien zur Entwicklung der Freien Gewerkschaften im Wilhelminischen Deutschland 1890 bis 1914*. Stuttgart, 1980.

______. *Reformismus und Radikalismus: Gespaltene Arbeiterbewegung im Weimarer Sozialstaat*. Munich, 1989.

Schorske, Carl E. *German Social Democracy 1905-1917: The Development of the Great Schism*. Cambridge, Mass., 1955.

Spencer, Elaine Glovka. *Management and Labor in Imperial Germany: Ruhr Industrialists as Employers, 1896-1914*. New Brunswick, 1984.

Sperber, Jonathan. *Rhineland Radicals: The Democratic Movement and the Revolution of 1848-1849*. Princeton, 1991.

Stachura, Peter. *The Weimar Republic and the Younger Proletariat: An Economic and Social Analysis*. New York, 1989.

Stachura, Peter, ed. *Unemployment and the Great Depression in Weimar Germany*. London, 1986.

Staritz, Dietrich. *Geschichte der DDR 1949-1985*. Frankfurt am Main, 1985.

Steinberg, Hans-Josef. *Widerstand und Verfolgung in Essen 1933-1945*. Hanover, 1969.

______. "Workers' Libraries in Imperial Germany." *History Workshop Journal* 1 (1976): 166-80.

Steinisch, Irmgard. *Arbeitszeitverkürzung und sozialer Wandel: Der Kampf um die Achtstundenschicht in der deutschen und amerikanischen Eisen- und Stahlindustrie 1880-1929*. Berlin, 1986.

Suckut, Siegfried. *Die Betriebsrätebewegung in der Sowjetisch Besetzten Zone Deutschlands (1945-1948)*. Frankfurt am Main, 1982.

Sywottek, Arnold. *Deutsche Volksdemokratie: Studien zur politischen Konzeption der KPD 1935-1946*. Düsseldorf, 1971.

Tenfelde, Klaus. "Mining Festivals in the Nineteenth Century." *Journal of Contemporary History* 13:2 (1978): 377-412.

______. *Proletarsiche Provinz: Radikalisierung und Widerstand in Penzberg/Oberbayern 1900-1945*. Munich, 1982.

______. *Sozialgeschichte der Bergarbeiterschaft an der Ruhr im 19. Jahrhundert*. Bonn-Bad Godesberg, 1977.

Tenfelde, Klaus, ed. *Arbeiter im 20. Jahrhundert*. Stuttgart, 1991.

Tenfelde, Klaus, and Heinrich Volkmann, eds. *Streik: Zur Geschichte des Arbeitskampfes in Deutschland während der Industrialiserung*. Munich, 1981.

Wachenheim, Hedwig. *Die deutsche Arbeiterbewegung 1844 bis 1914*. Cologne, 1967.

Weber, Hermann. *Die Wandlung des deutschen Kommunismus: Die Stalinisierung der KPD in der Weimarer Republik*, 2 vols. Frankfurt am Main, 1969.

______. *"Weiße Flecken" in der Geschichte: Die KPD-Opfer der Stalinschen Säuberungen und ihre Rehabilitierung*, 2nd ed. Frankfurt am Main, 1990.

Weitz, Eric D. *Creating German Communism, 1890-1990: From Popular Protests to Socialist State*. Princeton, 1997.

______. *Popular Communism: Political Strategies and Social Histories in the Formation of the German, French, and Italian Communist Parties, 1919-1948*. Western Societies Program Occasional Paper no. 31. Ithaca, NY: Cornell University Institute for European Studies, 1992.

______. "'Rosa Luxemburg Belongs To Us!': German Communism and the Luxemburg Legacy." *Central European History* 27:1 (1994): 27-64.

Wheeler, Robert F. "German Women and the Communist International: The Case of the Independent Social Democrats." *Central European History* 8:2 (1975): 113-38.

______. *USPD und Internationale: Sozialistischer Internationalismus in der Zeit der Revolution*. Frankfurt/Main, 1975.

Wickham, James. "Working-Class Movement and Working-Class Life: Frankfurt am Main during the Weimar Republic." *Social History* 8:3 (1983): 315-43.

Winkler, Heinrich August. *Der Schein der Normalität: Arbeiter und Arbeiterbewegung in der Weimarer Republik 1924 bis 1930*. Berlin, 1988.

______. *Von der Revolution zur Stabilisierung: Arbeiter und Arbeiterbewegung in der Weimarer Republik 1918 bis 1924*. Berlin, 1984.

______. *Der Weg in die Katastrophe: Arbeiter und Arbeiterbewegung in der Weimarer Republik 1930 bis 1933*. Berlin, 1990.

Zwahr, Hartmut. *Zur Konstituierung des Proletariats als Klasse: Strukturuntersuchung über das Leipziger Proletariat während der industriellen Revolution*. Berlin, 1978.

List of Contributors

David E. Barclay is Professor of History and Director of the Center for Western European Studies at Kalamazoo College. His publications include *Rudolf Wissell als Sozialpolitiker 1890-1933* (Berlin, 1984), *Frederick William IV and the Prussian Monarchy 1840-1861* (Oxford, 1995), and articles in a number of books and journals. He recently co-edited *Transatlantic Images and Perceptions: Germany and America since 1776* (New York, 1997) with Elisabeth Glaser-Schmidt. He is currently writing a biography of Ernst Reuter and a history of the revolutions of 1848 to 1850.

Eric D. Weitz is Associate Professor of History at St. Olaf College. He is the author of *Creating German Communism, 1890-1990: From Popular Protests to Socialist State* (Princeton, 1997) and *Popular Communism: Political Strategies and Social Histories in the Formation of the German, French, and Italian Communist Parties, 1919-1948* (Ithaca, NY, 1992), as well as "The Heroic Man and the Ever-Changing Woman: Gender and Politics in European Communism, 1917-1950," in *Gender and Class in Modern Europe*, ed. Laura Levine Frader and Sonya O. Rose (Ithaca, NY, 1996). He is currently writing a history of Weimar Germany.

Hermann Beck is Associate Professor of History at the University of Miami. He has written a number of articles on nineteenth-century German history and is the author of *The Origins of the Authoritarian Welfare State in Prussia: Conservatives, Bureaucracy, and the Social Question, 1815-70* (Ann Arbor, Mich., 1995). In 1997 to 1998 he is a member of the Institute for Advanced Study in Princeton, where he is working on a study dealing with the German educated elites and National Socialism.

Warren Breckman is Assistant Professor of History at the University of Pennsylvania, where he teaches courses on modern European intellectual history. He has recently completed a book entitled *Dethroning the Self: The Young Hegelians and the Political Theology of Restoration*, and he is now working on a study of French political theory after World War II.

David F. Crew is Associate Professor of History at the University of Texas at Austin. His most recent book, *Weimar Germans on Welfare*, was published by Oxford University Press in 1997. He has also edited *Nazism and German Society, 1933-1945* (London, 1994). His current research interests include German popular/mass culture in the twentieth century, the history of sexuality, and the politics of commemoration.

Geoff Eley is Professor of History at the University of Michigan. He is the author of *Wilhelminismus, Nationalismus, Faschismus: Zur historischen Kontinuität in Deutschland* (Munster, 1991) and editor of *Society, Culture, and the State in Germany, 1870-1930* (Ann Arbor, Mich., 1996). He has also co-edited *Becoming National: A Reader* (New York, 1996) with Ronald Grigor Suny, and *Culture/Power/History: A Reader in Contemporary Social Theory* (Princeton, 1994) with Nicholas Dirks and Sherry Ortner.

Anna-Sabine Ernst received her doctorate from the Humboldt University in Berlin. She is the author of *"Die beste Prophylaxe ist der Sozialismus": Ärzte und medizinische Hochschullehrer in der SBZ-DDR 1945-1961* (Berlin, 1997), and numerous articles on the DDR.

Atina Grossmann teaches modern European and German history and women's and gender studies at The Cooper Union and Columbia University in New York City. She is the author of *Reforming Sex: The German Movement for Birth Control and Abortion Reform 1920-1950* (New York, 1995) and numerous articles on "new women" and modernity in twentieth-century Germany. She co-edited *When Biology Became Destiny: Women in Weimar and Nazi Germany* (New York, 1984), and is currently working on a study of "Victims, Victors, and Survivors: War's End and Postwar Reconstruction, Berlin 1945-1949."

Donna Harsch is Associate Professor of History at Carnegie Mellon University. She is the author of *German Social Democracy and the Rise of Nazism* (Chapel Hill, NC, 1993) and is currently working on a social history of women in East Germany from 1945 to 1970. An aspect of this project has been published as "Society, the State, and Abortion in East Germany, 1950-1972," *American Historical Review* 102 (1997): 53-84.

Beatrix Herlemann is an independent scholar who has written widely on German communism and on the resistance against the Nazis. She has also curated museum exhibitions on the Third Reich. Among her publications are *Die Emigration als Kampfposten* (1982) and *Kommunal Politik der KPD im Ruhrgebiet 1924-1933* (1977).

Gerd-Rainer Horn is Assistant Professor of Modern European History at Western Oregon State College. His book, *European Socialists Respond to Fascism: Ideology, Activism, and Contingency in the 1930s*, was published by Oxford University Press in 1996. He has also published a number of articles on the political and social history of twentieth-century Europe in various European and American journals.

Peter Lösche is Professor of Political Science at the University of Göttingen, where he is also affiliated with the Zentrum für Europa- und Nordamerika-Studien. His most recent books include *Die SPD: Klassenpartei – Volkspartei – Quotenpartei* (Darmstadt, 1992), and *Die FDP: Richtungsstreit und Zukunftszweifel* (Darmstadt, 1996), both co-written with Franz Walter, and *Kleine Geschichte der deutschen Parteien*, 2nd ed. (Stuttgart, 1993).

William Carl Mathews is Associate Professor of History at the State University of New York – Potsdam College. He has published several articles on the Social Democrats and the inflation of 1914-23, most recently "The Social Origins of the *Noskepolitik*," *Central European History* 27: 1 (1994): 65-86.

Mary Jo Maynes is Professor of History at the University of Minnesota. Her recent works include *Taking The Hard Road: Life Course in French and German Workers' Autobiographies in the Era of Industrialization* (Chapel Hill, NC, 1995); *Gender, Kinship, Power: An Interdisciplinary and Comparative History* (New York, 1996), co-edited with Ann Waltner, Birgitte Soland, and Ulrike Strasser; and *Austrian Women in the Nineteenth and Twentieth Centuries* (Providence, RI, 1996), co-edited with David Good and Margarete Grandner.

Norman Naimark is Robert and Florence McDonnell Professor in East European Studies and Chair, Department of History, Stanford University. His books include, most recently, *The Russians in Germany: A History of the Soviet Zone of Occupation, 1945-1949* (Cambridge, Mass., 1995).

Toni Offermann lives in Kall-Wallenthal, Germany. He has written and edited many studies on the early history of labor movements in Germany, including *Arbeiterbewegung und liberales Bürgertum in Deutschland 1850-1863* (Bonn, 1979) and *Deutsche Handwerker- und Arbeiterkongresse 1848-1852: Protokolle und Materialien* (Berlin, 1983). With Dieter Dowe, he is currently co-editing a volume of *Materialien zur Sozialstruktur und Verbreitung von ADAV und LADAV 1867-1871.*

Dietrich Orlow is Professor of History at Boston University. He has published extensively in the area of contemporary German and European history, including *A History of Modern Germany, 1870-Present*, 3rd ed. (Englewood Cliffs, NJ, 1995), *Weimar Prussia, 1925-1933: The Illusion of Strength* (Pittsburgh, 1991), and *Weimar Prussia, 1918-1925: The Unlikely Rock of Democracy* (Pittsburgh, 1986). He is presently completing a monograph, "Three Paths to Pragmatic Reformism: A Comparative History of the Dutch, German, and French Socialists, 1945-1969."

Diethelm Prowe is Professor of History at Carleton College. Recent articles include "Economic Democracy in Post-World War I Germany," *Journal of Modern History* 57:3 (1985): 451-82; "Socialism as Crisis Response," *German Studies Review* 15:1 (1992): 65-85; and "'Classic' Fascism and the New Radical Right in Western Europe," *Contemporary European History* 3:3 (1994): 289-313.

Ralf Roth studied at the University of Frankfurt am Main and is currently associated with the Technical University of Berlin and the Deutsche Bahn

AG. He has published numerous articles as well as books, including *Gewerkschaftskartell und Sozialpolitik in Frankfurt am Main: Arbeiterbewegung vor dem Ersten Weltkrieg zwischen Restauration und liberaler Erneuerung* (Frankfurt am Main, 1991) and *Stadt und Bürgertum in Frankfurt am Main: Ein besonderer Weg von der ständischen zur modernen Bürgergesellschaft 1760 bis 1914* (Munich, 1996).

Adelheid von Saldern is Professor of Modern History at the University of Hanover. In 1989 she was Visiting Professor at Johns Hopkins University and in 1994 at the University of Chicago. Her most recent works include *Häuserleben: Zur Geschichte städtischen Arbeiterwohnens vom Kaiserreich bis heute* (Bonn, 1995) and *Neues Wohnen in Hanover* (Hanover, 1993).

Hanna Schissler is Associate Professor of History and German Studies at the University of Minnesota. Recent publications include *Geschlechterverhältnisse im historischen Wandel*, contributing editor (Frankfurt am Main, 1993); "Frauengeschichte vor Gericht: Der Rechtsstreit der amerikanischen Equal Employment Opportunity Commission mit der Firma Sears, and Co.," *L`Homme: Zeitschrift für Feministische Geschichtswissenschaft* (1995); "Gibt es eine Antwort auf Freuds Frage: Was will das Weib? Herrschaft und Unbewußtheit in den westdeutschen Geschlechterbeziehungen der fünfziger Jahre," *Potsdamer Bulletin für Zeithistorische Studien* (1997).

Jonathan Sperber is Professor of History at the University of Missouri, Columbia. His scholarly interests center around the social, political and religious history of nineteenth-century Germany. Major publications include: *Popular Catholicism in Nineteenth-Century Germany* (Princeton, 1984); *Rhineland Radicals: The Democratic Movement and the Revolution of 1848-1849* (Princeton, 1991); *The European Revolutions, 1848-1851* (Cambridge, Mass., 1994); and *The Kaiser's Voters: Electors and Elections in Imperial Germany* (Cambridge, Mass., 1997).

Index

C

D

E

F

I

J

K

L

S

T

U

V

W

Y

Z